Student-Centered Classroom Assessment

Second Edition

Richard J. Stiggins
Assessment Training Institute

Merrill,
an imprint of Prentice Hall
Upper Saddle River, New Jersey   Columbus, Ohio

Library of Congress Cataloging-in-Publication Data
Stiggins, Richard J.
    Student-centered classroom assessment / Richard J. Stiggins.—2nd ed.
        p. cm.
    Includes bibliographical references and index.
    ISBN 0-13-432931-7 (alk. paper)
    1. Educational tests and measurements—United States. 2. Examinations—United
States.   I. Title
   LB3051.S8536   1997
   371.2'6—dc20   95-53706
                                                                             CIP

Cover photo: © Jeffry W. Myers/The Stock Market
Editor: Kevin M. Davis
Production Editor: Alexandrina Benedicto Wolf
Copy Editor: Robert L. Marcum
Design Coordinator: Jill E. Bonar
Text Designer: Mia Saunders
Cover Designer: Russ Maselli
Production Manager: Patricia A. Tonneman
Electronic Text Management: Marilyn Wilson Phelps, Matthew Williams, Karen L. Bretz,
    Tracey Ward

This book was set in ITC Century by Prentice Hall and was printed and bound by R.R.
Donnelley & Sons. The cover was printed by Phoenix Color Corp.

© 1997 by Prentice-Hall, Inc.
Simon & Schuster/A Viacom Company
Upper Saddle River, New Jersey 07458

Earlier edition © 1994 by Macmillan College Publishing Company, Inc.

Printed in the United States of America

10 9 8 7 6 5

ISBN: 0-13-432931-7

Prentice-Hall International (UK) Limited, *London*
Prentice-Hall of Australia Pty. Limited, *Sydney*
Prentice-Hall of Canada, Inc., *Toronto*
Prentice-Hall Hispanoamericana, S. A., *Mexico*
Prentice-Hall of India Private Limited, *New Delhi*
Prentice-Hall of Japan, Inc., *Tokyo*
Simon & Schuster Asia Pte. Ltd., *Singapore*
Editora Prentice-Hall do Brasil, Ltda., *Rio de Janeiro*

For Nancy,
My Wife and Best Friend

An Important Welcoming Message

Greetings to you and welcome! We are about to take a very important journey together—a journey through the diverse and critically important world of educational assessment. Your success as a professional educator, whether as a classroom teacher or an administrator, will depend on your understanding of this world and your ability to work effectively within it. As you will see, both student achievement and academic self-concept are determined, by and large, on the basis of students' perceptions of their own success in the classroom. Students rely almost completely on the day-to-day, week-to-week, and term-to-term classroom assessments of their achievement to judge their current success and their hope for success in the future.

Students count on us, their teachers, to know what we're doing when it comes to assessing achievement. If we know how to assess accurately, we have the opportunity to contribute immensely to their success in school. But if we do not understand the principles of sound assessment, and therefore systematically mismeasure our students' academic achievement, we are likely to do great harm, in terms of both their actual achievement and their academic self-concept. For this reason, our journey through the world of classroom assessment is an important one indeed.

A Special Philosophy

The chapters that follow offer a special philosophy about classroom assessment—a philosophy that places *students* at the center of the assessment equation. To assist you in understanding this philosophy and in interpreting the assessment advice offered herein, let me spell out some of the values it is based on.

Without question, the single most important value any teacher must bring to the classroom assessment process is a very strong sense of caring about students' academic well-being. Our goal must be to be sure each student is free from academic harm in the classroom. As teachers, we must not just believe that all students can learn, but must really want each and every student to succeed in school and beyond. For this reason, we must be fanatics about the thoughtful, sensitive use of quality assessment within the instructional environment.

In our concern for the well-being of students, however, we must not make the mistake of lowering our academic standards merely to make school easy. On the contrary, a classroom environment centered on each student's academic well-being must hold those students accountable for the attainment of high academic standards that are both clearly articulated and not negotiable. Students must know that they are responsible for achieving in this place called school. Just trying hard, while critical for success, is not enough. Only achievement is enough. They must see the targets in full focus and know that we expect them to score bullseyes; finishing relatively high in a rank order of a group of low achievers will not suffice. We must help them develop the inner strength—the internal locus of control—to know they can succeed. I will offer a great many suggestions for how to use the assessment process as a teaching strategy to help them build that inner faith and sense of responsibility for their own learning.

Our classroom assessments should define for students precisely what we expect of them—they must define the truly important achievement targets. At the same time, those assessments will provide the basis of information for student, parent, teacher, principal, and community decision making. In addition, they can motivate students to try, or can discourage them from trying. They may screen students in or out of programs, giving them access to the special services they may need. Our classroom assessments often provide at least part of the basis for teacher and principal evaluation. Because of all the roles they play, day-to-day classroom assessments make major contributions to the effectiveness of schools and classrooms. For all of these reasons, they help students prosper and attain excellence, if we use them properly.

Experienced teachers and administrators know that these day-to-day classroom assessments are not the tests that command all of the public and political attention, or that consume the assessment budget each year. It is not our classroom assessments that draw all of the news coverage and editorial comment. All the visibility and political power honors go to our large-scale standardized tests. Nevertheless, anyone who has taught knows that it is classroom assessments—not standardized tests—that provide the energy that fuels the teaching and learning engine. For this reason, our classroom assessments absolutely must be of high quality.

A Collaborative Effort

We can achieve this goal together by collaborating in the process of understanding and applying a commonsense meaning of assessment quality. As my part of the collaboration, in the chapters that follow, I offer practical assessment ideas communicated in everyday language, with understandable classroom examples. You can fulfill your part of our bargain by studying these ideas, reflecting on them and/or discussing them with fellow students or colleagues, trying them out in your instructional context, and adapting the ideas to meet the needs of your students. You will not benefit from this book by simply reading it. It will not even suffice to read and discuss it with colleagues. To derive benefit, you must "do" this book. You must invest the mental time and energy needed to actually apply and experiment with the suggestions offered.

In other words, the success of our joint effort on behalf of sound classroom assessment will hinge on the extent to which you actively strive to construct your own personal meaning of the material presented. To aid you, I have inserted "Time for Reflection" activities throughout the text, and have concluded each chapter with a set of exercises designed to advance your learning. If you will take time to think about the issues at the time they are raised in the text, you will have a much easier time connecting the assessment ideas presented to your prior knowledge and experience. The effect will be a meaningful professional development experience. In fact, some readers have found it useful to keep a journal or portfolio of their responses to these brief "Time for Reflection" and end of-chapter exercise assignments. You might try this as a way to collect your expanding thoughts about applications of the assessment suggestions offered herein.

If you are teaching now, here is an engaging way to monitor your own improvement as a classroom assessor. Before you begin Chapter 1, select an assessment you have used recently in your classroom. Reflect on its quality—do you think it is a sound assessment? What are its strength and weaknesses? Answer these questions in a brief essay. Then, place both the assessment and your essay in a folder. This folder will be your "emerging assessment literacy portfolio." Repeat this activity after you have completed reading Part I, then again after you have finished Parts III and IV. When you have finished reading this book, return to your assessment literacy portfolio and reread the assessments and your four essays. Over the period of your professional development based on the study of this text, two things should change: (1) the quality of your assessments and (2) the depth and clarity of your evaluations of them as expressed in your essays. If you engage in this activity with a partner or as part of a learning team, you could share your portfolios, discussing and enhancing each other's growth.

Further, as we journey together, read critically. Ask tough questions about what you read in this book. Test the assessment strategies suggested against your own good judgment. In these ways, you will become a critical consumer of assessments and the information they provide.

A Tough Challenge

Be advised from the outset that the following chapters contain some challenging material. This goes with the territory. Nowhere in this text will you find me stating that the classroom assessment task is easy. But you will come to understand that it is critical to the well-being of your students.

Don't be put off by the complexity of the assessment process. Dig in and master it! If you do, both you and your students will benefit immensely. Assessment has a reputation for being quantitative, complicated, dry, and boring. This need not be the case. Assessment can be both challenging and empowering! Over the decades, many educators have faced assessment training with trepidation. Even today, most see assessment as merely the process of quantifying student achievement. Typically, this view leads to inferences about the mathematical nature of assessment, math anxiety may set in, and resistance to learning follows close on its heels. Please try to let that anxiety go right now. Assessment is a challenge in clear thinking and effective communication. High-quality assessment is well within the reach of every teacher.

A Special Note to Teachers in Training

If we are to travel together on this journey through the world of assessment during your teaching training program and if you have no prior classroom teaching experience, please keep two key points in mind. To begin with, you *are* experienced in the realm of classroom assessment. You have over a dozen years of firsthand real-life assessment experience from the student's point of view, from the perspective of the examinee. We will strive to take advantage of that experience whenever possible to help you assimilate the concepts and suggestions being offered. Your perception from the student's point of view is very relevant here.

Nevertheless, as is always the case, professionals-in-training must live through certain "academic" experiences before being given a license to apply their skills. So it is with teachers. Thus, your study of this book may occur before you experience life in the classroom. Sometimes this may make it difficult to understand and take command of assessment strategies—to see how those methods might fit into day-to-day instruction and affect students in positive ways. Since I can't magically infuse classroom experience into your structure of understanding, I will try to help you in a different way.

I have enlisted the support of two veteran teachers, Lynn and Casey, to travel with us through the realm of assessment and to serve as interpreters. Lynn has over a decade of elementary teaching experience and is a former state teacher of the year, a real pro. Casey has invested over twenty years in teaching multiple subjects at the intermediate and high school levels—here again, we have a veteran of outstanding reputation. Readers who have teaching experience will recognize them; we all have colleagues like them. From time to time during the presentation, Lynn or Casey, and sometimes both, provide insight as to "how it really is in schools." Sometimes they will speak directly to the inexperienced reader, offering advice about how to manage the assessment, evaluation, and grading processes when you finally arrive at your first school and teaching assignment. Other times we will eavesdrop on their conversations with each other, striving to understand how their perspectives bear on assessment life in their classrooms. Their assignment is to help light the way as we travel together.

A Roadmap of Our Journey Together

Our journey will unfold in four parts: Understanding the Classroom Assessment Context, Understanding Assessment Methods, Classroom Applications, and Communicating about Student Achievement. Each part offers unique perspectives on the classroom assessment process, yet the four parts present a unified overall picture of the assessment process and its place in day-to-day instruction.

Overview of Part I: Understanding the Classroom Assessment Context

Our journey begins by defining assessment roles and responsibilities and by describing the essential elements in the classroom assessment process. As Part I unfolds, you will see what it means to be a responsible, well-prepared classroom assessment professional, as we talk about what it really means to be assessment literate. What is quality assessment? How does a sound assessment differ form an unsound one? What competencies must one master to ensure sound assessment from the classroom to the boardroom?

We will delve deeply into the world of assessment in schools by exploring all of the different levels of users and uses of assessment. We will explore three different levels of assessment use: instructional uses, instructional leadership uses, and uses in setting policy. Through this discussion of the meaning of quality and various assessment roles and responsibilities, I will make it perfectly clear why the teacher lies at the heart of the assessment matter in school. You will also see why every teacher absolutely must do a solid job of assessing.

We will explore the two key elements in the classroom assessment quality-control equation: (1) knowing what is to be assessed and (2) knowing how to assess it. With respect to the *what* of the assessment equation, the critical question will become, Do you know what it means to succeed academically in your classroom or school? If you do not know the meaning and limits of this target, and cannot convey them in meaningful terms to your students, you minimize their chances of success.

With respect to the *how* of the classroom assessment equation, you will learn about the four different modes of assessment available for classroom use: selected response, essay, performance, and personal communication assessments. And most importantly, you will learn that no single assessment method can match all of our targets and serve all of our assessment purposes. You will see how these various methods can be aligned appropriately with the various kinds of achievement targets to produce assessments that make sense in your classroom.

Finally, we will finish framing the classroom assessment context by pointing out four troubling roadblocks to quality assessment. We will explore why it may be easier to define standards of quality assessment than to meet those standards in the classroom. These roadblocks arise from our adult emotions about the prospect of being assessed and evaluated, community assumptions about the meaning of sound assessment practice, a pervasive lack of time to assess well, and gaps in our assessment knowhow. And we'll see why a thorough knowledge of the principles of sound assessment is the key to removing all of these roadblocks.

Overview of Part II: Understanding Assessment Methods

Once the stage is set in Part I, we will begin an in-depth study of the assessment methods available for classroom use. Part II contains four chapters, one each on the design and development of selected response tests (multiple-choice, true/false, and the like); essay tests; performance assessments (assessments based on observation and judgment); and assessments that rely on direct personal communication with students, such as questioning during instruction, interviews, and conferences. I will make the point that—even in these trendy times emphasizing performance assessment—traditional modes of assessment still have major contributions to make in the classroom. We need to maintain a balanced perspective in our classroom assessment work.

Each of these chapters presents its assessment alternative in a manner calculated to help you understand how its contributions may lead to effective instruction. First, we discuss the kinds of achievement targets with which the method aligns. Then, we outline keys to effective development. We conclude each chapter by discussing productive ways to bring students into the assessment process as full partners, ways to use assessment as an effective teaching tool.

The bottom line is that we face an immense classroom assessment challenge as we move toward the twenty-first century. We have many different kinds of increasingly complex forms of achievement to assess that necessitate the use of all available tools. For this reason, each chapter in Part II communicates a decidedly positive point of view about the potential of the assessment method being discussed. This positive bent is tempered, however, by the resolute position that each method can and will reach its potential only if developers and users adhere to accepted guidelines for using it well. We spell out those rules, too, in Part II.

Overview of Part III: Classroom Applications

With a solid foundation of basic assessment methodology in hand, we will turn our attention to classroom applications. This part of the book consists of four chapters that deal with the assessment of different kinds of achievement targets. We will explore assessing student reasoning and problem solving in all of its many forms, assessing proficiency in demonstrating important skills and in creating products that meet standards of quality, and assessing students' development of certain important motivational dispositions regarding the need to meet high academic standards. In addition, we will explore the role of large-scale standardized testing in the classroom.

Each of these chapters will examine the potential match between the kind of target being addressed and the four kinds of assessment methods studied in Part II. In addition, you will find many examples in the union of method and target that reveal creative ways to use effective classroom assessment to generate accurate information about student achievement and to use assessment as a teaching strategy.

The goal in Part III is to make classroom assessment live in your mind, not as a set of abstractions, but as a real, potentially useful set of concepts, tools, and strategies that can bring students into the teaching and learning process in new and creative ways.

Overview of Part IV: Communicating about Student Achievement

This concluding section is divided into four relatively brief chapters, each dealing with a different form of communication about student achievement from various perspectives. A common theme underlies the chapters in this phase of our journey: If we're smart, we can use the communication process itself as a powerful source of positive student motivation.

We begin by understanding several keys to effective communication, building a "communication tower" from the ground up. Starting with clear achievement expectations, we will build quality assessment plans and carry out those plans to build a reservoir of high-quality information about each student's achievement. Then we must transform that information into an understandable form for a variety of users. Each of the last three chapters in Part IV describes one way to do that.

Report cards and grades are first. We will explore what it is we need to communicate via grades and how we can go about gathering and summarizing that information through report cards and grades most effectively in the future.

We then use report cards as a point of departure for exploring many other possibilities. Among these are portfolios, more detailed checklist and narrative reports, student-teacher conferences, and student-led parent-teacher conferences. These are presented as communication alternatives that show great promise for permitting us to effectively share greater detail about student achievement—to provide more information in this information age.

Keeping Our Targets Clear

As we study the classroom assessment process, we will refer consistently to the need for teachers to be able to define achievement targets in clear and specific terms. We will study the assessment of five different kinds of targets. To assist you in understanding these kinds of targets as they apply to your classroom, I will model this way of defining achievement expectations by categorizing the objectives of each chapter of this book in the same terms. Thus, as you study, you will be striving to do the following:

- *Master content knowledge*—be able to retrieve appropriate subject matter knowledge about assessment in an understandable form from memory or reference materials when needed.

- *Reason proficiently*—be able to pattern your thinking so as to use available content knowledge productively to solve classroom assessment challenges.

- *Become skillful*-be able to carry out steps in various processes such that you can apply procedural knowledge, reason productively, and actually do what is required to be considered proficient as a classroom assessor.

- *Develop quality products*—be able to use your skills to create tangible products that meet certain standards of quality, such as test instruments, scoring criteria, and so on.

- *Develop certain motivational predispositions*—as a result of study of, reflection on, and application of material presented, you will develop strong motivational dispositions to use assessment effectively in your classroom.

Through this modeling, I hope you will come to understand that you, too, must define your expectations of your students in these same terms so they can hit your targets, just as I want you to hit mine. Each chapter begins with objectives presented and classified in the preceding terms. Each chapter ends with a set of exercises intended to help you practice in attaining objectives thus categorized.

Keeping Perspective

As you study the material presented herein, strive to keep assessment in perspective. While I will argue that it is a continuous part of the instructional process that must command a great deal of a teacher's time and attention, it is by no means the only activity in the job of teaching. Therefore, you must keep assessment in balance in terms of your use of time and in terms of its imposition on learners. You can spend instructional time in many productive ways, including many different forms of direct instruction, cooperative learning, and self-study by students, among others. In fact, just providing students with some occasional unstructured time to "muck around" with materials and ideas without you evaluating them can lead to some very important learning experiences. This is by way of urging that you keep in check your natural teacher's impulse to judge students. Use it judiciously and wisely.

Just the Beginning

Let this book represent the beginning of a career-long exploration of discovery on your part. It is not possible to cover all critical elements of educational assessment in one introductory text. My challenge as author is to offer enough to be helpful—to get you started—while not overwhelming you. For this reason, I have selected for each chapter those ideas that are most likely to be most useful right away. But there is so much more that I wanted to say to you.

It is important that you regard our journey as a first excursion into the realm of assessment, to be followed by others as you move on to more advanced topics. I will give you a list of additional readings at the end of our trip. Now and always, you must endeavor to seek new understandings of assessment.

If you are ready, then, let our journey begin.

Acknowledgments

S*tudent-Centered Classroom Assessment, Second Edition,* represents the results of two decades of preparation under the tutelage of many outstanding primary, elementary, junior high, and high school teachers. In a very real sense, this book conveys the collective wisdom of those teachers who shared openly their assessment ideas, uncertainties, and frustrations. I wish to express my deepest appreciation for their willingness to share their students and classrooms with me so that I might learn. These teachers welcomed me into their world and helped me understand it.

Special thanks also to my wife and partner, Nancy Bridgeford, to whom this edition is dedicated. Nancy possesses the uncanny ability to ferret out writing that fails to convey clear meaning. Nowhere is effective communication more important or more challenging than in an introductory text on a technical topic like this one. Nancy's patient dedication to quality made effective communication possible here.

Sharon Lippert and Jennifer Dickey, members of the Assessment Training Institute staff, also made major contributions to the completion of this text. Sharon has spent her career helping me collect and present the ideas offered herein, preparing the dozens of manuscripts leading up to this one. Jennifer was responsible for preparing the manuscript for this edition. Their patience and sense of the importance of details contributed immensely to the final project.

Others contributed by reviewing the manuscript and providing constructive feedback. They include Susan M. Brookhart, Duquesne University; John R. Criswell, Edinboro University of Pennsylvania; David Frisbie, University of Iowa; Ronald M. Marso, Bowling Green State University; Douglas J. Mickelson, University of Wisconsin-Milwaukee; Paul Nichols, University of Wisconsin-Milwaukee (and his students); Richard Paul, Sonoma State University; Patricia A. Pokay, Eastern Michigan University; Sylvia Rosenfield, University of Maryland-College Park; Katherine

Ryan, University of Illinois; Emily Sagor, Assessment Training Institute intern; and Michael S. Trevisan, Washington State University. This text has been improved immeasurably by their insightful criticism.

And finally, I want to acknowledge once again the team from Merrill Education, who takes great pride in a job well done. Special thanks to Kevin Davis, Alex Wolf, and Lynn Metzger. To freelance copy editor Robert Marcum—a word crafter of immense talent—I simply say, we speak with one voice.

As educators, we know far more collectively than any of us does alone. When we pool our insights as a community of learners and combine this with a dedication to the academic and personal well-being of our students, we prepare ourselves to succeed as teachers.

Rick Stiggins
Portland, OR

Brief Contents

PART I   Understanding the Classroom Assessment Context   1

Chapter 1   Guiding Principles for Classroom Assessment   3
Chapter 2   Understanding the Critical Roles of Assessment   21
Chapter 3   Specifying Achievement Targets   43
Chapter 4   Understanding the Assessment Alternatives   73
Chapter 5   Facing the Barriers to Quality Assessment   91

PART II   Understanding Assessment Methods   111

Chapter 6   Selected Response Assessment: Flexible and Efficient   113
Chapter 7   Essay Assessment: Vast Untapped Potential   149
Chapter 8   Performance Assessment: Rich with Possibilities   175
Chapter 9   Personal Communication: Another
            Window to Student Achievement   223

PART III   Classroom Applications   251

Chapter 10 Assessing Reasoning Proficiency   253
Chapter 11 Performance Assessments of Skill and Product Targets   287
Chapter 12 Assessing Student Dispositions   319
Chapter 13 Classroom Perspectives on Standardized Testing   345

PART IV   Communicating About Student Achievement   381

Chapter 14 Understanding Our Communication Challenge   383
Chapter 15 Developing Sound Report Card Grading Practices   407
Chapter 16 The Role of Portfolios in the Communication Process   447
Chapter 17 Reports and Conferences That Highlight Achievement   473

Contents

PART I

Understanding the Classroom Assessment Context   1

CHAPTER 1   Guiding Principles for Classroom Assessment   3

Chapter Roadmap   3
A Vision of Success   4
Assessment Literacy Is the Key   7
A Set of Guiding Principles   10
Chapter Summary: The Critical Role of Assessment Literacy   19
Exercises to Advance Your Learning   20

CHAPTER 2   Understanding the Critical Roles of Assessment   21

Chapter Roadmap   21
Assessing for a Reason   23
Assessments That Inform Decisions   24
Contrasting Classroom and Large-scale Standardized Assessment   30
Using Assessment as a Teaching Tool   36
Chapter Summary: Sound Assessment Becomes Essential   39
Exercises to Advance Your Learning   40

CHAPTER 3   Specifying Achievement Targets   43

Chapter Roadmap   43

Our Mission and the Demand for Clear Expectations   45

The Benefits of Clear and Appropriate Targets   50

Types of Achievement Targets   54

Sources of Information About Achievement Targets   61

Communicating About Valued Achievement Targets   68

Chapter Summary: Clear Targets Are Key   69

Exercises to Advance Your Learning   70

CHAPTER 4   Understanding the Assessment Alternatives   73

Chapter Roadmap   73

The Assessment Options   75

Matching Methods with Targets   79

Chapter Summary: Targets and Methods Must Match   88

Exercises to Advance Your Learning   88

CHAPTER 5   Facing the Barriers to Quality Assessment   91

Chapter Roadmap   91

Understanding the Roadblocks   93

Chapter Summary: Clearing the Road to Quality   107

Exercises to Advance Your Learning   108

PART II

Understanding Assessment Methods   111

CHAPTER 6   Selected Response Assessment: Flexible and Efficient   113

Chapter Roadmap   113

The Role of Teacher Judgment in Selected Response Assessment   116

The Importance of Understanding Selected Response Assessment   116

Matching Selected Response Assessments to Achievement Targets   118

Developing Selected Response Assessments   122

The Steps in Test Development   123

Barriers to Sound Selected Response Assessment   143

Including Students in the Assessment Process   144

Chapter Summary: Productive Selected Response Assessment   145

Exercises to Advance Your Learning   146

CHAPTER 7   Essay Assessment: Vast Untapped Potential   149

Chapter Roadmap   149

Essay Assessment in a Productive Learning Environment   152

Ensuring the Quality of Essay Assessments   156

Developing Essay Assessments   161

Barriers to Sound Essay Assessment   171

Integrating Essay Assessment and Instruction   171

Chapter Summary: Tapping the Potential of Essays   173

Exercises to Advance Your Learning   173

CHAPTER 8   Performance Assessment: Rich with Possibilities   175

Chapter Roadmap   175

Using Performance Assessment to Advantage   178

Performance Assessment at Work in the Classroom   179

Ensuring the Quality of Performance Assessments   186

Developing Performance Assessments   191

Fine-Tuning Your Performance Assessments   212

Barriers to Sound Performance Assessment   217

More About Students as Partners   217

Chapter Summary: Thoughtful Development Yields Sound Assessments   219

Exercises to Advance Your Learning   220

CHAPTER 9   Personal Communication: Another
Window to Student Achievement   223

Chapter Roadmap   223

Personal Communication at Work as Assessment in the Classroom   226

Ensuring Quality Assessment   228

Matching Method to Target   231

Context Factors   234

The Many Forms of Personal Communication as Assessment   239

Integrating Assessment into Instruction   246

Chapter Summary: Assessment as Sharing, Person-to-Person   248

Exercises to Advance Your Learning   248

PART III

Classroom Applications   251

CHAPTER 10   Assessing Reasoning Proficiency   253

    Chapter Roadmap   253
    Five Guiding Principles   256
    Understanding Reasoning   258
    Matching Method to Target   265
    Judging Reasoning Proficiency   271
    Assembling the Parts   276
    Involving Students in Assessing Reasoning   279
    Chapter Summary: Finding the Path to Reasoning Power   284
    Exercises to Advance Your Learning   285

CHAPTER 11   Performance Assessment of Skill and Product Targets   287

    Chapter Roadmap   287
    Special Guidelines for Your Study of This Chapter   289
    Performance Assessment Examples from the Primary Grades   291
    Examples from Elementary Grades   298
    Examples from Junior High School   301
    Examples from High School   310
    Chapter Summary: Performance Assessment, a Diverse and Powerful Tool   315
    Exercises to Advance Your Learning   316

CHAPTER 12   Assessing Student Dispositions   319

    Chapter Roadmap   319
    Why Should We Care About Student Dispositions?   321
    Remain Mindful of the Five Standards of Quality   323
    Defining *Affect* as It Relates to Dispositions   327
    Exploring the Assessment Options   330
    Matching Method to Target   331
    Chapter Summary: Assessing Dispositions
    as a Path to Higher Achievement   342
    Exercises to Advance Your Learning   343

CHAPTER 13   Classroom Perspectives on Standardized Testing   345

    Chapter Roadmap   345
    A Brief History Lesson   347
    Troubling Contradictions   352
    A Guiding Philosophy   354
    Understanding the Purposes for Large-scale Assessment   355
    The Many Forms of Large-scale Assessment   356
    Matching Method to Target in Standardized Testing   362
    Test Development   364
    Interpretation of Commonly Used Test Scores   367
    Implications for Teachers   374
    Chapter Summary: Meeting the Challenges of Standardized Testing   378
    Exercises to Advance Your Learning   378

PART IV

Communicating About Student Achievement   381

CHAPTER 14   Understanding Our Communication Challenge   383

    Chapter Roadmap   383
    Maintaining the Quality of the Message   385
    Managing the Communication Environment   387
    Understanding Our Internal Barriers to Effective Communication   390
    Understanding Student-involved Communication   394
    Student-involved Communication and the Pursuit of Academic Excellence   396
    Chapter Summary: Meeting the Communication Challenge   404
    Exercises to Advance Your Learning   405

CHAPTER 15   Developing Sound Report Card Grading Practices   407

    Chapter Roadmap   407
    Understanding Our Current Grading Environment   409
    Selecting Targets for Grading Purposes   411
    Gathering Achievement Information for Grading Purposes   422
    Chapter Summary: Making the Grade   444
    Exercises to Advance Your Learning   445

CHAPTER 16   The Role of Portfolios in the Communication Process   447

Chapter Roadmap   447

The Popular Culture of Portfolios   450

Analyzing the Active Ingredients in Portfolios   453

Chapter Summary: Speaking Through Portfolios   469

Exercises to Advance Your Learning   469

CHAPTER 17   Reports and Conferences That Highlight Achievement   473

Chapter Roadmap   473

Detailed Written Reports   477

Conference Formats That Enhance Communication   492

A Final Thought About Your Communication Challenge   504

Chapter Summary: Finding Effective Ways to Communicate   505

For Further Reading   506

Exercises to Advance Your Learning   507

REFERENCES   509

INDEX   513

ABOUT THE AUTHOR   521

Understanding the Classroom Assessment Context

If measurement is to continue to play an increasingly important role in education, measurement workers must be much more than technicians. Unless their efforts are directed by a sound educational philosophy, unless they accept and welcome a greater share of responsibility for the selection and clarification of educational objectives, unless they show much more concern with what they measure as well as with how they measure it, much of their work will prove futile and ineffective.

E. F. LINDQUIST (1901–1978)

CHAPTER 1   Guiding Principles for Classroom Assessment

CHAPTER 2   Understanding the Critical Roles of Assessment

CHAPTER 3   Specifying Achievement Targets

CHAPTER 4   Understanding the Assessment Alternatives

CHAPTER 5   Facing the Barriers to Quality Assessment

1

Guiding Principles for Classroom Assessment

CHAPTER ROADMAP

We begin our journey together with an overall view of the challenges of classroom assessment. I highlight and illustrate several principles that will guide us along our way. As a result of studying the material presented in Chapter 1, reflecting on that material, and completing the learning exercises presented at the end of the chapter, you will master specific content knowledge:

1. Understand seven guiding principles of sound classroom assessment.
2. Learn five key attributes of sound assessments.

Further, as a result of our early travel together, you will be able to use this knowledge to reason by being able to do the following:

1. Translate the seven principles into terms that have personal meaning for you.
2. Identify examples from your personal experience of assessments that met and failed to meet the five attributes of sound assessment.

And finally, I hope you will develop the following dispositions:

1. See many different modes of assessment as useful—not just one or two.
2. See classroom assessment as the most important level of assessment for student academic well-being.
3. See students as the most important users of assessment results.
4. Value high-quality assessment under all circumstances both in the classroom and beyond.

The objectives of this opening orientation chapter do not include the mastery of any specific skills or product development capabilities. With this overview, then, let our journey begin.

A Vision of Success

Visualize yourself at a particularly important meeting of the school board in the district where you teach. The crowd is unusually large, the news media are present, and anticipation runs high. This is the once-a-year meeting at which the district presents the annual report of standardized test scores. Everyone wonders whether scores will be up or down this year. How will your school compare to all the others? How will your district compare to others in the area?

What most of those present don't realize as the meeting begins is that, this year, they are in for a big surprise with respect to both the achievement information to be presented and the manner of the presentation. To make the presentation, the chair of the school board introduces the assistant superintendent in charge of assessment.

As the presentation begins, the audience includes a young woman named Emily—a junior at the high school—sitting at the side of the room with her parents. She knows she will be a big part of the surprise but is only a little nervous. She understands how important her role is. It has been quite a year for her—unlike any she has ever experienced in school before. She also knows her parents and teacher are as proud of her as she is of herself.

The assistant superintendent begins by reminding the board and all present at the meeting that the standardized tests used in the district sample broad domains of achievement with just a few test items. Thus, they provide only the most general picture of student achievement. She points out that the only assessment format used is the multiple-choice test item—a format capable of reflecting only a small, but important, part of the total array of forms of achievement valued in this district. Much that we value, she points out, must be assessed by other means. She promises to provide an example later in the presentation. Emily's dad nudges her and they both smile.

Further, the presenter reminds the board that last year they approved an assessment policy changing district practice from a testing plan of administering the test battery to every pupil at every grade to a plan relying on a random sample of students at each grade level. The board had understood that the number of students tested would be greatly reduced. Thus, the cost of testing could be greatly reduced too. But this was to be done without sacrificing the average test scores that they wanted, both for individual school buildings and districtwide.

In this context, the presenter informs the board that the cost savings were used to develop and implement classroom-level assessments that provide greater detail on student achievement in performance arenas not testable by means of multiple-choice tests. Again, she promises examples later in the presentation.

Having set the stage, she turns to carefully prepared charts depicting average student performance in each important achievement category tested. Results are summarized by grade and building, concluding with a clear description of how district results had changed from the year before and from previous years. As she proceeds, board members ask questions and receive clarification. Some scores are down slightly; some are up. Participants discuss possible reasons. This is a routine annual presentation that proceeds as expected.

Next comes the break from routine. Having completed the first part of the presentation, the assistant superintendent explains how the district has invested its limited assessment resources to gather new information about one important aspect of student achievement. As the board knows, she points out, the district has implemented a new writing program in the high school to address the issue of poor writing skills among graduates. As part of their preparation for this program, the English faculty attended a summer institute on the assessment of writing proficiency and the integration of such assessments into the teaching and learning process. The English department was confident that this kind of professional development and program revision would produce much higher levels of writing proficiency.

As the second half of the evening's assessment presentation, the high school English department faculty will share the results of their evaluation of the new writing program.

As the very first step in this presentation, the English chair—who also happens to be Emily's English teacher—distributes copies of two samples of student writing to the board members (with the student's name removed), asking them to read and evaluate this writing. They do so, expressing their dismay aloud as they go. They are indignant in their commentary on these samples of student work. One board member reports in exasperation that, if these represent the results of that new writing program, the community has been had. The board member is right. These are, in fact, pretty bad pieces of work. Emily's mom puts her arm around her daughter's shoulder and hugs her.

But the chair urges patience and asks the board members to be very specific about what they don't like about this work. As the board registers its complaints, the faculty records the criticisms on chart paper for all to see. The list is long, including everything from mechanical errors to disorganization to incorrect word choice and vague ideas.

Next, the teacher distributes two more samples of student writing, asking the board to read and evaluate them. Ah, this, they report, is more like it! This work is much better! But be specific, the chair demands. What do you like about this work? Positive aspects are listed: good choice of words, sound sentence structure, clever ideas, and so on. Emily is ready to burst! She squeezes her mom's hand.

The reason she's so full of pride at this moment is that this has been a special year for her and her classmates. For the first time ever, they became partners with their English teachers in managing their own improvement as writers. Early in the year, her teacher made it crystal clear to Emily that she was, in fact, not a very good writer and that just trying hard to get better was not going to be enough. She was going to have to get better at this—and that was not negotiable. The teacher started the year by setting very high writing standards, expecting quality performance in word choice, sentence structure, organization, voice and some other factors, sharing some new "analytical scoring guides" written just for students. Each explained the differences between good and poor quality writing in understandable ways. When Emily and her teacher had profiled her first two pieces of writing using these standards, she got really low ratings. Not very good . . .

But she also began to study samples of writing supplied by her teacher that she could see were very good. Slowly, she began to see why they were good. The differences between these and her work started to become clear. Her teacher began to share examples and strategies that would help her writing improve—one part at a time. As she practiced with these and time passed, Emily and her classmates kept samples of their old writing to compare to their new writing—they began to keep portfolios. And thus, she began to see—literally see—her writing skills improve before her very eyes. At midyear, her parents were invited in for a conference at which Emily, not Emily's teacher, shared the contents of her portfolio and discussed her emerging writing skills. Emily remembers sharing thoughts about some aspects of her writing that had become very strong and some examples of things she still needed to work on. Now, the year was at an end and here she sat waiting for her turn to speak to the school board about all of this. What a year!

Now, having set the school board up by having them analyze, evaluate and compare these few samples of student work, the English chair springs the surprise: The pieces of writing they had just evaluated—first of dismal quality and then of outstanding quality—were produced by the same writer, two at the beginning and the others at the end of the school year! This, the chair reports, is evidence of the kind of impact the new writing program is having on student writing proficiency.

Needless to say, all are impressed. However, one board member wonders aloud, "Have all your students improved in this way?" Having anticipated the question, the faculty produces carefully prepared charts depicting dramatic changes in student performance over time on rating scales for each of six clearly articulated dimensions of good writing. They accompany their description of student performance on each scale with actual samples of student work illustrating various levels of proficiency.

Further, the chair informs the board that the student whose improvement had been so dramatically illustrated with the work they have just analyzed is present at this school board meeting, along with her parents. This student is ready to talk with the board about the nature of her learning experience. Emily, you're on!

Interest among the board members runs high. Emily talks about how she has come to understand the truly important differences between good and bad writing, differences she had not understood before, how she has learned to assess her own writing and to fix it when it doesn't "work well," and how she and her classmates have learned to talk with her teacher and each other about what it means to write well. Her teacher talks about the improved focus of writing instruction, increases in student motivation, and important positive changes in the very nature of the student-teacher relationship.

A board member asks Emily if she likes to write. She reports, "I do now!" This board member turns to Emily's parents and asks their impression of all of this. They report with pride that they had never been given so much quality information before about Emily's achievement—and most of it came from Emily herself. Emily had never been called upon to conduct the parent-teacher conference before. They had no idea she was so articulate. They loved it. Their daughter's pride in and accountability for achievement had skyrocketed in the past year.

As the meeting ends, it is clear to all in attendance that evening that this two-part assessment presentation—part from standardized test scores and part from students, teachers, and the classroom—reveals that assessment is in balance in this district. The test scores cover part of the picture and other assessment methods are needed to fill in more of that complex achievement picture. There is a good feeling in the air this evening. The accountability needs of the community are being satisfied and the writing assessment training and the new writing program are working to improve student achievement. Obviously, this story has a happy ending. Can't you almost visualize yourself walking out of the boardroom at the end of the evening, hearing parents wish they had had such an experience in high school? I sure can. Can't you just anticipate the wording of the memo of congratulations the superintendent will soon write to the English department? How about the story that will appear in the newspaper tomorrow, right next to the report of test scores? Everyone involved here—from Emily to her classmates to parents to teachers to assessment director to (at the end) school board members—knew what they were doing from an assessment point of view. They knew the meaning of quality assessment. This is an environment governed by an atmosphere of assessment literacy.

Assessment Literacy Is the Key

Because the staff and faculty in this particular district knew and understood the principles of sound assessment, because they knew how to translate those principles into sound assessments and quality information about students, and because they involved students in the assessment process as part of their effective instruction, a range of benefits accrued to all.

The Positive Results

To begin with, the students not only became more proficient as writers, but they also knew precisely when and why that happened. They were empowered by their teachers to use the assessment tools that allowed them to take responsibility for their own achievement. The mystery surrounding the definition of good writing was removed. Clearly, this openness paid off with higher achievement.

Similarly, the members of the English faculty were empowered to evaluate their own program. They were entrusted with the responsibility and were provided with the training and writing assessment tools needed to do that job. Not only did they use these new tools to fulfill their program evaluation responsibility, but they turned them into productive teaching tools, too.

Further, the faculty didn't retain the meaning of academic success as if it were some mystical treasure to be divined somehow by their students. Rather, they shared their vision of success openly and without reservation. There were no surprises here—and no excuses. As a result, students learned.

Other positive things happened, too. From an assessment point of view, limited district assessment resources were divided productively between those assessments that are likely to serve policy makers (districtwide assessment) and those that are likely to serve teachers and students in the classroom. The assessment environment is in balance in terms of users' needs.

Also from an assessment perspective, both during instruction and during the school board presentation, meaningful words and examples rather than just scores and grades were used as the basis for communicating about student achievement. And the resulting richness of mutual understanding of the real meaning of student success was compelling. Assessment is more than a set of numbers here. Things are in balance.

Still under the assessment heading, assessments that relied on observation and professional judgment (i.e., subjective assessments) were acknowledged to be of value in this context. You can bet that if our skillful assistant superintendent in charge of assessment had concluded the meeting by asking the school board if they would like to see more evidence of student achievement depicted in the form of performance assessments, she would have received a resounding *yes!* The assessment methods in use in this district are sensitive to all of the important forms of achievement, not to just a few.

And, one final positive aspect of this story is that a good part of the evidence that held sway with the policy makers was both generated by teachers in their classrooms and presented in a public forum in a way that established teachers' credibility as dependable sources of information on student achievement.

In one sense, their presentation revealed what good teachers they really are. I don't mean to say that it showed them to be good teachers because writing proficiency improved dramatically, although that obviously was a critically important result. Rather, I mean to point out that they were revealed to be good teachers of the school board, using hands-on applications of their newly acquired assessment methods to expand the horizons of the school board with respect to what represents sound assessment of student achievement. Common sense and a balance of perspectives on assessment ruled the day.

Things That Can Go Wrong

But for every such positive story in which sound assessment feeds into productive instruction and important learning, there may be another with a far less constructive—perhaps even painful—ending. For instance, some unfortunate students may be mired in classrooms in which they are forced to try to guess the meaning of academic success, because their teacher either lacks a vision of that meaning or chooses to keep it a mystery as a means of retaining power and control. When these students guess wrong and fail the assessment, not from a lack of motivation but for a lack of insight as to what they were supposed to achieve, permanent damage can be done to emerging academic self-concepts.

Then there are those students who prepare well, master the required material, and fail anyway, because the teacher prepared a test of poor quality, thus mismeasuring achievement. And, there are students whose achievement is mismeasured because the teacher placed blind faith in the quality of the tests that came with the textbook, when in fact that confidence was misplaced. Still further, some students fail not because of low achievement, but because their teacher's performance assessment judgments are riddled with the effects of gender or ethnic bias.

This list of problems could go on and on: School boards might make poor policy decisions because they fail to understand the limitations of standardized tests or the meaning of the scores these tests produce. Further, they may have had nowhere to turn for guidance in such assessment matters because of a lack of assessment literacy on the part of the school administrators who advise them.

When these and other such problems arise, an environment of assessment illiteracy dominates, assessments will be of poor quality, and students are placed directly in harm's way.

Our Common Mission

Our joint challenge in this book is to begin or to carry on with the professional development needed to assure high-quality assessment in your classroom. We must strive together to develop assessment literacy among all concerned about the quality of our schools and the well-being of students.

Assessment literates are those who understand the basic principles of sound assessment. But just understanding the meaning of sound assessment will not suffice. We must demand adherence to high standards by acting purposely to meet those standards in all assessment contexts and by pointing out to others when their assessments fail to measure up. As we implement assessments in the classroom or the boardroom, we must know how sound assessment relates to quality instruction and strive to maintain a balanced use of assessment alternatives.

We will continue to use both standardized tests *and* classroom assessment. We must appreciate the differences between the two, so as to be able to ensure quality assessments in both contexts and the appropriate applications of each.

These assessments will continue to serve both as providers of information for decision making and as teaching tools. We must understand the differences between these two uses if we wish to take full advantage of the power of assessment to promote learning.

There will continue to be paper and pencil *and* performance assessments. Each carries with it different rules of evidence for obtaining quality results. Know and follow them and you can assist students. Violate them and your students will suffer. Our task is to study and master those rules together.

Those who are assessment literate know the meaning of assessment quality with all of its nuances and know that we are never justified in settling for unsound assessments. That literacy is our goal as we visit the world of classroom assessment together.

A Set of Guiding Principles

In the chapters that follow, I will share a vast array of assessment tools, strategies, admonitions, and examples—all aimed at making assessment work well for you. As we proceed, you will find certain themes recurring. These are graphically portrayed in Figure 1–1, and are addressed in greater detail in the remainder of this chapter. They represent both important assessment realities teachers face in classrooms and important values that I personally have come to hold about classroom assessment. I share them with you here at the outset as interrelated themes that map the path to quality. The order in which they are presented is unimportant. All are profoundly important—together, they represent the foundation of your preparation to assess well in the classroom.

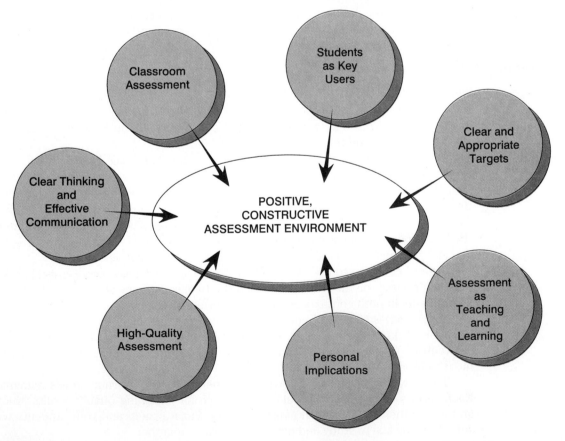

Figure 1–1
A Critical Blend of Guiding Principles

As you read, reflect back on Emily, the high school writing student in the opening scenario, and you will see why I started our journey together in that particular fashion.

Guiding Principle 1: Assessments Require Clear Thinking and Effective Communication

Those who will develop and use a high-quality assessment must share a highly refined focus. They must be clear thinkers, capable of communicating effectively both to those being assessed and to those who must understand the assessment's results.

Mention assessment and the first thoughts that come to mind are those of scores, numbers, and quantified indexes often attached to forms of achievement labeled very briefly, such as reading, writing, science, math, and the like. The underlying meaning of these single-word labels is rarely explicated. However, in our account of the school board meeting, the English faculty started with some clear thinking about the meaning of academic success in their classrooms and communicated that meaning effectively with their students, parents and school board members through the thoughtful use of performance rating schemes in combination with examples of student performance, both of which reflected that vision. Sound assessment requires clear thinking and effective communication—not merely the quantification of ill-defined achievement targets.

While many assessments do translate levels of achievement into scores, we are coming to understand two important realities more and more clearly. First, numbers are not the only way to communicate about achievement. We can use words, pictures, illustrations, examples, and many other means to convey meaning about student achievement. Second, the symbols used as the basis of our communication about student achievement are only as meaningful and useful as the definitions of achievement that underpin them and the quality of the assessments used to produce them.

Assessment literates are critical consumers of assessment information. They are constantly asking, Precisely what is being assessed here and how do I know what the results mean? They do not rest until they achieve a sharp focus: clear thinking and effective communication, both in their own assessments and those of others.

Guiding Principle 2: Classroom Assessment Is Key

Teachers direct the assessments that determine what students learn and how those students feel about that learning. In our opening account, the assessments that contributed to a stronger writing program were not the districtwide tests reported at the beginning of the board presentation. Rather, the critical assessments were those carried out by English teachers in their classrooms from the beginning to the end of the school year.

Yet, in most educational contexts, it is the standardized district, state, national, or even international assessment results that command all of the resources, news coverage, and political power, as though they were the only assessments that count. Nothing could be further from the truth. While these highly visible assessments do contribute to the quality of schools, they are not even in the same league as teachers' classroom assessments in terms of their direct impact on student well-being.

Nearly all of the assessment events that take place in students' lives happen at the behest of their teachers. The typical teacher can spend as much as one-third to one-half of his or her professional time involved in assessment-related activities (Stiggins & Conklin, 1992). Teachers make decisions about how to interact with their students at the average rate of one every two to three minutes—and most of those have antecedents in an assessment of student achievement—asking questions and interpreting answers, watching students perform, examining homework assignments, and using tests and quizzes, among other means (Shavelson & Stern, 1981). Assessment is almost continuous in many classrooms.

Clearly, classroom assessments are the assessments that are most available to teachers. They also are most closely aligned with day-to-day instruction and are most influential in terms of their contribution to student, teacher, and parent decision making (see Guiding Principle 3). Without question, teachers are the drivers of the assessment systems that determine the effectiveness of the schooling process.

Time for Reflection

It is not uncommon in the professional literature on assessment to see standardized tests referred to as the "high-stakes" assessments, while classroom assessments often are labeled "informal" assessments. In research completed at Stanford University (Haertel et al., 1984), high school students were asked how much importance they attached to their teachers' classroom assessments versus the district's standardized tests. Which do you think they see as "high stakes" and why?

Guiding Principle 3: Students Are Assessment Users

Students are the most important users of assessment results. In our opening vignette, Emily and her classmates learned to improve because their performance was directly compared to very high—and clearly stated—standards of quality performance. They learned to understand these standards through direct interaction with their teachers, based on practice in the presence of regular ongoing feedback on their progress via classroom assessments.

Consider the role of student as consumer of assessment results: Right from the time students arrive at school, they look to their teachers for evidence of their success. If that early evidence suggests that they are succeeding, what begins to grow in them is a sense of hopefulness and an expectation of more success in the future. This in turn fuels the motivation to try, which fuels even more success. The basis of this upward spiral is the evidence of their own achievement, which students receive from their teacher based on ongoing classroom assessments. Thus, classroom assessment information is the essential fuel that powers the learning system for students.

However, when the evidence suggests to students that they are not succeeding in this place called school, what can also begin to grow in them is a sense of hopelessness and an expectation of more failure in the future. This can rob them of the motivation to try, which in turn can lead to more failure and a downward spiral. Here again we see consequences of classroom assessment evidence, but this time as the fuel that drives the motivation not to try.

I do not mean to imply that all assessment results should be positive simply to keep students involved and motivated. On the contrary, if students are not meeting our high standards, our assessments must accurately reflect that fact. But if those results reflect a lack of academic success, we must act to change our instructional approach to prevent the pattern of failure from becoming chronic. We must find a different formula that brings to the student some hope of future success and we must use ongoing classroom assessments to reveal that success to our students.

There are many important assessment users at all levels of the educational process. We will study them in depth in Chapter 2. However, only students use the assessment results to set expectations of themselves. Students decide how high to aim based on their sense of the probability that they will succeed. They estimate the probability of future success based on their record of past success as reflected in their prior classroom assessment experience. No single decision or combination of decisions made by any other party exerts greater influence on student success.

Time for Reflection

What do you think are some other decisions students make based on classroom assessments of their achievement? Which of these do you think are most important? Why? Write down your ideas and save them to refer to when you get to Chapter 2, where we address assessment users and uses in detail.

Guiding Principle 4: Clear and Appropriate Targets Are Essential

The quality of any assessment depends first and foremost on the clarity and appropriateness of our definition of the achievement target to be assessed. In the opening vignette, a breakthrough in student writing achievement occurred because the English faculty returned from that summer institute with a shared vision of writing proficiency. They built their program, and thus the competence of their students, around that vision.

We cannot assess academic achievement effectively if we do not know and understand what that valued target is. There are many different kinds of valued achievement expectations within our educational system, from mastering content knowledge to complex problem solving, from performing a flute recital to speaking Spanish to writing a strong term paper. All are important. But to assess them well, we must ask ourselves: Do we know what it means to do it well? Precisely what does it mean to succeed academically? We are ready to assess only when we can answer these questions with clarity and confidence.

If my job is to teach students to become better writers, I had better start with a highly refined vision of what good writing looks like and a sense of how to help my students meet that standard. If my mission is to promote math problem solving proficiency, I had better be a confident, competent master of that performance domain myself. Without a sense of final destination reflected in my standards and sign posts along the way against which to check the progress of my students, I will have some difficulty being an effective teacher.

Guiding Principle 5: High-quality Assessment Is a Must

High-quality assessment is essential in all assessment contexts. Sound assessments satisfy five specific quality standards. All assessments must meet all standards. No exceptions can be tolerated, because to violate any of them is to place student academic well-being in jeopardy. These five standards, described here, are illustrated in Figure 1–2. This is the first of many discussions and illustrations of these quality standards that permeate this book. On this first pass, I intend only to give you a general sense of the meaning of *quality*.

Clear Targets.   First, sound assessments arise from and reflect clear achievement targets (as in Guiding Principle #4). You can ask this question about any assessment: Can the developer and user provide a clear and appropriate description of the specific achievement expectation(s) it is designed to reflect? If the answer is yes, proceed to the next standard. If the answer is no, realize that there is a very real danger of misassessment. As educators, we must all be confident, competent masters of the achievement targets we expect our students to master.

In the chapters that follow, we will define the teacher's classroom assessment challenge as including the need to assess four interrelated forms of achievement expectation, as well as dispositional expectations. We alluded to all of these in the chapter objectives. Most teachers expect their students to master content knowledge sufficiently to be able to use that knowledge productively to reason and solve problems. In addition, many teachers expect their students to develop specified skills and be able to use those skills productively to create products that meet certain standards of quality. Finally, most teachers hope their students will be predisposed to use their various academic proficiencies to meet the highest standards when presented with opportunities to do so within and beyond school. Assessment quality standard number one asks that those who develop or select classroom assessments begin that process with a refined sense of the specific knowledge, reasoning, skill, product, and disposition expectations they hold for their students. In other words, they must understand *what* they are assessing.

Focused Purpose.   This standard admonishes us also to begin the design process with a clear sense of *why* we are conducting the assessment. It is impossible to develop a quality assessment unless and until we know how we will use the results

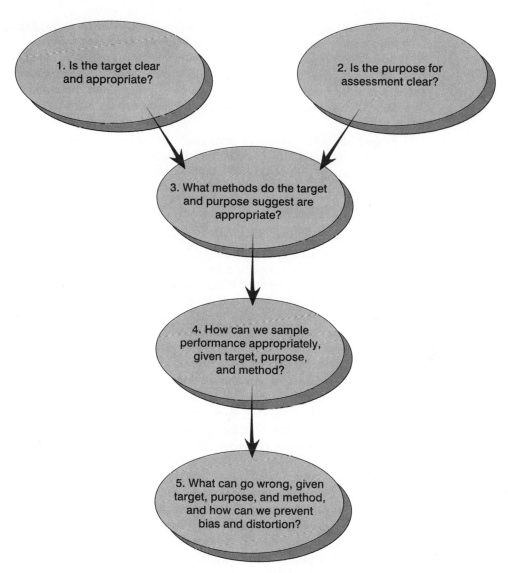

Figure 1–2
Keys to Sound Assessment

it produces. So again, about any assessment you can ask: Does the developer understand the intended uses and has the developer taken user(s') needs into account in developing and implementing the assessment?

In Chapter 2, we discuss the information needs of a dozen different assessment users at three levels of concern. First, there are those who use assessment results at the classroom level: students, teachers, and parents. Each user brings certain information needs to the classroom assessment table, and all needs must be met for schools to be effective. Then there are users at the instruction support level (principals, support teachers, curriculum personnel, etc.), and finally at the policy level (superintendents, school board members, state department personnel, etc.). Each brings unique information needs and has a right to have those needs met by our assessment systems. There is no single assessment capable of meeting all of these different needs. Thus, the developer of any assessment must start with a clear sense of whose needs the assessment will meet.

Proper Method.   A sound assessment examines student achievement through the use of a method that is, in fact, capable of reflecting the valued target. To test mastery of scientific knowledge, we might use a multiple-choice test. But when our challenge is to assess the ability to speak Spanish, we must turn to another method altogether. As stated, we have several different kinds of achievement to assess. As you will see in later chapters, we have several different kinds of assessment methods to use to reflect them. These include selected response methods (multiple choice, true/false, matching and fill in), essay assessments, performance assessments (based on observation and judgment), and direct personal communication with students (talking with them). Our classroom assessment challenge is to know how to match the method with the intended target. About any assessment, you can ask: Is the method used here capable of accurately reflecting the kinds of outcomes the user wishes to assess? If the answer is yes, proceed to the next standard. If it is no, be aware that student achievement is about to be misassessed.

Sound Sampling.   Almost all assessments rely on a sample of all the exercises we could have included if time were unlimited and the test could be infinitely long. A sound assessment offers a representative sample that is large enough to yield confident inferences about how the respondent would have done given all possible exercises. The realities of classroom life require that we generalize from our sample to the total performance arena being assessed. Each different classroom assessment context places its own special constraints on our sampling procedures. Our challenge is to know how to adjust our sampling strategies as context varies to produce results of maximum quality at minimum cost in time and effort. About any assessment, you can ask: Have we gathered enough information of the right kind, so we can draw confident conclusions about student achievement? If the answer is yes, proceed. If it is no, critical consumers of assessment information should be concerned about student well-being.

Accurate Assessment Free of Bias and Distortion.   Finally, this standard demands that we design, develop, and use assessments in ways that permit us to control for all sources of bias and distortion that can cause our results to misrepresent real student achievement. Again, each assessment context presents its own unique sources of interference with accurate assessment. Each assessment method permits errors to creep in when we let our guard down. With multiple-choice tests, for example, poorly written or culturally biased test items can harm the quality of resulting scores. With performance assessments, evaluator prejudice can bias judgments. And so it is with all methods. Our challenge is to know all sources of bias and distortion that can rob assessment results of clear and appropriate meaning and to know how to head off those problems before they get a foothold. About any assessment, you can ask: Have the important sources of bias been accounted for during development and use? If the answer is no, you must take or urge action to address unaccounted-for sources of error.

Violate any of these five criteria and you place students at risk. Problems arise when assessments are developed and used by those who fail to understand the valued outcome, fail to identify user needs, select an improper assessment method, sample achievement inadequately, or introduce bias. Unsound assessments can lead to misdiagnosed needs, failure to provide needed instructional support, use of inappropriate instructional approaches, counterproductive grouping of students, and misinformation provided to student and parent decision makers.

Guiding Principle 6: Understand Personal Implications

Assessment is an interpersonal activity. This principle has two important dimensions. The first has to do with one important reality of life in classrooms: Students are people, and teachers are people too, and sometimes we like each other and sometimes we don't. Because our assessment methods virtually always include a subjective aspect—where teacher judgment plays a role—there is always the danger that our personal feelings about students can creep into our judgments and bias the results. Unless we are aware of the dangers of this kind of distortion and remain vigilant to the need to remain as objective as possible, we stand the risk of inaccurately assessing the achievement of our students. Judgmental assessment is perfectly acceptable as long as we control for personal sources of bias. We will explore many ways to do this as our journey continues.

Second, assessment is a very complex interpersonal activity that is virtually always accompanied by personal antecedents and personal consequences. Classroom assessments are never the dispassionate, totally objective scientific acts some make them out to be. When we allow our students to be assessed, we expose them to the possibility of academic and personal benefit and harm. In the face of assessment and evaluation, as students or as adults, we are all vulnerable. Our assessments link our students to their constantly emerging academic and personal self-concepts. They provide students with the link to their sense of control over their own well-being in school. Students are more likely to feel in control when they know how to succeed and feel they can influence their own destiny (Messick, 1989). They lose control when they either don't understand the meaning of success or feel doomed to fail. Sound assessments can keep them feeling in control.

This means we must always strive for the highest-quality assessment, communicate results in a sensitive and private manner, and anticipate results so as to be prepared to offer specific support to students at any level whose achievement is low.

Time for Reflection

Think of a time in your life as a student when an assessment of your achievement made you feel good about yourself as a learner. What was it about that particular experience that left you feeling so good? Think of a time when an assessment left you with a negative academic self-concept. What was it about that experience that was so negative? What differentiated the two experiences?

Guiding Principle 7: Assessment as Teaching and Learning

Assessments and instruction can be one and the same if and when we want them to be. Sometimes, it's all right to conduct an assessment merely as a status check not linked to an immediate action. However, at other times it's a great idea to turn assessment events into powerful instructional tools. An excellent way to accomplish this is to involve students as partners in the assessment process.

Scriven (personal communication, 1995) provides us with a sense of the different levels of student involvement in the assessment process. Starting with very superficial involvement, each level brings the student further into the actual assessment equation. Students can do the following:

- take the test and receive the grade
- be invited to offer the teacher comments on how to improve the test
- suggest possible assessment exercises
- actually develop assessment exercises
- assist the teacher in devising scoring criteria
- create the scoring criteria on their own
- apply scoring criteria to the evaluation of their own performance
- come to understand how the assessment and evaluation processes affect their own academic success
- come to see how their own self-assessment relates to the teacher's assessment and to their own academic success

Perhaps the greatest potential value of classroom assessment is realized when we open the assessment process up and welcome students into that process as full partners. Please understand that I do not simply mean having students trade test papers or homework assignments so they can grade each other's work. That's strictly clerical stuff. This concept of full partnership goes far deeper.

Students who participate in the thoughtful analysis of quality work so as to identify its critical elements or to internalize valued achievement targets become better performers. When students learn to apply those standards so thoroughly as to be able to confidently and competently evaluate their own and each other's work, they are well down the road to becoming better performers in their own right. Consider Emily's case in the opening vignette. Her teacher helped her to internalize key elements of good writing so she could understand the shortcomings of her own writing, take responsibility for improving on them, and watch herself improve. Her confidence and competence in being a partner in assessment in her classroom came through loud and clear, both in the parent-teacher conference she led at midyear and in her commentary to the school board at the end of the year. I offer many specific suggestions for melding assessment and instruction in this way throughout this text on "student-centered" classroom assessment.

Time for Reflection

In your past, did you ever work with a teacher who succeeded in turning an assessment event into a positive constructive learning experience for you? Specifically, how did that teacher do so? What do you think might be some keys to turning assessment experiences into learning experiences for students? Brainstorm some ideas and save your list for later reference.

Chapter Summary: The Critical Role of Assessment Literacy

Considered together, the seven guiding principles discussed in this chapter form the foundation of the assessment wisdom all educators must master in order to manage classroom assessment environments effectively. Thus, in a sense, they underpin classroom assessment competence.

Those teachers who are prepared to meet the challenges of classroom assessment understand that they need to do their assessment homework and be ready to think clearly and to communicate effectively at assessment time. They understand why it is critical to be able to communicate their expectations to their students and their families and why it is essential that assessments be done well and also accurately reflect achievement expectations.

Well-prepared teachers realize that they lie at the heart of the assessment process in schools and they take that responsibility very seriously. Unfortunately, as you shall see in the next chapter, as a society and as a community of professional educators, we have not supported teachers over the decades in their preparation to fulfill this responsibility. But this is changing, as professional development in assessment is becoming an increasingly prominent educational priority.

Competent teachers understand the complexities of aligning a range of valued achievement targets with appropriate assessment methods so as to produce information on student achievement that both they and their students can count on to be accurate. They understand the meaning of sound assessment and they know how to use all of the assessment tools at their disposal to produce accurate information.

Effective classroom assessors-teachers understand the interpersonal dynamics of classroom assessment and know how to set students up for success, in part through using the appropriate assessment as a teaching tool. They know how to make students full partners in the processes of defining the valued outcomes of instruction and transforming those definitions into quality assessments.

As teachers bring students into the assessment process, thus demystifying the meaning of success in the classroom, they acknowledge that students use assessment results to make the decisions that ultimately will determine if school does or does not work for them. Our collective classroom assessment challenge is to be sure students have the information they need, in a form they understand, and in time to use it effectively.

Exercises to Advance Your Learning

Knowledge

1. Refer back to the seven guiding principles of sound classroom assessment often and keep them in mind throughout our journey into the realm of student-centered assessment.

2. Memorize the five key attributes of a sound assessment. Prepare to use them as the threads that bind together the rest of this book and the future of your classroom assessment work.

Reasoning

1. Translate the seven guiding principles into your own words and write a brief paragraph conveying your interpretation of each.

2. Translate the five key attributes of a sound assessment into your own words and write a brief paragraph conveying your interpretation of each.

Dispositions

1. Some contend that it has been a mistake to rely so completely on multiple-choice tests over the years as indicators of school achievement. They feel that we should turn to total reliance on performance assessments. What are your initial thoughts about the emphasis we should place on different assessment methods?

2. Guiding Principle 2 holds that classroom assessment is relatively more important than standardized tests to student well-being. Do you agree? Why?

3. Guiding Principle 3 holds that students are the most important users of classroom assessment results. Do you agree? Why?

4. Quality assessment is presented as essential in this chapter. Yet sometimes we just don't have the resources needed (time, materials, etc.) to achieve such quality. When a teacher knows this to be the case, what should she or he do, in your opinion?

2

Understanding the Critical Roles of Assessment

CHAPTER ROADMAP

The itinerary for this part of our journey leads us through an analysis of the different users and uses of assessment. We will explore not only who is served by assessments at various levels, but precisely how they are served (Figure 2–1). What kinds of information do they need and what kinds of assessment are likely to meet those needs? As you learn about instructional, instructional support, and policy level uses of assessment, you will master relevant knowledge by being able to do the following:

1. Identify the important users of assessment results.
2. Sample the most important uses of assessment.
3. List some of the key questions each user must answer with assessment results.
4. Specify the kind(s) of assessment information each user needs to make particular decisions.

As you shall see, this analysis of users and uses offers a balanced perspective regarding the need for quality at all levels. Both classroom and large-scale assessment serve important purposes. Both make contributions. So our reasoning objectives for this chapter are to make clear why standardized testing and classroom assessment are different and to promote clearer understanding of the implications of those differences. For this reason, after we analyze and compare users and uses, we will contrast classroom assessment and large-scale standardized testing in terms of the following:

1. The foundational assumptions from which they arise.
2. Their respective definitions of assessment quality.

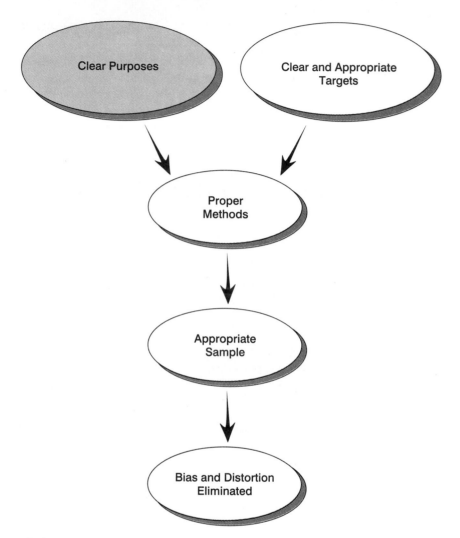

Figure 2–1
Key to Sound Assessment No. 1: A Sense of Purpose

3. The assessment methodologies used in each context.

4. Differences in interpretation and reporting of results.

Then, having framed classroom assessment in the larger context of all uses of assessment in schools, we will introduce a major theme of this text: How to use the classroom assessment process as a teaching strategy to promote higher levels of student motivation to strive for excellence, and ultimately achieve higher levels of achievement for more students.

Finally, having completed your work on this chapter, I hope you will be predisposed to do the following:

1. Value high-quality assessment and desire to work on behalf of quality classroom assessment for the sake of your students.

2. Acknowledge the contribution of quality assessment to student well-being at all educational levels.

3. See instructional value in student involvement in the classroom assessment process.

The objectives of this chapter do not include the mastery of any process skills or the creation of any products.

Our classroom assessment challenge is to understand the difference between sound and unsound assessment according to the five standards of quality listed in Chapter 1. Only by meeting these standards can we be sure we are accurately assessing achievement and using the results effectively to promote each student's academic well-being. To reiterate, then, sound assessments

- are designed to serve clearly defined purposes (i.e., to serve specific users in particular ways)
- arise from a clearly articulated set of achievement expectations
- rely on a proper assessment method capable of accurately reflecting the target(s)
- sample student performance in a representative manner with sufficient depth to permit confident conclusions about proficiency
- strive for accurate assessment by eliminating all relevant sources of bias and distortion that can lead to mismeasurement

Assessing for a Reason

In this chapter, we deal with the first of these standards of quality, the need to know our assessment purposes. As our discussion of purposes unfolds, you will learn how many users count on you to assess accurately.

High-quality assessments are specifically designed or selected to fit into the context for which they are intended. The context dictates the manner in which assessments are to be used—the purposes for assessing. Quality assessments arise from and serve clear and specific purposes. Therefore, if we are to devise effective assessments, we must begin with a refined answer to the questions, Why are we assessing? How will the assessment and its results be used? It is impossible to select or design and develop an assessment to serve a need unless and until we know what that need is: who is to be served and how.

As you shall see, assessments serve many masters in schools and there is no single assessment mode or event capable of serving all users. Different purposes require different assessment plans.

To understand the range of roles assessment plays in teaching and learning, we must appreciate how deeply assessment is woven into our educational fabric. With this broad view in mind, we can zero in on applications of assessment in the classroom, our primary focus. That big picture shows us that assessment serves policy makers, those who provide teachers with instructional support, and teachers, students, and parents—all users of assessment during the actual teaching and learning process in the classroom. Within the classroom, assessments serve two key purposes: The process serves as a powerful teaching tool, and the results inform instructional decision making. Each different level of use is important. Each has a profound impact on the nature and quality of instruction and therefore on student well-being. In this chapter, we examine why that impact is so great.

Assessments That Inform Decisions

If we are to plan instruction to meet student needs, we must ascertain what those needs are. If we seek to find the most effective instructional strategies, we must decide which have the most positive impact on achievement. To make these and other instructionally relevant decisions, we need accurate information on student achievement. Let's analyze the full array of decisions that can be informed with quality achievement information (Figure 2–2).

The many and varied ways that assessment results can inform decision makers are spelled out in Tables 2–1, 2–2, and 2–3. These presentations describe how each assessment user's roles and responsibilities contribute to student success, by depicting three levels at which assessment results can come into play.

The first level is that of instruction. Students, teachers, and parents gather and use the results of student achievement assessment to inform a variety of decisions that influence the effectiveness of instruction.

The second level is that of instructional support. Decision makers at this level back teachers up with whatever help they may need in the form of curricular, professional development, and/or resource support. Backup may come from the department, building, or district level, or beyond.

The final level of assessment use is the policy level. This is where the standards are put in place that govern practice in the school building and in the classroom. Policy influencers, policy makers, and those who enforce policy include the superintendent, the school board, public officials (appointed and elected), and citizens of the community.

Taken together, assessment users in these three categories make the decisions that determine whether schools work for any individual child, or for all children considered collectively. While I am of the opinion that decisions made at the classroom level contribute the most to student success, please understand that, in an

Figure 2–2
A Concrete Foundation for Maximum Learning

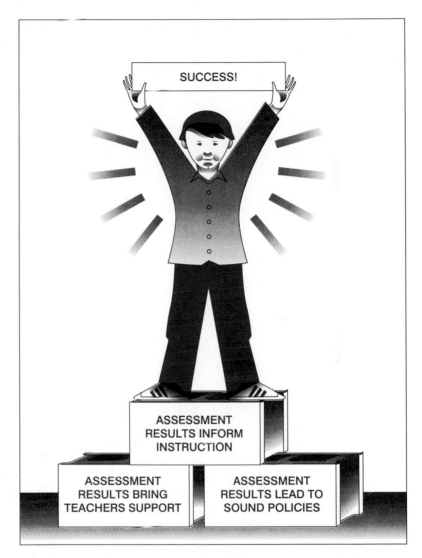

absolute sense, all parties listed in Tables 2–2 and 2–3 make important contributions too and their information needs all deserve careful attention.

Column one of each table lists the various decision makers whose decisions are (or can be) informed by assessment results. Column two lists samples of the kinds of decisions they make based at least in part on assessment results of some kind. These are not intended to be exhaustive. In column three, I translate each use into a sample question that the user might face in that decision-making context. Ideally, the answer will suggest which course of action to take—the ultimate decision.

To answer each question, the user needs certain kinds of information about students, information reflective of their achievement. Those information needs are identified in the fourth column. We will explore key dimensions of those information needs after you have an opportunity to examine the tables.

Table 2–1
Users and Uses of Assessment Results—Instructional Level

Users	Sample Uses	Key Question(s) to be Answered	Information Needed
Student	Track own success	Am I meeting the teacher's standards?	Ongoing assessment of mastery of required material
	Identify own needs	What help do I need to succeed?	Ongoing assessment of building blocks of competence
	Connect effort to results	Does my work pay off?	Continuous assessment of mastery of material student is trying to learn
	Plan for educational and vocational needs	What will be the next steps in my learning?	Assessment of targets that are prerequisites for later possibilities
Teacher	Identify needs of individuals	What does this student need help with?	Continuous assessment of individual mastery
	Identify needs of class or group	What do these students need help with?	Continuous assessment summarized over group
	Group students	Who among my students should work together?	Periodic assessment of individual mastery (if grouped by achievement)
	Grade	What grade should appear in the report card?	Summary of individual mastery of required material
	Evaluate instruction	Did my teaching strategies work?	Continuous assessment of group performance
	Evaluate self	How do I need to develop to be a better teacher?	Continuous assessment of group performance
Parent	Track child's success	Is my child succeeding in school?	Continuous feedback on student's mastery of material
	Identify needs	What does my child need in order to succeed?	Continuous feedback on student's mastery of material
	Evaluate teacher	Is my child's teacher(s) doing the job?	Continuous feedback on student's mastery of material
	Evaluate school	Is this school (district) working for my family?	Periodic comparison of school performance with that of other schools

Table 2-2
Users and Uses of Assessment Results—Instructional Leadership/Support Level

Users	Sample Uses	Key Question(s) to be Answered	Information Needed
Principal/ Vice Principal	Evaluate instructional program	Is instruction in particular areas producing results?	Periodic assessment of group achievement
	Evaluate teachers	Is the teacher producing results?	Periodic assessment of group achievement
		Does the teacher meet minimal performance standards?	Periodic assessment of group achievement
		What kinds of professional development would help this teacher?	Periodic assessment of group achievement
	Allocate resources	How shall we spend building resources in support of instruction?	Periodic assessment of group achievement
Support Teacher (mentor, lead teacher, department chair)	Assist new teachers	What does this teacher need to assure competence?	Continuous assessment of group achievement
	Support instructional program	Which teacher(s) need what help to do the job?	Periodic assessment of group achievement
Counselor/ Psychologist	Identify students with special needs	Who needs (can have access to) special support services such as remedial programs?	Periodic assessment of individual achievement
	Match students to program	What student should be assigned to which teachers to optimize results?	Periodic assessment of individual achievement
Curriculum Director	Evaluate program quality	Is the program in a particular area of instruction working?	Periodic assessment of group achievement

Table 2-3
Users and Uses of Assessment Results—Policy Level

Users	Sample Uses	Question(s) to be Answered	Information Needed
Superintendent	Evaluate program	Are programs producing student learning?	Periodic assessment of group achievement of district curriculum
	Evaluate principals	Is the building principal producing results?	Periodic assessment of group achievement of district/building curriculum
	Allocate resources	Which schools need/deserve more or fewer resources?	Periodic assessment of group achievement of district curriculum
School board	Evaluate program	Are students in the district learning?	Periodic assessment of group achievement
	Evaluate superintendent	Is the superintendent producing results?	Periodic assessment of group achievement
State department of education	Evaluate program	Are programs across the state producing results?	Periodic assessment of group achievement of state curriculum
Citizen/Legislator (state or national)	Evaluate program	Are students in our schools achieving in ways that will allow them to be effective citizens?	Periodic assessment of group achievement of valued achievement

Time for Reflection

Before continuing, study Tables 2–1, 2–2 and 2–3 carefully. What conclusions or generalizations can you draw from the contents of each? How are the stories told by each table the same? How do they differ? Jot down your thoughts on this before reading on.

The following generalizations seem warranted on the basis of Table 2–1:

- All three assessment users—students, teachers, and parents—make decisions that bear directly on whether instruction produces the desired achievement within each individual student.

- While we most often think of students as the examinees and not as examiners, they clearly are (or at least can be) assessors of their own academic progress and they use those results in some compelling ways.

- Given the manner in which assessment results fit into day-to-day classroom decision making, in all cases, assessment must be a continuous process. These are continuously recurring decisions. This is precisely why classroom assessment events are so much more frequent in a student's life than any other kind of assessment.

- At this level, assessment virtually always focuses on the individual student's mastery of specified material. Standards of acceptable achievement must be set by the teacher, if assessments are to show whether students have satisfied the requirements.

We see the following patterns in the information presented in Table 2–2:

- In almost every case, the focus of the decisions to be made is on the instructional program or the teacher, not on the individual student.

- Thus, attention at this level is given to assessments of student performance summarized over groups.

- Assessment need only be periodic, not continuous.

- At this level, heavy reliance is placed on the use of assessment results in which assessment instruments or procedures are held constant across classrooms. In other words, some standardization is required if sound decisions are to result.

We can make the following generalizations on the basis of the information in Table 2–3:

- The focus is on broad domains of achievement, not specific objectives of instruction.

- Also as with the support level, results summarized across students fill the need.

- As with the instructional support level, periodic assessment seems to suffice.

- And finally, at this level too, assessment procedures must be standardized to some degree across contexts and over time. The decisions to be made require it.

Having reflected on these three tables, do any general conclusions come to mind regarding the role of assessment in determining and enhancing the effectiveness of schools? Try these and see if you agree:

- Obviously, the assessment process is intricately woven into the effectiveness of school functioning. Often the degree of complexity of this portrait of the various assessments is surprising to educators. Nevertheless, as teachers and instructional leaders, we must all face the complexity and come to terms with it.

- Students count on many people to use sound assessment results in productive ways. All of the questions listed in column three of all the tables are critical to student well-being. This is why we must continually strive for the absolute highest-quality assessment. It is a moral, ethical, and professional imperative of the highest order.

- Considering the tables together, it is clear that both information gathered continuously on individual student mastery of specified material *and* information gathered periodically for the purpose of comparing students serve important roles. Thus, both must reflect sensitivity to the principles of sound assessment.

Given this summary of all of the decision-oriented users and uses of assessment, it becomes clear that any assessment policy, any educator, or any educational assessment practice that fails to acknowledge the critically important role of classroom and large-scale assessment places students *directly* in harm's way. We need to maintain a balanced perspective about the valuable role of assessment at all levels.

At the risk of appearing redundant, however, let me reiterate my belief that not all levels of assessment use are equally important. If teachers are devising and using poor-quality assessments on a day-to-day basis in the classroom, all other levels of assessment become irrelevant. If the instructional-level decisions are being made on the basis of inaccurate assessment results, sound assessments and decisions at instructional support or policy levels cannot overcome the damage that will result.

Contrasting Classroom and Large-scale Standardized Assessment

Classroom assessment and standardized testing are different disciplines within the educational assessment field. They serve users in different ways. Classroom assessments serve instructional purposes, as illustrated in Table 2–1. Large-scale standardized tests serve instructional support and policy-making purposes, as illustrated in Tables 2–2 and 2–3. These two kinds of assessments arise out of different assumptions about the assessment process, define quality assessment in different ways, and rely on fundamentally different assessment methods. They both are important—but they are different.

To explain some of the key differences, let's begin by reflecting on a message from the past. Over 50 years ago, Professor Robert Scates of Duke University wrote eloquently of the differences between the science of objective testing as it emerged in the late 1920s and the art of classroom assessment as carried out by teachers. The lessons he left for us are worth learning today.

A View from the Past

Scates (1943) points out critical differences in background and training between those test experts who apply the science of assessment in the standardized testing context and teachers who ply their assessment trade in the classroom.[1]

According to Scates, differences in training prepare them to attend to different things. For example, their purposes for measuring differ: The scientist seeks to describe, while the teacher seeks to control. The scientist seeks to extract single elements from complex reality, to assess parts, to isolate traits common to all subjects. The teacher, on the other hand, must both understand and describe the complex reality of the individual child, attending to what is unique and changeful. The scientist seeks data to classify, while the teacher seeks information to use in guiding the person to more learning.

In addition, Scates writes, measurement methods differ. The scientist most commonly relies on one-time test administration conducted uniformly across all students. Comparability of results is paramount so that conclusions can be drawn across students. Feedback to the student is often less important.

The teacher, on the other hand, relies on continuous observation to both assess and evaluate what is unique to the individual. Comparability of data across learners is less important to teachers than is immediate feedback to the student—a central ingredient in teaching and learning.

Scates asserts that the scientist attends to achievement that relates only to the discipline being studied, while the teacher attends to achievements that relate to the realities of students' lives beyond school. The scientist is concerned about how well the student will do on exercises. The teacher, in contrast, worries about how all the parts come together. As Scates writes:

> The teacher's task is that of the artist—to produce as well as his vision will permit him to see what ought to be produced and as well as his techniques and materials will permit him to follow what his vision pictures. In this process he can find some use for scientific measuring instruments, but they serve only a small portion of his needs, and they are likely to upset his perspective. They will serve, on occasion, as a check on certain limited aspects of what he is trying to do, but he dare not let them shift his attention from the whole picture to the elements that the tests are likely to cover. For he is an integrator, not a scientist. (p. 13)

---

[1]Adapted from "Differences Between Measurement Criteria of Pure Scientists and of Classroom Teachers" by R. E. Scates, from *Journal of Educational Research* (September 1943). Copyright 1943 by *Journal of Educational Research*.

A Connection to Today

One need not read Scates too deeply to understand that he was concerned about the centralized, standardized testing programs emerging in schools in the 1930s and 1940s. His was the perspective of the humanist concerned about the child and about the harm testing could do to the well-being of children and teachers. Today, five decades later, many also urge caution when using standardized tests because of their unintended consequences for schools and student well-being (Neil & Medina, 1991; Smith & Rottenberg, 1991).

My intent is not to enter into that argument, as I think this debate is counterproductive. As you saw above, a long list of assessment users need many different kinds of information to meet their various needs. We have a range of complex achievement targets to assess. We will need all the tools we have at our disposal to do this job. We cannot afford to throw any—including standardized tests—away. Our challenge is to find ways to use all of these tools well and to use them in balance, as in the school board meeting vignette in Chapter 1.

Because quality assessments are so essential for student success and academic well-being, I believe we must follow the trail marked by Scates some 50 years ago, pushing the comparison even further and highlighting additional differences. Only through this kind of analysis can we maintain the balance in assessment perspectives.

Different Goals and Roles

The underlying assumptions that guide classroom and large-scale assessment contain more differences than Scates noted. For instance, large-scale assessments are seen as the guardians of our educational standards. We use them as hallmarks, as we strive to keep those standards high. That is, we set as our public goal the desire to attain the highest possible test scores.

The role of assessment in the classroom, on the other hand, is to serve as an instructional tool helping teachers meet student needs. Teachers need accurate scores for each student, which may not be the highest possible scores.

This leads to profound differences in both the goal and the role of the assessor. Often, the covert political goal in the large-scale context, as defined by those in authority, is to attain scores that represent the school program, building, and system in the most positive light. The assessor's challenge often is to obtain the most positive data for the assessment resources invested. Frankly, this is calculated to keep those in authority looking effective in front of the community, their constituency.

The teacher's goal, on the other hand, is to make decisions that benefit students. The challenge in this case is to obtain the most usable data for the assessment resources invested.

Very often, the assessment specialist charged with conducting standardized tests acts as the servant of the decision makers, providing the results and then stepping aside. In essence, the data speak for themselves. The teacher, on the other hand, plays all roles, including those of assessor, interpreter, and user of the results. The teacher not only has a vested interest in the results, but the truly effective teacher also collaborates with the student and parent to attain the highest level of performance possible from each student (without violating standards of ethical practice, such as by cheating). In the case of classroom assessment, the data speak only when understood in the context of the student whose achievement is reflected therein.

Differences in the Meaning of Quality

This leads us to differences in the definition of *sound assessment*. The underlying basis of wisdom that defines the meaning of a quality assessment differs between the two contexts. In the large-scale assessment case, that wisdom is described in the professional journals of the test expert. A good test is one that satisfies clearly articulated validity standards (accurately reflects what experts say students should achieve), reliability standards (produces consistent scores), and efficiency standards (produces maximum-quality results for minimum investment of time and money). Testing experts have formulas that permit them to quantify these indexes of test quality. They judge a test to be of high quality if those mathematical indicators are sufficiently high.

In the classroom, however, the literature that defines a sound assessment is that which describes our understanding of the teaching and learning process. Sound assessments, in a teacher's mind, promote learning on the part of the student. Teachers often will say an assessment "worked" if that assessment promoted or provided evidence of growth. This is not to say validity, reliability, and efficiency standards are unimportant. Certainly, they are critical. But teachers virtually never quantify the technical quality of their assessments as psychometricians do. They strive to maximize the impact of their assessments.

To amplify just a bit, for the test technician, the quality of an assessment is a technical matter. The focus of the investigation of quality is on the test. There is the threat of negative sanctions from the measurement community (American Psychological Association, 1985) for those who fail to adhere to published professional standards of test quality.

But for the teacher, quality is not primarily a technical matter. Typically, for teachers it is a people matter. The focus of the investigation of quality is on its impact on students. Assessment works effectively, in the teacher's eye, when it reveals strengths and weaknesses in student performance—when it suggests concrete action on the part of teacher and/or student.

There is virtually never an external review of assessment quality in the classroom, because the sanctity of that classroom has generally been considered inviolate. The only standards normally involved are the teacher's own ethical ones and whatever standards of assessment quality the teacher acquired as a result of professional preparation to teach.

Please understand that this does not mean that teachers should not care about the technical quality of their assessments. They definitely should. The entire point of this book is that, given proper training and support resources, teachers can design and develop sound assessments. But for teachers, the meaning of quality often goes beyond technicalities to issues of student well-being.

More Differences in Methodology

Because classroom and large-scale assessment serve different purposes, they provide different forms of information and must, therefore, rely on different forms of assessment to deliver that information. Let's compare these methods just a bit more.

Large-scale assessments tend to rely on the objective paper and pencil test format to produce acceptable data at minimal cost. Huge numbers of tests can be machine-scored very quickly, and computers can generate interpretable score reports with relative ease. It is often the case, out of necessity, that the fidelity of large-scale assessment results be sacrificed somewhat for the sake of economy. Later, we will discuss some attempts to move beyond multiple-choice tests to the use of more complex and much more expensive methods.

Because of the broad scope and considerable cost of these assessments, they tend to occur infrequently, often no more than once a year. Also, the time allotted for completing them is quite limited, often allowing only minutes per subject matter area tested.

For this reason, very broad achievement targets are defined, often covering two or three grade levels of content with relatively few selected response items. Thus, the content coverage is very shallow. From these samples, then, extrapolations are drawn to broad achievement domains. These tests typically are not high-resolution microscopes.

Classroom assessment methods are different. In the classroom, assessment in one form or another is almost continuous. The amount of time allocated for classroom assessment is considerable, often rivaling direct instruction as the most time-consuming activity of the classroom (Stiggins & Conklin, 1992).

Teachers use paper and pencil instruments as soon as students are able to read and respond to them. These include teacher-developed and text-embedded tests and quizzes, homework and seatwork assignments, and even questionnaires. Teachers also rely extensively on observation of and professional judgments about achievement-related products and behaviors, as well as personal communication with students. Examples of the latter include instructional questions, interviews, informal one-on-one discussions, and conversations with others about students. The methods of classroom assessment are far more varied than are those of large-scale assessment, as they are used by teachers more frequently to gather more varied kinds of information.

For this reason, the achievement domains teachers assess are much more numerous and precisely defined than are those of the large-scale test developer. Compared to large-scale assessments, many classroom assessments may be regarded as high-resolution microscopes. The key difference is that, in the case of classroom assessment, the focus of any individual assessment is far narrower than that of the typical large-scale test. However, because teachers can rely on many methods for data collection applied in a continuous manner over time, they, too, can draw conclusions about broad domains of achievement—if each of the composite assessments is of high quality.

Differences in Administration

Beyond these considerable differences, the conditions of test administration often differ between large-scale and classroom contexts. In large-scale assessment, conditions of administration are standardized to assure comparability of results. Tests may be speeded; that is, all students may not finish all exercises. The pace at which students can answer test items is regarded as valuable information for indexing the student's achievement level relative to those of other students.

Classroom assessments, on the other hand, might be standardized for all within the classroom or might be individualized. They might be speeded or the teacher might regard assessments as power tests, allotting enough time for each student to attempt each exercise. For the teacher, comparability often gives way to maximizing the student's demonstrated level of achievement. Empathetic teachers often strive to give students the opportunity to succeed—to give them the benefit of the doubt—so as to maximize each student's motivation to continue. The result is a different assessment environment from that of the standardized test.

Differences in Interpreting Results

When an assessment has been administered and student responses analyzed, most often a score or profile of scores results. Those scores must then be evaluated in terms of some standard(s) of acceptable performance. Large-scale and classroom assessments often differ in the way this is done.

One of two different forms of interpretation is used, depending on the purpose for the assessment. Sometimes, each student's score is compared to a preset standard or criterion of acceptable performance: Attain a score of at least 90 percent correct and your score is interpreted to be an "A." All who meet the criterion get the grade. In other instances, a student's score is compared to the scores of other students: By attaining this score, you demonstrated a level of achievement that is higher than 90 percent of your classmates. The former is called *criterion-referenced* interpretation; the latter is labeled *norm-referenced* interpretation.

Because large-scale assessments sometimes serve the purpose of ranking students from the highest to the lowest achiever—as with college admissions tests—their scores often are interpreted by comparing each examinee to a norm group. These rely on norm-referenced interpretation. In addition, however, some large-scale districtwide or statewide tests compare student scores to preestablished standards of acceptable performance. These are said to be criterion-referenced tests. We will examine examples of these in greater detail in Chapter 11. So, large-scale assessments may be either criterion or norm referenced in their interpretation.

In the classroom, however, teachers almost always assess to see if students have hit the target. You will recall that virtually every decision listed in Table 2–1 required this kind of information. For this reason, classroom assessments typically are interpreted in criterion-referenced terms.

Differences in Reporting

Large-scale assessments virtually always produce results in the form of a score or profile of scores. All scores are comparable, assuming the test administrator adhered to the standardized procedures. As a result, scores can be aggregated from the individual student to the classroom, building, district, state, region, and the nation as a whole. Large-scale assessments report summary scores, often with interpretive aids that permit comparisons of student scores. Remember from Tables 2–2 and 2–3 that this is the kind of information that serves the needs of those responsible for instructional support and policy.

Also, since assessments are infrequent, reports of performance on those assessments are infrequent also. And reports often occur well after the assessment has been conducted, because of the complexities of scoring hundreds, thousands, or even tens of thousands of papers all at once, depending on the context.

Classroom assessments, on the other hand, may not translate into scores, although they frequently do. They may rely on symbols other than numbers that do not lend themselves to summary via mathematical operations. Further, they might result in judgments, insights, and immediate actions on the part of teachers. Not only might they not be comparable for each student, but also, some assessments might involve only one or a few students, depending on the context. Assessments often have immediate instructional applications. There is rarely a delay of more than a day or two between the assessment and the return of results, and feedback is often immediate.

Clearly, classroom and large-scale assessment methods are quite different. These differences are summarized in Table 2–4. Bear them clearly in mind, now, as we review the many users and uses of assessment throughout the educational process.

Time for Reflection

Think of a time in your life as a student when you took an important classroom test prepared and administered by your teacher. Now think of a time when you took an annual standardized test. Describe the differences between these two experiences. How did you prepare for each? How did you feel going into the assessment—confident, anxious, informed about why you were being assessed? What were the differences in how you were informed of results and in how the results were used?

Using Assessment as a Teaching Tool

You can see that assessment results help us refine instruction when they produce sound information for sound decision making. But Tables 2–1 to 2–3 don't provide the complete picture of the ways assessment can enhance learning in the class-

Table 2–4
Comparing Large-scale Standardized Assessment and Classroom Assessment

Point of Difference	Large-scale	Classroom
Goal	Understand and classify, maintain highest standards	Control and guide
	Obtain highest score	Obtain most accurate score
Focus	Isolated traits common to all students tested	Combination of traits within each student
	Achievement within disciplines	Skills related to life beyond school
	Traits stable over time	Traits that change over time
Role of Assessor	Uninvolved data collector	Data collector, interpreter, and user
Method of Assessment	One time, infrequent	Continuous
	Tend to be objectively scored	Objective and subjective
	Comparability critical across classrooms	Comparability less important
	A few very efficient methods	Greater variety of methods
Administration	Standard for all	May or may not be standard for all in classroom
	Tend to be speeded	Typically power assessments
Results	Scores	Scores, descriptions, judgements, profiles, etc.
	Feedback delayed, if offered at all	Feedback immediate
Meaning of Quality	Technical standards of validity and reliability	Positive impact on student learning
	Defined by assessment field	Defined by each teacher

room. Indeed, the very process of assessing—over and above the results it produces—can provide great motivation for students to learn and can promote that learning in many concrete and specific ways.

Methods That Have Stood the Test of Time

Some of the most useful ways of using assessment in instruction have been standard operating procedures for teachers for decades. In addition, we have recently seen a blossoming of exciting new ways of bringing students into the assessment process.

One of the most common and accepted ways to use assessment to promote learning is to use it as a source of motivation arising from the promise or threat of an examination in the future. For students who care to perform well, exam time is heavy-duty study time—time to cram, time for "all nighters." Clearly, we use assessments to motivate our students to behave in academically productive ways.

Another way to mix assessment and instruction is through the use of practice tests, which give students the opportunity to analyze their achievement and prepare for one final study push before the "real" test.

Yet another simple way to use the assessment process to enhance learning is by reviewing tests with students after they have been completed and scored. By carefully going over exams with students after returning them, we hope to reinforce important concepts and address misunderstandings, and thus continue their learning.

Three more ways in which we use assessment events as teaching and learning tools are open-book exams (where new material is learned during the process of preparing responses), take-home exams (which prolong the learning process, in effect, and urge students to tap resources found outside the classroom), and collaborative exam exercises (which permit students to continue learning from each other as they respond).

These strategies integrate assessment and instruction. In a sense, they make the two indistinguishable. However, the list of ways to accomplish this need not stop here.

Additional Methods for Changing Times

We set students up for success when we make sure they know and understand what it means to succeed and help them believe they can do so. We set them up for success when we show them the target, provide practice in shooting at it, and provide an assessment forum for them to see themselves demonstrating increasingly higher levels of proficiency. By the same token, we reduce their chances of hitting the target when we keep them from understanding what it looks like or keep them in the dark about how well they are meeting our expectations.

Time for Reflection

Can you think of a time in your school years when you were left in the dark about an achievement target you were supposed to hit? What was the effect of this lack of vision on your preparation for and/or success on the subsequent assessment?

Those concerned with student attainment of specific forms of achievement can take advantage of such open channels of communication by building a special kind of teacher-student working relationship, in which we supplant a lopsided power relationship with one of collaboration. The relationship in which the teacher is the possessor of mysterious wisdom and the student's job is to solve the mystery of the meaning of success is replaced by one in which student and teacher work together to find a common meaning of successful achievement and to help the student attain that goal. The teacher as holder and manipulator of all the power cards gives way to shared power and, as a result, the total amount of learning power brought to bear in the service of student achievement is greatly increased for both teacher and student.

This means that, when I teach my assessment course, I cannot succeed until I possess a clear vision of what my students must know and be able to do to become competent assessors. Further, neither my students nor I succeed until each of them not only shares my vision, but also can translate that vision into actions that help them produce the highest-quality assessments possible for use in their classrooms. I will not be the very best teacher I can be until every one of my students can hit the target *and knows it.*

We have many means at our disposal for setting students up for success in this way. For example, we may do any of the following:

- Bring them into the process of setting targets, such as letting them play a role in defining content to be mastered, skills to be demonstrated, and problems to be solved.

- Engage them in designing, developing, administering, scoring, and interpreting the results of practice assessments.

- Have them play a role in developing the performance criteria and rating procedures to be used in carrying out performance assessments—these are assessments that rely on observations and professional judgment to evaluate achievement, as you will see later.

- Set them to work cooperatively to internalize standards of quality and evaluate their own and each other's achievement.

This list could go on and on. As we progress, we will consider many examples of practical ways to turn the assessment process over to learners, to put the standards of quality in their hands, to eliminate the mystery of success in school, and to make them full partners in the assessment process. For now, suffice it to say that assessment is no longer merely a tool for collecting data.

Time for Reflection

Can you think of a time in your educational experience when your teacher involved you in the design of the assessment you would take? What role(s) did you play? What effect did this participation have on your motivation to work hard and succeed?

Chapter Summary: Sound Assessment Becomes Essential

Without question, effective, efficient, productive instruction is impossible without sound assessment. The very fabric of the American educational system, from the classroom to the boardroom to the halls of educational policy at the highest levels, is held together by threads of assessment. While our purposes for assessing and our assessment methods may differ across levels, the decisions they lead to must be made with the best interests of students clearly in mind.

We have explored the array of differences between and among the assessments used at both classroom and policy levels. They arise from different needs, rely on different procedures, lead to different interpretations and uses, and vary greatly in scope and depth. Nevertheless, all are important. All are useful. All must meet standards of quality.

As educators, we have a strong tendency to be parochial in our point of view about assessment, attending only to our own special corner of the teaching and learning world. This chapter is intended to represent and encourage a more worldly view. Those of us who teach must realize that other decision makers at other levels also need assessment results. While their tests tend to be different in form and tend to have less direct impact on student learning, they still are worth doing for all the reasons given herein.

By the same token, those in positions of school management and policy making must also acknowledge the supremely important role of classroom assessment. Students, teachers, and parents are decision makers too and are therefore critical users of assessment information. Our assessment traditions have neither included nor valued such a multifaceted view of the assessment process and its role in instruction. As a result, our allocations of assessment resources have not reflected a balance of concern for both large-scale and classroom assessment.

When we permit the breadth and depth of our vision of assessment to stretch from students in the classroom to policy makers in the boardroom to legislators in the chambers of political power, we begin to understand why assessment competence is so critical for professional educators and why basic assessment literacy is so important for those who support the educational enterprise. Sound assessment at all levels is critical to student well-being, and to effective schools.

Exercises to Advance Your Learning

Knowledge

1. Study Table 2–1 until you can reconstruct it from memory. Never lose this sense of the diversity of needs for assessment results at many levels and for many purposes.

2. Discuss Tables 2–2 and 2–3 with a colleague or fellow student to be sure you completely understand and can explain how each line contributes to effective schools.

3. Reread the section comparing standardized and classroom assessment and construct a simple summary table in your own words listing the differences between the two.

4. List as many ways as you can for making the assessment process a part of the learning process—not just a source of scores and grades. Learn this list—we will add breadth and depth to it as we proceed through this text.

Reasoning

1. Professor Scates noted key differences between standardized and classroom assessment some 50 years ago. He pointed out the dangers of overlooking these differences and urged that attention be given to assuring the quality of both. Yet, over the decades, we have neglected the quality of classroom assessment in favor of allocating immense resources for high-quality stan-

dardized testing. Why do you think this has been the case?

2. Those who advocate doing away with standardized tests often argue that they fail to reflect important outcomes. Find a sample of a commercially published standardized test battery, check its user's guide, and examine some test items. What kinds of achievement are tested? Are they important, in your opinion? Why?

3. Identify as many reasons as you can why involving students in the process of developing, administering, scoring, and interpreting results of classroom assessment might enhance their motivation to succeed.

Dispositions

1. Some contend that to assess student achievement at all is inhumane. "Judge not lest ye be judged," they might say. Others contend that the inhumanity arises out of poor-quality assessments and not out of the assessment act itself. With whom do you agree? Why?

2. Do you feel standardized tests are, in fact, overemphasized in our school culture and society? If you believe that, why do you think this might be the case?

3. Do you think students can or should be made more prominent players in school assessment processes? Why?

3

Specifying Achievement Targets

CHAPTER ROADMAP

In Chapter 1, we described high-quality assessments as those that arise from clearly articulated achievement targets, so we can reflect those targets with proper assessments. Thus, one challenge of educators in pursuit of quality assessments is to come to consensus on a clear set of achievement expectations for students, as highlighted in Figure 3–1.

Assessors who cannot define the student characteristic(s) to be assessed will have great difficulty picking a proper assessment method, defining a proper sample of performance, and minimizing problems within the assessment itself. Further, they will find it impossible to share a clear vision of success with their students or to select promising instructional strategies. A teacher faced with the responsibility of evaluating student writing proficiency who lacks a clear vision of what good writing looks like will be ineffective. Regardless of the subject or level of education, only those with sharp visions of valued outcomes can effectively and efficiently assess student attainment of those expectations.

For this reason, we devote this entire chapter to defining achievement targets for purposes of assessment. In this context, as you read the material presented, reflect upon it, discuss it with colleagues, and complete the exercises offered at the end of the chapter, you will gain control over knowledge that includes the following:

1. Understand the important benefits of specifying clear and appropriate targets.
2. Define the risks to the teacher of being explicit about achievement expectations.
3. Be able to identify five kinds of achievement targets valued in most classrooms.
4. Know where and how to access sources of information and guidance in selecting and defining valued targets.

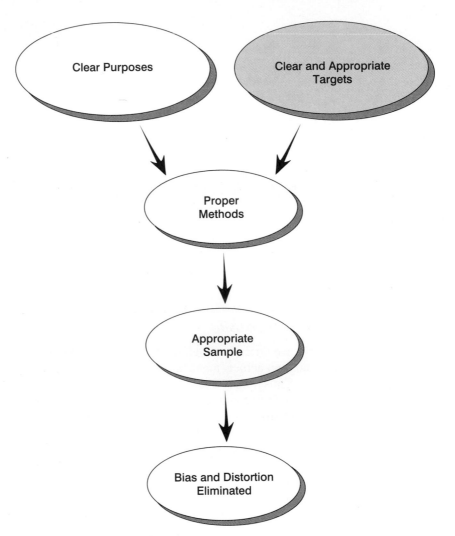

Figure 3–1
Key to Sound Assessment No. 2: Clear Targets

   5. Understand how to communicate achievement expectations to students and
      others.

Further, you will be able to build on this knowledge to reason productively about
different forms of achievement expectations in the following ways:

   1. Translate each of the five kinds of targets discussed in this chapter into real
      examples of significant targets from your own school experience.
   2. Infer what relationships exist between and among the five kinds of achieve-
      ment targets.
   3. Anticipate the impact on student well-being of trying to assess a target we, as
      teachers, do not understand.

In addition, by reading the chapter, and by pursuing the special project that begins at the end of this chapter and extends through the text, you will begin to develop skill in the process of analyzing a unit of instruction to ferret out its truly important achievement targets. The resulting product will be a set of targets ready to be aligned with appropriate assessment methods.

And finally, as a result of your work with this chapter, I hope you will become predisposed to

1. Rigorously define your achievement expectations of your students, attending to knowledge to be mastered, reasoning proficiencies, skills to be developed, and products to be created.
2. Strive to become a master yourself of any targets you must teach.

Just as we form a foundation of quality assessment by clarifying our purpose, so too do we shape that foundation by beginning the assessment process with a refined vision of the meaning of academic success. As we strive to define our achievement targets, both as guideposts for our instruction and as bases for our assessments, we benefit from the fact that the past decade has witnessed important breakthroughs in many disciplines in our understanding of the meaning of academic competence. The work of reading specialists, for example, permits teachers schooled in that work to produce more, and better readers today than ever before. And so it is with writing, and with reasoning and problem solving in math, science, and other disciplines. We will explore those developments and their assessment implications in depth in later chapters.

As we come to understand these refined visions, the added clarity will permit both teachers and students to experience higher levels of academic success than ever before. Our goal in this chapter is to understand what it means to clearly define achievement expectations in preparation for assessment.

Our Mission and the Demand for Clear Expectations

Let me set the stage for this facet of our journey with a brief history lesson about the evolution of schools in the United States and about corresponding changes in assessment priorities. In effect, this story places educators of today in the midst of rapidly changing societal, and therefore educational, needs. As you will see, the assessment implications are immense.

The Old Era

As schools evolved early in the twentieth century, they were assigned the mission of sorting students from the highest achiever (we call them *valedictorians*) to the lowest achiever. Society was satisfied to operate on the assumption that schools were working effectively if they assigned a "rank in class" to each student at the end of the educational experience. The absolute level of achievement attained by each student was less important.

This sorting process met many of society's needs during the 1920s and 1930s. It permitted students to find their way into the various levels of our social and economic system. Some would remain low in the ranking and would drop out and find work in our predominately agricultural and emerging industrial economy. Others would finish higher in the rank order and would continue into higher levels of education.

With the advent of compulsory education laws at roughly this same time, schools needed efficient ways to manage unprecedented numbers of students. By relying on a sorting process, limited resources could be put to the best use. The result was "assembly line schools," in which the amount of time allotted for learning was fixed at one year per grade, while the amount learned was left to vary across students. First graders started roughly equal in achievement. But by the end of the year, some had learned a great deal, while others had not. They took their varying levels of achievement on to second grade. There, those who had learned a great deal at the first stop on the assembly line learned a great deal more at stop two. Those who had learned little at stop one learned little more at stop two, leading to more variation in levels of achievement. And so it proceeded grade after grade, sorting students along a vast continuum of achievement. In this way, again, society could meet its need for citizens at different levels of academic achievement.

This system of education by rank order was locked into place in the 1930s with the advent of a new kind of test. This innovative assessment idea had several strong features. It was scientific in its rigor—controlling for the inherent biases and idiosyncrasies of the teacher's subjective judgment. It could be mass produced, mass administered, and mass scored very efficiently and inexpensively. But, most importantly, it could be specifically designed to provide the quintessential sorting criterion—a score that carried exactly the same meaning for all students who took the same test. If you have not guessed already, this new entry in the assessment arena was the objectively scored paper and pencil test. Because it served so many functions well, it quickly became the coin of the realm for documenting student achievement and dominated all thought about assessment for six decades.

Perhaps the most profound consequence of the simultaneous emergence of the sorting function and of this new form of assessment was the separation of two important educational functions. On one hand, teachers were assigned the responsibility of teaching. Their challenge was to master the technology of instruction. And on the other hand, assessors would measure student achievement. Their challenge would be to master and find ways to apply the rapidly emerging technology of objective testing. In effect, we assigned teaching and assessing to different people and built a huge wall between them. We said: Teachers, you teach and you don't need to know anything about assessment. And assessors, you assess and you don't need to know anything about teaching. Training programs, certification requirements, and job responsibilities were defined henceforth according to this functional differentiation.

But how, you might be asking, does this relate to the specification of achievement targets? The answer lies in understanding the freedom that the sorting system granted to teachers. They were to be accountable for ranking students. The fact is that one need not have a vision of the meaning of academic success or even a mastery of the principles of sound assessment to produce what appears to be an appropriate ranking of students. Remember, society never asked teachers for a dependable rank order. Until recently, society never checked into the underlying quality of the assessments teachers used to rank students. Appearances sufficed. During this era, we separated the assessment and teaching functions. Teachers were provided with little, if any, assessment training. That was someone else's job. In effect, no one seemed to care about the quality of classroom assessments. Instead, just in case teachers didn't do a good job, we backed them up with standardized tests designed specifically for the purpose of sorting.

The Forces for Change

This entire system appeared to function very smoothly for decades, seeming to meet society's needs, without clearly articulating any specific achievement expectations of students. However, this began to change in the 1970s and 1980s. Several forces came into alignment to call the blind sorting system into question. For one thing, society began to realize that schools that merely ranked left the bottom third of the student population—those who used to go off and work on the farm and in the factories— with no way to contribute to our economic system. We began to understand that workplace competence and other life skills are more important for these students than grade point averages. In response, we began to create programs for at-risk youth.

At about that same time in the 1980s, the business community became involved. Casey, an experienced high school teacher, remembers what that was like:

"I'll never forget that article in the local paper. The personnel director for a local business provided a reporter with examples of three letters of application submitted by our high school graduates. They were just filled with errors, lack of clarity—you name it. And we had to admit that they came from three of our better students. Wow—were we embarrassed.

"The next school board meeting was something to behold—covered, of course, by that same reporter. The superintendent invited the personnel director to attend. The bottom line for her was that her company had been hiring students who finished relatively high in the rank order and found later that they couldn't read or write well enough to do the job. She complained about students having no experience working on a team, solving complex problems, or being dedicated to hard work. Job-related competence, she said, should be as important as grade point averages and rank in class. She said other companies in town were saying the same things. I remember the school board being really clear about the need for change! We're still working on our high school curriculum to meet those needs.

"But not everyone on staff agrees with the need to change. Many of our kids score really high on the SAT and go on to do well in college. We're struggling with that. Nevertheless, anybody coming out of college today and joining this faculty had better be on top of their discipline, and they'd better be ready to help us fit it into our students' futures. No one wants any more bad press."

Through the late 1980s, society began to realize that only 30 percent of its high school students went on to universities. The remainder moved into the work force. Yet the entire high school experience, with its grade point average and ranking system, was tailored to meet only the needs of the college-bound student. We began to ask questions about the relevance of the high school experience for the majority of our students.

These concerns for competence among at-risk youth and job-related competence for all students have coalesced to make us realize that schools must become more than merely sorting institutions. They must become places in which students meet very high academic standards and acquire many of the life skills and job-related competencies needed to survive and prosper in a rapidly changing world. Schools, we decided, need to become achievement-driven institutions.

This does not mean we will stop being a competitive society. Some colleges and all employers will always seek to select the best candidates. But the selection process will be their responsibility. The mission of schools will be to provide them with the largest pool of highly qualified candidates possible. This demands that educators today, unlike those of the past, define the meaning of academic success in clear and specific terms and assess student attainment with a high degree of precision. Without such visions, we cannot provide society with the citizens it will need in the future.

Three Difficult Challenges for Teachers

In this changing context, educators are having to confront three challenges in defining those achievement expectations. The first is public debate about what it means to be a successful student. We are a pluralistic society, with diverse views regarding what should be the final product of schooling. As this debate rages on at many levels, as a classroom teacher or member of the instruction support team, you must keep one key point clearly in mind: Your students cannot wait for society to complete a long, drawn-out debate. They are counting on you to guide them to the targets that define success right now. They're expecting you to either (1) know where they are going, or (2) know how to help them figure it out for themselves.

For this reason, pending consensus about achievement expectations among our constituents, each of us must have a clear sense of what we believe our students need to know and to know how to do. Later in this chapter, I will offer suggestions for achieving this. But for now, just remember, the students who show up in classrooms tomorrow cannot wait for our lofty public dialogue to drag on indefinitely. They need to learn to read, write, speak, listen, do math, do science, speak second languages, and use computers *now*—not sometime in the uncertain future.

The second challenge we face in defining targets to be assessed is that our research on the meaning of academic success has revealed to us that many educational targets are in fact far more complex than we had previously realized. For example, we only recently have come to understand the multidimensional aspects of the reading, writing, and mathematics problem-solving processes. It is increasingly important that we strive to understand this complexity and learn to translate it into sound assessments and instruction. This will be an ongoing professional development challenge for every teacher. Be prepared to invest in your own future by remaining on top of changes in our understanding of the disciplines you teach.

The third challenge we face is an accelerating rate of change in both the number and complexity of school outcomes. The current pace of technological change is mind boggling, and all indications are that its momentum will accelerate. We have little idea what people will be hired to do in the twenty-first century, when today's kindergartners graduate from high school. For this reason, we must strive to help our students become lifelong, self-assessing learners who can keep track of their own alignment with changing times. As Figure 3–2 illustrates, successful students are those who believe in their own capabilities.

In the face of all of these challenges, it becomes your responsibility as a teacher to address these fundamental questions:

- Do you know what it is you want your students to know and to be able to do?
- Can you clearly define and defend your educational vision to yourself, your peers, and your community?
- Can you define success for your students in terms they understand?
- Can you provide an environment within which your students can understand their own success?

Figure 3–2
The Meaning of Academic Success

If your honest answer to all these questions is yes, you are ready to design assessments. If your response is no, or if you feel uncertain, you have more preparation ahead.

Time for Reflection

Take a few moments and reflect on the questions posed above. How clear is your vision of the meaning of academic success that you hold as important for your students? List the subjects you teach now or will teach in the future. Try to define concisely a few of your achievement expectations within each area. Can you specify what it means to do these things well?

The Benefits of Clear and Appropriate Targets

Any energy you invest in becoming clear about your targets will pay big dividends at assessment time. Three primary benefits will result if you can state your instructional responsibilities in clear terms.

Benefit 1: Limits to Teacher Accountability

One major benefit of defining specific achievement targets is that you set the limits of your professional responsibility. These limits provide you with a standard by which to gauge your own success as a teacher. In short, defining targets helps you control your own professional destiny.

With clearly stated student expectations in hand—expectations that have been verified as appropriate by your supervisors—if all goes well, you will be able to say, "I am a successful teacher. My students have attained the achievement targets that were assigned to me as my instructional responsibility." Hopefully, you will gain both the internal and external rewards of your own clearly defined and documented success.

From a slightly different point of view, in effect, this prevents you from being trapped with unlimited accountability where, by default, you are held responsible for producing in your students virtually any human characteristic that anyone has ever defined as desirable! No one can hope to succeed under the weight of such expectations. There will always be someone out there pointing to some valued outcome, claiming that schools failed them. This is a trap to which many educators fall prey. Clear targets set limits and set teachers and schools up for success by defining and delimiting responsibilities.

But Mind the Risks.   We would be naive if we failed to acknowledge that the clear and public definition of achievement expectations carries with it potential risks for teachers. Accountability is a double-edged sword. To the extent that you are clear and specific about the outcomes that you take on as your instructional responsibility, you open yourself up to the possibility that some of your students may not be able to hit the target after instruction, and there will exist concrete, irrefutable assessment evidence of this. There will be no hiding. In effect, your supervisor may be able to use your own focused, high-quality classroom assessment to muster evidence that you did not succeed in doing what you were hired to do—produce achievement results.

As a community of professionals, I think we need to face this possibility: If I succeed as a teacher and my students hit the target, I want credit and reward for that success. If my students fail to hit the target I want to know it, and I want to know why they failed.

I can think of at least five possible reasons why my students might not learn:

1. They lacked the prerequisites needed to succeed.
2. I didn't understand the target to begin with, and so could not convey it appropriately.
3. My instructional methods—strategies and materials—were inappropriate.
4. My students lacked motivation.
5. Some force(s) outside of school and beyond my control (such as home environment for example) interfered with and inhibited learning.

If I am a professional educator whose students failed to hit the target, I must know which problem(s) operated in my case if I expect to remedy the situation. Only when I know what went wrong can I make the kinds of decisions and take the kinds of action that will promote success for me and my students next time.

For example, if reason number one above applies, I need to talk with my colleagues at lower grades to discuss how our respective curricula mesh. If reasons two or three apply, I have to take responsibility for needing some pretty serious professional development. If reason number four applies, I may need to combine investigation of why my students lack motivation with self-analysis of my own professional development in motivating students. If reason number five applies, I need to contact the community beyond school to seek solutions.

Time for Reflection

What other reasons can you think of to explain why students might fail? What action might you take to counter each if it came up?

Note that I can choose the proper corrective action if and only if I take the risks of (1) gathering dependable information about students success or failure using my own high-quality classroom assessments, and (2) becoming enough of a classroom researcher to uncover the causes of student failure. If I as a teacher simply bury my head in the sand and blame my students for not caring or not trying, I may doom them to long-term failure for reasons beyond their control. Thus, when they fail, I must risk finding out why. If it is my fault or if I can contribute to fixing the problem in any way, I must act accordingly.

I believe that the probability of the risk ever coming into play is greatly reduced when I start out with clear and specific targets. If I can share the vision with my students, they can hit it! If I have no target, how can they hit it? When I start with a sharp vision of success, we both profit. This brings us to the next benefit.

Benefit 2: Limits to Student Accountability

Only when I have a clear sense of the following am I in a position to share the meaning of success with my students:

- knowledge my students need to master
- kinds of problems they need to be able to solve
- skills they must be able to demonstrate
- products they are to create
- dispositions I hope they will attain

If I can help them internalize these expectations, I set them up to take responsibility for their own success. The motivational implications of this for students can be immense.

Personalize this! Say you are a student facing a test. A great deal of material has been covered. You have no idea what will be emphasized on the test. You study your heart out—but, alas, you concentrate on the wrong material. Nice try, but you fail.

Time for Reflection

How do you feel when this happens? How are you likely to behave the next time a test comes up under these same circumstances?

Now, say you are facing another test. A great deal of material has been covered. But your teacher, who has a complete understanding of the field, points out the parts that are critical for you to know. The rest will always be there in the text for you to look up when you need it. Further, the teacher provides lots of practice in applying the knowledge in solving real-world problems and emphasizes that this is a second key target of the course. You study in a very focused manner, concentrating on the important material and its application. The result is a high score on the test. Good effort—you succeed.

Time for Reflection

Again, how do you feel? How are you likely to behave the next time a test comes up under these circumstances?

Given clear requirements for success, students are better able to gauge the appropriateness of their own preparation and thus gain control over their own academic well-being. Students who feel in control of their own probabilities of success are more likely to care and to strive for excellence.

Benefit 3: More Manageable Teacher Workload

As previously mentioned, in our research on the task demands of classroom assessment, my colleagues and I determined that typical teachers can spend as much as one-third to one-half of their available professional time involved in assessment-related activities. That's a lot of time! In fact, in many classrooms it may be too much time. Greater efficiency in assessment may be possible.

Clear achievement targets can contribute to that greater efficiency. Here's why: Any assessment is a sample of all the questions we could have asked if the test were infinitely long. But since time is always limited, we can never probe all important dimensions of achievement. So we sample, asking as many questions as we can within the allotted time. A sound assessment asks a representative set of questions, allowing us to draw inferences about student performance on the entire domain of material from that student's performance on the shorter sample.

If we have set clear limits on our valued target, then we have set a clear sampling frame. This allows us to sample with maximum efficiency and confidence (i.e., to gather just enough information on student achievement without wasting time overtesting). Let me illustrate.

If I want my students to master specific content knowledge, I can devise the most powerful (representative and efficient) test of that knowledge most easily when I have (1) set clearly defined limits on the size of that domain, (2) established which elements of that knowledge are most important for them to master for later learning, and (3) sampled those elements.

Similarly, if I select an achievement target in the arena of reasoning and problem solving, I will be confident of student mastery of those skills most quickly (i.e., based on the fewest possible exercises) if I am crystal clear about my definitions of *reasoning* and *problem solving*. If my vision of success is vague, I will need more evidence gathered over a longer period of time before I feel certain that my students have achieved.

Further, when I have a clear sense of the desired ends, I can use the assessment methods that are most efficient for the situation. In the next chapter, we will discuss four alternative assessment methods. I will argue that different methods fit different kinds of targets. It will become clear that some methods produce certain kinds of achievement information more efficiently than others. Skillful classroom assessors match methods to targets so as to produce maximum information with minimum invested assessment time. This is part of the art of classroom assessment. Your skill as an artist increases with the clarity of your vision of expected outcomes.

There you have three compelling reasons to invest energy up front to become clear about the meaning of success in your classroom. To make it easier for you to define success for yourself and your students, let's set some limits for the range of possible targets.

Types of Achievement Targets

But, you might now wonder, how do I specify my targets? What is it that I must describe about them? The first step in answering these questions is to understand that we ask our students to learn a number of different kinds of things. Our challenge as teachers is to understand which of these is relevant for our particular students at any particular point in time.

As my colleagues and I analyzed the task demands of classroom assessment, we tried to discern categories of targets that seemed to make sense to teachers (Stiggins & Conklin, 1992). We collected, studied, categorized, and tried to understand the various kinds of valued expectations reflected in teachers' classroom activities and assessments. The following categories or types of achievement targets—each of which I mentioned earlier—emerged as important:

- mastery of substantive subject matter knowledge, where mastery includes both knowing *and* understanding
- the ability to use that knowledge and understanding to reason, where reasoning leads to the ability to solve problems
- the development of certain skills, where it is the process of doing something that is important, such as reading aloud, speaking in a second language, or using psychomotor skills
- the ability to use those skills to create certain kinds of tangible products, such as samples of writing, reports, and art products, which exist independently of the performer but which provide concrete evidence of proficiency
- the development of certain kinds of dispositions or feelings, such as attitudes, interests, and motivational intentions

As you will see, these categories are quite useful in thinking about classroom assessment because they subsume all possible targets, are easy to understand, are related to one another in significant ways, and—here's the important part—have clear links to different kinds of assessment. But before we discuss assessment, let's understand these categories of achievement targets more thoroughly. We will discuss them briefly now, and then devote a chapter to the assessment of each in Part 3 of this text.

For clarity, I discuss these targets in the order I have just listed them. Because the targets build on one another, I can use this order to reveal important aspects of their interrelatedness. But there also is danger in doing this, because imposing an order can mislead us with respect to the totality of their relationships. Let me explain.

Because I refer first to knowledge and understanding (sometimes even calling them a "foundation") you may infer that your students must learn *content* before approaching any other targets. This is incorrect.

Students are natural thinkers, and sometimes they may use this natural thinking process to help them generate new *understanding*. As they become more proficient *reasoners* and problem solvers under your leadership, they become more capable of independently generating new *knowledge* and *understanding*; the two can interact, growing together. After all, isn't that our goal—to help our students attain this kind of independence, taking responsibility for managing their own learning?

Further, students can experiment with the application of new *skills,* as they try as beginners to create new *products.* As they refine their skills, their products improve in quality; again, the two grow together. In the process, they figure out how to *reason* through a problem more effectively, building on their existing *knowledge* and *understanding.*

These relationships among forms of achievement are important. They are dynamically interrelated targets that spiral toward academic excellence together. The order in which I discuss them is a useful but arbitrary construct. As a teacher, if I know how I'd like the parts to fit into a dynamic whole, when the need arises I can help my students pull out certain parts, examine them closely, and identify where difficulties may reside. For this reason, as a classroom assessor I must be prepared to assess any of the components of academic excellence: knowledge and understanding, reasoning, skills, or product development capabilities. This preparation frames our classroom assessment challenge.

Knowledge Targets

Teachers expect their students to master at least some content. Marzano, Pickering, and McTighe (1993) suggest that we differentiate between declarative and procedural knowledge:

> Declarative knowledge can be thought of as information and can be ordered somewhat hierarchically according to its generality. At the bottom of the hierarchy are facts about specific persons, places, things, and events; at the top are concepts and generalizations. For example, the statement "John Kennedy was assassinated on November 22, 1963" is a fact. The statement "People holding high political office put their lives in jeopardy" is a generalization. The phrase "political assassinations" is a concept. (pp. 17–18)

These authors suggest that facts, concepts, and generalizations are all important, with concepts and generalizations being capable of easier transfer to different situations. They offer several examples of content expectations that teachers might hold as important for students to master:

> *Science:* Understands that the universe is large and ancient on a scale staggering to the human mind.
>
> *Mathematics:* Understands the importance of geometry in the modern world.
>
> *History:* Recognizes that events in the past can inform the present.
>
> *Geography:* Recognizes that regions can be defined in cultural, physical or political terms.
>
> *English:* Recognizes the role literature plays in developing the principles governing the lives of people in a given society (p. 17).

Marzano and his associates differentiate between this form of knowledge and content centered on procedures: "Procedural knowledge can be thought of as strategies [and knowledge of] steps that must be executed in a set order" (p. 17). Some examples:

Science: Understands the steps to be carried out to complete an experiment.

Mathematics: Knows the algorithm for solving algebraic equations.

History: Uses the process of historical research to ask and answer questions about the past.

Geography: Understands how to accurately interpret and summarize information from a topographical map.

English: Understands each of the steps in the writing process and how they relate to one another.

We master these various forms of knowledge when we understand them. A foundation of knowledge underpins the attainment of academic competence, because all other forms of achievement arise out of a basis of knowledge and understanding on the part of the problem solver or skillful performer.

We cannot, for example, solve math problems—clearly a reasoning competence—without a foundational knowledge of math facts, number systems, and/or problem-solving procedures. Nor can we speak a foreign language skillfully without mastery of its vocabulary, syntax, and structure. It is impossible to write an essay in English without a practical knowledge of letters, words, sentences, paragraphs, and grammar, as well as an understanding of how to write in an organized manner. We cannot read with comprehension if we lack sufficient background about the material presented in the text. We cannot respond to an essay question on the Civil War in history class unless we know something about the Civil War! In every performance domain, there is a basis of knowledge underpinning competence.

Understand, however, that this foundation of knowledge is never sufficient for finding solutions to complex problems. It is merely one essential ingredient. The necessary knowledge must be combined with appropriate patterns of reasoning to succeed. But the essential point is that there is no such thing as content-free thinking. I will amplify this point in the next section.

At any point in the instructional process, a teacher concerned about student attainment of the building blocks of competence might legitimately hold as the valued target that students master some important basic knowledge (declarative or procedural). At such a time, assessment of student mastery of that knowledge might very well make sense.

Please notice that I have not once referred to the knowledge achievement target in terms of the teacher expecting students to *memorize* that knowledge. I said *master* important knowledge. The two are not the same. One masters content when one gains control over it, when one understands and is able to retrieve the specified material for use as needed. That control can be gained either by building it into one's structure of knowledge by learning it outright, or through the effective use of appropriate reference materials. In other words, I can use knowledge equally effectively from either source.

To be sure, there are things I need to know outright. I know I read faster and with better understanding if I don't have to look up every word—I need an appropriate sight vocabulary. Similarly, I know I write better if I possess a working knowledge of the grammatical structure of our language and if I know something about what I wish to write about. And so it is in science, math, social studies, the arts, and so on. The curriculum will include some content students must master outright.

Having said that, however, please keep this not-too-astounding thought in mind as you define your valued achievement targets: The world does not operate solely on information retrieved from memory. To see what I mean, just try to fill out your income tax return, operate a new computer, or use an unfamiliar transit system without referring to the appropriate user's guide. When we confront such challenges in real adult life, we rely on what we know to help us find what we don't know. The result is solutions to the complex problems of life. In fact, the older I get, the more I am aware of the differences between what I know and what I used to know! The material I have failed to retain has not left me, however, if I know where and how to find it when I need it.

In this information age, we're generating new information in almost all fields of study at incredible rates. The amount of available information doubles every few years in some disciplines. It is quite literally impossible for anyone to learn it all. But that does not mean that students cannot access all of it that they need—if they possess sufficient retrieval skills.

When we have learned to use computer information bases and know other reference technologies, we gain access to the most current knowledge on demand. Our intent is to maintain access to the important material only for as long as we need it, then to let the knowledge go. This must be regarded as a way of mastering (meaning *gaining control over*) some substantive subject matter knowledge that, in this day and age, is every bit as powerful and appropriate as being able to retrieve it from memory.

In short, this "knowledge" category of achievement targets includes both those targets (core facts, concepts, relationships, and principles) that students learn outright, and those targets that students tap as needed through research. Each presents special classroom assessment challenges. In both cases, knowing must be accompanied by understanding.

Time for Reflection

Identify the academic discipline you regard as your greatest strength. How strong is your underlying knowledge of facts, concepts, and generalizations in that area? Think about your weakest area of academic performance. How strong is your knowledge and understanding base there? How critical is a strong, basic understanding of facts, concepts, and generalizations to academic success?

Reasoning Targets

Rarely do we (or should we) ask students to master content merely for the sake of knowing it. It is virtually always the case that we want students to be able to use that information to reason and to solve certain kinds of problems. For example, we want them to analyze and solve story problems in math, compare current or past political events or leaders, reason inductively and deductively in science, and evaluate opposing positions on social and scientific issues. We want them to use what they know within the problem context to achieve a desired solution.

If we hold such targets as valuable for our students, it is incumbent upon us to define precisely what we mean by *reasoning* and *problem-solving proficiency*. Some teachers create their own definitions of different patterns of reasoning. Others rely on one or more of the many conceptual frameworks scholars have generated to define the thinking and problem-solving processes. Precise definition lays the foundation for meaningful assessment.

One conceptual framework has been advanced by Marzano (1992). Under the heading "Extending and Refining Knowledge," one of five such categories, Marzano lists such patterns of reasoning as comparing, classifying, inducing, deducing, constructing support, and abstracting. In another framework, Norris and Ennis (1989) include references to such patterns as analyzing arguments, judging the credibility of information sources, identifying assumptions, and deciding on an action, all of which call for the application of knowledge previously obtained in some manner. Similarly, Quellmalz (1987) searched the professional literature for all such frameworks and found analytical, comparative, inferential, and evaluative patterns of reasoning to be important.

We'll explore these patterns in later chapters. Obviously, they represent important forms of achievement. The key to our success in helping students master them is to understand that any form of reasoning can be done either well or poorly. Our assessment challenge lies in knowing the difference. Our success in helping students learn to monitor the quality of their own reasoning—a critical lifelong skill—is to help them learn the difference.

Paul (1995) provides us with guidance in this regard by offering a universal set of standards to apply when judging the quality of reasoning. All reasoning, he contends, arises from a purpose and focuses on a specific question. It is only within the context of that purpose and question that we can evaluate the quality of the reasoning completed. Thus our criteria hold that, to be sound, reasoning must be clear and accurate, relevant to the question at hand, and deep and broad enough to generate an answer to that question. (We discuss this further in Chapter 10.)

In the case of, as with all the other reasoning achievement targets, we who presume to help students master effective reasoning must first ourselves become confident, competent masters of the judgment criteria. We must strive to meet standards of intellectual rigor in our own thinking if we are to make this vision come alive in the minds of our students. We must be prepared to devise assessments that reflect not only the presence of valued patterns of reasoning, but also, the quality of that reasoning.

Skill Targets

In most classrooms, there are things teachers want their students to be able to do, instances for which the measure of attainment is the student's ability to demonstrate attainment of certain kinds of skills or behaviors. For example, at the primary-grade level, a teacher might expect to see certain fundamental social interaction behaviors or the earliest oral reading skills. At the elementary level, a teacher might observe student performance in cooperative group activities. In middle school or junior high, manipulation of science lab apparatus might be important. And at the high school level, public speaking or the ability to converse in a second language might represent valued outcomes.

In all of these cases, success lies in "doing it well." The assessment challenge lies in being able to define in clear terms, using words, examples, or both, what it means to *do it well*—to read fluently, work productively as a team member, or carry out the steps in a lab experiment. To assess well, we must provide opportunities for students to show their skills, so we can observe and evaluate while they are performing.

Note that two necessary conditions for performing skillfully are first, that the student master prerequisite procedural knowledge, and second, that the student have the reasoning power to use that knowledge appropriately in performance. Thus, knowledge and reasoning outcomes form the foundations of skill outcomes. However, it is critical that we understand that, in this category, the student's performance objective is to put all the foundational and reasoning proficiencies together and to be skillful. This is precisely why achievement-related skills often represent complex targets requiring quite sophisticated assessments.

Product Targets

Yet another way for students to succeed academically is through creating quality products—tangible entities that exist independently of the performer, but that present evidence in their quality that the student has mastered foundational knowledge, requisite reasoning and problem-solving proficiencies, and specific production skills.

For example, a high school social studies teacher might have students prepare a term paper. A middle school shop teacher might have students build a wooden table. An elementary school teacher might challenge students to prepare their first science lab reports. A primary-grade teacher might collect samples of student artwork. A classic example of this kind of target that crosses grade levels is the ability to create high-quality written products or writing samples—tangible products that contain within them evidence of the writer's proficiency.

In all cases, success lies in creating products that possess certain key attributes. The assessment challenge is to be able to define clearly and understandably in writing and/or through example, what those attributes are. We must be able to specify exactly how high- and low-quality products differ.

Note once again that successful performance arises out of student mastery of prerequisite knowledge and through the application of appropriate thinking and problem-solving strategies. In addition, the student will probably need to perform certain predefined steps in the process of creating the desired product. So certain achievement-related behaviors underpin the creation of quality products. But evidence of ultimate success lies in the product itself.

Dispositional Targets

This final category of valued targets is quite broad and complex. It includes those characteristics that go beyond academic achievement into the realms of affective and personal feeling states, such as attitude toward something, sense of academic self-confidence, or interest in something that motivationally predisposes a person to do or not do something.

Many teachers set as goals, for example, that students will develop certain dispositions, such as a positive self-concept, positive attitudes toward school and school subjects predisposing them to strive for excellence, strong interests that have that same effect, and a strong sense of internal control over their own academic well-being. Each of these can be defined in terms of three essential elements: Each disposition is directed at some specific object, each has a positive or negative direction, and each has a level of intensity, from strong to weak.

For instance, attitudes, values, and interests don't exist in a vacuum. Rather, they are focused on certain aspects of our lives. We have attitudes about self, school, subjects, classmates, and teachers. We hold values about politics, work, and learning. We are interested in doing, reading, and discussing certain things. Thus, dispositions are directed toward certain objects.

Further, our feelings about things are positive, neutral, or negative. Our academic self-concepts are positive or negative. We hold positive or negative attitudes. Our values are for or against things. We are interested or disinterested. Thus, direction is important. In school, we seek to impart positive dispositions toward productive academic practices.

And, our dispositions vary in their intensity. Sometimes we feel very strongly positive or negative about things. Sometimes we feel less strongly. Sometimes the intensity is too weak to ascertain its direction. Intensity varies. When teachers are in touch with the dispositions of their students (either as individuals or as a group) and when teachers can put students in touch with their own feelings about important issues, positive learning experiences can result. Obviously, however, we cannot know student feelings about things unless we ask. That requires assessment.

Since these affective and social dimensions of learners are quite complex, thoughtful assessment is essential. Success in assessing them is defined in exactly the same way as is success in assessing achievement: Sound assessment requires a crystal-clear vision or understanding of the characteristic(s) to be assessed. Only then can we select a proper assessment method, devise a sampling procedure, and control sources of bias and distortion so as to accurately assess direction and intensity of feelings about specified objects.

Summary of Targets

We have discussed five different but interrelated types of achievement targets. Knowledge and understanding are the foundation. Reasoning and problem solving require application of that knowledge. Knowledge and reasoning are foundations of successful skill performance and/or product development. And dispositions very often result from success or a lack of success in academic performance. But once again, remember that these can all grow and change in dynamic, interrelated ways within our students.

Step one in planning instruction or designing assessments is to specify the type(s) of target(s) to be hit by students. As you will see later, once a target is defined, the process of designing assessments is quite easy. The toughest part by far is coming up with the clear vision! We already have discussed the benefits of investing the effort required.

Time for Reflection

Think back through your experience as a student. Try to think of teachers in your school life who placed major emphasis on the five kinds of targets we have discussed. You may think of one teacher who stands out as emphasizing all, or your list might include a different teacher for each kind of outcome. But strive to think of someone who emphasized mastery of knowledge, someone who made you concentrate on using knowledge to solve problems, a teacher of skills, a teacher for whom the creation of quality products was paramount, and one who attended most to your dispositions—who promoted positive feelings on your part with respect to some subject. As you reflect back on each of these former teachers, how do you feel about the things you learned from them in relation to what you learned from other teachers? Do you regard these individuals as better teachers than others that you had?

Sources of Information About Achievement Targets

Teachers can search out, identify, and set limits on the achievement targets that are to represent their particular teaching responsibilities in three ways: through thorough professional preparation, community interaction, and thoughtful planning with colleagues. Let's explore each.

Professional Preparation

Solid professional preparation provides the foundation for clear and appropriate achievement targets. Put simply, if you intend to teach something, you had better understand it inside and out! Maximum teaching effectiveness arises from having a complete sense of the meaning of quality performance, including a complete understanding of the foundational knowledge and kinds of reasoning and problem-solving skills students need to master if they are to achieve success.

In my years of work in the arena of writing assessment, I have come across many teachers who have been given the responsibility of teaching students to write, but who haven't the slightest idea what it means to write well. They feel uncertain, and their students struggle. On the other hand, I also have met many teachers who possess a refined vision of success in this performance domain and have seen their students blossom as young writers. These two groups of teachers prepared differently to meet this professional challenge, and that difference showed in student achievement.

Those who would teach science concepts must first understand those concepts. Those who aspire to being math teachers must first develop a highly refined mental picture of those concepts, and so on. Those who would assess in these or any other performance domains must first become masters of the required material themselves. Three ways for you to reach this goal are to think of yourself as a lifelong learner, participate in professional training, and remain current with the literature of your profession.

Lifelong Learning.   Become the same kind of lifelong learner you want your students to become. Take personal responsibility to become good at what you expect your students to be good at. If you seek to help them become good writers, for example, become one yourself. Study, practice, strive to publish your work. Become a proficient performer yourself and commit to your own ongoing improvement, regardless of the target(s) you hold as valuable for your students.

Time for Reflection

In your lifetime, have you ever consciously made a commitment to yourself to become the very best you could possibly be at something? Did you succeed? Was the arena of your development related to your teaching? What if the next target you choose as this focus of your own excellence was the same as that of your students, and you set out together in search of that excellence?

Teacher Training.   If you are currently involved in an undergraduate or graduate-level teacher training program, be sure your methods courses reflect the latest thinking about definitions of academic success. Early on in each course, ask specific questions of your professors and evaluate their answers critically.

For example, ask them about their understanding of the alternative visions of student success that could govern teaching in this arena. They should be able to cite a number of options. Which of these alternatives do they hold as being most appropriate and why? They should be able to provide written descriptions of the visions they value, and they should be able to cite references from the professional literature to support the reasons they hold those particular values. How do your professors plan to assess your mastery of those visions of successful student achievement? They should be able to provide specific examples of the assessment instruments and procedures they plan to use.

Evaluate the meaning of student success conveyed by your professors. Does it make sense to you? Can you master this vision with sufficient depth to convey it to your students comfortably? I understand that I am asking you to do something that will require a stretch on your part to evaluate their responses to your queries. After all, you're there to learn about achievement targets. However, as a teacher, you must be able to evaluate ideas as you learn them.

I also realize that I am asking you to do something that will require diplomacy on your part, because you do not hold the power in this communication with your professors. But in one sense you do: Their job is to help you become a successful teacher. They have dedicated their professional lives to that effort. If your professors are committed to student well-being, they will welcome your "critical consumer" inquiries. (In fact, among the professors I know personally, you will gain great respect just for asking!)

Professional Literature.   While the ultimate responsibility for your preparation as a teacher falls to you and you alone, excellent support is available. As I noted in Chapter 2, our emergence into the era of achievement-driven education has spurred a great deal of high-powered reexamination of the valued outcomes of the educational process. This is a boon to teachers because in virtually every field, you have at your disposal definitions of achievement targets that hold the promise of allowing you to produce better achievers faster now than ever before—in reading, writing, science, math, reasoning and problem solving, foreign languages, and many other subjects.

To tap this wisdom, you need only contact the appropriate national professional association of teachers. Most have assembled commissions of their members to translate current research into practical guidelines for teachers, and many regularly publish journals to disseminate this research. Work with the resource personnel in your professional library if you have one. Often they can route special articles and information to you when they arrive. College and university libraries represent additional repositories of valuable information and support personnel. Further, each region of the nation is served by a regional educational laboratory. Check with your district office to identify yours. These agencies often offer information services.

You can also find support in understanding outcomes through study of textbooks, text support materials, and curriculum guides and frameworks. These might represent state, district, school, or even departmental statements of valued targets.

Tap all of these sources to build your own sense of understanding and confidence in the field of study in which you teach. I cannot overstate how much this will help when it comes to generating high-quality classroom assessment. In fact, it has been my experience in over 15 years of classroom assessment research that the single most common barrier to sound classroom assessment is the lack of vision of desired targets on the part of teachers.

Community Involvement in Setting Targets

As we proceed through the 1990s, one of the critical lessons we are learning is that schools are institutions that function in a larger social context. The tremendous challenge of understanding and meeting the many needs of youth today requires that educators collaborate with other service agencies. Thus, for our part, we in education must be in touch with our partners in the social service community as we establish the desired results of schooling.

Another lesson we are learning is that students can benefit from the restructuring of school organizations away from top-down hierarchies and toward school-based management models. This practice empowers schools to be in closer touch with their communities about expected results of schooling and it empowers local teachers and members of the instructional support team to take greater responsibility for and to feel greater control over student attainment of those valued results (Barbour & Barbour, 1997).

When we combine these lessons with the fact that we want schools to provide more than just a rank order of students—that is, we want them to provide competent citizens—what emerges is a pattern in which educators across the nation are meeting with local social, civic, and business communities to hammer out the desired outcomes expected from schools in the larger context of their communities.

This is another good thing for teachers, because it adds focus to school programs and sets useful limits on student, teacher, and school accountability. In addition, it enhances the clarity of our picture of the results that teachers and instructional leaders must translate into assessments. If these collaborative efforts have been started in your community, tap into them for valuable insights. If such local partnerships have not yet been established where you teach, take charge and play a role in initiating them. The richer sense that you will develop of what it takes to be a contributing member of the community will help immensely in your development of sound assessments of key proficiencies.

Any instructional team that has internalized these targets, determined the building blocks to competence, and divided responsibility for developing competence is preparing for student success. Figures 3–3 and 3–4 present two examples of final school achievement expectations generated through school-community collaboration. One arises from a school district in Oregon, the other from local efforts in a Washington school district.

Building a Team Effort

Once the broad goals have been established through communitywide planning, education professionals must take over to complete the next step: We must analyze each goal to determine the enabling objectives, the attainment of which builds to the accomplishment of the ultimate goal. If we want students to be competent communicators, for example, specific competencies they must attain include the abilities to read, write, speak, and listen. What does it mean to be a good reader? A good writer? What knowledge base must students master? What reasoning, skill, and product targets are relevant? We can learn the components of each of these from the professional literature and thus establish those critical building blocks of competence.

Once we identify those building blocks, then the various members of the professional team of educators must collaborate with one another—both within and across levels of instruction from primary to elementary to junior high to high school—to decide how to fit these into the curriculum at various levels of instruction and to define how they will support the ultimate goal: the development of competent communicators. What teachers will have responsibility for supporting student attainment of which of the building blocks? How shall teachers communicate with each other and with parents and students about progress? How shall all involved devise and conduct the assessments that inform instructional decision making? These are the classroom-level issues that teachers and instructional support personnel must address together to lay the foundation for student success.

Lynn, a veteran elementary teacher, has become sensitive to an important communication problem in the process of dividing responsibility in a continuous progress curriculum:

"It's really hard to get teachers at higher grade levels to meet and talk with us about this. Sometimes, they seem to have this attitude! Like they wouldn't lower themselves to talk with elementary teachers. And when we do meet—once a century—it's like they have a corner on the "truth" and dictate to us what we should do to support them. There's no mutual respect or collegiality—no thoughtful discussion and planning about how foundations shaped early lead to competence later. It's really frustrating sometimes.

"In fact, it goes even deeper than that. I really love what I do and I do it very well. Yet I have friends and others ask me: So, how long before you'll be good enough to become a high school teacher? It's like they think that the organizational ladder of schools ascends through grade levels. I'd like to see some of those upper-grade teachers come to my classroom and do what I do—they'd learn a lesson or two about the challenges of good teaching. It's frustrating. I just wish we could meet regularly across grade levels as peers to make sure our respective contributions are merged in terms of what's best for helping kids succeed academically."

On hearing this, Casey, our high school teacher friend, shares a different view:

"You know, Lynn, the frustration can go both ways. The problem I face is trying to teach algebra to students who lack the basic math skills, or trying to teach science when my students don't have the background knowledge they need. That's supposed to be your job. Sometimes I wonder what you folks do with these kids. We talk about it in math department meetings. Our teaching would be so much easier if we didn't think we had to start from scratch. It's really frustrating, here, too."

Obviously, there is a strong need for far better communication across the broad range of grade levels, from primary to elementary to junior high to high school. In fact, some have begun to suggest the need for an integrated continuous progress

---

OUTCOMES AND PERFORMANCE STATEMENTS

Our graduates will be:

1. Knowledgeable

    A. Demonstrate essential skills and knowledge in language: listening, speaking, reading, and writing.

    B. Demonstrate essential skills and knowledge in mathematics.

    C. Demonstrate knowledge of the geographies, histories, and cultures of the community, region, nation, and world.

    D. Demonstrate knowledge and skills in the basic principles, concepts, and language of the social sciences.

    E. Demonstrate knowledge and skills in the basic principles, concepts, and language of the natural sciences.

    F. Demonstrate knowledge and skills in the basic principles, concepts, and language of the arts.

    G. Demonstrate essential skills and knowledge in human movement, health, and fitness.

2. Capable Thinkers

    A. Use a variety of thinking processes to identify problems, make decisions, and resolve complex issues.

    B. Gather, evaluate, and use information from a variety of sources.

    C. Apply the strategies, techniques, and processes of the sciences, humanities, and arts.

    D. Apply concepts of natural, social, and organizational systems.

3. Effective Communicators

    A. Communicate through listening, speaking, reading, and writing, and through visual and symbolic forms.

    B. Communicate effectively with diverse audiences.

Figure 3–3
Outcomes and Performance Statements

curricula from primary grades through college. But no matter what the levels, such planned division of instructional responsibility is essential.

A Note of Caution

As a teacher, you may or may not practice your profession in a community that engages in the kind of integrated planning outlined above. You may or may not practice in a school in which staff collaborate in the articulation of achievement targets across levels. In short, you may or may not receive the kind of school and community support needed to do a thorough job of generating a continuous progress portrait of success for students.

C.   Communicate in at least one other language.

D.   Interpret human experience through literature and the arts.

E.   Use technology as a communication tool.

F.   Demonstrate effective interpersonal skills.

4.   Responsible Citizens

A.   Demonstrate responsibility as an individual and as a community member.

B.   Recognize and propose thoughtful solutions to local, national, and world problems.

C.   Demonstrate consideration for individual differences and for the contribution of diversity to society.

D.   Display positive health behaviors.

5.   Self-Directed Learners

A.   Create a positive vision for themselves and for their future.

B.   Set priorities and goals; construct and execute a plan for achieving those goals.

C.   Create options for themselves.

D.   Evaluate and manage their own progress toward goals.

E.   Demonstrate skills to get and keep a job.

6.   Collaborative Workers

A.   Participate as a member of a team and assume appropriate roles: lead, follow, and support others in a productive manner.

B.   Collaborate toward achieving a common goal.

C.   Resolve conflict effectively.

7.   Quality Producers

A.   Create products that achieve their purpose for the intended audience.

B.   Use craftsmanship, originality, and appropriate technology to produce high quality products.

Source: Corvallis, OR School District. Reprinted by permission.

Nevertheless, each of us has a responsibility to our particular students to be clear and specific about our achievement expectations. The point is, while all of the school and community planning work described above is being carried out (if it is conducted at all), tomorrow in your classroom, or as soon as you enter a classroom for the first time, there will be a group of students wanting and needing to master content knowledge, learn to solve problems, master important skills, create important products, and/or develop certain dispositions. They count on you to know what these things mean and to know how to teach and assess them. So when it comes to being clear about what it means to be successful in your classroom, the responsibility stops with you, regardless of what else is going on around you! Embrace that responsibility.

It is our expectation that students exiting South Kitsap School District will demonstrate a core of basic knowledge in order to be

* *creative thinkers* who develop and use a variety of resources to identify, assess, integrate, and apply a basic core of knowledge to effectively make decisions and solve problems.

* *self-directed learners* who set priorities, establish goals, and take responsibility for pursuing and evaluating those goals in an ever-changing society.

* *active citizens* who take the initiative to contribute time, energy, and talent to improve the quality of life for themselves and others in their local, national, and global environments.

* *effective communicators* who receive information in a variety of forms and present in various ways to a wide range of audiences.

* *quality producers* who create innovative, artistic, and practical products which reflect originality, high standards, and the use of appropriate technologies.

* *collaborative workers* who use effective group skills to manage interpersonal relationships within diverse settings.

Figure 3–4
South Kitsap School District Outcomes
Source: South Kitsap School District, Port Orchard, WA. Reprinted by permission.

Communicating About Valued Achievement Targets

If the driving force behind successful achievement-oriented schools is refined visions of success, then we must constantly strive to find more creative and effective ways to communicate our expectations to others. Over the years, we have found many ways to accomplish this and, without doubt, the most common is by using lists of instructional goals and objectives.

While this is an excellent option, it is just one of many ways to cast valued expectations in forms that allow us to communicate about them. We also can use other means to communicate targets.

For instance, a science teacher friend of mine presented a two-week biology unit on cells. As the unit unfolded, she engaged her students in some productive assessment-related activities. At the end of each day, she asked her students to identify what they thought was the most critical content covered that day. Using her thorough knowledge of the field, the teacher screened the ideas to be sure the students really hit on the important material. As a class, they kept a growing outline of important facts, concepts, and generalizations, adding a few each day. As the unit moved into week two, she made it clear to her students that these elements, among other things, were going to be covered on the unit test. She was making the target clear.

A writing teacher I know wanted her students to play a central role in defining their own writing achievement target. So she gave them two samples of student writing selected from previous years to illustrate two vastly different levels of proficiency. Working together as partners, they read the two papers and carefully analyzed their differences. Why is one so much better than the other, she asked? What makes them different? She was using examples of achievement-related products in conjunction with student assessments of proficiency to communicate her expectations to her students.

A primary school principal I know worked with her staff to devise a new program to help students apply their reasoning and problem-solving proficiencies. She knew the program would be challenging and that support from home would be essential, so she invited parents to school for an evening workshop. At that session, she and her staff posed for parents the same kinds of problems their children would be solving. In effect, she provided parents with an opportunity to come to understand their own and each other's reasoning and problem-solving skills. As a result, parents came to understand the kinds of achievement targets their children would be hitting. Everyone left that evening supportive and ready and able to help. The staff had succeeded in making their expectations clear to key members of their school community.

The bottom line is that we need not rely only on a list of objectives to describe our valued targets. We also can rely on summary statements of important learnings, examples of good work, and, indeed, the very assessment process itself as a means of communicating our vision to others.

Look for more examples of innovative ways to communicate expectations through the use of assessment as you read on. Assessment is not just for gathering data—it can be a valuable means for setting students up for success through clear thinking and effective communication about what it means to be successful.

Time for Reflection

If you expected your students to become proficient at assembling functional electrical circuits, which would be the most effective way for you to show them in advance what success looks like—reading them an instructional objective stating the outcome in behavioral terms or having them watch you do it successfully just once? In your opinion, why would one be more effective than the other?

Chapter Summary: Clear Targets Are Key

In this segment of our journey into the realm of classroom assessment, we have seen that the quality of an assessment rests on the clarity of the assessor's understanding of the student characteristic(s) to be assessed. We identified five kinds of interrelated targets as useful in thinking about and planning for assessment and its integration into the instructional process:

- mastering content knowledge
- using that knowledge to reason and solve problems
- demonstrating certain kinds of skills
- creating certain kinds of products
- developing positive dispositions

Each teacher faces the challenge of specifying desired targets in her or his classroom, relying on a commitment to lifelong learning, strong professional preparation, community input, and collegial teamwork within the school to support this effort.

I urge that you specify clear expectations in your classroom. Do so in writing and publish them for all to see. Eliminate the mystery surrounding the meaning of success in your classroom by letting your students see your vision.

If they can see it, they can hit it. But if they cannot see it . . .

When we do these things, benefits accrue for all involved. Limits of teacher accountability are established, setting teachers up to succeed. Limits of student accountability are established, setting students up for success. And, the huge assessment workload faced by teachers becomes more manageable because assessments can be sharply focused.

Exercises to Advance Your Learning

Knowledge

1. Go back and reread the important benefits of specifying clear and appropriate targets and restate them in writing in your own words. Make sure you understand them.

2. Identify the major risks to the teacher of being explicit about targets and be sure these make sense to you.

3. List and define the five kinds of achievement targets presented in this chapter. Make them part of that portion of your structure of knowledge that you learn outright—that you don't have to look up to recall.

4. Identify, in your own words, available sources of information and guidance in selecting and defining valued targets.

5. List in your own words three specific ways to communicate about expected outcomes. Look them up again in the chapter if necessary.

Reasoning

1. Translate each of the five kinds of outcomes into a real example of a significant target that you hit during your own school experience.

2. Explain in your own words the relationships that exist between and among the five kinds of achievement targets.

3. Turn to a current newspaper editorial page and read some of the editorials. Look for instances of the patterns of reasoning discussed in this chapter. Is there evidence of analytical reasoning in any of them? How about a relevant comparison? Do the authors draw generalizations (inferences)? Do they express opinions and defend them in terms of specific criteria? Make some judgments about the quality of the reasoning you read there. Is it clear, accurate, and relevant to the question at hand? Is it sufficiently deep and broad, in your opinion? Justify your responses.

4. What are the dangers to student academic self-concept of trying to assess an achievement you, the teacher, do not understand?

Skills and Products

See the Special Ongoing Assessment Project that follows this section.

Dispositions

1. Some educators divide reasoning into higher-order and lower-order kinds. Recall,

or knowledge-level targets often are regarded as "lower-order" thinking. Some regard these as "less important, less challenging." Do you agree? Does it make sense to you to label content mastery as less important or less valuable than the ability to use that knowledge to reason and solve problems? Why?

2. In our society today, heated debates continue regarding the kinds of achievement expectations our schools should help students attain. Opposing camps often include conservative and liberal political factions, religious communities of differing opinions, and business leaders seeking job competence as part of a broader view of the complete citizen. In your opinion, are these heated exchanges about valued targets good or bad for schools and students? Why do you feel that way? Do you think these differing points of view can be accommodated in our educational system? If so, how? If not, why not?

Special Ongoing Assessment Project: Part 1

This is the beginning of a special assignment designed to help you become assessment literate. It represents an extended and complex learning experience that starts here and continues, step by step, throughout the remainder of the text. Be advised in advance that this is a sizable project that will command a good deal of time on your part to complete well. But also be aware that the time will be well spent. As you apply what you learn through the completion of this project, you will expand and refine your sense of the meaning of quality assessment.

This assignment requires that you select a unit of instruction that is important to you and use its goals, objectives, instructional materials, and instructional interventions as the basis for a comprehensive classroom assessment design and development project. As you think about the instructional unit you might use, realize that ultimately you are going to be asked to identify its important achievement targets, devise an assessment plan for it, design and develop the actual assessments, devise systems for communicating with students about assessment results and, if feasible, carry out your assessment plan. As you select your focal unit, keep the following criteria in mind:

1. The best option is to focus this project on an already-developed unit for which you have clearly framed goals, objectives, and instructional interventions—with a starting point and a conclusion. In this way, you can concentrate your efforts on the assessment work to be done. However, you also can develop the unit of instruction from scratch, if you wish, simultaneously developing the assessment components right along with the unit. In real classroom practice, this is the way most assessments will be developed. Just be mindful of the greater time requirements of the latter option.

2. The unit should include at least several days or even weeks of instruction—thus covering a good deal of material. If possible, strive for a unit that includes all four forms of achievement: knowledge and understanding, reasoning, skills, and products. Factor in some dispositional targets if you wish. This will extend you into all dimensions of assessment, providing broad practice.

3. Your unit might be one you have taught or plan to teach, if you currently are a

teacher. Or it might be one that you have worked on in a methods class, if you are a student preparing to teach. If such sources are unavailable to you, select a unit of study that you recently completed as a student in one of your courses. Any of these will suffice.

4. If you currently are a teacher, it might be prudent to select a unit you teach regularly or plan to teach in the future. In that way, you take advantage of this learning experience to advance your real classroom agenda.

Once you have selected your unit, here is your first task: Using the lessons learned in this chapter, take a first pass at identifying the important achievement targets of your unit. What is the important knowledge students are to understand? Outline in detail the declarative knowledge to be mastered. Differentiate, if possible, that content you expect students to learn outright (the essential core) from content you expect them to be able to retrieve later if they need it. Then outline the procedural knowledge you expect students to master. Again, separate this content into that to be learned outright and that which can be retrieved later as needed.

After completing these outlines, reflect on the patterns of reasoning you might expect your students to need to acquire. Be careful here. We have not talked about this much yet. But just take a first pass at stating your valued reasoning and problem-solving targets—what might some of them be? We'll refine this list later.

Next, can you identify any skill or product development targets? What skills are your students to master—what things do you want them to be able to do? What kinds of products do you want them to create to show you they have met your expectations? Again, give yourself room here. We have not provided much detail yet about skill or product competence. Just take a first pass at these. We'll refine all of this as we travel on.

Finally, what dispositions do you hope your students will acquire? What is the instructional material you want them to have positive or negative feelings about?

Capture your thoughts about all these achievement targets in a written list and save it for later use. I suggest that you create a special assessment project portfolio to hold this list of targets and other documents. Since this project evolves throughout the text, your portfolio will prove an invaluable resource as you continue with me on our journey.

4

Understanding the Assessment Alternatives

CHAPTER ROADMAP

Having introduced the range of possible purposes for classroom assessment and the variety of different kinds of achievement targets to be assessed, we can now turn to the issue of selecting proper assessment methods. The assessment method of choice in any classroom context is a direct function of the purpose and the target. There are many possible reasons to assess. Different uses require different results. Different results require different modes of assessment. Further, there are many possible achievement targets. Different targets require different modes of assessment, too. Thus, without knowledge of purpose and target, it is impossible to devise a sound assessment. Now let's understand how assessment method fits into the puzzle (Figure 4–1).

By studying Chapter 4, you will have the opportunity to master the following content knowledge:

1. Understand the assessment formats that fall within each of the four basic assessment categories.
2. Identify the achievement targets best assessed with each method.

You will be able to use that knowledge to reason as follows:

1. In a real classroom assessment context, be able to select an assessment method that will make sense given the achievement target(s) to be assessed.
2. Understand why some assessment methods represent strong matches with achievement targets while others are weak.

And finally, I have set a goal that the following dispositions will emerge for you:

1. You will come to value all methods of assessment as useful and worthy of careful development and use.

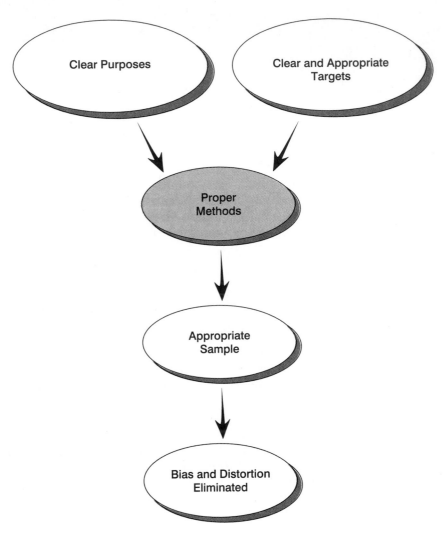

Figure 4–1
How Assessment Methods Fit In

2. You will seek the strongest possible matches between achievement targets and assessment methods on all occasions in the classroom.

The objectives of this chapter do not include the mastery of any process skills or the creation of any products.

We're going to study four basic assessment methods, all of which are familiar to you as a student and perhaps as a teacher: selected response assessments, essay assessments, performance assessments, and assessments that rely on direct personal communication with the student. Each provides its own special form of evidence of student proficiency. I introduce them in this chapter, and will devote an entire chapter to each method in Part 2, studying each in depth in terms of design, development, advantages, disadvantages, and keys to effective use in the classroom.

First, however, I am going to lay out the overall assessment plan that will guide the remainder of our journey together. In the second half of this chapter, we will analyze how each of these four assessment methods aligns with the five kinds of achievement targets discussed in Chapter 3. In essence, we will see which methods make sense with each target and which do not. We will do this by filling in the cells of Figure 4–2 with commentary on viable matches.

The Assessment Options

The artistry of classroom assessment requires that the teacher orchestrate a careful alignment among purposes, targets, and methods. For example, an assessment of instrumental music proficiency is likely to look very different from an assessment of scientific factual recall. One relies on the assessor to listen to and subjectively judge proficiency. The other requires the administration of a set of test items that are scored correct or incorrect, yielding a score reflecting proficiency. Different targets, different assessment methods.

Note also that an assessment of instrumental music proficiency for the purpose of planning the next lesson for a student demands a different kind of assessment

	SELECTED RESPONSE	ESSAY	PERFORMANCE ASSESSMENT	PERSONAL COMMUNICATION
Know				
Reason				
Skills				
Products				
Dispositions				

Figure 4–2
A Plan for Matching Assessment Methods with Achievement Targets

from one designed to determine who receives a scholarship to the conservatory. The former requires a narrowly focused, brief assessment; the latter a much larger, more diverse sampling of proficiency. As purpose varies, so does the definition of a sound assessment.

Once the requirements of a quality assessment are determined for a particular classroom assessment context (i.e., purpose and target have been specified), then and only then can a proper assessment method be selected, developed, and administered, so as to yield sound results for the user. The process is much like assembling a jigsaw puzzle—only those pieces that belong together will fit properly.

We're going to study the range of alternative assessment methods available to meet our combined purpose and target needs in the classroom. In addition, we will examine how to connect methods with outcomes—how to pick a method that really will reflect the target you wish to assess.

Keep the Options in Balance

As you read on, strive to maintain a balanced perspective regarding the viability of the assessment options covered. For decades, one method has dominated: objectively scored paper and pencil tests, such as multiple-choice formats. As a result, some very important achievement targets went unassessed, especially in the context of high-stakes assessments, where this method has been used extensively.

As we moved through the 1980s, we began to experience a backlash to those decades of domination. As pointed out earlier, we began to embrace a more complex array of valued achievement expectations, and this required the use of such alternatives as performance assessment methodology.

As a result of this swing in values, we face two dangers. If we are not cautious, we risk moving out of balance in our assessments once again, with the same kind of domination by a single (but different) assessment method. Or, we risk inadequate assessment of student achievement because we fail to understand or acknowledge the real costs of conducting sound performance assessments and thus end up doing a shoddy job of implementing this promising alternative.

We can prevent such problems only by acknowledging that the challenge we face is difficult, and by meeting this challenge by effectively developing and using all of the assessment tools we have at our disposal.

Selected Response Assessment

This category includes all of the objectively scored paper and pencil test formats. The respondent is asked a series of questions, each of which is accompanied by a range of alternative responses. The respondent's task is to select either the correct or the best answer from among the options. The index of achievement in this instance is the number or proportion of questions answered correctly.

Format options within this category include the following:

- multiple-choice items
- true/false items

- matching exercises
- short answer fill-in items

While I realize that fill-in-the-blank items do require a response that originates within the respondent, I include it in this category because it calls for a very brief answer that typically is counted right or wrong.

Standardized achievement test batteries often rely on selected response assessment methodology. So do the chapter tests that accompany many textbooks.

Time for Reflection

What is your most vivid memory of a selected response assessment from your school experience? What kinds of targets were assessed? How do you feel about these kinds of tests?

Essay Assessment

In this case, the respondent is provided with an exercise (or set of exercises) that calls for the preparation of an extended written answer. Respondents might be asked to answer a question or to provide an explanation of the solution to a complex problem. They might be asked to compare historical events, interpret scientific information, or solve open-ended math problems, where they are asked to show all work. The originally constructed responses are read by the examiner, who judges the quality of the responses in terms of scoring criteria.

Evidence of achievement is seen in the conceptual content of the response (i.e., ideas expressed and the manner in which they are tied together). The index of achievement typically is the number of points attained out of a total number of points possible.

Time for Reflection

Have you worked with a teacher who relied heavily on the essay form of assessment? What kinds of outcomes did this teacher value most? How do you feel about these kinds of tests?

Performance Assessment

In this case, the respondent actually carries out a specified activity under the watchful eye of an evaluator, who observes performance and makes judgments as to the quality of achievement demonstrated. Performance assessments can be based either on observations of the process while skills are being demonstrated, or on the evaluation of products created.

In the first case, evidence of achievement is seen in the respondent's ability to carry out the proper sequence of activities or to do something in the appropriate manner. Examples include musical performance, reading aloud, communicating conversationally in a second language, or carrying out some motor activity, as in the case of physical education or dance. In this case, it is the doing that counts. The index of achievement typically is a performance rating or profile of ratings reflecting levels of quality in the performance.

In the case of product evaluations, the respondent creates a complex achievement-related product that is intended to meet certain standards of quality. The product resulting from performance must exist as an entity separate from the performer, as in the case of term papers, science fair exhibits, and art or craft creations. The assessor examines the tangible product to see if those attributes are indeed present. In this instance, it is not so much the process of creating that counts (although that may be evaluated, too) but rather the characteristics of the creation itself. Again in this case, the index of achievement is the rating(s) of product quality. The classic example is the writing assessment, in which students produce samples that are evaluated not solely in terms of the content presented, but in terms of proficiency in using written language.

Time for Reflection

What is the most important performance assessment you ever participated in? What kinds of achievement targets were assessed? How effective was this kind of assessment for you?

Personal Communication as Assessment

One of the most common ways teachers gather information about day-to-day student achievement in the classroom is to talk with them! We don't often think of this as assessment in the same sense as the multiple-choice test or a performance assessment. But on reflection it will become clear to you that certain forms of personal communication definitely do represent assessments of student achievement.

These forms of personal communication include questions posed and answered during instruction, interviews, conferences, conversations, listening during class discussions, conversations with others (such as parents or other teachers) about student achievement, and oral examinations. The examiner listens to responses and either (1) tallies them right or wrong if correctness is the criterion, or (2) makes subjective judgments according to some quality criterion. Personal communication is a very flexible means of assessment that can be brought into play literally at a moment's notice. While it certainly is not as efficient as some other options when many students must be assessed, it can probe achievement far more deeply than can the other alternatives.

Time for Reflection

Have you ever had a teacher who always seemed to be able to ask just the right question at just the right time to reveal your own wisdom to you—wisdom you didn't even know you had? Or have you worked with a teacher who could always ask just the question you didn't know the answer to—and then always called on you? What effect did this have on you?

Some Thoughts About Methods

If you're tuned into 1990s assessment, you may be saying, "Wait a minute, what happened to the rapidly emerging alternative called portfolio assessment? Doesn't that represent a fifth method?"

I regard portfolios as a wonderful idea, and devote an entire chapter to their use in assessment and instruction in Part 4. However, I do not regard portfolios as a separate assessment method. Rather, they represent an excellent means of collecting diverse evidence of student achievement (probably gathered using a variety of the methods described in this chapter) and assembling it into a coherent whole. In short, portfolios are a means of communicating about student effort, growth, or achievement status at a point in time.

Note that three of the four assessment methods described call for complex responses in the form of original constructions by the student. They require the preparation of extended written responses, the performance of complex skills, the creation of multidimensional products, or participation in one-on-one communication—all of which take more time to administer and certainly more time to score than a set of true/false test items. Thus, if the amount of assessment time is held constant, selected response assessments can provide a much larger sample of performance per unit of assessment time.

Given this reality, you might ask, why not just use the most efficient option—selected response—every time? The reason is that selected response assessment formats cannot accurately depict all of the kinds of achievement we expect of our students. Different kinds of assessment methods align with different kinds of achievement targets. We shall explore these relationships now.

Matching Methods with Targets

The art of classroom assessment revolves around the teacher's ability to blend five kinds of achievement targets, with all of the forms and nuances of each, with four kinds of assessment methods, with all of the variations in format that come with each method. Sounds like a pretty big job! But, as it turns out, the recipes for creating these blends are not that complicated.

We will explore the blending process by crossing the five kinds of outcomes with the four methods to create a chart depicting the various matches of targets to methods, as shown in Figure 4–2. Within each cell of this table, we can explore the nature and viability of the match. The result, though not a simple picture, is both understandable and practical.

I present brief descriptions of the various matches in Table 4–1. As you read the table, please keep three key points in mind. First, remember that the various kinds of achievement targets we are discussing are interrelated, each building on and contributing to the others. Problem solving involves application of knowledge. Once attained, problem solutions can become part of our structure of knowledge. Skills represent procedural knowledge and problem-solving proficiencies in action.

And quality products result from combining knowledge, reasoning, and skills in the right ways. Teachers who are concerned with building competence might well need to assess any of these elements of success.

Second, remember that assessments provide us with external indicators of the internal mental states we call *achievement*. These indicators are visible manifestations that we can see and evaluate. In other words, we can't just lift off the top of the student's head and look inside to see if math problem-solving proficiency is in there. So, we administer an assessment in the form of several math problems to gather evidence of proficiency from which we infer mastery of the desired target. One important key to selecting an acceptable method for any particular form of achievement is to choose the method that permits us to draw the most accurate inference. Thus, the foundation for the selection of a method, once again, is a refined vision of the achievement target to be assessed.

And finally, as stated before, any assessment represents a sample of all the exercises we could have posed if the assessment were infinitely long. A sound assessment relies on a sample that is systematically representative of all the possibilities. We generalize from the sample to the infinite array. In effect, we can infer how much of the target students have mastered.

Our goal in assessment design is to use the most powerful assessment option we can. Power derives from the accuracy and efficiency with which a method can represent our valued target. We always want the highest-resolution picture of that valued target we can get using the smallest possible sample of student performance—maximum information for minimum cost.

As you read Table 4–1, I hope you can see more clearly why it is crucial to understand the achievement target in order to select a proper assessment method. This cannot be overstated: Different targets require different methods. Please study the table now and then read on.

A startling realization that came to me as I worked through the cells of this table, thinking about which methods matched what outcomes, was that almost every cell offered a viable match at some level. Some matches are stronger than others; that is, some get to the heart of the valued target better than others. For example, without question, the best way to assess writing proficiency is to rely on performance assessment and have students create written products. But we also can use selected response or personal communication to help students determine if they have mastered the knowledge base that underpins effective writing. This can help those who struggle to write well. Such assessments aren't intended to accurately depict writing. Rather, for the teacher striving to create writers, they provide accurate representations of key prerequisites to effective writing. Thus, for instructional purposes, they represent useful assessment alternatives.

The realization that all methods have the potential of contributing at least some useful information about most kinds of classroom outcomes is very good news, because it tells us that we have a variety of tools at our disposal to help us help students learn.

How, then, do we decide which one to use? In the best of all possible worlds where both our time to assess and our assessment resources are unlimited, we choose the cell that affords us the most accurate depiction of our desired target.

Table 4–1
Links Between Achievement Targets and Assessment Methods

TARGET TO BE ASSESSED	ASSESSMENT METHOD			
	SELECTED RESPONSE	ESSAY	PERFORMANCE ASSESSMENT	PERSONAL COMMUNICATION
KNOWLEDGE MASTERY	Multiple choice, true/false, matching, and fill-in can sample mastery of elements of knowledge	Essay exercises can tap understanding of relationships among elements of knowledge	Not a good choice for this target—three other options preferred	Can ask questions, evaluate answers, and infer mastery, but a time-consuming option
REASONING PROFICIENCY	Can assess application of some patterns of reasoning	Written descriptions of complex problem solutions can provide a window into reasoning proficiency	Can watch students solve some problems or examine some products and infer about reasoning proficiency	Can ask student to "think aloud" or can ask followup questions to probe reasoning
SKILLS	Can assess mastery of the knowledge prerequisites to skillful performance, but cannot rely on these to tap the skill itself		Can observe and evaluate skills as they are being performed	Strong match when skill is oral communication proficiency; also can assess mastery of knowledge prerequisite to skillful performance
ABILITY TO CREATE PRODUCTS	Can assess mastery of the knowledge prerequisite to the ability to create quality products, but cannot use these to assess the quality of products themselves		Can assess: (1) proficiency in carrying out steps in product development, and (2) attributes of the product itself	Can probe procedural knowledge and knowledge of attributes of quality products, but not product quality
DISPOSITIONS	Selected response questionnaire items can tap student feelings	Open-ended questionnaire items can probe dispositions	Can infer dispositions from behavior and products	Can talk with students about their feelings

81

But, in the real world, we must select the assessment methods that come closest to representing our valued targets and that at the same time fit into the resource realities of our classrooms. Though compromise is inevitable, we can work some pretty good tradeoffs between fidelity and cost of assessment if we know what we're doing.

To illustrate, let's move across the table left to right, one row at a time. Strive to see the big picture. We are looking at the forest now. We will spend the rest of this book examining the trees in rich detail.

Assessing Mastery of Content Knowledge

We all know we can use selected response, objective paper and pencil tests to measure student mastery of facts, concepts, and even generalizations. Typically, these assessments tend to test mastery of elements of knowledge in isolation, such as knowledge about the Civil War, spelling, vocabulary, Earth science, and the like. These tests are efficient in that we can administer large numbers of multiple-choice or true/false test items per unit of testing time. Thus, they permit us to sample widely and draw relatively confident generalizations from the content sampled. For this reason, when the target is knowledge mastery, selected response formats fit nicely into the resource realities of most classrooms.

But remember, even with this most traditional of all assessment methods, things can go wrong. For instance, what if respondents can't read? A nonreader might actually know the material but score low because of poor reading proficiency. If we conclude that his low score means a lack of knowledge, we would be wrong. We'll explore these and other potential sources of mismeasurement in later chapters.

When the domain of knowledge is defined not as elements in isolation but rather as larger structures of knowledge where elements relate in complex ways, we can test student mastery using the essay format. Examples of larger information chunks that students might be asked to know might include the causes of the Civil War or differences among igneous, metamorphic, and sedimentary rocks. In this case, we sample with exercises that provide relatively more information than any single selected response item and that require longer response times. So we typically administer fewer of them. Further, essay assessments present us with a more complex scoring challenge, and not just in terms of its time demands. Because we must judge response quality, not merely count it right or wrong, bias can creep in if we are not cautious. And remember, in this case, students also must bring writing proficiency into the assessment context. Thus, it is not useful in primary grades, before writing skills develop.

When it comes to the match between performance assessment and mastery of content knowledge, things quickly become complicated. The match is not always a strong one. To see what I mean, consider a brief example. Let's say we ask a student to complete a rather complex performance involving a process leading to a final product, as in the case of carrying out a science lab experiment to identify an unknown substance. If the student successfully identifies the substance, then we know that student possesses the prerequisite knowledge of science and lab procedures to solve the problem. In this case, the match between performance assessment and assessment of mastery of knowledge is a strong one.

However, to understand the complexity of this match, consider the instance in which the student fails to accurately identify the substance. Is that failure due to lack of declarative or procedural knowledge? Does the student possess the required knowledge and fail to use it to reason productively? Or does the student possess the knowledge and reason productively, but fail to use the lab apparatus skillfully? At the time the student fails to perform successfully, we just don't know.

Now here's the key point: We cannot know the real reason for failure unless and until we follow up the performance assessment with one of the other assessment methods (selected response, essay or personal communication—probably the natural choice in this case), ask a few questions, and find out if the prerequisite knowledge was there to start with. But if our goal to start with was to assess mastery of content knowledge, why would we go through all the hassle? Why not just turn to one of the other three options from the outset?

If my reason for assessing is to certify lab technicians, I don't care why the student failed. But if I am a teacher whose job is to help students learn to perform well in science, I must know why this student failed or I have no way to help her perform adequately in the future.

As an important aside, I submit that a primary reason why large-scale standardized assessments—whether objective tests or performance assessments—have historically had so little impact on teachers in classrooms is that they leave teachers not knowing the reasons for student failures. They reveal only high- or low-level performance, which from a public accountability point of view may be good enough. But, from the teacher's point of view, they fail to reveal which explanation for failure is correct. They fail to suggest actions the teacher can follow. Only sound classroom assessments can do this.

The final option for assessing mastery of knowledge is direct personal communication with the student—for example, by asking questions and evaluating answers. This is a good match across all grade levels, especially with limited amounts of knowledge to be mastered, few students to be assessed, and in contexts where records of performance need not be stored for long periods of time.

The reason I impose these conditions is that this obviously is a labor-intensive assessment method. So if the domain of knowledge to be assessed is large, the user is faced with the need to ask a large number of questions to cover it well. That just doesn't fit the resource realities in most classrooms. Further, if the number of students to be assessed is large, this option may not allow enough time to sample each student's achievement representatively. And, if records of performance must be stored over an extended period of time, written records will be needed for each student over a broad sample of questions. This, too, eats up a lot of time and energy.

Assessment via personal communication works best in those situations when the teacher is checking student mastery of critical content during instruction in order to make quick, ongoing adjustments as needed.

Assessing Reasoning and Problem Solving

In most classrooms, at all grade levels, we want students to be able to use the knowledge they master in productive ways to reason and solve problems. There are many ways to define what it means to be a proficient problem solver. We discuss many of these alternative conceptualizations and their assessment throughout this book. For now, let me cite a few sample patterns of reasoning as a point of departure for discussing assessment in this important arena.

One kind of reasoning we value is evaluative or critical thinking—the ability to make judgments and defend them through rigorous application of standards or criteria. Just as movie or restaurant critics evaluate according to criteria, so students can evaluate the quality of a piece of literature or the strength of a scientific argument.

Another commonly valued pattern of reasoning is inferential thinking—the ability to reason inductively and deductively, to draw generalizations from the evidence, or to predict outcomes from a set of initial circumstances. Yet another pattern involves using foundational knowledge to compare and contrast things, to infer similarities and differences.

How does one assess these kinds of reasoning targets? Our four methodological choices all provide excellent options when used by teachers who possess both a clear vision of what they wish to assess and sufficient craft knowledge of the assessment methods.

For example, we can use selected response exercises to determine if students can reason well. We can use them, for example, to see if students can analyze things, compare them, or draw inferences. Consider the following examples:

> Analytical reasoning: Which of the following sequences of plot elements properly depicts the order of events in the story we read today? (Offer response options, only one of which is correct.)
>
> Comparative reasoning: What is one essential difference between the story we read today and the one we read yesterday? (Offer response options, only one of which is correct.)
>
> Inferential reasoning: If you had to choose a theme from among those listed below for the story we read today, which would be best? Why do you think so? (Offer response options, more than one of which may be correct.)

Assuming that these are novel questions posed immediately after reading the story, so students had no opportunity to memorize the answers, they ask students to dip into their knowledge base (about the story) and use it to reason. More about this later in the book.

I continue to be surprised by how many educators believe that selected response exercises can test only recall of content. While they can do this very well, this assessment mode is more flexible than many people think, as the previous examples illustrate. There are limits, however. Evaluative thinking—expressing and defending a point of view—cannot be tested using multiple-choice or true/false items because this kind of thinking requires at least a written expression of the defense. Further, problems that are multifaceted and complex, involving several steps, the application of several different patterns of reasoning, and/or several problem solvers working together—as real-world problems often do—demand more complex assessment methods. But for some kinds of reasoning, selected response can work.

Essay tests represent an excellent way to assess student reasoning and problem solving. Student writing provides an excellent window into student thinking. In fact, very often, students can be encouraged to look through this window and assess their own reasoning and problem solving. Teachers can devise highly challenging exercises that ask students to analyze, compare, draw complex inferences, evaluate, or use some combination of these.

Of course, the key to evaluating the quality of student responses to such exercises is for the assessor to understand the pattern of reasoning required and to be able to detect its presence in student writing. Clear and appropriate scoring criteria are essential.

Performance assessment represents yet another excellent option in this arena that is applicable across all grade levels. We can watch students in the act of problem solving in a science lab, for example, and draw inferences about their proficiency. To the extent that they carry out proper procedures, they reveal their ability to carry out a pattern of reasoning.

However, again, drawing inferences about reasoning proficiency on the basis of the quality of student products can be risky. Certainly, strong performance (a high-quality product) is evidence of sound reasoning. But for classroom purposes, where assessment is used to promote student development, we have difficulty explaining and helping with weak performance—with a low-quality product. Did the student fail to perform due to a lack of foundational knowledge, failure to reason productively, or lack of motivation? As previously stated, without followup assessment by other means, we just don't know.

If we don't follow up with supplemental assessment, and thereby infer the wrong cause of failure, at the very least our remedy is likely to be inefficient. We may waste valuable time reteaching material already mastered or teaching reasoning skills already developed.

One of the strongest matches between target and assessment method in Table 4–1 is the use of personal communication to evaluate student reasoning. Teachers can do any or all of the following:

- Ask questions that probe the clarity, accuracy, relevance, depth, and breadth of reasoning.
- Have students ask each other questions and listen for evidence of sound reasoning.
- Have students reason out loud, describing their thinking as they confront a problem.
- Have students recount their reasoning processes.
- Ask students to reconstruct each other's reasoning.
- Simply listen attentively during class discussions for evidence of sound, appropriate reasoning.

Just talking informally with students can reveal so much, when we know what we're looking for! However, with this method, it will always take time to carry out the assessment and to keep accurate records of results.

Assessing Mastery of Skills

When our assessment goal is to find out if students can demonstrate achievement-related skills, such as speak in a second language, give a formal speech, or interact with classmates in socially acceptable ways, then there is just one way: Observe them while they are exhibiting the desired behaviors and make judgments as to their quality—performance assessment. There is no other choice. Each of the other options falls short for this kind of target.

But sometimes limited resources make it impossible to assess the actual skill. At those times, you may need to go for second best and come as close to the real target as you can. You have several options when you need to trade fidelity for greater efficiency in skills assessment. You can use selected response test items to determine whether the student can recognize the right behaviors. For example, given a number of performance demonstrations (on video, perhaps), can the respondent identify the best? Or, you may use a multiple-choice format to see if students know the proper sequence of activities to carry out when that is relevant to the outcome. Given several descriptions of a procedure, can the respondent identify the correct one? We can also use this method to ask if students have mastered the vocabulary needed to communicate about desired skills.

Realize, however, that such tests assess only prerequisites to effective performance—the building blocks to competence. They cannot assess that examinee's actual level of skill in performing.

With this same limitation, you could have students write essays about the criteria they might use to evaluate performance in a vocal music competition, knowledge that might well represent an important foundation for performing well in such a competition. But, of course, this will fall short of a real test of performance.

Finally, personal communication represents an excellent means of skills assessment when the skills in question have to do with oral communication proficiency. For such an outcome, this is the highest-fidelity assessment option.

For other kinds of skills, however, personal communication can only serve as a means to get at proficiency in describing sound performance. It falls short of providing direct data on the student's ability to perform.

Assessing Proficiency in Creating Products

The same limitations discussed for skills assessment apply here. If our assessment goal is to determine whether students can create a certain kind of achievement-related product, there is no better way than to have them actually create one. In fact, performance assessment represents the only means of direct assessment. The best test of the ability to throw a ceramic pot is the quality of the finished product itself. The best test of the ability to set up scientific apparatus is the completed arrangement. The best test of the ability to write a term paper is the finished paper.

Again, you could use a selected response assessment format to see if a student can pick out a quality product from among several choices. Or, you could test knowledge of a quality product's key attributes. But these are limited substitutes for assessment that actually asks students to create the product.

It is also possible to have students write essays about or discuss, with their teacher or other students, the key attributes of a carefully crafted object, such as a cabinet in shop class. Again, students who respond well to such an exercise might well possess the important prerequisite knowledge. But sometimes the real issue is whether students can create a carefully crafted cabinet. When that is the question, performance assessment is the answer.

Assessing Dispositions

It is instructive to note that the entries in the last row of Table 4-1 include no weak matches. The range of assessment methods available to tap the various dimensions of dispositions is wide indeed.

Let's take a minute to review some of the student characteristics that fall under this heading. Affective dimensions of individuals that might be the object of classroom assessment include attitudes, values, interests, self-concept, and motivation. Remember, as stated in Chapter 3, the focus of assessment in this case is to determine the direction and intensity of student feelings about different school-related issues. When it comes to dispositions, we seek strong positive affect: positive attitudes about school, subjects, classmates, and so on; strong values about hard work; a strong positive academic self concept; and strong positive motivation or seriousness of purpose.

The key to success in assessing these things—as usual—is a clear and appropriate definition of the characteristic to be assessed. Given a clear understanding, could we translate such targets into selected response questions? You bet! But our collection of such items won't be a test per se, it would more properly be considered a questionnaire. Many selected response item formats are very useful for such highly structured questionnaires. For instance, we could offer students statements and ask if they agree, disagree, or are undecided. Or, we could ask them to select from among a list of adjectives those that most accurately apply to themselves or to some other object. This assessment realm is rich with useful options.

Essay questions are another viable option for tapping dispositions. We can write open-ended questionnaire items that ask students to describe both the direction and intensity of their feelings about any particular object. After more than 15 years of in-school and in-classroom research on classroom assessment practices, one of the most startling insights for me has been how rarely teachers use questionnaires to gather affective information from their students—information that could make everyone's job much easier.

The match between affective targets and performance assessment is a bit more complex, however, because of the nature of the inferences that must be drawn. In this case, I urge caution. It certainly is possible to look at samples of student performance or at student-created products and draw conclusions about attitudes, values, and motivational dispositions with respect to that particular project. If students demonstrate high levels of achievement, their attitude was probably strongly positive, they probably valued the project and their work, and they probably were disposed to work hard to perform well.

However, care must be exercised at the other end of the performance continuum. When performance is poor, there are many possible explanations, only one of which is a poor attitude and lack of motivation. Only additional followup assessment will reveal the real reason for failure to perform.

One excellent way in which to conduct such a followup might be direct personal communication with the student. In the right atmosphere, students will talk openly and honestly about the strength and direction of their dispositions. The keys to success, of course, are to be able to establish that open, trusting environment and to know what kinds of questions to ask to tap important affect.

Chapter Summary: Targets and Methods Must Match

Sound classroom assessments arise from a clear and appropriate target and sample student performance with respect to that target using a proper assessment method. A strong assessment method is one that provides the most direct view of student performance—that permits the strongest inferences from the assessment results to the actual status of the achievement target.

In this chapter, we have described four assessment methods and discussed how they might be used selectively to tap student achievement on a range of school outcomes. A strong inference I would have you draw from now on is that the sound assessment of the full range of our valued school outcomes in the classroom will require applying all of the assessment tools we have at our disposal: selected response paper and pencil tests, essay exercises, performance assessments, and direct personal communication with students. No single method can serve all of our assessment needs at all grade levels. We must learn to use all methods applicable within our context.

Exercises to Advance Your Learning

Knowledge

1. List and define each of the four basic assessment methods. Identify format options within each method.

2. Scan the chapter again and create a new version of Table 4-1 in your own words.

Reasoning

1. If you were forced to select only one method for assessing each of the five kinds of achievement targets, which method would you choose for each and why?

2. Create another Figure 4-2 framework with empty cells. In each cell, if the union of

that target and method represents a match with the actual target, enter a plus sign. If the match is to prerequisites, enter an asterisk (*). What generalizations, if any, do you infer from the resulting pattern?

3. If our objective was to assess your teaching proficiency, what assessment method(s) should we use and why? (Pause to reflect on the active ingredients of good teaching before answering.)

Dispositions

1. Some in the education community condemn selected response tests as trivializing learning. Others condemn essay tests as too difficult to score dependably—as too subjective. Still others think performance assessment is too labor intensive and is as undependable as are essay tests. Then there are those who feel that personal communication is too biased a form of assessment because teacher-student personalities get in the way. If we listen to all critics, we are left without viable assessment options. To whom should we listen? What methods should we use? Why?

Special Ongoing Assessment Project: Part 2

At the end of Chapter 3, you listed the various kinds of achievement targets valued in your special unit of instruction. This might have included knowledge to master, reasoning proficiencies to develop, skills to attain, or product development capabilities to master. Please retrieve that list now from your special project portfolio so you can carry our special assignment work to the next level.

Your next assignment is to devise a very general assessment plan for this unit. This plan will detail the sequence of your important assessment events—what you plan to assess, when, and how as this unit unfolds. Realize that this is just a first pass at the planning process. You will have time to refine it later.

Reflect on your knowledge targets. During the unit, what content do you expect your students to learn? In what order do you expect them to master it and according to what general schedule? Remember to distinguish if you can between the content to be learned outright and that which can be retrieved later through the use of references. When in this process do you plan to check on their mastery of this material? Think about how you might stage appropriate assessments. What assessment method(s) might work best in this plan?

Reflect on your reasoning, skill, and product targets too, as appropriate. How does mastery of these targets unfold over time? What assessment methods might you employ to track student achievement of these targets and when would you use them during the instructional process?

When you have completed and recorded your preliminary plan of assessment events save your plan in your portfolio for later refinement.

Facing the Barriers to Quality Assessment

CHAPTER ROADMAP

In most classrooms, careful reflection will reveal what it means to do a good job of assessing. However, it can be quite another matter to actually attain a positive assessment environment that relies on quality tools. The reason for this difficulty is that our school culture routinely throws up imposing barriers to quality assessment. This chapter is about those barriers and how to remove them. As a result of studying the material presented in Chapter 5, reflecting on that material, completing the exercises presented at the end of the chapter, and hopefully interacting with colleagues, you will master a foundation of knowledge about key barriers to quality by understanding the following:

1. The origins of our common adult emotions about being evaluated and why these feelings can represent roadblocks to quality assessment.

2. How forces from within the school-community relationship can prevent educators from meeting standards of quality assessment.

3. Why time barriers can prevent teachers from being able to meet standards of quality assessment.

4. How a lack of assessment literacy blocks our progress toward effective schools by preventing us from removing these and other barriers to quality.

In addition, you will learn to use that foundation of knowledge to reason and solve problems in the following ways:

1. Relate your personal experiences with assessment to the emotions you feel about the prospect of being assessed and evaluated.

2. Draw generalizations about the proper course of action in addressing community assumptions about the status of assessment in their schools.

3. Infer proper courses of action to gain the time needed to assess well in the classroom.

Finally, I hope you emerge from your study of this chapter with the following dispositions:

1. Be willing to analyze and come to terms with your own personal assessment history, so it does not prevent you from considering ways to create positive, constructive assessment environments in your context.

2. See the value of encouraging and contributing to productive school and community partnerships as a means to achieve quality assessment in the classroom.

3. Be optimistic about the possibility of finding time to assess by understanding and applying sound assessment practices.

4. Feel strongly about the value of investing the time and energy required to develop sufficiently high levels of assessment literacy to be able to remove roadblocks to quality assessment within your own context.

This chapter does not include the development of any specific skills or product development capabilities.

We are well into our journey now, having discussed the first three quality standards, addressing the need for focused purposes, clear and appropriate targets, and proper assessment methods. We will spend the remainder of the text exploring these further and filling in the two remaining quality standards: the need to sample appropriately and the need for accurate, unbiased, distortion-free assessments. I hope by now your classroom assessment challenges are becoming clear to you: understand and remain sensitive to the difference between sound and unsound assessment. Only by meeting our quality standards can we assure students and their families that achievement is being accurately assessed and the results effectively used to promote each student's academic well-being.

Before we go further, however, we need to take a brief side trip to confront some realities of assessment life in schools. For several reasons, standards of quality assessment can be very easy to define but very difficult to meet in practice because, as I stated at the beginning of this chapter, our school culture presents us with several specific roadblocks to quality assessment.

I have chosen this point in our journey to diverge from the nitty-gritty details of assessment practice and confront these challenges for two reasons. First, chapters 1 through 4 have given you enough background to understand these roadblocks. Second, I plan to devote the rest of this book to helping you understand how to remove them.

If you are an experienced teacher, you will already have encountered each of these barriers and will know the frustration they can engender. My goal is to provide you with the insights and assessment tools you need to minimize that emotional stress.

If you are a teacher in training, believe me, you will face these barriers as soon as you reach the classroom. My goals with respect to your learning are (1) to help you begin to be aware of and anticipate these roadblocks and (2) to provide you with the foundation of assessment literacy you will need to successfully address them.

Regardless of your level of experience, *never* underestimate the power of the forces behind these roadblocks.

Understanding the Roadblocks

We will examine four roadblocks to quality assessment. I introduce them here, and will discuss them at length in the rest of the chapter.

The first barrier arises from within us—it is our own emotions about the assessment and evaluation process. The prospect of having our performance assessed and evaluated scares many of us, even as adults. The assessment part is not so much of a problem. This is the process of gathering information about our achievement. It's the evaluation part that triggers the strong feelings. This is the process of comparing our performance to standards of acceptable performance to see if we measure up—to determine if we are good enough.

As a result of many experiences in our youth and adult lives, many fear being evaluated, and for good reason. We will explore those experiences in this chapter. These strong negative feelings about assessment and evaluation are a barrier to quality assessment because they can prevent us from being willing to both take the risk and invest the mental energy needed to hold ourselves accountable for actual student achievement.

The second barrier arises from an external source, the communities within which schools function. It is not uncommon for parents and citizens to hold a set of beliefs about the state and status of assessment in their schools that can have the effect of preventing educators from being able to meet standards of quality. For example, they often believe that educators are trained to be competent assessors of student achievement. If this is a valid belief, high-quality assessments probably already are in use in their schools and there is no problem. But what if this assumption is in fact invalid and the community is unaware of it? Naive communities are unlikely to be willing to invest resources needed to fix inherent problems. This reluctance, in effect, deprives educators of the professional development resources needed to assure quality assessment.

The third barrier to quality classroom assessment is time. When teachers lack time to learn about quality assessment and time to carry out sound assessment practices, quality will suffer. The vast majority of teachers don't feel that they have time to participate in such professional development or time to assess well in the classroom. Given the broadening array of responsibilities assigned to teachers these days, finding time to carry out a whole new array of high-quality assessment strategies seems to them to be a huge challenge. Paradoxically, there are ways to overcome the "time to assess" barrier. But to learn about those ways we have to over-come the "time to learn" barrier. It's a catch-22 dilemma.

The final barrier to quality classroom assessment is our understanding of the meaning of quality and our lack of craft knowledge in how to meet standards of quality. As troubling as it is to admit, at the time of this writing in 1996, we remain a national faculty of teachers and administrators who completed undergraduate and graduate training programs almost completely devoid of any of the assessment training required to fulfill emerging classroom assessment responsibilities. With a few notable exceptions, it has been thus for decades. When we lack sufficient assessment literacy, we are unlikely to do a good job.

As it turns out, the knowledge of assessment methods needed to remove bar-rier four is also the key to removing the other three barriers. The reason many of us fear assessment and evaluation is that we don't understand it and therefore cannot gain control over it. When we feel vulnerable, we become anxious. When we gain assessment wisdom, that anxiety dissipates. The reason we have difficulty dealing with our communities about their assessment concerns is that we lack the under-standing and confidence to address key issues in a forthright manner. In effect, we have negotiated a treaty with them that in their eyes gives us license to do what we have always done because we have always done it, regardless of its appropriate-ness. The more we know about quality assessment practice, the easier it is to do the right thing for our students and help their families understand why our prac-tices are sound. The reason we have difficulty finding time to assess well is that we lack knowledge of assessment tactics that can make our teaching job faster, easier and better. With assessment literacy comes the time to do the assessment job we are hired to do within the time allotted to do it.

To reach any of these goals—to overcome any of the barriers—each of us must invest whatever time and energy it takes to develop sufficient assessment literacy to see our way clear of these roadblocks (Figure 5–1). This book is designed to help us negotiate the barriers. But first, let's understand each barrier more thoroughly.

Barrier 1: Our Emotions About Assessment and Evaluation

We are a society of adults that harbors some very strong emotions about the prospect of being evaluated. Most of us grew up in classrooms in which assessment almost always left us feeling like we were at risk. If we didn't study for an exam, we knew we risked being judged failures. Even if we did prepare carefully, there was always the chance that something could go wrong. I'm reminded of the bumper sticker I saw recently that read, "As long as there are tests in schools, there will be prayer in schools." These feelings of vulnerability form part of our foundation of adult feelings about the assessment and evaluation process.

These emotions run deep. I'm struck by how many teachers tell me that they have the recurring dream that they are back in school, they haven't been going to class and are far behind in their work, and the final exam is tomorrow. In this case, the residual emotion is one of guilt. Even if we prepare carefully, what if it isn't enough? And if we fail, we let everyone down—teacher, parents, grandparents, and so on. Guilt: the gift that keeps on giving! I'm reminded of another bumper sticker

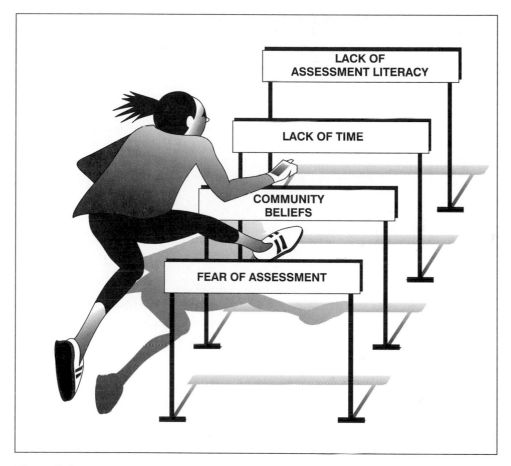

Figure 5–1
Overcoming the Barriers to Quality Assessment

that read, "My teacher was a travel agent for guilt trips." But where do these emotions come from?

Climb into your time machine and travel back in time with me and I'll show you. You are about to relive some assessment events of your youth. As you travel, tune into the emotions these experiences rekindle.

Return to your elementary years—fourth, fifth, or sixth grade—and bring back to memory one of your teachers from that time in your life. Visualize that classroom at the end of the day with everyone putting on coats to leave. Remember? Let say it's the end of the midyear semester. Before the final bell rings, your teacher issues one last instruction. As you recall your teacher saying something like this, recall the emotions you would have felt. Your teacher speaks in a loud voice: "Now remember, students, it's the end of the semester and of the grading period. So, remember— tomorrow is report card day! Be sure to remind your parents that report cards are coming home tomorrow. We want to be sure they're ready to sign them so you can bring them back to me. Have a good evening!"

Time for Reflection

As you recall this event, what emotions come to mind? Jot down the feelings you recall experiencing.

Now restart your time machine and drift forward to eighth grade. Recall science class. Let's say science is your first class early in the morning—the bell rings at 7:45 A.M. You're almost awake. Your science teacher, one of those superhigh-energy types, come bounding into the room, turns on those bright lights, and says (again, tune into the emotions this triggers): "Everyone clear your desks and take out a piece of paper and pencil. We're going to have a pop quiz this morning to see if you did the homework!"

Time for Reflection

Again, jot down the feelings this memory brings to mind.

Finally, ride your time capsule into high school, to the autumn of your senior year. It's the Friday night before or early Saturday morning of the day you are to take your college admission tests. What emotions do you recall feeling? What emotions do you feel now, just thinking about that event in your school life?

Time for Reflection

Write those feelings down. Compare the various emotions associated with these assessment events. Consider similarities and differences. Then think about this question: What were the key dimensions of the learning environments and evaluation experiences of our youth that left these emotions in our memories? Before reading on, list the contributing factors.

By and large, we are an adult society that looks back on assessment and evaluation during our school years with a sense of relief that we escaped. While this was not true for everyone, for many of us this was a negative, aggressive, anxiety-producing source of stress we had to live through because that was simply the way it was for us. Several specific dimensions of our classroom assessment realities contributed to these feelings. Sometimes we were called on to answer a question (without having volunteered!) and didn't know the answer. Remember the anxiety that this might happen, and the embarrassment when it did? Sometimes, achievement targets we were to hit on an upcoming test were not made clear to us. So we had to guess. If we guessed wrong, we suffered the consequences. Often, we got only one shot at it. We had to succeed because there was no second chance. Sometimes we'd concentrate on learning one thing and then were surprised with a test on something completely different.

In addition, it was not uncommon for our teachers to create an artificial scarcity of success by limiting the number of good grades available. In those cases, we could have achieved a great deal in an absolute sense but still not finish high enough in the rank order to get an A. Often the classroom assessment environment seemed to be an "us versus them" confrontation between students and teachers. They held all the power to evaluate. We were not in control of all the factors that determined our success and were frequently vulnerable at some level.

Please understand I do not contend that these were necessarily counterproductive emotions. They caused many of us to behave in academically responsible and productive ways. However, as I work with teachers and administrators—all of whom are former kids, by the way—I find few who want to return to those days. We wouldn't go back to being tested as we were in school on a bet! Our emotions on this subject are strong for very good reasons.

But for many of us, this was just the foundation of our collective emotions about assessment and evaluation. After we finished public school, we went on to college. Now there's a bastion of high-quality assessment! Those of you still in college know what I'm talking about. We continued to grow a victim's mentality about being evaluated (Figure 5–2). Then, as we began to train in college to become teachers, we confronted our first course in testing techniques. Virtually all of the research on the nature and impact of this training reveals that the content bore little relationship to the reality of assessment life in classrooms. Experienced teach-

Figure 5–2
The Fearsome Assessment Monster!

ers who took such courses know what I mean. If you are in training now, I hope you won't have to experience it.

The accumulation of these emotions led some to infer that assessment is a topic to be avoided. When educators draw this conclusion, the unfortunate consequence is that they become closed to the possibility of creating an assessment environment that is more positive and productive than the one we all grew up in. Casey, our veteran high school teacher, recalls this feeling:

"I remember when the education reformers began to tell us to state clear instructional goals. Back in the 1970s, it was *behavioral objectives*. Then we began calling them *minimum competencies*. Now, it's *clear outcomes*. They're all the same to me. And, right from the start, way back then, we were going to measure student success using 'criterion-referenced tests.' This type of test, we were told, was the key to totally effective schools.

"Then it hit me. 'Wait a minute,' I said to myself, 'what if I get explicit about my expectations and assess the right way, and the results reveal that my students didn't hit the target? Who's going to get blamed? Me!' But what if I did all in my power to help them learn? What if their failure was due to factors beyond my control? I still get the blame. I remember thinking how unfair that could be—and how risky for me.

"In fact, several of us concluded back in the 1980s that it was safer to remain vague about our achievement expectations and keep them to ourselves. So we just kept doing what we had always done. No one would ever see inside our gradebooks to find out who had learned and who had not. Even if they looked, we could rely on our testing and record-keeping procedures to present whatever image we wished of student learning.

"As long as some of our students scored really high on the SAT or the ACT at the end of high school, we'd be safe. Our goal was to avoid the risks. Personally, I just couldn't see any other way to survive."

Such fear of accountability for student learning can prevent us from building quality assessments into the classroom teaching and learning process. It is a barrier to sound assessment.

Time for Reflection

To capture a glimpse of a constructive classroom assessment environment, return to your time capsule once again and drift back again to your elementary, junior high, high school, or even college years. Does any teacher come to mind from your experiences who succeeded in taking classroom assessment—generally a negative, aggressive, anxiety-producing process—and turning it into a positive, productive learning experience for you? Specifically, what did that teacher do to accomplish that reversal? What was the effect of these events on your motivation to strive for higher levels of achievement for that teacher? Compare such experiences with those of colleagues or fellow students, if time and opportunity permit.

Barrier 2: Community Beliefs

It is not uncommon for parents and other citizens of a school community to believe that all is well with assessment, evaluation, and grading within their child's classroom. But when this is not the case and naive communities don't know it, there is a danger that they may not understand why specific action programs may be needed to address problems that inhibit school effectiveness. The unfortunate consequence of this oversight and lack of action can be poor quality assessment and academic harm to learners.

In this section, I will share some specific dimensions of classroom assessment environments that communities assume to be true, so you know what to expect from your school community and so we can explore their implications for the quality of assessments. But before listing and discussing these common beliefs, permit me an important note of caution.

I am about to raise questions about dimensions of educational practice that many educators would prefer not be asked. In fact, we have avoided asking them for decades for reasons that will become obvious. As a result, experienced teachers and administrators reading this may feel an increasing sense of uneasiness. If careful analysis reveals that any of the community beliefs listed below are indeed invalid, the result could be a public relations problem of immense proportions.

This leaves us on the horns of a painful dilemma. Do we ask questions about our traditional assessment practices that we may not want to have answered and deal with the results? Or do we continue to ignore these questions for the sake of community tranquility, jeopardizing student well-being due to the danger of ongoing mismeasurement of their achievement?

My point is clear and unequivocal: We can no longer avoid these issues. The risk to our students is too great. We must ask questions and then seek resources to address the needs revealed in the answers, for our students' sakes. Our communities are unlikely to support the allocation of those resources if they do not know there is a classroom assessment problem in their schools. We must help our communities investigate the validity of their beliefs so we can enter into partnership with them to achieve quality classroom assessments. Barbour and Barbour (1997) discuss at length the need for family-school-community partnerships to ensure quality education and assessment for all students.

We discuss here two common beliefs about the status of assessment in schools. They deal with our collective preparedness to assess well, asking: Are educators really ready to gather high-quality information about student achievement?

Community Belief 1. *Each teacher in each classroom is a competent, confident master of the achievement targets her or his students are to master.* Each district curriculum must have specified and each teacher must have internalized a vision of the meaning of academic success in her or his classroom to be able to translate that vision into quality assessments. If a community believes that its teachers are on top of their achievement targets and that belief is valid, then another necessary condition for quality assessment has been satisfied. But, if that belief is unfounded in any particular classroom, mismeasurement is assured.

We cannot prejudge any teacher in this regard. But neither should we blithely assume that all teachers are ready to meet this standard. In my years of research in classroom assessment, for example, I have come across many who are given responsibility for teaching students to write who have little sense of the attributes of quality writing. Further, as I train teachers in assessment processes, I often ask two questions: How many expect their students to become proficient reasoners and problem solvers in their classrooms? How many can tell me in specific detail the standards of effective reasoning they apply in evaluating student reasoning? Every hand goes up in response to the first question, while none remains up in response to the second.

Many in our society do not understand that we frequently ask new elementary teachers to teach math or science concepts and principles that they themselves have never been trained in and may not understand. We routinely place substitute teachers in teaching and assessment contexts for which they have insufficient academic backgrounds.

For many (and perhaps most) teachers this is not a problem. They are confident, competent masters of the disciplines within which they teach. But what of those who are not? And more importantly, what of their students? It is dangerous to assume that all is well. If communities don't understand that some teachers in their schools need help in this regard, they are not likely to be willing to allocate the resources necessary to provide the professional development required to overcome these problems. The implications for the quality of classroom assessments of their failure to act are obvious.

Community Belief 2. *Educators are thoroughly trained in and certified to apply the basic principles of sound classroom assessment.* From the outside, it appears that teachers are ready to assess. They do it all the time. And it is crucial that they do a good job of assessing. Everyone counts on their information to be accurate: students, other teachers, and parents. Given the importance of quality assessment to good teaching, one would naturally assume that a major part of the teacher preparation curriculum is devoted to helping them to get ready to fulfill this critically important responsibility.

In fact, however, this is often not the case. A series of studies carried out by several independent researchers over the past several decades reveals that assessment training has never been a prominent part of teacher training (summarized in Stiggins & Conklin, 1992). As I begin my classroom assessment workshops for practicing teachers, again, I ask two questions: How many took at least one course in assessment during their training to become a teacher? About half of the hands go up. For how many of you did this course meaningfully help you face the realities of life in classrooms? No hands will remain up.

This signals two obvious problems: Many practicing teachers were not trained in the principles of sound assessment, and those who did receive such instruction often found that it included few connections to the classroom. Because of these problems in teacher preparation, it is dangerous to assume that all teachers are ready to assess well. But most communities make just such an assumption. What are the implications for the well-being of children if the assumption is in fact invalid? Communities may be unwilling to support the allocation of resources for much-needed professional development in assessment practices because they are unaware that a lack of assessment skills represent a huge barrier to quality.

Further, just as with teachers, it is tempting to assume that principals, curriculum and project directors, associate superintendents, and superintendents are prepared to fulfill their considerable assessment responsibilities. Administrators not steeped in the basic principles of sound assessment will have considerable difficulty doing these jobs.

In reality, professional preparation to fulfill these responsibilities is almost nonexistent in administrator training and certification programs across the United States. Thus, unless they have developed a high level of assessment literacy on their own or through on-the-job training, the vast majority of administrators have not been prepared to deliver on this critically important job requirement. Yet as a society, we often blithely assume they have been. How can we protect the well-being of our students under these circumstances?

In summary, our communities tend to believe that our assessment house is in order—that the foundations are in place throughout our educational structure to accurately assess the achievement of students at all grade levels and in all classrooms. As it turns out, this is a very dangerous assumption to make. It may be true or not, depending on the context. When it is not, we place students *directly* in harm's way.

We cannot fix this problem unless our communities permit us to take time to find where such problems exist and to provide the professional development needed to increase our ability to assess well. If they assume there is no problem, there will be no solution. Schools and communities must work as a team to analyze which of these assumptions are valid and which are not (Figure 5–3). Only then can quality assessment be assured.

Time for Reflection

Now that you have seen the beliefs to be investigated, you can see how vulnerable school personnel could become to criticism about their assessment practices if communities were to begin to ask questions. This could cause— and, in fact, has caused—some to recoil from the prospect of encouraging school-community partnerships to investigate classroom assessment quality. Again the dilemma framed earlier comes to the fore. Do we ask questions about our traditional assessment practices we may not want to have answered and deal with the results? Or do we continue to ignore these questions for the sake of community tranquility, jeopardizing student well-being due to the danger of ongoing mismeasurement of their achievement? How do you answer? Do fellow students or colleagues agree with you?

1. Are our achievement targets defined and articulated across grades?

2. Have all teachers mastered the achievement expected of their students?

3. Do our teachers know how to assess accurately?

4. Are our administrators trained to assess well?

Figure 5–3
Questions for Schools and Communities to Ask About Assessment in Their Schools

Barrier 3: Lack of Time to Assess Well

Perhaps the most prominent barrier to quality assessment from the teacher's point of view is the lack of time to assess well. Listen as our two experienced teachers, Lynn and Casey, discuss the issues:

LYNN: I just can't handle any more of this school improvement stuff! First it's cooperative learning, then it's thematic instruction and integrated learning. Now they want us to muck around with the schedules. Now, we're "restructuring." Wow, so many changes. Oh, and by the way, when am I supposed to teach?

CASEY: I hear ya. And on top of those, there's all the new assessment practices we're supposed to be using. Like performance assessment—observe 'em and judge 'em. Why can't I just give 'em a test like I used to? I don't have time to do all that work.

LYNN: Have you tried it?

CASEY: I have some. And I can see how performance assessment fits sometimes. But where do I get the time?

LYNN: We just added a whole new emphasis on technology on top of the traditional curriculum. Now I've gotta learn all that stuff myself.

CASEY: You gonna do it?

LYNN: Not as a volunteer—no way. But I may get drafted.

CASEY: I know what you mean.

LYNN: (With a smirk.) I need a staff: a whole team of "assistant teachers" to delegate stuff to!

CASEY: Forget it—you're the only worker in your teaching world. Always have been, always will be!

LYNN: Which means I better get to work on these grades. Have you ever seen a gradebook like this? I've got 185 students this year!

This dialogue—an interchange any experienced teacher will recognize—touches on several specific issues that trouble teachers deeply. These issues are pertinent here because, if they're valid, each represents a strong barrier to assessment quality. Let's analyze them.

Issue #1. *The broadening scope of the curriculum means teachers must assess an ever-expanding array of forms of student achievement. Teachers don't have time to assess more.* Without question, the curriculum is evolving to include more achievement targets (such as with the addition of important technology and health-related topics), more complexity within the various targets we value (such as our enhanced understandings of what it means to be a proficient reader or writer), and more complex ways of integrating the curriculum across disciplines. Add to this mix a rapid expansion in recommended instructional imperatives, like cooperative learning and inclusion of diverse ability levels in the same classroom, along with the opportunity to be involved in school-based decision making and—whew!—one could be overwhelmed. How can we assess even more when we have too little time to cover it all, let alone assess it all, now?

There is only one answer: Find ways to assess less, not more. We accomplish this by focusing sharply on the truly critical material. As our presentation unfolds, we will advocate two specific ways to do this. I will introduce them now and explain them as we go.

The first way to focus is to begin to narrow the curriculum by differentiating content knowledge that students must know outright from that which they can be taught to retrieve later as they need it by using reference materials. Then we assess only mastery of the core for all and their skill in retrieving the rest. Once classroom assessments show students have mastered the core content, along with the retrieval skills needed to find the rest, the assessment challenge is met.

The second solution to the spreading curriculum is to carefully articulate the curriculum across grades by (1) starting with a vision of the final (end of high school) achievement, and (2) backing that vision down through the curriculum, so as to develop a smooth and complete transition from beginning student to competent student. If teams of teachers take seriously this division of responsibility, they can remove redundancy and irrelevance along the way while building in reinforcers of early material as a calculated part of the curriculum. Thus, each individual teacher's instructional (and therefore assessment!) contribution will become more focused and more manageable.

For those teachers who feel they simply have too much to assess and therefore cannot hope to assess it all well, issues of assessment quality are not likely to become sufficiently relevant to do anything about. But if we can assist teachers by narrowing and focusing and by collaborating with colleagues to divide the assessment responsibility, we may be able to encourage more conscientious attention to issues of assessment quality. This will be one of our goals as we work through subsequent chapters.

Issue #2. *The recommended assessment methods are the most labor-intensive kinds, like performance assessment. Teachers don't have time to do labor-intensive assessment.* The message many teachers are receiving in these assessment times is that the only acceptable way to assess student achievement is by means of performance assessment methodology—authentic exercises leading to observations and judgments of students. Advocates cite the richness of results they can derive from observations of complex performance and judgments based on complex performance criteria and standards. Hidden between the lines of such lofty prose for many teachers—like Lynn and Casey—is the subliminal message, "Lots of hard work!" Some respond by digging in their heels. I know of few teachers who are actively looking for more work to do.

The currently popular message about the primacy of performance assessment is wrong in several ways. First, performance assessment is not always the best way. In fact, sometimes it isn't even an acceptable way to assess. In certain instances with certain students and certain achievement targets, other methods, such as multiple-choice or true/false tests, must be brought into play in the classroom. When they fit, these are much more efficient options. And even when we turn to performance assessment as the best choice, those who possess a rich craft knowledge of the method know how to use it efficiently. This book offers that craft knowledge—not just for performance assessment but for many assessment methods.

If the assumption is that teachers don't have time to assess well because they don't have time to use these new labor-intensive methods, we must help them by invalidating that assumption. We do that by opening our classrooms up to the use of many methods of assessment. This, too, will be one of our goals as we work through this text.

Issue #3.   *Whenever student achievement is being assessed and evaluated, I—the teacher—must do all the work. Since I am in this alone, I don't have time to attend to assessment quality. My goal is just to do some assessment!*

The essence of this issue is this: The more I assess and the more labor intensive my assessment methods, the more work I, the teacher, am forced to do (Figure 5–4). I must make up the exercises. I must devise the scoring scheme. I must administer the exercises. I must do all of the scoring (tons of fun with essay tests or performance assessments!). I must record the results and try to summarize them all for the parent-teacher conference—which I must plan and conduct. Whew!

However, we can address this concern by considering a different way to structure the classroom assessment environment. There are many others very close by who can shoulder a great deal of this assessment responsibility. When they do, surprising things can happen in the amount of time you have available for teaching.

Number one on the list of helpers is students. They can become fully responsible partners in conducting the assessment activities listed in the preceding paragraph—and their involvement may represent some of the most focused, motivating and powerful instructional interventions we can possibly conceive. But there are other helpers too, such as fellow teachers, administrators, parents, and retired teachers, among others. We will discuss their role in overcoming the time barrier as our journey proceeds.

Issue #4.   *The district continues to demand that I store and summarize information about student achievement for communication to others in the grade-book and with report card grades. The record-keeping challenge that brings is immense. I know it doesn't work effectively, but I don't have time to consider alternatives.*

When teachers like Lynn and Casey think about an expanding list of achievement targets, expanding complexity within each target, and the need to communi-

Figure 5–4
Help Is on the Way!

cate greater detail about student achievement than has been demanded before, once again the prospect of early retirement begins to sound pretty attractive! The information gathering, processing, and communicating demands are imposing, to say the least. If we conceive of record keeping as a teacher-centered activity relying on Fred Flintstone technology, the time demands far outstrip anything a teacher can manage.

Again the solution to this problem lies in invalidating the assumptions—breaking an outdated mold. The realities of the information processing demands of achievement-driven schools are that 1920s information processing technology will not—indeed cannot—meet our needs. Each teacher must start with sharply focused visions of achievement targets, thoroughly developed assessment plans, highly efficient assessment methods, and recordkeeping strategies that rely on modern information management technology—yes, I mean computers. And on top if this, we must devise procedures for sharing summaries of student achievement with various audiences at various times and in a form the users of that information will understand.

All of this is within the reach of each and every teacher, but only if we invest the time and energy needed to develop the expertise to devise quality assessment plans and to take advantage of currently available information management technology. As this presentation continues, I will offer specific guidelines for how to reach these goals.

Barrier 4: Lack of Assessment Expertise

This is the easiest of the four roadblocks to quality to understand. We cannot meet standards of quality if we don't know what those standards are or how to meet them in any particular classroom assessment context. We remove this barrier by developing the expertise we need to meet the various challenges that emerge for teachers. The benefits of developing that expertise are immense.

After reflecting on the first three barriers to quality—our emotions, community beliefs, and lack of time—it should be clear that barrier four represents the key to a clear path to quality. Only through the attainment of a sufficiently high level of assessment literacy can teachers gain access to the equipment needed to remove the other three barriers. We remain fearful about assessment mysteries that we don't understand. We have difficulty assisting our communities in examining their beliefs if we remain fearful and lack the wisdom to help them understand the differences between sound and unsound assessment and evaluation practices. We can't use our assessment wisdom to make our assessment job faster, easier, and better if we don't understand the assessment economies we have at our disposal. *Assessment literacy is the key.*

But what does this really mean? Precisely what must teachers know, and what must we be able to do with that assessment knowledge to be successful? As a part of a statewide effort to support teachers in the classroom assessment process, the Washington State Commission on Student Learning, working through a committee of teachers, administrators, state department personnel, and representatives from higher education, has identified the specific competencies listed in Figure 5–5.

1. Teachers must be competent masters of each of the achievement expectations they hold as important for their students. That mastery must be to a sufficient level of understanding for teachers to be able to translate those expectations into quality assessments.

2. Teachers must understand all of the various purposes of assessment in schools and know how each level of assessment use (from classroom to building to district to state and beyond) impacts the quality of a student's schooling experience.

3. Teachers must understand and be able to apply standards of technical assessment quality.

4. Teachers must be able to identify an appropriate assessment method from among several available options, and they must be able either to (a) select previously developed assessments, or (b) design and develop new assessments that fit the contexts.

5. Teachers must be able to store, retrieve and communicate assessment results to users of that information in a timely manner that assures complete and accurate understanding of those results on the part of all relevant users.

6. Teachers must know and be able to meet standards of professional (fair, legal and ethical) practice in conducting classroom assessment practices.

7. Teachers must understand and remain sensitive to the personal consequences of their assessments for their students and the families of those students.

Figure 5–5
Washington State Classroom Assessment Competencies for Teachers
Source: Washington Commission on Student Learning. Reprinted with permission.

This text provides the kind of instruction and learning experiences needed to meet these standards of professional practice. We will explore achievement targets, assessment methods, and their alignment in greater depth in Parts 2 and 3. As we go, we will address the sampling and quality control guidelines needed to use each assessment method well. And we will explore the use of student-centered assessment as a motivational and teaching tool. Finally, we will conclude our journey in Part 4 with several chapters on strategies for effective communication about student achievement—strategies designed to meet the diverse information needs of all assessment users.

Chapter Summary: Clearing the Road to Quality

We have diverged from our detailed discussion of classroom assessment practices just enough to see that the path to quality classroom assessment is strewn with remnants of an assessment history that can keep us from reaching our goal. As we face our assessment future and strive to meet standards of quality, it is best that we proceed with our eyes wide open, aware of the considerable challenges we face.

Part of our assessment history is personal. Many of us have been taught to fear the prospect of being evaluated. Our automatic response is that we are at risk. Even if we prepare carefully and work hard to meet our goals and satisfy standards, something could go wrong and we could be victimized again. These feelings can force us to distance ourselves from the topic of assessment and evaluation, a topic we must master and understand thoroughly if we are to do the job we aspire to do: help learners succeed.

Part of that history involves the perceptions of those who view schools from outside and who exert influence on the manner in which schools do their work. If communities believe certain things to be true—that we know what to assess, how to assess, and how to use the results effectively—and those beliefs are in fact true, then schools and the needs of society are more likely to match, and the institution will fit smoothly into its place in that society. However, if society's beliefs about our preparedness to assess and the quality of our assessments are invalid and the community does not know this, problems lurk nearby. Communities unaware of a lack of preparedness to assess accurately are not likely to permit schools to spend resources to become more prepared.

Another relevant part of our assessment history has been the role of assessment practices in the larger context of task demands schools place on teachers. While assessment is one of the most prominent activities teachers engage in, it is by no means the only activity. If I as a teacher don't think I have enough time to be concerned about conducting quality assessments, then I am not likely to be willing (or able) to invest the time and energy needed to refine my assessment processes. The feeling of being overwhelmed with change can prevent me from even caring about quality assessment, let alone acting on that concern.

The fourth and final barrier to quality day-to-day classroom assessment is our chronic, decades-long practice of failing to provide teachers with the kind of assessment skills needed to reach that goal. Standards of quality that we do not understand are not standards at all—they are mysteries. And for many teachers and administrators today, assessment mysteries abound!

We prepare ourselves to clear the path to quality assessment by (1) learning those standards of quality, (2) understanding how to apply them in any classroom assessment context, and (3) using that wisdom to overcome our fear, establish honest school-community partnerships for quality assessments, and make the teaching job faster, easier, and better. This is our mission as we study together through this book.

Exercises to Advance Your Learning

Knowledge

1. List the four roadblocks to quality discussed in this chapter and in your own words describe how each could keep a teacher from meeting standards of assessment quality.

2. Describe in writing how forces from within the school-community relationship can prevent educators from meeting standards of quality assessment.

3. Teachers virtually always identify the time barrier as their major roadblock to quality. Recount in your own words what specific problems they encounter.

4. How can assessment literacy help us progress toward effective schools

by helping us remove barriers to quality?

Reasoning

1. Write a personal history of your assessment experiences in school. What were your most memorable experiences? How did they influence your schooling experience? What emotions do they trigger for you? What inferences would you draw about your emotions as a roadblock to your path to quality assessment in your classroom?

2. Given what you know about how communities might view the assessment environments in their schools, what generalizations do you draw about the proper course of action for a school or district to take in investigating the validity of these beliefs?

3. Assume you were talking to Casey, our high school teacher friend, who was complaining about the lack of time to meet emerging demands of assessment. Casey is expressing extreme frustration in terms of the four issues discussed in this chapter. What courses of action might you offer for dealing with each complaint?

Dispositions

1. Historically, assessment and evaluation during school years have carried a distinctly negative connotation. Most adults would not return to those experiences—they regard their escape into adulthood with immense relief. Yet some contend that this is the way school is supposed to be—it's a rite of passage. They made it through and others should be forced to deal with it, too. Do you agree? Is this the best way to encourage productive academic work on the part of students, in your opinion? Why?

2. If we encourage our communities to believe that all is well with the quality of assessments in their schools when all is not well, we purposely mislead them. To do otherwise is to leave ourselves vulnerable to intense criticism. But if we reveal potential inadequacies in our preparation to assess well, we may position ourselves to help more students to succeed. In your opinion, which should we do? Why? How do you think a superintendent would likely respond to the same question? A school principal? A school board member?

3. Do you believe it is possible to help teachers find the time to assess well? Can the time barrier be overcome? If so, how?

Understanding Assessment Methods

What makes a good test? This question concerns both students and instructors whenever a test is given. It is one of the most basic questions confronting those who make and use classroom tests. Too often it goes unanswered or is badly answered for lack of sound standards of quality and convenient techniques for applying them.

ROBERT L. EBEL (1910–1983)

CHAPTER 6   Selected Response Assessment: Flexible and Efficient

CHAPTER 7   Essay Assessment: Vast Untapped Potential

CHAPTER 8   Performance Assessment: Rich with Possibilities

CHAPTER 9   Personal Communication: Another Window to Student Achievement

Selected Response Assessment: Flexible and Efficient

CHAPTER ROADMAP

In this chapter, we will discuss four specific kinds of selected response test formats: multiple-choice, true/false, matching, and short answer fill-in. The great strength of these methods lies in their ability to tap certain kinds of student achievement with accuracy and efficiency, when skillfully developed. In this chapter, we will explore the origins of these strengths, what it means to develop and use them with care, and the limitations of these formats.

As we journey through this aspect of assessment, you will have the opportunity to master the following knowledge about selected response assessment formats:

1. Understand the roles of objectivity and subjectivity in selected response assessment.

2. Know three steps in the selected response assessment development process, including substeps in each.

3. Identify the kinds of achievement targets that can be reflected in selected response assessments.

4. List classroom assessment context factors to consider in deciding whether or when to use selected response assessments.

5. State considerations in sampling student performance with selected response exercises.

6. Know advantages and disadvantages of four selected response format options: multiple-choice, true/false, matching, and short answer fill-in items.

7. List specific guidelines for the construction of test items in these four formats.

In addition, you will have the chance to learn to use that knowledge to reason as follows:

1. Identify major categories of content and thinking for your selected response assessments.
2. Identify and state as propositions important ideas or learnings that can form the basis of sound test items.
3. Transform those propositions into high-quality selected response items.

The chapter will provide you with proficiency in developing the following skills:

1. Carry out the steps in the assessment development process.
2. Evaluate previously developed selected response assessments to ensure their quality.

And, you will learn to create selected response assessments that meet predefined standards for quality products.

Finally, I hope you will develop the following dispositions regarding selected response modes of assessment:

1. Sense the importance of knowing about sound selected response assessment.
2. Value selected response assessment as a viable option for use in the classroom.
3. See selected response assessment as a valuable instructional tool in which students should be and can be involved.
4. See selected response assessment as a means of increasing instructional efficiency.

As we go, keep the big picture in mind. Figure 6–1 is a duplicate of Figure 4–2, which matched our five achievement targets with four modes of assessment. We

	SELECTED RESPONSE	ESSAY	PERFORMANCE ASSESSMENT	PERSONAL COMMUNICATION
Know				
Reason				
Skills				
Products				
Dispositions				

Figure 6–1
Aligning Achievement Targets and Assessment Methods

will be dealing in depth with the shaded areas. Then, as we move through the remaining chapters of this book, we will cover more sections of the table until our comprehensive assessment picture is complete.

Consider the multiple-choice and true/false test—now there's a real test, the kind we've all come to know and love or fear, depending on our personal experiences. Have you ever noticed how many people contend that they were never good test takers in school? This usually is the kind of test to which they referred. Yet, many of the most important tests we took in school asked us to select the one right answer.

In Part 1, I tried to establish the balanced perspective that—even in these trendy performance assessment times—we can still rely on selected response assessment formats to provide very high-quality information about student achievement. But to take advantage of them, we must develop a strong sense of the targets for which they are appropriate. In addition, we must understand how to sample student achievement efficiently by means of test items and how to control for those bedeviling sources of distortion and bias that can creep into any assessment. Over the years, it has been difficult for many educators to delve into these matters, the lore and mystery of these tests rendering them unapproachable.

For most of us, our testing experience began with those once-a-year standardized achievement and/or intelligence tests. (Personally, I never seemed to finish those before my teacher called, "Time's up!" No one ever explained why they wouldn't let me finish. But rules were rules.) Soon, the scores came back and went into our "permanent record," even though no one ever seemed to know what those scores meant. It was all rather mysterious.

As we grew older, we came to care deeply about grades and grade point averages. As these aspects of the educational process grew in importance in our lives, our teachers tended to rely more and more on tests consisting of "right or wrong" items. Remember exchanging papers so we could score our neighbor's test as the teacher read the right answer? I guess they thought we'd cheat if we scored our own. And woe be unto the kid who happened to question a right answer—regardless of the reason!

Next came time for college admissions tests and even greater mysteries. No one seemed to know what was coming as test time approached, least of all our teachers. Nevertheless, we knew we had better be "on" that day. A whole Saturday morning—literally hours—of nothing but multiple-choice test items. And when you finished, you had no idea how well you had done. Remember? Then the scores came back and once again no one knew what they really meant—but they had to be high!

This is the lore of selected response tests. We've all experienced them, we have plenty of emotions tied to them and, to this day, we have lots of questions about them. My goal in this chapter is to eliminate the mystery surrounding this assessment method. We'll cover the basics of the various selected response formats. Then, in later chapters, we'll explore a variety of classroom assessment and standardized test applications of these formats.

The Role of Teacher Judgment in Selected Response Assessment

You may have been wondering why I have chosen the label *selected response assessments* for these four formats. Certainly, a more common label for these kinds of assessments is "objective test." I have chosen a less common label, paradoxically, to promote clearer understanding. The traditional label can mislead by suggesting that there is no subjectivity involved in these tests—that everything associated with this format is "scientific," and there is little danger of bias due to assessor judgment. The truth is that subjectivity enters into these methods, too.

Assessments are made up of (1) exercises designed to elicit some response from students, and (2) an evaluation scheme that allows the user to interpret the quality of that response. Let's be very clear about the fact that the "objectivity" in the selected response form of assessment applies *only* to the scoring system. It has nothing to do with the exercise side of the equation.

Well-written selected response test items frame challenges that allow for just one best answer or a limited set of acceptable answers. This leads to the "objective" evaluation of responses as being right or wrong. However, the process of developing exercises that form the basis of this kind of assessment includes a major helping of the test author's subjective professional judgment. When the test items are written and/or when they are selected for inclusion on the final test, someone is making a subjective judgment as to the meaning and importance of the material to be tested.

My point is that all assessments, regardless of their format, involve judgment on the part of the assessor. Therefore, all assessments reflect the biases or perspectives of that assessor. The key to the effective use of sound assessments as a part of the instructional process is to make sure those biases are clear and public from the outset, so that everyone has an equal chance to see and understand what it means to be successful.

Further, I have chosen the label *assessments* instead of *tests* to make the point that we are not talking only about traditional tests. Selected response formats also can appear on quizzes, homework assignments, and practice exercises during instruction. For this reason, they can be used *summatively* as final tests documenting achievement or *formatively* to promote learning along the way. In Chapter 2, we established that both uses are critical to student well-being and thus demand sound assessment.

The Importance of Understanding Selected Response Assessment

There are three specific reasons why it is important for you to understand how to design and use selected response assessments.

First and most obviously, there is a very good chance you will want to design and develop selected response assessments for use in your classroom. Most grade levels and school subjects include important achievement targets during the school year that can be translated into selected response assessments. When these times arise, you will need to know how to prepare and use such assessments.

The second reason for attaining a basic understanding of selected response assessment is that you may want to use tests developed by others. To do so, you will need to be able to review and evaluate the quality of these previously developed tests before using them.

For instance, you may want to use tests that come with your textbooks. Text publishers often ask their authors to develop tests to accompany their textbooks as an aid to the teacher and, frankly, as a marketing device to save teachers from the time-consuming work of developing their own tests. If these textbook-embedded tests are developed by those familiar with the achievement targets established for the book and knowledgeable about the development of sound tests, then everyone wins. The publisher sells books, the teacher saves time and effort, and students benefit from sound assessment during instruction.

Problems arise, however, if those who designed and developed these text-embedded tests did not understand the intended targets and/or were untrained in developing sound tests. When this occurs, unsound tests result and students will be inaccurately assessed.

What is the likelihood that this will occur? As a teacher, you will never know the skill level of those who designed the assessments that come with your textbooks. This leaves you with two choices: Trust the text author and publisher to have done a good job and assume that the tests are sound, or conduct your own quality control check on the tests. This choice should be an easy one; anyone who chooses option one simply is being naive or worse. But when you choose option two, you must be prepared to be a critical consumer and thoroughly carry out that quality control check.

Lynn, our experienced high school teacher, tells an interesting story that carries with it important advice about the assessment materials that come with textbooks:

"I served on a committee several years ago charged with adopting a new history textbook. As we reviewed all of the available options, publishers all made a big deal about the support they offered along with their texts. One such support was tests. I'll never forget one publisher's representative telling us, "Buy our product and you won't have to worry about tests. We have them all developed for you. Just copy and distribute them to your students." Luckily, we checked on these unit tests—they were a huge surprise. The text listed objectives and even included discussion questions that asked students to use their history knowledge in solving problems. This was one of the things we liked best about that particular book. But all we found on the tests were items measuring recall of trivial facts. It was as if the text and test authors never talked to each other. They were on completely different wavelengths—a total mismatch.

"Over the years, I've had many colleagues share variations on this same story. We have to be very careful. Just because a test comes with a really good textbook and happens to be typeset or even computerized is no guarantee of quality. Teachers have to be ready to verify that quality."

Lynn makes a critical point. Never forget that *you*, the teacher, are the last line of defense against the mismeasurement of student achievement using objectively scored paper and pencil tests. Whether you play the role of test developer or gatekeeper, in the final analysis, you are responsible for the quality of the tests used in your classroom.

The third reason why you need to be conversant with the meaning of quality as applied to selected response assessments is that you must be in a position to act in your own best interest when *your* achievement is being assessed. All undergraduate or graduate students face the prospect of taking tests. Even as a practicing teacher or administrator, at licensing or certification time, you may well find yourself confronted with selected response examinations. It is in your interest to know if these tests, which can influence your life in profoundly important ways, are sound or unsound.

When they are unsound, it is in your best interest and in the best interest of your classmates and others who will follow to identify any flaws in test design that are likely to render the score inaccurate as an estimate of real achievement.

I know this presents a challenge in diplomacy. It can be risky to point out these problems to those in power positions. But if we let obvious sources of mismeasurement go unchecked, not only do we allow ourselves to be mistreated, but we also miss golden opportunities to strike a blow on behalf of higher levels of assessment literacy throughout the educational system. When the opportunity presents itself, you can take advantage of such "teachable moments" to diplomatically help your professors understand and adhere to accepted standards of quality.

Time for Reflection

Have you ever been involved in an experience where you knew an assessment of your achievement was unsound and you knew why? What did you do about it? Was your action productive?

Matching Selected Response Assessments to Achievement Targets

In Chapter 4, we touched on strategies for aligning our various assessment methods with the different kinds of achievement targets. Let's continue that discussion now by examining the kinds of targets that we can effectively translate into selected response formats.

Example:

Select the best answer for the following question:

Which of the following test item formats can be used to assess both students' mastery of content knowledge and their abilities to use that knowledge to reason and solve problems?

    a.   Multiple choice
    b.   True/false
    c.   Matching
    d.   Short answer fill-in
    e.   All of the above
    f.   None of the above

The best answer is *e*, all of the above. All four formats can tap both knowledge mastery and reasoning, two of the five basic kinds of targets discussed in earlier chapters. In addition, however, these formats also can shed at least some light on the other three kinds of performance: skills, products, and dispositions.

Assessing Knowledge

Selected response test items can be used to test student mastery of subject matter knowledge. To fully understand this match, we must bear in mind four thoughts. First, mastery in this case includes both knowing and understanding the material in question. Second, students can master content knowledge in either of two ways: by learning it outright or by learning to retrieve it through the effective use of reference materials. Third, there are many ways to come to know something, including memorization, learning through frequent experience, and reasoning out a proposition or sequence. Fourth, useable knowledge takes many forms, including facts, concepts, principles or generalizations, and procedures.

Skillful selected response test item writers can use multiple-choice, true/false, matching, and fill-in test items to tap student mastery of knowledge in any or all of these forms, whether the material is known outright or must be retrieved through reference, and regardless of how students attained their mastery. Admittedly, we have used selected response over the decades far more often to test material supposedly learned outright than in any other form. But let's not lose sight of the fact that we can use interpretive exercises (a text passage, map, or data table with associated questions), open-book examinations, and take-home exams to see if students can gain access to information not learned outright when they need it. As stated earlier, this has become an important life skill.

Remember, though, that we have established that merely knowing, and even understanding, something is of little value if we are not proficient at using the knowledge productively.

Assessing Reasoning

Various reasoning and problem-solving outcomes also can be assessed with selected response formats. When we ask students to dip into their knowledge and understanding and use what they know in novel ways to figure something out, we ask them to reason. For example, we might ask students to decide how two things they know about are alike or different, or to read a story and glean the main idea (thus building a base of knowledge and understanding of that piece of literature), or to study a data chart (present them the essential knowledge) and draw a conclusion.

Skillful selected response test item writers can use multiple-choice, true/false, matching, and fill-in test items to tap these and many other forms of student reasoning.

Assessing Skills

While we cannot use selected response test formats to assess student mastery of skills such as speaking, performing (as in physical education), interacting socially, tuning an engine, and the like, we can use them to assess mastery of at least some of the procedural knowledge prerequisite to being able to demonstrate such skills. For instance, if a student fails on a performance assessment to communicate effectively in a second language, we might wish to follow up with a selected response test to see if the student knows the vocabulary. Or if a student is unable to adequately solve a math problem, we might follow up with an assessment of the student's knowledge of the algorithm for solving such problems. If a student fails to carry out a science lab procedure correctly, we can ask whether the student knows the steps in the process.

All proficiency is based on acquired knowledge. A student cannot write in an organized manner unless and until that student has mastered (i.e., knows) a variety of organizational alternatives. We can use selected response assessment to tap students' knowledge and understanding of the foundations of skillfulness, when it fits into instruction.

Assessing Products

Still further, we can construct selected response exercises that test student knowledge of the attributes of a quality product. Such knowledge is prerequisite to being able to create such a product. Students who don't know the attributes of a good term paper are unlikely to be able to reflect those characteristics in their own efforts. Students who cannot distinguish a quality product from an inferior one are unlikely to be able to produce quality. Selected response assessments can test all these prerequisites.

Time for Reflection

What are some of the things a student needs to know to be able to produce a quality term paper? List some of the procedural knowledge that you may need to cover during instruction to set students up for success on a term paper project. Further, what are the key attributes of a quality final product?

Please understand that these kinds of foundational knowledge—that is, knowing prerequisites—are typically not sufficient as results of instruction. Without question, ultimately, we are far more concerned with what students can do or create than we are with what they know. But knowledge foundations are absolutely necessary as outcomes. And, as a teacher charged with moving the student toward excellence, you may need to verify the presence of prerequisite knowledge in the student's bag of tools.

Also understand that I am not saying you must only or always assess knowledge foundations. My point is simply that you can if you wish, when it fits into your classroom context. And when you decide to do so, selected response formats can serve you well.

Assessing Dispositions

In a different vein, you can develop questionnaire items to tap student attitudes, values, motivational dispositions, and other affective states, items that ask the student to select from among a finite number of response options. Questions inquiring about preferred extracurricular activities, for example, might offer a series of choices. Attitude scales might offer a statement about a particular feeling, such as "School is a place where my academic needs are met," and then the responses might ask students if they agree, disagree, or are undecided. These formats can represent excellent ways to tap both the direction and intensity of student feelings about important aspects of school or classroom life.

Please note that the remainder of this chapter deals only with the design of selected response assessments of student achievement. In Chapter 12, we thoroughly discuss the design of assessment formats for use in assessing dispositions and affective states.

Summary of Target Matches

While we cannot reach all of the achievement targets we value with selected response exercises, we can tap parts of many of them. We can test student mastery of content knowledge, including that which is memorized and that which is secured through the effective use of reference materials. In addition, we can tap a variety of kinds of reasoning and problem solving, including analytical, comparative, and inferential thinking skills. And we can get at some of the underpinnings of successful performance in more complex arenas, assessing knowledge of appropriate procedures, and/or knowledge of the key attributes of quality products.

Thus, selected response assessment is versatile. In fact, it is a far richer and more useful methodology than most educators realize. The potential of this form of assessment to help teachers and students is often misunderstood and misrepresented. Some malign the multiple-choice format because it is the format used in standardized achievement tests. Critics sometimes contend that, since such tests are of little value in the classroom, the methodology must be flawed. This is not true, and represents a counterproductive position. In the classroom, where one important goal is to help students master the knowledge and thinking foundations of competence, the accurate and efficient assessment of that mastery can be a key to student growth and development. Selected response assessments have a role to play here; let us not discard the baby with the bathwater!

Developing Selected Response Assessments

Assuming that selected response assessment is appropriate for the target(s) you wish to assess, there are other realities of life in classrooms that can and should contribute to your decision to use this option. We consider those assessment context factors here, and then turn to the actual test development process itself, highlighting some simple, yet powerful keys to sound assessment.

Context Factors

It is appropriate to consider using selected response formats under the following conditions:

- *You are absolutely certain students have a sufficiently high level of reading proficiency to be able to understand the exercises.* Students' mastery of test material is always confounded with their ability to read the test items. Therefore, if you are administering a selected response test of knowledge mastery or problem solving to the poor reader or nonreader, you must give the examinee some kind of support in overcoming the reading difficulty. It is only through such adjustments that you can disentangle achievement and reading proficiency and obtain an accurate estimate of achievement.

- *You can take advantage of already-developed, available, high-quality tests.* Why waste time on new development when others already have done the work for you? But again, you must verify quality—you cannot and should not assume it. Also be advised that some publishers have begun to produce computerized banks of test items out of which teachers can develop their own tests. If well written (read on to find out what this means), these can be very helpful.

- *You plan to take advantage of the efficiency of the format.* Once developed, you can administer the selected response test to large numbers of students at the same time and score it very quickly. These tests can be very efficient.

- *You use this format when the scope of the knowledge and reasoning achievement target is broad.* When there is much material to be mastered and tested, you will need relatively large samples of test items to do it justice. These tests can cover a broad array of information in limited testing time.

- *Time permits students to respond to all test items.* In the old era of assessment, we ranked students on the basis of speed and accuracy. Very often, tests carried tight time limits by design. Not all students finished the test. However, as we are now concerned more about competence, assessment must focus on mastery of material, with less emphasis on speed. Test items not attempted fail to contribute useful information about the students' level of learning. For this reason, it is best to opt for "power" tests, which permit every student to at least attempt each test item.

- *Computer support is available to assist with item development, item storage and retrieval, test printing, and optical scan scoring.* You can save immense amounts of time and effort through the thoughtful use of personal computer and optical scanning technology with selected response assessments. I expand on this idea in the following section.

Using Technology in Assessment

Today's technology can greatly ease the workload associated with selected response assessment. One time- and labor-saving device of immense potential is the personal computer. Many text publishers and other service providers have developed computerized test item banks. The packages often include disks full of developed test exercises grouped and coded by content, type of reasoning involved, grade level, and subject. Software packages are also available to ease the word processing load of test construction, should you choose to create your own.

Ward (1991) provides a compilation of nearly one hundred currently available computerized test-item banking and test-analysis software packages. To illustrate the level of sophistication of this technology, IPS Publishing of Vancouver, Washington, has developed thousands of computer algorithms, or routines, capable of automatically generating millions of high-quality mathematics test exercises on command. Exercises generated reflect specific learning objectives cross-referenced to nearly all of the texts used across the United States and Canada in elementary arithmetic through advanced college level mathematics.

Another application of technology that demands mention here is optical scanners—those scoring machines that produce results so quickly. The fact is that any teacher who uses selected response formats other than fill-in and is scoring by hand is wasting a great deal of time. Not only can these machines generate test scores, but in their currently available versions, they also can analyze test items to tell you how your students did collectively on each item. If that is not diagnostic of your instruction and students' learning, diagnosis will never be possible! Further, companies such as ABACUS in Portland, Oregon, have combined scanning technology with other computer hardware and software to link objectives, assessments, and student records in new and efficient ways. And the good news is that these optical scanners and the associated forms for automatic test scoring such as those supplied by NCS of Eden Prairie, Minnesota, are now quite inexpensive.

I will continue to refer to applications of technology in classroom assessment as our journey progresses, particularly in Part 3, dealing with classroom applications. But for now, let's examine the nature of the test development process itself.

The Steps in Test Development

Described in its simplest form, the selected response test is developed in three steps—each of which requires the application of special professional competence. Those three basic steps require that the developer do the following:

1. Devise a test plan or blueprint that identifies an appropriate sample of achievement.

2. Identify the specific components of knowledge and thinking to be assessed.

3. Transform those components into test items.

The steps of test planning and identifying elements to be assessed are the same for all four test item formats, so we will deal with those together. Then we will discuss how to write quality test items using each individual format.

Step 1: Preparing a Test Plan

Building a test without a plan is like building a house without a blueprint. Two things are going to happen and both are bad! First, the construction process is going to take much longer than it would if you had a plan, and second, the final product is not going to be what you had expected or hoped for. In the development of selected response assessments, a carefully developed blueprint is, as you shall see, virtually everything. Plan well and the test will almost automatically develop itself.

Besides making the test development process easier and more efficient, test blueprinting offers an opportunity for teachers and students to clarify achievement expectations—to sharpen their vision of what it means to be successful. As you will see, this planning process absolutely requires that the test developer delve deeply into the material to be learned, so as to understand the deep structure of the knowledge to be mastered and the complexity of the problem solving to be accomplished using that knowledge. Without this clarity and depth of vision, it will be impossible to develop sound assessments.

We have two types of test plans from which to choose. One is called a *table of test specifications*. The other relies on a list of *instructional objectives* to guide test construction. Each holds the promise of providing the foundation for a sound test and helping integrate selected response assessment into your teaching and learning process. Choose whichever you like—both work. They are essentially equally effective as test planning devices, as you shall see.

The Table of Specifications.   To explain how the table of test specifications works, we must begin with the basic unit of the objectively scored test, the individual test item. Any test item requires the respondent to do two things: to gain access to a specific piece of information (either from memory or reference materials), and to use that knowledge to carry out a cognitive operation (i.e., to solve some kind of problem).

For example, I might construct a test item based on knowledge of a piece of literature and ask the respondent simply to recall it:

Who were the main characters in the story?

Or, I might ask the respondent to recall two elements of content knowledge from literature and relate one to the other, as in this comparison item:

What is one similarity between the antagonist and the protagonist?

In this case, the respondents must dip into their reservoir of knowledge about the two characters (prerequisite knowledge), analyze the component elements of each, and find elements that are similar (comparative thinking). So it is in the case of all such test items: Elements of knowledge are carried into some thinking process.

Time for Reflection

Find a test you have developed or taken that relies on selected response items. Analyze 5 or 10 items to determine the knowledge and cognitive processing skills the respondent must possess to answer correctly. Save the test and your analysis of it for later work.

The table of test specifications takes advantage of this combination of knowledge retrieval and its application to permit the development of a plan that promises to sample both in a predetermined manner. Table 6–1 is a simple example of such a table. In this table, we find a plan for a unit test in history, focusing on the Civil War. The test is to include 30 items worth one point each.

On the left, we have subdivided the content knowledge into three basic categories: causes, major battles, and effects of the war. Each category obviously contains many elements of knowledge within it, some of which will be transformed into test items later. But for now, note in the last column that we have decided to include 5 items testing knowledge of causes, 10 on battles, and 15 on effects. These numbers reflect our sense of the relative importance of these three categories of material.

Time for Reflection

Think about how a teacher might establish test item priorities. Why might some categories receive more items than others? How have you set these priorities in the past, if you are now a classroom teacher?

The differences in the number of items assigned to each category might reflect any or all of the following:

- the amount of instructional time spent on each
- the amount of material in each category
- the relative importance of material in each category for later learning

This is an important part of the art of classroom assessment: As a teacher, your special insights about the nature and capabilities of your students and the nature and amount of material you have covered must come into play in setting these priorities. Given this particular body of material, as a teacher-test developer, you must ask, What should be the areas of greatest emphasis if I am to prepare students for material to come later in their education?

Table 6–1
Table of Specifications for Civil War Unit Test

Content Category	Number of Points			
	Know	Compare	Infer	Total
Causes	2	2	1	5
Major battles	6	2	2	10
Effects	7	4	4	15
Total	15	8	7	30

To be able to answer this question—to develop this achievement target vision—you must know and understand the content and kinds of reasoning that form the foundations of your special arenas of instructional responsibility. You must be a master of the content and thinking that students need to learn. In the absence of such a vision of the meaning of success for students, how do you design instruction to promote that success and how do you devise assessments reflective of that success? You cannot.

Notice the columns in Table 6–1. Three kinds of thinking are listed—three different kinds of cognitive actions to be required of respondents: *recall* elements of knowledge, *compare* them, and *draw inferences* (meaning to draw generalizations using the knowledge in the reasoning process). Once again, outcome priorities are reflected on the bottom: 15 recall items, 8 comparison items, and 7 inference items. If the test is to accurately and fairly test the results of instruction, students need to have been provided with opportunities to practice these patterns of thinking. That is, instruction should have reflected these priorities, too.

Once the categories are defined and row and column totals are specified (which does not take very long for a teacher who *knows* the material), you need only spread the numbers of items through the cells of the table so that they add up to the row and column totals. This will generate a plan to guide the writing of a set of test items that will systematically sample both content and thinking priorities as established.

But how do you decide how many rows and columns to include in a table of test specifications? How do you decide what those rows and columns should reflect? There are no rigid rules. You can include as many rows and columns as make sense for your particular unit and test. This aspect of the development process is as much art as it is science. You should consider the following factors with respect to content categories:

1. Look for natural subdivisions in the material presented in a text, such as chapters or major sections within chapters. These are likely to reflect natural subdivisions of material that are generally accepted by experts in the field. Each chapter or section might become a row in a table of specifications.

2. Be sure categories have clearly marked limits and are large enough to contain a number of important elements of knowledge within each. As you will see, these elements are to be sampled during item writing and you need a clear sampling frame.

3. Use subdivisions of content and kinds of thinking that are likely to make sense to students as a result of their studies. Ultimately, they must see the vision too if they are to meet your expectations.

With respect to reflecting the kinds of thinking to be assessed, categories included in the table should have the following characteristics:

1. Categories should have clear labels and underlying meanings. There are many options out there that have been carefully researched and are highly refined. I will say more about these, and provide examples, in Chapter 10.

2. Categories should be so familiar and comfortable that you can almost automatically pose exercises that demand student thinking in those terms.

3. Each category should represent kinds of thinking and problem solving that occur in the real world.

4. All categories should represent kinds of thinking students can understand and converse about as a result of experience and practice during instruction.

The bottom line is this: The categories of content, kinds of thinking tested, and proportion of items assigned to each should reflect the target priorities communicated to students during instruction. Remember, students can hit any target they can see and that holds still for them!

Instructional Objectives as Test Plans.   You can reach this same end of building a quality test plan by generating a list of instructional objectives, if you assume each objective, like each cell in a table of specifications, specifies the knowledge to be brought to bear and the action to be taken (recall it, analyze it, compare it, and so on) by the student. Here are examples of such objectives:

The student will be able to compare and contrast the battle strategies of the Union and the Confederacy.

The student will know (i.e., be able to recall) the causes of the Civil War.

Note that you need not write each objective so as to define targets at a high level of specific detail. Rather, like cells in a table of specifications, they can set frames around categories that contain many possible test items within them. Sound objectives answer the question, What knowledge is to be used to perform what cognitive activity? Later, you can prepare test items that ask your students to retrieve these required knowledge and use it to figure out the right answer. But more about that later in this chapter.

Plans Really Help.   For now, simply realize that the frames placed around content and reasoning by tables of specifications and lists of instructional objectives are very important for three reasons. First and foremost, they define success for students, giving those students control over their own fate. They know that, if they master the material, they will score high. Those who know this going into the test are more likely to succeed. Turn the spotlight on your expectations so all can see them.

Second, clearly written expectations in the form of tables of test specifications and lists of objectives set limits on teacher accountability for student learning. With thoughtful plans in place, for example, you are no longer responsible for seeing to it that every student knows every single fact about the Civil War. Rather, students need to know causes, battles, and effects, and know how to reason using that information. When your students can hit such a complex target, you are a supreme success as a teacher—and there can be no question about it.

Third, once the overall plan is assembled, it becomes possible for you to develop comparable forms of the same test. This can be very useful when you need to protect test security, such as when you need another form for students who were absent or who must retake the test for some reason. You can assemble another set of items that samples the same content and kinds of thinking, and develop a test of different items that you know represents identical material. This means that all students are provided with the same chances of success.

Summary of Step 1.   The first step in test development is to formulate a plan—a blueprint for the test, if you will. Sound plans can be developed only by those who have attained complete mastery over the material (content and thinking) to be assessed. Given that foundation, you can either (1) design a table of test specifications, or (2) prepare a list of instructional objectives. Any cell of the table or any objective will represent the union of two essential elements: some content knowledge to be retrieved via memory or reference and some cognitive act to be carried out using that material.

Using tables of specifications or lists of objectives allows you to connect the test directly to instructional priorities. In this way, these plans also set limits on the meaning of student and therefore teacher success, thus maximizing the chances that you and your students will each achieve the levels of excellence that you seek.

Step 2: Selecting Material to Test

After developing the table of specifications or list of objectives, the test designer faces the challenge of selecting the combined elements of knowledge and thinking to test. In Table 6–1, the cell crossing battles with recall requires the construction of six test items. The next key test development question is, Can these items test recall of *any* six battles during the Civil War? How does one decide which of the huge number of facts about Civil War battles to test?

There are two factors to consider in answering this question: the need to sample representatively the different components of material in the unit, and the relative importance of those components. Let me explain how these come into play.

Sampling Considerations.   As previously stated, any selected response assessment is really only a sampling from an ideal, infinitely long test. Clearly, if we were to test student mastery of every event of the Civil War, we'd be talking about an impossibly long test! The most efficient way to prevent this problem and create tests that fit into reasonable time limits is to select a sample of the important material, test it, and assume that the score on that sample reflects student mastery of what is important in that body of knowledge.

To understand this, think about commonly used polling techniques. Pollsters cannot afford to ask every citizen's opinion. So they select a sample of voters, ask them to express their opinions, and then estimate from this carefully selected sample how the general population feels on key issues.

In test development, we do exactly the same thing with test items. If we thoughtfully sample larger bodies of content and thinking (assessment specialists call these *domains*), then performance on the sample can lead to inferences about the proportion of material in those larger domains that students have mastered.

But precisely what is it that we are to sample on our test on the Civil War, for example? Can we pick just any set of facts, test them, and then generalize? The answer is no, not just any facts. Here is another place where classroom assessment becomes an art. We must select a sample of all possible *important* elements of knowledge in combination with *important* cognitive challenges.

Who decides what is important, and how do they do it? If you are to develop the test, you do! If the textbook publisher developed the test and you are charged with evaluating it, you must establish the achievement target priorities in your classroom, so you can see if the text-embedded test covers your valued targets.

This is yet another reason why the assessor must possess a carefully refined vision of the achievement target. Those who have immersed themselves in the material know what is important. But there are other places to turn to for advice in finding the important material. For example, the textbook's author will highlight and emphasize its most important material in lists of objectives and chapter summaries, as will any accompanying teacher's guides.

In addition, state, district, building, and/or department curriculum guidelines typically spell out priorities at some level. Sometimes, just taking time to talk with colleagues about instructional priorities can help.

Other valuable sources of guidance in articulating valued knowledge and thinking outcomes are the various national and state professional associations of teachers, such as of science, mathematics, English, and so on. Nearly every such association has assembled a commission within the past five years to identify and spell out in writing standards of excellence for student achievement in their domains. You should be familiar with any national standards of student performance held as valuable by teachers in your field.

Out of all of this *you* must decide what is important to test within each cell of your table of specifications or within each instructional objective you specify in your classroom. And so it is that, even though you might use an "objective test" format, the material tested is very much a matter of professional judgment on your part.

But please understand that this subjectivity is not a problem as long as you are in touch with priorities in your field and specify your valued outcomes carefully. No one can do this work for you. You must possess the vision, and it must be a sound and appropriate one, given the students you teach and the latest thinking about the disciplines you teach and assess.

Identifying Important Propositions.   In this section, I offer a practical and efficient means of transforming your vision, whether expressed in a table of specifications or a list of objectives, into quality test items. This strategy promises to save you more test development time and have a greater impact on the quality of your tests than any other single test development suggestion in this chapter. Just be advised from the outset that this tactic is subtle, another aspect of the *art* of test development. But with practice, anyone can master it.

Capture the elements to be tested in the form of clearly stated sentences that reflect important elements of content and stipulate the kind of cognitive operation to be carried out. In the test development field, we call these statements *propositions.* As you shall see, propositions save time.

But before I illustrate them, I need to ask you to accept something on faith now, which I will verify for you later through example: When you have identified and listed all of the propositions that form the basis of a test, the test is 95 percent developed! While the work remaining is not trivial, I promise you that it will go so fast it will make your head spin. When your goal is high-quality selected response tests, if you invest your time up front in identifying the important elements of success—finding those targets that top your list of things students should know and be able to do—the rest of the test development process will be automatic.

To collect these propositions, or basic units of test development, we begin by reviewing the material to be sampled on the test, keeping the table of specifications or instructional objectives close at hand.

Refer to Table 6–1 once again. We need 15 recall test items in total. Two of these must address causes of the war. So as we review the material on causes of the war, we seek out and write down, say, five or six causes that we think every student should know.

Remember, we don't need to gather a large number of causes-recall propositions, because we're going to use only two of them on the test. But those collected must reflect the most important material. As we collect propositions, we use clearly stated sentences:

> *One major cause of the Civil War was the desire of the North to abolish slavery.*

> *A contributing cause of the Civil War was conflicting economic priorities of the industrial North and the agricultural South.*

Once we have written the causes-recall propositions, we move on to find key elements of the battles-recall cell. Note from the blueprint that we need six of these. Given this expectation, we should try to find and state 10 or 12 important propositions. That way, if we need to replace some later or if we want to develop two forms of the same test, we have our active ingredients (additional propositions) ready to go. (And by the way, item writing is easier when you state propositions in your own words. Do not lift them verbatim from the text.)

Besides, we want to have enough test propositions to confidently generalize that student performance on the sample reflects mastery of the universe of material we could have included on the test. We know we can't ask everything. But we need to be sure to ask enough. It's a matter of judgment. If we err at all, we want to err in the direction of including too many rather than too few items for a given cell.

And so we would proceed through all nine cells of the table, seeking out and writing down more propositions than we will need. In effect, we are creating a list of important learnings. Note that we have attempted no test items yet.

Table 6–1 tells us we need a total of eight comparison propositions, two each on causes and battles and four on effects. Here's a possible battle proposition requiring comparative thinking:

> *The 1864 battles of The Wilderness and Cold Harbor were similar in that both brought generals Lee and Grant into direct confrontation and resulted in huge casualties on both sides.*

Here is an example requiring inferential thinking:

> *Superior weaponry and training were primary reasons for the ultimate victory of the Union Army in the Civil War.*

This proposition includes possible inferences about effects for that cell of the table of specifications. Please note that these inferences may not have been explicitly covered in class; that is, we may not have expected students to know them outright. Rather, they may represent the kinds of inferences we want them to be able to draw *using* their own knowledge of the Civil War. To test their ability to think on their feet, then, we must present cognitive challenges in test items that demand more than recall.

This idea bears further discussion, as it is critical to sound test development. As shown in Table 6–1, we need test items that reflect the student's ability to think comparatively (column 2) and to draw inferences (column 3). To reach this goal, a very special relationship must exist between the items that appear on the test and the preceding instruction: The item must, at test time, present a problem that calls for applying knowledge in a way *not* specifically covered during instruction. Thus, it must present a problem for which students have not had the opportunity to learn the answer. They must be given the challenge of reasoning it out right there on the spot.

Certainly, students must dip into their reservoir of available knowledge—that is, must recall information—to reason productively. But the aim of some propositions should be to assess more than recall, when the goal of instruction is more than recall. If we want students to make the leap, for example, from just knowing something to analyzing, comparing, or inferring—that is, to reasoning—we must rely on novel questions at test time to make them do so.

The most practical implication of this perspective on test development is that it makes it perfectly acceptable to include material on the test not explicitly covered in class, if we wish to tap student reasoning and problem solving. However, we also have an obligation to the students to be sure they have had the opportunity to

(1) have access to the knowledge required to answer such test items, and (2) practice with similar kinds of reasoning and problem-solving propositions. I will say more about these issues in Chapter 10, where we will discuss assessing student thinking and problem solving.

Summary of Step 2.   Step two calls for selected response test developers to march back through the material to assess, blueprint in hand, in search of the important learnings to be tested. These form the basis of propositions—sentences that capture the essence of things worth knowing and reasoning activities worth doing. These propositions are what you will translate into actual test items, discussed in step three.

But before making those translations, it is wise to step back from this list of propositions and review them one more time, asking yourself, Does this collection of sentences really provide a composite picture of what I think are the important knowledge and reasoning outcomes of this unit? If you really know and understand the material and know how the material relates to that which the student will confront in the future, weak propositions will jump out at you. If you find weak entries, replace them. When the list meets your highest standards of coverage, you are ready to make a selected response test.

Additional Thoughts on Steps 1 and 2

Without question, these are complex test development steps. And, reasonably, you may be asking, How does he expect me to do all of this and teach, too? My answer is for you to stick with me through the final test development step, where it will become apparent why all of this planning saves you a great deal of time and effort.

Also, this kind of test development process quickly becomes second nature to those who practice and master it. I promise you, if you are not confident that you have mastered all of the content or thinking processes before you start, by the time you finish designing some tests in this way, you will have mastered them. In this sense, the very process of test development is an excellent professional development experience.

And finally, let me plant a small seed of an idea in the following "Time for Reflection," so we can grow this idea together as we travel on.

Time for Reflection

If this test development process involves too much work for one teacher to do all alone, can you think of any helpers that you might bring into the process to lighten the workload associated with developing tables of specifications, lists of objectives, and propositions? Who could help you and what sort of work might they do? Jot down some thoughts now and we will come back to this later.

Step 3: Building Test Items from Propositions

Earlier, I noted that developing a high-quality test plan and specifying propositions represent 95 percent of the work in selected response test development. Complete the list of propositions and the test will almost develop itself from that point on. The reason lies in the fact that the proposition captures a complete and coherent thought. Professional test developers understand that the key to fast and effective item writing is to be sure to start with a complete and coherent thought about each fact, point of information, or matter of inference that you intend to test.

Once we have a proposition in hand, we can spin any kind of selected response item out of it that we wish. Let me illustrate with the following inference proposition. (Remember, I want my students to think through the answer to this. It was not explicitly covered in class.)

> *If the Union Army had followed up its defeat of Lee and his Army of Northern Virginia at Antietam, the Civil War would have been shortened.*

To generate a true/false item out of this proposition that is true, we can simply include the proposition on the test as stated! The proposition is a true true/false test item as written. This is always the case in well-stated propositions.

If we want a true/false item that is false, we simply make one part of the proposition false:

> *A Union Army follow up of its defeat of the Confederacy at Antietam would have had no effect on the outcome of the Civil War.*

To convert this proposition to a fill-in item, we simply leave out the phrase dealing with the effect and ask a question:

> *What would have happened if the Union Army had followed up its defeat of Lee's Confederate forces at Antietam?*

If we desire a multiple-choice item, we add a number of response options, only one of which is correct.

Mark my words: Every well conceived and clearly stated proposition—whether requiring recall or some other kind of thinking—is an automatic source of test items.

Invest your time and effort up front learning the underlying structure of the material you teach, and finding the *important* propositions. These are the keys to the rapid development of sound selected response assessments.

Item Writing Tips.   Once you have identified the format(s) you plan to use, a few simple keys will aid you in developing sound test items. Some of these guidelines apply to all formats; some are unique to each particular format. They all have the effect of helping respondents understand exactly what you—the item writer—are going for in posing the exercise.

General Guidelines.   These tend to focus on the form of the item. The simplicity of their advice belies their power to improve your tests, believe me.

1. *Write clear and sharply focused test items.* Good item writing is first and foremost an exercise in clear communication. Follow the rules of grammar—tests are as much a public reflection of our professional standards as any other product we create. Include only material essential to framing the question. Be brief and clear. Our goal is to test mastery of the material, not the student's ability to figure out what we're asking!

Not this:

When scientists use magnets they need to know about the poles, which are?

But this:[1]

What are the poles of a magnet called?
   a.   Anode and cathode
   b.   North and south
   c.   Strong and weak
   d.   Attract and repel

2. *Ask a question.* In using multiple-choice and fill-in, minimize the use of incomplete statements as exercises. When you force yourself to ask a question, you force yourself to express a complete thought in the stem or trigger part of the item, which usually promotes the respondent's clear understanding.

Not this (you might present these items with a graph depicting interest rate patterns):

Between 1950 and 1965
   a.   Interest rates increased
   b.   Interest rates decreased
   c.   Interest rates fluctuated greatly
   d.   Interest rates did not change

But this:

What was the trend in interest rates between 1950 and 1965?
   a.   Increased only
   b.   Decreased only
   c.   Increased, then decreased
   d.   Remained unchanged

3. *Aim for the lowest possible reading level.* This is an attempt to control for the inevitable confounding of reading proficiency and mastery of the material

---

[1]Item adapted from *Handbook on Formative and Summative Evaluation of Student Learning* (p. 592, Item A.4-n-2.211) by B. S. Bloom, J. T. Hastings, and G. F. Madaus, 1971, New York: McGraw-Hill. Copyright 1971 by McGraw-Hill, Inc. Reprinted by permission of the publisher.

in the student's score. Minimize sentence length and syntactic complexity and eliminate unnecessarily difficult vocabulary.

4. *Eliminate clues to the correct answer either within the item or across items within a test.* When grammatical clues within items or material presented in other items give away the correct answer, students get items right for the wrong reasons. The result is misinformation about the student's true achievement.

Not this:

All of these are examples of a bird that flies, *except* an
- a.   Ostrich
- b.   Falcon
- c.   Cormorant
- d.   Robin

(The article *an* requires a response beginning with a vowel. As only one is offered, it must be correct.)

Or this:

Which of the following are examples of birds that do not fly?
- a.   Falcon
- b.   Ostrich and penguin
- c.   Cormorant
- d.   Robin

(The question calls for a plural response. As only one is offered, it must be correct.)

5. *If you write the items, have them read at least once by a knowledgeable colleague.* This is especially true of the really high-stakes tests, such as big unit tests and final exams. No one is perfect. We all overlook simple mistakes. Having a willing colleague review your work takes just a few minutes and can save a great deal of time and eliminate problems in the long run. Don't get your ego so tied up in your test that you can't take needed constructive criticism.

6. *And please, double-check the scoring key for accuracy before scoring.* Enough said!

Multiple-choice Items.   When developing multiple-choice test items, keep these few simple, yet powerful, guidelines in mind:

1. *Ask a complete question to get the item started, if you can.* This has the effect of placing the focus on the item in the stem, not in the response options. (See the previous interest rate example.)

2. *If you find yourself repeating the same words at the beginning of each response option, reword the stem to move the repetitive material up there.* This will clarify the problem and make it more efficient for the respondent to read. (Again, see the interest rate example.)

3. *Be sure there is only one correct or best answer.* This is where that colleague's independent review can help. Remember, it is acceptable to ask respondents to select a best answer from among a set of answers, all of which are correct. Just be sure to word the question so as to make the respondent's task clear.

4. *Word response options as briefly as possible and be sure they are grammatically parallel.* This has two desirable effects. First, it makes items easier to read. Second, it helps eliminate grammatical clues as to the correct answer. (See the second bird example.)

Not this:

Why did colonists come to the United States?
   a.   To escape heavy taxation by their native governments
   b.   Religion
   c.   They sought the adventure of living among Native Americans in the new land
   d.   There was the promise of great wealth in the new world
   e.   More than one of the above answers

But this:

Why did colonists migrate to the United States?
   a.   To escape taxation
   b.   For religious freedom
   c.   For adventure
   d.   More than one of the above

5. *Vary the number of response options presented as appropriate to create the item you want.* While it is best to design items around three or four response options, you can develop some very effective items by offering two to five response options. Further, it is permissible to vary the number of response options offered across items within the same test. But please, try not to use "all of the above" or "none of the above" to fill up spaces just because you can't think of viable incorrect answers. In fact, sound practice suggests limiting their use to those few times when they fit comfortably into the item context. Some teachers find it effective to include more than one correct answer and ask the student to find them all, when appropriate. Give credit for all correct answers.

By the way, here's a simple, yet crafty, multiple-choice item writing tip: If you compose a multiple-choice item and find that you cannot think of enough plausible incorrect responses, include the item on a test the first time as a fill-in item. As your students respond, those who get it wrong will provide you with the full range of viable incorrect responses you need to include it next time as multiple choice!

True/False Items.   You have only one simple guideline here: Make the item *entirely* true or false *as stated.* Complex "idea salads" including some truth and some falsehood just confuse the issue. Precisely what is the proposition you are testing? State it and move on.

Matching Items.   When developing matching exercises, which are really complex multiple-choice items with a number of stems offered along with a number of response options, follow all of the multiple choice guidelines offered previously. In addition, observe the following guidelines:

1. *State the matching challenge up front* with a clear and concise set of directions specifying what is to be matched.

2. *Keep the list of things to be matched short.* The maximum number of options is ten. Shorter is better. This minimizes the information processing and idea juggling respondents must do to be successful.

3. *Keep the list of things to be matched homogeneous.* Don't mix events with dates or with names. Again, idea salads confuse the issue. Focus the exercise.

4. *Keep the list of response options brief in their wording and parallel in their construction.* Pose the matching challenge in clear, straightforward language.

5. *Include more response options than are needed and permit response options to be used more than once.* This has the effect of making it impossible for the respondent to arrive at the correct response purely through a process of elimination. If a student answers correctly using elimination and you infer that student has mastered the material, you will be wrong.

Fill in Items.   Here are three simple guidelines to follow:

1. *Ask a question of the respondent and provide space for an answer.* This forces the expression of a complete thought on your part. The use of incomplete statements as item stems is acceptable. But if you use them, be sure to capture the essence of the problem in that stem.

2. *Try to stick to one blank per item.* Come to the point. Ask one question, get one answer, and move on to the next question. Simple language, complete communication, clear conclusions. Does the student know the answer or not?

3. *Don't let the length of the line to be filled in be a clue as to the length or nature of the correct response.* This may seem elementary, but it happens. Again, this can lead to misinformation about the student's real level of achievement.

Mixing Formats Together.   The creative test developer also can generate some interesting and useful assessment exercises by mixing the various formats.

1. Mix true/false and multiple-choice formats to create exercises in which the respondent must label a statement true or false and select the response option that gives the proper reason why.

   Example:

   As employment increases, the danger of inflation increases.
   a.   True, because consumers are willing to pay higher prices
   b.   True, because the money supply increases

    c.   False, because wages and inflation are statistically unrelated to one another

    d.   False, because the government controls inflation

2. Mix multiple-choice or matching and fill-in questions to create a format in which the student must select the correct response and fill in the reason why it is correct. As a variation, we can ask why incorrect responses are incorrect too.

Time for Reflection

Can you recall any variations of these formats used by your own teachers that you found to be challenging, creative, or especially effective? Can you think of combinations of these formats that might be useful?

Interpretive Exercises.   Here's another simple but effective test development idea: If you wish to use selected response items to assess student reasoning and problem-solving proficiency, but (1) you are not sure all of your students have the same solid background in the content, or (2) you want to see them apply content you don't necessarily want them to memorize, you can turn to what is called an *interpretive exercise.* In this case, you provide information to respondents in the form of a brief passage, chart, table, or figure and then ask a series of questions calling for the interpretation or application of that material.

    Example:[2]

Here is a graph of Bill's weekly allowance distribution.

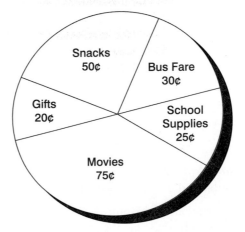

---

[2]Reprinted from "Measuring Complex Achievement: The Interpretive Exercise" (p. 198, Example III) in *Measurement and Evaluation in Teaching* (6th ed.) by N. E. Gronlund and R. L. Linn, 1990, Englewood Cliffs, NJ: Merrill/Prentice Hall. Copyright 1990 by Prentice Hall Publishing Co. Reprinted by permission of the publisher.

1. What is the ratio of the amount Bill spends for school supplies to the amount he spends for movies?
   A. 7:2
   B. 1:3
   C. 2:7
   D. 3:1

2. What would be the best title for this graph?
   A. Bill's weekly allowance
   B. Bill's money graph
   C. Bill's weekly expenditures
   D. Bill's money planning

More General Guidelines.   And finally, here are a few simple guidelines for setting up the test as a whole that will improve the quality of the results:

1. *Provide clear directions and specific indications of the point value for each exercise.* This helps students use their time wisely.

2. *Start each test with some relatively easy items.* This will give students both some time and the means to get their test anxiety under control.

3. *Present all items of like format together.*

4. *Keep all parts of an item on the same page.*

5. *Make sure all copies are clear and readable.*

Summary of Step 3.   In this step, you transformed propositions into test items. This need not be a complex process. Regardless of the item format, you must write test items as clearly and as simply as possible, ask questions whenever possible, eliminate inappropriate clues to the correct answer, seek one clearly correct answer whenever possible and appropriate, ask a colleague to review important tests, and follow just a few simple format-specific guidelines for item construction. Figure 6–2 presents these guidelines collected for convenient use.

Further, we help students perform up to their potentials when we provide clear and complete instructions, let students know how each exercise contributes to the total test score, start with easy items, and make sure the test is readable.

Selecting from Among the Four Formats

An important issue we have yet to address is, How do we decide which selected response format—multiple-choice, true/false, matching, or fill-in—to use within each assessment context?

Figure 6–2
Test Item Quality Checklist

General guidelines for all formats
_____ Items clearly written and focused
_____ Question posed
_____ Lowest possible reading level used
_____ Irrelevant clues eliminated
_____ Items reviewed by colleague
_____ Scoring key double checked

Guidelines for multiple-choice items
_____ Item stem poses a direct question
_____ Repetition eliminated from response options
_____ One best or correct answer is provided
_____ Response options are brief and parallel
_____ Number of response options offered fits item context

Guideline for true/false items
_____ Statement is entirely true or false as presented

Guidelines for matching exercises
_____ Clear directions given
_____ List of items to be matched is brief
_____ List consists of homogeneous entries
_____ Response options are brief and parallel
_____ Extra response options offered

Guidelines for fill-in items
_____ A direct question is posed
_____ One blank is needed to respond
_____ Length of blank is not a clue

In general, the first three are preferable when scoring efficiency is an issue, especially when you have an optical scan machine scoring service available. When achievement targets fit these formats, students are old enough to respond by bubbling in answer sheets (generally from grade 4), and scoring can be automated, multiple-choice, true/false, and matching formats can be big time savers. Unfortunately, until computer technology allows us to scan and evaluate stud8ent writing, short answer fill-in items are going to take longer to score. (Incidentally, the technology exists today to scan actual student work into the computer. But its evaluation still requires the human eye and mind.)

On the other hand, fill-in exercises are preferable when we wish to control for guessing. And make no mistake about it, guessing can be an issue. If a student guesses an item right and we infer that the right answer means the student has mastered the material, we are wrong. This means we have mismeasured that student's real achievement.

Given a true/false test, respondents who rely on blind guessing alone will answer about half of the items correctly. With multiple-choice, it depends on the number of response options: Four-choice tests yield a guessing score of about 25 percent correct; five-choice, roughly 20 percent. Notice that any respondent who can confidently eliminate two or three options in a multiple-choice item before guessing raises the odds of guessing correctly! Fill-in items, on the other hand, greatly reduce the chances of success through guessing alone.

Our heart must go out to students who score below the chance or guessing score on a selected response test. Not only are such students misinformed, but they're unlucky!

Multiple-choice items are recommended when the author can identify one correct or best answer and at the same time identify a number of viable incorrect responses. On its surface, that might sound obvious. But think about it. If we formulate our incorrect responses carefully, we can use multiple-choice items to uncover common misunderstandings and to diagnose students' needs. Let me illustrate.

If we were to start with a math problem and solve it correctly, we have identified the correct response (response option 1). Next, we can solve that same problem making a common mistake on purpose. Say we carry that mistake all the way to an answer. This yields response option 2, and it will be incorrect. But if anyone chooses that incorrect response option when they take the test, we will know what mistake they made. Next, we solve the same problem making another kind of common mistake, and another viable incorrect response results (response option 3). We continue until we have as many incorrect response options as needed. Thus, each incorrect response can provide useful information about the students who choose it, if you develop the item thoughtfully.

If we administer such a test and analyze how many students selected each response option (which we may do very easily with currently available optical scan test scoring technology and item analysis software packages), we gain clear insights into common misconceptions among our students. Multiple-choice exercises developed in this way can serve to identify student needs with a minimum investment of testing time.

True/false exercises are most useful when we have a great deal of material to cover and want to ask a large number of questions per unit of testing time, or when we have much to cover and limited testing time. These items require very short response times. They also are usable when we either cannot think of or don't want to take the time to generate lists of viable incorrect response options for multiple-choice items.

The greatest strength of matching items lies in their efficiency. When carefully developed to include homogeneous elements, they are in effect several multiple-choice items presented at once. Each premise statement to be matched triggers a new multiple-choice test item and all items in a matching exercise offer the same set of multiple response options. They can be used to assess mastery of knowledge and/or thinking and problem solving, although most tend to center on recalling associations.

Working Backwards to Verify Test Quality

We have come a long way in this chapter depicting a three-step test development process, from blueprints to propositions to test items. Before we leave this topic, let's discuss a natural extension of this process. This is an idea that may already have occurred to you.

We can reverse this entire process in order to evaluate previously developed tests, such as those that come with a textbook or those we have developed in previous years. To do this, we begin at the test item level: Do the items themselves adhere to the few critical guidelines presented previously? If they do not, there is obvious reason for concern about test quality. If they do, we proceed to the next level of analysis.

At that next level, we can transform the items into the propositions that they reflect. We accomplish this by doing the following:

- Combining the multiple-choice item stem with the correct response.

- Adding true true/false items to the list of propositions.

- Making false true/false items true.

- Matching up elements in matching exercises.

- Filling in the blanks of short answer items.

We then analyze the resulting list of propositions, asking, Do these reflect the priorities in our instruction? In addition, we can collect the propositions into like groups to generate a list of instructional objectives or to create a table of specifications depicting the overall picture of the test, including the proportional representation of content and thinking. Again we can ask, Do these reflect priorities as we see them?

This backward analysis can both reveal the flaws in previously developed tests and help us understand the nature of the revisions needed to bring the test up to important standards of quality.

Barriers to Sound Selected Response Assessment

Recall that, in earlier chapters, we listed five key attributes of a sound assessment: clear target, clear purpose, proper method, appropriate sample, and extraneous interference controlled. These also reflect the things that can go wrong, that can keep a student's test score from being an accurate reflection of that student's real level of achievement. Listed below, by way of summary, are many of the sources of mismeasurement touched on in this chapter. Also listed are actions we can take to prevent these problems. We offer these remedies in the service of helping you develop sound selected response assessments.

Potential Sources of Problems	*Suggested Remedies*
Lack of vision of the target priority	Carefully analyze the material to be tested to find the knowledge and reasoning targets.
	Find truly important learning propositions.
Wrong method for the target	Use selected response methods to assess mastery of knowledge and appropriate kinds of reasoning only.
	Selected response can test prerequisites of effective skill and product performance, but not performance itself.
Inappropriate sampling:	
• Not representative of important propositions	Know the material and plan the test carefully.
• Sample too small	Include enough items to cover key concepts.
• Sample too large for time available	Shorten cautiously so as to maintain enough to engender confidence in generalizing to the total domain.
Sources of Extraneous Interference	
• Student-centered problems	
• Cannot read well enough to respond	Lower reading level of test or offer reading support.
• Insufficient time to respond	Shorten test or allow more time.
• Poor-quality test items	Learn and follow both general and format-specific guidelines for writing quality items.
	Seek review by a colleague.
• Scoring errors	Double check answer key; use it carefully.

Including Students in the Assessment Process

We have said from the outset that classroom assessment can serve two important purposes. One is to provide information for teacher, student, and parent to use in informing the various decisions they must make. The other is as a teaching tool. Figure 6–3 presents specific ways to weave selected response assessment develop-

---

- Develop a table of test specifications for a final unit test *before* the unit is ever taught. A clear vision of the valued outcomes will result and instruction can be tailored to promote student success.

- Share a copy of that plan with every student. Review it carefully at the beginning of the unit and explain your expectations at that time. Now students and teacher share the same vision.

- Involve students in the process of devising the test plan, or involve them from time to time in checking back to the blueprint (1) to see together—as partners—if you might need to make adjustments in the test plan and/or (2) to chart your progress together.

- Once you have the test plan completed, develop a few test items each day as the unit unfolds. Such items certainly would reflect timely instructional priorities. Further, at the end of the unit, the final exam would be all done and ready to go! This eliminates the last-minute anxiety of test development and improves test quality.

- Involve students in writing practice test items. Think of the benefits: the students will have to evaluate the importance of the various elements of content, and they will have to become proficient in using the kinds of thinking and problem solving valued in your classroom. Developing sample test items provides high-fidelity practice in doing these things.

- As a variation on that theme, provide unlabeled exercises and have students practice (1) placing them in the proper cell of the test blueprint, and (2) answering them.

- As another variation, have students evaluate the quality of the tests that came with the textbook— do they match your plan developed for instruction?

- Have students use the test blueprint to predict how they are going to do on each part of the test before they take it. Then have them analyze how they did, part by part, after taking it. If the first test is for practice, such an analysis will provide valuable information to help them plan their preparation for the real thing.

- Have students work in teams, with each one given responsibility for finding ways to help everyone in class score high in one cell, row, or column of a table of specifications or one objective.

- Use lists of unit objectives and tables of test specifications to communicate with other teachers about instructional priorities, so as to arrive at a clearer understanding of how those priorities fit together across instructional levels or school buildings.

- Store test items by content and reasoning category for reuse. If the item record also included information on how students did on each item (say, the percentage that got it right), you could revise instruction next time for items students had trouble with. Incidentally, this represents an excellent place to use your personal computer to advantage as a test item storage and retrieval system.

Figure 6–3
Strategies for Connecting Assessment to Instruction

ment and use into the very fabric of your teaching and learning environment. Many of these suggestions reflect an idea planted earlier in the chapter. Remember when I asked you who else might become involved in the process of assessment development and use, in order to lighten your classroom assessment workload? The coworkers to whom I referred are your students.

Figure 6–3 represents only the beginning of a practically endless list. You can and should generate ideas to add to it. These uses of the selected response assessment development process all contribute to one huge key to student success: *Students can hit any target that they can see and that holds still for them.* These strategies serve to remove the mystery surrounding the meaning of academic success. They bring students into the process of defining that meaning and give them control over their own well-being.

Time for Reflection

Can you think of other specific ways to use assessment development, administration, scoring, or interpretation as an integral part of the teaching and learning process? Brainstorm more options. Did any of your own teachers integrate assessment into instruction? What did they do?

Chapter Summary: Productive Selected Response Assessment

During this phase of our journey through the realm of educational assessment, we have considered multiple-choice, true/false, matching, and fill-in selected response test item formats. We established at the beginning of the chapter that these options often are labeled *objective tests* because of the manner in which they are scored. Answers are right or wrong—there is no judgment involved. However, subjective professional judgment does play a major role in all other facets of this kind of assessment, from test planning, to the selection of material to be tested, to the process of item writing itself. For this reason, it is essential that all selected response test developers adhere conscientiously to procedures for creating sound tests. Those procedures were the topic of this chapter.

We discussed the match between selected response assessment methods and the five basic kinds of achievement targets that are serving as signposts for our journey. These selected response formats can serve to assess student mastery of content knowledge, ability to reason in sophisticated ways, mastery of some of the procedural knowledge that underpins skills and the development of complex products, and presence of certain dispositions.

As we examined the test development process itself, we explored several context factors that extend beyond just the consideration of match to target that must be taken into account in choosing selected response assessment. These included factors related to the students' reading abilities and to the kinds of support services available to the user.

Also under the heading of test development, we explored a three-step developmental sequence: test planning, identifying propositions to be tested, and test item writing. We reviewed a limited number of specific item and test development tactics within each step that promise to decrease test development time and increase test quality.

We closed with a list of specific ways to bring students into the assessment as full partners. Note that we are not referring simply to exchanging papers at test scoring time; rather, we are talking about a full partnership in assessment, with students assisting in identifying valued targets, designing assessments, creating those assessments, and interpreting and using assessment results. Note this last segment well! It presents a theme that will dominate the remainder of our travels together.

Exercises to Advance Your Learning

Knowledge

1. In your own words, describe the specific kinds of achievement targets that can be transformed into selected response formats and those that cannot.

2. Make a checklist of factors to take into account when considering use of the selected response option.

3. What are the key considerations in devising a sound sample of selected response items?

4. Make a chart listing the four selected response formats as rows and the following as columns: principle advantages, limitations, and when to use. Review this chapter and fill in the cells of the table.

5. Make a one-page chart listing your own abbreviations of the general and format-specific guidelines for item writing presented in Figure 6–2. Keep them handy for reference if and when you consider selected response assessment.

Reasoning

1. Identify 10 important propositions from this chapter. Include some knowledge and some reasoning propositions. When you have done so, review the list and ask yourself, Do these represent the most important learnings from this chapter? Evaluate and comment on each.

2. Transform each of your propositions into true true/false, false true/false, fill-in, multiple-choice, and (where appropriate) matching items.

Skills and Products

See the Special Ongoing Assessment Project following this section.

Dispositions

1. Some have argued that these are times for performance assessment and that selected response assessments are remnants of bygone times—that selected response assessment formats have no place in the future of school testing. Do you agree? Why?

2. How do you feel about the idea of using selected response exercises and tests as teaching tools? Can they be helpful? If so, how? If not, why not?

3. I argue in this chapter that the suggested test development procedures would save you time in your test development process, if you use these kinds of assessment in your classroom. Do you agree? Why?

Special Ongoing Assessment Project: Part 3

For the unit of instruction you selected, practice applying the suggestions offered in this chapter. Focus on your important knowledge and reasoning expectations and devise a table of specifications for this unit. Then find the key propositions for each cell in your table, and construct test items for your propositions. As you go, be sure to follow the item construction guidelines outlined in this chapter. When you have completed your work, evaluate the test you created in terms of the attributes of sound assessment.

Then, select a previously developed test, either from your files or from a text series you may have used, and apply these principles in evaluating it. Have the item writing and test development guidelines been followed? Can you see how to fix whatever problems you find?

Essay Assessment: Vast Untapped Potential

CHAPTER ROADMAP

As with selected response assessments, each of us may find that we must develop our own essay tests. Further, we may need to evaluate an essay test developed by others, and/or find ourselves on the examinee side of an essay test. Under all of these circumstances, it is important that we understand how we can meet standards of assessment quality using this form of assessment.

To assist you in developing this understanding, we will address four aspects of essay assessment in this segment of our journey: the critical role of subjective judgment in essay assessment; the match of essay assessment to the five kinds of achievement targets; the essay assessment development process, covering both exercise development and the specification of scoring criteria; and strategies for drawing students into the essay assessment process as a means of raising both their levels of motivation to learn and their actual achievement.

As a result of studying the material presented in Chapter 7, reflecting on that material, and completing the learning exercise presented at the end of the chapter, you will be knowledgeable about the following:

1. The roles of objectivity and subjectivity in essay assessment.

2. The kinds of achievement targets that can be reflected in essay assessments.

3. Three key steps in the essay assessment development process.

4. Classroom assessment context factors to consider in deciding whether or when to use essay assessments.

5. Important considerations in sampling student achievement through the use of essay exercises.

6. Specific guidelines for the construction of essay exercises and scoring schemes.

7. Specific ways to bring students into the essay assessment process as a teaching strategy.

In addition, you will be able to use that knowledge to reason as follows:

1. Select appropriate content and reasoning targets for translation into essay assessments.
2. Translate those outcomes into quality exercises and scoring criteria.

You will become proficient in carrying out the following skills, resulting in quality assessment products:

1. Carry out the steps in the assessment development process.
2. Evaluate previously developed essay assessments to ensure their quality.
3. Create essay assessments that meet predetermined standards.

And, I hope you will become predisposed to do the following:

1. Feel that it is important to know about sound essay assessment.
2. Value essay assessment as a viable option for use in the classroom.
3. See essay assessment as a valuable instructional tool in which students should be and can be full partners.
4. See essay assessment as a viable alternative to performance assessment in contexts where authentic performance assessment is not possible.

As we proceed through this phase of our journey, keep the big picture in mind. From our chart matching achievement targets with modes of assessment, we will be dealing with the sections darkened in Figure 7–1 as we proceed through this chapter.

The essay form of assessment may have the greatest untapped potential of any of the four assessment methods discussed in this book. The time has come for us to begin to take greater advantage of this rich assessment option.

As mentioned earlier, our changing social and economic circumstances and our increasingly technical world demand that schools assist students in attaining increasingly complex forms of achievement. As a result, during the 1980s, these more sophisticated targets spawned interest in assessment methods able to tap the greater depth of our achievement expectations. We began to sense the insufficiency of selected response assessment. In response, we began to explore richer assessment methods, such as performance assessment, to tap student proficiency. This is one important reason why performance assessment gained immense popularity in schools in the late 1980s and throughout the 1990s. At the same time, however, this exploration has brought us to startling realizations regarding the expense of authentic performance assessments. Those costs are detailed in the next chapter. This leaves us on the horns of a troubling dilemma. Do we ignore the complexity of performance assessments and turn to efficient selected response

	SELECTED RESPONSE	ESSAY	PERFORMANCE ASSESSMENT	PERSONAL COMMUNICATION
Know				
Reason				
Skills				
Products				
Dispositions				

Figure 7–1
Aligning Achievement Targets and Assessment Methods

assessments or embrace the complexity and pay the price of labor-intensive assessment?

Essay assessments may represent an alternative approach to this dilemma, one that gets us off the hook. As you shall see in this chapter, essays permit us to tap at least some of our most highly valued, yet complex, achievement targets at a fraction of the cost of performance assessments. Further, as we begin to see students as partners in the assessment, we will come to regard labor-intensive assessment methods such as essays as more feasible than we have in the past because of their immense power as teaching tools—not merely as sources of data.

For all of these reasons, essay assessments can become an increasingly useful alternative as we move through the 1990s. This chapter explores the untapped potential of the essay assessment alternative and reviews this assessment methodology's three major strengths:

- Essays can delve into student attainment of some complex and sophisticated achievement targets.

- They can assess these outcomes at a relatively low cost in terms of teacher time and energy.

- Essay assessment can be integrated productively into the teaching and learning process.

Be advised, however, that this assessment method brings risks with it too. For instance, it can be very time consuming, because of the time required to score student responses. Further, users can mismeasure student achievement if they do any or all of the following:

- lack a sufficiently clear vision of the kinds of outcomes to be learned and therefore assessed
- do not connect the essay format to the proper kinds of achievement targets
- use this method with students who lack sufficient writing skills to convey their achievement of content or reasoning skills
- do not representatively sample the target forms of achievement
- disregard the many sources of bias that can invade subjective assessments

Those schooled in the efficient use of essay assessment and in methods of avoiding these pitfalls, however, can use essay assessment to great advantage.

Time for Reflection

Please take a few minutes to reflect on your past experience with essay assessments. How often have your teachers relied on this method? If you teach currently, how much do you use this option? When you have come into contact with essay assessment as a student or teacher, what has the experience been like? Has it been positive or negative? Why?

Essay Assessment in a Productive Learning Environment

A professor acquaintance of mine uses essay exercises exclusively for his final examinations in the classroom assessment course that he teaches for teachers and school administrators. He reports that he likes the essay format because it allows him (1) to present exercises that depict relatively complex real-world classroom assessment dilemmas, and (2) to ask his students to use their assessment methodology knowledge and reasoning abilities to describe how they would resolve each dilemma if confronted with it in their classroom.

Obviously, he could obtain a more "authentic" assessment of their proficiency if he could place his students in a real classroom, and observe their performance in solving the identified problems. But since that kind of authenticity is beyond reach, he turns to an essay test and effectively gains insight into their achievement.

The Assessment

The professor samples the achievement of his students using 10 essay exercises on each final exam. He chooses those that appear on any one exam from a pool of exercises that he and his students have devised over the years to represent the broad array of classroom assessment challenges teachers face in real classrooms. Since time will not permit testing for all eventualities, the professor must compromise by administering a limited set of exercises and inferring from every student's performance how much of the important material they have mastered. He feels 10 exercises are enough to give him confidence in making these inferences.

For each exercise, he has established performance expectations in advance by specifying either one best solution or a set of acceptable solutions to the classroom assessment problem presented. The professor carefully translates these expectations into a predetermined scoring scheme. His students are told up front how many points are associated with each exercise and they strive to attain as many of those points as they can.

Following is a sample of one of his exercises, along with its scoring scheme. It reveals the kind of real-world complexity he can attain with this assessment format.

Sample Essay Exercise

Assume you are a French teacher with many years of teaching experience. You place great value on the development of speaking proficiency as an outcome of your instruction. Therefore, you rely heavily on assessments where you listen to and evaluate performance. But a problem has arisen. Parents of students who attained very high scores on your written tests are complaining that their children are receiving lower grades on their report cards. The principal wants to be sure your judgments of student proficiency are sound and so has asked you to explain and defend your assessment procedures. Describe three specific assessment-related procedures you would want to follow in this instance and explain how you would defend each. (2 points for each procedure and rationale, total = 6 points.)

Criteria Used to Score Responses to This Exercise:

Assign points to each response as follows: 2 points if the student's response lists any of these six procedures and defends each as a key to conducting sound performance assessments:

- specify clear performance criteria
- sample performance over several exercises
- apply systematic rating procedures
- maintain complete and accurate records
- use published performance assessments to verify results of classroom assessments
- use multiple observers to corroborate

Also award 2 points if the response lists any of these and defends them as attributes of sound assessments:

- specifies a clear instructional objective
- relies on a proper assessment method
- samples performance well
- controls for sources of rater bias

All other responses receive no points.

The professor claims that, over the years, these final exams have become very much a part of the teaching and learning process in his classes. I explain below how he has been able to achieve this.

The Process

These essay finals are take-home exams, so as to maximize the amount of time students spend reflecting and learning. His students report that they do, in fact, spend a considerable amount of time preparing their responses. Further, students receive the exercises a few at a time throughout the term, as the professor presents the material needed to address the various problems. This has the effect of making the achievement targets perfectly clear to the students, thus helping to focus learning and reduce test anxiety. It also focuses study and spreads the extra learning time and effort over the entire term.

As take-home exams, these obviously are open-book exams. The professor covers a great deal of material about assessment in this course and reports that he does not expect students to memorize it all, anymore than he expects his physician to memorize all of the treatment options she has at her disposal.

Rather, each student receives a full set of text materials assembled into an easy reference presentation format. Over the course of instruction and as they work on the exercises, students learn how to use these reference materials. Hopefully, after the course is over, they will keep their "library" of assessment ideas handy for classroom use. The open-book exam format encourages them to learn the overall organizational structure of these materials.

The Scoring

At the end of the term, when students hand in their final exam for scoring (all 10 exercises come in together), the professor applies the predetermined scoring guides in evaluating each response to each exercise. Since enrollment can exceed 50 students per class, he has had to find ways to maximize reading and scoring efficiency. The single biggest time saver, he reports, is to have the scoring criteria clearly in mind before beginning the scoring process. Next is to score all responses to one exercise at one time and then move on to the next exercise. We'll review more time-saving ideas later in the chapter.

The Feedback

Students receive feedback on their performance in the following forms:

- points assigned to each part of each response
- brief written rationale for the score, suggesting factors they might have overlooked
- the total number of points summed over all exercises
- a grade based on comparing the total score to a predetermined set of cutoff scores for each grade

Students who attain grades that are lower than their expectations for themselves can rework any exercise(s) any time and resubmit their exam for reevaluation. If a reevaluation of their written work and a personal discussion with the professor reveals that they have completed more productive study and have attained a higher level of proficiency, the professor submits a change of grade at once. This procedure has the effect of extending the learning time beyond the limits of a single term when necessary.

Time for Reflection

If you took a course from a professor who practiced these assessment procedures (and perhaps you have), what would you expect to be the effect on your learning? Try to think of as many effects as you can.

The Impact

The professor reports that scoring all responses to a single exercise together helps him to integrate assessment into instruction in another important way. After reading 50 attempts to solve a relatively complex classroom assessment problem, he assures me that he knows which facets of his instruction were effective and which were not. When his students are ready to resolve the classroom assessment dilemma presented in an exercise, he reports, it shows—almost all of them provide acceptable solutions. But when the professor has failed to set them up for success, it becomes painfully obvious in paper after paper. He knows without question which phase of instruction did not work. Next term, he revises instruction in the hope that his students will perform better on similar exercises.

The impact on students is clear, too. A high percentage of them do very well on these exams. They report that they spend more time on these exercises than on other exams, and that they really have to study, analyze, and reflect deeply on the material covered in class and required readings to find solutions to the problems presented. And, they welcome the opportunity to rework the material when necessary to score higher.

Context Is Critical

Without question, this particular professor's assessment and grading procedures will not work in all contexts. In a very real sense, he works in what most teachers would regard as an ideal world: a manageable number of students and few preparations.

However, my point in telling you this story is *not* to convince you to adopt his procedures. Rather, it is to make the point that essay assessment can contribute to the effectiveness of a learning community in which teacher and students enter into a partnership with a mutual goal of maximum achievement.

We will explore how this might be done in your classroom, given your realities.

Ensuring the Quality of Essay Assessments

Essay assessments represent the first of three assessment methods to be discussed over the next few chapters that are subjective by their very nature. You may recall that selected response assessments, we said, rely on matters of professional judgment in the setting of the target and design of the assessment exercises, but scoring typically is not a matter of judgment. By design, answers to well-constructed test items are right or wrong. The number of right answers produces a score that is not a matter of judgment, either. With essay assessments, professional judgment plays a bigger role. Let's examine that expanded role.

Subjectivity in Essay Assessment

In the case of essay tests, professional judgment plays a role in both development and scoring. This means there are more ways for unwanted bias to creep into the assessment results, placing the attainment of meaningful scores in jeopardy. That, in turn, means that users of this methodology must be doubly vigilant against potential problems. However, we know how to create "subjective" (or judgmental) assessment tools in a systematic way that can ultimately make them one of the most versatile tools at our disposal.

Perhaps the most critical message of Part 2 of this book is this: **Assessments such as essays, that rely on professional judgment to evaluate student work, can produce quality results leading to effective instruction and high achievement only if they are carefully developed according to known rules of evidence using proper procedures.**

In the case of essay assessments, teacher judgment is involved in the following aspects:

- establishing the underlying achievement target
- selecting the component parts of that guiding target to include in the assessment
- preparing essay exercises themselves
- devising scoring criteria
- conducting the scoring process itself

If teachers are not versed in the discipline being assessed or are not in command of the achievement targets they will assess, they obviously run the risk of mismeasurement and it is their students who will feel the effects—frustration, misconceptions, and reduced learning.

In the case of essay assessment, as with any form of assessment, the responsibility for avoiding such problems and for assuring quality rests squarely with *you*, the teacher! Those who thoroughly comprehend the content and patterns of reasoning to be mastered are in an excellent position to plan exercises and scoring schemes that fit the valued outcomes of instruction. It is only through developing and using strong exercises and appropriate scoring criteria that you may avoid errors in measuring student achievement attributable to evaluator or rater bias. Let's look at specific ways to reach this goal.

Matching Method to Target

Essay assessments have a potential contribution to make in assessing key dimensions of student learning in all five categories of valued targets—knowledge, reasoning, skills, products, and predispositions (affect).

Assessing Knowledge.   Most experts advise against using essays to assess student mastery of subject matter knowledge, when the targets are conceived of as specific facts or concepts students are to learn. The primary reason is that we have better options at our disposal for tapping this kind of outcome. Selected response assessment formats provide a more efficient means of assessment that, at the same time, allow for a more precise and controlled sampling of the achievement domain.

Selected response test formats are more efficient than essays in this case for two reasons. First, you can ask more multiple-choice questions than essay questions per unit of testing time because multiple-choice response time is so much shorter. You can provide a broader sample of performance per unit of time with selected response items than with essay exercises. Second, scoring of selected response items is much faster than scoring of essays.

Selected response methods allow for a more confident sampling of student mastery of material in part because many more items can be included in the test, and in part because the inclusion of those items forces the student to address all key elements of knowledge within the target domain.

As an example, say we want to evaluate students' spelling. If we do so by assessing their spelling as it appears in the papers they write, students can mislead us with respect to their real spelling achievement. Student writers are more likely to use words that they are confident they know how to spell. They will avoid words they are not sure about. Thus, left to their own devices, they can keep us from finding the words they cannot spell by leaving them out of their writing. In this way, a writing-based assessment of spelling will provide us with a biased sample of all the words students may need to know how to spell.

Selected response assessments counteract this problem by forcing the respondent to answer a set of items that systematically sample the target achievement. Such assessments force the examinee to demonstrate mastery of all relevant material. If we ask students to attempt every word on the list (i.e., rely on a short answer fill-in test), we will find out which they can spell and which they cannot. In this way, selected response formats offer a greater degree of control in sampling their spelling proficiency.

Even though all of this is true and important, however, I argue in favor of using the essay format for the assessment of student mastery of a specific, important form of content knowledge. Let me explain.

In discussing the design and development of selected response items, I described a planning process that began with a broad domain of content, divided that into categories for the table of specifications, and divided categories even further into collections of individual propositions, any one of which might be transformed into a specifically focused test item. In this scenario, elements of knowledge become quite narrow and individual (i.e., unrelated to one another).

However, this is not the only way to conceive of knowledge to be mastered. We may also conceive of units of knowledge that are larger, each containing numerous important smaller elements within it, all of which relate to one another in some important way. For example, we might want students to know all of the parts of a particular ecosystem in science and to know how they are related to one another. An essay assessment can help us evaluate student attainment of this kind of knowledge.

Following is an example of such an exercise that a science teacher might use on a final exam in a biology course to find out if students know and understand the water cycle.

> *Describe how the concepts of evaporation and condensation as studied in class come into play in the context of the water cycle. Be sure to include all key elements in the cycle and how they relate to one another. (20 points)*

We can use such exercises in an open-book exam, too, if we wish to assess mastery of such complex knowledge through the use of reference materials. With essay assessments, we are seeking a readout of the more complex cognitive map of the learner. One of the most common complaints against the selected response form of assessment is that it compartmentalizes learning too much—students demonstrate knowledge but are not asked to integrate it into a larger whole. Students familiar with and expecting essay assessments know that such integration is important and are more likely to prepare in that way.

Assessing Reasoning.   Assessment experts agree that this is the real strength of essay assessment. At testing time, we can present complex problems that ask learners to bring their subject matter knowledge and reasoning skills together to find a solution. In instances where we cannot see this knowledge retrieval and reasoning process unfold, we ask students to describe the results of their reasoning in their essays. From this, we make inferences about the state of their knowledge and their ability to use it in problem-solving contexts.

We can ask them to analyze, compare, draw inferences, and/or think critically in virtually any subject matter area. Furthermore, we can pose problems that require integrating material from two or more subjects and/or applying more than one pattern of reasoning. The key question we ask is, Do students know how and when to use the knowledge they have at their disposal to reason and solve problems? Here is an example from a "science, technology, and society" course taught by a middle school teacher:

> *Using what you know about the causes of air pollution in cities, propose two potentially useful solutions. Analyze each in terms of its strengths and weaknesses. Compare them in terms of their social and scientific consequences and therefore their acceptability to inhabitants of cities. (20 points)*

Remember, however, the keys to the successful assessment of student thinking through the use of the essay format are the same as the keys to success with the selected response format:

1. Assessors must possess a highly refined vision of what they mean by the terms *reasoning* and *problem solving*. (We discuss this in detail in Chapter 10.)

2. Assessors must know how to translate that vision into clear, focused essay exercises and scoring criteria.

3. The exercises must present problems to students that are new at the time of the assessment (i.e., problems for which students must figure out a response).

We will discuss how to meet these standards later in this chapter.

Assessing Skills.   If the valued achievement target holds that students become proficient in demonstrating specific skills, then there is only one acceptable way to assess proficiency: observation of actual performance. For instance, say we want to find out if students can carry out certain complex behaviors, such as participating collaboratively in a group, communicating orally in a second language, debating a controversial issue in social studies, or carrying out the steps in a science experiment. In these cases, standards of sound assessment require that we give students the opportunity to demonstrate group participation skills, speak the language, debate, or conduct an actual lab experiment.

There is no way to use an essay test format to assess these kinds of performances. An essay exercise would not be "authentic"—it would not, could not, accurately depict real performance.

However, there are some important skill-related outcomes that we can tap with the essay format. For instance, we can use the essay to assess mastery of some of the complex knowledge and even problem-solving skills that are *prerequisite* to performing the skill in question.

For example, if a student doesn't *know* how the functions of different pieces of science lab equipment relate to one another in an experimental context, there is no way that student will successfully complete the lab work. We could devise an essay question to see if she had mastered that prerequisite knowledge.

Thus, we could use the essay format to assess student attainment of some of the building blocks of competence. The results of such assessments can be enlightening to a teacher planning future lessons aimed at helping students to attain ultimate competence.

Assessing Products.   Again in this case, if the valued target holds that students be able to create a specified kind of product that reflects certain attributes, the only high-fidelity way to assess the outcome is to have them actually create the product so we can evaluate it according to established standards of quality.

However, essays can provide insight into whether the student knows and understands the process of creating a quality product. Or, essays might provide insight into the respondent's awareness of the criteria or key attributes of a quality product. These might be useful assessments in a classroom context where the foundations of competence are being built. We can use essay assessments in these contexts, however, only if we remain constantly aware of the fact that being able to write about a good product and being able to create that product are different outcomes.

Assessing Writing as a Product.   One kind of product we often ask students to create is samples of their writing. We do this with essay tests, research report assignments, term papers, and so on. It is tempting to think of a term paper as just a long essay assessment tapping mastery of larger knowledge structures and/or complex thinking.

However, these bigger writing projects are different from responses to essay exercises, largely because of subtle but important differences in the nature of the criteria used to evaluate each.

When students write in response to an essay exercise, we evaluate in terms of criteria that focus on the respondent's mastery of the kind(s) of content and/or reasoning needed to answer the question adequately. Thus, it is the *substance* of the writing—the ideas expressed—that go under the microscope.

But when writing is the medium used to produce such a product as a term paper or research report, the criteria used to evaluate performance typically include issues of *form* as well as those of content and reasoning. When students use written language as a medium of communication, we also may evaluate their writing in terms of organization, sentence fluency, word choice, voice (i.e., the extent to which the writer's personality comes through to the reader), and other important factors.

Further, we can evaluate research reports and term papers in terms of presentation format, use of graphs and tables, and use and citation of references. When matters of form come into play, I think of writing as an achievement-related product and my list of key aspects of good performance begins to grow. We will discuss this more in Chapter 8.

A key lesson to learn is that subjective assessment, whether judging content or form, requires clear thinking and effective communication of the performance criteria you will use to evaluate performance.

Assessing Dispositions.   Student writing can also provide a window into students' motivations or attitudes. When we ask them specific questions about the direction and intensity of their feelings about focused aspects of their schooling, in an environment where honesty is accepted, students can and will inform us about their attitudes, interests, and levels of motivation. Questionnaires containing open-ended questions can produce student responses that are full of profoundly important insights into the affective and social climate of a school or classroom.

Chapter 12 deals in detail with issues and procedures related to the assessment of dispositions using this and other methods.

Summary of Target Matches.   On the whole, essay assessment is a very flexible format. It can provide useful information on a variety of targets. We can use it to evaluate student mastery of larger structures of knowledge, whether learned out-right or mastered through the use of reference materials. We certainly can tap student reasoning and problem solving skills. We can assess mastery of the complex procedural knowledge that is prerequisite to skilled performance and/or the creation of quality products. And finally, we also can explore student motivations and attitudes in rich and useful ways through student writing.

But again, I caution that a student's foundation of prerequisite knowledge of the steps to take to appear skilled or to create a quality product, while necessary for attaining required levels of performance, may not be sufficient to guarantee success in actually demonstrating skill or creating that product.

Time for Reflection

We are about to begin the section of this chapter dealing with the design and development of sound essay exercises and scoring criteria. Before we do, please do the following: Draft an essay exercise that could appear on a final exam on this chapter that asks the respondent to describe the relationships between essay assessment and the various achievement targets—knowledge, problem solving, and so on. Also, draft a proposed scoring scheme for your exercise. Keep these drafts handy, and refer to them as we discuss procedures for developing and scoring essay assessments. The purpose for this exercise is to provide you with an opportunity to try this before learning some of the intricacies of essay development. This will provide you with a context within which to understand the design suggestions offered below. So don't read on until you do this work!

Developing Essay Assessments

The design and development process for essay assessments includes three steps:

1. assessment planning
2. exercise development
3. preparation to score

Test planning for this form of assessment is very much like planning selected response assessments, while exercise development is a bit easier, and preparation to score is much more challenging. After considering important context factors to take into account in deciding whether or when to use this option, we will turn to the test planning phase.

Context Factors

You will need to consider the classroom context factors delineated in Figure 7–2 before deciding whether the essay format is appropriate for the particular achieve-

- *The respondents' level of writing proficiency*. This is absolutely critical. If students lack writing skill, it is impossible to use this mode of assessment to gather useful information about their achievement. Writing proficiency is always confounded with achievement in this format. If students cannot write, we must select another mode of assessment. It is the only fair way.
- *The availability of already developed high-quality essay exercises with associated scoring criteria*. If the work has already been done by you, your colleagues, or by the textbook author, and essays are ready to go, then go with them. Just be sure to verify quality.
- *The number of students to be evaluated*. The smaller the group, the shorter the overall time needed to do the scoring. The larger the group, the more time you need. Plan accordingly.
- *The number of exercises needed to sample the material and the length of responses to be read and scored*. The smaller the number of exercises needed to provide an adequate sample of material and the shorter the response, the less time will be needed for scoring. Most assessment experts recommend the use of more shorter exercises rather than fewer exercises requiring longer responses. The more exercises you use, the easier it is to sample the domain representatively.
- *The amount of person time available to read and evaluate responses*. This need not be only teacher time, although your time should be a major consideration. Sometimes, essay scoring support can come from students, teacher aides, or even from qualified parents. Be advised, however, of the two keys to being able to take advantage of such scoring assistance:
  1. Develop clear and appropriate scoring criteria and procedures.
  2. Train all scorers to apply those standards fairly and consistently.

Figure 7–2
Context Factors in the Use of Essay Assessments

ment target you are assessing. Attention to these factors will help you use this format most effectively.

Assessment Planning

The challenge, as always, is to begin with clearly articulated achievement targets. In this case, the target will reflect both the components of knowledge and the patterns of reasoning to be mastered by the respondent. Consequently, once again we have the option of starting with either a table of test specifications or a list of instructional objectives.

Tables of specifications for essay tests are like those used for selected response assessments in some ways, and different in others. The similarities lie in the basic framework. Table 7–1 is an example of such a table for an essay test covering some of the material on a series of short stories read in class. As the developer of such a table, I must specify the categories of knowledge to be used on one axis and the patterns of reasoning expected on the other. Row and column totals, and therefore entries in the cells of the table, once again represent the relative emphasis assigned to each.

Table 7–1
Table of Specifications for an
Essay Test

Content	Number of Points			
	Know	**Infer**	**Evaluate**	**Total**
Setting	10 pts	10	10	30
Plot	10	10	10	30
Characters	0	20	20	40
Total	20	40	40	100

However, with the essay table of specifications, cells each contain the number of points on the test that I have assigned to that content-reasoning combination, not the number of individual test items, as was the case in Chapter 6. When I actually construct the test, I might spread those points over one or more exercises associated with each cell.

Given 100 points for the entire exam, this plan obviously emphasizes the understanding of characters relative to the other two categories, requiring that respondents rely on that understanding to infer and evaluate. If I were to use exercises valued at 10 points each, I would need 10 exercises distributed so as to reflect these priorities.

I could translate these same values into instructional objectives, if I wish, as shown in the following list. I list these sample objectives simply to illustrate a second way of capturing and communicating the meaning of academic success reflected in the cells of the table. You need not do both the table and the objectives. Select one or the other as a means of reflecting your valued outcomes.

- Students will know the settings of the stories.
- Students will be able to draw inferences based on their knowledge of the plots and characters in the stories.
- Students will be able to carry out a systematic evaluation of the quality of the plot and character development.

Sampling Student Achievement with Essays.   Just as with selected response items, essay exercises represent a sampling of two key elements: some knowledge to be retrieved (either from memory or reference) and some kind(s) of cognitive act to be carried out using that knowledge. In the case of essay exercises, the units of knowledge involved are bigger, more inclusive entities than those that might form the basis of a multiple-choice test item.

Also as with selected response test plans, each cell in Table 7–1, or each instructional objective, establishes a sampling framework. That is, each captures components of knowledge and examples of the application of kinds of thinking. For instance, under the first objective, I might ask about several plots. For the second objective, the range of possible inferences and contexts within which to reason about characters is large, spanning several characters and stories. For the third objective, again, I have available a number of sample plots that I might present for evaluation.

Clearly, it would be impossible to include in one assessment all of the possible instances of the union of rows and columns as depicted in the table of specifications or in these kinds of objectives. Rather, the preferred method is to sample from all of these possibilities, picking a representative sample of the most important instances to present as exercises. And then, based on student performance on this sample, we generalize to the domain of all possible exercises. If the student does well on these, that student would probably do well on any other set of similar exercises. Thus, in this sampling sense, essay tests are just like selected response tests.

But who identifies the knowledge and reasoning components to be considered as important for classroom assessment? This is *your* responsibility as the expert on valued outcomes in your classroom. Thus, you must possess an in-depth understanding of the full range of material that you could assess. As soon as you have identified the range of possibilities, you are ready to select a representative sample of these for use in devising the exercises and scoring schemes that will comprise your test.

Note also that a table of test specifications designed to reflect the number of points allocated to each row, column, and cell can serve as the basis for an assessment made up of both selected response and essay exercises. While selected response items might count one point each, essay responses might count more.

Developing Essay Exercises

Essay exercises should pose problems for students to solve. But what are the attributes of a sound exercise?

One of my graduate students once described an exercise he received on a final exam at the end of his undergraduate studies. He had majored for 4 years in Spanish language, literature, and culture. His last final was an in-class essay exam with a 3-hour time limit. The entire exam consisted of one exercise, which posed the challenge in only two words: "Discuss Spain."

Obviously, he would have preferred a bit more detail. But haven't we all had experiences like this? One of the advantages often listed for essay tests relative to other test formats is that essay exercises are much easier and take less time to develop. I submit that many users turn that advantage into a liability by assuming that "easier to develop" means you don't have to put much thought into it—as evidenced in the above example.

Another common mistake teachers make is trying to turn an essay exercise into a demonstration of their creativity. A scientist friend offered an example from his experience as a college student: "Take a walk through a late Mesozoic forest and tell me what you see." This is better than "Discuss Spain." However, even more specification is needed to set the respondent up for success.

To succeed in the use of this assessment format, we must invest thoughtful preparation time in writing exercises that challenge respondents by describing a single complete and novel task. Sound exercises do three things:

1. *Identify the knowledge to be incorporated.* They specify the knowledge the student is supposed to command in preparing a response.

Example: During the term, we have discussed both the evolution of Spanish literature and the changing political climate in Spain during the twentieth century.

2. *Specify the kind(s) of reasoning or problem solving to be carried out by the respondent.* Sound exercises specify what respondents are to write about.

   Example: During the term, we have discussed both the evolution of Spanish literature and the changing political climate in Spain during the twentieth century. Analyze these two dimensions of life in Spain, citing three instances where literature and politics may have influenced each other. Describe the mutual influences in specific terms.

3. *Point the direction to an appropriate response without giving away the store.* Good exercises list the key elements of a good response without cueing the unprepared examinee on how to succeed.

   Example: During the term, we have discussed both the evolution of Spanish literature and the changing political climate in Spain during the twentieth century. Analyze these two dimensions of life in Spain, citing three instances where you think literature and politics may have influenced each other. Describe the mutual influences in specific terms. In planning your response, think about what we learned about prominent novelists, political satirists, and prominent political figures of Spain. (5 points per instance, total = 15 points.)

Let's analyze the content of the example provided at the beginning of the chapter, reproduced below.

Assume you are a French teacher with many years of teaching experience. You place great value on the development of speaking proficiency as an outcome of your instruction. Therefore, you rely heavily on assessments where you listen to and evaluate performance. But a problem has arisen. Parents of students who attained very high test scores on your written tests are complaining that their children are receiving lower grades on their report cards. The principal wants to be sure your judgments of student proficiency are sound and so has asked you to explain and defend your assessment procedures. Describe three specific assessment-related procedures you would want to follow in this instance and explain how you would defend each. (2 points for each procedure and rationale, total = 6 points.)

Here's the challenge to the student in a nutshell:

Demonstrate knowledge of:	performance assessment methodology
By using it to reason:	draw inferences about the proper applications of methods to a specific instance
Adhering to these standards:	list three appropriate ones and defend them

Time for Reflection

Please return to the essay exercise you developed at the beginning of this section of the chapter. Did you specify the knowledge to be used, kinds(s) of reasoning to be employed, and standards to be applied? Adjust your exercise as needed to meet these standards.

Another good way to check the quality of your essay exercises is to try to write or outline a quality response yourself. If you can, you probably have a properly focused exercise. If you cannot . . . you see what I mean.

Incidentally, when I use essays, I like to make it clear to my students that I care far more about the content of their answer than the form. I urge them to communicate their ideas as efficiently as they can, so I can read and score their responses as fast as possible. I urge them to use outlines and lists of ideas, examples, illustrations—whatever it takes to come to the point quickly and clearly. I do not require the use of connected discourse unless it is needed to communicate their solution to the problem. I explain that I do not want them beating around the bush in the hope that somewhere, somehow, they say something worth a point or two. Believe me, this suggestion makes scoring so much easier!

Figure 7–3 presents a checklist of factors to think about as you devise essay exercises. Answering these questions should assist you in constructing effective essay exercises.

In regard to the inclusion of the last point in Figure 7–3, don't offer choices: The assessment question should always be, "Can you hit the agreed-on target?" It

Figure 7–3
Factors to Consider When
Devising Essay Exercises

_____ Do exercises call for *brief, focused responses*?

_____ Are they written at the *lowest possible reading level*? Double check at the time of administration to ensure understanding—especially among poor readers.

_____ Do you have the confidence that qualified *experts in the field would agree with your definition* of a sound response? This is a judgment call.

_____ Would the elements in your scoring plan be *obvious to good students*?

_____ Have you presented one set of exercises to all respondents? *Don't offer optional questions* from which to choose.

should never be, "Which part of the agreed-on target are you most confident that you can hit?" This latter question always leaves a teacher uncertain about whether the student has in fact mastered the material covered in exercises not selected—some of which may be crucial to later learning. When students select their own sample of performance, it can be a biased one.

Here is a final idea for exercise development: If you wish to use the essay format to assess reasoning skills, but you are not sure all students have a sufficient or equal grasp of the underlying body of knowledge, provide the knowledge needed to solve the problem and see if they can use it appropriately. This is another instance where you can use the interpretive exercise format discussed in Chapter 6. Simply provide a chart, graph, table, or paragraph of connected discourse and spin an essay or essays out of the material presented, as shown in the following example.

Map Skills: The Compromise of 1820

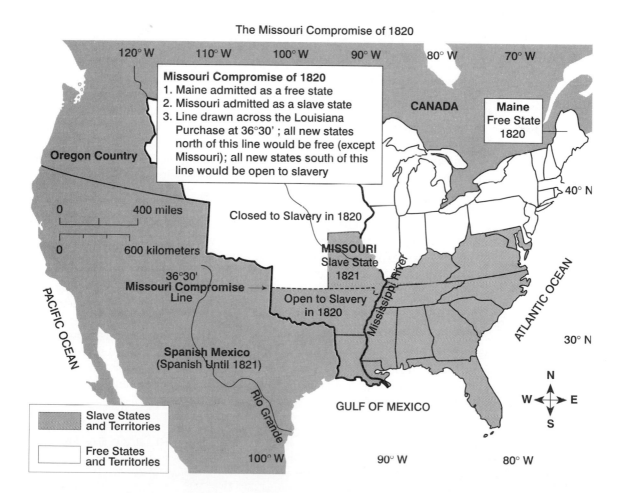

Study the map. Then decide whether these statements are true or false. Explain your answers.

1. Most of the Louisiana Purchase was open to slavery.
2. Missouri was south of the line marked at 36 degrees, 30 minutes.
3. Missouri was admitted to the United States as a slave state.
4. The Mississippi River divided the free and slave territories.
5. The southwest boundary of the United States in 1820 was the Rio Grande.[1]

Developing Essay Scoring Procedures

Many teachers score essays by applying what I call "floating standards," in which you wait to see what responses you get to decide what you wanted. The cynic in me says users of this method of scoring simply adjust internally held standards and invisible score scales downward during scoring to produce scores that indicate high levels of achievement regardless of whether those levels were attained. The perceived benefits of this method, I fear, are that students always appear to have achieved, and no one will ever know otherwise—no one will be able to detect the underlying manipulation that occurred.

No one, that is, except the perpetrator! The only standards of ethical practice that will ever come to bear on your essay scoring practices are those that you hold for yourself. In that regard, I hope you will adhere to the instructional and assessment philosophy that has guided everything we have discussed up to this point: **Students can succeed if they know what it means to succeed.** That means we state the meaning of success up front, design instruction to help students succeed, and devise and use assessments that reflect those prestated standards. That includes formulating essay scoring criteria in advance and holding yourself and your students accountable for attaining those standards.

Essay scoring is a classic example of evaluative or critical thinking. In evaluative thinking, we express an opinion about something and defend it through the logical application of specified criteria. Theater critics evaluate plays according to certain (rarely agreed on!) criteria and publish their reviews in the newspaper. Movie critics give thumbs up or down (an evaluative judgment) and use their criteria to explain why.

These are exactly the kinds of evaluative judgments teachers must make about responses to essay exercises, as presented in this chapter, and to observed performance and achievement-related products, as discussed in Chapter 8. In all cases, the key to success is the clear articulation of appropriate performance criteria.

---

[1]Reprinted from *Explaining American History* (p. 303) by M. Swartz and J. R. O'Connor, 1986, Englewood Cliffs, NJ: Globe. Copyright 1986 by Globe. Reprinted by permission.

Scoring Options.   Typically, we convey the evaluative judgment in terms of the number of points attained on the exercises. Here are two acceptable ways to do this:

- *The Checklist Option*—Assign points to specific ingredients in an answer, and award points when the respondent includes those active ingredients.

- *The Rating Scale Option*—Define achievement in terms of one or more performance continuums in the form of rating scales; for example, a five-point scale defines five levels of performance and the rater subjectively places students' responses along that scale.

The French teacher example examined earlier in this chapter illustrates the checklist option. A rating scale for the evaluation of more features of an essay response, such as the quality of content and ideas, might look as follows:

5	The response is clear, focused and accurate. Relevant points are made (in terms of the kinds of reasoning sought by the exercise) with good support (derived from the content to be used, again as spelled out in the exercise). Good connections are drawn and important insights are evident.
3	The answer is clear and somewhat focused, but not compelling. Support of points made is limited. Connections are fuzzy, leading to few important insights.
1	The response either misses the point, contains inaccurate information, or otherwise demonstrates a lack of mastery of the material. Points are unclear, support is missing, and/or no insights are included.

With a rating scale such as this, it is perfectly acceptable to leave points 2 and 4 for the evaluator to interpolate if the response falls in between two given scores.

The idea is to develop as many such scales as make sense for the evaluation of the particular material you are rating. Other criteria for ratings, for example, might include these factors:

- demonstrated mastery of content
- organization of ideas
- soundness of reasoning

Obviously the rating scale option is more subjective than the checklist option for awarding points. However, if you have done the following three things, your rating scales can serve as excellent tools for evaluating essay responses:

1. Define the meaning of student success in terms of such scales in advance of the assessment.

2. Provide examples to your students illustrating the differences between sound and unsound performance.

3. Provide students with practice in performing successfully according to those standards.

Experts in assessment urge also that you adhere to the additional guidelines presented in Figure 7–4 when developing essay scoring procedures.

Time for Reflection

Please return to the scoring scheme you developed for your exercise at the beginning of this discussion. Did you devise a clear and appropriate set of standards? Adjust them as needed.

- Set *realistic expectations and performance standards* that are consistent with instruction and that promise students some measure of success if they are prepared.
- Check scoring guides against a few real responses to see if any *last-minute adjustments* are needed.
- *Refer back to scoring guidelines* regularly during scoring to maintain consistency.
- *Score all responses to one exercise* before moving on to the next exercise. This does two things: It promotes consistency in your application of standards, and speeds up the scoring process.
- Score all responses to one exercise *in one sitting without interruption* to keep a clear focus on standards.
- Evaluate responses *separately for matters of content (knowledge mastery and reasoning) and matters of form (i.e., writing proficiency)*. They require the application of different criteria.
- Provide feedback in the form of *points and written commentary* if possible.
- If possible, keep the *identity of the respondent anonymous* when scoring. This keeps your knowledge of their prior performance from influencing current judgments.
- Although it is often difficult to arrange, try to have *two independent qualified readers score* the papers. In a sense, this represents the litmus test of the quality of your scoring scheme. If two readers generally agree on the level of proficiency demonstrated by the respondent, then you have evidence of relatively objective or dependable subjective scoring. But if you and a colleague disagree on the level of performance demonstrated, you have uncovered evidence of problems in the appropriateness of the criteria or the process used to train raters, and some additional work is in order. When very important decisions rest on a student's score on an essay assessment, such as promotion or graduation, double scoring is absolutely essential.

Figure 7–4
Guidelines for Essay Scoring

Barriers to Sound Essay Assessment

To summarize, there are many things you can do to cause a student's score on an essay test to represent that student's real level of achievement with a high degree of accuracy. Potential sources of mismeasurement are listed here, along with the action you can take to ensure sound assessment.

Source of Error	*Counteraction*
Lack of target clarity:	
• Underlying knowledge unclear	Carefully study the material to be mastered and outline the knowledge structures to be assessed.
• Patterns of reasoning unspecified	Define forms of reasoning to be assessed in clear terms (see Chapter 10 for examples).
Wrong target for essay	Limit use to assessing mastery of larger knowledge structures (where several parts must fit together) and complex reasoning.
Lack of writing proficiency on part of respondents	Select another assessment method or help them become proficient writers.
Inadequate sample of exercises	Select a representative sample of sufficient length to give you confidence, given your table of specifications.
Poor-quality exercises	Follow guidelines specified above.
Poor-quality scoring:	
• Inappropriate criteria	Redefine criteria to fit the content and reasoning expected.
• Unclear criteria	Prepare explicit expectations—in writing.
• Untrained rater	All who are to apply the scoring criteria must be prepared to do so.
• Insufficient time to read and rate	Find more raters (see Figure 7-5 for examples), or use another method.

Integrating Essay Assessment and Instruction

With all assessment methods, the first and most obvious way to integrate assessment into the teaching and learning process is to match assessment to instruction by being sure that what is taught and learned is what is assessed. In the context of achievement-based education, students deserve practice hitting the very targets for which they will be held accountable. Similarly, teachers deserve to be held accountable for their students' success in attaining those prespecified and agreed-on outcomes.

Beyond this essential perspective, Figure 7–5 presents additional ways to integrate assessment with instruction by involving students as full partners in the process of assessing their own and each other's achievement.

This figure is intended to present enough ideas to prime the pump—it's just a start. The list of ways to bring students into the assessment equation is as endless as your imagination. Please reflect, experiment, and find more ways. These uses of the essay assessment development process all contribute to that huge key to student success: making the target crystal clear for them to see and hit. These strategies serve to remove the mystery surrounding the meaning of good performance on an essay and in the classroom. They put students in control of their own academic well-being.

- As with selected response assessment, develop a blueprint for an essay test before a unit is ever taught, share that plan with the students, and keep track of how well instruction is preparing them to succeed on the exam.

- Present students with unlabeled essay exercises and have them practice fitting them into the content and reasoning cells of the table of specifications.

- Have students join in on the process of writing sample exercises. To do so, they will need to begin to sharpen their focus on the intended knowledge and thinking targets—as they do this, good teaching is happening! Be careful, though, these might best be used as examples for practice. Remember, to assess student thinking, the exercises that actually appear on a test must present novel problems.

- Give students some sample exercises and have them evaluate their quality as test exercises, given the test blueprint.

- Have students play a role in developing the scoring criteria for some sample exercises. Give them, for example, an excellent response and a poor-quality response to a past essay exercise and have them figure out the differences.

- Bring students into the actual scoring process, thus spreading the work over more shoulders! Form scoring teams, one for each exercise on a test. Have them develop scoring criteria under your watchful eye. Offer them advice as needed to generate appropriate criteria. Then have them actually score some essays, which you double check. Discuss differences in scores assigned. Students find this kind of workshop format very engaging.

- Have students predict their performance in each cell in the table of specifications or objectives and then compare their prediction with the actual score. Were they in touch with their own achievement?

- Save essays and scoring criteria for reuse. A personal computer can help with this. If you keep information on student performance on each record (say, average score), you can adjust instruction next time to try to improve learning.

- Exchange, trade, or compare tables of specifications and/or exercises and scoring criteria with other teachers to ease the workload associated with assessment development.

Figure 7–5
Involving Students in the Assessment Process

Chapter Summary: Tapping the Potential of Essays

We all have heard those stories about the same essays being given to several college professors, who assigned vastly different grades to the same pieces of work. These stories often are cited as indictments of the essay form of assessment. This is unfair.

The reasons the professors disagreed on the level of proficiency demonstrated were that they had no opportunity to discuss and arrive at common expectations—there was no development of a common view of what it meant to perform well, no communication, no preparation to devise sound exercises and to score dependably. As a result, there was no common basis for assigning grades.

These stories reflect supremely poor application of a potentially sound, rich, and powerful assessment method. When placed in the hands of teachers and students who know what they are doing, essay assessments—like selected response assessments and the other methods that remain to be discussed—can unlock and promote effective teaching and learning.

In this chapter, we have explored ways to tap this power by preventing many of the quality control problems that can arise in the context of naive use. We began by exploring the prominent role of subjectivity and professional judgment in the essay assessment process. This prominence means that this method carries with it dangers of bias. We studied specific ways to prevent these dangers from becoming realities. One is to connect the essay assessment method to appropriate kinds of achievement targets. These include mastery of complex structures of knowledge, complex reasoning processes, some of the knowledge foundations of skill and product proficiencies, and affective outcomes.

However, the heart of the matter with respect to quality assessment is adherence to specific assessment development procedures. We studied these in three parts: assessment planning, exercise development, and preparation to score. In each case, we reviewed specific procedural guidelines.

And, as in Chapter 6, we closed with an array of strategies to engage students as full partners in the assessment process, from design and development of exercises, to scoring, to interpretation and use of essay assessment results. These strategies connect assessment to the teaching and learning process in ways that can maximize both student motivation to learn and actual achievement.

Exercises to Advance Your Learning

Knowledge

1. Refer back to the text and list three reasons for using essay assessments.

2. Summarize from memory three basic steps in the essay assessment development process.

3. What kinds of achievement targets can be transformed into the essay assessment format and what kinds cannot? Review the text if necessary to find the answer, then memorize it.

4. What factors should one take into account in considering use of the essay assessment

option? Again, learn this outright. These considerations are very important.

5. Make a one-page chart with three columns listing your own tailor-made abbreviations of the information presented in Figures 7–3, 7–4, and 7–5. Keep this handy for easy reference when you use essay assessment.

Reasoning

1. Write five essay exercises that tap dimensions of this chapter. When you have done so, review the list and ask yourself whether these really represent the most important learnings from this chapter.

2. Devise scoring schemes for each of your exercises.

Skills and Products

See the Special Ongoing Assessment Project following this section.

Dispositions

1. Some have argued that these are times for performance assessment and that such paper and pencil assessments as essay tests are remnants of bygone times—that these assessment formats have no place in the future of school testing. Do you agree? Why?

2. Throughout the chapter, I argue that the assessment development procedures outlined here will help those who use these kinds of assessments to connect their essay assessments directly to their instruction. Having completed the chapter, do you agree? Why?

3. I also argue that the assessment development and use procedures suggested herein could save you time, if you use these kinds of assessments in your classroom. Do you agree? Why?

Special Ongoing Assessment Project: Part 4

From your selected unit of instruction, identify complex structures of content and patterns of reasoning you regard as important. Devise a table of specifications, find key elements for each cell in your table, and construct essay exercises and scoring criteria for these. When you have completed your work, evaluate the assessment you have created in terms of the attributes of sound assessment discussed in this and earlier chapters. How did you do?

Then select a previously developed essay test, either from your files or from a text series you may have used, and apply the principles learned in this chapter in evaluating it. Have the guidelines been followed? Can you see how to fix any problems you find?

Performance Assessment: Rich with Possibilities

CHAPTER ROADMAP

In these times of intense interest in alternative forms of assessment, you will need a strong background in performance assessment—assessment based on observation and judgment. Virtually all teachers observe and evaluate the achievement of their students. Further, our professional literature, published instructional materials, and published tests offer teachers already developed performance assessments to consider for use in the classroom. As always, we are the gatekeepers. Our job as teachers is to check these for quality and appropriateness before permitting them into our classrooms.

To help you meet these challenges, we will conduct a thorough analysis of the basic elements of a performance assessment in this chapter, detailing a step-by-step assessment development process. Our joint mission is to help you learn how to avoid the many pitfalls to sound performance assessment.

Again, as in previous chapters, be sure to keep the big picture in mind. We will be addressing the performance assessment column of our targets-by-methods chart, as shown in Figure 8–1.

As a result of studying the material presented in this chapter, reflecting on that material, and completing the learning exercises presented at the end of the chapter, you will master important content in the form of knowing and understanding:

1. The roles of objectivity and subjectivity in performance assessment.
2. The kinds of achievement targets that can be reflected in performance assessments.
3. Nine design decisions in performance assessment development.
4. Key considerations in sampling student performance via performance exercises.
5. How to construct performance exercises and scoring schemes.

	SELECTED RESPONSE	ESSAY	PERFORMANCE ASSESSMENT	PERSONAL COMMUNICATION
Know				
Reason				
Skills				
Products				
Dispositions				

Figure 8–1
Aligning Achievement Targets and Assessment Methods

6. Ways to bring students into the performance assessment process as a teaching strategy.

In addition, you will be ready to use that knowledge to reason as follows:

1. Infer when performance assessment is the best choice for a classroom assessment context.
2. Find specific reasoning, skill, and product targets that can form the basis of performance assessment exercises.

You will become skillful at the following:

1. Carrying out the steps in designing performance assessments.
2. Evaluating previously developed performance assessments to determine their quality.

Under the heading of product development capabilities, you will be able to create performance assessments that meet standards of quality.

And finally, I hope you will complete your work with this chapter predisposed to do the following:

1. Understand the importance of knowing about sound performance assessment.
2. Value performance assessment as a viable option for use in the classroom.
3. See performance assessment as a valuable instructional tool in which students can and should be full partners.
4. Regard performance assessment with caution, valuing the need to adhere to rigorous standards of quality in development and use.

Important Notice—Please read this carefully! This chapter is just the first of several discussions of performance assessment in this book. It describes and illustrates the basic design structure of these assessments. In later chapters, we will explore many more classroom applications. For example, Chapter 10 addresses performance assessment of reasoning proficiency, while Chapter 11 illustrates using performance assessment to evaluate a variety of skills and products. Your understanding of performance assessment is contingent on mastering material covered in all of these chapters.

Over the past decade, the education community has discovered the great potential of performance assessment. These assessments involve students in activities that require them to demonstrate the mastery of certain skills. They must show us that they can do certain things or that they can create products that meet certain standards of quality. This assessment methodology permits us to rely on evaluator judgment to tap many complex achievement targets that cannot be translated into paper and pencil tests. Across the land, educators have been in a frenzy to learn about and use this "new" assessment idea.

With performance assessments, we observe students while they are performing or we examine the products they create, and we judge the level of proficiency demonstrated. As with essay assessments, we make subjective judgments about the level of achievement attained by comparing student performance to predetermined standards of excellence.

For example, a primary-grade teacher might watch a student interacting with classmates and draw inferences about that child's level of development in social interaction skills. If the levels of achievement are clearly defined in terms the observer can easily interpret, then the teacher, observing carefully, can derive very useful information from watching—information that will aid in planning strategies to promote further social development. Thus, this is not an assessment where answers are counted right or wrong. Rather, like the essay test, we rely on teacher judgment to place the student's performance somewhere on a continuum of achievement levels ranging from unable to perform to very high levels of proficiency.

Or, as another engaging example, a middle school science teacher might examine "mousetrap cars" students have built to determine if they have followed certain principles of energy utilization. Mousetrap cars are vehicles powered by one snap of a spring-loaded mousetrap. One object is to see who can design a car that can travel the farthest by converting that amount of energy into forward motion. When the criteria are clear, the teacher can help students understand why the winning car meets the standards.

Performance assessment methodology has arrived on the assessment scene with a flash of brilliance unprecedented since the advent of selected response test formats earlier in this century. For many reasons, this "new discovery" has struck a chord among educators at all levels. Recent popular applications carry such labels as *authentic assessments, alternative assessments, exhibitions, demonstrations,* and *student work samples,* among others.

Please understand from the outset, however, that there is nothing new about performance assessment. This is not some kind of radical invention recently fabricated by opponents of traditional tests to challenge the testing industry. Rather, it is a proven method of evaluating human characteristics that has been in use for decades (Linquist, 1951), for centuries, maybe even for eons. For how long have we selected our leaders, at least in part, on the basis of our observations of and judgments about their performance under pressure? Further, this is a methodology that has been the focus of sophisticated research and development both in educational settings and in the workplace for a very long time (Berk, 1986).

Besides, anyone who has taught knows that teachers routinely observe students and make judgments about their proficiency. Admittedly, some of those applications don't meet accepted standards of assessment quality (Stiggins & Conklin, 1992). But we know performance assessment is common in the classroom, and we know what it takes to do it well. Our challenge is to make sure we know and meet those quality standards.

Using Performance Assessment to Advantage

Keeping Perspective

Performance assessments are seen as providing high-fidelity or "authentic" assessments of student achievement (Wiggins, 1993). Proponents contend that, just as high-fidelity musical reproductions provide rich and accurate representations of the original music, so too can performance assessments provide high-resolution representations of complex forms of achievement—achievement that stretches into life beyond school.

On the other hand, however, some urge great caution in our rush to embrace this methodology, because performance assessment brings with it great technical challenges. They correctly point out that this is a very difficult methodology to develop and use well (Dunbar, Koretz, & Hoover, 1991). Virtually every bit of research and development done in education and business over the past decades leads to the same conclusion: Performance assessment is a complex way to assess. It requires that users prepare and conduct their assessments in a thoughtful and rigorous manner. Those unwilling to invest the time and energy needed to do it well place their students directly in harm's way.

In this sense, performance assessment methodology is best kept in perspective. It is neither the savior of the teacher nor the key to assessing the "real" curriculum, as some would have us believe. It is but one tool among many capable of providing effective and efficient means of assessing our most highly valued achievement targets. In that sense, it is a valuable tool indeed.

Just be advised that it is not easy to design and use performance assessments. To be sure, there is nothing in this and other chapters on this topic you cannot master. But don't take this methodology lightly—we're not talking about "assessment by guess and by gosh" here. There is no place in performance assessment for "intuitions" or ethereal "feelings" about student achievement. It is not acceptable for a teacher to claim to just "know" a student can do it. Credible evidence is required. Neither is this a mystical mode of assessment, nor are keys to its proper use a mystery. It takes thorough preparation and meticulous attention to detail to attain appropriate levels of performance assessment rigor.

Adhere to the rules of evidence when developing performance assessment as spelled out in this chapter and you can add immeasurably to the quality and utility of your classroom assessments of student achievement. Violate those rules—which is very easy to do in this case!—and you place your students' academic success in jeopardy.

Time for Reflection

Performance assessments are based on observation and judgment. Can you think of instances outside of the school setting where this mode of assessment comes into play in your life? In the context of hobbies? In work settings? In other contexts? Please list five or six examples.

Performance Assessment at Work in the Classroom

To appreciate the true potential of performance assessment, we need to explore the range of design alternatives couched within this methodology. I will briefly describe and illustrate the range of applications in this section. Then, after analyzing performance assessment's match to different types of targets, we will delve deeply into the development process.

We initiate the creation of performance assessments just as we initiated the development of paper and pencil tests in the previous two chapters: with a plan or blueprint. And, as with selected response and essay assessments, the performance assessment plan includes three components. In this case, each component contains three specific design decisions within it.

First, performance assessment developers must *clarify the performance* to be evaluated. Second, they must prepare *performance exercises*. Third, they must devise systems for *scoring and recording* results. The immense potential of this form of assessment becomes apparent when we consider all of the design options available within this three-part structure.

As we explore that structure, we will examine how one group of teachers selected from among the array of performance assessment design possibilities to find the design they needed to serve their purposes. Remember Emily, the high school English student in the school board meeting scenario that opened Chapter 1? Let's explore the assessment challenges that her English teachers faced as they endeavored to put her and her classmates in touch with their emerging proficiency as writers.

As we discuss how Emily's teachers used performance assessments of writing proficiency, bear in mind that they assessed for two reasons, or to serve two purposes: (1) to help their students become better writers, and (2) to gather information on improvement in student writing as part of their evaluation of the impact of their new instructional program.

Clarifying the Performance to Assess

The first challenge faced by the English faculty in Emily's high school was that of defining their vision of academic success—of stipulating what it meant to be a good writer within their program. With performance assessment, we have the freedom to select from a broad range of achievement target possibilities, as you shall see. In specifying the target, we must make three design decisions: What type of performance are we assessing? Whose performance will be assessed? And, specifically, what does good performance look like? Let's consider these three design decisions in a bit more detail.

The Type of Performance.   To make this design decision we answer the basic question, How will successful achievement manifest itself—where will we most easily find the evidence of proficiency? That evidence might take the form of a particular set of skills or behaviors that students must demonstrate. In this case, we watch students "in process," or while they are actually doing something, and we evaluate the quality of their performance. In that instance, success manifests itself in the actions of the student.

On the other hand, sometimes evidence of having done well means that the student has created a particular kind of product—a tangible entity that exists independently of the student—that we may then examine to find evidence of proficiency. Note also, that some assessments might combine assessments of skills and the product that results, such as when we assess computer operations and the quality of the resulting program.

Since Emily's teachers wanted to evaluate their students' writing proficiency, they needed to see and make judgments about the quality of actual samples of student writing. Since we cannot peer inside their heads as they compose, we must read their written products and draw inferences from these about writing proficiency.

Time for Reflection

Based on your experience as a student and/or teacher, can you think of additional classroom contexts where it might be relevant to assess student products? How about instances in which teachers might observe students in action demonstrating mastery of specific skills? Finally, can you conceive of assessments that might focus both on skills or processes and products?

Whom to Assess.   Understand that performance assessments can focus the judge's attention on the performance of individual students or of students working in groups. Without doubt, most classroom assessments attend to the performance of students working alone. But in these times of cooperative learning, evaluating teamwork also can require the use of performance assessment. For instance, we might observe and judge group interaction behaviors, tracking the manner in which the group works as a whole.

In the case of Emily and her English class, the focus of attention is on the writing proficiency of each individual student. Each student must learn to write. If the individual improves, the program is working for that student. But when it comes to evaluating the impact of their instructional program, the faculty must look first at each individual and then summarize individual performance over all students within and across classes.

Defining Success.   Once we have decided on the type of performance and performer on which to focus, the real work begins. Attention then shifts to (1) specifying all key elements of quality performance, and (2) defining a performance continuum for each element so as to depict what student achievement is like when it is of very poor quality, when it is outstanding, and at levels of proficiency in between. These key elements or dimensions of performance are called the performance criteria.

In terms of the writing program in which Emily is engaged, performance criteria answer the following questions: Specifically, what does good writing look like? How shall we know good writing when we see it? What will we accept as evidence of having become proficient as a writer?

Clear and appropriate answers to these questions—that is, sound performance criteria—are critical to sound performance assessment. When we can provide sound criteria, we are in for an easy and productive application of this methodology. Not only will we be ready to focus instruction sharply on the expected outcomes, but also, with clearly articulated performance criteria, both students and teachers can learn to share a common language in which to converse about the student's evolving proficiency.

The English faculty at Emily's high school participated in a summer professional development program that helped them understand and learn to apply a vision of the meaning of quality writing that included six performance criteria. Figure 8–2 presents these key dimensions of good writing in the form of six 5-point rating scales. This is the very informal, student-friendly version that the faculty created to help make these ideas come alive for their students. Their instructional challenges were to (1) help Emily and the others see and understand how and why their own writing was strong or weak in these terms, and (2) show them how to build on strengths to overcome weaknesses. High ratings on these scales, the faculty said, was reflective of very good writing in their classrooms.

Time for Reflection

The concept of establishing performance criteria should not be a new one to you. We do it all the time in our daily lives. When you are evaluating a movie, what criteria do you apply? How about a restaurant? Write down criteria you think should be used as the basis for evaluating a teacher. The principles are always the same: identify the key elements in successful performance.

Word Choice

5 I picked *just* the right words to express my ideas & feelings.
- Every word seems exactly right.
- Colorful, fresh & snappy--yet nothing's overdone.
- Accurate & precise: that's me!
- Vivid, energetic verbs enliven every paragraph.

3 It might not tweak your imagination, but hey--it gets the message across.
- It's functional, but it's not a stretch for me.
- O.K., so there's a cliche here and there.
- You'll find some originality, too!
- I *might* have over-utilized my thesaurus . . .

1 My reader is likely to ask, "Huh?"
- I'm a victim of vague wording and fuzzy phrasing.
- It's hard to picture what I'm talking about.
- Maybe I misused a word or two . . .
- Some redundant phrases might be redundant.

Voice

5 I've put my personal stamp on this paper!
- My paper shines with personality.
- The writing is lively and engaging.
- I speak right to my readers.
- The writing rings with confidence.

3 What I truly think and feel shows up *sometimes*.
- You might not laugh, cry or pound on the table.
- Right on the edge of finding its own voice.
- My personality pokes through here & there.
- Pleasant & friendly--cautious, though!

1 I'm not comfortable letting the real me show through.
- It could be hard to tell who wrote this.
- I kept my feelings in check.
- Safe & careful--that's my paper.
- Audience? What audience?

Sentence Fluency

5 My sentences are clear, varied, and a treat to read aloud!!
- Go ahead--read it aloud. No rehearsal necessary!
- Sentence variety is my middle name.
- Deadwood has been cut.
- Smooth as a ski run in December.

3 My sentences are clear and readable.
- Pretty smooth & natural--with just a bump or two.
- Some sentences could merge; some need to be cut in two.
- A little deadwood--but it doesn't bury the good ideas!
- Yeah, I got into a rut with those sentence beginnings.

1 I have to admit, it's a challenge to read aloud!
- You might have to stop or re-read to make sense of this.
- It's hard to tell where one sentence stops and the next begins.
- Bumpity, bump, bump, bump . . .

Conventions

5 I made so few errors, it would be a snap getting this ready to publish!
- Caps are in the right places.
- Great punctuation--grammar, too.
- Spelling to knock your socks off.
- Paragraphs are indented--you gotta love it.

3 Some bothersome mistakes show up when I read carefully.
- Spelling's correct on SIMPLE words.
- Caps are mostly there.
- Grammar's O.K., though not award-winning.
- Yeah, you might stumble over my innovative punctuation.
- Reads like a first draft, all right.

1 Read it once to decode, then again for meaning.
- Mistakes make the going rough.
- I've forgotten some CAPS--otherS aren't Needed.
- Look out four spelling mysteaks.
- Want the truth? I didn't spend much time editing.

Ideas and Content

5 It's clear, focused, & jam-packed with details.
- You can tell I know a LOT about this topic.
- My writing is bursting with interesting tidbits.
- My topic is small enough to handle.
- Every point is clear.
- The paper "shows" -- it doesn't "tell."

3 It has its intriguing moments, but it could use some details.
- I know just enough to write.
- Some of my details are too general.
- My topic might be a little too big to handle.
- Now and then it grabs your attention.

1 I'm just figuring out what I want to say.
- I just don't know enough about this topic yet.
- It's hard to picture anything.
- I'm still thinking on paper--looking for an idea.

Organization

5 Clear & compelling direction makes reading a BREEZE.
- My beginning gets you hooked.
- Every detail is in the right place.
- You won't feel lost.
- My paper ends at just the right spot--& it leaves you thinking.

3 You can follow it pretty well.
- I have a beginning.
- Most details fit where I put them.
- The paper has an ending, but it needs some work.

1 Where are we headed?
- You could get dizzy trying to follow this.
- Beginning? Oops . . .
- My ideas seem scrambled, jumbled, confusing--even to me.
- It doesn't have a real ending. It just stops.

Figure 8–2
Analytical Writing Assessment Rating Scales
Source: Spandel, V. and Stiggins, R. J. (1996) *Creating Writers, 2nd Ed.* New York: Addison Wesley-Longman. Reprinted with permission.

Developing Performance Exercises

Next, we must think of ways to ask students to perform in a manner that will reveal their level of proficiency. How can we have them create and present a sample product for us to observe and judge? What instructions can we give them that will permit them to demonstrate mastery of essential skills? In this case, we must decide on the nature of the exercises, the number of exercises needed, and the actual instructions to give to students.

Nature of Exercises.   Performance assessment offers two exercise choices that, once again, reveal the range of potential applications of this methodology. One option is to present a structured assignment in which we provide students with a predetermined and detailed set of instructions as to the kind of performance desired. They are completely aware of the assessment, they reflect on and prepare for this assignment, and then they provide evidence of their proficiency. For example, we might ask them to prepare to give a certain kind of speech, perform some kind of athletic activity, build a mousetrap car or, in Emily's case, write about a particular topic for a particular purpose.

But here's another performance assessment option: Sometimes, we can observe and evaluate performance during naturally occurring classroom events and gather useful information about "typical" student performance. For example, a primary-grade teacher interested in the social interaction skills of one student obviously would disrupt the entire assessment by instructing the student, "Go interact with that group over there, so I can evaluate your ability to get along." Such an exercise would run completely counter to the very essence of the assessment. Rather, the teacher would want to stand back and watch the student's behavior unfold naturally in a group context to obtain usable information. Assessments that are based on observation and judgment allow for this possibility. Just try to be unobtrusive in this way with a true/false test!

In addition, we can combine observations derived from structured assignments and from the context of naturally occurring events to generate comparable information about the same achievement target. For example, Emily's English teacher might evaluate writing proficiency gathered in responses to required assignments and in the context of student daily writing journals done for practice. The combined information thoughtfully evaluated over time in terms of the six performance criteria offered in Figure 8–2 can help students and teachers alike to watch writing improve.

Time for Reflection

Can you think of an instance outside of school in which observation of naturally occurring performance serves as the basis for an assessment—in the context of a hobby, in a work setting, or in some other context? What is observed and judged and by whom?

Exercise Content.   The final design decision we must make about exercises is to formulate the actual content of the assignment; that is, when structured assignments are used. Like the essay exercise discussed in Chapter 7, instructions for structured exercises should include the kind(s) of achievement the respondent will demonstrate, conditions under which that demonstration is to take place, and standards of quality the rater will apply in evaluating performance. Here is a simple example of a complete exercise:

> *Achievement:* Please write dramatic dialogue depicting a conversation between the two main characters in the short stories we read last week and this week. Be sure the conversation illustrates their similarities and differences in perspective.
>
> *Conditions:* Work with your study team to carry out the prewriting work of analyzing and preparing to write. Draft your dialogue on your own. Submit your draft to your teammates for review and evaluation and then revise as needed. Turn the finished product in for evaluation and conference with me by the end of the week.
>
> *Standards:* Remember, your product will be evaluated according to the criteria we developed together in class, dealing with content and ideas, voice, sentence fluency, and word choice. As you know, these will be the focus of my review and so they should command your attention and that of your review team also.

When you think of the array of behaviors and products we ask students to master in school, the infinite range of conditions under which we ask them to perform, and the huge number of different visions of excellence we must apply from primary grades through high school, you begin to sense the immense potential of performance assessment methodology. This extreme flexibility is why everyone is so excited about it.

Number of Exercises.   Once we determine the nature of the exercise, we must decide how many exercises we need to lead to confident conclusions about student proficiency. This is a sampling issue. How many examples of student performance are enough? Remember, we must decide how many exercises provide a representative sample—given our classroom time and resource constraints.

For example, if you want to know if students can speak French, how many times do they have to speak for you to be reasonably certain you could predict how well they would do given one more chance? How many samples of Emily's writing must her teachers see to be confident about her writing proficiency? In fact, the answers to these questions are a function of the assessment context. To answer them, we must consider the reasons for assessment, the scope of the target, and other issues. We will review these factors later in the chapter. For now, just be aware of the need to sample in a thoughtful manner.

Scoring and Recording Results

Once we have defined the target and developed exercises, we must decide how we will collect and manage the assessment results. We must select a level of detail in our scores that will serve the intended purpose of assessing, choose a proper record keeping method, and decide who will actually observe and evaluate performance.

The Form of Results.   First, we must select one of two ways of scoring performance. Option one is to evaluate performance *analytically*, making independent judgments about each of the performance criteria. In this case, performance is profiled in terms of multiple judgments or ratings of achievement—as with the six writing assessment scales presented earlier. Option two is called *holistic* scoring. In this case, we judge performance by making one overall judgment that combines all criteria into one evaluation. Our choice—analytical or holistic—is a function of the context within which assessment results are to be used. More about that later, too.

In Emily's class, because the purpose for assessing is to help teacher and student identify specific strengths and weaknesses in writing, an analytical scoring scheme is best. The six attributes of quality writing represent an analytical system of scoring when each scale is applied independently of the others, resulting in a profile of six different ratings.

Recording Procedures.   Here, we must ask how we can transform our judgments (defined in terms of our performance criteria) into records that convey usable information. Once again, the great flexibility of performance assessment methodology comes through as we begin to examine our choices:

- checklists of desirable attributes present or absent in performance
- various kinds of performance rating scales (such as those used in Emily's writing instruction)
- anecdotal records, which rely on written descriptions of and judgments about performance
- mental records, which capture images and records of performance in the memory of the evaluator for later recall and use (to be used cautiously!)

As you shall see later, our choice is a function of the assessment context—the purpose for assessing and the nature of the performance being evaluated.

Identifying the Rater(s).   And finally, performance assessment users must decide who will observe and evaluate performance. In most classroom contexts, the most natural choice is the teacher. Since performance evaluators must possess a clear vision of the desired achievement and be capable of the rigorous application of the performance criteria, who could be more qualified than the teacher? Another option is to bring in another qualified expert, such as another teacher or someone from the community.

Beyond these, however, if we expect students to construct their own meaning from learning experiences and to feel in control of their own academic well-being, we must help them learn to conduct self-assessments. The instructional potential of preparing students to apply performance criteria to evaluate their own work should be obvious. We will discuss this at length later in this and other chapters.

Time for Reflection

As a student, have you ever been invited to observe and evaluate your own skill or product performance or that of other students? What did you observe? What criteria did you use? Were you trained to assess? What was that experience like for you?

Summary of Basic Components

Figure 8–3 summarizes the nine design decisions faced by Emily's teachers—in fact, by any teacher who wishes to use performance assessment in her or his classroom.

Design Ingredient	Options	Writing Assessment Application in Emily's High School
1. Clarify Performance		
Nature of performance	Skill to be demonstrated Product to be created	Assess written products
Focus of assessment	Individual Group	Individual's writing proficiency
Performance criteria	Reflect key aspects of successful performance	Six analytical rating scales
2. Develop Exercises		
Nature of exercises	Structured assignment Naturally occurring event	Structured writing assignment
Content of exercises	Define target, conditions of performance and criteria	Specify kind of writing, conditions under which it is to be produced, and which of the six scales will apply to each assessment
Number of exercises	One to several, depending on context	Several exercises used over time helped students see improvement
3. Score and Record Results		
Level of detail	Holistic Analytical	Analytical
Method of recording	Checklist Rating Anecdotal Mental record	5-point rating scales
Identify the rater	Teacher Student (peer) Student (self) Outside expert	Teacher Student (peer and self)

Figure 8–3
Performance Assessment Design Framework

Ensuring the Quality of Performance Assessments

If we are to apply the design framework shown in Figure 8–3 productively, we need to understand where pitfalls to sound performance assessment can hide. For instance, if we are not careful, problems can arise from the inherently subjective nature of performance assessment. Other problems can arise from trying to use this methodology in places where it doesn't belong.

Let's explore these and other challenges that accompany this assessment format. If we can anticipate them, we can avoid them.

Subjectivity in Performance Assessment

Professional judgment guides every aspect of the design and development of every performance assessment. For instance, as the developer or user of this method, you establish the achievement target you will assess using input about educational priorities expressed in state and local curricula, your text materials, and the opinions of experts in the field. You interpret all of these factors and decide what you will emphasize in your classroom—all matters of your professional judgment. But I cannot emphasize enough how critical it is for you to preare for this by mastering the discipline you teach. You cannot simply pull criteria out of a hat.

Once you have identified your target, you select the assessment method to reflect that target. Based on your vision of the valued outcomes and your sense of the assessment options available to you, you make the choices. This certainly qualifies as a matter of professional judgment.

In the classroom, typically you create the assessment, either selecting from among some previously developed options or generating it by yourself. If you generate it yourself, you choose whether to involve students or other parties in that design process. You devise performance criteria, formulate performance exercises, and observe and evaluate student proficiency. Every step along the way is a matter of your professional and subjective judgment.

For decades, the assessment community assigned performance assessment to second-class citizenship because of the danger of biased judgment that could result from all of this subjectivity. The possibility of inaccurate assessment due to subjective judgment simply left this methodology too risky for many.

More recently, however, we have come to understand that carefully trained performance assessment users, who invest the clear thinking and developmental resources needed to do a good job, can use this methodology effectively. Indeed, many of the increasingly complex achievement targets that we ask students to hit today demand that we use performance assessments and use them well. In short, we now know that in certain contexts we have no choice but to rely on subjective performance assessment. So we had better do our homework and be prepared to do a good job!

Here I must insert as strong a warning as any presented anywhere in this book: In your classroom, *you* will set the standards of assessment quality. It is *your* vision that you will translate into performance criteria, exercises, and records of student achievement. For this reason, it is not acceptable for you to hold a vision that is wholly a matter of your personal opinion about what it means to be academically successful. Rather, your vision must have the strongest possible basis in the collective academic wisdom of experts in the discipline within which you assess and of colleagues and associates in your school, district, and community.

In other words, systematic assessment of student performance of the wrong target is as much a waste of time as a haphazard assessment of the proper target. The only way to prevent this is for you to be in communication with those who know the right target, so you can become a serious student of their vision of academic excellence. Strive to know the patterns of reasoning, the skills, and the products that constitute maximum proficiency in the disciplines you teach and assess.

Time for Reflection

What specific sources can teachers tap to be sure they understand skill and performance outcomes for their particular subject matter areas?

Matching Method to Target

As your definition of the meaning of academic excellence becomes clear, it will also become clear whether or when performance assessment is, in fact, the method of choice in that context. While the range of possible applications of this methodology is broad, it is not infinitely so. Performance assessment can provide dependable information about student achievement of some, but not all, kinds of valued targets. Let's examine the matches and mismatches with the five kinds of targets we have been discussing: knowledge, reasoning, skills, products, and dispositions.

Assessing Knowledge.   If the objective of your instruction is to have students master a body of knowledge, observing and judging performance or products may not be the best way to assess if they have succeeded. Three difficulties can arise in this context, one related to potential sampling errors, another to issues of assessment efficiency, and a third related to the classroom assessment and instructional decision-making context.

Consider, for example, asking students to participate in a group discussion conducted in Spanish as a means of assessing mastery of Spanish vocabulary and rules of grammar. While this is an apparently authentic assessment, it might lead you to incorrect conclusions. First, the students will naturally choose to use vocabulary and syntax with which they are most comfortable and confident. Thus, they will naturally select biased samples of all possible vocabulary and usage.

Second, if this is an assessment of the level of knowledge mastery of a large number of students, the total assessment will take a great deal of time. This may cause you to collect too small a sample of the performance of each individual, leading to undependable results. Given this achievement target, it would be much more efficient from an achievement sampling point of view to administer a simple objectively scored vocabulary and grammar test. Then, once you are confident that students have mastered the foundational knowledge and the focus of instruction turns to real-world applications, you might turn to the group discussion-based performance assessment.

Consider this same issue from a slightly different perspective. If you use the performance assessment as a reflection of knowledge mastery, it will be difficult to decide how to help the student who fails to perform well. It will not be clear what went wrong. Is the problem a lack of knowledge of the vocabulary and grammar, and/or an inability to pronounce words, and/or anxiety about the public nature of the demonstration? Since all three are hopelessly confounded with one another in this case, it will be difficult to decide on a proper course of action. Thus, once again, given this target and this context, performance assessment may not be the best choice.

When assessing student mastery of content knowledge, whether learned outright or with the use of references, a selected response format may be the best choice. When larger structures of knowledge are the target, the essay format may be preferable. When the context permits direct questioning of the student person-to-person, asking questions and listening to answers may be the method of choice. All three of these options offer greater control over the material sampled in the assessment than does performance assessment.

Assessing Reasoning.   Performance assessment can provide an excellent means of assessing student reasoning and problem-solving proficiencies. Given complex problems to solve, students must engage in reasoning processes that include several steps. While we cannot directly view the thought processes, we can use various assessment procedures that reveal to us students' patterns of reasoning.

For example, we might give chemistry students unidentified substances to identify and watch how they go about setting up the apparatus and carrying out the study. The criteria might reflect the proper order of activities. Those who reason well will follow the proper sequence and succeed. Those whose reasoning is flawed will go awry. Some might classify this as a selected response test: Students identify the substance correctly or they do not; they are right or wrong. While that is true in one sense, think about how much richer and more useful the results are when the assessment is conceived and carried out as a performance assessment—especially when the student fails to identify the substance accurately. A comparison between the student's actual reasoning with the reasoning spelled out in the performance criteria will reveal when the problem solver is on track. Specific incorrect results will suggest specific actions that are likely to help the student do better the next time.

Performance assessments structured around products students create also can provide insight into the reasoning process. The resulting product itself is a reflection of sound or unsound reasoning during its development. One simple example might be the production of a written research report by students who carried out the previous experiment. That report would reflect and provide evidence of their problem-solving capabilities.

Another example of a product-based performance assessment would be the physics challenge of building a tower out of toothpicks that will hold a heavy load. One performance criterion certainly will be the amount of weight it can hold. But others might focus on whether the builder adhered to appropriate engineering principles. The product-based performance assessment can help reveal the ability to apply those principles.

In fact, the thoughtful development and use of this performance assessment can help students achieve such a problem-solving goal. For example, what if you gave students two towers built purposely to hold vastly different amounts of weight? You might tell them to analyze each in advance of the load-bearing experiment to predict which would hold more. Further, you might ask them to defend their prediction with specific design differences. After the experiment reveals the truth, the students are more likely to be able to infer how to build strong towers. In essence, you will have made the problem-solving criteria clear.

Assessing Skills.   The great strength of this assessment methodology lies in its ability to ask students to perform in certain ways and to provide a dependable means of evaluating that performance. Most communication skills fall in this category, as do all forms of performing, visual, and industrial arts. The observation of students in action can be a rich and useful source of information about their attainment of very important forms of skill achievement. We will review many examples of these as our journey continues.

Assessing Products.   Herein lies the other great strength of performance assessment. There are occasions when we ask students to create complex achievement-related products. The quality of those products indicates the creator's level of achievement. If we develop sound performance criteria that reflect the key attributes of these products and learn to apply those criteria well, performance assessment can serve us as both an efficient and effective tool. We may evaluate in this way everything from written products, such as term papers and research reports, to the many forms of art and craft products. Again, many examples will follow.

Assessing Dispositions.   To the extent that we can draw inferences about positive attitudes, strong interests, motivational dispositions, and/or academic self-concept based either on the actions of students or on what we see in the products they create, then performance assessment can assist us here, too.

However, I urge caution. Remember, sound performance assessment requires strict adherence to a preestablished set of rules of evidence. Sound assessments must do the following:

- Reflect a clear target—We must thoroughly understand and develop sound definitions of the affective targets to be assessed.

- Serve a clearly articulated purpose—We must know precisely why we are assessing and what it is we intend to do with the results—especially tricky in the case of affective targets.

- Rely on a proper method—The performance must present dependable information to us about disposition.

- Sample the target appropriately—We must collect enough evidence to give us confidence in our conclusions.

- Control for key sources of bias and distortion—We must understand the potential sources of bias in our judgments about student attitudes, values, interests, and so on and neutralize them in the context of our assessments.

When applying these standards of quality to the assessment of achievement outcomes—those discipline-based targets we are trained to teach—it becomes somewhat easier to see the keys to assessment success. That is, hopefully, we have immersed ourselves far enough in a particular field of study to attain a complete understanding of its inherent breadth and scope. We should know when a sample of test items, a set of essay exercises, a particular performance assessment, or a product evaluation captures the meaning of academic success.

When it comes to student dispositions, however, most of us have had much less experience with and therefore are much less comfortable with their meaning, depth, and scope. That means successfully assessing them demands careful and thoughtful preparation.

We can watch students in action and/or examine the things they create and make inferences about their affective states. But we can do this only if we have a clear and practiced sense of what it is we are looking for and why we are assessing it. I will address these issues in depth in Chapter 12.

Summary of Target Matches.   There are many important achievement targets that we can translate into performance assessments. That is, if we prepare carefully, we can develop performance criteria and devise exercises to sample the following:

- application of knowledge in a variety of problem-solving contexts

- proficiency in a range of skill arenas

- ability to create different kinds of products

- some motivational dispositions of our students

In fact, the only target for which performance assessment is not recommended is the assessment of simple elements or complex components of subject matter knowledge. Selected response, essay, and personal communication formats work better here.

Developing Performance Assessments

As you learned earlier, we develop performance assessments in three steps. Each step corresponds to one of the three basic design components introduced earlier. Developers must specify the performance to be evaluated, devise exercises to elicit the desired behavior, and develop a method for making and recording judgments. Let's analyze these in detail.

Defining Performance and Devising Criteria

Remember, our goal in this case is to describe the important skills students are to demonstrate or to identify the important attributes of the products they will create. Our basic challenge is to describe the underlying basis of our evaluations.

More specifically, in designing performance assessments, we must find a vocabulary to use in communicating with each other and with our students about the meaning of successful performance. The key assessment question comes down to this: **Do you, the teacher, know what you are looking for in performance?** But the more important instructional question is this: **Do you know the difference between successful and unsuccessful performance and can you convey that difference in meaningful terms to your students?** Remember, students can hit any target that they can see and that holds still for them. In performance assessment contexts, the target is defined in terms of the performance criteria.

Shaping Your Vision of Success.   Without question, the most effective way to be able to answer these two questions in the affirmative is to be a master of the skills and products that reflect the valued academic achievement targets in your classroom. Those who teach drama, music, physical education, second languages, computer operations, or other skill-based disciplines are prepared to assess well only when they possess a refined vision of the critical skills involved. Those who instruct students to create visual art, craft products, and various written products face both the teaching and assessment challenges with greatest competence and confidence when they are masters at describing the high-quality product to the neophyte.

Connoisseurs can recognize outstanding performance when they see it. They know a good restaurant when they find it. They can select a fine wine. They know which movies deserve a thumbs-up and which Broadway plays are worth their ticket price. And connoisseurs can describe why they believe something is outstanding or not. However, because the evaluation criteria may vary somewhat from reviewer to reviewer, their judgments may not always agree. For restaurants, wines, movies, and plays, the standards of quality may be a matter of opinion. But, that's what makes interesting reading in newspapers and magazines.

Teachers are very much like these connoisseurs in that they must be able to recognize and describe outstanding performance. But this is where the similarity ends. Not only can well-prepared teachers visualize and explain the meaning of success, but they also can impart that meaning to others so as to help them become outstanding performers. In short, they are teachers, not just critics. Often, it is easy to criticize, but difficult to inspire improvement.

In most disciplines, there are agreed-on skills and products that proficient performers must master. The standards of excellence that characterize our definitions of high-quality performance are always those held by experts in the field of study in question. Outstanding teachers have immersed themselves in understanding those discipline-based meanings of proficiency and they understand them thoroughly.

Even when there are differences of opinion about the meaning of outstanding performance in a particular discipline, well-prepared teachers understand those differences and are capable of revealing them to their students.

It is this depth of understanding that we must capture in our performance expectations so we can convey it to students through instruction, example, and practice. Because they must be shared with students, our performance criteria cannot exist only in the intellect of the assessor. We must translate them into words and examples for all—especially our students—to see.

Finding Help in Shaping Your Vision.   In this regard, since we now have nearly a decade of significant new discipline-based performance assessment research and development behind us, many fields of study already have developed outstanding examples of sound criteria for critical performance. Examples include reading proficiency, writing proficiency, foreign language, mathematics, and physical education. The most accessible source of information about these developments is the national association of teachers in each discipline. Nearly every such association has advanced written standards of student achievement in their field of study within the past 5 years. Any association that has not completed that work by now is conducting such studies at this time and will have them completed soon. I will illustrate the results of this work later, in Part 3.

But this is not the only source to tap. Many contend that most of the important advances in the development of new assessment methods achieved over the past decade, including innovative performance assessment designs, have come from assessment departments of state departments of education. For this reason, it may be useful to contact your state education agency to see if they have either completed development of performance criteria in your discipline or know of other states that have. Again, I will share examples of these later.

In addition, consider the possibility that your local district or school curriculum development process may have resulted in the creation of some new performance assessments. Or perhaps a colleague, completely unbeknownst to you, developed an evaluation of a kind of performance that is of interest to you, too. You will never know unless you ask. At the very least, you may find a partner or even a small team to work with you in your performance assessment development.

And finally, many newly published textbooks and packages of instructional materials include the expectation that students will develop reasoning, skill, or product capabilities as one result of study in that context. As a result, many include their own performance assessments. Check this source too. But be careful! Be sure to verify the quality of these assessments before using them. Let the consumer beware. . . .

Six Steps in Developing Your Own Criteria.   If you wish to develop performance criteria yourself, you will need to carry out a thoughtful skill or product analysis. That means you must look inside the skills or products of interest to find the active ingredients. In most cases, this is not complicated.

A member of the faculty of a college of education whom I know decided to develop a performance assessment of her own teaching proficiency. She wanted to model the performance assessment design process to help her students understand the details. So the performance she chose to evaluate was her teaching. This meant that they needed to start by defining the key attributes of a good teacher. I want to show you how she did this. But remember, while this particular example happened at the postsecondary level, both the process and the lessons it teaches can be applied in any classroom at any level. Note particularly the manner in which this teacher engaged her students as partners in the process of devising these criteria.

Incidentally, the details of this illustration come directly from the actual classroom where this work was done. They are not intended to represent exemplary work or the best possible representation of the attributes of good teaching. I merely use them to illustrate a real-world application of an excellent teaching and assessment process.

As you study the steps described, consider other contexts where this process might come into play in your classroom. For example, how might you use these steps to help your students devise performance criteria for some form of their achievement to be evaluated? I once watched a class of third graders go through this same process to devise criteria for the assessments of upcoming dramatic presentations of historical characters they were planning for their parents. A middle school social studies teacher I know used these steps to help his students devise criteria for evaluating research reports they were about to write. As you read on, see if you can see applications of this six-step process that might be relevant in your context.

Step 1: Brainstorming.   The process began by having students engage in reflective brainstorming. The professor talked with her students a few moments about why it is important to understand how to provide sound instruction in assessment methods, and then asked, "What do you think might be some of the factors that contribute to effective teaching?" They listed suggestions on the board, trying to capture the essence of each with the briefest possible label. That list looked something like this:

know the subject	poised
use humor	flexible
organized	on schedule
enthusiasm	good support materials
fresh ideas	appropriate text
relevant content	monitor student needs
clear objectives	voice loud, clear, varied
be interactive	comfortable environment
use visuals well	be interesting
material connected	materials readily available
appropriate pacing	challenging
believe in material covered	personalize communication
professional	effective time management
credible information	in control

From time to time, the teacher would dip into her own reservoir of ideas about effective teaching and offer a suggestion, just to prime the pump a bit.

As the list grew, the brainstorming process slowed. When it did, she asked another question: "What specific behaviors could teachers engage in that would help them be effective—what could they do to maximize the chances of making instruction work?" The list grew until everyone agreed that it captured most of what really is important. The entire process didn't take more than 10 minutes.

Time for Reflection

Think about your experience as a student and/or teacher. What other keys to effective teaching can you think of?

Step 2: Condensing.   Next, they had to condense the long list. She told them that they needed to be able to use all of these excellent suggestions to evaluate her class and her effectiveness. However, given the list they had just brainstormed, they just wouldn't have time to evaluate on the basis of all those criteria. They would have to boil them down to the truly critical factors. She asked how they might do that.

Some students thought they should review the list and pick out the most critical entries—concentrate on those first, they suggested. Others urged condensing the long list into a smaller number of major categories within which to group elements. The professor asked, "What categories might we use to subsume the long list into to reach these goals?" She asked the class if they could define four or five categories—capturing the essence of each category with the briefest possible label. (Remember, these category headings need to represent truly important aspects of performance, because they form the basis for the performance criteria, as you will see.)

The five categories the students came up with after about five minutes of reflection and discussion were Content, Organization, Delivery, Personal Characteristics, and Classroom Environment.

Time for Reflection

Based on the list presented, supplemented with your additions, what other categories would you suggest?

Remember, the goal of this entire activity is to build a level of understanding and a vocabulary both students and teacher can use to converse with each other about performance. This is why it is important to engage students in the process of devising criteria, even if you already know the criteria you want to use. **When you share the stage with your students—when they get to play a role in defining success and in choosing the language to describe it—in effect, you begin right away to connect them to their target.** (Please reread that sentence. It is one of the most important in the entire book. It argues for sharing your vision and thus your power to evaluate with your students. The motivational and achievement consequences can be immense.)

Step 3: Defining.   After identifying the categories, they had to define each one. To accomplish this, class members collaborated in generating definitions of each of the five categories (or, as it turns out, major dimensions of effective teaching). The professor assigned responsibility for writing concise definitions of key dimensions to groups of students, one dimension per group. She advised them to consider the elements in the original brainstormed list by reviewing it and finding those elements subsumed within each category. When each group had drafted its definition, a spokesperson read its definition to the class and all were invited to offer suggestions for improvement. Here are some of the definitions they composed:

Content:	quality of presentation of research, theory, and practical applications related to the topic of assessment; appropriateness of course objectives
Organization:	order or structure within which material is presented—does it aid learning?
Delivery:	deals with the presentation and interaction patterns in terms of conveying material and helping students learn it
Personal characteristics:	the personal manner of the instructor in relating to the material and the students, and the interaction between the two
Class environment:	all physical aspects of the learning atmosphere and setting that support both students and teacher

Step 4: Contrasting.   The class had to contrast levels of proficiency to find keys to success. With labels and definitions for key performance dimensions in hand, they turned to the next challenge: finding words and examples to describe the range of possible teaching performance within each dimension. They had to articulate what teaching looks like when it fails to meet standards of quality, when it is outstanding, and points in between. By establishing a sense of the underlying continuum of performance for each dimension of effective teaching (that is, by developing a common meaning of proficiency, ranging from none to totally proficient), in effect, they would be laying a foundation for being able to observe and evaluate teaching across several dimensions and levels of proficiency.

In preparation for this activity, the professor used brief, 10-minute videos of two teachers in action, one faltering badly and the other hitting on all cylinders. She showed the video of outstanding performance to her students and asked the question, "What makes this performance so good—what do you like about this work?" They listed keys to success in terms of their major categories of performance. Then she played the video of very poor performance. "What," she asked, "makes this performance inferior—in terms of our major categories of teacher performance?" This time, they listed the problems. "What," she asked next, "do you see that makes them different in terms of the five key dimensions defined earlier?"

They rewound and reviewed the examples several times while defining those differences for each dimension.

It has been my experience over the years that this process of asking students to contrast examples of vastly different performances virtually always helps students zero in on how to describe performance, good and poor, in clear, understandable language. But remember, if you are having them devise criteria for evaluating performance that is unfamiliar to them, you will need to provide some support. For instance, a high school teacher I know wanted students to devise criteria for a term paper. Since the students had not written a term paper before, she provided examples of high- and low-quality work for them to analyze and compare.

Step 5: Adding Detail.   The next challenge was to describe success in detail. As the students began to become clear on the language and examples needed to describe performance, they searched for ways to capture and quantify their judgments, such as by mapping their continuum descriptions onto rating scales or checklists. (We'll learn more about this in a later section on scoring and recording.) The class decided to develop 3-point rating scales to reflect their thinking. Figure 8–4 presents some of these scales.

Content	3	outcomes clearly articulated challenging and proactive content highly relevant content
	2	some stated outcomes content somewhat interesting and engaging some relevance to content
	1	intended outcomes not stated content boring irrelevant content
Delivery	3	flow and pace move well humor used checks for clarity regularly feedback used to adjust extensive interaction with students
	2	pacing acceptable some of the time material and/or delivery somewhat disjointed some checking for clarity some student participation
	1	pacing too slow or too fast delivery disconnected much dead time no checking for clarity no interaction—one-person show

Figure 8–4
Sample Score Scales for Effective Teaching

Time for Reflection

See if you can devise a 3-point rating scale for one or two of the other crite-ria defined.

Step 6: Refining.   The process of revising and refining never stopped. The professor was careful to point out that even when they arrived at a definition of academic success—whether as a set of performance criteria, rating scales, or whatever form it happened to take—the work was not yet done. They needed to practice applying their new standards to some teaching samples to see whether they really fit, or whether they might need to more precisely define key aspects of performance. We can learn a general lesson from this: We should never regard performance criteria as "finished." Rather, with time and experience in applying our standards to actual samples of student work, our vision of the meaning of success will grow and change. We will sharpen our focus. As this happens, we are obliged to adjust our performance expectations to reflect our most current sense of the keys to academic success.

Summary of the Six Steps.   When it comes down to you devising your own performance criteria, follow the steps listed in Figure 8–5. And remember, when students are partners in carrying out these six steps, you and your students join together to become a learning community. Together, you open windows to the meaning of academic success, providing your students with the words and examples to see that vision.

Partnership Is the Key.   By now, you may have realized that the entire performance criteria development sequence we just reviewed represents far more than just a preparation to assessment. This sequence can involve participants in serious, highly motivated questioning, probing, and clarifying. In fact, assessment and instruction are indistinguishable when teachers involve their students in the process of identifying performance criteria.

However, for various reasons, you may not wish to involve your students. Perhaps the students are too young to comprehend the criteria or the process. Or perhaps the target requires the development and application of highly technical or complex criteria that would be out of reach of the students. I have seen kindergartners work productively with their teacher to define some simple targets. But it may not always be appropriate.

When this happens, at least consider another option for carrying out this same set of activities: Rather than engaging your students as your partners, devise criteria with a group of colleagues. If you do, you may argue about what is really important in performance. You might disagree about the proper language to use to describe performance. And you may argue with each other about key differences between sound and unsound performance. But I promise you these will be some of the most engaging and productive faculty meetings of your professional life. And out of that process might come long-term partners in the performance assessment process.

Step 1. Begin by reflecting on the meaning of excellence in the performance arena that is of interest to you. Be sure to tap your own professional literature, texts, and curriculum materials for insights, too. And don't overlook the wisdom of your colleagues and associates as a resource. Talk with them! Include students as partners in this step too. Brainstorm your own list of key elements. You don't have to list them all in one sitting. Take some time to let the list grow.

Step 2. Categorize the many elements so that they reflect your highest priorities. Keep the list of categories as short as possible while still capturing the essence of performance.

Step 3. Define each category in clear, simple language.

Step 4. Find some actual performance to watch or examples of products to study. If this step can include the thoughtful analysis of a number of contrasting cases— an outstanding term paper and a very weak one, a student who functions effectively in a group and one who is repeatedly rejected, and so on—so much the better.

Step 5. Use your clearest language and your very best examples to spell out in words and pictures each point along the various continuums of performance you use to define the important dimensions of the achievement.

Step 6. Try your performance criteria to see if they really do capture the essence of performance. Fine tune them to state as precisely as possible what it means to succeed. Let this fine tuning go on as needed for as long as you teach.

Figure 8–5
Steps in Devising Performance Criteria

Even if everyone doesn't agree in the end, each of you will have reflected deeply on, and be able to defend, the meaning of student success in your classroom. We all need that kind of reflection on a regular basis.

Attributes of Sound Criteria.   Quellmalz (1991), writing in a special issue of a professional journal devoted to performance assessment, provides us with a simple list of standards against which to compare our performance criteria in order to judge their quality. She points out that effective performance criteria:

1. reflect all of the important components of performance—the active ingredients in target attainment.

2. apply appropriately in contexts and under conditions in which performance naturally occurs.

3. represent dimensions of performance that trained evaluators can apply consistently to a set of similar exercises; that is, they are not exercise specific.

4. are developmentally appropriate for the examinee population.

5. are understandable and usable by all participants in the performance assessment process, including teachers, students, parents, and the community.

6. link directly to our instructional objectives; that is, we teach what we preach.

7. provide a clear and understandable means of documenting and communicating about student growth over time.

We might expand this list to include one additional standard: The development of performance criteria should be seen as an opportunity to teach. Students should be given the opportunity to analyze work of varying quality and *figure out* what makes outstanding work outstanding. This will help them understand keys to success. They will become more proficient performers faster, given the chance to see the criteria come into play in their own work and that of others.

Figure 8–6 details rating scales that depict key dimensions on which to base judgments of student problem-solving proficiency. Note the simple, yet clear and specific nature of the communication about important dimensions of performance. With these kinds of criteria in hand, we definitely can help students become better performers.

Designing Performance Exercises

Performance assessment exercises, like selected response test items and essay exercises, frame the challenge for the students and set the conditions within which they are to meet that challenge. Thus, performance assessment exercises clearly and explicitly reflect the desired outcomes. Like essay exercises, sound performance assessment exercises outline a complete problem for the respondent: achievement to demonstrate, conditions of the demonstration, and the applied standards of quality.

As specified earlier in this chapter, we face three basic design considerations when dealing with exercises in the context of performance assessment. We must determine the following:

1. the nature of the exercise(s), whether they are preplanned exercises or naturally occurring events

2. the specific content of structured exercises, defining the tasks performers will carry out

3. the number of exercises needed to provide a sufficient sample of performance

We will now delve into each in some detail.

Nature of Exercises.   The decision about whether to rely on structured exercises, naturally occurring events, or some combination of the two should be influenced by several factors related to the assessment target(s) and the environment within which we conduct the assessment.

When we want to maintain tight control over the range of performance we see and evaluate, to ensure evaluation of specific important skills, we need structured exercises. If, for example, I want to see and hear a student communicate in a second language in a variety of social situations, I must strategically sample those instances. I cannot simply leave to chance which situations the student performs in.

Further, structured exercises and naturally occurring events can help us get at slightly different targets. When we announce in advance a pending performance

Problem Solving Scoring Rubric

	Accurately identifies constraints or obstacles	Identifies viable and important alternatives for overcoming the constraints or obstacles.	Selects and adequately tries out alternatives.	If other alternatives were tried, accurately articulates and supports the reasoning behind the order of their selection and the extent to which each overcame the obstacles or constraints.
4.	Accurately and thoroughly describes the relevant constraints or obstacles. Addresses obstacles or constraints that are not immediately apparent.	Identifies creative but plausible solutions to the problem under consideration. The solutions address the central difficulties posed by the constraint or obstacle.	Engages in effective, valid, and exhaustive trials of the selected alternatives. Trials go beyond those required to solve the problem and show a commitment to an in-depth understanding of the problem.	Provides a clear comprehensive summary of the reasoning that led to the selection of secondary solutions. The description includes a review of the decisions that produced the order of selection and how each alternative fared as a solution.
3.	Accurately identifies the most important constraints or obstacles.	Proposes alternative solutions that appear plausible and that address the most important constraints or obstacles.	Puts the selected alternatives to trials adequate to determine their utility.	Describes the process that led to the ordering of secondary solutions. The description offers a clear, defensible rationale for the ordering of the alternatives and the final selection.
2.	Identifies some constraints or obstacles that are accurate along with some that are not accurate.	Presents alternative solutions for dealing with the obstacles or constraints, but the solutions do not all address the important difficulties.	Tries out the alternative, but the trials are incomplete and important elements are omitted or ignored.	Describes the process that led to the ordering of secondary solutions. The description does not provide a clear rationale for the ordering of the alternatives, or the student does not address all the alternatives that were tried.
1.	Omits the most significant constraints or obstacles.	Presents solutions that fail to address critical parts of the problem.	Does not satisfactorily test the selected solutions.	Describes an illogical method for determining the relative value of the alternatives. The student does not present a reasonable review of the strengths and weaknesses of the alternative solutions that were tried and abandoned.

Figure 8–6
Sample Performance Assessment Rating Scales
Source: From *Assessing Student Outcomes Using the Dimensions of Learning Model* (pp. 79–80) by R. Marzano, D. Pickering, and J. McTighe, 1993, Association for Curriculum Supervision and Development. Reprinted by permission.

assessment and give students instructions as to how to prepare, we intend to maximize their motivation to perform well. In fact, we often try to encourage the best possible performance by attaching a grade or telling students that observers from outside the classroom (often parents) will watch them perform. When we take these steps and build the assessment around structured exercises, we set our conditions up to assess students' best possible performance, under conditions of maximum motivation to do well.

However, sometimes our objective is not to see the student's "best possible" performance. Rather, what we wish is "typical" performance, performance under conditions of the students' regular, everyday motivation. For example, we want students to adhere to safety rules in the woodworking shop or the science lab all the time (under conditions of typical motivation), not just when they think we are evaluating them (maximum motivation to perform well). Observation during naturally occurring classroom events can allow us to get at the latter.

From an assessment quality-control point of view, we still must be clear about our purpose. And, explicit performance criteria are every bit as important here. But our assessment goal is to be watching closely as students behave spontaneously in the performance setting.

Time for Reflection

Identify a few achievement targets you think might be most effectively assessed through the unobtrusive observation of naturally occurring events. In your experience as a teacher or student, have you ever been assessed in this way? When?

In addition to motivational factors, there also are practical considerations to bear in mind in deciding whether to use structured or naturally occurring events. One is time. If normal events of the classroom afford you opportunities to gather sound evidence of proficiency without setting aside special time for the presentation of structured exercises and associated observations, then take advantage of the naturally occurring instructional event. The dividend will be time saved from having to devise exercises and present and explain them.

Another practical matter to consider in your choice is the fact that classrooms are places just packed full of evidence of student proficiency. Think about it—teachers and students spend more time together than do the typical parent and child or husband and wife! Students and teachers live in a world of constant interaction in which both are watching, doing, talking, and learning. A teacher's greatest assessment asset is the opportunity to observe student achievement continuously over time. This permits the accumulation of bits of evidence—for example, corroboration of past inferences about student proficiency and/or evidence of slow, gradual growth—over extended periods of time, and makes for big samples. It offers opportunities to detect patterns, to double check, and to verify.

Everything I have said about performance assessment up to this point has depicted it as rational, structured, and preplanned. But teachers know that assessment also is sometimes spontaneous. The unexpected classroom event or the briefest of unanticipated student responses can provide the ready observer with a new glimpse into student competence. Effective teachers see things. They file those things away. They accumulate evidence of proficiency. They know their students. No other assessor of student achievement has the opportunity to see students like this over time.

But beware! These kinds of spontaneous performance assessments based on on-the-spot, sometimes unobtrusive observations of naturally occurring events are fraught with as many dangers of misassessment as any other kind of performance assessment. Even in these cases, we are never absolved from adhering to the basic principles of sound assessment: clear target, clear purpose, proper method, sound sample, and controlled interference.

You must constantly ask yourself: What did I really see? Am I drawing the right conclusion based on what I saw? How can I capture the results of this spontaneous assessment for later use (if necessary or desirable)? Anecdotal notes alone may suffice. The threats to sound assessment never leave us. So by all means, take advantage of the insights provided by classroom time spent together with your students. But as a practical classroom assessment matter, do so cautiously. Create a written record of your assessment whenever possible.

Time for Reflection

Can you think of creative, realistic ways to establish dependable records of the results of spontaneous performance assessments that happen during an instructional day?

Exercise Content.   Like well-developed essay exercises, sound structured performance assessment exercises explain the challenge to the respondent and set them up to succeed if they can, by doing the following:

- identifying the specific kind(s) of performance to be demonstrated
- detailing the context and conditions within which proficiency is to be demonstrated
- reminding students of the standards (criteria) to be applied in evaluating performance

Here is a simple example of an exercise that does all three:

Achievement: You are to use your knowledge of how to convert energy into motion and your knowledge of simple principles of mechanics to reason through the design for a mousetrap car. Then you are to build that car.

Conditions: Using materials provided in class and within the time limits of four class periods, please design and diagram your plan, construct the car itself, and prepare to explain why you included your key design features.

Standards: Your performance will be evaluated in terms of the specific standards we set in class, including the clarity of your diagrammed plan, the performance and quality of your car, and your presentation explaining its design features. If you have questions about these instructions or the standards of quality, let me know.

In this way, sound exercises frame clear and specific problems to solve.

In a comprehensive discussion of the active ingredients of sound performance assessment exercises, Baron (1991) offers us clear and thought-provoking guidance:

- If a group of curriculum experts in my field and a group of educated citizens in my community were to infer my educational values from what they see in my exercises, would they be pleased with what they saw?

- As students prepare for my assessment exercises and I structure my curriculum and pedagogy to enable them to be successful in these tasks, do I feel assured that they will be making progress toward becoming academically successful as defined in my classroom?

- Do my tasks clearly communicate my standards and expectations to my students?

- Are some of my tasks designed to have students make connections and forge relationships among various aspects of the curriculum?

- Do my tasks encourage students to access prior knowledge and problem-solving skills to perform well?

- Do some exercises ask students to work collaboratively to solve complex problems?

- Are my students sometimes expected to sustain their efforts over a period of time to succeed?

- Do my exercises expect self-assessment and reflection on the part of my students?

- Are my tasks likely to be meaningful and challenging for my students?

- Do some of my exercises present problems that are situated in real-world contexts?

These guidelines define the art of developing sound performance exercises.

Time for Reflection

What might a performance assessment exercise look like that could test your skill in developing a high-quality performance assessment? What specific ingredients would you include in the exercise?

The Number of Exercises—Key Sampling Considerations

The Sampling Challenge.   How do we know how many exercises we need within any particular assessment to give us confidence that we are drawing dependable conclusions about student proficiency? This can be somewhat tricky with performance assessments, because it can take quite a bit of time to develop, administer, observe, and score any single exercise. In a half-hour of testing time you can administer lots of multiple-choice test items, and thus cover much territory with your sample, because each item demands so little response time. But what if the performance assessment exercise—which typically requires a more complex demonstration—takes 15 minutes? Clearly we cannot administer as many per unit of testing time. As a result, sometimes it can be very difficult to sample using a number of different exercises, given our classroom workload and time constraints. Consider writing assessment, for example. Because writing takes so many forms and takes place in so many different contexts, assessing overall writing proficiency can be very complex. A quality sample of writing proficiency allows one to make generalizations about student proficiency across the entire performance domain. As a result, the sample of writing exercises must include assignments calling for various kinds of writing, such as narrative, expository, and persuasive. In other words, because a student skilled in expository writing may not manage persuasion effectively, we must tap each with our sample of exercises. This takes time. This is the performance assessment sampling challenge.

Practical Guidance.   Sampling always involves trade-offs between quality of resulting information and the cost of collecting it. Few have the resources needed to gather the perfect sample of student performance. We all compromise. The good news for you as a teacher is that you must compromise less than the large-scale assessor, primarily because you get to have more time with your students. This is precisely why I feel that the great strength and future of performance assessment lies in the classroom, and not in large-scale standardized testing.

Let's define *sampling* as the purposeful collection of information about student achievement in order to support conclusions about that achievement. In the classroom, often we have the luxury of being able to gather that information strategically in bits and pieces over time. If we plan assessments carefully, these bits can form into a representative sample of performance that is broad enough in its coverage to lead us to confident conclusions about student achievement.

Unfortunately, there are no hard and fast rules to follow in determining how many exercises it takes to yield dependable conclusions. That means we must once again speak of the *art* of classroom assessment. Casey, our elementary teacher friend, offers practical guidance on this matter:

"I use a simple decision rule to tell me if I know enough about a student's achievement—if my sample of exercises has covered enough ground—to justify a final conclusion about how the student is doing. Now remember, this is really a matter of my judgment based on prior experience with the targets and with kids—we're not exactly talking scientific decision making here! So, here goes: I feel that I have presented enough exercises and gathered enough instances of student performance when I am quite certain that I can accurately predict how well the student would do if I gave him or her one additional exercise. You know, I guess there is a rational part to it, because I do try to sample student achievement more than once and under a number of different circumstances. So I know I'm not guessing. After a while a teacher compiles enough information to know whose getting it and who isn't."

An Illustration.   Let's explore a real-world assessment situation to see how sampling comes into play. Let's say we are a licensing board charged with responsibility for certifying the competence of commercial airline pilots. One specific skill we want them to demonstrate, among others, is the ability to land the plane safely. So we take a candidate up on a bright, sunny, calm day and ask her or him to land the plane—clearly an authentic performance assessment. And let's say this pilot does an excellent job of landing. Are you ready to certify?

If your answer is yes, I don't want you screening the pilots hired by the airlines on which I fly. Our assessment reflected only one narrow set of circumstances within which we expect our pilots to be competent. What if it's night—not bright, clear daylight? A strange airport? Windy? Raining? An emergency? These represent realities within which pilots must operate routinely. So the proper course of action in certifying competence is to see the pilot land under various conditions, so we can ensure safe landings on all occasions. To achieve this, we hang out at the airport waiting for the weather to change, permitting us to quickly take off in the plane so we can watch our candidate land under those conditions. And over the next year we exhaust the landing condition possibilities—right?

Of course not. Obviously, I'm being silly here. We have neither the time nor the patience to go through all of that with every candidate. So what do we do? We compromise. We operate within our existing resources and sample pilot performance. We have the candidate land the plane under several different conditions. And at some point, the array of instances of landing proficiency (gathered under strategically selected conditions) combine to lead us to a conclusion that each pilot has or has not mastered the skill of landing safely.

This example frames the performance assessment sampling challenge in a real-world situation that applies just as well in your classroom. How many "landings" must you see under what kinds of conditions to feel confident your students can perform according to your standards? The science of such sampling is to have thought through the important conditions within which you will sample performance. The art is to use your resources creatively to gather enough different instances under varying conditions to bring you and the student to a confident conclusion about proficiency.

In this context, I'm sure you can understand why you must consider the seriousness of the decision to be made in planning your sample. Some decisions bear greater weight than others. These demand assessments that sample both more deeply and more broadly to give you confidence in the decision that results—such as certifying a student as competent for purposes of high school graduation, for example. On the other hand, some decisions leave more room to err. They allow you to reconsider the decision later, if necessary, at no cost to the student—for example, assessing a student's ability to craft a complete sentence during a unit of instruction on sentence construction. When the target is narrow and the time frame brief, we need sample but few instances of performance.

Figure 8–7 identifies six factors to take into account in making sampling decisions in any particular performance assessment context. Even within these guidelines, however, remember Casey's sampling decision rule: "I feel that I have presented enough exercises and gathered enough instances of student performance when I am quite certain that I can accurately predict how well the student would do if I gave him or her one additional exercise." In your classroom, if you sense that you have enough evidence, draw your conclusion and act on it.

Your professional challenge is to follow the rules of sound assessment and gather enough information to minimize the chance that you are wrong. The conservative position to take in this case is to err in the direction of oversampling to increase your level of confidence in the inferences you draw about student competence. If you feel at all uncertain about the conclusion you might draw regarding the achievement of a particular student, you have no choice but to gather more information. To do otherwise is to place the well-being of that student in jeopardy.

Time for Reflection

Based on your experience as a student, can you identify one skill target that you think would take several exercises to sample appropriately and another that you think could be sampled with only one, or very few, exercises? What are the most obvious differences between these two targets?

- *The Reason for the Assessment*—The more important the decision, the more sure you must be about the student's proficiency. The more sure you must be, the bigger should be your sample. Greater coverage leads to more confident conclusions about achievement.

- *The Scope of the Target*—The more narrowly focused the valued achievement target, the easier it is to cover it with a small sample. Targets broad in their scope require more exercises to cover enough material to yield confident conclusions.

- *The Coverage of Any One Exercise*—If the student's response is likely to provide a great deal of evidence of proficiency, you need not administer many such exercises. How many term papers must a student prepare to demonstrate that he or she can do it?

- *Time Available to Assess*—If you must draw conclusions about proficiency tomorrow, you have too little time to sample broadly. But as the time available to assess increases, so can the scope of your sample.

- *Consistency of Performance*—If a student demonstrates consistently very high or very low proficiency in the first few exercises, it may be safe to draw a conclusion even before you have administered all the exercises you had intended.

- *Proximity to the Standard*—If a student's performance is right on the borderline between being judged as competent or incompetent, you might need to extend the sample to be sure you know which conclusion to draw.

Figure 8–7
Practical Considerations in Performance Assessment Sampling

Scoring and Recording Results

Three design issues demand our attention at this stage of performance assessment development, if we are to make the entire plan come together:

1. the level of detail we need in assessment results
2. how we will record results
3. who will do the observing and evaluating

These are straightforward decisions, if we approach them with a clear target and a clear sense of how the assessment results are to be used.

Level of Detail of Results.   We have two choices in the kinds of scores or results we derive from our observations and judgments: holistic and analytical. Both require explicit performance criteria. That is, we are never absolved from responsibility for having articulated the meaning of academic success in clear and appropriate terms.

However, these two scoring procedures use the criteria in different ways. If we score *analytically,* we make our judgments by considering each key dimension of performance or criterion separately, thus analyzing performance in terms of each of its elements. If we make our judgments *holistically,* we consider all of the criteria simultaneously, making one overall evaluation of performance. The former provides a high-resolution picture of performance but takes more time and effort to accomplish. The latter provides a more general sense of performance but is much quicker.

Your choice of scoring procedure will turn on how you plan to use the results (whether you need precise detail or a general picture) and the resources you have available to conduct the assessment (whether you have time to evaluate analytically).

Some assessment contexts demand analytical evaluation of student performance. No matter how hard you try, you will not be able to diagnose student strengths or weaknesses based on holistic performance information. As teachers, we cannot help students understand and learn to replicate the fine details of sound performance by scoring their work in holistic terms.

But on the other hand, it is conceivable that you may find yourself involved in an assessment where you must evaluate the performance of hundreds of students with few resources on hand, too few resources to score analytically. Holistic scoring may be your only option.

As a personal aside, I must say that I am minimizing my own use of holistic scoring as a single, stand-alone judgment of overall performance in classroom assessment. I see few applications for such a score *in the classroom.* Besides, I have begun to question the meaning of such scores. I have participated in some writing assessments in which students whose analytical profiles of performance using the six different rating scales described earlier in the chapter were remarkably different and yet ended up with the same holistic score. That gives me pause to wonder about the real meaning and interpretability of holistic scores. I have begun to think holistic scores mask the kind of more detailed information needed to promote classroom-level student growth. In the classroom, the benefits of quick scoring carry heavy costs in the loss of precision in our assessment information.

When you need a holistic score, generate it by summing or averaging analytical scores. Or, if your vision of the meaning of academic success suggests that some analytical scales are more important than others, then assign higher weights to some (by multiplying by a weighting factor) before summing. However, you must spell out in advance a rational basis for determining those weights.

It may also be acceptable to supplement a set of analytical scores with an "overall impression" rating, if you can define and describe to your students how the whole is, in fact, equal to more than the sum of the individual parts of performance.

Recording Results.   Performance assessors have the freedom to choose from among a wonderful array of ways to record results for later communication. These include checklists, rating scales, anecdotal records, and mental record keeping. Each of these is described in Table 8–1 in terms of definition, principal strength, and chief limitation.

Figure 8–8 presents a sample writing proficiency checklist. It reflects three early levels of skill, with each further subdivided into a series of attributes that the teacher checks as present or absent in student work. Earlier in the chapter we presented examples of writing and reasoning rating scales. Anecdotal records simply describe in writing how the students' performance compared to standards of acceptable performance.

Table 8–1

Options for Recording Performance Judgments

	Definition	Strength	Limitation
Checklists	List of key attributes of good performance checked present or absent	Quick; useful with large number of criteria	Results can lack depth
Rating scales	Performance continuum mapped on several-point numerical scale ranging from low to high	Can record judgment and rationale with one rating	Can demand extensive expensive development and training for raters
Anecdotal records	Student performance is described in detail in writing	Can provide rich portraits of achievement	Time consuming to read, write, and interpret
Mental records	Assessor stores judgments and/or descriptions of performance in memory	Quick and easy way to record	Difficult to retain accurate recollections, especially as time passes

Preconventional

			Makes marks other than drawing on paper (scribble writing)
			Primarily relies on pictures to convey meaning
			Sometimes labels and adds "words" to pictures
			Tells about own writing
			Writes random recognizable letters

Emergent

			Sees self as writer
			Copies names and familiar words
			Uses pictures and print to convey meaning
			Pretends to read own writing
			Prints with upper-case letters
			Uses beginning/ending consonants to make words

Developing

			Takes risks with writing
			Begins to read own writing
			Writes names and favorite words
			Writing is from top-bottom, left-right, front-back
			May interchange upper- and lower-case letters
			Begins to use spacing between words
			Uses beginning, middle, and ending sounds to make words
			Begins to write noun-verb phrases

Figure 8–8
Writing Proficiency Checklist

Note that checklists, rating scales, and anecdotal records all store information that is descriptive in terms of the performance criteria. That is, each element of performance checked, rated, or written about must relate to our judgments about student performance as captured in our criteria.

In using mental record keeping, we store either ratings or images of actual performance in memory. I included this option to provide an opportunity to urge caution when using this notoriously undependable storage system! Most often, it is not a good idea to rely on mental records of student achievement. When we try to remember such things, there are five things that can happen and four of them are bad. The one good possibility is that we might retain an accurate recollection of performance. The bad things are that we could do any or all of the following:

- forget, losing that recollection forever

- remember the performance but attribute it to the wrong student

- allow the memory to change unconsciously over time due to more recent observations of performance

- retain a memory of performance that serves as a filter through which we see and interpret all subsequent performance, thus biasing our judgments inappropriately

The chances of these problems occurring increase in proportion to the length of time we try to maintain accurate mental records, the number of students involved, and the complexity of the target and therefore the memories we must maintain. Thus, I urge you to limit your use of this filing system to no more than a day or two at most and to sharply focused targets for very few students. If you must retain a record of performance, write it down—as a checklist, a set of rating scales, or an anecdotal record!

Identifying the Rater(s).   The purpose of the assessment drives the selection of observers and evaluators. When the goal is to certify that students have met performance standards for important grading, promotion, or graduation decisions, then you, the teacher, must be the assessor. The only acceptable alternative in these contexts is for you to bring into the classroom another adult rater (a qualified outside expert). Schools that ask students to do exhibitions and demonstrations, such as senior projects, science fairs, and music competitions, routinely rely on outside expert judges. In all cases, it is essential that raters be fully trained and qualified to apply the performance criteria that underpin the evaluation—high-stakes decisions hang in the balance.

On the other hand, as we have established, we can use assessments as far more than simply sources of scores to inform decisions. We can use them as teaching tools. We can accomplish this in one way by using performance assessments to teach students to evaluate their own and each other's performance. The very process of learning to dependably apply performance criteria helps students become better performers, as it helps them to learn and understand key elements of sound performance. So when the assessment is to serve instructional purposes, students can be raters, too.

And remember, some classroom situations may require relying on multiple raters to serve multiple purposes. For example, students can learn to evaluate their own work with teacher supervision, thus helping themselves and each other to improve. Then, when the summary judgment is needed, such as to assign a final grade, the teacher/expert can evaluate the final performance.

Fine-Tuning Your Performance Assessments

Clearly, the prime consideration in the selection of an assessment method is the match of performance assessment methodology to your target. In addition, however, it is prudent also to consider some other practical questions when deciding if or how to use performance assessment in your classroom.

Approximating the Best

Remember, while we can use performance assessment to assess reasoning, we also can use selected response and essay formats to tap this kind of achievement. In addition, while performance assessment is the best option for measuring attainment of skill and product outcomes, again, we can use selected response and essay formats to assess student mastery of important prerequisites of effective performance. In this sense, they represent approximations of the best.

Further, as you will see in Chapter 9, sometimes we can gain insight into achievement by having students talk through hypothetical performance situations. Admittedly, these are second best when compared to the real thing. But they can provide useful information at lower cost.

These "proxy" measures might come into play when we seek to size up a group of students very quickly for instructional planning purposes. In such a case, we might need only group performance information, so we could sample a few students from the group and assess just a few aspects of the performance of each. By combining information across students, we generate a profile of achievement that indicates group achievement strengths and needs. We can use such information to plan instruction. Under these circumstances, it may be unnecessary to use costly, full-blown performance assessments of every student. Rather, we might turn to simpler, more efficient paper and pencil or personal communication-based approximations of the best assessment to get what we need.

In effect, you can use proxies to delve into the prerequisites of skill and product performance to determine individual student needs. Remember that the building blocks of skill and product development competence include knowledge to be mastered and reasoning power—both of which you can assess with methods far more efficient than performance assessment. Not only can proxy measures serve as a means of such formative assessment, but also, to the extent that you involve your students in the assessment process, they can introduce students to the various prerequisites before they need to put them together.

Further, when time resources are too limited to permit a full-blown performance assessment, you might be forced to think of alternatives, to come as close as you can to the real thing, given your resources. While the resulting paper and pencil or personal communication assessments will fall short of perfection, if they are thoughtfully developed, they may give you enough information to serve your needs.

If you do decide to use approximations, however, never lose sight of their limitations; understand the targets they can and cannot reflect.

Time for Reflection

Can you remember a paper and pencil test you have taken that was a proxy measure for an achievement target that would have been more completely or precisely assessed with a performance assessment? How close did it come to the real thing, in your opinion?

The Order of Development

In explaining the basic three-part performance assessment design framework, we began by defining performance, then developing exercises, and finally devising scoring practices. However, this is not the only possible order of development of the parts of a performance assessment.

For instance, we might begin developing a performance assessment by creating rich and challenging exercises. If we can present complex but authentic, real-world problems for students to solve, then we can see how they respond during pilot test administrations and devise clear criteria for evaluating the achievement of subsequent performers.

On the other hand, it is difficult to devise exercises to elicit outcomes unless and until we have specified precisely what those outcomes are. In this case, we could start by selecting the target, translate it into performance criteria, and then develop performance rating procedures. Then, given a clear vision of the desired performance, we can devise exercises calculated to elicit samples of performance to which we can then apply the criteria.

In a sense, we have a chicken-or-egg dilemma here. We can't plan to evaluate performance until we know what that performance is—but neither can we solicit performance properly until we know how we're going to evaluate it! Which comes first, the performance criteria or the exercises?

As luck and good planning would have it, you can take your choice. Which you choose is a function of your level of understanding of the valued outcomes you will assess.

When You Know What to Look for.   Those who begin the performance assessment development process with a strong background in the discipline to be evaluated probably possess a highly refined vision of the target and can develop performance criteria out of that vision. If you begin with that kind of firm grounding, you may be able simply to sit at your desk and spell out each of the key elements of sound performance. With little effort, you may be able to translate each key element into different levels of achievement proficiency in clear, understandable terms. If you have sufficient pedagogical knowledge in your area(s) of expertise, you can use the procedures discussed in this chapter to carry out the necessary professional reflection, spell out your performance criteria, and transform those into scoring and recording procedures. Then you will be ready to develop exercises to strategically sample the performance you desire.

When You Have a Sense of What to Look for.   However, not everyone is ready to jump right in in this manner. Sometimes you have a general sense of the nature of the performance but are less clear on the specific criteria. For example, you might want your students to "write a term paper," but not have a clear sense about the standards of term paper quality you want to apply.

When this happens, you need a different starting place. One option is to give students a general term paper assignment and use the resulting papers—that is, actual samples of student work—as the basis for defining specific criteria. You can select a few high-quality and a few low-quality papers to compare as a means of generating clear and appropriate performance criteria. One way to do this is to sort them into three or four piles of general quality, ranging from poor to excellent, then carefully and thoughtfully analyze why the papers differ. Why do some work, while others don't? In those differences are hidden the performance criteria you seek.

The major shortcoming of starting with general exercises, of course, is that it puts students in the unenviable position of trying to perform well—write a good term paper, for example—without a clear sense of what good performance is supposed to look like. But remember, you need do this only once. From then on, you will always have well-developed criteria in hand to share with students in advance.

You can avoid this problem if you can recover copies of previous term papers. The key is to find contrasting cases, so you can compare them. They needn't come from your current students. Or, if you are assessing a demonstrated skill, perhaps you can find videotapes of past performance or can locate students practicing and observe them. One excellent way to find the right performance criteria, your vision of the meaning of academic success, is by "student watching." You can derive the critical elements of student success from actual samples of student work. But to take advantage of this option, you first need to get them performing somehow. That may mean starting with the development of exercises.

When You're Uncertain About What to Look for.   Other times, you may have only the vaguest sense of what you want students to know and be able to do within a particular discipline. In these instances, you can use performance assessment exercises to help identify the truly important learnings. Here's how this works: Begin by asking yourself, What kinds of real-world challenges do I want students to be able to handle? What are some sample problems I hope students will be able to solve? Using creative brainstorming, you and your colleagues can create and collect numerous written illustrative sample exercises. When you have assembled enough such exercises to begin to zero in on what they are sampling, then step back from the array of possibilities and ask, What are the important skills that seem to cross all or many of these problems? Or, if products are to result, What do all or many of the products seem to have in common? In short, ask, What are these exercises really getting at?

In other words, we draw inferences about the underlying meaning of success by examining various examples of how that success is likely to manifest itself in real-world problems. Out of these generalizations, we can draw relevant and explicit performance criteria.

One thing I like about this strategy is the fact that the resulting performance criteria are likely to be usable for a number of similar exercises. Good criteria generalize across tasks. They are likely to represent generally important dimensions of sound performance, not just those dimensions that relate to one narrowly defined task. They capture and convey a significant, generalizable portion of the meaning of academic success.

Checking for Errors in Judgment

Subjective scoring—a prospect that raises the anxiety of any assessment specialist—is the hallmark of performance assessment. I hope by now you see why it is that we in the assessment community urge caution as educators move boldly to embrace this option. It is fraught with potential danger and must be treated with great care.

We already have discussed many ways to ensure that our subjective assessment process is as objective as it can be:

- be mindful of the purpose for assessing

- be crystal clear about the target

- articulate the key elements of good performance in explicit performance criteria

- share those criteria with students in terms they understand

- learn to apply those criteria in a consistent manner

- double check to be sure bias does not creep into the assessment process

Testing for Bias.   There is a simple way to check for bias in your performance evaluations. Remember, bias occurs when factors other than the kind of achievement being assessed begin to influence rater judgment, such as the gender, age, ethnic heritage, appearance, or prior academic record of the examinee. You can determine the degree of objectivity of your ratings by comparing them with the judgments of another trained and qualified evaluator who independently observes and evaluates the same student performance with the intent of applying the same criteria. If, after observing and evaluating performance, two independent judges generally agree on the level of proficiency demonstrated, then we have evidence that the results reflect student proficiency. But if the judges come to significantly different conclusions, they obviously have applied different standards. We have no way of knowing which is the most appropriate. Under these circumstances the accuracy of the assessment must be called into question and the results set aside until we have thoroughly explained the reasons for those differences.

Time for Reflection

It's tempting to conclude that it is unrealistic to gather corroborating judgments in the classroom—to double check ratings. But before you read on, can you think of any helpers who might assist you in your classroom by playing the role of the second rater of a performance assessment? For each, what would it take to involve them productively? What benefits might arise from their involvement?

Practical Ways to Find Help.   While this test of objectivity, or of evaluator agreement, promises to help us check an important aspect of performance assessment quality, it seems impractical for classroom use for two reasons: It's often difficult to come up with a qualified second rater, and we often lack the time and expertise required to compare evaluations.

In fact, however, this process need not take so much time. You need not check all of your judgments for objectivity. Perhaps a qualified colleague could double check just a few—just to see if your ratings are on target.

Further, it doesn't take a high degree of technical skill to do this. Have someone who is qualified rate some student performance you already have rated, and then sit down for a few minutes and talk about any differences. If the performance in question is a product students created, have your colleague evaluate a few samples. If it's a skill, videotape a few samples. Apply your criteria to one and check for agreement. Do you both see it about the same way? If so, go on to the next one. If not, try to resolve differences, adjusting your performance criteria as needed.

Please understand that my goal here is not to have you carry out this test of objectivity every time you conduct a performance assessment. Rather, try to understand the spirit of this test of your objectivity. An important part of the art of classroom performance assessment is the ability to sense when your performance criteria are sufficiently explicit that another judge would be able to use them effectively, if called on to do so. Further, from time to time it is a good idea to actually check whether you and another rater really do agree in applying your criteria.

On those occasions, however, when you are conducting very important performance assessments that have significant impact on students (i.e., for promotion decisions, graduation decisions, and the like), you absolutely must at least have a sample of your ratings double checked by an independent rater. In these instances, remember you do have access to other available evaluators: colleagues in your school or district, your building administrative staff, support teachers, curriculum personnel, experts from outside the field of education (when appropriate), retired teachers in your community, qualified parents, and others.

In addition, sharing your criteria with your students and teaching them to apply those standards consistently can provide you with useful insights. You can be assured that they will tell you which criteria they don't understand.

Just remember, all raters must be trained to understand and apply your standards. Never assume that they are qualified to evaluate performance on the basis of prior experience if that experience does not include training in using the criteria you employ in your classroom. Have them evaluate some samples to show you they can do it. If training is needed, it very often does not take long. Figure 8–9 presents steps to follow when training raters. Remember, once they're trained, your support raters are allies forever. Just think of the benefits to you if you have a pool of trained evaluators ready to share the workload!

- Have trainees review and discuss the performance criteria. Provide clarification as needed.
- Give them a sample of work to evaluate that is of known quality to you (i.e., which you already have rated).
- Check their judgments against yours, reviewing and discussing any differences in terms of the specifics of the performance criteria.
- Give them another sample of work of known quality to evaluate.
- Compare their judgments to yours again, noting and discussing differences.
- Repeat this process until your trainee converges on your standards, as evidenced by a high degree of agreement with your judgments.
- You and the trainees evaluate a sample of work of unknown quality. Discuss any difference.
- Repeat this process until you have confidence in your new partner(s) in the evaluation process.

Figure 8–9
Steps in Training Raters of Student Performance

Barriers to Sound Performance Assessment

There are many things in the design and development of performance assessments that can cause a student's real achievement to be misrepresented. Many of the potential problems and remedies are summarized in Table 8–2.

More About Students as Partners

Imagine what it would mean if your helpers—your trained and qualified evaluators of skills or products—were your students. Not only could they be participants in the kind of rater training spelled out in Figure 8–9, but also, they might even be partners in the process of devising the performance criteria themselves. And, once trained, what if they took charge of training some additional students, or perhaps trained their parents to be qualified raters, too? The pool of available helpers begins to grow as more participants begin to internalize the meaning of success in your classroom.

Without question, the best and most appropriate way to integrate performance assessment and instruction is to be absolutely certain that the important performance criteria serve as the goals and objectives of the instruction. As we teach students to understand and demonstrate key dimensions of performance, we prepare them to achieve the targets we value. We prepare in sound and appropriate ways to be held accountable for student learning when we are clear and public about our

Table 8–2
Barriers to Sound Performance Assessment

Potential Source of Problems	Remedy
Inadequate vision of the target	Seek training and advice needed to clarify the vision. Collaborate with others in this process.
Wrong method for the target	Stick to skill and product targets when using performance assessment.
Incorrect performance criteria	Compare contrasting cases to zero in on key differences. Use quality criteria devised by others.
Unclear performance criteria	Study sample of performance more carefully. Rely on qualified experts whenever necessary.
Poor-quality exercises	Think about and specify achievement to be demonstrated, conditions, and standards to be applied.
Inadequate sample of exercises	Define the domain to be sampled as precisely as possible. Gather as much evidence as resources permit.
Too little time to evaluate	Add trained evaluators—they are available!
Untrained evaluators	Use clear criteria and examples of performance as a starting point in training them.
Inappropriate scoring method selected (holistic vs. analytical)	Understand the relationship between holistic and analytical scoring and assessment purpose.
Poor record keeping	Strive for accurate written records of performance judgments. Don't depend on memory.
Keeping the criteria and performance assessment process a mystery to students	Don't!

performance criteria, and when we do all in our power to be sure students have the opportunity to learn to hit the target.

In addition, we can make performance assessment an integral part of the teaching and learning process by involving students in assessment development and use in the following ways:

- Share the performance criteria with students at the beginning of the unit of instruction.
- Collaborate with students in keeping track of which criteria have been covered in class and which are yet to come.
- Involve students in creating prominent visual displays of important performance criteria for bulletin boards.
- Engage students in the actual development of performance exercises.
- Engage students in comparing and contrasting examples of performance, some of which reflect high-quality work and some of which do not (perhaps as part of a process of developing performance criteria).

- Involve students in the process of transforming performance criteria into checklists, rating scales, and other recording methods.

- Have students evaluate their own and each other's performance, one-on-one and/or in cooperative groups.

- Have students rate performance and then conduct studies of how much agreement (i.e., objectivity) there was among student judges; see if degree of agreement increases as students become more proficient as performers and as judges.

- Have students write about their own growth over time with respect to specified criteria.

- Have students set specific achievement goals in terms of specified criteria and then keep track of their own progress.

- Store several samples of each student's performance over time, either as a portfolio or on videotape, if appropriate, and have students compare old performance to new and discuss in terms of specific ratings.

- Have students predict their performance criterion-by-criterion, and then check actual evaluations to see if their predictions are accurate.

These activities will help increase students' control of their own academic well-being and will remove the mystery that too often surrounds the meaning of success in the classroom.

Time for Reflection

Have you ever been involved in any of these ways of assessing your own performance—as a partner with your teacher? If so, what was the experience like for you?

Chapter Summary: Thoughtful Development Yields Sound Assessments

This chapter has been about the great potential of performance assessment, with its vast array of design options. However, the presentation has been tempered with the admonition that we all develop and use this assessment format cautiously. Performance assessment, like other methods, brings with it specific rules of evidence. We must all strive to meet those rigorous quality control standards.

We began with a brief overview of the three steps in developing performance assessments: clarifying performance (dealing with the nature and focus of the achievement to be assessed), developing exercises (dealing with the nature, content, and number of exercises), and scoring (dealing with kinds of scores, recording results, and identifying and training the evaluator). As we covered each step, we discussed how students could become full partners in performance assessment design, development, and use. The result will be better performers.

To ensure quality, we discussed the need to understand the role of subjectivity in performance assessment. We also analyzed the match between performance assessment and the five kinds of achievement targets, concluding that strong matches can be developed for reasoning, skills, and products. We discussed the key context factors to consider in selecting this methodology for use in the classroom, centering mostly on the importance of having in place the necessary expertise and resources.

We devised six practical steps for formulating sound performance criteria, urging collaboration with students and/or colleagues in the process. We set standards for sound exercises, including the need to identify the achievement to be demonstrated, the conditions of the demonstration, and the standards of quality to be applied. And finally, we spelled out scoring options, suggesting that analytical evaluation of student work is likely to be most productive, especially when students are trained to apply standards of quality to their own and each other's work.

As schools continue to evolve, we will come to rely on performance assessment as part of the basis for our evaluation of student achievement. Hopefully, we will find even more and better ways of integrating performance assessment and instruction. Let us strive for the highest-quality, most rigorous assessments our resources will allow.

Exercises to Advance Your Learning

Knowledge

1. Memorize the three basic parts and nine design decisions that guide the performance assessment development process. These are essential to the thoughtful application of this assessment format.

2. Referring back to the text, list the aspects of performance assessment design that require professional judgment and the dangers of bias associated with each.

3. Again, rereading the text, specify in writing the kinds of achievement targets that can be transformed into the performance assessment format and those that cannot.

4. Working with a colleague or fellow student, brainstorm the key considerations in devising a sound sample of performance exercises.

5. Memorize the six steps in the design of performance criteria and the basic ingredients of sound exercises. If you know them, you can apply them automatically as appropriate.

6. In your own words and without referring to the text, list as many ways as you can to bring students into the performance assessment process as partners. Then check your list against the ideas offered herein.

Reasoning

1. Based on what you now know about selected response, essay, and performance assessment, write a comparative analysis of the active ingredients in each method, as well as the strengths and weaknesses.

Skills and Products

1. Turn to the list of attributes of sound performance criteria provided by Quellmalz on pages 199–200. Using these as the basis of your work, develop a set of performance rating scales that teachers might use to evaluate the quality of their performance criteria.

2. Turn to the list of attributes of sound performance exercises provided by Baron on page 204. Using these as the basis of your work, develop a set of performance rating scales teachers might use to evaluate the quality of their exercises.

Dispositions

1. Some have argued that performance assessments are too fraught with potential bias due to evaluator subjectivity to justify the attention they are receiving these days. Do you agree? Why?

2. Throughout the chapter, I argue that the assessment development procedures outlined here will help teachers who use performance assessments to connect those assessments directly to their instruction. Having completed the chapter, do you agree? Why?

3. I also argue that the assessment development and use procedures suggested herein, while apparently very labor intensive, could save you valuable teaching time in the long run. Do you agree? Why?

Special Ongoing Assessment Project: Part 5

From your selected unit of instruction, identify a skill achievement target—where students are expected to do something proficiently. Go through the step-by-step process of designing a performance assessment of this skill proficiency. Articulate performance criteria, devise appropriate exercise(s), and plan for scoring and recording.

Then identify a product you expect your students to create. Devise a performance assessment of these student products, in terms of criteria, exercise, and scoring.

When you have completed this work, evaluate the quality of your work using the rating scales you devised for skill exercises 1 and 2 above.

Finally, write a brief outline of steps you might use to involve your students in developing and using these assessments as a part of the teaching and learning process.

9

Personal Communication: Another Window to Student Achievement

CHAPTER ROADMAP

Teachers gather a great deal of valuable information about student achievement by talking with them. We seldom think of this personal communication as assessment, but it often is. At different times during the teaching and learning process, we might ask questions during instruction, listen to answers, and evaluate achievement, or we might conduct conferences with students that, in effect, serve as interviews that yield information about achievement. These kinds of assessment formats are the focus of this chapter.

As a result of studying the material presented in Chapter 9, reflecting on that material, and completing the learning exercises presented at the end of the chapter, you will master content knowledge in the following forms:

1. Understand the roles of objectivity and subjectivity in assessments based on personal communication.

2. Know the kinds of achievement targets that can be reflected in personal communication–based assessments.

3. Be able to cite the strengths, limitations, and keys to effective use of several forms of personal communication assessment: instructional questions and answers, class discussions, conferences and interviews, oral exams, conversations with others about students, and student journals.

4. Understand key considerations in sampling student performance via personal communication.

5. List specific ways to engage students in the assessment process using personal communication.

Further, you will be able to use that knowledge to reason about the following:

223

1. When and where to turn to assessment based on personal communication.
2. Potential contributors to mismeasurement when relying on personal communication and how to control them.
3. How to sample student achievement properly using personal communication as the assessment method.

The skills you will develop as a result of your work in Chapter 9 will center on the ability to pose questions and interact with students in ways that permit the collection of quality information about mastery of knowledge and reasoning proficiency.

Further, you will become proficient at creating products such as record-keeping systems for storing information about student achievement gathered via personal communication.

Finally, I hope you will become predisposed to do the following:

1. Regard personal communication with caution, valuing the need to adhere to rigorous standards of quality in development and use.
2. Value personal communication as an assessment option in the classroom.
3. See assessment via personal communication as a valuable instructional tool in which students should be and can be full partners.

You will find that the tenor of this chapter is somewhat different from that of the three previous methodology chapters. My intent is not so much to provide extensive detail on concrete procedures as it is to inform you of the factors to be aware of as you interact with students and draw inferences about their achievement based on what you hear from them. If you interact in a focused manner, listen attentively, and are cautious in the conclusions you draw, your personal communications with students can provide a clear window into student learning.

Those who teach understand that although personal communication as assessment virtually never informs the momentous decisions in students' lives, or commands the attention of highly visible standardized testing programs, it nevertheless, as you will see in this chapter, always has been and always will be a critical form of classroom assessment.

In terms of our big picture, the shaded cells in Figure 9–1 indicate the material covered in this chapter.

Our personal exchanges with students can be packed with useful information about their achievement, and thus can serve a variety of important and often interwoven purposes in the classroom. For example, sometimes our communications with students simply provide information that corroborates or calls into question assessment results secured through other, more structured means. That is, some teachers use this form of assessment to double check assessments. Sometimes, teachers use question and answer exchanges during instruction to find out if the class as a whole or individual students are on track or tuned in—to monitor and adjust, if you will. In addition, teachers often use various forms of personal communication to encourage and evaluate student reasoning and problem solving. Clearly

	SELECTED RESPONSE	ESSAY	PERFORMANCE ASSESSMENT	PERSONAL COMMUNICATION
Know				
Reason				
Skills				
Products				
Dispositions				

Figure 9–1
Aligning Achievement Targets and Assessment Methods

these uses of the personal communication assessment process are very important to student well-being in the classroom.

Many of our most common ways of interacting with students turn out to be productive sources of insight into student learning. Often, teachers do the following:

- Ask questions during instruction, listen to answers, and evaluate achievement.
- Conduct conferences with students that, in effect, serve as interviews yielding information about achievement.
- Listen carefully for student contributions during class discussions to evaluate student reasoning.
- Conduct oral examinations to assess mastery of required material.
- Converse with others (students, teachers, and parents) to gather information about a student's achievement.
- Request that students collect their thoughts about their learning in various forms of journals, diaries, and logs.

When we use these forms of assessment with care, we can tap dimensions of achievement not easily accessed through other means. For example, an effective questioner can use properly sequenced questions to probe deeply into students' reasoning processes to help them tune in to and understand their own problem-solving approaches. Further, thoughtful questioners can effectively link assessment to instruction by using questions to uncover and immediately correct students' misconceptions or faulty reasoning.

By the same token, if we are not careful in our use of personal communication as assessment, we can mismeasure achievement every bit as easily with this as with any other mode. As you shall see, the list of potential pitfalls is as long as that for performance or paper and pencil assessments. In fact, in some senses, the list of challenges to the effective use of personal communication assessment is even longer than those of other modes because this one often is carried out casually in an informal context, where bias can creep in without even being noticed. But the good news is that we know how to overcome these potential problems.

Nowhere is classroom assessment more of an art than in the use of personal communication to track student growth and development. Typically, there is no table of test specifications to match against our intended target. There are no test items to check for quality, no score results. We can't check for agreement among observers to see if judgments are consistent. These are the artifacts of preplanned, structured classroom assessments. Often, personal communication is not like that. It's more spontaneous, more personal.

Nevertheless, we must understand and appreciate the fact that even this more artistic mode of assessment carries with it specific rules of evidence. Understand and adhere to those rules and you can derive valuable information about the attainments of your students. Disregard those rules and—just as with other forms of assessment—you can do great harm. With this form of assessment, just as with the others, we must vigilantly pursue quality.

Personal Communication at Work as Assessment in the Classroom

Casey, our high school teacher friend, has agreed to help us begin this phase of our journey with an analysis of an instructional-assessment strategy that relies heavily on personal communication as its source of achievement data. It's called *scored discussions* (Zola, 1992). Here's how it works:

"My goal is to help students learn to make productive contributions to public discussions of important, social issues. So the focus of my assessment is the quality of student contributions during class discussion. Depending on the context, I sometimes alter the particular achievement targets I'm aiming for. Sometimes the assessment and evaluation might focus on the nature and quality of the content contained within each student's contributions. Other times the form of their social interaction during discussion is more important.

"I begin by informing my students that they will read a brief essay on a controversial social topic and then discuss it, analyzing key elements of the controversy and evaluating different points of view. I tell them that the discussion may become 'spirited' from time to time, as opinions are expressed and challenged. However, I'm really clear about my expectation that each discussant's contributions be substantive—based on accurate knowledge and appropriate reasoning—and that the interaction remain civil.

"We prepare for the discussion with a set of interrelated brainstorming questions: From the perspective of personal interactions, how might we judge the substantive quality of someone's contributions? What discussion skills are most likely to contribute to a "civil" class discussion? What positive behaviors are truly effective discussants likely to exhibit? We brainstorm these together. Often the list of keys to success begin like this:

- Background facts included in comments are accurate and relate to the topic.
- The reasoning employed by the contributor is clear for all to see (and to challenge if necessary).
- Contributions contain evidence of listening attentively to others.
- Effective contributors ask clarifying questions of others—questions that make sense.
- Class members are not afraid to take a position and defend it.
- Discussants make their points clear and brief.

"When the idea well begins to run dry, we move to the next stage, where I ask them to identify three of the listed attributes of quality contributions they feel are most crucial to achieving a productive discussion. We highlight those. They then select three more from the remaining skills that they consider important, but not quite as important as the first set. We set these aside for the moment.

"Next, we brainstorm personal interaction patterns that might be counterproductive in a discussion. This list includes the following:

- relying on personal opinion or inaccurate information to make points
- reasoning in faulty, illogical ways
- not contributing to the discussion
- failing to listen attentively
- interrupting others
- putting down others for their ideas
- dominating the discussion
- making contributions that are off-topic

Again, we set priorities among these counterproductive patterns.

"From these lists, we make up a scoring sheet that lists the important aspects of productive contributions, each of which earns 2 points if exhibited during discussion. Next, we list the less important productive contributions, giving these a point value of 1. Counterproductive contributions are then listed, with point values of –2 and –1. Each discussant's goal, we agree, is to contribute to the discussion in ways that result in them attaining the highest (positive!) score."

The Discussion and Assessment Process

Now here's a twist that I think is terrific in Casey's application of this strategy: Students are paired randomly. One member of each team is labeled an "innie," the other an "outie." The innies sit in a circle, with their outie partner sitting right behind them, scoring sheet in hand. Innies read a brief piece on a controversial topic (perhaps a newspaper editorial on a volatile political issue) and discuss it among themselves. Every time his or her partner exhibits one of the behaviors listed on the scoring sheet, the outie tallies it. Later, tallies are counted to find the frequency of occurrence of the various targets. These are multiplied by points to yield a score.

Innies and outies then reverse roles. Outies read an essay on a controversial topic and discuss. Their partners observe, evaluate, and summarize in exactly the same way, arriving at a profile of performance for later discussion.

When discussions are finished, partners meet to share and discuss results. Their assignment is to talk with each other about the quality and impact of their contribution to the group interaction. They identify positive, productive patterns, as well as ways to improve, providing specific examples of things that seemed to work well and those that did not. If any misinterpretation occurs, discussants have a chance to explain what they were trying to do. In short, partners provide feedback on results, not just as scores, but as personal communication about the assessment and its results.

Later, the class as a whole discusses the implications of this activity for attaining goals of civic responsibility. As they are debriefed on this activity, of course, they strive to adhere to good discussion techniques!

Casey is considering a variation on this idea for next year—videotaping two class discussions. The first taped discussion will take place before they brainstorm and learn about productive interaction strategies. After brainstorming a list of keys to effective contributing, they will tape the discussion of another controversial topic, striving to meet the standards of effective practice and scoring each other's contributions. Finally, the class will view both videos and compare and contrast group performance, asking, Was the discussion conducted at the end of the lesson more civil and productive than the beginning discussion?

Time for Reflection

Obviously, the scored discussions activity will span considerable time, with the preparation to assess, multiple discussions, partner feedback and debriefing, and whole-class debriefing. If you were to plan this for your classroom over several days, what would your lesson plan look like? Please devise a sample plan—in writing.

Ensuring Quality Assessment

Assessment via personal communication is yet another assessment method that is subjective by its very nature. In this section, we explore the role of subjectivity in this form of assessment. We then deal with other practical quality control matters, including issues of match between personal communication and the five kinds of outcomes we've been exploring, classroom realities to take into account with this method, and more sampling considerations.

Subjectivity in Personal Communication

Professional judgment, and therefore subjectivity, permeates all aspects of assessments that rely on personal communication. Each of these factors is a matter of our professional judgment:

- the achievement targets we set for students
- the questions we pose (and sometimes generate on the spot)
- the criteria we apply in evaluating answers (often without a great deal of time to reflect)
- the performance records we store (sometimes in memory!)
- the manner in which we retrieve those results for later use
- interpretations we make of the results
- the various ways in which we use those results

The presence of subjectivity makes it imperative that, as when using other assessment methods, you know and understand the achievement target and know how to translate it into clear and specific questions and other probes to generate focused information.

Potential Problems.   Let's be specific about the three reasons not to take personal communication as assessment too lightly as a source of information and as a teaching strategy.

Reason 1: The Problem of Forgetting.   The first reason for caution is that we must remain mindful of the fallibility of the human mind as a recording device. Not only can we lose things in there, but also, the things we put in can change over time for various reasons, only some of which are within our control. These are aspects of subjectivity to be aware of when using personal communication as assessment, where we often store our recollections in memory. We must act purposely to counteract these dangers. The scored discussion idea described previously did so by having students carefully develop and use their scoring sheets.

Time for Reflection

Have you ever been the victim of an assessment in which you demonstrated some important proficiency, but because of your teacher's mental lapse, the record of your accomplishments was lost? If so, what was that experience like for you?

Reason 2: The Problem of Filters.   We also must remain aware of and strive to understand those personal and professional filters, developed over years of experience, through which we hear and process student responses. They represent norms or standards, if you will, that allow us to interpret and act on the achievement information that comes to us through observation and personal communication. We have discussed them before—they are our personal biases.

These filters hold the potential of improving or harming assessment quality. On the good side, if we set achievement expectations based on a thorough understanding of a particular field of study and if we interpret the things students say with those clearly held and appropriate standards, we can use personal communication as a positive and productive form of assessment.

Further, if we set our expectations for individual learners on the basis of accurate information about their current levels of achievement, we maximize the chances that we will be able to assist them in achieving more. These represent appropriate uses of norms and expectations.

However, there is a dark side to these interpretive filters. They can be the source of inappropriate bias. If we set our expectations for students, not on the basis of a clear understanding of the discipline or not on the basis of careful assessment of student capabilities, but on the basis of stereotypes or other convenient categories of people that are in fact unrelated to real academic achievement, we risk doing great harm indeed. If, for example, we establish professional filters by holding predetermined expectations of learners according to gender, ethnic heritage, cultural background, physical appearance, linguistic experience, our knowledge of a student's prior achievement, or any of a wide variety of other forms of prejudice—unrelated to actual achievement—we allow bias to creep into the assessment process. The scored discussion class described previously countered these dangers by adhering to one of the basic rules of sound assessment: Develop clear targets. They were careful to spell out the specific behaviors they labeled productive and counterproductive.

Time for Reflection

As a student, have you ever been on the losing end of a biased assessment— where for some reason, your teacher's inappropriate personal or professional filters led to an incorrect assessment of your proficiency? What was that like? What effect did it have on your learning?

Reason 3: The Challenge of Sampling.   Just as with other forms of assessment, we can make sampling mistakes. One is to gather incorrect information by asking the wrong questions, questions that fail to reflect important forms of achievement. Another mistake is to gather too few bits of information to lead to confident conclusions about proficiency. In our scored discussion example, this problem would arise if the discussions were too short for everyone to have a chance to demonstrate the ability to contribute productively.

Still another sampling mistake is to spend too much time gathering too many bits of information. This is a problem of inefficiency. We eventually reach a point of diminishing returns, where additional information is unlikely to change the conclusion about proficiency. This would occur in the scored discussion example if the group interactions went on longer than necessary.

To avoid such sampling problems, we must seek just enough information without overdoing it. In the classroom, this is very much a matter of subjective judg-

Attribute of Quality	Defining Question
Arise from a clear and specific achievement target	Do my questions reflect the achievement target I want my students to hit?
Serve clear purposes	Why am I assessing? How will results be used?
Assure a sound representation of that target	Can the target of interest to me be accurately reflected through personal communication with the student?
Sample performance appropriately	Do I have enough evidence?
Control for unwanted interference	Am I in touch with potential sources of bias, and have I minimized the effects of personal and professional filters?

Figure 9–2
Defining Issues of Quality for Personal Communication as Classroom Assessment

ment. Thus, it represents another example of a place where the *art* of classroom assessment—your professional judgment—comes into play. More about this soon.

Avoiding Problems Due to Subjectivity.   We can avoid problems due to the fallibility of the human mind and bias only by attending to those five ever-present, important, basic attributes of sound assessment as they apply in the context of personal communication. Whether we plan or are spontaneous in our personal communication with students, we must bear these quality standards in mind. Figure 9–2 reviews these standards as they apply to personal communication as assessment.

When we meet these standards of quality, personal communication holds the promise of providing rich and useful data about student attainment of important educational outcomes. Obviously, as with other methods, one prominent key to our success is the match of our method to the various outcomes we need to assess. We discuss how to find sound matches next.

Matching Method to Target

Personal communication-based assessments can provide direct evidence of proficiency in three of our five kinds of targets and can provide insight into the student's readiness to deliver on the other two. This is a versatile assessment option.

Assessing Knowledge

This can be done with personal communication, but you need to be cautious. Obviously, you can question students to see if they have mastered the required knowledge or can retrieve it through the effective use of reference materials. To succeed, however, you must possess a keen sense of the limits and contents of the domain of knowledge. Once again, since you cannot ask all possible questions, especially using this labor-intensive method, you must sample and generalize in a representative manner in the questions you pose. I'll say more about the critical importance of careful sampling.

Assessing Reasoning

Herein lies the real strength of personal communication as a means of assessment. Skillful questioners can probe student reasoning and problem solving, both while the very thinking process is underway and retrospectively, to analyze how the student reached the solution. But even more exciting is that you can use the questioning process to help students understand and enhance their own reasoning.

For example, you can ask them to let you in on their thought processes as they analyze events or objects, describing component parts. You can probe their abilities to draw meaningful comparisons, to make simple or complex inferences, or to express and defend an opinion or point of view. There is no more powerful method for exploring student reasoning and problem solving than a conversation while the student is actually trying to solve the problem. By exploring their reasoning along with them, you can provide students with the kinds of understanding and vocabulary needed to converse with you and with each other about what it means to be proficient in this performance arena.

Asking students to "think out loud" offers great promise for delving deeply into their reasoning. Mathematics teachers often ask a student to talk about his or her thinking while proceeding step-by-step through the solution to a complex math problem. This provides a richness of insight into the student's mathematical reasoning that cannot be attained in any other way.

Further, as students talk through the process, you also can insert follow-up questions: Why were certain steps taken or omitted? What would have happened if you had . . . ? Do you see any similarities between this problem and those we worked on last week? When students are unable to solve the problem, tactical questioning strategies can tell you why. Did the student lack prerequisite knowledge of number systems? Analyze the problem incorrectly? Misunderstand the steps in the process? These probes permit you to find student needs and link the assessment to instruction almost immediately—there is no need to wait for the score reports to be returned!

Time for Reflection

One of the popular ways of assessing reading comprehension these days is to have students retell a story they have just read. As the retelling unfolds, the teacher is free to ask questions as needed to probe the student's interpretation. Why do you think this kind of assessment has become so popular? What does it offer that, say, a multiple-choice test of reading comprehension does not?

Assessing Skills and Products

In the previous chapter, we established that the only way to obtain direct information about student skills or proficiency in creating quality products is to have them actually "do or create" and compare their work to preestablished standards of quality.

However, if you are a skilled teacher of "doing or creating" (i.e., a teacher who possesses a highly refined vision of such targets), you can ask your students to talk through a hypothetical performance, asking a few key questions along the way, and know with a certain degree of confidence whether the students are likely to be proficient performers, and what aspects of their performance are likely to fall short of expectations.

This can save assessment time in the classroom. Let's say, for example, the kind of performance to be assessed is complex and the cost of time and materials required to conduct a full-blown performance assessment is quite high, as in an assessment of repairing an expensive piece of electronic equipment in a technology education class. If this teacher has some question about a particular student's proficiency and, therefore, is hesitant about investing the time and equipment needed to carry out the assessment, she could simply sit down and talk with the student, ask a few critical questions, and, based on the level of achievement reflected in the student's answers, infer whether it would be proper to conduct the actual assessment or offer additional instruction and more time to prepare.

In this same performance-related sense, you can ask students strategic questions to examine the following:

- prior success in performing similar tasks
- confidence in their ability to deliver sound performance
- knowledge and understanding of the criteria to be used to evaluate performance (i.e., key skills to be demonstrated or key attributes of quality products)
- awareness of the steps necessary to create quality products

Based on the results of such probes, you can infer about competence. But again, talking is not doing. Without question, some may be able to talk a better game than they can actually deliver. So clearly, personal communication is inferior to actual performance assessment when it comes to evaluating skill and product outcomes. But under certain circumstances, it can be an inexpensive, accessible, and instructionally relevant form of classroom assessment.

Assessing Dispositions

Herein resides another strength of personal communication as a form of assessment. Perhaps the most productive way to determine the direction and intensity of students' school-related attitudes, interests, values, or motivational dispositions is to simply ask them. An ongoing pattern of honest exchanges of points of view between you and your students can contribute much to the creation of powerful learning environments.

The keys to making personal communication work in the assessment of student affect are trust and open channels of communication. If students are confident that it's all right to say what they really think and feel, they will do so.

Time for Reflection

What kinds of questions might you ask a student to tap the direction and intensity of that students' real, honest feelings about the learning environment in your classroom?

Context Factors

Obviously, in the hands of an experienced user, personal communication has much to offer as an assessment technique.

First, you can forge a clear and complete link between your questioning strategies and the focus of instruction. Even as the teaching and learning process is progressing, a few strategically placed questions can help you to monitor and adjust.

Second, unlike some other forms of assessment, a questioner who is startled or puzzled by a student response can ask follow-up questions to dig more deeply into student thinking. In other words, you can get beyond a particular response to explore its origins. If you find misconceptions, you can take immediate action to correct them.

Third, also unlike some other forms of assessment, personal communication can be spontaneous, allowing you to take advantage of unexpected opportunities to assess and promote achievement. That is, when you sense a need for a bit more information on student thinking, you can strike while the iron is hot and take advantage of a teachable moment.

Fourth, personal communication is almost infinitely flexible in its range of applications as classroom assessment. It can focus on a range of valued outcomes. It can focus the assessment microscope on individual students, or on students as a group. It can sample students and/or the material being covered. Students may volunteer to respond, or you can call on anyone. Interaction can be public or private. Questions and answers can come from either you or the student. Assessment can be structured or informal. Considering the flexibility indicated here, you must agree that this is a versatile mode of assessment.

And fifth, to the attentive user, the student's nonverbal reactions can provide valuable insights into achievement and feelings about the material learned (or not learned). These indicators of confidence, uncertainty, excitement, boredom, comfort, or anxiety can lead you to probe more deeply into the underlying causes. This kind of perception checking can result in levels of student-teacher communication not achievable through other assessment means.

Other Factors to Consider

However, given even these strengths, the fact that almost all classroom assessment using personal communication is not subject to outside verification means that no one but you will ever be able to check to see if you are doing a good job. The standards of sound practice here are yours, and yours alone. Remember, your students and their parents will assume that you are constantly applying the highest standards of professional practice.

In that regard, there are several potential pitfalls to sound assessment using personal communication about which you must remain constantly aware.

A Common Language Is the Foundation.   Teacher and student must share a common language to communicate effectively. This factor has become more and more critical through the 1980s and 1990s, as ethnic and cultural diversity have increased markedly in our schools. By common language, I don't just mean a shared vocabulary and grammar, although these obviously are critical to communication. I also mean a common sense of the manner in which a culture shares meaning through verbal and nonverbal cues. Ethnicity and cultural heritage may differ between student and teacher. If you assess by means of personal communication, you must know how to make meaning in the language and culture of your students. When you lack that understanding, you ensure mismeasurement.

Sufficient Verbal Fluency Is Essential.   This is not the same as common language. If this method is to provide accurate information about achievement, students must be both willing and able to express themselves fluently. The danger of mismeasurement lies in both directions here. If the student is not fluent, you may misinterpret and draw incorrect inferences. And if the student is "too fluent" (if you know what I mean) you can be bamboozled—Beware!

Personality Is Important, Too.   Shy, withdrawn students simply may not perform well in this kind of assessment context, regardless of their real achievement. To make these methods work, two people must connect in an open, communicative manner. For some students, this simply is too risky—often for reasons beyond your control.

This coin has two sides: There also is the danger that students with very outgoing, aggressive personalities will try to lay down a "smoke screen" to mislead you with respect to their real achievement. But, this works only with assessors who have not prepared carefully, and who cannot stay focused. You fall prey to the dangers of bias in assessment when you allow yourself to be distracted by irrelevant factors.

We Must Allow Sufficient Time.   There must be enough time available to carry out this one-on-one form of assessment. When the target is narrow in scope and you are assessing only a few students, time may not be a factor. A question or two may suffice to provide a quick glimpse into achievement. No problem.

However, as the target broadens and the number of students increases, two time dimensions become more important. First, there must be enough time to permit you to interact with each student whose achievement you are assessing in this manner. Second, there must be sufficient time available with each student to allow you to properly sample achievement. If this time is not available, it is better to turn to another strategy that does not require such intense one-on-one contact.

Create a Safe Environment.   Personal communication works best as assessment when students feel they are in a safe learning environment. There are many ways to interpret this. One kind of safety permits them to succeed or fail in private, without an embarrassing public spotlight. Another kind of safety takes the form of a peer environment sensitive to the plight of those who perform less well and supportive of their attempts to grow. Still another kind of safety comes from having the opportunity to learn more and perform again later with the promise of a higher level of success. Nowhere is personal safety more important to sound assessment than when that assessment is conducted through public personal communication.

Students Must Understand the Need for Honesty.   Personal communication works best as assessment when students understand that sometimes their teacher needs an honest answer—not their attempt at a best possible answer or the answer they think their teacher wants to hear. This mode of assessment provides its best information most efficiently when a sound interpersonal relationship exists between you and your students. Again, the key is trust. Students must know that if they give you the "socially desirable" response to a question—a response that misrepresents the truth about their achievement or feelings—then you will be less likely to help them.

Accurate Records Are Key.   Because there are no tangible results with assessments conducted via personal communication, records of achievement can be lost. Over a span of a few moments or hours when the communication focuses on narrow targets, this may not be a problem. But when the context includes many students, complex targets, and a requirement of extended storage, you absolutely must maintain tangible records—written or taped records of some kind. If you have no means or hope of doing so when necessary, you would do better to revise your assessment plans.

Figure 9–3 summarizes the five benefits of and seven practical keys to the effective use of assessment by means of personal communication discussed above.

More About Sampling

Remember, any assessment represents only a sample of an ideal assessment of infinite length. The key to successful sampling in the context of personal communication is to ask a representative set of questions, one that is long enough to give you confidence in the generalizations drawn to the entire performance domain.

Example of an Easy Fit.   Lynn, our elementary teacher friend, tells this story illustrative of a time when sampling challenges were relatively easy to meet:

"I was about to start a new science reading activity on fish with my third graders. As a prereading activity, I wanted to be sure all my students had sufficient

Benefits:

- Personal communication can be quick and efficient.
- Immediate connections are possible between assessment and instruction.
- The user can be opportunistic—taking advantage of teachable moments.
- The method is flexible.
- Assessment can attend to nonverbal responses, too.

Things to investigate:

- Do teacher and students share a common language?
- Have students attained a sufficiently high level of verbal fluency to interact effectively?
- Do students have personalities that permit them to open up enough to reveal true achievement?
- Is there sufficient time for assessment?
- Do students see the environment as safe enough to reveal their true achievement?
- Do students understand the need to reveal their true achievement?
- Can accurate records of achievement be kept?

Figure 9–3
Factors to Consider in the Use of Personal Communication as Assessment

background information about fish to understand the reading. So I checked the story very carefully for vocabulary and concepts that might be stumbling blocks for my students. Then I simply asked a few strategic questions of the class, probing understanding of those words and ideas and calling on students randomly to answer. As I sampled the group's prior knowledge through questions and answers, I made mental notes about who seemed not to know some of the key material. This time there were only three or four. Later, I went back and questioned each of them more thoroughly to be sure. Then I helped them to learn the new material before they began reading."

In this scenario, the performance arena is quite small and focused: vocabulary and concepts from within one brief science story. Sampling by means of personal communication was simple and straightforward, and there are no real record-keeping challenges presented. Lynn simply verified understanding on the part of the students before proceeding. After that, most records of performance could go on the back burner. Lynn did make a mental note to follow up with those students who had the most difficulty, but decided that all other records could be "deleted."

Example of a More Challenging Fit.   Now here's a scenario in which the assessment challenges are more formidable: A high school health teacher who relies extensively on small- and large-group discussion of health-related social issues as her instructional technique wants to encourage student participation in class discussions. To accomplish this, she announces at the beginning of the year that 25 percent of each student's grade will be based on the extent and quality of their participation in class. She is careful to point out that she will call on people to participate and that she expects them to be ready.

This achievement target is broader in two ways: It contains many more elements (the domain is much larger), and it spans a much longer period of time. Not only does the teacher face an immense challenge in adequately sampling each individual's performance, but also, her record-keeping challenge is much more complex and demanding. Consider the record-keeping dilemma posed by a class schedule that includes, say, four sections of eleventh-grade health, each including thirty students! And remember, mental record keeping is not an option: When we try to store such information in our gray matter for too long, bad things happen. These are not unsolvable problems, but they take careful preparation to assess. In this sense, they represent a significant challenge to the teacher.

These two scenarios capture the essence of the quality control challenge you face when you choose to rely on personal communication as a primary means of tracking student achievement. You must constantly ask yourself: Is my achievement target narrow enough in its scope and short enough in its time span to allow for conscientious sampling of the performance of individual students or students as a group? If the answer is yes, in your opinion, proceed to the next question: Is the target narrow enough in its scope and short enough in its time span to allow me to keep accurate records of performance? If the answer again is yes, proceed. If the answer to either question is no, choose another assessment method.

Time for Reflection

A PE teacher is about to start a new game with a class of 30 fourth graders. She thinks the rules are familiar to all, but decides to check just to be sure. So she picks a student and asks what that student should do, according to the rules, if a particular situation arises. The student answers correctly. She calls on another, seeking a second interpretation. Correct again. She infers that the class knows the rules. Soon, the game falls into disarray due to rules violations. What mistake(s) did the teacher make? What should she have done?

Assessing Individuals or the Whole Class.   Personal communication assessments are useful in tapping the level of achievement of students both individually and as a class or group. Experienced teachers know how to sample a class of students by (1) selecting a small number representative of the various levels of achievement in the group, and (2) asking a small but representative sample of key questions of this "test" group, so as to infer about student mastery of material just covered. Results of such assessments of group status can tell teachers whether to reteach or move on.

But to make this work, we must remember that the samples of students and achievement must both be representative and have sufficient depth to justify our conclusions. The PE teacher in the previous "Time for Reflection" did not. She checked the knowledge of too few students to support her inference about the knowledge level of the class as a whole. And, she asked too few questions about the rules of the game to correctly infer about student knowledge of all the rules. Both problems conspired to misinform her about her students' readiness to play the game.

Time for Reflection

What could the PE teacher have done to sample student achievement more dependably?

Before leaving sampling issues, let me restate in explicit terms a critical point in sampling individual student achievement through personal communication: Beware of the natural tendency to undersample. Often a teacher will pop two or three quick questions at a student, hear wrong answers, and make a snap judgment about overall achievement. Two questions is a pretty short test!

When relying on personal communication to assess—especially when using this mode—be sure to take time to gather enough information. Remember that tip I offered earlier about the art of determining when you have enough information to decide? You know you have asked enough questions and heard enough answers to infer about student achievement when you can anticipate with a high degree of confidence how students would answer if you gave them one more. Keep this tip in mind and don't sell your students short.

Summary of Quality Control Issues

Personal communication in its many forms can supply useful information to teachers about a variety of important educational outcomes, including mastery of subject matter knowledge, reasoning and problem solving, procedural knowledge that is prerequisite to skill and product creation proficiency, and dispositional outcomes. To create effective matches between this method of assessment and these kinds of targets, however, the user must start with a clear vision of the outcomes to be attained, know how to translate that vision into clear, focused questions, share a common language and open channels of communication with students, and understand how to sample performance representatively. But none of these keys to success is powerful enough to overcome the problems that arise when teachers' interpretive filters predispose them to be inappropriately biased in deciphering communication from students.

The Many Forms of Personal Communication as Assessment

Throughout the previous discussion of quality control, we have addressed personal communication as a class of assessment formats. We now conduct a thorough analysis of six formats of personal communication: questioning, conferences and interviews, class discussions, oral examinations, journals and logs, and conversations with others. We will define each format and identify several keys to its effective use in the classroom.

Please bear with me through this section, as I rely heavily on lists as a concise form of presentation. They allow me to share many thoughts in little space.

Instructional Questions and Answers

This has been a foundation of education since before Socrates. As instruction proceeds, either the teacher or the students themselves pose questions for others to answer. This activity promotes thinking and learning, and also provides information about achievement. The teacher listens to answers, interprets them in terms of internally held standards, and draws inferences as to the level of attainment of the respondent.

These keys to successful use will help you take advantage of the strengths of this as an assessment format, while overcoming weaknesses:

- Plan key questions in advance of instruction, so as to ensure proper alignment with the target and with student capabilities.
- Ask clear, brief questions that help the student focus on a relatively narrow range of acceptable responses.
- Probe various kinds of reasoning, not just recall of facts and information.
- Ask the question first and then call on the person who is to respond. This will have the effect of keeping all students on focus.
- Call on both volunteer and nonvolunteer respondents. This, too, will keep all students on task.
- Keep mental records of performance only for a few students at a time and over no more than a day or two. Written records are essential for large numbers of students over longer periods.
- Acknowledge correct or high-quality responses; probe incorrect responses for underlying reasons. Also regarding incorrect or low-quality responses, remember that the public display of achievement (or the lack thereof) links closely to self-concept. Strive to leave the respondent with something positive to grow on.
- After a question is posed, wait for a response—let the respondent know that you expect a response.

While this last suggestion—allowing time for students to respond—turns out to be surprisingly difficult to do, research reviewed and summarized by Rowe (1978) reveals many benefits. These effects appear to be most positive when we give traditionally low-achieving students time to respond:

- The length of student responses increases.
- The number of unsolicited but appropriate responses increases.

- Failure to respond decreases.
- Student confidence increases.
- The incidence of creative, speculative responses increases.
- Student-centered interaction increases, while teacher-centered teaching decreases.
- Students defend inferences better.
- The number of questions asked by students increases.
- Slow students contribute more.
- Discipline problems decrease.
- Teachers tend to view their class as including fewer academically weak students.
- Teachers are less likely to expect only their brighter students to respond.

If we can force ourselves *not to fill the silence with the sound of our own voices* and can wait for responses to brief, clearly focused questions, not only do we obtain sound assessment information, but also, in effect we integrate assessment deeply into the instructional process.

Conferences and Interviews

Some student-teacher conferences serve as structured or unstructured audits of student achievement, in which the objective is to talk about what the student has learned and has yet to learn. The teacher and student talk directly and openly about levels of student attainment, comfort with the material to be mastered, specific needs, interests, and desires, and/or any other achievement-related topics that contribute to an effective teaching and learning environment. In effect, teachers and students speak together in the service of understanding how to work effectively together.

Remember, interviews or conferences need not be conceived as every-pupil, standardized affairs with each event a carbon copy of the others. You might meet with only one student, if it fills a communication need. And, interviews or conferences might well vary in their focus across students who have different needs. The following are keys to successful use of conference and interview assessment formats:

- Both participants must be open to honest communication and willing to examine the real, important aspects of teaching and learning.
- Interview questions must be sharply focused on the achievement target(s) and the purpose for meeting.
- Questions should be carefully thought out and planned in advance. Remember, students can share in the preparation process.
- Plan for enough uninterrupted time to conduct the entire interview or conference.
- Be sure to conclude an interview with a summary of the lessons learned and their implications for how you and the student will work together in the future.

One important strength of the interview or conference as a mode of assessment lies in the impact it can have on the student-teacher relationship. When conducted in a context where the teacher has been up front about expectations, students understand the achievement target, and all involved are invested in student success, the conference has the effect of empowering students to take responsibility for at least part of the assessment of their own progress. Conducted in a context where everyone is committed to success and where academic success is clearly and openly defined, interviews are both informational and motivational in their outcomes.

Class Discussions

When students participate in class discussions, as in the example at the beginning of this chapter, the things they say reveal a great deal about their achievements and their feelings. Discussions are teacher- or student-led group interactions in which the material to be mastered is explored from various perspectives. Teachers listen to the interaction, evaluate the quality of student contributions, and draw inferences about individual student or group achievement. Clearly, class discussions have the simultaneous effect of promoting both student learning and their ability to use what they know.

To take advantage of the strengths of this method of assessment, while minimizing the impact of potential weaknesses, follow these keys to successful use:

- Prepare questions or discussion issues in advance to focus sharply on the intended achievement target.

- As with the scored discussions example at the beginning of the chapter, be sure to differentiate between achievement targets that are a matter of substance of contributions and targets that are a matter of form of communication. Be clear about the meaning of success in both cases.

- Involve students in the process of preparing, being sure their questions and key issues are part of the mix.

- Rely on debate formats or other team formats to maximize the number of students who can be directly involved. Pay special attention to involving low achievers.

- Formalize the discussion format to the extent that different roles are identified, such as moderator, team leader, spokesperson, recorder, and so on, to maximize the number of students who have the opportunity to present evidence of their achievement.

- Remember, the public display of achievement represents a risk that links that achievement (or the lack thereof) to self-concept. Be aware of those times when that risk must be controlled a bit for student good.

- Provide those students who have a more reserved personal style with other equally acceptable means of demonstrating achievement.

- Contexts where achievement information derived from participation in discussion is to influence high-stakes decisions, such as a grade, require dependable written records of performance.

The great strength of class discussion as assessment is in its ability to reveal the depth and quality of students' thinking—their abilities to analyze, compare, infer, and defend their points of view. The great danger of this method is the difficulty in sampling student performance in a complete and equitable manner. Care must be taken to structure discussions thoughtfully if we are to use them as assessments.

Oral Examinations

In European educational traditions and current assessment practices, the oral examination still plays a strong role. Teachers plan and pose exercises for their students, who reflect and provide oral responses. Teachers listen to and interpret those responses, evaluating quality and drawing inferences about levels of achievement.

In a very real sense, this is like essay assessment, discussed in Chapter 7, but with the added benefit of being able to ask follow-up questions.

While the oral examination tradition lost favor in the United States with the advent of selected response assessment, it still has great potential for use today—especially given the increasing complexity of our valued educational outcomes and the complexity and cost of setting up higher-fidelity performance assessments.

You can take advantage of the strengths of this format by adhering to some simple keys to the successful use of this method. You accomplish this in effect by adhering to all of the quality control guidelines listed in Chapter 7 for the development of quality essay assessments:

- Develop brief exercises that focus on the desired target.
- Rely on exercises that identify the knowledge to be brought to bear, specify the kind of thinking to be used, and identify the standards that will be applied in evaluating responses.
- Develop written scoring criteria in advance of the assessment.
- Be sure criteria separate content and thinking outcomes from facility with verbal expression.
- Prepare in advance to accommodate the needs of any students who may confront language proficiency barriers.
- Have a checklist, rating scale, or other method of recording results ready to use at the time of the assessment.
- If possible, record responses for later reevaluation.

Clearly, the major argument against this format of assessment is the amount of time it takes to administer oral exams. However, you can overcome part of this problem by bringing students into the assessment process as partners. If you adhere to the guidelines listed above and spread the work of administering and scoring over many shoulders, you may derive great benefit from oral assessment.

Journals and Logs

Sometimes personal communication-based assessment can take a written form. Students can share views, experiences, insights, and information about important learnings by writing about them. Teachers who frame writing assignments that cause students to center on particularly important achievement targets can derive clear and useful information by reading what students have written. Further, they can provide written feedback to their students.

Four particular forms of such written communication bear consideration: response journals, personal writing journals, diaries, and learning logs. These are infinitely flexible ways of permitting students to communicate about their learning, while at the same time practicing their writing and application of valued patterns of reasoning. In addition, because these written records are accummulated over time, we can use them to help students reflect on their improvement as achievers.

Response Journals.   Response journals are most useful in situations where you ask students to read and construct meaning from literature, such as in the context of reading and English instruction. As they read, students write about their reactions. Typically, you would provide structured assignments to guide them. Assignments include such tasks as the following:

- analyzing characters in terms of key attributes or contribution to the story
- analyzing evolving story lines, plots, or story events
- comparing one piece of literature or character to another
- anticipating or predicting upcoming events
- evaluating either the piece as a whole or specific parts in terms of appropriate criteria
- suggesting ways to change or improve character, plot, or setting, defending such suggestions

Teachers who use response journals report that it is an excellent way to permit students to practice applying reasoning patterns, and to increase the intensity of student involvement with their reading. Further, it can provide a means for students to keep track of all the things they have read, building in them a sense of accomplishment in this facet of their reading.

Personal Writing Journals or Diaries.   This is typically the least structured of the journal options. In this case, you would give students time during each instructional day to write in their journals. The focus of their writing is up to them, as is the amount they write. Sometimes the writing is evaluated, sometimes it is merely for practice. When you evaluate it, either you, or the student, or both, make judgements. Often young writers are encouraged to use their journals to experiment with new forms of writing, such as dramatic dialogue, poetry, or some other art form. Some teachers suggest to their students that they use personal journals as a place to store ideas for future writing topics. In one sense, this represents an excellent way to gain insight into the quality of student writing when students are operating at typical levels of motivation to write well. Since there is no high-stakes assessment under way, they do not have to strive for excellence. They can write for the fun of it and still provide both themselves and their teachers with evidence over time of their improvement as writers.

Learning Logs.   Students use learning logs to keep ongoing written records of the following aspects of their studies:

- achievement targets they have mastered
- targets they have found useful and important
- targets they are having difficulty mastering
- learning experiences (instructional strategies) that worked particularly well for them
- experiences that did not work for them
- questions that have come up along the way that they want help with
- ideas for important learnings or learning strategies that they might like to try in the future

The goal in the case of learning logs is to have students reflect on, analyze, describe, and evaluate their learning experiences, successes, and challenges, writing about the conclusions they draw. We have the freedom to be more or less structured in using learning logs. Certain circumstances may benefit from a high degree of structure, such as when you want students to center on and practice with a particular pattern of reasoning. In these cases, you would carefully structure learning log assignments. Under other circumstances, you may give students a great deal of freedom in logging their learning experiences. In any case, you can learn a great deal about students' academic self-concepts and achievements by viewing them through this window.

Conversations with Others

We also can derive useful information about student achievement by talking with others about the achievement of the student in question. However, this form of personal communication must be used very carefully to produce quality information.

If you ask the right questions of those who have reason to know about the achievement of a particular student, then they may be able to provide insights you are unable to generate on your own. Possible sources may include other students, other teachers, other school staff, parents, and siblings. Since these people might have sampled student performance in ways you have not, in effect, you broaden your awareness of achievement and add confidence to your assessments if you add their inferences to your information base.

If you rely on conversations with others to derive information about the achievement of your students, be sure to be a critical consumer of the information you receive. Probe the nature and quality of the evidence mustered by the information provider. Be sure you share a common understanding about the discussed achievement targets. Be sure the person with whom you converse used sound assessment methods, sampled appropriately, and controlled for his or her own biases. In other words, ask only those who are in a position to know about the achievement of your students. Further, especially in contexts where critical decisions hang in the balance, solicit information from more than just one other source, to guard against hidden bias.

Integrating Assessment into Instruction

Since instruction is conducted in large part through personal interaction between teacher and student, integrating personal communication forms of assessment into the teaching and learning process can be quite easy and very useful. One way to do this is to remain keenly aware of the nature of the role of questioning in a productive learning environment and of the nature and function of the questions we ask. The other is to take advantage of the array of possible ways of involving students in the assessment process. Let's analyze these a bit more.

The Nature of Questions

Hunkins (1995) provides a concise summary of the various ways the questioning process can draw students into constructing their own meaning from the material they study. Figure 9–4 presents a list of questioning techniques that serve specific learning functions and that have particular instructional implications. In effect, each of these techniques turn the questioning process into a partnership between teacher and student, making students responsible in part for the success of the interchange. In these ways, we encourage students to begin to evaluate the quality of their own responses.

Student Involvement in Assessment

Over and above the nature of the questions we ask our students, we have other practical means to draw them into personal communication-based assessment that have the effect of helping them become better achievers. As before, we strive to open up the process and welcome students as fully responsible partners in meeting the challenges of monitoring and maximizing their academic success. Following is a brief list of ways to do this (some of which I mentioned earlier in the chapter):

- Minimize the number of questions posed that simply require yes or no answers. Seek more complex responses as a matter of routine, so students come to expect it.
- Tap the full range of kinds of reasoning, not just recall of facts.

Technique	Function	Instructional Implications
Probing	Encourages in-depth response; clarifies respondent's intent	Must demand and provide time for response; encourages respondent to dig deeper in processing the question
Clarification	Probes the precise meaning of response and prevents misinterpretation	Sets the expectation that "vague" responses are unacceptable and encourages thoughtful, precise answers
Elaboration	Adds depth to response; encourages respondent to bring in more information	Curriculum must offer enough depth of information on key topics to permit elaboration
Redirection	Encourages respondents to approach a problem from a different perspective	Instruction must encourage flexibility in thinking, so respondents know when and how to redirect
Supporting	Furnishes respondent with cognitive and affective encouragement	Classroom assessment environment must help students feel that it is safe to take risks and that they are valued as questioners

Figure 9–4

Questioning Techniques That Draw Students into Learning

Source: Adapted from *Teaching Thinking Through Effective Questioning* (p. 216) by F. P. Hunkins, 1995, Norwood, MA: Christopher-Gordon Publishers, Inc. Adapted by permission.

- Wait for a response. Let students know that you expect an answer and will not let them off the hook by allowing them to remain silent. Once they speak, the channels of communication are open.
- Keep the whole class involved by calling on nonvolunteers, asking students to add to what someone just said, and asking them to signal if they agree or disagree.
- Turn responsibility for questioning over to students; they can ask them of each other or of you (put your own reasoning power on the line in public once in a while).
- Ask students to paraphrase each other's questions and responses.
- Ask students to address key questions in small groups, so more students can be involved.
- Offer students opportunities to become discussion leaders, posing questions of their own.
- Ask students to keep track of their own performance, such as through the use of tally sheets and diaries.
- Designate one or two students to be observers and recorders during discussions, noting who responds to what kinds of questions and how well; other teachers can do this too.
- Engage students in peer and self-assessment of performance in discussions.

- Schedule regular interviews with students, one-on-one or in groups.
- Schedule times when your students can interview you to get your impressions about how well things are going for them as individuals and as a group.

Time for Reflection

Have you studied with teachers who relied heavily on some form of personal communication as described in this chapter? How did they assess? Did they do it well?

Chapter Summary: Assessment as Sharing, Person-to-Person

The key to success in using personal communication as assessment of student achievement is to remember that, just because assessment is sometimes casual, informal, unstructured, and/or spontaneous, this does not mean we can let our guard down with respect to standards of assessment quality. In fact, we must be even more vigilant than with other forms of assessment, because it is so easy to allow personal filters, poor sampling techniques, and/or inadequate record keeping to interfere with sound assessment.

When we attend to quality standards, we use our interactions with students to reach important achievement targets, including mastery of knowledge, reasoning, knowledge and reasoning prerequisites of skill and product development competence, and affective targets. Thus, like the other three modes of

assessment, this one is quite flexible. Even though we typically don't refer to personal communication as assessment, if we start with a clear and appropriate vision, translate it into thoughtful probes, sample performance appropriately, and attend to key sources of bias, we can generate quality information in this manner.

So can students. Whether in whole class discussions, smaller collaborative groups, or working with a partner, students can be assessors, too. They can ask questions of each other, listen to responses, infer about achievement, and communicate feedback to each other. Beware, however. The ability to communicate effectively in an assessment context is not "wired in" from birth. Both you and your students must practice it, to hone it as an assessment skill.

Exercises to Advance Your Learning

Knowledge

1. Referring to the text, specify the roles of objectivity and subjectivity in assessments based on personal communication.

2. Study the section in this chapter on the kinds of achievement targets that can be

reflected in personal communication-based assessments. Learn which targets fit this mode, which do not, and why.

3. Refer to the text and list the strengths, limitations, and keys to effective use of the six formats of personal communication assessment: instructional questions and

answers, conferences and interviews, class discussions, oral exams, journals and logs, and conversations with others about a student's achievement.

4. Referring to the text, identify and describe in your own words the key considerations in sampling student performance via personal communication.

5. Learn the list provided at the end of the chapter of ways to engage students in the assessment process using personal communication.

Reasoning

1. Assume that, as a first-grade teacher, you are about to read a story about volcanoes. To ensure that your students will understand the story, you want to be sure they know the meanings of several key words used by the author. You decide to ask a few questions of the class before beginning. How would you handle this assessment situation? Would personal communication play a role? If so, how? How might you appropriately sample achievement?

2. Assume you are a high school chemistry teacher needing to verify student adherence to safety rules in the science lab. How would you do so? What role might assessment via personal communication play? How might you appropriately sample performance?

3. In the scored discussion example at the beginning of the chapter, Lynn, the teacher, turned assessment and feedback responsibility over to the students. Students worked together to devise a set of expectations, observe each other, and share feedback. Do you think, therefore, that this represented a high-quality assessment? Why?

4. Identify three specific purposes each for assessment, achievement targets, and

classroom contexts in which you would turn to personal communication as your method of assessment.

5. For each instance identified in exercise 4, identify any potential sources of interference that might lead to mismeasurement. How would you control each?

Skills

1. Enlist a colleague, friend, or classmate as a subject for this activity. Find a topic of mutual interest, such as a piece of literature, a hobby, a professional activity, or a favorite place. Plan and conduct an interview of your subject to find out how much that person really knows about this topic. Prepare your specific questions and/or other interaction ideas in advance. Your goal is to elicit information about their knowledge and their abilities to use that knowledge to reason effectively. Before the interview, think of any potential problems that could arise and take action to prevent them. Keep a list of both ideas and problems. Conduct your interview, then analyze your work. Were you able to collect quality information from your interaction? Why? If not, why not?

Dispositions

1. Some have argued that assessments that arise out of personal communication are too fraught with danger of bias due to subjectivity to justify their use as a source of classroom assessment information. Do you agree? Why?

2. Do you feel that assessment based on personal communication could be more beneficial to students and their academic well-being when used for some purposes than others? If so, for what classroom assessment purposes might they be most helpful? Why? Please be specific.

Special Ongoing Assessment Project: Part 6

From the unit of instruction you selected for your ongoing development project, identify an achievement target or set of targets that could provide a basis for an assessment that relies on personal communication in one of the forms described in this chapter. Refine your vision of the target(s) to a sufficient level of precision to be able to create the assessment instruments and procedures needed to sample student performance in a manner that avoids the common sources of bias and distortion that can creep into such assessments.

Classroom Applications

For the teacher alone to know and understand the criteria is not sufficient. The student must also know what the teacher expects, how to demonstrate satisfactory completion of the requirements, and how to achieve outstanding performance. . . . Whatever the level of the student or the content of the class, the student should always be able to expect that there will not be any hidden rules.

BRENDA LOYD, 1949–1995

CHAPTER 10 Assessing Reasoning Proficiency

CHAPTER 11 Performance Assessments of Skill and Product Targets

CHAPTER 12 Assessing Student Dispositions

CHAPTER 13 Classroom Perspectives on Standardized Testing

Assessing Reasoning Proficiency

CHAPTER ROADMAP

In earlier chapters, we established the critical importance of reasoning proficiency both as a target in its own right and as a foundation for other competencies. Virtually every national analysis of and commentary on the state of education completed in recent years has referred to the need to develop proficient problem solvers if we are to be competitive in the world economy of the twenty-first century. For this reason, the 1980s and 1990s have become the decades of the reasoning and problem-solving curriculum. In this chapter, we will explore the objectives of this curriculum and the transformation of reasoning targets into quality assessments.

As a result of studying the material presented in Chapter 10, reflecting on that material, and completing the learning exercises presented at the end of the chapter, you will gain control over important content knowledge, as evidenced by your ability to do the following:

1. List guidelines for selecting or developing a vision of reasoning and problem solving for use in your classroom.

2. Summarize some important ways of reasoning and their interrelationships.

3. Specify assessment formats capable of tapping student reasoning.

4. Identify keys to effectively translating reasoning into assessment exercises and scoring criteria.

5. Articulate ways to integrate the assessment of reasoning into day-to-day classroom teaching and learning.

In addition, you will be able to use that knowledge to reason as follows:

1. Be in touch with the quality of your own reasoning, self-assessing according to high intellectual standards.

2. Translate various kinds of reasoning and problem solving into assessment methods usable in your own classroom.

Further, you will master the following skills, resulting in the following products:

1. Carry out the steps required to create assessments that tap various forms of reasoning and problem solving and that meet the five standards of quality.

Finally, it is my hope that you will become predisposed to do the following:

1. See reasoning as an essential achievement target for your students.
2. Appreciate the role of foundational knowledge and understanding—retrieved both from memory and through reference materials—in the reasoning process.
3. See focused, high-quality assessments of reasoning and problem solving as essential.
4. Feel the need to launch your own personal professional search for a vision of reasoning proficiency to which you can make a commitment.

As you read this chapter, continue to keep in mind our big classroom assessment picture. The shaded areas of Figure 10–1 indicate the relevant achievement targets and assessment methods.

Teaching and assessing reasoning proficiency represent significant challenges for many teachers. The challenges come in two parts. The first is defining what it means to reason well, and the second is transforming that vision into quality assessments.

I encounter the depth of the challenge of defining the target as I travel the continent offering workshops on the assessment of reasoning. I start every workshop with three questions. First, I ask participating teachers, How many of you expect your students to become proficient at reasoning as a result of the time spent in your classroom? Virtually every teacher in every audience will raise her or his hand. I then ask question two: How many of you can define for me *precisely* what it means to be an effective thinker in your classroom? Almost no hands remain raised.

Given this response, my third question becomes moot: How many of you can assure me that you use quality assessments to gather dependable information about student reasoning proficiency? In the absence of a sharply focused vision of this target, quality assessment remains beyond reach.

The key question is, What does it mean to reason? How is reason evidenced, for example, by students who perform the following acts?

- Write a good critical review of a piece of literature.
- Solve a complex math problem.
- Successfully debate an issue.
- Predict the results of a science experiment.

	SELECTED RESPONSE	ESSAY	PERFORMANCE ASSESSMENT	PERSONAL COMMUNICATION
Know				
Reason				
Skills				
Products				
Dispositions				

Figure 10–1
Aligning Achievement Targets and Assessment Methods

- Combine insight from science and social studies to solve an environmental problem.

And, as an additional, equally critical question, How do we determine if students have met appropriate standards of excellence in reasoning?

These questions illustrate the targets and classroom assessment issues we face in this chapter. But there is good news for those who face this challenge. As we endeavor to define and assess reasoning and problem-solving proficiencies, we can stand on the shoulders of clear thinkers who have worked to define them and to create sound assessment ideas. Their work has revealed a very important set of achievement targets in far richer detail than ever before. So the good news is that we are now in a position to help more students become more effective and proficient reasoners and problem solvers today than at any time previously.

But, to reach this goal, each and every teacher must develop (1) a highly refined vision of reasoning and problem-solving proficiencies, (2) a clear sense of what it means to reason effectively, and (3) skill in translating his or her vision into quality assessment exercises and performance criteria. Then and only then will we be ready to integrate those assessments into the teaching and learning process, and to give students responsibility for monitoring the quality of their own reasoning.

As you shall see, all four basic forms of assessment—selected response, essay, performance assessment, and personal communication—have important contributions to make in the assessment of reasoning. We can comfortably translate a variety of important forms of reasoning into selected response formats. Others are better triggered with carefully crafted essay exercises, performance exercises, or thoughtful dialogue with students. We will examine examples of all of these.

Five Guiding Principles

But before we begin our examination, let me share some guidelines that should influence your work in this arena.

Guideline 1: Formulate Clear Targets

By now, you're probably growing weary of hearing this. But the fact is, of all the kinds of achievement targets discussed in this book, none places a greater premium on your sharp vision of the valued target than does reasoning. Each of us must enter our classroom with a refined conceptual understanding of the reasoning process, the vocabulary needed to communicate effectively, and the strategies needed to share both the vision and its vocabulary with our students. Without such a clear sense of the kinds of reasoning students are to master and the standards of quality we will apply, both we and our students will remain adrift in uncertainty about their success. Here's why: Remember how the various kinds of achievement targets discussed in this book work together to promote academic success? Only when requisite *knowledge* is available can we use that knowledge to *reason* and solve problems. Remember also that we can reason things through to generate new insights, thus building new knowledge and understanding through good thinking. Reasoning is the process of generating understanding. So these targets are intertwined.

Further, knowledge and reasoning proficiencies underpin complex *skills* that, in turn, lead to the ability to create quality achievement-related *products*. And by successfully figuring out how to use our skills to make something new, we gain new understanding of how to be successful. So once again, we see the interrelationship among these four achievement targets. Each is indispensable. In essence, they all grow together. As students gain access to and come to comprehend ever more complex and differentiated arrays of knowledge, they can solve more and more complex problems, permitting them to master increasingly sophisticated skills and to create products of increasing complexity. And, as they grow, our students gain confidence as problem solvers, predisposing them to strive for further excellence. Thus it becomes clear that sound *reasoning* represents a critical building block in the development of academic competence.

As you study the reasoning process presented here and in other professional literature and plan how to share it with your students, keep the following three selection criteria in mind:

1. Develop a vision of the reasoning achievement target that you can believe in and invest time in mastering yourself—a framework you can become so comfortable with that you can effortlessly integrate its valued reasoning processes into every nook and cranny of your classroom. I urge you—**take this responsibility seriously.**

2. Be sure your vision of reasoning makes sense in the real world, that it reflects the manner in which individuals solve important everyday problems. The standards we apply in evaluating the quality of our reasoning are the same as those we use in adult life.

3. You must be able to translate the forms of reasoning you teach and the standards of quality you apply into terms that make sense to your students. You also must be able to translate the reasoning and problem-solving process into terms they can integrate and use in their academic and personal lives. You must share with them both a conceptual understanding of your expectations and a vocabulary they can use to converse with you about reasoning.

Guideline 2: Beware of the Label "Higher-order Thinking"

I believe that the common practice of differentiating between higher- and lower-order thinking is dangerous. When we differentiate in this manner, unfortunately, the honor of being labeled "lower-order thinking" always goes to the mastery and understanding of *knowledge,* of content. As a result, students come to see this kind of achievement as unimportant and don't gain access to the very content understandings they need to solve the complex problems we expect them to handle.

But, you might argue, we needed to correct our prior overemphasis on rote memorization of content to the exclusion of other important ways of achieving. I wholeheartedly agree. Perhaps the most valuable lesson we have learned in recent years from those studying cognitive processes is that rote memorization doesn't ensure understanding, and thus is not a powerful way to promote learning. But that does not mean it is unimportant to be able to gain access to knowledge from one's memory or through the use of reference resources in a problem-solving context. We can balance our targets if we continue to place curricular emphasis on the development of complex reasoning power arising out of the need to apply knowledge and understanding. A balanced sense of the relationship between these targets is critical to academic success.

Guideline 3: Acknowledge Two Ways of Knowing

Knowledge retrieved through the effective use of reference is every bit as powerful as knowledge retrieved from memory, when the objective is to solve problems. Most of us grew up in an educational environment in which one was defined as a master of content if one knew it outright and understood it. But to reiterate a key point made earlier in this book, it is far from being the only way of knowing and understanding.

I am also the master of knowledge when I can retrieve it when I need it, efficiently and in a useable form. Thank heaven my physician, my tax accountant, and my auto mechanic have learned this lesson! They cannot know outright all that they need to know to help me solve my problems. But it is crucial to my well-being that they know where to go to get the answers they need to questions that concern my health, my relationship with the IRS, and my transportation.

There are two ways for me to be a master of knowledge—know it outright and know where to get it when I need it. Hopefully, my mind will always hold much for me to tap and use productively. But in this information age, I must now acknowledge that my library and my computer will always hold more. As we discuss the meaning and assessment of reasoning proficiency in this chapter, let's agree to allow for both ways of knowing as the basis for success as a problem solver.

Guideline 4: Remember, Students Are Natural Thinkers

This may surprise some readers too—especially those with classroom experience! But seriously, we don't need to teach most students to think. The majority of students are natural thinkers from the time they arrive at school. That is, they possess those cognitive abilities they need to survive and even prosper in school and beyond. They are capable of interacting purposefully with their world, confronting problems, reflecting on solutions, solving problems, and deriving or constructing personal meaning from experience. Further, most students will use these inherent abilities as long as we don't discourage them and/or prevent them from doing so.

But here's the problem, according to critical thinking expert Richard Paul (1995): The human mind is a mixed bag of good and bad thinking, of sharp focus and fuzzy thinking, of ignorance and sound knowledge, of accurate conceptions and misconceptions, of misunderstanding and important insight, of open-mindedness and prejudice. Our challenge as teachers is to help our students learn to clean out their mental houses—to clear out the garbage and let sound reasoning prevail. With certain exceptions, our students bring with them all the tools they need to reason effectively. We must help them understand how to use those tools and how to assess when they have done it well.

Time for Reflection

Find some young children at play. Just watch them solve problems. See if you can identify some of the reasoning and problem-solving strategies they use. Look for insights, prejudices, and productive and unproductive thinking. Are they reasoning well? From your observations, what inferences do you draw about the thinking tools they bring with them to school?

Guideline 5: Share Assessment Responsibility

Teachers do not have to take complete responsibility for the assessment of students' reasoning proficiencies. Given conceptual understanding of reasoning processes, standards of quality, and a way to converse about their thinking, students can monitor their own and each other's reasoning, enjoy being part of the process, and learn a great deal along the way! Our job as teachers is to begin with a vision of how one organizes reasoning in productive ways, to share that vision with our students, to teach them to monitor their own reasoning, and to offer positive support as they come to terms with that reasoning.

Understanding Reasoning

In a very real sense, this chapter is simply a continuation of our work during the prior nine chapters to understand how to help students become critical thinkers. The whole idea of student-centered classroom assessment is one of introducing students to standards of high performance and showing them how to apply those standards to evaluate their own academic success. I intend to shift ultimate responsibility for assessing degree of success from the teacher to the student. I intend to help you see how to turn your students into lifelong evaluators and managers of the quality of their own performance. In this chapter, we will explore standards of effective reasoning and see how to turn them over to our students so they can monitor their own success in this arena of performance.

Over the past decade, many educational researchers, psychologists, and philosophers have reflected on the reasoning and problem-solving process, putting forth a dazzling array of useful ways of describing it. With the help of my teachers (identified in the next section), I have tried simply to get you started. Even so, be advised that the forms of reasoning presented may appear complex. Please don't be put off by the apparent complexity. There is nothing here you cannot master and put to very productive use in your classroom. But to gain control over these forms of reasoning, you must become a student of effective reasoning. To learn to reach this goal, you must practice. Use this chapter merely as a starting place. Then follow up, reading the references discussed herein. Do this and your students will prosper as reasoners and problem solvers. Fail to invest properly in your own understanding and your students will suffer the consequences.

Some Organizing Structures

A review of the professional literature on the topic of reasoning reveals a variety of conceptual frameworks detailing an even wider variety of useful forms of reasoning, all of which can come into play in a problem-solving context. For example, Bloom, Englehart, Furst, Hill, and Krathwohl (1956) present a taxonomy of seven "higher-order thinking skills," Marzano (1992) describes 18 "dimensions of learning" that detail different ways of reasoning, while Quellmalz (1987) simplifies these to five kinds of reasoning. These and other such frameworks receive frequent reference in our professional literature, as educators strive to assemble the problem-solving curriculum.

These ways of understanding the intricacies of reasoning can either enhance or hinder our attempts to help students become effective thinkers. They help by revealing various ways to organize our thinking productively. Sometimes we reason analytically, striving to see how the elements of a larger whole fit together. Other times we reason comparatively, seeking to understand similarities or differences. I will illustrate several of these organizing structures.

These taxonomies hinder us because many educators have interpreted them to list several independent ways of thinking, inferring that when we are reasoning in one way we are not reasoning in another. They lead us to believe that life presents challenges that call for one best kind of reasoning. If we hit on it we succeed; if not, we fail. The key to success thus would lie in knowing what pattern of reasoning to apply in what context. In fact, both school and life are far more complicated than that.

How then should we understand what it means to reason well? The answer lies in understanding various ways to organize our thinking and how those ways must come together to solve problems. Let's start by exploring a few of the commonly referenced forms of reasoning. Then we'll explore their dynamic interrelationships.

Those who have written of ways to conceptualize reasoning point out that we can reason *analytically, comparatively,* or *evaluatively.* In addition, we *synthesize, classify,* and *draw inferences.* Let's think about what these mean.

Time for Reflection

As you read about these different ways of reasoning, you will see that each possesses its own definition and each can be uniquely illustrated in understandable terms. Nevertheless, as you may have guessed, I am going to argue that they virtually never function independently of one another. Rather, these patterns work together to bring us to problem solutions. For now, as you read about these, take a few seconds with each to see if you can identify some of the ways they fit together. Note those connections for later reflection.

Analytical Reasoning.   Remember in our earlier discussions of performance assessment and writing assessment where we drew the distinction between holistic and analytical scoring? In holistic scoring we consider all of the performance criteria together and assign one score to overall performance. In analytical scoring we break performance down into its component parts (word choice, organization, voice, and the like), evaluating and assigning a score to each part. It is this sense of the meaning of *analytical* that we are speaking of here. When we reason analytically, we reason through the component parts of something: its ingredients, internal functioning, and how its parts fit together. When reporters do "news analysis" they go into a story in greater depth to study its parts.

In this case, our instructional challenges are to be sure that our students have access to whatever knowledge they need to see inside something and that they have guided practice in exercising their thought processes in this manner.

Our assessment challenge is to ask them to tap into that knowledge base and apply their reasoning skills to a novel analytical task. For example, in literature, we might provide practice in doing character analysis by having students read a new story (gathering knowledge of a new character) and asking them to generate an original analysis of this character they have just "met."

Synthesizing.   Let's say we have just finished studying the structure of the short story as a literary form. In addition, we have just finished reading a short story. We now have two different sources of knowledge and understanding about short stories to tap as we strive to integrate them. This integration process is one of *synthesizing.*

This context presents fertile ground for exploring ways to combine these various sources of information to glean insights and to draw conclusions about this form of literature. How, for example, did the author's work reflect what we learned about the structure of the short story? To answer, respondents must reason by combining knowledge of the literary form with knowledge of the story just read to draw defensible conclusions.

Incidentally, we hear a great deal of interest being expressed these days in the development of "integrated" or "thematic" instruction or curriculum. This often is described as being different from discipline-based instruction, in which students study math, science, writing skills, and so on, separately. Thematic instruction encourages students to bring knowledge and productive patterns of reasoning together from several disciplines, as they explore their particular theme, whether it be the study of a particular culture, scientific problem, or social issue. Such curricula place a premium on synthesizing insights from divergent sources and present wonderfully rich opportunities to develop and assess student mastery of this way of reasoning.

Comparative Reasoning.   *Comparative* reasoning refers to the process of figuring out how things are either alike or different. Sometimes we compare in terms of similarities, other times we contrast in terms of differences, still other times we do both. To understand this kind of reasoning, we must see that a proficient reasoner begins with a clear sense of those things to compare and then identifies the basis or bases of similarity or difference before proceeding to draw out specific points of comparison, highlighting why those particular points are important. Here are simple examples: In what way are these two poems alike and different? Given this early and this late work by this particular author, what changes do you see in style?

Classifying.   Sometimes, life presents us with reasoning challenges that ask us to categorize or *classify* things. When we budget, we classify expenses. When we analyze how we use our time, we organize events into different categories. In science, we classify plants and animals. In politics, we categorize issues and candidates. To reason productively in this manner, we must first know the categories and the attributes of things found within each, as well as the attributes of those things to be classified. Then we can compare each thing to be classified with the categorical options and place it in its appropriate group.

Inferential Reasoning.   In this case, we reason productively when we can *infer* principles, draw conclusions, or glean generalizations from accumulated evidence. Reasoning travels from particular facts to a general rule or principle. Here are two examples: Now that you have read this story, what do you think is its general theme or message? Given the evidence provided in this article about the stock market (notice, an example of using knowledge gained through reference), what is the relationship between interest rates and stock values? We help our students gain control over their inferential reasoning proficiency when we make sure they have the opportunity to access the proper knowledge from which important rules or principles arise and when we provide guided practice in drawing conclusions or generalizations.

We also reason inferentially when we apply a general rule or principle to find the solution to a problem. Reasoning here travels from the general to the specific. Given what you know about the attributes of good persuasive writing, does this piece represent good work? If this really is an example of a tragic hero in literature, what should happen next in the story? Obviously, the key instructional challenge is to be sure students have the opportunity to learn and understand the rules, generalizations, or principles we want them to apply. Then and only then can we present them with novel contexts within which to apply those rules in order to assess their reasoning proficiency.

Evaluative Reasoning.   We reason *evaluatively* when we judge the value or appropriateness of something by logically applying proper judgmental criteria. Within the context of our journey together, do you understand that the very process of evaluating the quality of student work in terms of some predetermined standards, such as writing assessment, is a classic example of evaluative reasoning? When we express and defend a point of view, we reason evaluatively.

Our instructional task is to help students understand the criteria they should be applying when they defend their point of view on an issue. Who is the best candidate for mayor? That's a matter of opinion. What are the important characteristics of a good mayor? These are the things we discuss in class. And we must address how to apply those standards in a logical manner.

Our assessment challenge is to determine if our students are able to apply those criteria appropriately, given a *novel* evaluative challenge. Do you understand, therefore, that students who are able to appropriately evaluate a piece of writing they have never seen before using a learned set of analytical rating scales are demonstrating proficiency in evaluative reasoning? It is in this sense that I say this entire book is about developing critical thinkers.

Time for Reflection

Before you read on, please be sure you completed the task framed in the previous Time for Reflection. This is a critically important reflection on your part. If you did not do it, please reread the descriptions and see if you can compare them and infer how they relate to each other. If you have noted connections, take a few minutes now to see if you can identify additional relationships between or among them.

Relationships Among Parts

As I wrote about the preceding organizing structures, I tried very hard to use descriptive vocabulary that permitted you to see connections. Please check your Time for Reflection notes about the relationships among these forms of reasoning as I discuss some of these connections. I hope that that reflection activity and your study of the six organizing structures brought you to see many important relationships. I plan here merely to share a few of my own inferences, to establish the dynamic nature of the reasoning process. Your reasoning may be different. If you are seeing rich relationships, you are reasoning in a productive manner.

- Synthesis requires inductive inference; we do it well when we see the unity arising from divergent parts.

- Complex comparisons require a prior step of analyzing the things to be compared to identify potential points of similarity and difference.

- Comparison is a form of inferential reasoning, where we must see how comparative criteria manifest themselves in each case.

- Classification involves comparison of each thing to be classified to the attributes of each category to infer which goes where.

- Inductive inference requires that we compare the pieces of evidence at hand to see what they have in common.

- Evaluation requires analysis and comparison of different points of view before coming to judgment.

- We can make evaluative judgments about the quality of any reasoning, if we have standards for what it means to do it well.

- Knowledge is not merely a prerequisite of good thinking, it also can be the *result* of good thinking. We can rely on reasoning to help us generate new understandings. A thoughtful analysis once completed can be retained for later use. An inference drawn once through careful reasoning can become a strong part of one's structure of knowledge and understanding.

So it is that different ways of reasoning form a puzzle whose pieces fit together to permit us and our students to figure things out. It is appropriate to help students see and understand the different organizing structures. In fact, we can generate some compelling assessment exercises by structuring them around these forms. It is not appropriate to promote the misconception that one can respond to those exercises merely by applying one form of reasoning. These forms are not independent; students must use them in combination to achieve well-reasoned solutions. As you will see, the key to the effective evaluation of reasoning is to identify those universal standards of sound reasoning within each structure.

Students who encounter a new math problem, debate a volatile social issue, or confront an unknown substance in a science lab bring all of these ways of reasoning into play in a rapid-fire manner, analyzing the problem to infer what knowledge bases they must bring to bear. Beyond school, when students are confronted with a drug pusher, an angry classmate, or the demands of peer pressure, they must think clearly and select a proper course of action. Those who are masters of their own reasoning and who know how to use their minds effectively have a strong chance of generating productive responses to such circumstances.

As teachers, how do we determine what learning experiences will set our students up for this success and how do we know if those experiences worked? We must assess their reasoning, at the same time preparing them to take charge of monitoring the quality of their own reasoning.

Before we address the assessment side of this equation, let's collect our thoughts with a few additional insights about what it means to be a proficient reasoner.

Summary of Reasoning Processes

I hope it is clear by now that, if we have nothing to think about, there will be no thinking. In other words, we cannot reason productively without access to the knowledge and understanding needed to solve the problem at hand. Imagine trying to analyze, compare, synthesize, or evaluate something that you know nothing about. To be sure, there are many productive ways to come to know and understand. But what is essential is that we rely on these ways as part of the reasoning process.

If the meaning of this process we call *reasoning* is becoming clear to you, you will understand the following:

- Reading doesn't just *require* reasoning—reading *is* reasoning. As you gather new information from the text you are reading at this second, you are comparing its message to your existing structure of knowledge and understanding, evaluating what I am saying to you, inferring what to retain and change in that structure, synthesizing what you know already with what you are learning, and building your own understanding. You are reasoning.

- Writing is reasoning. When we compose new text, we analyze what it is we wish to say, infer how to say it well, and evaluate our results to see if we have met standards of effective communication.

- Math problem solving is reasoning. The problem presents a challenge to be analyzed, so we can infer what math rules and principles apply. We use those procedures to generate a solution—something we may then evaluate in terms of its appropriateness.

- Science is reasoning. We pose hypotheses, make predictions, gather data, analyze them, and draw conclusions. These are the key steps in the scientific reasoning process. And remember, we use these steps most productively when we are masters of the science *knowledge* needed to solve complex problems.

- The creation of art is reasoning. The musician is constantly evaluating performance in relation to the demands of the music and drawing inferences about how to improve. The painter creates visual images by comparing the emerging painting to some internal or external standards of quality and inferring how to improve it.

One Final Point

One question often posed by primary-grade teachers during my workshops on assessing reasoning is, How do I know what is developmentally appropriate for my students? At what age can students be expected to think? Lynn, our elementary teacher friend, has some thoughts on this topic:

"I'll never forget when I first started my career as a first-grade teacher. I thought my job was to begin to fill their little heads with the knowledge of the world. Somewhere, I had learned that they weren't ready to figure things out yet.

That was not "developmentally appropriate." Someone told me that Piaget said there were stages they go through and my kids weren't there yet. The textbooks we used and the curriculum outline I was given said, in effect, that I needed to rely pretty much on direct instruction and rehearsal to teach them what they needed to know. I was into lots of rote learning.

"But something began to trouble me right from the start. I remember Amy. One time I just happened to walk past her desk while she was working on a simple word puzzle. She was stumped, so I filled in a blank for her. Well, you'd think I had just insulted her best friend. 'No,' she complained, pushing me away, 'I wanted to figure it out myself. I can do it. Don't help me.'

"Then there was the time Bart was really frustrated with a math problem. Unlike Amy, he wanted my help. But I was busy with other students on another project and asked him to be patient. Patience was never Bart's long suit. Right then, Esteban came up and said he could help Bart figure it out. They'd work together.

"Several other such incidents finally helped me get it through my thick head that I had been wrong about these kids. When the light finally went on in my mind, I began to realize that they *are* thinkers. Their growing little brains are working just fine, thank you very much. They aren't just empty boxes for me to fill with knowledge. They can be problem solvers if I just give them a chance. From then on, we began to have some real fun and to do some serious learning by reasoning things through."

Lynn is right. The conventional wisdom is that the vast majority of students can reason from the day they arrive at school. From the outset, they can figure out what things are made up of (analysis), how ideas can fit together (synthesis), how things are alike and different (comparison), how to categorize, and how to draw simple inferences. However, they are severely limited in the range of knowledge and understanding they bring to their reasoning challenges—especially when it comes to school subjects. Further, as mentioned above, misconceptions and prejudices may abound. For these reasons, we must help our students clean out and rebuild their understandings and show them how to use their abilities to figure things out as they confront increasingly complex challenges through their schooling years.

Matching Method to Target

The transformation of reasoning targets into selected response test items, essay exercises, performance tasks, or discussion or interview questions is straightforward, once we understand the reasoning process. In all cases, we must pose challenges that ask students to tap what they know and to use that to figure something out. Before we examine some examples, let me share a set of related insights that I have found useful.

The Question Is Key to Success in Assessing Reasoning

When it comes to selecting an assessment method for reasoning targets, the question is everything. The context from which the question arises suggests the proper assessment method and tells us whether we will, indeed, tap students' reasoning, or merely their rote recall. Let me explain.

Type of Question Is Key to Method.   Paul (1995) suggests that the questions we pose in reasoning contexts fall into three categories:

1. those with one right answer
2. those with better or worse answers, depending on the quality of the reasoning used
3. those with as many different answers as there are human preferences

Questions that fall into category one arise from disciplines within which we have an acknowledged system for determining one correct answer, such as mathematics. Questions that are matters of recall or that call for the application of established bodies of knowledge and reasoning principles fit here:

Combining what this map tells you about average rainfall with your knowledge of how plants grow, where on the map would you expect to find the highest-yielding agricultural regions?

These types of questions permit the effective use of selected response assessment because they lead to a right answer. Personal communication may also be a suitable assessment method if the context is right.

Questions in category two require that respondents understand the issue at hand, bring accurate and appropriate knowledge to bear, and figure out a sound answer:

How did differences in the economies of the North and South contribute to the outcome of the Civil War?

In this case, there is no single correct answer. Rather, the quality of the response turns on the quality of the respondent's reasoning. This type of question lends itself to essay assessment, or to performance assessment if the context is right. Both will require subjective evaluation criteria reflective of the relevant reasoning quality. We will consider some of these criteria later in this chapter.

This second category also can include selected response questions that call for the best answer from among several correct answers. These cases require effective reasoning to make the important differentiation among response options.

Category three questions are matters of personal opinion or personal preference:

Which car do you prefer?

What kind of vacation do you wish to take?

In this case, even though the answers require evaluative reasoning, there is no basis for determining appropriateness either in terms of correctness or rationality of underlying reasoning. Thus, while they are related to our personal well-being, they have no place in classroom assessment of academic success.

Novel Exercises Trigger Reasoning.   Sound assessment requires that respondents see assessment exercises for the first time at the time they are to respond. You may have noticed in the previous section that I made consistent reference to this need to present novel exercises if we wish to gain insight into student reasoning. Casey, our high school teacher friend, explains why:

"In one of my classes, we study various forms of government. My students are expected to master specific knowledge about different governmental structures. As they are learning about the various structures, from time to time I ask them to brainstorm a list of similarities and differences between and among different governments—to compare them. Other times, I ask them to use what they know to draw conclusions about the functions of government. As they do so, we write their ideas on the chalkboard. These both require complex reasoning—right? I regard these as challenging, but always engaging, exercises. Sometimes, my kids struggle with them.

"But let's say we do the brainstorming comparison exercise to glean important similarities and differences between two countries' governments. After we list their responses on the chalkboard, I tell my students how important that list of similarities and differences is, and inform them that they had better learn it because it will be on the final exam next week. When this same exercise, which tapped rich comparative and inferential reasoning during class, appears as an essay exercise on the final, what kind of reasoning is it assessing?

"I hope your answer is 'recall.' Any time my instruction asks my students to respond from rote memory, the assessment of those responses taps nothing more than that—regardless of what the exercise looks like. So how do we get beyond recall at testing time? By posing questions that the students have never seen before. These are the only kinds of exercises that engage the wheels of the reasoning process."

Casey's in-class brainstorming task assesses more than recall because the students are forced to do more than simply remember what they know about government. When the challenge is new, the students must dip into their knowledge, retrieve the right information, and use it in practiced, productive reasoning. If they have seen the question before, there is no guarantee that these steps will be required.

Please do not infer from this that turning an in-class reasoning exercise into recall items on a test is necessarily a bad idea. Sometimes, you might regard results of such classroom activities as well-worth knowing outright. When this happens, by all means put them on the test—but as recall exercises, nothing else.

Time for Reflection

Casey's comments trigger an important assessment question. What if I posit an exercise on an exam that requires both the retrieval of useful knowledge and the ability to use it productively in a complex reasoning activity and the student fails to respond appropriately? Because both knowledge and reasoning are mixed up in the exercise, I cannot explain the failure in a manner that permits me to plan how to help that student. If failure was due to a lack of knowledge, I do one thing. If it was due to flawed reasoning, I do another. If I assess merely to certify competence and for no other reason, I don't care why the student failed. But if I assess to further student success, I care deeply why this failure occurred. Let's say you were assessing to promote success. Can you think of any ways to prevent this dilemma from arising?

Selected Response

Sometimes we can effectively and efficiently assess student reasoning proficiency by posing questions that lead the respondents to one best answer if they reason appropriately. We can translate five of the six ways discussed at the beginning of the chapter into such test exercises, if we wish. The one exception is evaluative reasoning, which requires that the student formulate and present an original defense of the judgment made. More about this soon. Study the examples offered in Table 10–1.

Table 10–1
Sample Selected Response Exercises That Require Reasoning

Reasoning	Illustration
Analysis	Of the four laboratory apparatus setups illustrated below, which will permit the user to carry out a distillation? (Offer four diagrams, one of which is correct.)
Synthesis	If we combine what we know about the likely impact of strong differences in barometric pressure and in temperature, what weather prediction would you make from this map? (Accompany the exercise with a map and several predictions, one of which is most likely.)
Comparison	What is one important difference between igneous and sedimentary rocks? (Offer several differences, only one of which is correct.)
Classification	Given what you know about animal life of the arid, temperate, and arctic regions, if you found an animal with the following characteristics, in which region would you expect it to live? (Describe the case and offer regions as choices.)
Inference	From the evidence provided to you in the graph, if water temperature were to go up, what would happen to the oxygen content of that water? (Provide a graph depicting the relationship between the two and offer conclusions as choices.)

In all such cases, the questioner must anticipate the form(s) of reasoning the respondent will use and frame the anticipated inference in advance. There may be just one or more than one defensible answer, but the array of possibilities must be clear. If there is more than one, respondents must be advised to use their reasoning skills to find the best one or all correct responses. The questioner must know the answer(s) expected of the reasoner before asking the question.

Having said this, however, I hasten to point out that we must always remain open to the possibility that our students might out-think us! They may come up with solidly defensible inferences that we had not considered. When this happens, we should give them credit for their insight.

In any event, the evaluation of the quality of student reasoning is based on the correctness of their answers. If the exercise is well constructed and respondents reason well, they answer correctly. In the context of assessing reasoning, the strengths of selected response assessment are the same as those of all applications of this method: tight control over the reasoning sampled within test items, the possibility of obtaining comparable results across multiple students, and great efficiency in doing so. We can administer a large number of test items per unit of testing time, permitting us to sample broadly. But always remember, if they are to tap *reasoning* proficiency, our exercises must offer new challenges.

One major limitation of this format is its inability to tap multistage, complex reasoning completed over a period of time. Another problem is our inability to identify and help the misinformed student who selects the incorrect response but relies on sound reasoning processes.

Essay

We can pose essay exercises that ask our students to convey the nature and quality of their reasoning in brief written responses. For instance, we might tap their abilities to reason by asking them to figure out this analytical problem:

> *Break air pollution down into its different sources, detailing how they can combine with each other to lead to an air stagnation alert.*

Or we could investigate reasoning in the context of evaluative probes:

> *Evaluate arguments for and against irrigating deserts to produce food. Take a position on this issue and defend it. Make explicit the criteria you are using as the basis for your position and be sure to apply them in a logical manner.*

We may use similar probes to determine if our students can use their reasoning proficiencies to compare, categorize, or infer.

However, in this case, the evaluation of the quality of the student's response is not quite as straightforward as it was with selected response. We have entered the realm of subjective assessment and so must devise appropriate scoring schemes. More about that later in the chapter.

Clearly, the strength of this method for assessing reasoning is the richness of insight it can offer, provided respondents are proficient writers. Not only can we determine if the underpinning knowledge and understanding are present, but also, we can determine if students have reasoned well. The major drawback is the complexity and time demands of scoring. We have already discussed in earlier chapters how to get around both problems. We will review them again later in this chapter.

Performance Assessment

In this case, our exercises must ask students to reveal their proficiency either by (1) reasoning in some publicly visible manner so the nature and quality of their thought processes are apparent for all to see, or by (2) creating a tangible product that contains within it evidence of the reasoning that led to its creation. One way to accomplish option two is to ask for a public display reflective of the embedded reasoning. Marzano, Pickering, and McTighe (1993) offer an example:

> You have volunteered to help out at your local library with their literacy program. Once a week after school, you help people learn how to read. To encourage your student to learn, you tell her about the different kinds of literature you have read, including poems, biographies, mysteries, tall tales, fables, and historical novels. Select three types of literature and compare them using general characteristics of literature that you think will help your student see the similarities and differences. Be ready to present a visual presentation of the comparison. (p. 98)

Or, by simply changing the display of reasoning prowess from a visual presentation to a speech detailing the comparison, we switch to option one. Those familiar with science fairs will recognize that they require a combination of a public display of the reasoning carried out and public commentary on that thinking.

However, a completely different approach to conducting a skill-based performance assessment of reasoning skill might be to pose a problem, such as a science challenge, and observe students as they set about solving it. A science teacher friend of mine presents students with two seemingly identical glasses of soda, but one is the diet version. Their task is to identify which is which. She observes carefully as they proceed, specific performance criteria in hand.

Her product-based performance assessment version of this exercise asks students to prepare a written report detailing how they solved the problem, including (1) the steps they completed to solve the problem, (2) the results of each step, and (3) how they decided on each succeeding step. She sees their analytical, comparative, inductive, deductive, and other forms of reasoning come alive in these reports.

In all of these cases, the key to assessment success is to apply performance criteria that reflect the quality of reasoning demonstrated.

Personal Communication

This assessment option, like performance assessment, is labor intensive because of the need to conduct direct interactions with students; nevertheless, many contend that it provides the clearest window into student reasoning. To begin with, it allows us to ask those follow-up questions that probe more deeply into student reasoning. We can ask why they responded or thought as they did. When we ask focused questions, exploring the depths of student responses, we can both highlight good thinking and uncover misconceptions and inadequate reasoning.

In another form, this kind of assessment permits us to listen to students "think aloud" as they solve the problems we pose. Math teachers often report that the easiest way to see and understand the mistakes their students are making in solving problems is to have them talk about their reasoning as they do it. Many reading teachers ask students to retell the story in their own words. By interspersing strategic questioning, these teachers generate insights into analytical, comparative, or other forms of reasoning.

A great advantage of this option is that we can tap reasoning proficiency with our students one-on-one or through group discussions. Just remember, to assess reasoning skills, the questions we pose during these interchanges must require that students address novel problems.

With personal communication-based assessments, sometimes our questions might have right answers. If students reason effectively, they will get them right. Other times, reasoning proficiency is reflected in extended, more complex discussions. In these cases, we face the challenge of subjectively applying more complex evaluative criteria like those that characterize essays or performance assessments. Let's discuss that next.

Time for Reflection

As you look back over these applications of our four basic assessment methods to the assessment of reasoning proficiency, what do you see that those applications have in common? What are the most prominent differences among them?

Judging Reasoning Proficiency

As our students respond to our reasoning challenges, we must be prepared to judge the quality of those responses. Indeed, we must be prepared to teach them to judge the quality of their own responses. The essential point is that it is insufficient for our students to demonstrate that they can reason analytically, comparatively, or evaluatively if they attempt to reason in these ways and do it badly. Rather, our goal and theirs must be to reason *well*.

As stated, when we rely on carefully constructed, high-quality selected response test items or on direct questions posed to students that have right answers, evaluation is not a problem. In fact, if we develop our multiple-choice items carefully, as mentioned earlier in the book, we can actually use the students' incorrect responses to reveal the very nature of the flaws in their reasoning. You will recall that we do this by building the distractors (incorrect response options) around common misconceptions and common mistakes in reasoning. Students who choose those answers reveal to us how we can help them do better next time.

But, as mentioned, when we turn to essays, performance assessments, and complex personal interactions for our evidence of proficiency, we face real difficulties. Here again, however, we have good news. In recent years, several clear thinkers have been working on this problem and can offer us some real solutions.

One of these is Paul (1995), whose analysis of the critical-thinking process leads us to important evaluation insights. Essentially, Paul's basic premise is that all reasoning has a universal underlying structure and can therefore be evaluated in terms of a universal set of quality standards. Because his excellent analysis of reasoning is very broad and complex, I am unable to cover it all in this introductory text. However, with his permission, I offer here a simplified version that retains the basic integrity of Professor Paul's total model.

The Elements of Reasoning

To begin with, all reasoning, regardless of its form, takes place for a *purpose*. We reason well when we consistently center on that purpose. Why are we comparing, analyzing, or classifying? In addition, all reasoning is focused on a *central problem* to be solved, question to be answered, or issue to be resolved. What is it that we are reasoning about? Third, the reasoning process virtually always is conducted from a particular *perspective* or point of view, typically that of the reasoner. In addition, those who reason virtually always bring background experience and data, in the form of *information,* concepts, and ideas, to bear. And finally, reasoning leads to *conclusions,* which have their own *implications* and consequences. Essentially, Paul suggests that it is within these parts that we can assess the quality of student reasoning. Let's see how.

Purpose.   The criteria by which we might evaluate a student's essay, public presentation, or product (such as a term paper or exhibit) in terms of that student's attention to a central purpose for reasoning might include the following:

- clarity of the statement of purpose
- significance of that purpose
- achievability of the purpose
- consistency of attention to the stated purpose throughout the presentation

Poor-quality performance would be evidenced by a lack of clarity, a trivial purpose, and/or unrealistic or contradictory purposes.

Central Problem.   All reasoning represents someone's attempt to answer an important question, figure out the solution to some problem, or resolve some central issue. In this case, we seek the following:

- a clearly articulated question
- subject matter of some significance
- an answerable question
- a relevant issue

Our students fall short of the target if their central question is unclear, insignificant, unanswerable, or irrelevant.

Perspective.   Reasoning is virtually always carried out from some point of view. Accordingly, reasoning is better when "multiple, relevant points of view are sought out, articulated clearly, empathized with fairly and logically and applied consistently and dispassionately" (Paul, 1995, p. 159). This suggests evaluative criteria that center on the following:

- flexibility of point of view
- fairness of perspective
- clarity of perspective
- breadth of point of view

If the point of view taken carries with it assumptions that are unclear, unjustified, or contradictory, the quality of the resulting reasoning will suffer.

Information, Concepts, and Ideas.   Reasoning is only as sound as the background facts, concepts, and ideas brought into the problem-solving process. We reason well when we rely on evidence that is all of the following:

- clearly presented
- relevant to the issue at hand
- sufficiently deep, given the problem
- accurate
- consistently applied

Students fail to perform adequately if their reasoning is based on supportive material that is unclear, irrelevant, superficial, inaccurate, biased in a self-serving manner, or not carefully applied to the problem.

Conclusions and Implications.   Reasoning is only as sound as the conclusions it leads us to. If we fail to understand the implications of those conclusions, we attain an incomplete result. We seek conclusions that are all of the following:

- clearly stated
- justifiable and justified in the presentation
- compelling, given the purpose and the problem at hand

Time for Reflection

Take a few minutes to review the listed elements and create a simple checklist of key attributes of sound reasoning you might give to students to guide their work.

Universal Standards

This analysis of keys to success across the various elements of reasoning has led Paul to articulate "intellectual standards that apply to thinking in every subject" (1995, p. 63). Those expectations are listed in Table 10–2.

Performance Criteria for Reasoning.   But how do we complete the translation of these performance continuums into a set of performance criteria that we can use to evaluate student performance and that we can teach students to apply to their own reasoning? Once again, Paul (1995) provides concrete guidance. Table 10–3 depicts his version of those criteria for the evaluation of a student's treatment of *purpose,* the first of his elements of reasoning. Note that he describes performance characteristics of both good and bad reasoners and illustrates what positive and constructive negative feedback might look like in each case.

Time for Reflection

This activity is best completed by teams working together and sharing the task. Given the five-part outline of elements of reasoning provided and the model performance criteria and feedback just presented, complete a set of descriptions of high- and low-quality performance for the central problem, perspective, information, and conclusion elements. Also generate examples of feedback you might provide to students. As an extension of this work, refer if possible to Paul (1995), where he too has completed this task. Compare his work to yours. (If you do this, remember that we simplified a bit here. Paul's work is more comprehensive.)

Table 10–2
Paul's Standards of High- and Low-quality Reasoning

Thinking that is:		Thinking that is:
Clear	vs	Unclear
Precise	vs	Imprecise
Specific	vs	Vague
Accurate	vs	Inaccurate
Relevant	vs	Irrelevant
Plausible	vs	Implausible
Consistent	vs	Inconsistent
Logical	vs	Illogical
Deep	vs	Superficial
Broad	vs	Narrow
Complete	vs	Incomplete
Significant	vs	Trivial
Adequate *(for purpose)*	vs	Inadequate
Fair	vs	Biased or One-Sided

Source: From *Critical Thinking: How to Prepare Students for a Rapidly Changing World* (p. 63) by R. Paul, 1995, Santa Rosa, CA: Center for Critical Thinking. Reprinted by permission.

Table 10–3
Sample of Paul's Performance Criteria of Effective Reasoning

Purpose *(All reasoning has a purpose.)*		
Fundamental Standards:	1) Clarity of Purpose, 2) Significance of Purpose, 3) Achievability of Purpose, 4) Consistency of Purposes	
Failures of Purpose:	1) Unclear Purpose, 2) Trivial Purpose, 3) Unrealistic Purpose, 4) Contradictory Purposes	

Good Reasoners:	*Bad Reasoners:*	*Feedback to Students:*
take the time to state their purpose clearly	are often unclear about their central purpose	(–) You have not made the purpose of your reasoning clear. What are you trying to achieve? Whom are you trying to persuade? (+) Your paper reflects an excellent sense of unity of purpose. It all fits together like pieces of a puzzle.
distinguish it from related purposes	oscillate between different, sometimes contradictory, purposes	(+) You do a good job of distinguishing different but related goals. (–) You seem to have a number of different purposes in mind. I am not sure how you see them as related. You seem to be going off in somewhat different directions.
periodically remind themselves of their purpose to determine whether they are straying from it	lose track of their funda-mental end or goal	(–) After the second paragraph you seem to wander from your purpose. How do your 3rd and 4th paragraphs relate to your central goal? (+) I like the way you periodically show the reader how the points you are making all add up to a central conclusion.
adopt realistic purposes and goals	adopt unrealistic purposes, set unrealistic goals	(+) You make a wise decision not to try to accomplish too much. Accomplishing a little, well, is almost always better than failing in a grand and sweeping design. (–) You try to accomplish too much in so short a paper.
choose significant purposes and goals	adopt trivial purposes and goals as if they were significant	(–) Your paper would have been stronger if you had chosen a more important goal. (+) The goal of your paper is worthwhile and well-chosen.

Source: From *Critical Thinking: How to Prepare Students for a Rapidly Changing World* (p. 157) by R. Paul, 1995, Santa Rosa, CA: Center for Critical Thinking. Reprinted by permission.

Summary of Judging Reasoning Proficiency

We are free to assess reasoning proficiencies using all of our available methods. Successful use of each, as always, requires a clear sense of the target. We can rely on exercises that ask our students to reason in any of a variety of directions, such as comparative or analytical reasoning. We must remain constantly aware of the need to present novel exercises and of the fact that many forms of reasoning will come into play as our students respond to any particular exercise. We may ask questions that require effective reasoning to find the one correct or best answer, or we may pose open-ended essay or performance exercises that elicit original responses. When we do the latter, we need performance criteria that reflect sound reasoning with all of its various dimensions considered.

Assembling the Parts

Now that we have covered the basic ingredients of assessing reasoning, including the development of exercises and evaluative criteria, let's consider two other examples that address the assessment process from slightly different points of view.

The Norris-Ennis Framework

Norris and Ennis (1989) suggest that we can capture the essence of "critical thinking" in five steps:

1. Clarify the issue by asking critical questions.
2. Gather critical information about the issue.
3. Begin to reason through the various sides or points of view.
4. Gather further clarifying information and conduct further analysis as needed.
5. Make and communicate the decision.

In addition, Norris and Ennis expand our notion of the effectively functioning thinker and problem solver by including in their framework an important array of dispositions that define a "critical spirit," or the propensity to use one's critical thinking abilities when needed.

Critical Abilities.   Norris and Ennis (1989) contend that "critical thinking is reasonable and reflective thinking that is focused upon deciding what to do or believe" (p. 3). It is reasonable in that it is not arbitrary—it does not lead to just any conclusion but rather brings the critical thinker to the best conclusion for that context, given the information available. It is reflective in that the thinker consciously and assertively seeks the best possible solution. Thus, critical thinking, according to Norris and Ennis, is consciously directed at a goal. That goal is to find the best action or belief.

Thus, Norris and Ennis focus their analysis of the reasoning process on gathering information and applying proper criteria to judge different courses of action or points of view. Several reasoning steps come into play, as shown in Table 10–4. In this case, a student is trying to determine a proper course of action.

Time for Reflection

Following the steps shown in Table 10–4, including the practical example, proceed through Norris and Ennis's reasoning process to pose an important question in deciding this issue: Should primary-grade teachers be encour-

Table 10–4
Norris and Ennis's Critical Thinking Framework

Step in the Process	Thinking Required	Practical Example
Carry out elementary clarification of the problem	Understand the issue at hand	Should I stay home and study or visit friends?
	Analyze the points of view or positions	If I stay home, that means . . . If I go, that means . . .
	Ask and answer questions that clarify and challenge	What are the benefits of each action? What are the costs of each?
Gather basic information	Judge the credibility of various sources of information	Who can most effectively help me?
	Gather and judge information	When asked, my friends said . . . When asked, my parents said . . .
Make inferences	Make and judge deductions using available information	If I go, these will be the implications: If I stay, these will be the implications:
	Make and judge inductions	How can I meet both sets of needs?
	Make and judge value judgments	Which set of needs is most important?
Carry out advanced clarification	Define terms and judge definitions as needed	What does punishment mean? What does friendship mean?
	Identify assumptions	Study is good. I have to study now. Friends are important.
Come to best conclusion	Decide on an action	You decide!
	Communicate decision to others	And tell everyone.

Source: Adapted from *Evaluating Critical Thinking* (n.p.) by S. P. Norris and R. H. Ennis, 1989, Pacific Grove, CA: Critical Thinking Books & Software. Copyright 1989 by Critical Thinking Books & Software, 800-458-4849. Reprinted by permission of the publisher.

aged to use performance assessments in their classrooms? When you have finished, try a science issue: Should the United States continue developing a space station? And finally, think through the questions contained within any issue of special importance to you. Does the Norris and Ennis framework represent a useful process for deciding on a proper course of action or belief, in your opinion? (Think critically!)

The Critical Spirit.   Those with a critical spirit, Norris and Ennis (1989) tell us, demand sound thinking from themselves and from those around them. They strive to stay well informed from the most credible sources, remain open-minded, and take personal pleasure in dealing as completely as possible with complex problems. These are values and attitudes that predispose us to think critically, and we will see how to assess them in Chapter 12, where we discuss assessment of dispositions. For the time being, just realize that Norris and Ennis emphasize that reasoning proficiencies can go to waste in the absence of a sense of responsibility to use them.

Time for Reflection

What do you think might be some of the instructional keys to helping each of your students develop a "critical spirit?" How might you help them recognize their own critical dispositions?

Matching Method to Target.   The Norris and Ennis (1989) critical reasoning process is complex, and calls for the integrated use of various thought processes. Because of this complexity, it does *not* lend itself to selected response assessment. However, we could use the essay format to evaluate student proficiency in applying the Norris and Ennis reasoning processes. We might ask them to reason through issues that are matters of opinion, such as, "Who is the best candidate for governor?" Since there is no right answer, the quality of a student's response, according to Norris and Ennis, should be judged in terms of the five parts described previously.

Based on student responses, we could evaluate not only the quality of criteria they consider and the support they muster for their points of view, but also the nature and quality of the inferences they draw and their abilities to select credible sources of information and identify underlying assumptions made by those espousing certain points of view, among other reasoning powers.

In addition, of course, performance assessment could serve us well in assessing critical thinking. We could pose an issue for students to address individually or in groups and observe the process from a distance with clear "critical thinking skills" performance criteria in mind. We saw examples of these criteria earlier in the chapter. More follow later. We also might probe their reasoning via personal communication with a few strategically placed questions as they work through an issue, or have students reason aloud as we listen and evaluate them.

Or better yet, we could engage students in devising essay or performance assessment scoring criteria, or a checklist of key steps in the Norris and Ennis critical thinking process. We could turn at least some of the responsibility for the evaluation of their own and each other's reasoning over to our students. As they internalize the vision and reflect on their own work, they become critical thinkers.

The Quellmalz Framework

Quellmalz and Hoskyn (1988) offer us relevant help in assessing student reasoning as demonstrated in their writing, by providing performance criteria developed to evaluate analytical, comparative, inferential, and evaluative thinking as presented in that writing. An example appears in Figure 10–2, depicting their four inferential reasoning rating scales.

When students are given writing exercises that require this kind of reasoning, these criteria can prove useful. Both students and teachers can learn to apply them: students when they write and evaluate their own writing, and teachers in evaluating and providing feedback on student writing.

An application of these criteria is presented in Figure 10–3, showing an example of student work and a set of ratings of that sample using the criteria given in Figure 10–2. The student was given a passage to read about a Native American boy who had found a wounded bear cub, nursed it back to health, and then released it. The boy missed the cub, so went with his grandfather to try to see if the cub was doing well. This student was then asked to infer and write about the mood that the author was trying to create, citing information from the text supporting her conclusion.

Before you read on, please be sure to complete the following Time for Reflection exercise.

Time for Reflection

Find a colleague or classmate to work with on this activity. Both of you study and discuss the criteria spelled out in Figure 10–2 until you are quite sure you understand them. Help each other to see their meaning. Then cover up the ratings at the bottom of Figure 10–3 and independently read the sample of student writing. Each of you rate this student's reasoning performance according to the Figure 10–2 criteria, again working independently. Then compare your ratings. Do they agree? Explore any differences you find. Why did they occur? Check your work against the ratings listed at the bottom of Figure 10–3. Do they agree? What does this exercise suggest to you about how to successfully apply this subjective kind of assessment?

Involving Students in Assessing Reasoning

Our ultimate challenge is to teach students to understand, organize, and monitor their own reasoning. They come to us already thinking—it's wired in, so to speak. Our job is to point out how they can use those natural thinking processes to advan-

Inference essays are evaluated according to four features: (1) stating a valid conclusion; (2) presenting evidence in support of the conclusion; (3) explaining why the evidence supports the conclusion; and (4) when appropriate, considering alternative interpretations. The fourth feature is optional in evaluating students' written work, although it should routinely be considered in the lesson discussion.

Each feature is rated on a scale from 1 (low) to 4 (high). A score of one generally indicates that the feature is absent or inaccurate, while a score of four indicates that the feature is fully developed. Do not score the essay if it is off task. An explanation of the basis for each score point follows:

Conclusion/Generalization

4   The essay states a valid, acceptable conclusion. The conclusion is specific and accurate. The statement of the conclusion is elaborated by a fuller introduction that may include background, context, importance, or the types of information or evidence to be presented as support.

3   The essay simply states a specific, valid conclusion.

2   The essay implies the conclusion or generalization, but does not state it. Wrong conclusion with some evidence.

1   The conclusion is either not stated at all or it is inaccurately stated.

Supporting Evidence/Information

4   The essay presents evidence of information that is specific, accurate, relevant, and more than sufficient to support the conclusion.

3   The essay presents just enough evidence or information to support the conclusion. There may be some general descriptions of evidence or something slightly questionable. Most of the evidence is specific, accurate, relevant, and adequate to support the conclusion.

2   The evidence is not strong enough to support the conclusion. Some of the evidence may be specific, but most of it may be general or vague. Some evidence may be questionable. Evidence supports wrong conclusion.

1   Little or no evidence supports the conclusion. The evidence may be mostly vague, confusing, and inaccurate.

Figure 10–2

Criteria for Assessing Inference in Student Writing

Source: From *Multicultural Reading and Thinking Program Resource Notebook* (n.p.) edited by J. Hoskyn and E. Quellmalz, 1993, Little Rock, AR: Arkansas Department of Education. Copyright 1993 by Arkansas Department of Education. Reprinted by permission of the publisher.

tage to reason and solve problems both in school and beyond. The way to do this is to provide them with (1) an understanding of their reasoning processes, (2) a vocabulary with which to communicate about those processes, and (3) the skills and insights they need to evaluate their own reasoning.

To reach this goal, students must understand what it means to reason well in their classrooms. They must master the language needed to converse about that process and they must develop the ability to reflect on their own thinking and problem solving. But perhaps most importantly, as Norris and Ennis (1989) have shown us, we must help them to take charge of their own reasoning and problem-solving proficiencies—to have a "critical spirit."

Explanation

4 The essay explains clearly, accurately, and thoroughly why the evidence presented supports the conclusion. Explanatory statements may summarize the relevance of the body of evidence, or may explain each type of evidence.

3 The essay presents some explanations of why most of the evidence supports the conclusion.

2 The essay may attempt an explanatory statement, but clear reasons are not given for the relevance of the evidence to the conclusion.

1 No explanations are offered, or they are confusing or inaccurate.

Alternative Interpretations

4 The essay discusses how additional evidence or the same evidence may lead to different conclusions.

3 The essay states one or more alternative interpretations that may derive from the same or additional evidence; however, there is no discussion.

2 The essay asserts that there may be alternative interpretations, without specifying what they are.

1 No mention is made of alternative interpretations or the alternative offered seems completely inappropriate.

(The authors also offer scales for the remaining inference criteria. However, those listed here will suffice to illustrate the kinds of judgments made.)

We can take advantage of several ways to do this. Note that some of these elaborate on ideas presented in previous chapters.

- Have students think aloud or write out steps when problem solving. This allows them to hear or see their thought processes, and makes those processes easier to think and talk about.

- Be sure your students learn to label and understand the various ways in which they reason. This provides a language to use in self-reflection and in communication about reasoning. As a matter of classroom routine, constantly and explicitly model, label, and explain your reasoning.

- Ask students to question each other's reasoning in terms of Paul's (1995) universal standards. The process of searching for the proper questions to ask classmates about their reasoning helps students understand their own reasoning more completely.

- Offer students repeated opportunities to participate in developing assessment exercises that tap different kinds of reasoning, and to interpret assessment results in terms of the information they provide about performance in different problem-solving contexts.

- When asking questions that require reflection and thought, be sure to wait for a response. Reasoning takes time.

- Avoid questions during instruction that call for yes or no answers. Pose questions that require more complete thought and communication.

I am infering the modd of a story about an Indian boy looking for a cub. I think the modd is joyful. Here is why.

First, it said Red Bird could hardly control his exitment, a sign of happiness can be noticed by ones exitment.

Next, it is said that the singing of the birds echoed the singing of the Red Birds heart, Pink, yellow, and blue flowers danced in the breeze. That tells me that it was cheerful all around them.

Last, it said grandfather's eyes twinkled as they turned back toward the village. This meant that he was happy or joyful inside.

I think other conclusions are possible. I could have chosen peaceful. But I think there is more evidence that this story is joyful.

It is important to know the mood of the story so I can have a better understanding of the story and I can become a better reader.

Conclusion: 4-
The writer briefly describes the story and states a valid conclusion, based on the evidence available in the story.

Evidence: 3+
Of the descriptions available in the text, the writer cites evidence which is sufficient, accurate, and relevant.

Explanation: 4
The writer provides convincing explanations why each citation implies happiness.

Alternative Interpretation: 3-
The writer proposes a plausible alternative interpretation; however, s/he does not explain why the alternative is not as good.

Figure 10–3
Sample of Student Writing with Inference Ratings
Source: From *Multicultural Reading and Thinking Program Resource Notebook* (n.p.) edited by J. Hoskyn and E. Quellmalz, 1993, Little Rock, AR: Arkansas Department of Education. Copyright 1993 by Arkansas Department of Education. Reprinted by permission of the publisher.

- Use "concept mapping" (Novak & Gowin, 1984) to assess reasoning proficiency. In this approach, students create bursting diagrams to convey their understanding of concept relationships. Figure 10–4 shows a sample concept map about assessment as we are studying it. These maps reflect the complexity and ingredients in students' structures of knowledge, and efficiently evaluate reasoning.

- Have students develop and apply scoring criteria to evaluate responses to reasoning exercises.

- Keep the whole class involved in the reasoning process during instruction by calling on nonvolunteers, by asking students to paraphrase each other's responses, and by asking them to add to each other's responses.

- Have students keep journals in which they describe the effectiveness of their reasoning and problem solving. This provides experience using the language of reasoning and in being reflective.

- Have students build portfolios of examples of their own reasoning that provide evidence that they are becoming more and more proficient in terms of the nature and complexity of the reasoning they can carry out and the problems they can solve.

- Most importantly, remember that the assessment of students' abilities to reason and solve significant problems requires the presentation of novel challenges at assessment time. This means we must set students up for success by being sure they have access to essential knowledge via memory or reference materials and by providing practice with essential reasoning processes. Then, at assessment time, we must present brand-new exercises, so they can put their reasoning tools to work.

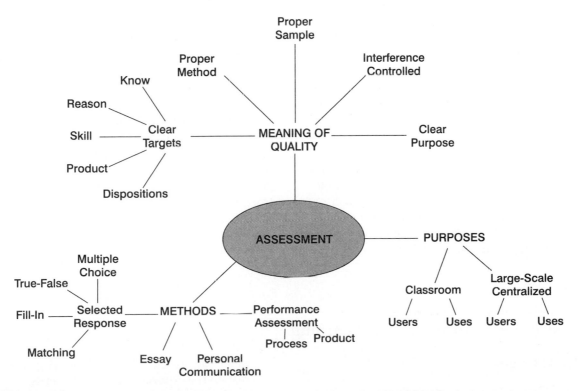

Figure 10–4
A Bursting Concept Map of Assessment

Chapter Summary: Finding the Path to Reasoning Power

If students are to hit important reasoning and problem-solving targets—if they are to become enthusiastic, confident, and competent users of their own reasoning power—they must be in touch with their own capabilities in this critical performance arena. We need not teach them to think, but we must help them understand, clean up, and organize their thinking so they can use it to maximum advantage. We must remember that the human mind does not come with a user's guide. Part of our job as teachers is to provide that guidance.

If we are to assist students, each of us must establish for ourselves that vision of the proficient problem solver that will guide instruction in our classroom. In effect, we must become comfortable with ourselves as thinkers. To the extent that we can agree across classrooms and grade levels about what it means to succeed at this, we maximize the chances of developing ever more advanced levels of student proficiency over time.

How do you choose a vision to share? First, you need a conceptual definition of *reasoning* that you are willing to master completely—so completely that it becomes second nature to you in teaching and in assessing.

Second, your vision needs to make sense in the real world. Your challenge is to understand reasoning so completely that you can translate it into real-world examples easily and comfortably. You will need many examples to share with your students of ways real-world

problems can be addressed using whatever ways of thinking you choose. It is only through these applications that you can help your students both to see the relevance of becoming more capable problem solvers, and to be motivated to take responsibility for their own reasoning and problem solving.

Third, your vision must be one that you can bring to life for your students. It must be made up of component parts that students can understand, translated into a vocabulary they can use in conversation with you and with each other. One excellent way to share the meaning of success with students is to teach them to reflect on, understand, and evaluate their own reasoning.

Our professional development challenge in preparing to assess reasoning is to understand how to translate the reasoning models we value into appropriate forms of assessment. All four basic methods—selected response, essay, performance assessment, and personal communication—can reflect valuable kinds of reasoning if users understand and adhere to the key attributes of sound assessments: Start with a complete vision of the kind of reasoning to be assessed, select an appropriate method, sample student reasoning with enough exercises to give you confidence in assessment results, control for all those sources of extraneous interference discussed in earlier chapters, and be sure assessments align with clear purposes for assessing.

Exercises to Advance Your Learning

Knowledge

1. What criteria should educators apply in selecting or developing a vision of the reasoning process to use in their classrooms?

Refer back to the chapter if you wish and restate the criteria in your own words.

2. Write a brief essay or create a simple diagram revealing that you understand the

relationships that exist among the six ways of reasoning described at the beginning of the chapter.

3. List five specific keys to the effective assessment of reasoning found in this chapter.

4. List the strengths and weaknesses of each of the four basic assessment methods when applied to the assessment of reasoning.

5. List as many different ways as you can to integrate the assessment of reasoning into day-to-day classroom teaching and learning.

Reasoning

1. Review samples of your academic work from your past and identify a paper you have written on a topic that was of interest to you. Applying Paul's (1995) universal standards of sound reasoning, evaluate your own work. Did you reason well?

2. Select a content area of interest to you in which you have developed a strong background. Within that context, develop three exercises that tap reasoning as discussed in this chapter.

3. In the content area you chose in reasoning exercise 1, select an important issue about which there might be differences of opinion and analyze that issue according to Norris and Ennis's (1989) conceptual framework.

Skill and Products

See the Special Ongoing Assessment Project following this section.

Dispositions

1. Throughout this chapter, I have argued that access to knowledge and understanding are essential components of sound reasoning. Do you agree or disagree? Why?

2. It has been common in schools in the past to make "higher-order reasoning" a special emphasis of talented and gifted programs. At the same time, it has rarely been a special thrust of remedial programs. Do you think such differentiation across program lines is appropriate? Why?

3. Obviously, reasoning is not a simple process to understand or master. It takes a keen mind and a commitment to standards of excellence. Yet I have argued that because the success of our students hinges on mastering it, we must master it ourselves. Otherwise, we can neither devise learning experiences nor provide accurate assessments. Do you agree with these statements? Has my reasoning been sound? Has it been convincing? Explain your answers.

Special Ongoing Assessment Project: Part 7

From the unit of instruction that you selected for your assessment development project, you have already identified knowledge and reasoning targets to be assessed in response to early exercises and you have devised at least one assessment of these targets. Based on the material covered in this chapter, go back to that previous work and do the following:

- Identify specific patterns of reasoning you expect students to master.

- Transform those patterns into sample exercises. Include selected response, essay, and performance exercises.

- For your selected response items, prepare brief written descriptions of why the right answer is right. What reasoning should bring the respondent to the correct answer? What flaws in reasoning will bring them to incorrect responses?

- For your essay and performance assessments, devise appropriate scoring criteria.

If you were to develop exercises and scoring standards like these and assemble them into assessments of the reasoning you expect your students to master in this unit of instruction, what would you need to do to be sure those assessments met each of our five attributes of a quality assessment?

11

Performance Assessment of Skill and Product Targets

CHAPTER ROADMAP

This chapter is made up of examples of performance assessments selected to reveal the diversity of possible applications of this rich form of assessment. These illustrations cross grade levels from primary through high school, include disciplines ranging from language arts to math and science and on to the performing arts, and cover such scoring options as rating scales and checklists of individual and group performance scored holistically and analytically. Each example teaches an important lessons about how to develop and use performance assessments. In addition, I have selected examples that help us see inside some important targets. The beauty and the curse of performance assessment lie in the clarity it demands of us.

As a result of studying the material presented in Chapter 11, reflecting on that material, and completing the learning exercises presented at the end of the chapter, you will add richness to the knowledge and understanding you developed in studying Chapter 8 about the basic performance assessment design. Specifically, you will be prepared to do the following.

1. Identify strengths, limitations, and keys to the effective development of performance tasks and criteria.
2. Understand the range of achievement targets that performance assessments can reflect.
3. Understand the full range of different forms of performance assessment.

Our goal is to be sure you are able to use that knowledge to reason as follows:

1. Select skills and products that can form the basis of quality performance assessments.
2. Evaluate performance assessments to determine if they meet standards of quality.

In addition, you will become even more skillful than you were at the end of Chapter 8 at carrying out the steps in performance assessment development. The quality of the performance assessments you design and develop will improve.

And finally, I hope you will develop an even stronger set of positive dispositions about this assessment format than you developed in studying Chapter 8. Specifically, I hope you come to believe the following:

1. Performance assessment is a viable option for collecting achievement information in the classroom.
2. Performance assessment is a valuable instructional tool in which students can and should be full partners.
3. This assessment option deserves to be used with caution and only by those schooled in and committed to meeting the most rigorous standards of quality.

No assessment method can surpass performance assessment for flexibility and range of useful classroom applications. Its potential for tapping valuable yet complex and important achievement targets is immense. Referring once again to our big picture, we will journey through that region of our targets-by-methods chart darkened in Figure 11–1.

As our journey spirals once again through the domain of performance assessment, it is important that we revisit lessons learned earlier. In Chapter 8, you will recall, we developed a three-part performance assessment design framework. We began by defining the performance to be evaluated, then devised exercises to elicit instances of that performance, and finally, we developed scoring and recording pro-

	SELECTED RESPONSE	ESSAY	PERFORMANCE ASSESSMENT	PERSONAL COMMUNICATION
Know				
Reason				
Skills			▓▓▓	
Products			▓▓▓	
Dispositions				

Figure 11–1
Aligning Achievement Targets and Assessment Methods

cedures for capturing our judgments. Because it may have been a while since you studied the basic design structure in Chapter 8, I recommend that you return to the section, "Developing Performance Exercises," in that chapter to refresh your understanding. Keep this design framework in mind as you proceed through this chapter.

You may also recall examples of performance assessment studied in earlier chapters. In Chapter 8, we delved into writing assessment and in Chapter 10 examined the assessment of reasoning proficiency. We will continue our study of such examples here.

Special Guidelines for Your Study of This Chapter

As you analyze, compare, draw generalizations about, and evaluate these examples, be a critical consumer and keep our standards of performance assessment quality in mind.

Keeping Perspective

Remember, the performance assessment examples are intended to serve only as illustrations. I offer them to trigger your imagination, stimulate your curiosity, and encourage you to learn more about this methodology. In that regard, I remind you not to simply read through this chapter and move on. Rather, reflect on the examples as a means of widening your perspectives about performance assessment. If you are teaching, consider adapting some as needed for experimental use in your classroom.

Further, while several appear to be highly refined applications, still, think of them as works in progress. One of the great lessons we are learning from our experiences in designing and developing performance assessments is that the very process of devising exercises and performance criteria helps us to refine our vision of the meaning of academic success. As a result, it is best to think of any set of performance criteria as the latest version of an ever-sharpening portrait of that success.

If you use these assessments, remember your students. It is very important that they develop a sense of both understanding and ownership of the performance criteria. This argues against the wholesale installation of other people's criteria in the classroom. Rather, even when using criteria developed by others, it is wise to "lead" students to your adopted standards of quality through the use of the student-centered performance assessment development procedures specified in the section, "Developing Performance Assessments," in Chapter 8. Again, review these before continuing.

In addition, remember that an appropriately focused set of performance criteria, although certainly necessary for quality performance assessment, is far from sufficient. The key to the effective application of those criteria in the classroom is carefully prepared observers/raters. Skillful performance assessors are trained, not born. And training them is very challenging work—whether they're Olympic figure skating judges, assessors of student writing, evaluators of learning disabled students, or students preparing to evaluate their own performance. Aspiring performance assessors must remain open-minded and willing to learn as they strive to master achievement standards. Unless we invest in thoughtful preparation, we cannot expect our observations of and judgments about student performance to be dependable, regardless of the quality of the performance criteria we start with.

And finally, remember to maintain a balanced perspective. Performance assessment represents just one of four viable methods of assessment that we have at our disposal. We can use selected response, essay, and personal communication formats to tap student mastery of many of the important dimensions of knowledge and reasoning prerequisite to becoming skillful in performance. In addition, we can use the essay format to approximate some very sophisticated forms of performance. Classroom teachers faced with growing assessment challenges and shrinking assessment resources cannot overlook these options.

Standards of Performance Assessment Quality

As you review the examples of performance assessment exercises, scoring criteria, student responses, and teacher ratings, keep in mind the specific standards of quality Baron and Quellmalz offered in Chapter 8. Baron (1991) provided us with questions to ask when evaluating our performance exercises or tasks:

- If a group of curriculum experts in my field and a group of educated citizens in my community were to infer my educational values from what they see in my exercises, would they be pleased with what they saw?

- As students prepare for my assessment exercises and I structure my curriculum and pedagogy to enable them to be successful on these tasks, do I feel assured that they will be making progress toward becoming academically successful as defined in my classroom?

- Do my tasks clearly communicate my standards and expectations to my students?

- Are some of my tasks designed to have students make connections and forge relationships among various aspects of the curriculum?

- Do my tasks encourage students to access prior knowledge and problem solving skills to perform well?

- Do some exercises ask students to work collaboratively to solve complex problems?

- Are my students sometimes expected to sustain their efforts over a period of time to succeed?

- Do my exercises expect self-assessment and reflection on the part of my students?

- Are my tasks likely to be meaningful and challenging for my students?

- Do some of my exercises present problems that are situated in real-world contexts?

Quellmalz (1991) advised us to check our performance criteria to see if they do the following:

- Reflect all of the important components of performance—the active ingredients in target attainment.

- Apply appropriately in contexts and under conditions in which performance naturally occurs.

- Represent dimensions of performance that trained evaluators can apply consistently to a set of similar exercises; that is, they are not exercise specific.

- Are developmentally appropriate for the examinee population.

- Are understandable and usable by all participants in the performance assessment process, including teachers, students, parents, and the community.

- Link directly to our instructional objectives; that is, we teach what we preach.

- Provide a clear and understandable means of documenting and communicating about student growth over time.

Check to see if the illustrations provided in this chapter meet these standards.

Performance Assessment Examples from the Primary Grades

Checklists of Beginning-writer Skills

In Chapter 8, you will recall, we studied a set of writing assessment criteria reflective of the work of the mature writer. Remember, we used such labels as word choice, sentence fluency, organization, voice, and the like to capture these criteria. But writers don't spontaneously appear in classrooms as mature writers. How do we judge emerging writing skills—those skills that lead up to a place where we can begin to apply the mature writer criteria? In her training guidebook for assessing new writers, *Seeing with New Eyes*, Spandel (1994) provides us with checklists for each of five developmental stages for young writers. We present these in Figure 11–2.

For our purposes, the particular stages are less important than the way each stage is described. Always remember that our goal in devising performance criteria is to describe—not merely to judge. In this case, Spandel has devised a focused set of indicators in checklist format that permit teachers to locate their students in a developmental continuum. With these lists in hand, teachers can encourage and support the emergence of those prewriting proficiencies that naturally come next.

From an assessment perspective, one positive feature of checklists of attributes present or absent is that their application requires less refined discrimination by judges. These observations are easier to make objectively than are some of the more refined judgments required of more precise ratings scales illustrated later in the chapter. In that sense, checklists are easier to turn over to students, so they can become dependable raters of their own and each other's work. For these reasons, I encourage the use of checklists in performance assessment when working with beginners. It helps them get focused. You can add specificity as they become

Stage 1: Readiness

The student

- Scribbles
- Notices print in the environment
- Shows interest in writing tools
- Likes to make marks on paper
- Begins to recognize the power of print
- Likes listening to stories, poems, etc.
- Begins connecting writing/pictures with self-expression
- Likes expressing himself/herself orally

Stage 2: Drawing

The student

- Draws pictures with recognizable shapes
- Captures more feeling in art through motion, color, facial expressions
- Enjoys dictating or recording stories, poems, etc.
- May dictate or record stories to accompany pictures
- Begins labeling and using titles
- Plays with words and letters
- Feels confident to "write by myself"
- Enjoys writing
- Adds details that might have been overlooked earlier
- Uses words or pictures to express personal feelings

Stage 3: Experimentation

The student

- Feels more confident imitating environmental print
- Writes more
- Experiments with letters and rudimentary words
- Attempts longer expressions (two or more words)
- Shows more awareness of conventions of print: spaces between words, spaces between lines, use of capital letters, up-down orientation, left-right orientation, use of punctuation
- Begins using some capital letters, though not necessarily appropriately placed
- Begins to experiment with punctuation, though not necessarily appropriately placed

Figure 11–2

Five Achievement Stages for Beginning Writers

Source: Spandel, V. (1994) *Seeing with New Eyes: A Guidebook on Teaching and Assessing New Writers.* Portland, OR: Northwest Regional Educational Lab. Reprinted by permission.

Stage 4: Moving Toward Independence

The student

- Becomes a keen observer of environmental print
- Feels increasing confidence copying and using environmental print
- Enjoys writing words, phrases and short sentences on his/her own
- Expands oral stories and all-about essays
- Enjoys drawing pictures—then creating accompanying text
- Writes longer, more expansive text
- Asks more questions about conventions
- Includes more conventions of writing in own text, including periods, question marks, commas, quotation marks, capital letters—which may or may not be appropriately placed
- Likes to share—may ask others to read text

Stage 5: Expanding & Adding Detail

The student

- Writes more—up to a paragraph or more
- Experiments with different forms: lists, recipes, how-to papers, all-about essays, stories, poems, descriptions, journals, notes
- Begins using some conventions (spaces between words, capitals, periods, title at the top) with growing consistency
- Shows increasing understanding of what a sentence is
- Adds more detail to both pictures and text
- Expresses both ideas and feelings purposefully and forcefully through pictures and text
- Shows increasing confidence experimenting with inventive spelling—especially if inventive spelling is encouraged
- Increasingly uses writer's vocabulary to ask questions or discuss own writing—especially if traits are taught

comfortable. Checklists also work well when proficiency can be defined in terms of a list of several key attributes that comprise success.

Time for Reflection

Let's say you planned to use checklists like these to help students begin to write and you wanted to share your expectations with their parents. What strategies can you think of for doing so? How could you help parents see where their child is in the development of emergent writing skills?

Rating Reading Fluency

Along with its assessment of oral reading proficiency, the National Assessment of Educational Progress (NAEP) assembled a team of reading researchers and educators to develop the Integrated Reading Performance Record, or IRPR. Among other things, this interview-based assessment sequence included a performance assessment of reading fluency (Pinnell et al., 1995). The developers focused their attention on three key elements of reading in order to define fluency. It is instructive to review their thinking for the lessons this analysis can teach us about the depth of understanding it takes to devise quality performance criteria and rating scales.

First, the apparent grouping of words or phrasing is evident in oral reading through the intonation, stress and pauses that are exhibited by readers. The beginning and ending of a phrase may be emphasized by the perceived rise and fall of pitch, or simply by the hesitation or pause between phrase endings and phrase beginnings.

A second element of oral reading that was part of rating students' fluency was adherence to the author's syntax or sentence structure. Recognizing the author's syntax can be critical since identical groups of words may represent various meanings when read with different syntactical patterns displayed through intonation, stress placement, or insertions of pauses. Adhering to the author's syntax during oral reading requires the reader to be aware of the ideas that are expressed in the text. Reading a phrase or sentence with a syntactical structure that differs from the one intended may indicate that the reader has lost track of the meaning in the passage.

The third element that played a role in how fluency was described was the expressiveness of the oral reading. While the IRPR development committee felt that [beginning readers] should not be expected to provide consistently expressive oral presentations, there was agreement that fluent readers naturally provide some expression in their reading and this should be accounted for in the overall fluency rating. Therefore, the presence of at least some expressiveness was required of the highest fluency-level readers. For example, a minimal attempt to interject a sense of feeling, anticipation, or characterization was expected for the highest level of fluency.

The accuracy of students' reading was one element of oral reading that was not considered as a part of the fluency scale. Although an analysis of students' deviations from text was conducted [as part of this assessment], it was determined that word recognition accuracy should not be considered in fluency. A major reason for this decision was that all readers—even the most fluent—make errors as they read. (pp. 15–16)

Figure 11–3 presents the reading fluency rating scale that resulted from these deliberations. Note particularly how the sense of the meaning of proficiency described is translated into the four levels of ratings. These kinds of thoughtful understandings and connections are central to the development of quality performance assessments.

Time for Reflection

*Given the previous discussion of reading fluency, and the holistic rating scale shown in Figure 11–3, can you develop a set of **analytical** rating scales for reading fluency? Take a moment and give it a try.*

Level 4 — Reads primarily in larger, meaningful phrase groups. Although some regressions, repetitions, and deviations from text may be present, these do not appear to detract from the overall structure of the story. Preservation of the author's syntax is consistent. Some or most of the story is read with expressive interpretation.

Level 3 — Reads primarily in three- or four-word phrase groups. Some smaller groupings may be present. However, the majority of phrasing seems appropriate and preserves the syntax of the author. Little or no expressive interpretation is present.

Level 2 — Reads primarily in two-word phrases with some three-or four-word groupings. Some word-by-word reading may be present. Word groupings may seem awkward and unrelated to larger context of sentence or passage.

Level 1 — Reads primarily word-by-word. Occasional two-word or three-word phrases may occur—but these are infrequent and/or they do not preserve meaningful syntax.

Figure 11–3
NAEPs's Integrated Reading Performance Oral Reading Fluency Scale
Source: From *Listening to Children Read Aloud* by G. S. Pinnell, J. J. Pikulski, K. K. Wixen, J. R. Campbell, P. B. Gough, & A. S. Beatty, 1995, Washington, DC: Office of Educational Research and Improvement, U.S. Department of Education.

Assessing Emerging Math Skills

Math teachers also have been at work in recent years analyzing the meaning of mathematical problem solving proficiency. One particularly interesting example is provided in a teacher's classroom assessment guide developed by the Illinois Department of Education (1995). Here is a sample of a grade 3 math computation performance exercise:

> An activity class for children was held last Saturday, and 20 children attended. The instructor brought 12 apples and 15 bananas as a snack for the children. One helper passed out the apples to the students while another helper passed out the bananas. Every student received at least one of the fruits. If all the apples and bananas were given out, how many students got more than one fruit? Show all your work and explain in your own words how you found your answer. (p. 23)

Figure 11–4 presents the scoring criteria used. Note that each criterion is labeled, then it is defined, and finally, it is transformed into specific ratings. The focus is sharp here and that's what it takes to conduct quality performance assessments. After you review these, study the samples of student work offered in Figure 11–5. See if you understand the rationale for the ratings offered.

Time for Reflection

How might this strategy of having students write about their solutions to math problem be transformed into a productive way of conferring with stu-

Score Level	Mathematical Knowledge	Strategic Knowledge	Communication
	Knowledge of mathematical principles and concepts which result in a correct solution to a problem	Identification of important elements of the problem and the use of models, diagrams and symbols to systematically represent and integrate concepts	Written explanation and rationale for the solution process
4	• shows complete understanding of the problem's mathematical concepts & principles • uses appropriate mathematical terminology & notation (e.g., labels answer as appropriate) • executes algorithms completely and correctly	• identifies all the important elements of the problem and shows complete understanding of the relationships among elements • reflects an appropriate and systematic strategy for solving the problem • gives clear evidence of a complete and systematic solution process	• gives a complete written explanation of the solution process employed; explanation addresses what was done, and *why* it was done • if a diagram is appropriate, there is a complete explanation of all the elements in the diagram
3	• shows nearly complete understanding of the problem's mathematical concepts and principles • uses nearly correct mathematical terminology and notations • executes algorithms completely; computations are generally correct but may contain minor errors	• identifies most of the important elements of the problem and shows general understanding of the relationships among them • reflects an appropriate strategy for solving the problem • solution process is nearly complete	• gives nearly complete written explanations of the solution process employed; may contain some minor gaps • may include a diagram with most of the elements explained

2	• shows some understanding of the problem's mathematical concepts and principles • may contain major computational errors	• identifies some important elements of the problem but shows only limited understanding of the relationships among them • appears to reflect an appropriate strategy but application of strategy is unclear • gives some evidence of a solution process	• gives some explanation of the solution process employed, but communication is vague or difficult to interpret • may include a diagram with some of the elements explained
1	• shows limited to no understanding of the problem's mathematical concepts and principles • may misuse or fail to use mathematical terms • may contain major computational errors	• fails to identify important elements or places too much emphasis on unimportant elements • may reflect an inappropriate strategy for solving the problem • gives minimal evidence of a solution process; process may be difficult to identify • may attempt to use irrelevant outside information	• provides minimal explanation of solution process; may fail to explain or may omit significant parts of the problem • explanation does not match presented solution process • may include minimal discussion of elements in diagram; explanation of significant elements is unclear
0	• no answer attempted	• no apparent strategy	• no written explanation of the solution process is provided

Figure 11–4
Illinois Mathematics Scoring Criteria

Source: From *Performance Assessment in Mathematics: A Guide to Scoring Open-ended Items* (p. 19), by Illinois State Board of Education, 1995, Springfield, IL: Author. Reprinted by permission.

Goal 1: Computation

An activity class for children was held last Saturday, and 20 children attended. The instructor brought 12 apples and 15 bananas as a snack for the children. One helper passed out the apples to the students, while another helper passed out the bananas. Every student received at least one of the fruits. If all the apples and bananas were given out, how many students got more than one fruit? Show all your work and explain in words <u>how</u> you found your answer.

Overall Score = 1

MATHEMATICAL KNOWLEDGE	STRATEGIC KNOWLEDGE	COMMUNICATION
Score = 1	Score = 2	Score = 0
Incorrect answer. Shows limited understanding of the mathematical concepts involved. Does not set the problem up correctly (each child should receive at least one piece of fruit).	Identifies some important elements (apples and bananas); however, children are not represented in diagram.	No written explanation of how problem was solved.

Overall Score = 4

MATHEMATICAL KNOWLEDGE	STRATEGIC KNOWLEDGE	COMMUNICATION
Score = 4	Score = 4	Score = 4
Problem is solved correctly. Shows complete understanding of the concepts needed to solve this problem.	Clear evidence of a solution process is given. Identifies important elements (number of bananas, apples, and children). Diagram reflects systematic approach.	Complete explanation of solution process and complete diagram with elements labeled.

Figure 11–5
Application of Illinois Mathematics Scoring Criteria
Source: From *Performance Assessment in Mathematics: A Guide to Scoring Open-ended Items* (p. 19), by Illinois State Board of Education, 1995, Springfield, IL: Author. Reprinted by permission.

dents as a personal communication-based assessment and as a teaching method?

Examples from Elementary Grades

An Estimation Problem

Alberta Education (1994) developed a math performance assessment in which students are given a set of materials to manipulate and a problem to solve. They then communicate their solutions in the form of brief written responses for evaluation. In one such problem, students are asked to use estimating strategies and population sampling techniques to estimate the number of beans in a large bucket. In addition to the bucket of beans, they're given magic markers, a tray, and a small cup. The accompanying worksheet lists only two directives: Explain the strategy you used to estimate the number of beans. State how many beans are in the bucket.

In this case, the performance assessment does not center on the work of students while they solve the problem. That would necessitate the use of very time consuming one-on-one observation and judgment schemes. Rather, the evaluator focuses on the results of having attempted to solve the problem. In that sense, as writing assessment, this is a product-based performance assessment. This greatly increases the efficiency of the judgment process. Written responses are evaluated in terms of two performance criteria: problem solving and communication. These have been defined and translated into 4-point rating scales, presented in Figure 11–6.

Time for Reflection

If you were in charge of this assessment and found a lack of agreement among raters of the math performance, what procedures would you implement to increase agreement? Where might the problems be? Be specific, listing as many possible causes as you can and procedures you might take to correct them.

Evaluating a Science Experiment

In contrast, some performance assessors define in much greater detail their vision of academic success. For instance, the Kansas Science Assessment relies on a highly-refined set of scoring criteria to tap four dimensions of student performance. The achievement target in this case is the ability to design an experiment to answer a question presented by the teacher. Here's an example of one of their performance exercises:

Imagine that you are using your parent's computer and you accidentally knock over a glass of pop. You run to the pantry for paper towels and find four brands on the shelf. You have no idea which will do the best job in cleaning up the mess. After you deal with the emergency, you decide to find out which one will clean up such a mess in the shortest amount of time.

1. Design and conduct a study to show which paper towel is the best to use. The best towel may be the fastest at absorbing liquid, it may hold the most liquid, or it may do both of these.

2. To conduct this experiment you will need to use some or all of these materials: paper towels, a balance scale, measuring cups, water, weights and eyedropper.

3. As a conclusion, describe how you tested the towels and how and why you decided which product was best.

Your teacher will judge your project in terms of your ability to judge the quality of the towels based on the information you get from your study, appropriateness of information gathering procedures, accuracy of information gathered, whether enough information was gathered, and whether someone not involved in your study could understand your findings. (Fort Hays Educational Development Center, n.d.)

		PROBLEM SOLVING	COMMUNICATION
3	B E Y O N D	Analyzed and readily understood the task. Developed an efficient and workable strategy. Showed explicit evidence of carrying out the strategy. Synthesized and generalized the conclusion.	Rich, precise and clear all the time (mathematically correct, correct symbolism). Representation is very perceptive (chart, diagram, graph). Explanations are logical and appropriate.
2	A T L E V E L	Understood the task. Developed a workable strategy. Inferred (some evidence) but not always clear. Connected and applied the answer.	Appropriate most of the time, accurate, mostly clear. Representation is accurate and quite appropriate. Explanations are mostly clear and logical.
1	N O T Y E T A T	Partially understood the task. Appropriate strategy some of the time. Possible evidence of a plan—not clear. Partial connection of answer.	Appropriate some of the time, but may not be clear. Uses representation but not too precisely. Explanations have some clear parts.
0		Totally misunderstood. Inappropriate, unworkable strategy. No evidence of carrying out a plan. No connections of answer. Blank.	Unclear or inappropriate use of symbolism. Incorrect use of representation. Explanation is not clear. Blank.

Figure 11–6
Alberta Education Mathematics Scoring Criteria
Source: Reprinted from "Science Performance Assessment and Standards." G. Hall, 1994, St. Alberta, Alberta, Canada. Reprinted by permission.

I like the fact that students are reminded of the performance criteria right within the context of the exercise description. If instruction has been aligned appropriately with this assessment, there are no surprises here. Students have been given the opportunity to learn to succeed on such an assessment. But it never hurts to remind them of the target.

In the Kansas assessment, students worked in teams to devise and conduct their experiment and prepare their results. Further, they were instructed to maintain one log or journal for the team documenting decisions made, hypotheses tested, methods used, analyses carried out, findings, and conclusions. The performance ratings focus on the journals. Four 5-point rating scales were developed for scoring Recognizing and Defining the Problem, Designing the Problem Solving Strategy, Implementing the Strategy, and Interpreting and Communicating Findings and Conclusions. Figure 11–7 presents the first- and last-mentioned of these scales.

Note that only points 1, 3, and 5 are defined in this example. Raters still can use points 2 and 4 if they feel performance rests between the other points. This practice is not uncommon, as carefully trained judges using clearly defined criteria can make these discriminations.

Note also the immense detail of the Interpreting and Communicating scales. This is as close as I have seen developers come to using checklists to define the various points on a rating scale. Users can scan these lists of indicators seeking reference points to determine the level of proficiency exhibited. But more to the point, if science instruction in this context really prepares students to understand all of these reference points and provides students with practice in evaluating their own and each other's work, I think we'd be talking about some very high-quality teaching and significant student learning!

Time For Reflection

Devise another performance exercise or task that could elicit performance for which these performance criteria might be relevant.

Examples from Junior High School

Assessing Artistic Performance

During the late 1980s, a project emerged in the Pittsburgh, Pennsylvania schools that both sharpened our thinking about the meaning of success in the arts (including music) and started us down the road to rigorous, student-centered art assessment. The project, called Arts Propel, operates on the assumption that learning requires interaction among production, perception, and reflection:[1]

---

[1]The quotation is reprinted from *Arts Propel: A Handbook for Music* by Lyle Davidson, Carol Myford, Donna Plasket, Larry Scripp, Spence Swinton, Bruce Torff, & Janet Waanders. Copyright 1992 by Educational Testing Service, Princeton, NJ (on behalf of Project Zero, Harvard Graduate School of Education). Reprinted by permission of the publisher.

Recognizing and Defining the Problem

1	3	5
Recognizes limited unique characteristics of an event or happening	Recognizes some unique characteristics of an event or happening	Recognizes all unique characteristics of an event or happening
Classifies items using irrelevant characteristics	Classifies items using a single pertinent characteristic	Classifies items using several pertinent characteristics
Does not recognize problems in information from media and other sources	Recognizes problems in information from media and other sources but does not see connection to testing	Recognizes problems in information from media and other sources as testable
Does not understand information in symbolic form and/or is unable to assess appropriateness of problems to scientific method	Understands information in symbolic form but is not able to integrate this information with other resources to assess appropriateness of problem solving to testing with scientific method *or* Misinterprets some symbolic information but is able to integrate this information with other resources to assess appropriateness of problem solving to testing with scientific method	Understands information in symbolic form and is able to integrate with other information to assess appropriateness of problem to testing with scientific method

Figure 11–7

Kansas Science Assessment Scales

Source: From staff development materials (pp. 7, 10, & 35) by the Fort Hays Educational Development Center, 1994, Hays, KS: Author. Reprinted by permission.

Interpreting and Communicating Findings & Conclusions

5	3	1
Makes clear reasonable predictions based on the observed or recorded information	Makes predictions but they lack some clarity or are somewhat unreasonable based on the observed or recorded information	Unable to make understandable predictions
Identifies the parts of a system and the interaction of those parts	Identifies the parts and interactions of a system, but understanding is incomplete or unclear	May recognize the parts of a system, but does not recognize or understand the interactions
Communicates meaning of results clearly and concisely	Communicates meaning of results in a somewhat clear fashion though some ambiguity is present	Unable to clearly communicate meaning of results
Relates interpretations and findings to everyday environment appropriately and accurately	Shows some ability to connect interpretations and findings with everyday environment	Does not make pertinent connections between interpretations and finding and everyday environment
Reports information clearly using charts, graphs or tables	Reports information using charts, graphs or tables, but report is somewhat ambiguous	Charts, graphs or tables are very ambiguous
Makes clear reasonable predictions, using various forms of data and understands the lack of precision/reliability with predictions	Makes predictions using various forms of data but either the predictions or their understanding of the precision/reliability of predictor lacks clarity to some degree	May make a reasonable prediction but unable to explain/convey understanding of precision/reliability issues
Explains phenomena in terms of their interactions, with clarity and understanding	Explains phenomena in terms of their interactions, but explanation lacks clarity	Unable to explain phenomena in terms of their interactions in understanding manner
Identifies and explains the strengths and weaknesses of decisions, design, or information presented	Identifies strengths/weaknesses but explanation is incomplete	Limited identification and explanation of strengths/weaknesses
Generates relevant, new hypotheses based on current interpretation of information	Generates new hypotheses but they either lack relevance or are not accurate extensions of information	Unable to generate new alternative hypotheses based on current information
Synthesizes information to understand the big picture as well as important details	Has some understanding of going beyond component parts but has not yet "put it all together"	Lacks understanding of the "big picture" though may understand some or all component parts
Uses statistical analyses to interpret results of research	Use of statistical analyses in interpretation is either incomplete or somewhat inaccurate	Does not understand the application of statistical analyses to interpretation
Relates findings to appropriate scientific laws or theories	Has some understanding of scientific laws or theories relevant to current findings	Unable to make the connection between findings and scientific law or theories

303

Production [is] a perspective taken by the music maker or performer. This involves two strands: knowledge of the domain (how to play an instrument or critique a performance) and what we call authorship, or a willingness to take personal responsibility for work in that domain (ranging from eager citizenship in the ensemble to original or prolific arranging, improvising, or composing).

Perception [is] a broad-based dimension that includes the perspective of the active listener as well as the maker of art. The perceptual skills of the active listener involve particular aural skills (e.g., ability to match pitch, or hearing that a pitch or rhythm is incorrect) applied to one's own performance or that of others. Perception is also more general (e.g., awareness of form and style or sensitivity to interpretations) and even extends to one's social perception (e.g., understanding critiques of one's work or listening and then planning revisions of work with others).

Reflection also has a broad meaning. It includes reflection as the perspective of the evaluation of productions and perceptions and as the interpersonal aspect of understanding work in the domain. Reflection is thinking over what one has grasped perceptually. It involves both self-knowledge ("What am I after?") and self-assessment ("Did I get there?"); and self-correction in a content of knowledge of the materials of music ("How do I get closer?").

This very healthy student-centered classroom assessment philosophy led these educators to define key elements of sound performance (pun intended!) and to share that definition with performers for purposes of self-assessment. Figure 11–8 shows a sample Arts Propel rating sheet, in this case for instrumental music performance.

Four parts of this are interesting. First of all, notice the precise use of language to describe performance in an individual music lesson. This lays the foundation for effective communication among all concerned with student success. Second, the rating form permits the collection of repeated judgments over time. This permits both student and teacher to track improvement (or the lack of it) over the course of several lessons. When we discuss portfolios in Part 4 of this book, we will discuss how this can serve as an important source of motivation for all involved. Third, the form combines rating scales on the top with a comments section on the bottom. Such combinations are not only acceptable in the same assessment, but they make sense when the nature of the performance expectations include continuums that involve artistic interpretation.

Fourth, notice that each rating scale begins at 1.0 and proceeds to 3.9 or 4.9 in tenths of points. In the latter case, the result is a 49-point rating scale! The apparent power of this microscope belies the underlying precision of the raters. Precisely what is the difference between performance at the 3.2 level and performance at the 3.3 level? We are not capable of making this level of refined discrimination in judging most human performance. Indeed, it's very difficult for most raters to make dependable differentiations in levels of proficiency using even a 7-point scale. We must strive to build our rating scales around the assumption that evaluators (and, we hope, students too) are going to understand the precise meaning of each point of the scale. Otherwise they will not be able to do their job of discriminating levels and promoting progress toward ever higher levels of proficiency. Keep the number of scoring points under control.

Time for Reflection

If you are not an instrumental music teacher, find one on the faculty of your training program if you are a student or in the schools of your community if you are a practitioner. Search out a music teacher of some experience. Ask if you could meet with this person to discuss assessment. Take Figure 11–8 with you and ask this teacher to review and explain it to you. What does each criterion mean? How does the evaluator know the student's level of proficiency? Simply listen to the way he or she talks about performance and strive to get a sense of the depth of this teacher's vision of what it means to be a good musician. What generalizations does this suggest about the foundations of strong performance assessment?

Oregon Math Assessment Project

Refinements in our understanding of achievement targets in math led by the National Council of Teachers of Mathematics (NCTM, 1989) have given rise to an impressive array of experiments in performance assessment in this achievement domain. NCTM contends that all students must attain appropriate levels of mathematical literacy by meeting five basic standards:

- learn to value mathematics
- become confident in their ability to do mathematics
- become mathematical problem solvers
- learn to communicate in mathematics
- learn to reason mathematically

One example of an innovative assessment of these kinds of math targets is under development in Oregon. For over a decade, the state of Oregon has pioneered the development of analytical writing assessment schemes and has led efforts to integrate such performance assessments into instruction. It continues in this leadership role by being among the first to generalize this technology into the realm of math performance assessment. Oregon also used the NCTM standards as its vision of success, assembled experienced math teachers, and engaged them in devising performance assessment criteria to be used in evaluating written student solutions to complex, open-ended math problems.

Four such criteria are applied: Conceptual Understanding, Processes and Strategies, Interpret Results, and Communication. Definitions are shown in Figure 11–9, along with analytical rating scales. Here again we see examples of 5-point rating scales with points 1, 3, and 5 specifically defined. Scores of 2 and 4 are available for use also, if the rater determines that a response lies between two points on the score continuum.

DOMAIN PROJECT: INDIVIDUAL LESSON

Ensemble or Class: _____ [Voice]

Grade Level(s) _____

(7–90 version)

Date: _____

Teacher: _____

Student: _____

Date: _____

Condition: _____

Vocal Performance Execution Dimensions	Teacher Scoring Student Performance				
	1	2	3	4	5

Vocal Performance
Execution Dimensions
Score = NA If Not Applicable   **Music Performed**

Pitch Production*

[1.0–1.9] = seldom performs pitches accurately or securely;

[2.0–2.9] = sometimes performs with accurate pitch but with frequent or repeated errors

[3.0–3.9] = mostly accurate and secure pitches but with a few isolated errors;

[4.0–4.9] = virtually no errors and very secure pitches;

Rhythm/Tempo Production*

[1.0–1.9] = seldom performs durations accurately or with a steady tempo

[2.0–2.9] = sometimes performs durations accurately but with an erratic pulse or with frequent or repeated durational errors;

[3.0–3.9] = mostly accurate rhythm and pulse with a few durational errors;

[4.0–4.9] = secure pulse and rhythmically accurate;

Diction*

[1.0–1.9] = seldom able to regulate vowel colors or consonants;

[2.0–2.9] = generally consistent vowel color with some attempt to regulate sound;

[3.0–3.9] = consistent vowel colors with increased control of consonants;

[4.0–4.9] = maintains consistent control of diction;

Figure 11–8

Arts Propel Performance Rating Sheet

Source: From *Arts Propel: A Handbook for Music* (n.p.) by Lyle Davidson, Carol Myford, Donna Plasket, Larry Scripp, Spence Swinton, Bruce Torff, & Janet Waanders. Copyright 1992 by Educational Testing Service, Princeton, NJ (on behalf of Project Zero, Harvard Graduate School of Education). Reprinted by permission of the publisher.

Dynamics (if applicable) [1.0–1.9] = seldom able to control dynamics; [2.0–2.9] = generally controls dynamics with some responses to score markings; [3.0–3.9] = consistent dynamics and responses to score markings;					
Timbre or Tone Quality* [1.0–1.9] = uncontrolled tone production throughout all registers of voice; [2.0–2.9] = occasionally controls timbre in one register; [3.0–3.9] = generally controls timbre in more than one register; [4.0–4.9] = maintains consistent control throughout registers;					
Posture (if applicable) **(Observed By Teacher During Performance)** [1.0–1.9] = seldom attempts to use appropriate posture or diaphragm support; [2.0–2.9] = poor posture or support sometimes interferes with sound production; [3.0–3.9] = mostly consistent posture or support only within limited range; [4.0–4.9] = maintains consistent control and support throughout registers;					
Breath Control* [1.0–1.9] = no use of support mechanism; [2.0–2.9] = inconsistent use of support mechanism; [3.0–3.9] = consistent use of support mechanism; [4.0–4.9] = manipulates support mechanism for a variety of musical effects;					
[*Most conservative scoring = assign lowest possible score based on any or all of the factors listed] (make additional comments on back)					

	Conceptual Understanding	Processes and Strategies	Interpret Results	Communication	
	Demonstrates an indepth understanding of the concepts, processes, principles, and skills.	**Selects effective procedures/strategies or modifies existing ones presenting work logically and coherently.**	**Inference/interpretations answer the question posed and verify the solution.**	**Communicates thinking effectively and clearly to various audiences, using dynamic and diverse means.**	
5	• Articulates the problem from multiple perspectives selected from a variety of sources • Connects prior knowledge to the task • Uses effective scientific/mathematical processes/concepts to analyze the problem	• Shows effective questioning and originality • Displays evidence of clarity, organization, continuity and reasoning • Consistently applies creative applications of concepts and strategies • Uses more than one method (when appropriate)	• Results are verified, interpreted and lead to a meaningful conclusion • Interpretations and conclusions show strong evidence of reasoning • Possible alternative explanations of the task or the results are presented	• Uses appropriate terminology/vocabulary and a variety of forms to communicate thinking processes (when the context expects it) • Presentation clearly displays the thinking throughout • Communicates effectively to the target audience • Reflects on the concepts required, process used, and results drawn to conclusions	
4					

3	• Displays an understanding of major concepts and/or processes • Assumptions about the purposes may be flawed • Makes partial connections between/among the concepts	• Uses imprecise scientific, mathematical, principles and/or procedures • Some strategies may be ineffectual, not appropriate, or only partially useful • Work is clear and focused, but may not be applicable to the problem	• Results are interpreted and brought to a partially meaningful conclusion • Interpretations and conclusions show evidence of focus • Verification may not connect the results to the original task	• Limits communication to some important ideas • Partially communicates the thinking involved during the task • Presentation may lack organization • Communication is effective only with a limited audience • Uses adequate vocabulary/terminology
2				
1	• Presents fragmented understanding of concepts and/or processes • Translates the problem/situation into inappropriate concepts or processes • Makes minimal connections • Attempts to solve problems using inappropriate processes/concepts	• Skills and strategies lack a central focus • Procedures are ineffective and/or not recorded • Strategies and/or procedures are not brought to completion	• Only the conclusion and verification are present • Inferences are implied and not supported • Alternative explanations although required are not presented • Unsuitable methods or solutions are not eliminated	• Does not successfully communicate thinking • Misuses appropriate terminology • Logical focus is missing • Results are poorly communicated • Communication focuses solely on the solution

Figure 11-9
Oregon Math Assessment Rating Scales
Source: from "CIM Outcome: Apply Science and Mathematics" by Office of Assessment and Technology, Oregon Department of Education, 1994, Salem, OR: Oregon Department of Education. Reprinted by permission.

Criteria such as these permit the creation of the same kind of collaborative environment in math classrooms that we find these days characterizing writing instruction. Students can be given complex, open-ended math problems to solve, be taught to understand and apply these kinds of performance criteria, and then evaluate their own and each other's work while the teacher plays the role of coach and advisor. The result is a kind of math workshop environment.

Examples from High School

Foreign Language Assessment

Whenever possible, it is best to devise performance criteria applicable to student responses to multiple exercises. That is, criteria ought not to be exercise specific. When criteria are generalizable, users can apply them repeatedly, drawing confident conclusions about student achievement. Performance criteria that are specifically applicable to only one exercise can be too narrow in scope to lead to confident conclusions.

Perhaps the best examples of generalizable performance criteria are those devised by the American Council on the Teaching of Foreign Languages (ACTFL) for use with their Oral Proficiency Interview (ACTFL, 1989). The Oral Proficiency Interview is a standardized procedure for the global assessment of speaking ability that relies on a trained examiner to carry on a conversation with the examinee, rating oral proficiency during the interaction, as well as afterward, via audiotape recording.

The most unique and special feature of this assessment is that the proficiency guidelines that guide the rating process, developed originally by the government's Interagency Language Roundtable Testing Committee, are generic. That is, the same criteria can be applied to the evaluation of language proficiency in many languages. In fact, ACTFL currently offers training in the application of the criteria in eleven languages: Arabic, Chinese, English as a second language, French, German, Hindi, Italian, Japanese, Portuguese, Russian, and Spanish.

Another useful feature of the ACTFL rating system is that it begins with four major levels of proficiency and then further subdivides and defines each level in a straightforward manner, as seen in Figure 11–10. The result is a nine-level rating scale that teachers can use to track student progress over several years.

Although foreign language proficiency is a complex achievement target, these teachers and assessors have captured that complexity with thoughtful, clearly descriptive language. These kinds of criteria represent far more than rating scales. They represent the basis for communication and shared meaning about assessment between teacher and student.

Time for Reflection

Let's say you want to create a student-friendly version of the ACTFL criteria. What might it look like? (You needn't create the entire set. Start at the

Novice	*The Novice level is characterized by the ability to communicate minimally with learned material.*
Novice-Low	Oral production consists of isolated words and perhaps a few high-frequency phrases. Essentially no functional communicative ability.
Novice-Mid	Oral production continues to consist of isolated words and learned phrases within very predictable areas of need, although quality is increased. Vocabulary is sufficient only for handling simple, elementary needs and expressing basic courtesies. Utterances rarely consist of more than two or three words and show frequent long pauses and repetition of interlocutor's words. Speaker may have some difficulty producing even the simplest utterances. Some Novice-Mid speakers will be understood only with great difficulty.
Novice-High	Able to satisfy partially the requirements of basic communicative exchanges by relying heavily on learned utterances but occasionally expanding these through simple recombinations of their elements. Can ask questions or make statements involving learned material. Shows signs of spontaneity although this falls short of real autonomy of expression. Speech continues to consist of learned utter-ances rather than of personalized, situationally adapted ones. Vocabulary centers on areas such as basic objects, places, and most common kinship terms. Pronunciation may still be strongly influenced by first language. Errors are frequent and, in spite of repetition, some Novice-High speakers will have difficulty being understood even by sympathetic interlocutors.
Intermediate	*The Intermediate level is characterized by the speaker's ability to:* • create with the language by combining and recombining learned elements, though primarily in a reactive mode; • initiate, minimally sustain, and close in a simple way basic communicative tasks; and • ask and answer questions.
Intermediate-Low	Able to handle successfully a limited number of interactive, task-oriented and social situations. Can ask and answer questions, initiate and respond to simple statements and maintain face-to-face conversation, although in a highly restricted manner and with much linguistic inaccuracy. Within these limitations, can perform such tasks as introducing self, ordering a meal, asking directions, and making purchases. Vocabulary is adequate to express only the most ele-mentary needs. Strong interference from native language may occur. Misunder-standings frequently arise, but with repetition, the Intermediate-Low speaker can generally be understood by sympathetic interlocutors.

Figure 11–10
ACTFL Foreign Language Proficiency Guidelines for Speaking
Source: From *Oral Proficiency Interview: Tester Training Manual* (n.p.) by the American Council on the Teaching of Foreign Languages, 1989, Yonkers, NY: Author. Reprinted by permission.

Intermediate-Mid	Able to handle successfully a variety of uncomplicated, basic and communicative tasks and social situations. Can talk simply about self and family members. Can ask and answer questions and participate in simple conversations on topics beyond the most immediate needs; e.g., personal history and leisure time activities. Utterance length increases slightly, but speech may continue to be characterized by frequent long pauses, since the smooth incorporation of even basic conversational strategies is often hindered as the speaker struggles to create appropriate language forms. Pronunciation may continue to be strongly influenced by first language and fluency may still be strained. Although misunderstandings still arise, the Intermediate-Mid speaker can generally be understood by sympathetic interlocutors.
Intermediate-High	Able to handle successfully most uncomplicated communicative tasks and social situations. Can initiate, sustain, and close a general conversation with a number of strategies appropriate to a range of circumstances and topics, but errors are evident. Limited vocabulary still necessitates hesitation and may bring about slightly unexpected circumlocution. There is emerging evidence of connected discourse, particularly for simple narration and/or description. The Intermediate-High speaker can generally be understood even by interlocutors not accustomed to dealing with speakers at this level, but repetition may still be required.
Advanced	*The Advanced level is characterized by the speaker's ability to:* • *converse in a clearly participatory fashion,* • *initiate, sustain, and bring to closure a wide variety of communicative tasks, including those that require an increased ability to convey meaning with diverse language strategies due to a complication or an unforeseen turn of events.* • *satisfy the requirements of school and work situations; and* • *narrate and describe with paragraph-length connected discourse.*
Advanced	Able to satisfy the requirements of everyday situations and routine school and work requirements. Can handle with confidence but not with facility complicated tasks and social situations, such as elaborating, complaining, and apologizing. Can narrate and describe with some details, linking sentences together smoothly. Can communicate facts and talk casually about topics of current public and personal interest, using general vocabulary. Shortcomings can often be smoothed over by communicative strategies, such as pause fillers, stalling devices, and different rates of speech. Circumlocution which arises from vocabulary

Figure 11–10, *continued*

lowest level and try translating it for high schoolers who are just beginning to learn to speak a foreign language.)

Assessing Discussion Skills

The Ministry of Education in Alberta, Canada, has devised a set of performance standards to apply in evaluating student participation in small-group discussions.

	or syntactic limitations very often is quite successful, though some groping for words may still be evident. The Advanced-level speaker can be understood without difficulty by native interlocutors.
Advanced-Plus	Able to satisfy the requirements of a broad variety of everyday, school, and work situations. Can discuss concrete topics relating to particular interests and special fields of competence. There is emerging evidence of ability to support opinions, explain in detail, and hypothesize. The Advanced-Plus speaker often shows a well-developed ability to compensate for an imperfect grasp of some forms with confident use of communicative strategies, such as paraphrasing and circumlocution. Differentiated vocabulary and intonation are effectively used to communicate fine shades of meaning. The Advanced-Plus speaker often shows remarkable fluency and ease of speech but under the demands of Superior-level, complex tasks, language may break down or prove inadequate.
Superior	*The Superior level is characterized by the speaker's ability to:* • *participate effectively in most formal and informal conversations on practical, social, professional, and abstract topics; and* • *support opinions and hypothesize using native-like discourse strategies.*
Superior	Able to speak the language with sufficient accuracy to participate effectively in most formal and informal conversations on practical, social, professional, and abstract topics. Can discuss special fields of competence and interest with ease. Can support opinions and hypothesize, but may not be able to tailor language to audience or discuss in depth highly abstract or unfamiliar topics. Usually the Superior-level speaker is only partially familiar with regional or other dialectical variants. The Superior-level speaker commands a wide variety of interactive strategies and shows good awareness of discourse strategies. The latter involves the ability to distinguish main ideas from supporting information through syntactic, lexical, and suprasegmental features (pitch, stress, intonation). Sporadic errors may occur, particularly in low-frequency structures and some complex high-frequency structures more common to formal writing, but no patterns of error are evident. Errors do not disturb the native speaker or interfere with communication.

These are presented in Figure 11–11. Three 5-point scales capture the student's Interaction Skills, Comprehension Strategies, and Performance Skills. As you see, they deal with far more than the participant's speech patterns, focusing the observer on the quality of the student's involvement with the group and comprehension of the ideas being discussed. In fact, actual speaking proficiency is defined simply in terms of vocabulary and language usage—keeping them in perspective in the larger context of productive discussion.

Scoring Guide for Small Group Discussion

[Talk will be characterized by pauses as students grapple with new ideas; the more thoughtful students may exhibit more pauses. False starts and repetitions will characterize talk until comprehension and linguistic control develop toward the end of the activity. Sentences may not be completed; students will interrupt one another, completing ideas begun by others.]

Interaction

5   **Excellent:** The student is attentive, open-minded, courteous and sensitive to the ideas, tone, and purpose of the activity; intellectual curiosity, attention to the task, and sensitivity to others helping to create a productive climate in the group. The student confidently shares ideas and feelings, actively builds on the ideas of others, and is an effective member or leader of the group.

4   **Proficient:** The student is attentive and courteous; purposefully and confidently undertakes the task assigned; thoughtfully handles the ideas offered by others, willingly offers own ideas, and is an efficient member or leader of the group.

3   **Satisfactory:** The student is courteous and willing to share with and listen to others; relies on the momentum of the group to motivate his inquiry into the topic; accepts ideas of others, offers own ideas, and is a courteous member or leader of the group.

2   **Limited:** The student is easily distracted; lacks the confidence to receive and express ideas easily and clearly; looks for confirmation of initial biases and may use language, tone, or nonverbal behavior inappropriate for the occasion or purpose; is a guarded, insecure member of the group and is uncomfortable in the role of leader.

1   **Poor:** The student is uninvolved in the activity and lacks the confidence to explore ideas orally; contributes almost nothing to discussions which is appropriate for the occasion and purpose; is uninvolved in the group and is unwilling to act as leader.

Figure 11–11
Alberta Education Group Performance Rating Scales
Source: From *Oral Communication Evaluation* by Alberta Education, Student Evaluation Branch, 1990, Edmonton, Alberta, Canada: Author. Reproduced with the permission of the Minister of Education, Province of Alberta, Canada, 1995.

Time for Reflection

Let's say you wanted these rating scales to guide instruction and assessment in your classroom. But, you wanted your students to be partners in that process and wished to also use these performance assessment ingredients in the teaching process. Specifically how might you involve your students in (1) understanding these criteria and (2) learning to apply them to their own and each other's work? Share your ideas among classmates or colleagues.

Comprehension Strategies
5   **Excellent: The student's discussion is perceptive, thorough, and insightful. Support is substantial and logical.** The student shows perception while actively developing understanding of themes, main ideas, and supporting details; selects details from the text to support interpretations and revises interpretations to accommodate all details in the text; has a clear idea of the shape of the task and sustains inquiry until the task is thoroughly completed.
4   **Proficient: The student's discussion is thoughtful and methodical. Support is appropriate and substantial.** The student shows thoughtfulness as understanding of themes, main ideas, and supporting details develops; selects details from the text to support interpretations; has a clear idea of the shape of the task and sustains inquiry until the task is substantially completed.
3   **Satisfactory: The student's discussion is on topic and sustained. Support is offered.** The student shows a developing understanding of themes, main ideas, and supporting details; accepts ideas with little question but can explain and support ideas when asked by others to elaborate; has a mechanical understanding of the task and sustains inquiry until the task is completed.
2   **Limited: The student's discussion is sporadic. The student struggles to provide ideas or support.** The student has difficulty developing an understanding of themes and distinguishing between main ideas and supporting details; may frequently ask for repetition of ideas but shows little evidence of understanding; may have a limited understanding of the task or may understand the task but be unable to sustain the inquiry to adequately fulfill the task.
1   **Poor: The student's discussion is weak and unfulfilling.** The student does not develop an understanding of themes, main ideas, and supporting details; may passively accept ideas offered by others; involvement detracts from the activity rather than enhances it.
Performance Skills (Vocabulary, Language Use)
5   **Excellent:** The student uses precise vocabulary and economical syntax.
4   **Proficient:** The student uses precise vocabulary and expresses ideas clearly.
3   **Satisfactory:** The student uses general vocabulary and expresses ideas wordily.
2   **Limited:** The student uses vocabulary that is too general and immature to allow for adequate discussion beyond a fairly literal level.
1   **Poor:** The student's vocabulary and sentence skills are too deficient to support ideas required by the level of discussion.

Chapter Summary: Performance Assessment, a Diverse and Powerful Tool

The examples in this chapter, combined with those presented in Chapters 8 and 10, reveal the immense flexibility and potential of performance assessment. They remind us, too, of the great depth of information we can generate about student attainment of complex skill and product outcomes.

They also lead us to a few conclusions about the effective use of performance assessment:

- Start with a sharply focused vision of the meaning of academic success. A thorough understanding is essential. Imagine what it would be like to try to develop performance criteria to evaluate a skill or product you knew nothing about.

- Use precise language to label and define all key dimensions of performance before trying to devise a scoring scheme.

- Use the full range of scoring options: rating scales, checklists, and anecdotal records.

- Develop rating scales so as to describe performance at all points along the continuum. This is how we can help students see themselves becoming more proficient.

- Devise exercises that ask respondents to prove they can use what they know. Be sure to remind them of the scoring criteria to be used with each performance—no surprises.

- Even when relying on holistic scoring, we must go through the process of developing a complete set of performance criteria. What are the elements of performance to be combined into the overall judgment? Don't let holistic scoring be a license to be sloppy.

- We can also focus our performance assessments on group performance. In real life, we are team members much of the time.

- Invest in thorough rater training (whether those assessors be teachers or students). Remember, our goal is high interrater agreement. We want two independent observers to agree on the level of proficiency demonstrated.

Remember that our professional journals are presenting more and more performance assessments, including descriptions of exercises and performance criteria. Thus, very often, those who wish to assess performance need not start from scratch. Help may be readily available from colleagues and associates across the country who may already have designed exercises and devised scoring criteria. Learn to tap these sources.

Also, if you don't have the time or other resources available to develop and use a full-blown performance assessment, proxy measures, such as the essay format described in Chapter 7, may help you come very close to your intended outcome. As in the examples provided in Chapter 9, learning logs, diaries, and notebooks provide students with an opportunity to write about their thinking. Although these options may not be as "authentic" as real performance assessments, they, too, can provide a clear view of important forms of student achievement.

Finally and most importantly, remember that students can be full partners in designing, developing, and using performance assessments like those presented above in their classrooms. And when they do play key roles in the assessment process, they will think of creative and engaging exercises, and will define performance criteria that have value for them. They may well need guidance and leadership from their teacher. But with that help, they can contribute, learn a great deal, and enjoy doing so.

Exercises to Advance Your Learning

Knowledge and Reasoning

1. List the key attributes of sound performance criteria. Analyze four or five of the examples provided in this chapter. Did they meet these standards?

2. Review all of the examples of performance assessments provided in Chapters 8, 10, and 11 and analyze them according to the following categories:

List all of the achievement targets covered.

How many assess skills; products?

How many assess individuals; groups?

How many focus on structured exercises; naturally occurring events?

How many yield holistic scores; analytical scores?

How many transform results into rating scales; checklists?

How many rely on criteria that the student could learn to apply? If it depends, what does it depend on?

What generalizations can you make about performance assessment from these analyses?

Skills and Products

1. Find an example of a performance assessment developed by others that covers targets from a discipline familiar to you. Evaluate it in terms of the attributes of a sound assessment. Is it a quality assessment?

Dispositions

1. Some have argued that performance assessments are too subjective and potentially biased to justify the attention they are receiving these days. Now that you have studied the methodology itself and many examples of its application for classroom use, do you think it is possible to devise assessments that minimize bias? How might you convince skeptics?

2. I have argued that, even when a teacher is adopting or adapting other people's assessment criteria and procedures, that teacher can connect the performance assessments directly to instruction by involving students in developing the criteria, and by guiding them in the right direction as needed. Do you think this represents sound practice? Why or why not?

Special Ongoing Assessment Project: Part 8

From your selected unit of instruction, in conjunction with Chapter 8, you identified some skill or product targets of interest to you and developed a performance assessment. For further practice, go back and evaluate that work, making adjustments in that assessment as needed based on the new lessons you learned in this chapter. If possible, also identify patterns of reasoning you expect your students to master and develop an additional performance assessment out of those achievement expectations.

12

Assessing Student Dispositions

CHAPTER ROADMAP

From the beginning of our journey, we have spoken of the need to assess five kinds of targets. Yet our conversation has centered most directly on those four dealing with interrelated forms of academic achievement. When we assess mastery of subject matter knowledge, we seek to know how much of the material the student has learned. When we assess reasoning, we seek to know how effectively the student can use that knowledge to solve problems. When we assess skills, we evaluate what a student can do. When we assess products, we evaluate the quality of the things the student creates. Now we turn to the fifth target: student dispositions, the feeling dimensions of students in school—the inner motivations or desires that influence their thoughts and their actions. In this case, we center not on what students know and can do, but on what they *feel* about key aspects of their schooling—the attitudes, motivations, and interests that predispose students to behave in academically productive ways.

More specifically, our mission in this chapter is to make this affective target understandable and accessible to teachers and students in the classroom. We will define and examine strategies for assessing students' dispositions, or their prevailing tendencies or inclinations to act in academically and intellectually productive ways.

As a result of studying the material presented in Chapter 12, reflecting on that material, and completing the learning exercises presented at the end of the chapter, you will master the following knowledge:

1. State reasons why all teachers should attend to student dispositions.
2. List attributes of high-quality assessments of dispositions.
3. Understand differences between assessments of achievement and assessments of disposition.

4. Know ground rules for the productive assessment of student feelings in the classroom.

5. State definitions of specific dispositional targets.

6. Specify alternative methods of assessing those targets, detailing strengths, limitations, and keys to effective use of each.

7. List specific ideas for developing and using each method.

You will be able to use that knowledge to reason as follows:

1. Transform certain dispositions into probes that tap both direction and intensity of student feelings, using paper and pencil formats, performance assessment, and direct personal communication.

2. Evaluate assessments developed by others to determine if they meet standards of quality.

You will become skillful at carrying out the steps required to develop sound dispositional assessments. Thus, you will be able to produce questionnaires, performance assessments, and interview protocols that meet standards of quality.

And finally, you will, I hope, come to believe the following:

1. Student dispositions are important results of classroom instruction and are key contributors to high levels of student achievement.

2. High-quality assessment of student dispositions can be developed in classrooms.

In terms of the big road map, as shown in Figure 12–1, we will be concentrating on the darkened dispositions line at the bottom.

	SELECTED RESPONSE	ESSAY	PERFORMANCE ASSESSMENT	PERSONAL COMMUNICATION
Know				
Reason				
Skills				
Products				
Dispositions				

Figure 12–1
Aligning Achievement Targets and Assessment Methods

Schools are about more than academic achievement. Our aspirations for our students extend beyond achieved competence. We do little good to teach students to be competent writers if, in the end, they do not see themselves as competent, or worse, if they hate to write. If they fail to see the value of writing, they will not be disposed to use the skills they have acquired. Similarly, we fall short of our goal of developing competent readers if we fail to impart the great joy and power of reading. If those feelings are missing, our students will not be disposed to weave reading into their lives. Indeed, we can do great harm if the schooling process leaves our students feeling as though they are incapable of learning. Regardless of their actual ability to learn, if they don't perceive themselves as in charge of their own academic well-being, they will not be predisposed to become the lifelong learners they will need to be in the twenty-first century. Attitudes about writing and reading, as well as academic self-concept, are important targets of classroom instruction.

Thus, in this chapter we deal with the feeling dimensions of students in school—the inner motivations or desires—the dispositions that influence thought and action. In this case, we center not on what students know and can do, but on what they feel about key aspects of their schooling. We term these *affective* targets. Like achievement, affect is a multidimensional human characteristic, including such subcategories as attitudes, motivations, and interests. We will discuss student affect about the many ingredients of school: teachers, classmates, school subjects, extracurricular activities, instructional methods, themselves as learners, and others.

I hope you will be pleased to learn that our assessment challenge in this case is quite easy to understand. Feelings about school vary both in their direction (from positive through neutral to negative) and intensity (from very strong to moderate to very weak). Our assessment task is to tap both direction and intensity.

With these two features in mind, I can share why I have adopted the label *dispositions* in this chapter. Our instructional goals for developing student affect are not value neutral. Often, we hope for strong, typically positive feelings in our students when it comes to learning. We strive to develop learners who are predisposed to behave in certain academically productive ways in school. We seek a strong work ethic, positive motivation, intense interests, positive attitudes, and a positive academic self-concept—that is, a strong sense of internal control over one's own academic success. Sometimes we seek to develop strong negative dispositions that influence students to behave in certain ways, such as the disposition not to use drugs or engage in other unhealthy, unsafe, or inconsiderate behaviors. We can know if we are succeeding in achieving these goals only if we are ready to assess student dispositions or affect within the context of our own schools and classrooms.

Why Should We Care About Student Dispositions?

There are those who contend that school is, in fact, only about academic achievement—that student feelings, or their dispositions, should be off-limits. They feel that attitudes and interests are the responsibility of family, church, and community. And in a sense, I must agree with them. Families and communities differ widely regarding the "proper" attitudes and values to hold. Given those differences of opinion, it becomes very difficult for schools to decide which ones should be factored into the school curriculum.

One approach to resolving such a dilemma would be to leave the matter of values, attitudes, and such out of the educational equation altogether. Render those unto the family, community, and religious institutions.

But there remains one equally compelling reason why, as teachers, we absolutely must address dispositions in the classroom. The fact is that motivational predispositions go a long way toward determining whether any given student will or can achieve. In other words, affect and achievement cannot be separated from one another in the classroom. Given this reality, then, as a teacher I must know how to help students develop academically empowering dispositions and I must be ready to teach them how to use those dispositions to promote their own success.

Students who have positive attitudes, the motivation to try, and a sense of internal control of their own academic well-being are more likely to achieve at high levels than those who are negative, lack desire, and see themselves as victims of a hostile school world. Very often, students fail not because they cannot achieve, but because they don't want to achieve. Often, they have given up and are not motivated to learn. Why? There may be many reasons: They don't understand the work, find it too hard to do, lack prerequisite achievement, and so on. And so they fail, which in turn robs them of (1) the prerequisites for the next learning and (2) a sense that they could succeed if they tried. This can become a vicious cycle—a self-fulfilling prophecy. They feel academically powerless and thus become powerless. This negative academic self-concept drives out of students any motivation to try. This is the downward spiral that can result from the complex interaction between achievement and affect. These students become predisposed to fail.

Remember, however, that this spiral also has a positive version. Right from the time students arrive at school, they look to their teacher for evidence of the extent to which they are succeeding in this place called school. If that early evidence (from their teacher's classroom assessments) suggests that they are succeeding, what can begin to grow in them is a sense of hopefulness for the future and an expectation of further success down the road. This, in turn, fuels the motivation to strive for excellence, which spawns more success and results in an upward spiral of positive dispositions and academic achievement that every parent and teacher dreams of for their children. These students become predisposed to succeed.

Clearly, there are many forces in a student's life that exert great influence on attitudes, values, interests, self-concept—indeed, dispositions to try to achieve excellence. Chief among these are family, peer group, church, and community. But schools are prominent on this list of contributors, too, especially when it comes to dispositions to invest the energy required to learn. To the extent that you wish to help students to take advantage of affect as a driving force toward greater achievement, it will be important for you to know how to define and assess it well.

In a very real sense, the theme of this book is that students' willingness to take responsibility for their own learning and their ultimate academic success go hand in hand. We can use the assessment process to engender in our students strong motivation to try by using assessment to do the following:

- reveal the affective target to them in rich detail
- show the students how to get there from here
- provide focused practice
- permit students to monitor their progress along the way

Thus, student-centered assessment can fuel a strong sense of hope for success on the student's part, predisposing that student to pursue academic excellence.

Time for Reflection

From a personal point of view, which of your school-related feelings (positive or negative) seem to have been most closely associated with your achievement successes in school? Were there subjects you liked or disliked? Instructors who motivated or failed to motivate? Positive or negative values that you held? How have your dispositions toward school related to your achievement? Discuss these with colleagues or classmates.

Remain Mindful of the Five Standards of Quality

During the course of my decade of classroom assessment research, and as I offer workshops across the country on classroom assessment topics, I find a pervasive tendency to take lightly the assessment of affective student characteristics. Many seem to assume that, because it is not achievement ("It's only affect"), we don't have to plan for or conduct rigorous assessments. As a result, many fail to attend carefully to standards of assessment quality in this endeavor. If your assessments of student dispositions are to be useful, they too must arise from clear targets and reflect those targets with proper methods. In fact, as you shall see, everything you have learned about quality assessment up to this point remains relevant in assessing student dispositions:

- Start with a clear vision of the affective target—what dispositions will you assess?
- Establish a clear reason for assessing—why will you assess them?
- Rely on proper assessment methods—which method provides the most accurate reflection?
- Sample appropriately—how can you gather sufficient information to make dependable inferences about student dispositions?
- Control for extraneous interference—what factors could bias or distort results and how do we prevent these problems?

The range of available assessment methods is the same as it is for achievement targets. You can opt for paper and pencil methods (selected response or essay), performance assessments, and/or personal communication. While the assessments themselves may look different in format, the basic methodology remains constant, as do the attributes of sound assessment. The keys to success are to start with a clear vision and to know how to translate it effectively into quality assessments.

But There Is One Critical Difference

There is one very important difference between student achievement and student affect that bears directly on differences in the manner in which we use assessment. That difference has to do with the reasons for assessing. Let me explain.

It is perfectly acceptable to hold students accountable for the mastery of knowledge, reasoning, skill, and/or product targets. In this context, we assess to verify that students have met our expectations. However, it is *not* acceptable to hold students accountable in the same sense for their dispositions. It is never acceptable, for example, to lower a student's grade because of an attitude that we regard as negative or because a student has a poor academic self-concept. Nor, conversely, is it acceptable to raise a student's grade just because of a positive attitude, regardless of achievement.

Rather, we assess dispositions in the hope of finding positive, productive attitudes, values, and sense of academic self—strong positive academic values, positive attitudes about particular subjects, strong interests in particular topics, and things students say they like to do and can do well—so we can take advantage of these to promote greater achievement gains.

But if our assessments reveal negative affect, then we have an obligation to plan educational experiences that will result in the positive dispositions we hope for. In fact, such experiences may or may not succeed in producing the positive motivational predisposition we desire. But, if we do not succeed in this endeavor, we cannot place sanctions on students with negative affect in the same way we can for those who fail to achieve academically. We cannot hold them accountable for positive affect in the same way we do for positive achievement.

On the contrary, I think responsibility for school-related affect should rest with us educators. As a teacher, I hold myself accountable for the dispositions my students develop about classroom assessment as a result of the training I offer. If I don't turn them on to the critical importance of quality assessment, if they don't leave my classes feeling a strong sense of responsibility to learn about and create quality assessments, I regard that as my fault. I must strive to find better ways to motivate my students to act responsibly with respect to the quality of their classroom assessments.

Time for Reflection

In your experience as a student, have you ever had a report card grade greatly influenced (i.e., raised or lowered) by some aspect of your attitudes or motivations? What was that experience like? What impact did it have on your motivational dispositions?

Three Ground Rules

Before we begin to define and to discuss ways to assess dispositions, let's pause briefly and agree on three critically important ground rules for dealing with these targets in the classroom.

Ground Rule 1.   *Always remain keenly aware of the sensitive interpersonal nature of student feelings and strive to promote positive dispositions through your assessment of these.* The process of assessing feelings of any sort yields vulnerability on both sides. When you assess, you ask students to risk being honest in an environment where honesty on their part has not always been held at a premium. They may be reticent to express honest feelings because of a lack of experience in doing so and because of the risk that the results somehow could be used against them. It takes a teacher who is a master of human relations to break through these barriers and promote honest expression of feelings in classrooms. One way I have done this is to permit respondents to my queries to remain anonymous. More about that later.

And for your part, you risk asking for honesty in a place where the honest response just may not turn out to be the one you had hoped to hear. Negative feedback is never easy to hear and act on. So many avoid this danger by simply not asking. If you ask how students are feeling about things in your classroom, listen thoughtfully to the answers, and act on the results in good faith, the reward will be worth the risk you take. The result will be a more productive student-teacher relationship—a working partnership characterized by greater trust.

Time for Reflection

Under the best of circumstances, teachers become anxious when the time comes to ask students what they think about their teaching. Can you think of specific actions a teacher might take in preparing for, conducting, and interpreting the results of such an assessment to minimize the personal risk? List as many ideas as you can. Discuss them with colleagues or classmates.

Ground Rule 2.   *Know your limits when dealing with affective dimensions of instruction.* There are two important interrelated limits of which you should be aware. First, as you come to understand and assess affect, you will occasionally encounter students who are deeply troubled, personally and/or socially. Be caring but cautious in these instances. These are not occasions for you to become an amateur psychologist. If you find yourself in a situation where you feel uneasy with what you are learning about a student or about your ability to help that student deal productively with feelings or circumstances, you may well be reaching the limits of your professional expertise. Listen to your instincts and get help.

The most caring and responsible teachers are those who know when it is time to contact the principal, a counselor, a school psychologist, or a physician to find competent counseling services for students. Do not venture into personal territory for which you are not trained. You can do harm if you fail to respond appropriately—even with the most positive intentions.

The second set of limits is a corollary to the first. I urge you to focus your attention on those classroom-level dispositions over which you are likely to (and in fact should) have some influence. When assessing and evaluating student feelings, stick with those feelings as they relate to specific school-related objects: dispositions toward subjects or classroom activities, interests they would like to pursue, personal dispositions as a learner in an academic setting, and so on. These have a decidedly school-oriented bent and they represent values families and school communities are likely to agree are important as parts of the schooling experience.

I urge you to avoid those aspects of personal circumstance or personality that stretch beyond the classroom, such as family values, anxiety, or personal self-concept. These can either take you beyond your capacity as a professional, or take you into value arenas that your students' families or communities may regard as out of bounds for school personnel.

Please understand this: You need not go too far over those classroom-related limits before members of your community may begin to see your actions on behalf of positive, productive affect as invading their turf. Some families and communities are very protective of their responsibility to promote the development of certain strongly held values and will not countenance interference from schools. This is their right.

You must decide how to deal with these limits within your community. Just be advised that the conservative approach is to focus in your classroom on those dimensions of affect that we all agree are the legitimate purview of the teacher—dispositions toward school-related matters. As the chapter progresses, you will attain a clearer sense of what this means.

Time for Reflection

How might a teacher, or even an entire school, work with the community to establish parameters for dealing with affective targets—to divide responsibility for assuring positive student feelings about school and school-related topics without stepping out of bounds? What specific strategies come to mind for heading off problems in advance?

Ground Rule 3.   *If you care enough to understand affect and to develop quality assessments in this arena, then care enough to take the results seriously and change your instruction when results suggest there may be a need for change.* In other words, don't ask how students are feeling about things just to appear to care. The more you act on the results of these assessments, the greater the potential that students will share feelings in the future that will allow you to improve the nature and quality of your learning environment. When done well, assessment of school-related dispositions can be a productive classroom activity for students and teachers. It can lead to specific actions on the part of teachers and students that promote constructive learning and maximum achievement.

Defining *Affect* as It Relates to Dispositions

To make sense of the range of possible targets that might be included under this heading, I will follow Anderson's (1981) lead and discuss several kinds of affect that have relevance in the school setting: attitudes, interests, motivation, school-related values, academic self-concept, and locus of control.[1] These represent significant dimensions of classroom affect that are relatively easy to define and understand. But more importantly, they represent attributes of students that predispose them to behave in academically productive ways that at the same time can be assessed in the classroom using relatively straightforward procedures.

However, be advised that these are not the only forms of affect referred to in the professional literature. Sometimes, for example, educational goals may refer to such attributes as interpersonal sensitivity, honesty, morality, responsibility, and self-assurance, among others. In this chapter, we will not delve into all of these forms of affect for three reasons: Our available space is limited, the definitions of these additional options are not as clear and sharp as those listed above, and sometimes these kinds of affect can take us dangerously close to the limits of our professional and community responsibility (in my opinion). We will therefore limit our discussion to the six kinds of affect listed.

Defining Our Focus

If we are to assess these affective characteristics, we must begin with clear and specific definitions. In this section, we will learn some basic definitions that will suffice for you to be able to design simple assessments for use in your classroom. However, please realize that our education literature contains a large body of knowledge about each of the various kinds of outcomes defined here. The more deeply you can tap into that literature and understand these concepts, the easier it will be for you to address them in your assessment and instruction. Please take seriously your professional responsibility to become a student of the kinds of affect you seek for your students.

Attitudes.   Anderson defines *attitudes* as "feelings that . . . can be either unfavorable or favorable, positive or negative, and are typically directed toward some specific object. The association between the feelings and a particular object are learned. And once learned, the feelings are consistently experienced in the presence of that object" (p. 33).

Obviously, the range of attitudes we can hold is as broad as the array of experiences or objects to which we react emotionally. In schools, students might have favorable or unfavorable attitudes about each other, teachers, administrators, school subjects, instructional activities, and so on. Hopefully, success can breed

---

[1] All quotations from and references to Anderson's work in this chapter are from *Assessing Affective Characteristics in the Schools,* by L. W. Anderson, 1981, Needham, MA: Allyn & Bacon. Used by permission of the publisher.

positive attitudes, which then fuel the desire for greater achievement, which in turn breeds more positive attitudes. Thus, positive attitudes predispose students to academic success.

Interests.   These represent feelings that can range from a high level of excitement to no excitement at all at the prospect of engaging in, or while engaged in, some particular activity. Once again, the relationship between the object and level of interest is learned. A student might be very interested in drama, but completely disinterested in geography. Strong interests, like positive attitudes, can link students to the greater potential for success. In this sense, they too relate to student dispositions.

Motivation.   We will define this form of affect as the need within a student to achieve or to act favorably toward school activities and/or school-related work. It is the willingness to follow through, the disposition to seek success, to avoid failure, and to aspire to performance norms and expectations. For example, students can be highly motivated or not motivated at all to participate in some learning activity or to pursue some direction of study.

School-related Values.   Anderson thoughtfully defines these feelings as "beliefs as to what should be desired, what is important or cherished and what standards of conduct or existence are personally or socially acceptable . . . values influence or guide things: behavior, interests, attitudes, satisfactions. . . . [They] are enduring. That is, values tend to remain stable over fairly long periods of time" (p. 34). Again, the objects of our values can range far and wide and are learned. They seem to find anchor points deep in our beings. Among the values related to academic success are a strong work ethic and a sense that a learned society is likely to be productive. These, then, are values that predispose students to succeed in school.

Academic Self-concept.   No affective characteristic is more school-related than this one. It is the sum of all evaluative judgments one makes about one's possibility of success and/or productivity in an academic context. In essence, it is an attitude (favorable or unfavorable) about one's self when viewed in a classroom setting. Academic self-concept, writes Anderson, is a learned vision that results largely from evaluations of self by others over time. Quite simply, those who see themselves as capable learners are predisposed to be capable learners.

Locus of Control.   This represents a sufficiently important part of academic self-concept to justify considering separately. In this case, the characteristic of interest is the student's attributions or reasons for academic success or failure. One kind of attribution is defined as internal: "I succeeded because I tried hard." Another possible attribution is external, where chance rules: "I sure was lucky to receive that A!" Yet another attribution also is external, but someone else rules: "I performed well because I had a good teacher." At issue here are students' perceptions of the underlying reasons for the results they experienced. This, too, is a learned self-perception arising from their sense of the connection of effort to academic success.

In school, our aspiration must be to help students see the connection between their efforts and their levels of academic success. Those who perceive themselves as being in control of their own academic destiny, and who at the same time see the goal as being within their grasp, are predisposed to succeed.

Variations Within Kinds of Affect

As mentioned earlier, these various kinds of affect vary along three important dimensions: focus, direction, and intensity. They focus our feelings about specific aspects of the world around us. Some, like attitudes and values, can focus outside of ourselves. Others, like academic self-concept and locus of control, focus on our inner views.

Affect also can vary in direction—stretching from a neutral point outward in both directions along a continuum from positive to negative.

And finally, feelings vary in their intensity, from strong to moderate to weak. As you visualize the continuum for each type of affect, as you move further and further away from neutral, think of feelings as increasing in intensity. In the extremes, feelings become either strongly positive or negative.

Always bear in mind, also, that feelings can be very volatile—especially among the young. Student feelings can quickly change both in direction and intensity for a large number of reasons, only some of which are rational or understandable by adults. I mention this only to point out that it may be important to assess dispositions repeatedly over time to keep track of them. The results of any one assessment may have a very short half-life.

Anderson provides a simple table depicting these variations, reproduced in Table 12–1. Given our discussion so far, I'm sure you can begin to understand why our assessment challenge is to focus our attention on the school-related interests or concerns and to gather information on the direction and intensity of school related feelings. We capture the essence of student dispositions to success in school when we focus on the right-hand column of the table. It is quite possible to determine how closely students approximate these desired feelings, if we understand and apply some relatively straightforward assessment tactics.

Time for Reflection

Read through the entries in Table 12–1, and for each line, think of some current aspect of your life that comes close to each end of that continuum: something you have a very positive attitude about and something about which your attitude is very negative, something you're very interested in and something in which you have little interest, and so on, all the way to the bottom. Your students have feelings too—just as strong as yours. The key question is, how can we tap those feelings to improve achievement and student competence?

Table 12–1
Range of School-related Affect

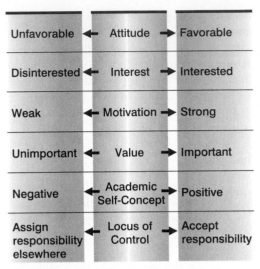

Unfavorable ←	Attitude →	Favorable
Disinterested ←	Interest →	Interested
Weak ←	Motivation →	Strong
Unimportant ←	Value →	Important
Negative ←	Academic Self-Concept →	Positive
Assign responsibility elsewhere ←	Locus of Control →	Accept responsibility

Source: Adapted from *Assessing Affective Charac-teristics in the Schools* (n.p.) by L. W. Anderson, 1981, Needham, MA: Allyn & Bacon. Copyright 1981 by Allyn & Bacon, Inc. Adapted by permission of the publisher.

Exploring the Assessment Options

So, how do we assess the focus, direction, and intensity of feelings about school-related objects? Just as with achievement, we rely on standard forms of assessment: paper and pencil methods that rely on selected responses or essays, performance assessment, and personal communication with students.

In this case, I group selected response and essay into a paper and pencil form of assessment because the two options represent different forms of questions that can appear on one of our basic affective assessment tools: the questionnaire. We can ask students questions about their feelings on a questionnaire and either offer them a finite range of response options from which to select, or ask them open-ended questions and request brief or extended written responses. If we focus the questions on affect, we can interpret responses in terms of both the direction and intensity of feelings.

Performance assessment of affective targets is like performance assessment of achievement targets. We conduct systematic observations of student behavior and/or products with clear criteria in mind and draw inferences about the direction and intensity of students' feelings. So, once again, observation and professional judgment provide the basis for this form of affective assessment.

Assessments of dispositions via personal communication typically take the form of interviews, either with the student or with others who know about the student. These can be highly structured or very casual, such as in a discussion or conversation with a student. The questions we ask and the things we talk about reveal the direction and intensity of feelings.

The remainder of this chapter is devoted to examining each of these basic assessment options and to exploring how each can help you tap the six kinds of affective targets defined for this discussion.

Matching Method to Target

Each of the methods for tapping student affect can be cast in many forms and each carries with it specific advantages, limitations, keys to success, and pitfalls to avoid. Let's examine these, then review a few tips for the effective development and use of each. As we go, I will try to illustrate how the various forms of questionnaires, performance assessment, and personal communication can be used to tap our six defined kinds of affect.

Table 12–2 shows an overview analysis of the assessment methods. As you can see, each method offers its own special set of strengths. These can help you fit each into your context as needed. Notice also that the keys to success and potential pitfalls are consistent across the bottom part of the table. Students who fail to understand and appreciate the purpose for the assessment and/or are feeling vulnerable are less likely to communicate feelings honestly. By the same token, it is critical that they understand that their task is not to create responses to please their teacher. There are no "right" answers, only honest answers. This can be a surprisingly difficult concept to get across to students whose only experience has been to strive to be correct—to try to please the teacher.

Time for Reflection

What specific actions can a teacher take to help students understand the meaning of a "socially desirable response"? This is when students give us the answer they think we want to hear or will be comfortable with, regardless of how they really feel. How can we help them see why truly honest answers are more appropriate under some circumstances?

In addition, the assessment should not be so long that motivation lags among respondents. And it should not include questions that "lead" students to the response you want to receive. Here are two out-of-balance items that lead the respondent:

1. You really do like math, don't you?
2. Which response best reflects your attitude toward math?
   a. I love it
   b. I like it a lot
   c. I find it very challenging
   d. I really enjoy it

You should instead ask focused questions in a value-neutral manner:

Table 12–2
Tools for Assessing Disposition and Affect

	Selected Response (Structured) Questionnaire	Open-ended (Nonstructured) Questionnaire	Performance Assessment	Personal Communication
Strengths	Can be sharply focused Easy to administer Easy to summarize results Results comparable across respondents Can be anonymous Can sample consistently over time	Focus can be sharp Relatively easy to develop Relatively easy to administer Reasons for feeling can be probed Can be anonymous Can sample consistently over time	Inferences can be drawn by observing behavior or products Can focus on nonverbal cues Can be unobtrusive Can observe groups or individuals	Can be highly focused Can be casual, nonthreatening Can be highly structured or not Can attend to verbal and nonverbal cues Can ask follow-up probes Respondents like attention Can produce greater depth
Limitations	No follow-up probes Reasons for feelings may not be apparent Reading proficiency required	No follow-up probes Labor-intensive processing of results Scorer can misinterpret Reading proficiency required Writing proficiency required	Can unwittingly observe atypical behavior (i.e., nonrepresenta-tive sample) Sometimes may not be anonymous Can misinterpret behaviors seen Can be time consuming	Withdrawn student may not communicate Interviewer can misinterpret Cannot be anonymous Can be time consuming
Best Results When	Purpose is clear Affective target defined Students understand and value the purpose Administration is relaxed Instructions are clear Questions worded clearly	Purpose is clear Affective target defined Students understand and value the purpose Administration is relaxed Instructions are clear Questions worded clearly Students are proficient writers	Purpose is clear Criteria are clear and appropriate Multiple observations are made Students understand and value the purpose Instructions are clear	Purpose is clear Affective target defined Students understand and value the purpose Interaction is relaxed Instructions are clear Questions worded clearly
Pitfalls to Avoid	Students don't take it seriously or feel threatened Students offer socially desirable response Too long Ambiguous questions Leading questions	Students don't take it seriously or feel threatened Students offer socially desirable response Too long Ambiguous questions Leading questions	Unclear criteria Too few observations Assessment triggers socially desirable behaviors that misrepresent real affect	Students don't take it seriously or feel threatened Students offer socially desirable response Too long Ambiguous questions Leading questions

1. How confident are you that you can solve this kind of math problem appropriately: (fill-in some math problem-solving challenge)?

And, you should offer response options that combine direction and intensity:

    a. Very confident
    b. Quite confident
    c. Somewhat confident
    d. Not confident at all

We will now consider procedural guidelines that can enhance the quality of questionnaire, performance assessment, and interview planning and design.

Questionnaires

Questionnaires represent one of the most convenient means of tapping important student dispositions. And yet, in all of my years involved in classroom assessment research, I cannot remember more than a handful of teachers who used this method in their classrooms. There are many possible reasons. Perhaps for some the risk of tapping student feelings within the learning environment is too high. Others may lack confidence in questionnaire development. Still others may think of achievement as so important that they give no attention to affect. Some may simply feel that students won't take it seriously.

The best way I know to get students to take questionnaires seriously (i.e., to provide complete and honest responses) is to let them know that they have everything to gain and nothing to lose by being honest. That means focusing on topics students care about and establishing a reputation for acting on results in ways that benefit them.

Within the questionnaire itself, we must strive to ask questions that are relevant—about which students are likely to have an informed opinion. We must avoid ambiguity; ask brief, precise, complete questions; and offer response options that make sense.

Whenever I develop a questionnaire, I strive to combine all of these ideas in a way that enlists the support of the respondent as an ally, a partner in generating useful information—that is, information that promises to help us both. Sometimes that means permitting responses to be offered anonymously, to reduce the risk to the respondent. Sometimes it means promising to share results or promising to act purposefully and quickly based on those results. Sometimes it just means urging them to take the questionnaire seriously, to care as I do about the value of the results for making things better for all. In any event, I try to break down the barriers between us.

Time for Reflection

What ways can you think of to develop and use questionnaires in the classroom in a manner that encourages students to become partners in the process and to use results to create a better classroom for all?

Selected Response Formats.   We have a variety of formats to choose from as we design questionnaires. For example, Gable (1986) suggests that we can ask students if they agree with specific statements, how important they regard specific things, how they would judge the quality of an object of interest, or how frequently an event occurs. The following examples demonstrate possible response options for these kinds of scales. Note that each scale represents both direction and intensity of feelings. Let's see how they apply to our defined kinds of affect.

We might wish to assess student attitudes toward a specific instructional strategy. One way to do this is to present a positive statement:

Do you agree or disagree with the following statement in respect to your own learning?

The group project we did in class yesterday helped me learn more about my leadership skills.
  a.   Strongly agree
  b.   Agree
  c.   Undecided
  d.   Disagree
  e.   Strongly disagree

Or, we might assess student interest in participating in certain activities:

Would you like to do more collaborative group projects in the future? How important are such projects to you?
  a.   Very important
  b.   Important
  c.   Undecided
  d.   Unimportant
  e.   Very unimportant

Other such selected response scales tap the perceived quality of some object or activity:

How would you judge your performance in preparing your term paper?
  a.   Excellent
  b.   Good
  c.   Fair
  d.   Poor
  e.   Very poor

Some may determine perceived frequency of occurrence of a particular event:

How frequently do you feel you understand and can do the math homework assignments you receive in this class?
  a.   Always
  b.   Frequently
  c.   Occasionally
  d.   Rarely
  e.   Never

One of the most common forms of selected response questionnaire items asks the student to choose between or among some forced choices. The following examples are designed to help us understand a student's locus of control:

If I do well on a test, it is typically because
  a.   my teacher taught me well.
  b.   I was lucky.
  c.   I studied hard.

or

I failed to master that particular skill because
  a.   I didn't try hard enough.
  b.   my teacher didn't show me how.

Yet another kind of selected response format, one that I use extensively, is a scale anchored at each end by polar adjectives and offering direction and intensity options in between. Here's an example focused on student interest and motivation:

Use the scales provided below to describe your feelings about participating in the school subjects listed. Place an X on the line that best reflects your feelings:

Math

very interested __ __ __ __ __ completely disinterested
very motivated __ __ __ __ __ completely unmotivated

Science

very interested __ __ __ __ __ completely disinterested
very motivated __ __ __ __ __ completely unmotivated

Time for Reflection

Let's say you want to tap the attitudes of your students about the textbook you are using. Your task is to gather information about the direction and intensity of their most important feelings about this book. Create 5 to 10 bipolar scales like those above that reflect key elements of a textbook. Once gathered, how might such information be used to advantage?

An easy adaptation of the selected response format can provide a means of tapping the attitudes of very young students. Rather than using words to describe feeling states, we can use simple pictures:

Given an object about which to express their feelings, such as free reading time, for example, you would instruct the students to circle the face that tells how they feel about that object.

If you focus these kinds of response scales on specific school-related objects, students can have a relatively easy time revealing their attitudes, interests, school-related values, academic self-concept, and the like. Further, it is usually easy to summarize results across respondents. The pattern of responses, and therefore the feelings, of a group of students is easily seen by tallying the number and percent of students who select each response option—a straightforward summary of results.

Written Response.   Another kind of question we might pose on a questionnaire is the essay, in which the respondents are free to write in their response. If we ask specific questions eliciting direction and intensity of feelings about specific school-related issues, we may readily interpret responses to even unstructured questions:

> Write a brief paragraph describing how you feel about our guest speaker today. Please comment on your level of interest in the presentation, how well informed you thought the speaker was, and how provocative you found the message to be. Also, express any other feelings you might have had during the presentation. As you write, be sure to tell me how strong your positive or negative feelings are. I will use your reactions to plan for guest speakers for the future.

We may combine some assessment of affect with some practice in evaluative thinking:

> As you think about the readings we did this month, which three did you find most worthwhile? For each, specify why you found it worthwhile.

A thoughtful reading of the responses to these kinds of questions will reveal similarities or differences in students' opinions and can be useful in planning for future instruction.

Some Additional Thoughts About Questionnaires.   To maximize the efficiency and value of the results obtained, always connect your questions to direct action. By this, I mean ask only those questions that will provide you with the specific and significant information you need to make your decisions. For each question you pose, you should be able to anticipate the course of action you will take given each possible response: "If my students respond this way, I will do this. . . . If they respond the other way, the results will mean that I should instead do that. . . . " Discard any query that leaves you wondering what you'll do with the results.

I have one more critical piece of advice: If you promise respondents that the information will be gathered anonymously, stick with that promise under *all* circumstances. Never try to subvert such a promise with invisible coding or other identification systems. Students need be caught in that trap only once to come to believe that neither teachers nor administrators can be trusted. We face a hard enough challenge establishing open channels of communication without having to overcome this kind of obstacle, too.

Time for Reflection

Have you ever been promised anonymity and then had that trust violated? If so, what was that experience like for you? What impact did it have? If you have not had this experience, ask around and find someone who has. Ask that person to describe the experience, and listen to his or her affect!

And remember, if you plan your selected response questionnaire carefully and coordinate the response modes with a mark-sensing optical-scan response sheet, you can use scanning technology to save time and effort in summarizing the questionnaire results for you. Very often, these machines can produce frequency-of-response tallies in record time, making your job much easier. If there is one mistake I see inexperienced questionnaire designers make, it is failing to comprehend the time it will take to summarize the results. Check with your district computer personnel to see if this technology is available.

Performance Assessments

In one sense, using observations and judgments as the basis for evaluating student dispositions is a practice that is as old as humankind. In another sense, it is an idea that has barely been tried.

The sense in which performance assessment has been a standard indicator of dispositions has to do with the inferences we tend to draw when we see students doing certain things. Adhering to classroom rules, for example, is often cited as evidence of a "positive attitude." Or, tardiness is seen as evidence of a lack of respect for school or as evidence of irresponsibility. Sometimes we observe and reflect on our interactions with students, such as when they appear not to be trying or not seeming to care, and we infer that they are "unmotivated" and "have a bad attitude."

While these inferences may be correct, they also can be dangerous. What if our casual observations and intuitive conclusions are wrong? What if adhering to the rules reflects a low willingness to take risks, tardiness is due to some factor beyond the student's control, or the apparent lack of motivation is not a result of low self-esteem, but rather an indication that we were not clear in helping that student understand the task to be completed? If our inferences are wrong, we may well plan and carry out activities that completely miss the point.

A Very Important Note of Caution.   My point is that the cavalier manner in which we observe and draw inferences about student attitudes, values, interests, and the like very often reflects our own lack of regard for the basic principles of sound assessment. The rules of evidence for observing and judging don't change just because the nature of the target changes. Vague targets, inappropriately cast into the wrong methods, that fail to sample or control for bias lead to incorrect assessments of dispositions just as they lead to incorrect inferences about achievement. The rules of evidence for sound assessment are *never* negotiable.

For this reason, developing performance assessments of affect requires that we follow exactly the same basic design sequence used for performance assessment of achievement. We must specify the performance to be evaluated, select a context and method within which to observe, and devise a method to record and store results.

This does not mean spontaneous observations and judgments are unacceptable. But we must remain vigilant, for many things can go wrong with such on-the-spot assessments. That awareness can serve to make us appropriately cautious when making snap judgments.

Time for Reflection

Have you ever been the victim of a performance assessment in which a teacher's observation and judgment of your actions led to an incorrect inference about your affect? What were the circumstances? What impact did this mismeasurement have on you?

As developers of affective performance assessments, we face the same design decisions that we spelled out in detail in Chapters 8 and 10. They are translated into design questions for the assessment of affect in Figure 12–2.

I know this list of design questions looks imposing in this context. You might read it and ask, Why be so formal? It's not as if we're conducting an assessment for a final grade or something! In fact, many regard it as instinctive for teachers to observe some behavior and infer almost intuitively about student attitudes, motivations, school-related values, and so on.

But this is exactly my point. We often think that, just because this is "only affect," we can disregard all of the requirements of sound assessment. I promise you, if you disregard the rules of evidence in conducting assessments based on observation and judgment—whether assessing attitude or writing proficiency—your assessment will almost always produce questionable and/or unreliable results. For this reason, it is *always* important to strive for quality assessment.

A Classroom Application.   Here is an example of a productive performance assessment of student dispositions in the classroom: Let's say we want to assess students' motivational predispositions to apply their best critical thinking skills when they are needed. Remember when we spoke of the concept of the "critical spirit" defined by Norris and Ennis (1989) in Chapter 10? Let's plan to assess the direction and intensity of this affective characteristic.

To conduct this assessment, we plan to focus on individual student performance in a team problem-solving context. To make the assessment as efficient as possible, we randomly select a few students to observe each day.

Further, let's say that we know from prior assessments that the students have mastered critical thinking skills and that they know how and when to bring these skills into play in group work contexts. So the essential procedural knowledge is in place. Now the question is, Will they use appropriate skills when needed?

1. How shall we define the disposition to be assessed?
    What shall we focus on to evaluate student feelings?
    •   A behavior exhibited by the student?
    •   A product created by the student?
    Who will our assessment focus on?
    •   Individual students?
    •   Students in groups?
    What specific performance criteria will guide our observations and inferences about student affect?

2. How shall we elicit performance to be evaluated in terms of the disposition it reflects?
    Which format will we use?
    •   Structured exercises?
    •   Observe students during naturally occurring classroom events?
    How many instances of performance will we need to observe to make confident generalizations about student feelings?
    If we use structured exercises, what will we tell students to do under what conditions, according to what standards of performance?

3. What method will we use to record results of our observations?
    Which do we wish to obtain?
    •   A single overall judgment about student affect?
    •   Are there specific aspects of their feelings we wish to tap?
    What record will we create of student affect?
    •   Checklist?
    •   Rating scale?
    •   Anecdotal record?
    Who will observe and judge?
    •   The teacher?
    •   Students themselves?

Figure 12–2
Designing Performance Assessments of Affect

Our primary source of evidence will be student interaction behaviors. That is, when students work in groups, do they exhibit proper critical thinking skills at appropriate times? If so, we can infer that they are, in fact, motivated to display the desired "critical spirit."

Our performance criteria, therefore, will list group interaction skills indicative of critical reasoning. We will look for their application during teamwork time. And so, in this case—just as with performance assessment of achievement—we must know in advance how a high-level performer differs from a low-level performer. If we cannot specify that difference, we cannot dependably assess the desired dispo-sitions.

Because we want to observe performance under normal conditions, we will conduct our assessment unobtrusively by watching and evaluating interaction skills during our regularly scheduled teamwork time. Thus, we will rely on naturally occurring events to trigger performance.

Our record-keeping method will be a simple checklist of attributes of those who demonstrate "critical spirit" behaviors, as shown in Figure 12–3. We will ran-domly select several students and watch their interactions. Every time a certain skill should have come into play, we check that skill. If the student comes through and delivers as needed, we check that, too. The question is, What proportion of invitations to exhibit specific critical thinking skills actually elicits the required skill? The higher the proportion, the stronger the "critical spirit." But remember, all of this is contingent on verifying in advance that students know how and when to behave as critical thinkers. If that knowledge base is not in place, performance is beyond reach.

This example of performance assessment of affect reveals the subtlety of this evaluation process: We observe behaviors or examine products to infer about stu-dent attitudes, values, interests, and so on. Thus, we analyze performance for signs of the direction and intensity of attitude, interest, school-related values, or self-concept. In that sense, this is an indirect assessment method. We rely on exter-nal indicators to infer about internal states of mind. When we use questionnaires or interviews, we ask students direct questions about their feelings. This typically is not the case with performance assessment. That means we could easily draw incor-

Figure 12–3
Checklist for Evaluating Critical Spirit
Source: Adapted from *Evaluating Critical Thinking* (Chapter 1) by S. Norris and R. Ennis, 1989, Pacific Grove, CA: Critical Thinking Books & Software. Copyright 1989 by Critical Thinking Books & Software. Adapted by permission of the publisher.

Critical thinkers
____ seek a statement of the question
____ seek reasons and explanations when they need them
____ act purposely to be well informed
____ use and refer to credible sources of information
____ keep their thinking relevant and to the point
____ look for alternatives
____ remain open minded
    ____ seriously consider points of view other than their own
    ____ disagree without letting disagreement interfere with their reasoning
    ____ withhold judgment when evidence is insufficient
____ take a position but change it when evidence requires it
____ bring order to complex parts
____ are sensitive to feelings, level of knowledge, and degree of sophistication of others

rect inferences if we have not planned carefully and carried out a thoughtful assessment, according to the rules of performance assessment evidence described earlier in this text. Beware here—danger lurks if you violate our standards of assessment quality.

Personal Communication as a Window to Student Feelings

Most regard direct communication as an excellent path to understanding student feelings about school-related topics. We can interview students individually or in groups, conduct discussions with them, or even rely on casual discussions to gain insight about their attitudes, values, and preferences.

This method offers much. Unlike questionnaires, we can establish personal contact with the respondent, and can ask follow-up questions. This allows us to more completely understand student feelings. Unlike performance assessment, we can gather our information directly, avoiding the danger of drawing incorrect inferences. This assures a higher level of accuracy and confidence in our assessment results.

Keys to Success.   One key to success in tapping true student feelings is *trust*. I cannot overemphasize its critical importance. Respondents must be comfortable honestly expressing the direction and intensity of their feelings. Respondents who lack trust will either tell us what they think we want to hear (i.e., give the socially

---

- *Don't overlook the power of group interview.* Marketing people call these *focus groups*. Sometimes students' feelings come clear to them and to you by bouncing them off or comparing them to others. Besides, there can be a feeling of safety in numbers, allowing respondents to open up a bit more.

- *Rely on students as interviewers or discussion leaders.* Often, they know how to probe the real and important feelings of their classmates. Besides, they have credibility in places where you may not.

- *Become an attentive listener.* Ask focused questions about the direction and intensity of feelings and then listen attentively for evidence of the same. Sometimes interviewers come off looking and acting like robots. Sometimes just a bit of interpersonal warmth will open things up.

- *Be prepared to record results in some way.* Often we use tape recorders in interview contexts, but this is certainly not the only way to capture student responses. For example, you could create a written questionnaire form but ask the questions personally and complete the questionnaire as you go. Or, you could just take notes and transcribe them into a more complete record later. In any event, students will appreciate that you asked how they felt, but only if you seem to remember what they said and take it into consideration in your instructional planning.

Figure 12–4
Guidelines for Conducting Interviews to Assess Disposition

desirable response) or they will shut us out altogether. For many students, it is difficult to communicate honest feelings in an interview setting with the real power sitting on the other side of the table, because all hope of anonymity evaporates. This can seem risky to them.

Another key to success is to have adequate time to plan and conduct high-quality assessments. This is a labor-intensive means of soliciting information.

In many ways, the remaining keys to success in an interview setting are the same as those for questionnaires:

- Prepare carefully.
- Make sure respondents know why you are gathering this information.
- Ask focused, clear, brief questions that get at the direction and intensity of feelings about specific school-related topics.
- Act on results in ways that serve students' best interests.

In other ways, this assessment format brings with it some unique challenges. Figure 12–4 offers guidelines to help you meet those challenges.

Chapter Summary: Assessing Dispositions as a Path to Higher Achievement

Our fifth and final target for students is the development of positive dispositions about learning. The assessment question is, Are students developing the positive attitudes, strong interests, positive motivations, positive school values, positive academic self-concept, and internal locus of control needed to succeed in school and beyond? These are affective targets reflecting student tendencies to behave in academically productive ways during the schooling process. They vary both in intensity and direction, ranging from strongly positive to strongly negative. Our assessment challenge is to track their intensity and direction.

There are two basic reasons why we should care about student dispositions. First, they have value in their own right. They represent personal characteristics that we in the United States value as a society. It is the American way to want all citizens to feel as though they are in control of their own destinies. Second, student attitudes, motivation, interests, and preferences are closely related to achieve-

ment. While it may be arguable which comes first, achievement or positive affect, we know that they both support each other in important ways.

Our assessment options in this case are the same as those we use to track student achievement: paper and pencil, performance assessment, and personal communication. Paper and pencil alternatives take the form of questionnaires. We reviewed several different question formats for use in these instruments. Performance assessments have us observing student behaviors and/or products and drawing inferences about affective states. The careful development of these observation-based assessments may help us draw strong inferences about dispositions. Personal communication using interviews, discussions, and conversations can clarify student attitudes and often give the clearest insights.

We began the chapter with three specific ground rules intended to prevent the misassessment of these important student characteristics and prevent the misuse of the results. They bear repeating as final thoughts on this topic.

- Always remain keenly aware of the sensitive interpersonal nature of student feelings and strive to promote positive dispositions through your assessment of these outcomes.

- Know your limits when dealing with student affect. Assess school-related feelings only and get help when you need it.

- If you care enough to learn about these affective student characteristics and to develop quality assessments of them, then care enough to take the results seriously and change your instruction when needed.

Exercises to Advance Your Learning

Knowledge

1. Explain in your own words two specific reasons why all teachers should attend to student feelings in their classrooms.

2. Without referring to the text, describe the key attributes of quality assessments of student dispositions.

3. Referring to the text, describe the essential differences between classroom assessments of achievement and assessments of dispositions.

4. Learn the three ground rules for dealing with the assessment of student feelings in the classroom so you can repeat them without referring to the text. In your own words, state why each is important.

5. Referring to the text as needed, list and define the specific kinds of affect discussed in this chapter.

6. Create your own personal version of a chart identifying alternative methods of assessing those targets. In your own words, detail strengths, limitations, and keys to effective use of each method.

7. For each method, list five practical development and use ideas from material presented in this chapter.

Reasoning

1. Return to Table 12–1 in the text. For each type of affect listed, select a focus or object of interest to you and develop two simple questions that you might use either on a questionnaire or in an interview to assess the direction and intensity of the feelings of your students.

2. Find a previously developed questionnaire and evaluate it to determine if it meets our five standards of quality.

Skills

See the Special Ongoing Assessment Project following this section.

Products

1. We have spoken in Chapters 8 and 11 of key attributes of sound performance criteria. When you have completed development of the performance criteria for the following Special Ongoing Assessment Project exercise, evaluate your work in terms of those standards.

2. Evaluate the questionnaire you develop for the following Special Project exercise in terms of the attributes of a sound assessment.

Dispositions

1. Write about the direction and intensity of your feelings about the value of affect (1) as a target of classroom instruction, and (2) as one key contributor to high levels of student achievement.

2. Write about the direction and intensity of your feelings about the need for high-quality assessment of student dispositions in the classroom.

Special Ongoing Assessment Project: Part 9

Identify some dispositions you hope your student will develop as a result of completing the special unit of instruction you have been working on. Devise a questionnaire to tap some of these dispositions. Also, create a blueprint of a performance assessment of others, including a complete set of performance criteria reflecting the feelings you intend to assess. Finally, develop a set of questions you might use in an interview context to probe some of those dispositions.

Classroom Perspectives on Standardized Testing

CHAPTER ROADMAP

Thus far, our journey through the realm of assessment has focused exclusively on assessments developed and used by the teacher in the classroom. In this chapter, however, we will veer away from that track to provide some insight into the world of large-scale standardized achievement tests. Our mission will be to review their purposes, study the complex array of assessment forms used, and understand how to interpret and use test results. We will study the standardized test development process, revealing techniques test developers use to create quality assessments. And we will develop specific lists of responsibilities to be fulfilled by teachers and administrators who administer, interpret, and use standardized testing

As a result of studying the material presented in Chapter 13, reflecting on that material, and completing the learning exercises presented at the end of the chapter, you will come to know and understand the following:

1. The various uses educators make of standardized test scores.

2. The various levels at which standardized tests are administered.

3. How the four basic forms of assessment come into play in the standardized testing context.

4. The steps in the standardized test development sequence.

5. The meaning and proper interpretation of the commonly used test scores.

Further, you will be prepared to use that knowledge to reason productively in the following ways:

1. Understand the contradictions and misconceptions that permeate the realm of standardized testing.

2. Evaluate the match between local curriculum and standardized test coverage of content, reasoning, and other skills.

3. Interpret and use standardized test scores correctly.

4. Evaluate whether standardized test results are likely to provide information relevant to a particular decision.

You will become proficient at the following skill:

1. Analyzing standardized tests for local use.

And on completing this work, I hope you will hold the following dispositions:

1. Be balanced in your opinions about the proper use of standardized tests, both in terms of their impact on student well-being relative to classroom assessment, and with respect to the various targets to be assessed and assessment methods to be used.

2. Value an assessment-literate school culture and community that understands standardized tests.

3. See a clear sense of purpose as central to effective use of standardized tests.

4. Value high-quality assessment in the standardized test context.

The objectives for this chapter do not include the creation of any products.

I have included this chapter specifically to address the classroom teacher's primary standardized testing question: What should the conscientious teacher do in response to unrelenting tendency for school administration and the community to "evaluate test scores"? The darkened cells in Figure 13–1 indicate that portion of the comprehensive assessment picture discussed in this chapter.

The contemporary educational system has included a strong standardized test tradition for decades. Standardized testing programs use their resources to develop and implement assessments in which large numbers of students respond to the same or similar sets of exercises under approximately the same conditions. Thus, it is test exercises, conditions of test administration, scoring procedures, and test score interpretation that are "standardized" across all examinees. As a result, the scores can be interpreted to mean the same for all examinees and thus can be compared across students and classrooms.

Often, school districts participate in several layers of standardized testing, from districtwide to statewide to national and sometimes even international programs. Some districts may administer a dozen or more different standardized testing programs in a given year involving different students for different purposes. Some districts test every pupil at every grade, while others sample students or grade levels.

Some standardized tests are *norm referenced;* they permit us to interpret each student's performance in terms of how it compares with that of other students who took the same test under like conditions. These tests permit us to rank students in terms of their achievement. Other standardized tests are *criterion ref-*

	SELECTED RESPONSE	ESSAY	PERFORMANCE ASSESSMENT	PERSONAL COMMUNICATION
Know	■			
Reason	■			
Skills			■	
Products			■	
Dispositions				

Figure 13–1
Aligning Achievement Targets and Assessment Methods

erenced; they permit us to compare a student's performance with a preset standard of acceptable performance—no reference is made as to how that student compared to other students. These tests permit us to detect specific strengths and weaknesses in achievement. Standardized tests have been developed to cover many different school subjects. Further, they can involve the use of any of our four basic forms of assessment, although nearly all rely on selected response formats because of the scoring efficiency with large numbers of examinees.

The purposes of this chapter are to provide you with enough background information about large-scale standardized assessment to permit you to understand how such assessments fit into the classroom and the larger world of educational assessment in general, and to help you comprehend your own professional responsibilities with respect to these testing programs.

A Brief History Lesson

To set the stage, let's travel back to the 1920s and 1930s, when we first began to rely on these comprehensive achievement testing programs. By examining social and educational forces at work at that time, we can gain important insights into the emergence of educational assessment as a prominent feature of school life.

In the Beginning

In the early 1900s, the United States was built on an agricultural economy, with some heavy industry emerging in the northeast. As a result, Americans could secure economic well-being without a great deal of formal education. For this reason, school dropout rates in those days were three times those of today. However, those leaving the educational system were not labeled "at-risk youth" as they are today, because our society and economy offered them diverse opportunities to contribute and succeed.

During the 1920s and 1930s, America's post-World War I ethnic population was becoming increasingly diverse, with immigrants from the world's cultures arriving at all borders in huge numbers. It was popular to conceive of the United States as the great melting pot. We aspired to a common language, culture, national experience, and heritage. To achieve this end, we sought a homogenizing experience, and believed that schools might provide that common ground. So we conceived of the standard curriculum for all students, and we sent out word via compulsory attendance laws that everyone would have to come to school and be educated.

And so, to school they came—in unprecedented numbers, thus presenting educators of those times with the immense challenge of schooling the masses with very limited resources. To meet this challenge, educational leaders conceived of "assembly line schools," schools in which young children entered the system and stopped at the first point on the assembly line. They allowed a fixed amount of time—one year—for students to master the required standard curriculum. In that kind of system, there would be variations in the amount learned by every individual by the end of first grade.

Students then moved on to stop two. By the time they reached the end of their time at stop two, those who mastered a great deal at stop one on the assembly line would have learned much more. Those who learned little at stop one would learn little more at stop two. The amount of variation in achievement among students increased. And so it would go through several years of public school education. The range of student achievement would continue to expand.

Sorting, society decided, would be an important social function of schools. By spreading students out along a continuum of achievement, schools could facilitate merging them into the various segments of the economic and social structure. In effect, this sorting function formed the foundation for the era of assessment that was about to begin in the 1930s and would extend into the 1990s.

Juxtaposed with this evolution of schools as sorting institutions in the 1930s was another revolutionary change that brought educational assessment into the forefront of school functioning. As it happened, at precisely this same time, there appeared on the educational scene a new kind of achievement test—a format that appeared to fill several critical needs.

A "New" Kind of Test Appears on the Scene

Educators writing in the professional literature referred to this new kind of test as "scientific" (Scates, 1943) in that it was capable of controlling for inherent biases and idiosyncrasies of teachers' subjective judgments, which prior to this time had formed the basis for assessment in schools. Also, as advocates pointed out, this new kind of test could be mass produced, mass administered, and mass scored very efficiently—and efficiency was seen as essential in those times of rapid growth in education and of limited resources to accomplish it.

This test also brought with it an even more important advantage: It was able to produce the quintessential sorting criterion—a score had exactly the same meaning for every student who took the same test. It offered concrete, apparently "scientific" support for the sorting function of schools.

This new entry in the assessment arena was, as you may have deduced, the objectively scored paper and pencil test. Because of its great efficiency and the comparability of its scores, this assessment option became so popular that it dominated our conception of educational assessment for 60 years.

A Time of Disconnected Efforts

The era of assessment that began in the late 1920s can be characterized in terms of three very important patterns of professional practice, one involving teachers, another involving assessment personnel, and a third involving administrators and policy makers.

First, very early in this era, educators separated two critical functions. On one hand, teachers would have responsibility for teaching. Their challenge would be to master and apply the technology of instruction. On the other hand, professional assessment experts would assess. Their professional challenge and role would be to master and apply the rapidly emerging technology of testing.

In effect, local teachers and administrators entrusted responsibility for assessment to the measurement community, thus in effect separating assessment and instruction and assigning them to different parties. This amounted to saying, "Teachers, you teach and you don't need to know anything about assessment. And assessors, you test and you need not know anything about teaching." Training programs, certification requirements, and job responsibilities were defined according to this difference in function.

This led to the second important pattern of professional practice that characterized this era. Once in charge, the assessment community launched a 60-year-long program of psychometric research and development that had some very important characteristics. Assessors began to define *assessment* as the quantification of student achievement. This permitted the introduction and use of sophisticated mathematical models to describe student achievement and to summarize achievement information. As a result, the world of testing quickly became quantitatively complex and highly technical in its vocabulary. This technical assessment vocabulary made communication among assessment specialists efficient and effective. However, few outside the field could understand it. As a result, assessment experts could communicate clearly among themselves, but outsiders (teachers, administrators, and policy makers, in this case) were left out of the assessment equation. In effect, an impenetrable wall was constructed between assessment and instruction due to a lack of common understanding, and that wall grew very high very quickly.

The March Toward Layers of Standardized Testing

Once school officials began to understand the great efficiency of these new objectively scored paper and pencil tests, they took the first steps in what also turned out to be a 60-year march, toward ever-more centralized assessment of student achievement, which resulted in layers of standardized testing programs.

Scholarship and College Admissions Testing.   This march began modestly in the late 1920s with a few local scholarship testing programs, which relied on essay tests to serve their sorting and selecting needs. Thus, right from the outset, quality tests were those that maximized individual differences in student achievement. These differences would serve to rank examinees for the award of scholarships.

These local applications were so effective that, by the late 1930s, they had given rise to our first national college admissions testing programs, the College Boards. While the earliest of tests relied on essay assessment, in the 1940s the huge volume of national testing soon forced a change as the College Board turned to multiple-choice testing technology as a more efficient format. With this change dawned the era of selected response testing for sorting purposes. Late in that decade, the second college admissions test appeared on the scene, the ACT Assessment Program. It relied on the same technology for the same sorting and selecting purposes.

Published Test Batteries.   The new objective testing technology continued to evolve as a sorting and selecting tool. By the late 1940s, test publishers were selling standardized versions of objective paper and pencil tests to schools for use at all grade levels. The test user guides were careful to point out that scores on these tests were intended to serve as one additional piece of information to be used by teachers to supplement their classroom assessments and help sort students into proper instructional treatments. Remember this purpose; it is a critical issue in the whole historical picture.

In the 1960s, society began to raise serious questions about the effectiveness of schools. With the former Soviet Union first into space in the late 1950s, for example, our society began to question the quality of math and science education in schools. In addition, the upheavals surrounding the Vietnam War, the Civil Rights Movement, student protests, and the like gave rise to and fueled an environment of questioning and challenge. Many social institutions came under scrutiny, including schools. This general reexamination of our social priorities and institutions gave birth to the sense that schools (and the educators who run them) might need to be held accountable for more than just providing quality opportunities to learn—for more than just sorting students according to achievement. Rather, they might also be held responsible for producing real student learning and for ensuring that all students attain certain specified levels of achievement.

Testing for Accountability.   In response to the 1960s challenge that schools might not be "working," administrators, to evaluate their programs, were forced to turn to their only source of believable student achievement data: scores from commercially available standardized objective paper and pencil achievement tests.

This represented a profoundly important shift in our perceptions of these tests. They changed from being seen as just one additional piece of information for teachers, to being seen as standards of educational excellence. The underlying testing technology did not change. These were still tests designed to sort students based on assessments of very broad domains of content. All that changed was our perceptions of the tests and the meaning of their scores. They came to be seen as the guardians of our highest academic expectations—a use their original developers had never intended.

Remember that these changes in the manner of viewing and using these tests were motivated by the laudable desire for school improvement. Besides, these changes occurred in the midst of an assessment era that had differentiated the teaching and assessing functions. Neither teachers nor administrators were trained in or expected to understand the basic principles of sound assessment. They could not have been expected to understand the limitations of standardized tests or how inappropriate these changes actually were.

However, throughout the 1960s, as testing for accountability grew in popularity, we saw little change in the nature of our schooling experience or its results. As a matter of fact, some social critics continued to see a decline in the quality of schools.

Statewide Testing.   So society began to ask, If local district testing programs do not promote school improvement, why not try statewide testing programs? Surely, policy makers said, if we have a statewide criterion of excellence, schools will improve.

During the 1970s, statewide testing programs spread across the country; the decade began with very few such tests and ended with nearly 40 states conducting their own testing programs. And significantly, many states opted to develop their own tests to be sure they focused on important educational outcomes in that state. They tended to move from tests designed to sort to tests reflective of student attainment of specific achievement targets (i.e., from norm- to criterion-referenced tests). Even so, the addition of large numbers of state-level testing programs has not been accompanied by marked changes in the nature or quality of schools.

National and International Assessment.   So, in the 1970s and 1980s, we added the National Assessment of Educational Progress, along with international testing programs, in the hope that testing achievement at ever-more centralized levels would somehow lead to school improvement. But alas, while evidence of student achievement abounded, little evidence of school improvement was forthcoming.

You can see the pattern of practice that emerged over these decades. Our collective view of the path to school improvement told us that, if we just find the right level at which to test, schools will improve. To illustrate the strength of this view, as we moved into the 1990s as concerned as ever about the quality of schools, we were poised to repeat the same behavior as we faced the prospect of the mother of all centralized, standardized tests: the national every-pupil examination. Once again, advocates of a complex national testing program repeated the by-now hollow admonition: Just test it and schools will get better, as though the addition of yet another layer of testing would somehow succeed where others have not. At the time of this writing in 1996, however, the political winds are blowing in the direction of state and local control of educational priorities, and a national every-pupil examination program seems unlikely.

Troubling Contradictions

Throughout this evolution, standardized testing has been troubled with apparent contradictions. The conflicting perspectives usually have arisen out of a general lack of understanding of these tests, both within and around our school culture. Let me illustrate.

As a society, we have placed great value on standardized tests. We assign great political visibility and power to the results they produce at local, state, and national levels. The paradox is that, as a society (both within and outside schools), we seem to have been operating on blind faith that these tests are sound, and that educators are using them appropriately. As a society, almost to a person, we actually know very little about standardized tests or the scores they produce. It has been so for decades. This blind faith has prevented us from understanding either the strengths or the important limitations of standardized tests. As a result, the discrepancy is immense between what most educators and the public think these tests can do and what they actually are capable of delivering.

We have tended to ascribe a level of precision to test scores that belies the underlying reality. Many believe we can use standardized test scores to track student acquisition of new knowledge and skills so precisely as to detect deviations from month-to-month norms; so precisely that we can use them to predict success at the next grade level or success in college or life after school. But, as you shall see later in the chapter, standardized tests typically are not the precision tools or accurate predictors most think they are. They do not produce high-resolution portraits of student achievement. Rather, they are designed to produce broad general indicators of that achievement. This is their often misunderstood heritage.

In addition, because we have tended to grant such power to these tests and to the scores they produce, we have been relentless in our attempts to make them powerful instructional tools that are relevant in the classroom. The problem here is that they provide little information of value for day-to-day instruction. There are two reasons for this. First, the tests often are so broad in their coverage that they are too imprecise for teacher use. Second, tests are administered only once a year, while teachers must continually make decisions. For these reasons, standardized tests typically are of little value at the instructional level. But, of course, this does not preclude their use at instructional support and policy levels of decision making.

In the 1980s, some noticed these problems and concluded that we should do away with standardized tests, arguing that the problems meant that the tests were of poor quality. In fact, standardized tests generally do a good job of assessing the characteristics they are intended to measure. They are designed to sample student achievement in broad classifications of content and to tap specific kinds of reasoning and problem solving. Typically, a careful analysis by an assessment literate educator will reveal that a good standardized test does this very well.

Our long-term societal habits of assigning great power to standardized tests, ascribing unwarranted precision to the scores they produce, striving against all odds to make them instructionally relevant, and generally misunderstanding them even while attacking them have conspired to create a major dilemma in education today: We have permitted these tests to form the basis of a school accountability system that is incapable of contributing to much-needed school improvement efforts. Sadly, our general lack of understanding of these tests from classroom to boardroom to legislative chamber has prevented us from achieving the *real* accountability that we all desire.

Addressing the Contradictions

To achieve the goal of real school accountability for student learning, we need to untwist the seemingly paradoxical standardized testing circumstances in which we find ourselves.

First, we must acknowledge that standardized tests as we have defined them in the past really only cover a small part of our most valued targets. They assess mastery of broad domains of content knowledge and some patterns of reasoning. But by the same token, they have tended not to assess complex multipart reasoning and problem solving. They have failed to assess student mastery of achievement-related skills or the ability to create complex achievement-related products—all critical outcomes. As a result, we must acknowledge that the scope of coverage of most standardized tests is insufficient to warrant dependable inferences as to the overall effectiveness of our teachers or schools.

Second, we must press forward on our 1990s agenda of discovering better ways to assess a broader array of valued targets. We must invest the resources needed to experiment with and devise assessments and record-keeping systems that permit us to produce high-quality multidimensional portraits of student achievement, as that achievement grows from grade to grade. These systems will require the commonsense application of all four assessment methods, developed and used by an education community schooled in the basic principles of sound assessment.

And that leads directly to our third course of action: We must strive to create a society (both within and outside of schools) that understands the differences between sound and unsound assessment. Whether we advocate or oppose large-scale standardized assessment, we can hope for a positive result of our national testing debate only if we argue from an informed perspective. Comprehensive professional development in assessment is a must for all educators, and in-depth dialogue with our communities about the basic principles of sound assessment is equally important.

If we fail to take these steps, we will continue to risk harm to our students due to the inept use of standardized testing. If we are going to administer standardized tests on a broad scale and wish to use the results productively, we must think and act within the framework of a usable, fair, and consistent philosophy or set of principles. In the following section, I share what I believe to be such a productive standardized testing philosophy.

A Guiding Philosophy

Our challenge as a school culture and as a larger society is to keep these standardized tests in perspective in terms of their potential impact on student learning. Large-scale assessment results do not have as big an impact on student learning as do classroom assessments. Yet our allocation of resources, media attention to scores, and political emphasis on standardized tests would lead one to believe that they represent the only assessments worth caring about. In this regard, our priorities have been out of balance.

If we are to establish a more balanced set of assessment priorities, we must give far greater attention to ensuring the quality of classroom assessments. Having said this, let me remind you that a balanced perspective encourages the effective use of *all* of the assessment tools we have at our disposal. This includes standardized tests. In the hands of informed users who know and understand both the strengths and limitations of these tests, they can contribute useful information to educational decision making. Besides, they are so deeply ingrained in our educational fabric that our communities have come to expect to see scores from these tests periodically.

For these reasons, I believe that districts that abandon this kind of testing altogether, as some are doing, make a serious mistake. The reason is that the vast majority of districts are unable to develop and implement the kinds of sound assessment alternatives needed to provide quality information for policy-level decision making. And similarly, most districts lack the expertise needed to develop assessments in which their communities are likely to have confidence.

Therefore, I think sound practice is conveyed through behavior such as that displayed in the opening vignette of Chapter 1, in which the district did the following:

- Continued to use their traditional standardized testing program, but
- Changed from testing every pupil to sampling methods that reduced the number of students tested, and thus reduced testing costs.
- Used the savings to begin the kind of professional development needed to begin to assess specific aspects of student achievement not currently measured.

This is the kind of plan that can permit us to introduce the full array of assessments needed to profile the full set of achievement targets we expect of students. But, we need to complete several years of solid professional development and serious local assessment development to achieve this goal. So, as a nation, we had better get started. In the meantime, most of our communities will demand that we continue with some form of standardized testing.

This leads me to the following philosophy: We should continue the limited use of standardized tests where relevant to inform instructional support and policy decisions, but we must at the same time make absolutely certain each and every user of the assessment results (from the classroom to the living room to the boardroom to the legislature) is thoroughly schooled in the meaning and limitations of the scores. Ill-prepared users misunderstand, misinterpret, and misuse test results.

From the perspectives of student well-being, sound public policy, and effective instructional practice, this is unacceptable.

If, as educators, parents, and policy makers, we presume to make decisions that affect student well-being based on scores on these tests, we absolutely must know what we are doing. This means that everyone involved must understand both the strengths and the real limitations of standardized tests. Your preparation to provide leadership in this effort begins here and now.

Understanding the Purposes for Large-scale Assessment

Standardized testing, as noted, arose in the 1930s and 1940s from a desire to assist schools in their social function of sorting students along a continuum of achievement. Tests designed to serve these sorting functions highlighted achievement differences between and among students to produce a dependable rank order of achievers from lowest to highest. Such tests refer each individual student's performance back to a norm group for interpretation—how that student compared to other examinees who took the same test under the same conditions. This is called *norm-referenced* test interpretation.

Time for Reflection

What are some instructional support and policy decisions we make that necessitate ranking students (individually or in groups) so as to compare them?

Beginning with the accountability movement of the 1960s, however, the function of assessment started to shift from sorting to verifying student attainment of specific educational outcomes. As this shift in our large-scale assessment purpose has unfolded through the 1970s, 1980s, and 1990s, we have seen steady emergence of a different way of interpreting student performance. Rather than referral of scores back to a norm group for comparative interpretation, each student's score is compared with a preset standard of acceptable performance, or a criterion. Assessments interpreted in this way are said to be *criterion referenced*.

Time for Reflection

What are some of the kinds of decisions that require a criterion-referenced interpretation of test results?

Neither norm-referenced nor criterion-referenced score interpretation is inherently superior or more appropriate. Each fits into certain assessment contexts. Therefore, issues of large-scale standardized test quality must be discussed first and foremost in terms of purpose.

Revisiting Users and Uses

In Chapter 2, we analyzed the users and uses of assessment at three levels: instruction, instructional leadership, and policy. We revisit those here, to establish a context for this chapter.

The prime assessment users at the instructional level are students, teachers, and parents. Nearly all of the key questions they face require the continuous collection of fairly precise individual student achievement information. Of the 15 instructional uses of assessment listed in Table 2–1 for students, teachers, and parents, only 2 called for the kind of periodic assessment typically provided by standardized testing. At this level of assessment, the need for comparable test scores is not nearly as strong as the need for precise detail on specific student attainments.

However, you may recall that those in instructional support positions, including building principals, curriculum personnel, counselors, support teachers, and the like, need general achievement information that is comparable across all students, so scores can be summarized to inform key decisions (see Table 2–2). Periodic assessments of group achievement provided by standardized testing programs administered about once a year often can provide sufficient achievement information for these users.

Depending on the particular decision to be made, some users at the instructional support level may require norm-referenced (comparative) information. For instance, selecting students for special remedial or gifted programs often requires comparative scores. But most require criterion-referenced results reflecting student attainment of targets included in the school, district, or state curriculum.

Finally, think about the policy level of assessment use, involving superintendents, school board members, state department of education personnel, legislators, and citizens. Their decision-making frameworks are spelled out in Table 2–3. Here again, we find strong need for general information on group achievement—comparable scores gathered periodically and aggregated at various levels, such as school, district, and state. As at other levels, we find a prominent place for criterion-referenced information among those concerned with student attainment of specific state, district, or building targets.

Consider the key differences among assessment users in information needs as depicted in Tables 2–1, 2–2, and 2–3. Clearly, large-scale standardized tests are tools for instructional support and policy, where decisions require information summarized over large numbers of students. They do not serve classroom-level decision makers well, because of their relative infrequency and the low-resolution picture of student achievement they convey.

The Many Forms of Large-scale Assessment

Large-scale standardized testing programs come from many sources and take different forms. In fact, they can be developed by a department- or grade-level team within an individual school building, by district or state assessment personnel, or by test publishers for general sales and distribution or under contract for a particular client. To use these various forms well, we must understand them and how they differ.

Local Assessment Programs

Locally developed districtwide tests typically are designed to reflect valued outcomes within that district. As such, they most often take the form of criterion-referenced tests. An excellent example of such a program is the Portland Levels Test designed, developed, and managed by the Portland, Oregon, Public Schools. Mathematics, reading, and English usage tests have been developed using selected response exercises, and a direct writing assessment has been added using performance assessment methodology. All assessments are specifically designed to reflect valued district outcomes. Further, each selected response test item is placed on a numerical scale in terms of content and degree of difficulty to track student development continuously across grade levels.

This is just one example of many such assessments developed at the local level. These kinds of assessments typically are developed by larger districts, which have the resources needed to support the technical staff required to build such a program.

It is not uncommon for districts to conduct their local standardized testing programs in two parts. They might administer both a norm-referenced standardized achievement test battery districtwide and locally developed criterion-referenced tests reflecting some priority targets in their particular community. A variation on this theme that is growing in popularity is to administer the norm-referenced test battery to a random sample of students—because this can produce the group achievement data needed for policy-level decisions at greatly reduced cost—and use the cost savings for local criterion-referenced assessment at the instructional level.

It has been my experience that those who know the basic principles of sound test development can meet the challenge of local criterion-referenced test development very well. However, those who attempt local development of standardized tests without expertise have great difficulty developing sound assessments.

Published Achievement Tests

The most commonly used form of assessment in districtwide programs is the commercially published, norm-referenced standardized achievement test battery. Test publishers design, develop, and distribute these tests for purchase by local users. Each battery covers a variety of school subjects, offering several test forms tailored for use at different grade levels. Users purchase test booklets, answer sheets, and test administration materials, as well as scoring and reporting services. It is not uncommon these days for districts with their own response sheet scanning technology to also purchase test scoring software from the test publisher to analyze their own results.

The unique feature of these tests is the fact that they are nationally *normed* to facilitate test score interpretation. This simply means that the designers administered the tests to large numbers of students before making them available for general purchase by users. Test results from this preliminary administration provide the basis for comparing each subsequent examinee's score. The resulting scores are given percentile rank, grade equivalent, normal curve equivalent, and other labels. In a later section of this chapter, we will see exactly how these scores and labels are interpreted.

In addition, most test publishers now report at least some criterion-referenced information on score reports. Items in the battery that test the same skill or objective are collected into a small test within a test, allowing the publisher to generate a score for that specific objective. The publisher typically sets a cutoff score of, say, 80 percent correct to conclude that the student has mastered that objective. Results are reported in terms of whether the objective has been mastered. Typically, results are reported for several such objectives.

Such information summarized across students can help districts identify skills or objectives in need of more attention within the curriculum. Another way districts analyze student performance that helps to identify student needs is by requesting item analysis data as part of their score reporting service. Given information on how students tended to perform on items in specific performance categories, instructional leaders can zero in on needed adjustments in instructional priorities.

Table 13–1 lists some of the currently available multisubject norm-referenced standardized achievement test batteries. Also, test publishers develop and distribute a variety of single-subject tests designed for use at various grade levels. Publishers provide catalogues of their products on request.

The key issue faced by consumers of these products is, Which test battery should we buy and use? To answer this question, a district must compare coverage of the various tests available with its local curriculum priorities at the grade level(s) at which the test is to be used. The user's guide for each test will present tables of test specifications, like the ones we studied in Chapter 6, representing the specific content knowledge and the specific patterns of reasoning tapped by every test in the battery. That coverage will vary greatly for the same grade levels across test batteries. Since there is no universally accepted national curriculum in the United States, test publishers test different content under the same subject label aimed at the same grade levels. For this reason, each district must compare and decide which test battery most closely aligns with its curriculum. Only this kind of analysis can assure sound sampling of student achievement. We will discuss this further.

State Assessments

The development of state assessments over the past 20 years has paralleled the emergence of concern over the effectiveness of schools, both in its timing and in the nature of the assessments that have emerged. As the accountability movement

Table 13–1
Partial List of Published Multisubject Standardized Test Batteries

Test	Tests for Grades Ranging	Publisher
California Achievement Test	K–12.9	CTB Macmillan/McGraw-Hill Del Monte Research Park 2500 Garden Road Monterey, CA 93940
Comprehensive Tests of Basic Skills	K–12.9	CTB Macmillan/McGraw-Hill Del Monte Research Park 2500 Garden Road Monterey, CA 93940
Iowa Tests of Basic Skills	K–12	Riverside Publishing Co. 8420 Bryn Mawr Ave. Chicago, IL 60631
Metropolitan Achievement Tests Survey	K–12	Psychological Corporation 555 Academic Court San Antonio, TX 78204
SRA Achievement Series	K.5–12.9	CTB Macmillan/McGraw-Hill Del Monte Research Park 2500 Garden Road Monterey, CA 93940
Stanford Achievement Tests	K–12.9	Psychological Corporation 555 Academic Court San Antonio, TX 78204

gained momentum in the late 1960s and early 1970s, statewide assessments appeared with increasing frequency. Beginning with just a handful of assessments, by 1995, 46 states had their own assessment programs.

Because these tests were created to see if students were meeting state standards of educational attainment, many statewide tests include criterion-referenced components. Norm-referenced tests also continue in use, however, as the summary of current testing programs in Figure 13–2 shows.

In the beginning, most states relied on selected response formats because of the large numbers of students being tested. Machine scoring made the job easier and relatively inexpensive. Recently, however, state assessments have been experimenting with large-scale applications of performance assessment methodology, as they strive for more accurate representations of the complex targets articulated during the 1980s. Clearly, the most popular applications of performance assessment have been in writing assessment, where writing prompts are standardized for administration across the state, scoring criteria have been devised, and raters are trained to evaluate performance. States also are experimenting with large-scale performance assessment in math, science, social studies, the arts, and other performance arenas.

Figure 13–2

1995 Summary of State Testing Programs

Source: Adapted from *State Student Assessment Program Database* (n.p.) by L. Bond and E. Roeber, 1995, Oakbrook, IL: North Central Regional Educational Laboratory and Council of Chief State School Officers. Copyright 1995 by North Central Regional Educational Laboratory and Council of Chief State School Officers. Reprinted by permission of the publishers.

Total Number of States Testing	45
Subjects Tested	
Math	45
Language arts, including reading	42
Writing	34
Science	30
Social Studies	27
Vocational Topics	4
Aptitude	2
Grades Tested	
Kindergarten	2
1	3
2	5
3	23
4	32
5	24
6	22
7	17
8	40
9	15
10	25
11	30
12	5

National Assessment

Yet another level of large-scale assessment that reflects our growing concern over school quality is the National Assessment of Educational Progress (NAEP). This federally funded testing program periodically samples student achievement across the nation to track the pulse of changing achievement patterns. Results are intended for use by policy makers to inform decisions. Since its first test administration in 1969, NAEP has conducted criterion-referenced assessments of valued outcomes in reading, writing, math, science, citizenship, literature, social studies, career development, art, music, history, geography, computers, life skills, health, and energy. NAEP assessment procedures have used all four assessment methods, with selected response methods dominating.

These biannual assessments gauge the performance of national samples of 9-, 13-, and 17-year-olds, as well as young adults, reporting results by geographic region, gender, and ethnic background. In recent years, the U.S. Congress has authorized NAEP to experiment with a voluntary state-level sampling plan permitting a state-by-state comparison of achievement results.

Forms of Assessment Used

Origin
    Commercially developed (off the shelf)   23
    Modified commercial test   9
    Custom test developed under contract   8
    State developed   38

Form of Interpretation
    Norm-referenced components   31
    Criterion-referenced components   33

Writing Assessment
    Based on student writing sample   34
    Based on work accumulated in portfolio   2

Using performance assessment   18

Purposes Cited for Assessment

Instructional Process
    Student diagnosis   27
    Improvement of instruction   44
    Program evaluation   39

Student Accountability
    Student recognition   12
    Student promotion   5
    Honors diploma   3
    Endorsed diploma   3
    High school graduation   17

School Accountability
    School recognition   8
    School performance reporting   35
    High school skills guarantee   8
    School accreditation   12

College Admissions Testing

Yet another form of standardized testing is the college admissions test, norm-referenced assessments of student achievement conducted near the end of high school for purposes of selection into college, placement in college courses, and awarding of scholarships. Two such admission tests are currently in use in the United States: the ACT Assessment, conducted by the American College Testing Program of Iowa City, IA, and the Scholastic Assessment Test (SAT), conducted by the College Board.

While these tests are often cited as classic examples of norm-referenced tests, most don't realize that they have a strong basis in mastery of content and reasoning skills, too. The ACT Assessment, for example, includes four separate selected response tests, each of which yields several scores reflecting content mastery as well as reasoning skills. The scores reported include English (with usage and rhetoric subscores), Mathematics (with pre-algebra and elementary algebra, intermediate algebra, algebra/geometry, and plane geometry/trigonometry subscores), Reading (with social studies/science and arts/literature subscores), and Science Reasoning subscores. This strong discipline-based coverage allows the scores to serve educational and vocational planning, as well as course placement, purposes.

The Scholastic Assessment Test, developed by the Educational Testing Service for the College Board, defines scores in a different manner, starting with two general examinations that result in Verbal and Math scores and then adding a variety of advance placement examinations in many subjects.

Scores on these tests serve college admissions, as well as guidance and placement, purposes. Examinees direct that their scores be sent to the colleges of their choice. Admissions officers use these data, along with high school grade-point averages and a variety of other information about students, to select their freshman class. Scores also are passed along to course placement personnel for assigning students to the level of instruction that will best meet their needs. Performance on the College Boards and the ACT Assessment also feed into various local, state, and national scholarship award programs, including the National Merit Scholar program.

Summary of the Forms of Standardized Testing

Clearly, large-scale standardized tests come in many shapes and sizes. They can be developed at district, state, national, and even international levels to inform a variety of decisions. Many are intended for purposes of comparing and sorting students and for use at district, state, and national levels of decision making. However, as schools become achievement-driven institutions, criterion-referenced interpretations are becoming more prominent.

Matching Method to Target in Standardized Testing

Across these many applications, all four of the commonly used forms of assessment—selected response, essay, performance assessment, and personal communication—have their roles.

Selected Response

The most popular form is and always has been the selected response format. It is relatively easy to develop, administer, and score in large numbers. When the achievement targets are content mastery and/or certain kinds of thinking and problem solving, its great efficiency makes this the method of choice for large-scale test developers. Its major drawback, as we have discussed, is the limited range of targets that can be translated into this format.

Essay

The essay format, a dominant form of assessment in European testing tradition, is rarely used in standardized testing in the United States. The one exception has been its recent popularity in writing assessments. But this application, in which it is the form of communication and not the content mastery or reasoning that counts, is really an example of product-based performance assessment. However, the future may hold a larger role for traditional essay tests in large-scale assessment contexts, as the high costs of full-blown performance assessments become clear. Time will tell.

Performance Assessment

This option is the focus of much current discussion and experimentation in large-scale assessment. The assessment research and development community is exploring applications in writing, mathematics problem solving, science, reading, foreign languages, interdisciplinary programs, and other performance areas. The great strength of this methodology is its ability to capture useful information about student performance on complex targets. Its limitations are the complexity of sampling and costs of the scoring process.

Sampling can be a problem because of uncertainty regarding the number of performance samples needed to lead to confident generalizations about student mastery. This problem is exacerbated by the amount of time needed to respond to each contributing exercise.

For example, if we wish to assess writing proficiency, how many samples of student writing do we need to draw confident generalizations about student achievement in this complex area? The answer depends on how broadly or narrowly we define the target. Broad definitions will require sampling student performance across many forms of writing (narrative, persuasive, expository, etc.). If each writing sample requires an hour or two for the student to generate, the cumulative cost of test administration can be high. When these costs are added to the costs of labor-intensive performance assessment scoring, the overall price tag can become frightening.

The two most attractive solutions to this problem from a cost-effective perspective (always an issue in these contexts) can have decidedly negative affects on the interpretability of the resulting scores. One is to sample broad targets with very few exercises, yielding results that do not systematically reflect the content domain of interest (assess writing proficiency with one 20-minute writing sample). The other is to define targets very narrowly (assess grammar and spelling only), thus failing to reflect real-world complexity in the assessment and its results.

In these times of limited assessment resources and increasing demand for the higher-fidelity results of performance assessments, assessment experts continue to experiment with new and better ways to solve these problems. This experimentation is likely to continue, as we seek more efficient means of using this methodology in large-scale assessment.

Time for Reflection

Why do you think this experimentation is continuing in the face of the extremely high costs of large-scale applications of performance assessment methodology?

Personal Communication

The role of personal communication in large-scale assessment is beginning to change too, as researchers begin to discover the strengths of interviews as a method of data collection. By having students "think aloud" about what they have read, reading specialists gain insight into student comprehension (Wade, 1990). Math and science assessments also can take advantage of this idea. By having students reason out loud as they solve complex problems and respond to carefully crafted questions, assessors can gain insight into the reasoning processes of respondents and into their ability to communicate effectively. Of course, the drawback of this labor-intensive assessment method is the time required to interview large numbers of students. For this reason this method will be most attractive when assessing relatively small samples of students. But it is an idea with great potential.

Test Development

While standardized tests may differ in coverage from publisher to publisher, they all rely on the same basic test development process. If we understand that process, we may appreciate how much work must be done, and how dedicated to quality local, state, and national large-scale test developers must be.

Clarifying Targets

Typically, standardized test developers begin with the thoughtful study of valued achievement targets in the context in which the test is to be used. Since most published norm-referenced tests still rely on selected response exercises, the targets of interest include student mastery of content knowledge and the ability to use that knowledge to reason and solve specified kinds of problems. In the context of state and local assessments, targets also may include skills and products. In either case, test development typically begins with comprehensive studies to identify achievement target priorities. Curriculum materials and commonly used textbooks also are tapped for information as to what should be tested. Most test developers place a priority on involving practicing teachers and experts in the disciplines to be tested in their planning process, in order to be sure the resulting assessments connect with the appropriate targets.

The objective of these studies is to plan or blueprint the assessments to be developed. In those cases where selected response exercises are to be used, a table of specifications like those presented in Chapter 6 are created for each test. When performance assessments are to be developed, the skills to be demonstrated or products to be created are outlined.

In terms of our five attributes of sound assessment, therefore, these tests typically arise from very clear targets. But most users don't realize that these targets are very broad in scope, often including several grades' worth of content in a single 40-item test. That means the coverage of any single topic may be very shallow, including no more than a few items to cover a year's worth of material. Indeed, given this constraint, you can see why the vast majority of material covered in any textbook or local curriculum will not be tested. But these tests cannot be made too long, or they will take up too much instructional time.

Time for Reflection

In what way could this limited content coverage become a problem for the test publisher? On the surface, it appears to be the user's problem, demanding cautious interpretation. From what perspective(s) is it more than that?

Translating Target to Method

Developers of large-scale standardized tests typically know how to match their target with a proper assessment method. In the past, they have relied on selected response formats because these formats have allowed them to easily tap the valued knowledge and reasoning targets. Now, however, these same test publishers are beginning to turn to performance assessment for more complex skill and product targets.

When assessment plans are ready, test construction begins. Some developers use their own in-house staff of item writers; others involve qualified practicing teachers to create exercises. In either case, item writers are trained in the basic principles of sound item construction. Further, in most cases, those who are trained must still demonstrate an appropriate level of proficiency on a screening test before being asked to contribute to test development.

Attention to Sound Sampling and Control of Interference

Typically, test developers write two times more test exercises than will be used on the final test. They then carefully screen the items to select the best, taking great care to sample performance with enough exercises to represent the test plan or blueprint fairly and completely.

Once items have been selected, qualified test-development experts, content-area experts, and members of appropriate minority groups review the exercises for accuracy, appropriateness, and bias. Poor-quality or biased exercises are replaced. Through this review and evaluation process, extraneous sources of bias and distortion are, ideally, cleared out of the test.

To uncover and eliminate other potential problems, the next step in test development is to pretest or pilot-test the items; developers recruit classrooms, schools, or districts to administer the exercises under conditions as similar as possible to those in which the final test will be used. Their objectives are to find out if respondents interpret exercises as the authors intended and to see how well the exercises "function." Test developers also want to know how difficult the items are and how well they differentiate between those who know and do not know the material. All of this helps them retain only the most appropriate exercises for the final test.

After selecting items to match the content and reasoning targets of the test, yet another external review takes place. Item-development specialists, content-area experts, and minority representatives examine the final collection of test items again to ensure quality and appropriateness.

Test Norming

The result of this creation, selection, and review process is a sharply focused, high-quality new test. But the work doesn't stop there. Many test development plans call for the administration of the final test as a whole for further quality control analysis and, in the case of norm-referenced tests, to establish norms for score interpretation.

As soon as a test is ready, the publisher launches a national campaign to recruit school districts to be part of the norming sample. The aim is to involve large and small, urban and rural districts in all geographic regions, striving to balance gender and ethnicity—in short, to generate a cross section of the student population in the United States.

Even though thousands of students may be involved, understand that these norm groups are voluntary participants. For this reason, they *cannot* be regarded as systematically representative of the national student population. Thus, when we compare a student's score to national norms, we are not comparing them with the national student population, but to the norm group recruited by that test publisher for that particular test.

Because of the voluntary nature of norm group selection, different test publishers end up recruiting different districts to serve in the norming process for their particular tests. Because none is randomly equivalent to the national student population nor to any norm group used by another publisher, norm-referenced scores attained on different test batteries cannot be meaningfully compared to one another.

Norm-referenced standardized tests are revised and renormed every few years to keep them up to date in terms of content priorities, and to adjust the score scale. This is necessary because, as the test remains on the market, districts align their curricula to the material covered. This is how they meet the accountability challenge of producing high scores. Over time, however, more and more students will score higher on the test. This makes it difficult for the test to differentiate among top-end students, so publishers rewrite the test and renorm periodically to adjust the difficulty of the test. Users are advised to keep track of the occurrence of such "restandardizations," as they can affect the interpretation of test scores. Ask your test publisher about this.

Summary of Test Development

Clearly, standardized tests are products of hard work and careful attention to detail on the part of professional test developers working hand-in-hand with subject matter experts. As traditionally conceived, these tests have limitations. Paramount among those limitations has been their heavy reliance on selected response formats and the narrowness of the definition of academic success this engenders. But one thing that is typically not a limitation is test quality. These tests are carefully developed.

Interpretation of Commonly Used Test Scores

Standardized tests that rely on selected response items can report any of a variety of kinds of scores. We will review the five most common of these in this section by explaining how each score is derived and suggesting how evaluators may use each score to understand and interpret test performance. We will study raw scores, percent correct, percentile ranks, stanines, and grade equivalents.

While these do not represent the only scores you will confront as a test user, they are the ones you are most likely to use and have to interpret for others. You must be conversant with these scores to interpret and use them appropriately.

Raw Score

When students take a test, the number of items they answer right is called a *raw score*. In the standardized test context, this forms the basis of all the other scores. This score is important for two reasons. First, as you shall see, all other scores are derived from it. Second, it should be the starting point in the interpretation of standardized test score reports, because the raw score tells interpreters whether they can meaningfully interpret and use the other scores reported.

To illustrate, if the items on a multiple-choice test offer four response options, a student who simply guesses will answer about a quarter of the items right. Thus, the guesser will attain a raw score very close to a quarter of the highest possible raw score.

This means that every selected response test has a *chance or guessing score* that you can calculate in advance. Take the number of items on the test and multiply it by the proportion of items a blind guesser could be expected to get right. For a four-choice multiple-choice test, that figure is .25. For a five-choice format, it is .20. So for a 40-item test with four choices per item, a person who was purely guessing would receive a score of about 10.

Time for Reflection

What is the chance score for a true/false test? Given this, what is the effective range of the test in terms of possible scores, calculated in terms of percent correct?

If you know that chance score for your standardized test, you can scan the score report for raw scores within a point or two of that chance score and identify students who either may have guessed or whose academic development may be far below that assessed by the test you used. For those students, you may need follow-up testing at a lower level to obtain accurate information on their true level of achievement. Only a careful analysis of student scores close to the chance score can lead you to these students.

Percent Correct

This score is as familiar and easy to understand as the raw score. *Percent correct* reflects the percent of test items answered correctly by the examinee: raw score divided by total items on the test. This is the kind of score we use in the classroom to promote a common understanding and interpretation of performance on classroom tests. As the total number of items changes from test to test, we can always convert raw scores to percent correct and obtain a relatively standard index of performance.

There are two reasons why this kind of score is important in the context of standardized tests. First, this is the kind of score large-scale test developers use to determine mastery of objectives for a criterion-referenced score report. Examinees are judged to have mastered the objective if they answer correctly a certain percentage of the items covering that objective. The exact cutoff varies at around 70 to 80 percent correct across standardized tests.

The second reason for addressing this kind of score is to differentiate it from percentile. Very often, test users confuse percent correct with percentile scores or percentile rank. They are fundamentally different kinds of scores bringing completely different interpretations to the meaning of test performance. To understand the differences, we must first understand each.

Percentile Rank

For me, this represents the essence of a norm-referenced test score. The reason we compare student performance on standardized tests to that of other students (i.e., in the norm group) is to see how that student's score ranked among others who have taken the same test under the same conditions. Does the student score higher than most? Lower? Somewhere in the middle? This is the question addressed by this score.

Specifically, the *percentile rank* tells us what percent of the norm group a student with any given raw score *outscored*. A student with a percentile rank of 85 outscored 85 percent of the examinees on whom the test was normed.

Our objective in the following analysis is to create a conversion table that will allow us to convert every possible raw score on a test to a percentile, thus depicting what percent of the norm group scored below that particular raw score. This will permit us simply to check an examinee's raw score and know instantly what percent of the norm group that examinee outscored.

Table 13–2 provides the information we need to understand how a student's raw score can be converted to a percentile score. It describes the performance of our norm group on a new test. We will study this table column-by-column to describe this conversion process.

Column one tells us we will be analyzing student performance on a 30-item test. Let's say it's a four-choice multiple-choice test. Possible raw scores range from 0 to 30, although the principle of chance suggests that a score of 7 or 8 represents the functional floor of the performance continuum.

Table 13–2
Understanding Percentile Scores

(1) Raw Score	(2) Number of Students	(3) Percent of Students	(4) Cumulative Percent	(5) Percentile Score
30	10	0.5	99.5	99
29	10	0.5	99.0	98
28	20	1.5	98.5	97
27	20	1.5	97.0	96
26	30	2.0	95.5	94
25	20	1.5	93.5	92
24	40	2.5	92.0	90
23	60	4.0	89.5	86
22	80	5.5	85.5	80
21	120	8.0	80.0	72
20	150	10.0	72.0	62
19	180	12.0	62.0	50
18	170	11.5	50.0	39
17	130	8.5	38.5	30
16	120	8.0	30.0	22
15	90	6.0	22.0	16
14	80	5.5	16.0	11
13	70	4.5	10.5	6
12	40	2.5	6.0	4
11	20	1.5	3.5	2
10	10	0.5	2.0	2
9	10	0.5	1.5	1
8	10	0.5	1.0	1
7 (Chance)	10	0.5	0.5	0
6				
5				
4				
3				
2				
1				
Total	1,500	100		

Column two tells us how many students in our 1,500-person norm group actually attained each raw score. For instance, 20 students scored 25 on the test, 70 scored 13, and so on.

Column three presents a simple conversion of column two; it simply presents the percentage of students who attained each raw score. Look at raw score 20. One hundred and fifty students actually achieved this score, which represents 10 percent of the total of 1,500 examinees in the norm group.

Column four is where it begins to get tricky. This column presents the percentage of students attaining each raw score or any raw score below that score. Start at the bottom of the column. What percent of students attained a raw score of 7? One-half of one percent. Move up the column. What percent of students attained a raw score of 17 or lower? 38.5 percent. So, a student who attains a raw score of 17 scored equal to or higher than 38.5 percent of those in the norm group.

But remember, that's *not* our definition of percentile score. For each raw score, we need to know what percentage of those who took the test were outscored by those attaining each raw score. Look at raw score 26. These students outscored everyone with scores of 25 or lower. We see that 93.5 percent of examinees attained a score of 25 or lower. If we round to whole numbers, then the percentile score for a raw score of 26 is 94. Anyone attaining that score outscored 94 percent of those in the norm group. These percentiles appear in column five.

So, in effect, we can create the conversion table we need for comparing raw scores of all future examinees who take the same test under the same conditions with the performance of the norm group—that is, for ranking students in terms of performance—simply by matching the raw score to the percent from column five, and reading it into the computer to make all future conversions for us. This is exactly what test publishers do. A raw score of 29 reflects a level of achievement on this test that is higher than 98 percent of the examinees in the norm group. This will remain true until the test is renormed.

Time for Reflection

Let's say a test is renormed every seven years. That means the conversion table will remain unchanged over those years. While the test is on the market and in use in a school culture that values high scores, teachers will naturally strive to learn about and cover what it tested. Over the long haul, what effect is this likely to have on average raw scores? On average percentile scores?

When test publishers norm a test, they create conversion tables for their national norm group, and typically also offer percentile conversions based on geographic region, gender, race/ethnicity, and local performance only. This means that exactly the same kind of conversion table is generated for students who are like one another in these particular ways.

You can see why I refer to percentile as the quintessential norm-referenced score. It provides a straightforward comparison of student performance as the basis for score interpretation.

It also should be clear how percent correct and percentile differ. The former refers scores back to the number of items on the test for interpretation, while the latter compares the score to those of other examinees for interpretation. Their points of reference are fundamentally different.

Stanine

This score represents a basic reduction of the broad conversion of the scores given in Table 13–2, as depicted in Table 13–3, from 24 points (raw scores 7 to 30) down to 9 score points, thus the name *stanine,* short for "standard nine." This conversion is done by dividing the percentile column into nine parts and assigning a numerical score to each part. Thus a student is assigned a stanine based on percentile rank. It simply represents a less precise score scale, each point of which can be interpreted quite easily. When interpreted in terms of the general descriptors listed in the right-hand column on the table, this score is easy to understand. A student who attains a stanine of 3 on a test is interpreted to have scored below average in terms of the performance of the norm group.

Grade Equivalent Scores

This score scale represents yet another way to describe the performance of a student in relation to that of other students. The basis of the comparison in this case is students in the norm group at specified grade levels.

For instance, an examinee with a raw score of 20 on a test might have achieved the same raw score as students in the norm group who were just beginning fourth grade. This examinee would be assigned a *grade equivalent score* of 4.1: "fourth grade, first month." These scores are said to place students on the performance continuum in terms of a grade and month during the school year. But how does the publisher go about creating a conversion table for such scores?

Let's say the publisher is norming a newly developed 40-item test of fifth- and sixth-grade math. It administers its test to large numbers of students in those two

Table 13–3
Understanding Stanines

Stanine	Percent of scores	Percentile range	Descriptor
9	4	96–99	well above average
8	7	89–95	
7	12	77–88	above average
6	17	60–76	
5	20	40–59	average
4	17	23–39	
3	12	11–22	below average
2	7	4–10	
1	4	1–3	well below average

grades at the very beginning of the school year. Each student receives a raw score ranging from 10 to 40. On further analysis of test results, let's say that the average score for fifth graders is 23, while sixth graders score an average of 28 correct. With this information, as represented graphically in Figure 13–3, Graph A, we can begin to create our conversion table. The first two conversions from raw to grade equivalent scores are those for the average raw scores. Because 23 was the average score for fifth graders, we assign that raw score a grade equivalent of 5.0. Because 28 was the average raw score of sixth graders when we administered our test, it is assigned a grade equivalent of 6.0. That accounts for 2 of the 30 raw score points to be converted. What about the rest?

Under ideal circumstances, the best way to convert the rest would be to administer our new test to students each month, so we could compute averages for them and complete more of our conversion table. Unfortunately, resources are limited and few schools would put up with that much test administration.

So, as an alternative, we can simply make the assumption that students grow academically at a predictable rate and then interpolate. By connecting the two averages, we create a mathematical equation that allows us to convert the scores between 23 and 28 to grade equivalents, as in Figure 13–3, Graph B. By projecting each raw score point over to the linear function on the graph and then down to the corresponding point on the grade scale, we find the grade equivalent to assign to each raw score.

But what about scores above and below this range? How shall we convert these? We have two choices: (1) Administer the new test to students at higher and lower grade levels, compute averages, and complete the table, or (2) rely on our assumption that students grow at a predictable rate and simply extend our mathematical function down from 23 and up from 28. Option 2 is depicted in Figure 13–3, Graph C, where a raw score of 40 converts to a grade equivalent of 8.5. This provides a means for completing the raw score conversions.

Once the conversion table is completed and read into the computer, henceforth, any student who attains a given raw score will be assigned the corresponding grade equivalent. Thus, the grade equivalent score reflects the approximate grade level of students in the norm group who attained that raw score.

The strength of this kind of score is its apparent ease of interpretation. But this very strength also turns out to be its major flaw. Grade equivalent scores are easily misinterpreted. Here is an example of what can go wrong:

Let's say a very capable student scores a perfect raw score of 40 on our new math test. As you can see from Figure 13–3, graph C, this will convert to a very high grade equivalent score. For the sake of illustration, that score is 8.5. An uninformed parent is going to see that and say "We must start my fifth grader using the eighth-grade math book at once!"

Time for Reflection

From the foregoing discussion, you may be able to see the two critical fallacies in this parent's reasoning. Before you read on, see if you can identify them.

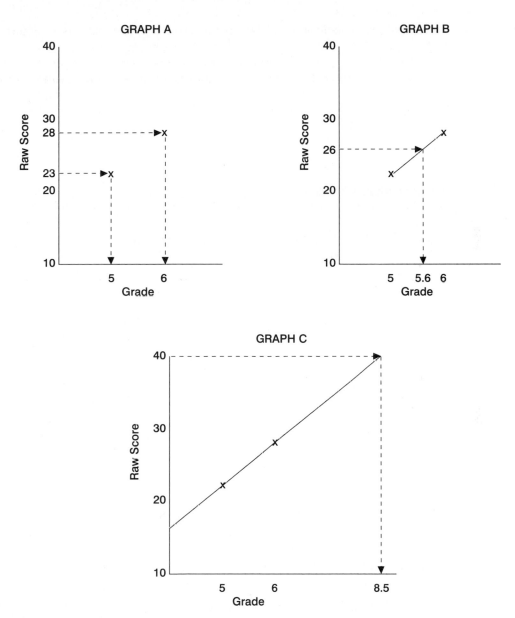

Figure 13–3
The Derivation of Grade Equivalents

First of all, no information whatever was gathered about this student's ability to do seventh- or eighth-grade math. All that was tested was fifth- and sixth-grade math. No inference can be made about the student's proficiency at higher levels. Second, eighth graders have probably never taken the test. The score represents an extrapolation on the part of the test score analyst as to how eighth graders would be likely to score if they took a test of fifth- and sixth-grade math.

Thus, again no conclusion can be drawn about any connections to eighth-grade math.

The bottom line is that grade equivalent scores are *not* criterion-referenced scores. There is no sense in which the grade equivalent score is anchored to any body of defined content knowledge or skill mastery. It is only a comparative score referring a student's performance back to the typical performance of students at particular grade levels in the norm group.

Real-world Test Score Interpretation

A less abstract way to understand these scores and their interpretation is to see how they look in the real world. Typically, test publishers provide a variety of different presentations of test scores tailored to the information needs of different users. Figure 13–4 shows an example of one useful reporting form. In this case, Riverside Publishing provides a "Profile Narrative Report" of scores on the Iowa Test of Basic Skills. Note that national percentile scores are presented in both numerical and bar graph form. Take a moment to examine these scores and then read the narrative score interpretation to the right.

Implications for Teachers

So what does all of this mean for those concerned primarily with classroom assessment? For educators, it means understanding that you have some large-scale assessment responsibilities that revolve around the need to use these tests appropriately. In that regard, you have a simple, yet demanding, three-part responsibility.

Responsibility 1: Student Well-being

Your first and foremost responsibility is to see to the well-being of your students—to keep them from being harmed. That means you must do everything you can to be sure all students come out of large-scale assessment experiences with their academic self-concepts intact. You can do several specific things to fulfill this professional obligation:

- *Be constantly mindful of when standardized tests are likely to contribute useful information and when they are not.* You can do this only if you understand the meaning of test results and how that meaning relates to the reasons for testing. In my opinion, we have entirely too much standardized testing being conducted merely as a matter of tradition and with no sense of purpose. Always insist on attention to purpose: What are the specific decisions to be made, by whom, and what kind(s) of information do they need? Will the test provide useful information?

- *Participate in the standardized test selection process within your district whenever possible.* And be sure to bring your knowledge of the attributes of

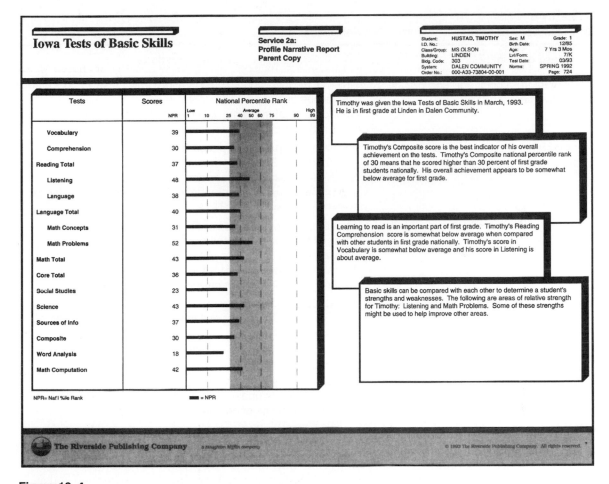

Figure 13–4
Sample Score Report from Iowa Test of Basic Skills
Source: Reprinted from *Iowa Tests of Basic Skills: Interpretation Guide for Teachers and Counselors.*
Chicago, IL: The Riverside Publishing Company. 1996. Reprinted by permission.

sound assessments to the process. You know the standards of quality. Table
13–4 translates those standards into critical consumer questions you can ask.
Demand quality.

- *Be sure your instructional program sets students up for maximum
  achievement.* Make sure the areas to be tested are covered. But keep this in
  perspective. If the standardized tests you are using represent only a fraction
  of your total curriculum, allocate a fraction of your instructional time to its
  particular targets. To do otherwise is to permit the standardized test to inappropriately narrow your instructional program. Make sure everyone knows
  what proportion of your curriculum is covered so they can keep these tests
  in perspective!

Table 13–4
Key Questions to Ask in Standardized Test Selection

Standard of Quality	Critical Questions
Tests arise from clear and appropriate achievement targets	Which of the tests under consideration most closely approximates local curriculum priorities? What percent of the items to be used at a given grade level actually test material our district teaches at that level?
Assessments serve clear and appropriate purposes	What are our specific purposes for standardized testing—who are the users and what information do they need? Which of the tests under consideration is most capable of providing the needed information, in understandable terms and in a timely manner?
Method accurately reflects the valued outcomes	What are all of our valued school and/or district targets? Which of these targets require the use of which methods of assessment? Which of the standardized tests under consideration rely on proper methods for our targets and purposes?
Assessments sample achievement appropriately	How does each test under consideration sample student achievement and how does that plan relate to our local achievement targets? Which test samples our curriculum most completely?
Assessments control for bias and distortion	What sources of interference present potential problems, given our standardized testing context? Which of the tests under consideration allow us to control for the most sources of potential problems?

- *Prepare your students to participate productively and as comfortably as possible in large-scale testing programs.* Take time to be sure they understand why they are taking these tests and how the results are to be used. Be sure they know going into the testing situation what the scores mean and do not mean. Provide practice with the kinds of test items they will confront, so they know how to deal with those formats. Communicate with parents about the importance of a settled home environment during the times of standardized testing. Be sure they, too, are advised on how to keep these tests in perspective. And above all, be positive and encouraging to all before, during, and after these assessments. All of these steps help students become "test-wise."

- *When asked to participate in administering standardized tests, take the responsibility seriously and follow the prescribed instructions.* You must follow standards of ethical practice. Anything you may do to cause students to misrepresent their real levels of achievement has the potential of doing harm to them, to you as a professional, and to the integrity of the educational community as a whole. If you are opposed to a particular set of standardized testing practices, bring all of your assessment literacy tools to bear during the debate. That is your right and your responsibility. But when assessment begins, adhere to prescribed procedures so users can accurately interpret the results.

- *Whenever standardized test results are being reviewed, discussed, or used in a decision-making context, urge for complete understanding and proper interpretation and use of those results.* If you determine that users do not understand the meaning and/or limitations of the scores in question, strive to explain them, or, if necessary, urge that users seek professional assessment expertise. Be diplomatic in this effort, but assertive. Do not permit misinterpretation. The well-being of your students hangs in the balance.

If you are a teacher or support person who is not in charge of planning or carrying out the standardized program, obviously you cannot dictate your district's course of action. But you can always be a voice for reasoned use of these tests. The higher your level of assessment literacy, the more persuasive you can be.

Responsibility 2: Community Awareness

Promote understanding within your community of the role of standardized testing and the meaning of test results. Members of the school board, parents, citizens, and members of the news media may need basic assessment literacy training to participate productively in the proper use of results. Only when they, too, understand the meaning of sound assessment will they be in a position to promote the wise use of these tests. Here are some suggestions:

- *Encourage those responsible for district staffing to create a position for an assessment specialist* (if there is no such person now). This position will provide a focal point for leadership and services in this arena. Experience dictates that such staff members will be kept very busy—with both professional development activities and public relations!

- *Ask those test publishers who provide you with standardized testing services to assist you in your efforts to promote more complete community understanding of both the strengths and limitations of standardized tests.* You should regard this as a legitimate part of their professional responsibility.

- *Seek out and take advantage of agencies that provide assessment training services.* These may include assessment service units of state departments of education, professional development units within intermediate educational service districts, staff developers from regional laboratories, other local private or public service agencies, and nearby colleges and universities.

Responsibility 3: Maintain Perspective

We must all constantly urge those who support, design, and conduct standardized testing programs to keep these tests in perspective in terms of their relative importance in the larger world of educational assessment. We must constantly remind ourselves and others that these tests represent but a tiny fraction of the assessments in which students participate and that they have little influence on day-to-day instruction. While standardized tests should continue to command resources, we must begin to move rapidly toward a more balanced expenditure of those very limited resources so as to support quality classroom assessment, too.

This chapter appears in this book on student-centered classroom assessment to provide you with the motivation, understanding, and tools you need to follow these simple guidelines. I urge you to be a critical consumer of standardized tests and the scores they produce and to encourage others to do likewise.

Chapter Summary: Meeting the Challenges of Standardized Testing

Our purpose in this chapter has been to understand and learn to negotiate the challenges presented to teachers and those in positions of instructional support by standardized testing. Throughout our discussion, we spoke of the need for a balanced perspective on all fronts: leave traditional tests in place; economize whenever possible; use the cost savings to develop greater local assessment capacity; and experiment with innovative new assessment methodologies. But always with a sense of the need to meet standards of quality (clear targets, clear purpose, proper methods, proper samples, and interference controlled).

We reviewed the array of assessment purposes introduced in Chapter 2, emphasizing again the place of standardized testing in the larger context of educational assessment. These tests serve both policy and instructional support functions. They tend to be of little specific value to teachers, because the assessment demands of the classroom require greater frequency of assessment and higher resolution pictures of student achievement than the typical standardized test can generate. The one part of the score report teachers are likely to find useful are the criterion-referenced scores reflecting student mastery. While once a year is not frequent enough to be comprehensive, at least teachers get some detail with these scores.

We studied the various levels of standardized testing, from local to state to national to college admission testing, pointing out that all four assessment methods are used at some level. And we discussed their development.

Next, our attention turned to understanding and interpreting commonly used standardized test scores: raw scores, percent correct, percentile, stanine, and grade equivalent. These and other such scores are safe and easy to use when the user understands them. But, by the same token, they can be easily distorted by the uninformed. Your challenge is to become informed.

We ended with a quick summary of our professional responsibilities. We emphasized that our concern first and foremost should be for the well-being of students. Under all circumstances, we must demand quality assessment of our local curricula. Each of us should strive to be an activist with a voice of reason in this arena. Only then will we be able to keep this form of assessment in proper perspective.

Exercises to Advance Your Learning

Knowledge

1. Based on your review of material presented in Chapter 2 and reexamined in this chapter, list the decisions informed by standardized test results and identify the various decision makers who use these results.

2. Review the chapter and identify as many different forms of large-scale standardized tests as you can.

3. List the various steps in the standardized test development process, explaining how test publishers attend to issues of test quality at each step.

4. After studying the section in this chapter on score interpretation, identify and define the kinds of standardized test scores discussed.

5. Commit to memory the basic standardized testing responsibilities of the classroom teacher.

Reasoning

1. Turn to the section in this chapter, "Troubling Contradictions." List each of the contradictions identified and explain why it represents a potential problem in our effective use of standardized tests in schools.

2. Assume that your careful analysis of commercially available standardized tests reveals that only one-half of the items in any subtest covers material specified in your curriculum at the specified grade levels you had planned to test. That is, the best overlap you can get between what you want to test and any available test is 50 percent. This means that you will not have taught one-half of the material tested during the year you test it. Yet your school board and administration compel you to choose and administer a test anyway. How should you proceed? What should you do to maximize the value of assessment and minimize harm to students?

3. Compare and contrast norm-referenced and criterion-referenced interpretation of test scores.

4. Compare and contrast percent correct and percentile rank scores.

5. Give one example of each type of score and explain how it should be interpreted.

6. Assume a student attains a raw score at the chance level on a particular test. The computer converts that score to a grade equivalent score that turns out to be 3 grades below the student's current assigned grade. The next year that same student scores at the chance level again. Again the conversion reveals the student still to be 3 years behind. The student's teacher the second year notes that the two grade equivalent scores reveal the student (1) remains 3 years behind, but (2) shows 1 year of growth over the past year. On reflection, this second teacher concludes that "this student is 3 years behind but growing." Is this a proper conclusion? Why?

Skills

1. Assume that you are to chair a committee to reevaluate and, if necessary, revise your district's standardized testing program. Other committee members are a member of your school board, the district curriculum director, a parent, a principal, and three teachers (elementary, middle school, and high school). Describe the scope of the work facing your committee. List in order the steps your group should take to complete its task. Specify why each step is relevant, and why you have placed them in your chosen order.

Dispositions

1. Do you believe there is a legitimate role for standardized tests in the schooling process? In your opinion, do they serve

important users and purposes? Defend your answers.

2. For decades, we have been a society willing to place blind faith in test scores, never inquiring into the nature of the tests that produced them. Why do you think we have done this? Do you think this attitude is healthy for schools and for students? Why? Why not?

3. We have consistently centered in this text on five standards of assessment quality. Do you believe that these standards should also apply to standardized tests? Why? Why not?

Communicating About Student Achievement

We are concerned not only with improving assessment of what students know but also with how differences in what they know come from the educational experiences we provide. . . . Everyone ought to be thinking about [students'] opportunity to learn as part of interpreting assessment results.

LEE BURSTEIN (1947–1995)

CHAPTER 14   Understanding Our Communication Challenge

CHAPTER 15   Developing Sound Report Card Grading Practices

CHAPTER 16   The Role of Portfolios in the Communication Process

CHAPTER 17   Reports and Conferences That Highlight Achievement

14

Understanding Our Communication Challenge

CHAPTER ROADMAP

This is the first of four chapters dealing with the process of sharing assessment results. In this opening discussion, we set standards of sound practice in communicating about student achievement. Then, in the subsequent chapters, we explore how these standards affect us when we strive to communicate using report card grades, portfolios, and various other written and conference-based strategies.

As a result of studying the material presented in this chapter, reflecting on that material, and completing the exercises offered at the end of the chapter, you will know and understand the following:

1. Three key steps in preparing to communicate effectively about student achievement.

2. Four key steps in establishing and maintaining an effective communication environment.

3. How open, student-involved communication differs from more traditional teacher-centered communication.

4. The relationship between student-involved communication and student motivation.

In addition, you will be able to take advantage of that knowledge base to reason in the following ways:

1. Analyze previously developed communication systems to determine if they satisfy standards of effective communication.

2. Analyze the active ingredients in inclusive, student-involved communication processes.

3. Draw inferences about communication practices that are likely to have positive and negative consequences for student motivation.

This chapter does not include any skill or product targets. But I do hope you will come to appreciate the immense contribution effective communication makes to the academic well-being of students. I hope this will predispose you to take very seriously your responsibility to use the communication process to motivate students to strive for academic excellence.

Throughout our journey, we have spoken consistently of two reasons for assessing. One centers on the use of assessment results to inform decisions and the other on the use of the assessment process as a teaching strategy. Neither use can be fulfilled unless lines of communication between teacher and student are open, with accurate information about student achievement flowing from message senders to message receivers. In the classroom, our communication mission is twofold:

- Make sure all message receivers understand the meaning of assessment results.
- Be sure students are in a position to use those results effectively and efficiently to promote their own academic well-being.

Recall from Chapter 2 that there are many users of assessment results who make key decisions that directly affect the nature and quality of the student's schooling experience. At the classroom level, students, teachers, and parents represent these key users. At the level of instructional support, principals, support teachers, guidance personnel, and curriculum staff make important decisions. At the policy-making level, superintendents, school board members, citizens, and public officials often rely on assessment results to inform their decision making. Refer to Tables 2–1 through 2–3 to refresh your sense of the many ways assessment results bear on the academic well-being of students. Effective communication systems provide information to all of these users in a form they understand and in a timely manner to serve their intended purposes.

As you will see, our discussion of the principles of effective communication represents a review of our journey up to this point. As we know, effective communication about student achievement is only possible if we start with accurate information about student achievement derived from quality assessments. If we mismeasure student achievement to begin with and thus initiate communication with inaccurate information, we are virtually assured of miscommunication no matter what mode of communication we use. We must start with clear and appropriate targets and quality assessments *and* we must adhere to certain principles of effective communication, if our work is to be valuable to those who must make decisions based on the information we provide.

We begin with a discussion of how we maintain the quality of the message we wish to send. To explain this, I have selected the metaphor of constructing communication towers—structures that can support the lines of communication between assessor and the user(s) of assessment results. Without strong towers, I will argue, key lines of communication will not be properly supported.

We then consider the interpersonal environment within which the message is to be sent and received. Unless we consider the needs and perspectives of both message sender and receiver in setting up lines of communication, significant sources of "noise" can interfere with the clarity of the signal. Our challenge is to find ways to filter out that interference so we can convey clear, interpretable meaning.

By the time we finish describing the complex and demanding requirements of a sound communication environment, you may be wondering if it's even possible, let alone desirable, to try to manage all of the important contingencies. Most teachers decide that it is—that the effort required to communicate effectively is justified for student well-being. But sometimes it's tempting to conclude that the barriers to truly effective communication are too imposing to overcome. Since this has direct consequences for our students, we will analyze those barriers very carefully so as to understand how to remove them.

Our ultimate goal in this phase of our journey is to expand our discussion of student-centered classroom assessment to include the possibility of open, student-involved communication of assessment results. As you know, student-centered assessment opens the assessment process up and welcomes students into a partnership in order to generate the motivation needed to strive for excellence. So it is with student-involved communication. We seek to involve students in the communication process to generate the expectation that they can succeed. For this reason, we conclude the chapter with a thoughtful analysis of the relationship between the communication process and student motivation.

Maintaining the Quality of the Message

We establish the foundation of effective communication long before any achievement information changes hands. We build strong foundations by attending to the principles of sound assessment in formulating our message. Therefore, everything we have covered in the first 13 chapters of this book forms the foundation to effective communication. Let's review and see why.

A Foundation of Clear Targets

If we are to communicate effectively about student achievement, we must first identify the achievement targets we wish to communicate about. Both message sender and message receiver must be aware of these achievement expectations. If we can't agree on the targets that are to be the focus of our assessment and communication systems, we're sure to have some difficulty arriving at a mutually agreeable set of symbols to use to convey information about student success. If message receivers don't know what targets underpin our assessments, then grades based on those assessments will be devoid of meaning for them.

This means that, if we seek effective communication, we must analyze the learning context to decide if we want students to master content *knowledge*. If we do, we must assess and prepare to communicate about their success in doing so. We must also decide if we wish to promote the development of *reasoning* and problem-solving proficiencies. If we do, again, we must build our assessment, information management, and communication systems around that set of expectations. And, as I'm sure you're anticipating, if we expect students to develop *skills,* to learn to create *products,* or to develop certain *dispositions* toward school and learning, we must define these targets also.

In other words, we should not assume that all parties to the communication network hold a common understanding about what it means to succeed in any particular classroom, school, or district over any particular time frame. Rather, we must make a conscious effort to establish that common vision. If we do not invest that effort, we risk miscommunication and all that goes with it.

A Framework of Quality Assessments

Given a common vision, the next essential ingredient in a strong foundation for effective communication is the transformation of our targets into quality assessments—assessments capable of producing accurate information about student achievement. As you know, sometimes those assessments may take the form of assignments, projects, tests, or any classroom event that provides evidence of achievement. They might be *selected response, essay assessments, performance assessments, or assessments based on personal communication,* depending on which option best matches with the target and with available resources. Also, as you know, each assessment that is to contribute information to our communication must adhere to five standards of quality, by reflecting the agreed-upon *target,* arising from a clear sense of *purpose,* relying on a proper *method, sampling* achievement appropriately, and controlling for all relevant sources of *bias and distortion* that can cause our assessments to be inaccurate.

We can communicate effectively only if we can depend on our assessment results to accurately reflect student achievement. This requires high-quality design and development of every assessment created to contribute information to our communication system. No communication system can transform inaccurate information into an accurate message.

A Record of Accurate Information

The result of our administration and scoring of these high-quality assessments will be a reservoir of accurate information about the extent to which each individual student has met the established achievement expectations. If the time period over which we gather information is relatively brief and the target relatively narrow, this reservoir may include just one or two tests or projects. But if it spans a longer period covering broader targets—such as a quarter, semester, or full year—our record may include numerous pieces of information we must consider together to draw our conclusions. It is this accumulated academic record of student success that we must summarize and share with those who must consider it in their decision making.

If the assessment and communication context calls for sharing information about just one student's performance, as it typically does in the classroom, then we must be prepared to convey the accumulated record of each individual either in total or in some summary form. If the context necessitates sharing information about several (perhaps many) students, as instructional support and policy level decisions often do, then we must be prepared to summarize evidence from the accumulated records of all who are to contribute to the profile of group performance.

In short, when we agree on the meaning of academic success, develop quality assessments of those expectations, and carefully accumulate, store, and summarize appropriate information about student achievement, we build a support structure that underpins effective communication. On the other hand, if we are vague about our targets, inept in our use of assessments, and sloppy in our record keeping, then effective communication about student achievement will remain beyond our reach. It is only when we have satisfied these necessary conditions that we can begin to discuss how to communicate effectively.

Managing the Communication Environment

While we are developing the underlying structure of quality assessment and information storage, we must also attend to the thoughtful preparation of the interpersonal communication environment. Message sender and message receiver(s) must be ready to share information in an environment conducive to hearing and understanding each other.

Clear Reasons for Sharing Information

Message sender and message receiver(s) must understand and agree on the expected consequences of communicating. If communication is to "work" in the desired ways, we must know what this means both from the sender's and receiver's points of view.

What motivates the message sender to share the achievement information? What do the receivers expect to do with the assessment results? These questions must be thought out in advance for communication to be effective.

But the questions don't stop there. What motivates the message receivers? Are their motivations likely to leave them open to hearing the message being sent? Do the message receivers regard the sender as a credible source of information? Are all users clear about how to use the information most productively? Take these issues for granted and risk miscommunication. Take time to clarify them and we build a foundation of accurate communication.

Time for Reflection

Here's one way to probe the keys to effective communication from the message receiver's point of view: Let's say the message to be delivered to a student is negative—a disappointing performance on an assessment. What conditions need to exist within that student for him or her to be ready to receive and act productively on the information? What conditions are likely to inhibit his or her ability to hear and respond to negative feedback? List as many elements of each as you can.

A Shared Language with Which to Communicate

Effective communication is possible only if all participants assign the same meanings to the symbols used to convey information, whether words, pictures, examples, grades, scores, graphs, charts, or something else. We address part of this requirement when we agree in advance on the forms of academic achievement we will communicate about. But that's not enough. When we transform those expectations into assessments, then transform the assessments into scores or other indicators, and then transform the results into evaluative judgments about proficiency (such as grades), there is ample opportunity along the way for the true meaning of achievement to be lost. Accurate communication about levels of achievement is possible only if we prevent a loss of meaning (1) by carefully explaining the nature of all transformations to users, and (2) by making sure message receivers understand our intended meaning of the symbols we use to communicate *before we ever use them.*

As educators, we suffer from a "disease" that makes it very difficult for us to contribute to the development of a shared language with our student and parent message receivers: We are afflicted with the dreaded "jargon." It's true! We maintain a closed system of words and phrases that is often unfathomable by the lay public. This vocabulary is made even more uninterpretable if we combine it with the "technospeak" of the assessment community. We avoid miscommunication with our various publics by striving to use their vocabulary—not ours—when addressing them. When writing narrative descriptions of student performance, generating checklists of competencies, or explaining grades or test scores, we must remain aware of the fact that everyone does not understand teacher language. Most, however, do understand the English language. The basic guideline, therefore, is to communicate using simple, straightforward language whenever possible.

Time for Reflection

One set of symbols we use to deliver messages about student performance in the classroom is report card grades: A, B, C, D, and F. The teacher formulates that message and enters it into the academic record. Who are the people whom we assume will understand the meaning of that message down the road? List as many intended receivers of this message as you can. What conditions do you think need to be satisfied for all of these users to under-stand the teacher's intended message? Is it feasible to meet all of these condi-tions, in your opinion? Why?

An Opportunity to Share

If we are to effectively communicate messages about student achievement, there must be a designated time, place, and set of circumstances where message sender and message receiver(s) agree to attend without distraction to the information being shared. This might take the form of a conference between sender and receiver, a written report of achievement, a public presentation of achievement information, the delivery of an anticipated report card, or other communication method. To work effectively, these opportunities must permit participants time to suspend other activities and attend to information being conveyed. To be most effective, they also should include time to interpret the meaning of the message, check for understanding, and devise action plans if needed.

Without this agreed time to focus on the matter at hand—that is, a student's attainment of designated achievement expectations—our hectic worlds of compet-ing priorities can interfere with our communication. For instance, we might not take time to be sure the symbols we are using have the same meaning for both sender and receiver. Or we might not take time to clarify the interpersonal dynam-ics of the situation, leaving the message receiver too vulnerable to hear or act on the message. Or we might fail to see that sender and receiver(s) value differently the different forms of academic achievement and are incorrectly assuming that it is their vision that is being reflected.

We prevent these problems only by devoting the time needed to address both the achievement and the interpersonal dynamics of the assessment, evaluation, and communication context as summarized in Figure 14–1.

Keys to Managing Message Quality
- Clearly articulated and thoroughly understood achievement targets
- High-quality assessments of those targets
- Accumulation and storage of accurate information about achievement

Keys to Managing Interpersonal Dynamics
- An agreed upon sense of the purpose for the communication
- A common language of symbols understood by both sender and receiver
- An opportunity for sender and receiver to attend to the message
- Verification that the message was received and understood

Figure 14–1
Summary of Keys to Effective Communication

Checking for Understanding

But our list of keys to effective communication is not yet complete. We still have one key step to consider: How will we know if the receiver understands the communication? How shall we know if it serves its intended purpose?

Violations of this standard are common, sometimes occurring in the midst of games we play trying to convince ourselves that we are checking. We place letter grades on report cards and send them home with the request that parents sign the back of the cards as evidence of having seen them. But we rarely ask them to explain back to us what the grades mean to see if they understand the message being sent. We rarely check to see if they know how to act purposefully to deal with grades. We just assume . . .

We must check both for understanding and to find out if the communication has served its purpose. If we fail to follow up, how will we know if the message has gotten through, if we need to repeat it, or if we need to provide it in a different form? And remember, it is impossible for us to verify if the message got through if we were unsure what message we intended to send.

Understanding Our Internal Barriers to Effective Communication

As you can see, there is a great deal of work associated with preparing to communicate effectively about classroom assessment results. Nevertheless, given the critical role of accurate information about student achievement, it is clear that the work must be done. That is, most practicing or prospective educators reading the foregoing analysis of the underpinnings of effective communication acknowledge its critical contribution to student well-being and pledge to devote the needed time and energy needed to do a good job.

But by the same token, we would be naive if we assumed that this kind of careful analysis of the keys to success has driven the design of our grading and other communication systems in the past. The fact is that schools have not worked hard to establish communication over the decades. There are specific reasons for this. I will say this as gently and diplomatically as I can, but it must be said: Not everyone involved in the schooling process wants all parties to share accurate information about actual student achievement. The reality is that we can face significant downside risks by building information management and communication systems that reveal the truth about student achievement in vivid detail. Let's examine why.

The Risk of Being Held Accountable

As a teacher, I could risk being judged professionally incompetent if I permit others to evaluate my competence on the basis of the success of my students. What if I teach, but they just don't learn? What if I try very hard, but they don't? After all, I am not in control of all the variables that determine whether my students will learn, so there is always the chance that they won't achieve. If I'm clear and public about my expectations and rigorous and public about my assessments, evidence might abound of my students' lack of achievement. As a teacher, I have a great deal on the line here.

To keep from being victimized by this, I may conclude that it is safer for me to remain vague about achievement expectations and to cloak my assessments of student success in the mysteries of highly complex and technical testing practices and grading procedures—especially if I lack confidence as a teacher. Because few educators or citizens understand what those test scores mean anyway and no one will ever be able check my grade book or know my real underlying report card grading practices, the fact is that I can put forth a very convincing case for having taught well, whether I did so or not. No one except me will ever know if my instruction really worked or if my students learned anything. Thus, as a teacher, I can escape any real accountability for student learning if I wish. I can minimize my risk and maximize my safety by hiding behind a smoke screen of assessment and grading complexity.

Why, you might ask, would a teacher think this way? Consider the practicalities. If, as a teacher, I am clear and public about my achievement targets, am rigorous and public about my assessments of student performance, and communicate achievement results in a complete and honest manner, I open myself to possible criticism on several fronts. For instance, there may be some parents or taxpayers out there who will disagree with and will challenge my vision of the meaning of academic success. If I don't feel that I am a true master of those targets, I might want to avoid that discussion. Worse yet, what if some of my students don't happen to succeed at hitting the target after I had a chance to teach them to do so? If I've been public about all of this, the citizenry might be able to use my own assessments as evidence to indict me for not doing the job I was hired to do. Indeed, my own students might turn on me—portfolios in hand —demanding that I provide them with more effective help. In short, I stand to lose control, to lose power, to lose my sense of personal professional safety. If I am feeling vulnerable about any of this, why would I do such a thing?

But on the other hand, if I am a confident teacher whose goal is to help the highest possible proportion of my students attain the highest possible levels of academic achievement, my reasoning might be somewhat different. The reason why I would communicate openly would be clear. I cannot reach my teaching goal unless I take this risk. Which students are more likely to succeed academically: those striving to hit clearly defined standards of excellence or those for whom those standards remain a mystery? Those who see a clear path to success or those for whom that path remains a mystery? Those who get to take advantage of effective communication to watch their work improving or those who are forced to remain in the dark about their learning due to the absence of feedback or the inability to interpret the feedback they receive? As a confident teacher devoted to student success, I must risk being open to public review of my success.

One final point about this issue. Let's not be so naive as to think that only teachers face this kind of risk. It reaches all levels of educational responsibility. If I am a superintendent who is unclear about the mission of my schools, unclear about our valued achievement targets, fearful that my teachers might not be successfully promoting student learning, and one who knows little about assessment, I might feel somewhat insecure about developing and implementing an assessment management and communication system that ensures the public will learn the truth about student achievement. The results might be very good or very bad. If I sense that the risks of the latter occurring are too high, I might opt to keep achievement expectations vague and to put forth the appearance of rigorous assessment more than the reality of rigor. When the public is naive, it is very easy to project the image that all is well. Often, it is the politically smart thing to do.

Time for Reflection

Can you think of any concrete actions we might take in the classroom, school, and community to help teachers (and superintendents) make the decision that it is worth taking the risk of being accountable for student learning? Discuss this with classmates or colleagues and list as many ideas as you can.

The Challenge of Too Little Time

Perhaps the most prominent internal barrier to best practice from the teacher's point of view is the lack of time to communicate well. As a teacher, several specific time issues might trouble me deeply. For instance, the past decade has seen an explosion in the scope of the school curriculum, with new targets being added and the old targets acquiring greater complexity. This broadening of the curriculum means I have more to assess and more to communicate about. I might simply feel that I don't have time to communicate about everything. Further, many of the new communication methods advocated these days, such as portfolios, conferences, and narrative reports, are labor intensive. I might conclude that I simply don't have time to carry out such time-consuming communication processes. And to top this off, whenever student achievement is being assessed and communicated about, I—the teacher, the only laborer in this classroom—must do all the work. I don't have an "assistant teacher" to delegate this activity to.

The bottom line might be that all of this talk about effective communication leaves me frustrated about the apparent lack of concern for my workload. The more I have to communicate about and the more labor intensive my communication methods, the more work I am forced to do. I must make up the assessments, devise the scoring scheme, administer the exercises, and do all of the scoring. Then I must record the results and try to summarize them all for the parent-teacher conferences—which I must plan and conduct. That's a lot of work for one person to do! Better to keep it simple, even if the results might be imperfect.

What If the Message Receiver Can't or Won't Listen?

Another troubling barrier to effective communication can be the lack of willingness or ability of the message receiver to hear or accept the message being delivered. Obviously, this is rarely a problem when the message is positive, when grades or test scores are high, or when sincerely felt words of praise are flowing forth. But it is a problem when the message is about disappointing student achievement. For example, students may simply avoid or dismiss the feedback or parents may simply not show up for parent-teacher conferences. The "turn off" can happen for any of a number of reasons, most of which have to do with the receiver's self-concept or view of the message sender.

Sometimes it's difficult to remain mindful of the conditions under which individuals may actually listen to and accept negative information about themselves. For instance, students may need to hold certain attitudes and perspectives to be able to receive and act on such messages. They may need to see themselves as key players in the search for information about their own achievement. They may need assistance in developing a sufficiently strong academic self-concept so they can acknowledge their shortcomings and not feel defeated. Further, students must see the provider of the feedback as credible, honest, and helpful. And finally, they must come to see the benefits of the message very quickly, so they can muster the resources needed to act purposefully. These are very challenging standards to meet.

From the other point of view, as the giver of the feedback, you must be able to present it constructively, delivering a clear, focused, and understandable message. You must be able to communicate acceptance of the students while critiquing their achievement. Even more importantly, you must help students understand that you share a common mission: greater achievement for them.

Clearly, it is no simple task to communicate to students that they have missed the target but still have the hope of success and reason to stay motivated. But as teachers-communicators, that is exactly what we must do. We will return to this issue.

The Risk of Failing to Meet Parent or Community Expectations

But, you might ask, what if I try to communicate in different ways and some families or even whole segments of the community don't like my changes? Some parents cling tenaciously to the view that sound educational practice is delimited only by the experiences they recall having when they were in school. These critics sometimes hold that "anything you do to my child by way of assessment or grading that was not done to me represents unsound practice." To be sure, if the practices they experienced in their youth were sound, they are to be respected for their views. However, if the practices they experienced were unsound, their demands that those practices be continued represent barriers to effective communication. In this situation, if parents expect one form of communication and you deliver something different, the consequences could be dire.

As a result, some educators contend that it is best to avoid controversy and take the conservative approach of sticking with the tried and true, regardless of its appropriateness or effectiveness as a communication practice. This is the third issue you must face in formulating your communication systems. And once again, it involves an aspect of risk. How can you devise information-sharing strategies that keep all parties feeling that their needs are being met? Should we stick with established norms? If we consider new options, do we have the time and expertise needed to convince and retrain a community? The risk is that we might create distracting controversies.

To Risk or Not to Risk

The bottom line is that classrooms and schools cannot function effectively unless decision makers (students, teachers, parents, etc.) can count on ongoing access to accurate information about student achievement. We either communicate effectively or we fail at our mission. We can do so only by becoming confident, competent assessors prepared to (1) help our communities understand the differences between sound and unsound communication practices, (2) become skillful in delivering tough messages in ways that leave students able to respond, (3) find smarter ways to communicate to overcome time barriers, and (4) make a commitment to the use of effective communication in the service of greater student achievement. We can do this, as I contend in the next section, only by relying on open, student-involved forms of communication.

Understanding Student-involved Communication

As we visualize lines of communication in school settings, it is tempting to see the teacher at the head of the communication network, conducting assessments, entering the results in a grade book, and periodically delivering information to those who need it—mostly parents and students who receive this information in the form of grades and test scores. We tend to think of teachers as message senders and others as message receivers. And to be sure, if we follow the guidelines for effective communication described earlier, this can be an effective way to share achievement information.

However, we make a mistake if we assume that this always represents the only or even the most effective way to deliver messages about student success. We have an array of additional communication options at our disposal—many of which can be distinctly more productive, depending on the context.

For example, it has become the custom in our most visible communication systems, such as report cards and test score reports, to define our achievement targets very simply, using such one-word labels as *reading, mathematics, spelling, science,* and so on, with no accompanying information about underlying meaning. Typically, we have assumed that both message senders and receivers understand and agree on the meaning of each label. But if this is an invalid assumption, the message is lost.

There is a way to avoid this risk. We can devise more inclusive communication systems that still value reading, math, spelling, science, and other domains of achievement but that describe them in richer detail, permitting the sharing of more precise information about student success. For instance, *reading* may be more than a generic label. The word actually refers to a process made up of component parts, all of which must come together for the reader to construct meaning from the text. In this context, relevant assessment questions would include the following: Are readers able to use context to determine word meaning? To comprehend and monitor their own understanding? To alter reading strategies to fit the material? We can assess to gather answers to such questions, and we can devise information management systems to reflect the extent to which students have demonstrated the component proficiencies in each academic subject area, if we wish. Such systems are likely to be far more useful than simple labels and associated grades to teachers helping students to achieve ever-higher levels of proficiency.

Further, our traditions have assigned textbook authors, standardized test publishers, and teachers the role of "keepers of the vision," placing them in charge of defining the meaning of academic success, and of deciding if, when, and with whom to share that meaning. If they fail to share with students, or do it poorly, students will not see or understand the target. In this context, any information shared about student success will be devoid of meaning for the student.

The alternative is to open lines of communication so all participants—students, teachers, and (to the extent possible) parents—share a common understanding of the relevant vision of success. Only when all individuals involved actually understand that vision can they communicate about its attainment. Further, if students can play even a small role in setting the target (under the teacher's leadership), we can gain considerable motivational, and therefore achievement, benefits. I will explain why toward the end of the chapter.

Our traditional communication systems have relied on test publishers and teachers to be the assessors. In open, inclusive systems, *all* share responsibility for assessing and interpreting results, again under the teacher's leadership. All three key players in the classroom assessment process—students, teachers, and parents—understand the meaning of academic success, the standards to be met, and the meaning of results.

Our traditions also have made teachers directors of communication, with all information emanating from them and going to students and parents. In more inclusive communication, teachers, students, and parents trade responsibility for delivering information to others. Sometimes students take charge, sending information to teachers and parents. Sometimes parents deliver information to students and teachers. Still other times, teachers run the show. Sometimes, members of the networks team up to inform the other. Information about student achievement can pass in all directions.

Our primary communication symbols traditionally have been grades and test scores. Inclusive systems might rely on these, too, but in a context of deeper mutual understanding of what they mean. More importantly, participants also use other forms of communication, such as words, pictures, and examples conveyed in narratives, lists of goals attained, and so on.

Finally, our traditions have us relying on report cards, test score reports, and parent-teacher conferences as primary vehicles for sharing achievement information. To be sure, when used appropriately, such vehicles can help us convey meaningful information. But, again, we have choices. We also can rely on more complete written reports, conferences that involve students, and portfolios as treasure troves of information about and reflections on student achievement. In the remaining chapters of this book, we will explore both traditional and more inclusive commnication.

Time for Reflection

Now that we have considered differences between traditional and more student-involved communication, center your thoughts on the student-involved side. From a teacher's point of view, what would you think would be the major advantages or benefits of creating this communication environment in the classroom? What would the major disadvantages be? List as many as you can of each and save your lists for later reference.

Student-involved Communication and the Pursuit of Academic Excellence

If we expand our thinking, we can use inclusive communication methods to encourage our students to strive for the highest levels of academic excellence. Without doubt, we have a long history of trying to motivate students to put forth maximum effort through the use of grades as rewards and punishments. However, social psychologists now tell us why those efforts have been insufficient, if not counterproductive. They also point out that we have at our disposal far better methods of motivating. Let's explore these dynamics of the communication process.

Reward and Punishment as a Path to High Achievement

The theory of learning that has exerted greatest influence on school efforts to motivate is known as *behaviorism*. Proponents of this theory explain how or why we learn as a function of schedules of rewards and punishments (Skinner, 1974). We tend to repeat behavior that is regularly reinforced within our environment. Behavior that is repeatedly punished is likely to be extinguished and to disappear. Therefore, by manipulating rewards and punishments we can encourage learners to repeat academically productive behavior and to eliminate behavior unlikely to result in learning. This theory of motivation has spread so deeply into our classrooms and into society at large that it has now become an unquestioned "truth." In the classroom, one part of our communication tradition has served as the primary source of those rewards and punishments: grades. High grades are thought to reinforce the behavior that resulted in substantial learning, while failing grades are supposed to extinguish the behavior that resulted in insufficient learning. Sounds like a pretty straightforward way to promote the pursuit of academic excellence, doesn't it?

However, another social psychologist, Kohn (1993), cautions that this seductive simplicity belies the underlying truth that motivation is not all that straightforward. That is, using grades as rewards and punishments does not motivate learning in productive ways. Indeed, he contends, they have just the opposite effect. Relying on a comprehensive review of decades of research, Kohn concludes that the use of extrinsic sources of motivation, such as stars, stickers, trophies, and grades, can bring students to believe that learning activities are not worth doing in their own right, thus undermining students' natural curiosity to find out how and why things work as they do. In fact, from the learner's point of view, Kohn concludes that, "the more you want what has been dangled in front of you, the less you may come to like whatever you have to do to get it" (p. 83).

While admitting that one can gain a high degree of immediate control over the classroom using relatively simple behavior management methods, Kohn (1993) feels that the following occurs over the long haul:

- Students lose sight of the value of things learned (i.e., will come to value the grade rather than what it represents).

- Students become dependent on the reward as payment, on the need to be controlled, and on the controller ("If I don't get credit in the form of a grade, I just won't do the work.").

- Students become unwilling to take risks in the learning environment because it might cost them some reward (e.g., opting for less rather than more challenging courses in high school to maintain a high GPA).

All of these perceptions, and others that Kohn identifies, carry with them obviously and profoundly negative consequences for student achievement.

Besides, he holds, there is compelling evidence that a carrot-and-stick approach to learning simply doesn't work:

> "Do this and you'll get that" turns out to be bad news whether our goal is to change behavior or to improve performance, whether we are dealing with children or adults, and regardless of whether the reward is a grade, a dollar, a gold star, a candy bar, or any of the other bribes on which we routinely rely. Even assuming we have no ethical reservations about manipulating other people's behavior to get them to do what we want, the plain truth is that this strategy is likely to backfire. (Kohn, 1993, p. 47)

Among others, Kohn cites the research findings of Condry (1977), who concluded that people do the following when offered rewards:

> . . . choose easier tasks, are less efficient in using the information available to solve novel problems, and tend to be answer oriented and more illogical in their problem-solving strategies. They seem to work harder and produce more activity, but the activity is of a lower quality, contains more errors, and is more stereotyped and less creative than the work of comparable nonrewarded subjects working on the same problems. (quoted in Kohn, 1993, pp. 471–472)

Assuming that these researchers correctly describe what turns out to be a confusing relationship of behaviorism and student motivation—and they provide a compelling body of research to defend their position—we are forced to ask the question, If grades don't necessarily result in greater learning, how then shall we encourage our students to strive to attain academic excellence?

Time for Reflection

Think about your own schooling experiences. Can you think of an instance in which your pursuit of a reward in school carried with it negative consequences for your actual level of achievement? Discuss these experiences and their consequences among a group of classmates or colleagues.

Causal Attributions as a Path to High Achievement

Part of the answer may lie in the work of Weiner (1974), who developed a theory of motivation that expands on the idea of reward and punishment in a very interesting manner. He contends that we are driven by an internal reality or filter that helps us interpret who is in control of or responsible for our personal successes and failures. This is called *attribution theory*. You may recall that we spoke briefly of it in Chapter 12 relative to the assessment of student dispositions.

Basically, those students who attribute their academic successes to their own ability and hard work are said to have an *internal locus of control* over those successes. They see themselves as able. Thus, when faced with a learning challenge, they are likely to feel in control of the situation, to anticipate future success, and to invest whatever it takes to succeed.

However, there also are those who attribute the reasons for their successes to others. Their interpretation holds that success in school probably resulted from good luck or the hard work of a good teacher. In their minds, they are not in control of the reward and punishment contingencies—someone else is. These students have an *external locus of control.*

As we face the challenge of encouraging students to put forth the effort required to become productive learners, we must strive to develop within them a sense of pride at having tried hard. If we can use the communication system to show them that hard work can pay off with success (you can get high grades for putting forth effort), they will be in control of the reasons for their success. This will prepare them to face new challenges with confidence and the motivation to succeed. In this sense, our goal is to help students feel as though they are in charge of their own academic successes—if they try, they have the resources to learn.

In a very real sense, this represents the school version of the American dream. Hard work is its own reward. Pull yourself up by your bootstraps with hard work. We value this because we feel—logically—that those who try to learn succeed more than those who don't try. In reality, however, just as with behaviorism, life is more complicated than this set of values would imply.

The connection of effort to achievement is relatively easy to make for the academically successful student. But what about the students who fail to achieve and who attribute that failure to their own lack of ability? What do we do with students who try hard and fail anyway? How do we keep them from giving up in the face of insurmountable odds? How do we keep these students from feeling unable to control their own well-being in school? The bottom line is, how do we keep them from giving up on themselves and on their teachers?

Further, how do we deal with students who attribute the reasons for academic failure to a system that is "out to get them"—to drive them from school? Or students who lack the courage to risk trying out of fear that they might not succeed—because of uncertainty about who really is in control? Where does the motivation come from for these students to invest whatever it takes to find some level of academic success?

Maintaining Self-worth as a Path to High Achievement

The answer to these questions may lie in the work of Covington (1992), centering on the concept of student self-worth. He points out that school presents students with a special "ability game" that can be difficult to win. "In this game, the amount of effort students expend provides clear information about their ability status. For instance, if students succeed without much effort, especially if the task is difficult, then estimates of their ability increase; but should they try hard and fail anyway, especially if the task is easy, attributions to low ability are likely to follow" (pp. 16–17). Covington's perspective is that students' prime objective in schools is to maintain a sense of ability—a sense that they can do it, if they try. But in a cruel twist of this perspective, many students consciously chose to not study and not achieve because if they try and fail they damage that internally held and publicly perceived sense of capability, the basis of their self-worth. They feel it is better to maintain at least some degree of uncertainty, and therefore some degree of self-esteem, by not investing in the system.

Of course, not all students see themselves or school in this self-doubting way. Some are distinctly more positive in asserting an internal locus of control. Covington (citing Skinner, Welborn, & Connell, [1990]) differentiates between success- and failure-oriented students. This orientation influences how they see themselves in the competitive arena of the classroom:

> When children believe that they can exert control over success in school, they perform better on cognitive tasks. And, when children succeed in school they are more likely to view school performance as a controllable outcome. . . . Children who are not doing well in school will perceive themselves as having no control over academic success and failures and these beliefs will subsequently generate performances that serve to confirm their beliefs. (Skinner et al., 1990, as cited in Covington, 1992, p. 38)

So far, this sounds just like Weiner (1974). However, Covington (1992) then departs from his predecessors in offering us a trichotomy of student perceptions of self-worth: (1) *success-oriented* students, those who are academically competent; (2) *failure avoiders*, who are uncertain about the probability of success; and (3) *failure acceptors*, who see themselves as doomed from the outset. He describes the first two orientations through the following examples of Losa and John.

Losa believes in herself as capable of success in the classroom. Her frequent success reaffirms this self-concept. But when failure does occur in school (a rare occurrence), she quickly infers that she didn't try hard enough or didn't understand the task well enough to perform well on it. In this sense, failure is not a threat. It does not lead to a sense of incompetence but rather one of ignorance: "There must be something I missed—something correctable if I just work harder and smarter." In the face of failure, she relies on her sense of her own ability to infer a problem that leaves her feeling guilty but optimistic. As a result, she does better the next time. The steps in her reasoning are depicted in Figure 14–2. Under all circumstances, she's safe because she has desensitized herself to the potentially negative effects of evaluation. She has the inner resources to risk comfortably.

But the failure-avoiding student responds to success and failure differently. John is a self-doubting, apathetic high school senior. When faced with an academic challenge, his first thought is that he just isn't smart enough to succeed. This pessimism contributes to a lack of effort. So his performance is likely to be borderline, at best, which reinforces his feelings of inadequacy, and so on. To make matters worse, John can even extend this counterproductive self-concept into those occa-

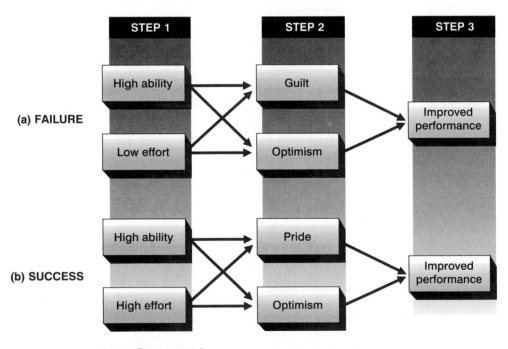

Figure 14–2
The Steps in the Reasoning of Losa, a Success-oriented Student
Source: From *Making the Grade: A Self-worth Perspective on Motivation and School Reform* (p. 56) by Martin V. Covington, 1992, New York: Cambridge University Press. Reprinted by permission of Cambridge University Press.

sions when he succeeds. His internal sense of low ability can leave him worrying that he really didn't deserve the high grade. Further, he might be concerned that someone might discover that he's really only a high-achieving impostor. He lacks any sense of pride in accomplishment that would be reassuring about his future prospects of high grades, thinking instead that he was just lucky to do well this time. His reasoning is depicted in Figure 14–3. In effect, John can snatch defeat from the jaws of imminent victory, resulting once again in a kind of pessimism that promises more poor performance in the future. Under no circumstances is he safe, making it very difficult to risk trying something new or something that might require a stretch on his part.

This is where John's apathy comes from. Covington (1992) points out that John is not "unmotivated" at all. Rather, he is highly motivated, but to do the counterproductive thing from an academic achievement point of view.

And, to complete the picture, in a similar situation we also can find *failure-accepting* students. They are even more trapped than John. These students have experienced so much failure over such a long period of time that they have given up completely on themselves and school. There is no desire to "try" left in them and thus they are assured of virtually never succeeding academically. As a result,

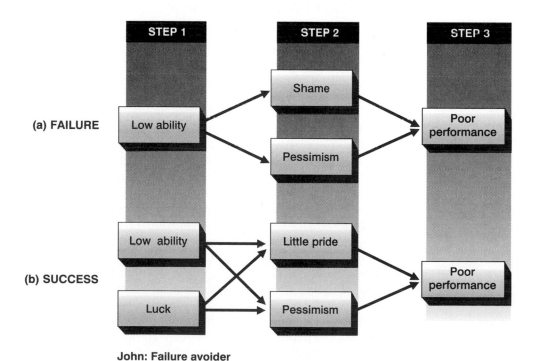

John: Failure avoider

Figure 14–3

The Steps in the Reasoning of John, a Failure Avoider

Source: From *Making the Grade: A Self-worth Perspective on Motivation and School Reform* (p. 58) by Martin V. Covington, 1992, New York: Cambridge University Press. Reprinted by permission of Cambridge University Press.

they are constantly bombarded with compelling evidence of their own "stupidity." Soon they become numbed to the onslaught and become mental dropouts. Covington refers to this as *learned helplessness*. Even if they happen to succeed at something, these students are sure to credit blind luck, disregard any message of possible competence, and remain enmeshed in a tangle of doom. Such students feel absolutely no control over what happens to them in school and therefore are always vulnerable. Taking the risks needed to learn is not only beyond their reach, it's also beyond their frame of reference.

Time for Reflection

As you reflect on your own school experiences, which of these categories do you fall into now? Can you remember classmates that fell into the other two categories? If you are teaching now, who among your students fit into these categories? Take some time to share your self-perceptions with classmates or colleagues.

How Can Student-involved Communication Help?

Clearly, our goal must to be to help our students maintain the internal sense that (1) they can do the work and (2) the work is worth doing. But we must be very careful here, on two fronts.

First, neither we nor they should interpret this to mean that the academic work to be done is easy. The subtle but critical difference is this: We must convince them that the work to be done is challenging—that there is always a risk of failure, but that risk is not a reason to stop. We must help them understand that they cannot succeed unless they face the fact that they are going to fail sometimes. We all do. But if they learn to manage that risk, they will come to see that persistence is the key to success. We must convince them that the risk is worth taking.

Second, we must remain aware of the fact that many forces impinge on a student's academic self-concept. Primary among these are early childrearing practices. Obviously, as teachers we have no control over these. Further, even during the school years, many things are happening in students' lives that affect their perceptions of self-worth. Most of these happen outside of the classroom—again beyond our control. For these reasons, it is imperative that we maintain perspective on the extent to which we alone can help a student overcome a sense of a lack of academic ability. But if we team up with parents in a common mission of trying to help, the combined forces can be quite powerful. Communication strategies that include both student and parent in the process can tap that power.

Covington (1992) offers practical advice about how to do this. He points out that whether any particular student will risk trying is a function of three things: the learner's motivational tendency (success oriented, failure avoider, or failure acceptor), the learner's internal sense of the probability of achieving the goal, and the attractiveness of that goal for the learner. This leads to the "commonsense observation that individuals are stirred to action if there is a reasonable chance that they will get something they want" (p. 33).

The entire basis of the concept of student-centered classroom assessment is to keep students feeling that they can control what they achieve. We do this by being crystal clear about the meaning of success (no surprises) and through the use of understandable (not necessarily easy) assessments. We help them develop a clear sense of what it takes to succeed.

Then, by involving them in the assessment process itself—by teaching them to monitor the accumulating evidence of their own increasing proficiency—we help them understand the very high probability that they will continue to succeed if they continue their current level of effort. To the extent that we can show them where their success is leading in terms of their ultimate competence, we can help them believe that the targets are indeed worth hitting. Also, to the extent that we bring their families into the assessment and evaluation process, such that students can reveal often unexpected success to those whose opinions they care about, we can build a sense of pride in achievement that they may have rarely felt in their school lives. Finally, to the extent that we can bring students into the process of setting the learning targets, we can also maximize the chances that they will be "stirred to action."

Student-involved communication can help us motivate students by clarifying their understanding of the meaning of success, by helping them feel empowered to risk failure while expecting success, and by instilling in them a sense of pride in achievement. We can help them develop strong achievement aspirations. We can generate this motivation by building communication systems that *describe* student performance consistently and understandably over time in ways that teachers, students, and their families understand.

We all find it impossible to be success oriented—to risk trying harder even in the face of possible failure—when success and failure have no clearly interpretable reference points. Involving students in communication makes those reference points clear for all to see, as we discuss in the following chapters. Such clarification addresses each of the four barriers to quality assessment identified earlier in the chapter: fear of accountability, lack of time, message receiver "turn off," and parental expectations. By enhancing students' internal locus of control and raising their self-expectations, we increase the chances that large proportions of our students will achieve as expected. This makes it easier to face the need to be accountable for achievement. By involving students in the process, we spread the work of communicating across more shoulders. This has the effect of returning time dividends to teachers. And by involving parents directly in the assessment and communication processes, we alleviate any confusion about their information desires. This ensures that they will be satisfied with the achievement information they receive about their children.

Said another way, we must aspire to the development of learning-oriented versus performance-oriented classroom environments. Overemphasis on competition for grades, reduction in grades for misbehavior, or building the expectation that virtually everything will be translated into a grade have the effect of telling the student that what's important here is the immediate performance. As a result, the aspiration to get the grade can become a light so brilliant in students' lives that it blinds them to what really counts. In this environment, as the desire to perform increases, the motivation to learn decreases. Thus, paradoxically, the very motivational strategy we have used to get students to care and try hard can have just the opposite effect.

The use of many student-involved assessments, all of which help learners to see themselves learning but only a few of which translate into grades per se, can keep the brilliance of the grade from blinding. The use of communication strategies that maintain within all learners a full sense of what they are achieving—that keep them feeling in control of their own success—can result in a far more productive classroom environment for all students.

In the following three chapters, we will explore how to use student-involved communication in conjunction with student-centered classroom assessment to take advantage of the resulting motivational dividends. In effect, we will explore how to maintain each student's success orientation in a positive way and how to help John overcome self-doubt and apathy. In Chapter 15, we'll address communication via grades. Some are ready to abandon report card grades in light of the aforementioned dangers. I am not yet ready to give up on them for many reasons. But there are certain rules that we must follow for grades to serve our student-centered purposes. We'll spell those out in the next chapter.

Chapter 16 will deal with portfolios, a very popular communication idea. Once again, for this exciting and productive information management system to reach its potential—to provide an accurate record of achievement and be a powerful motivator of learners—we must carry out specific procedures. We'll outline them.

And finally, in Chapter 17 we'll wrap up our journey together by providing examples of alternative communication ideas, such as narrative reporting, checklists, rating scales, and various kinds of conferences, all of which can energize students and teachers to aspire to academic excellence. Just remember as we explore these applications that student-involved communication can serve us well only if it arises from a foundation of high-quality classroom assessment.

Chapter Summary: Meeting the Communication Challenge

This introduction to the underlying principles of student-involved communication began with a thorough analysis of the active ingredients of an effective information management and communication system. Three of these ingredients address fundamental considerations about maintaining the quality of the message itself. These demand that we prepare to communicate effectively by clarifying achievement tar-

gets, by devising quality assessments, and by compiling accurate records of student achievement. Four more active ingredients center on effective management of the communication environment. These ask us to be clear about our reason(s) for communicating, to develop a language both message sender and message receiver understand, to schedule an opportunity where both agree to attend to the information-sharing process, and to check for understanding of the information shared.

But if it's so easy to define effective communication in these terms, why is it so difficult to attain effective communication in schools? We explored four possible answers: fear of being accountable for student learning, lack of time to meet standards of quality assessment and effective communication, lack of willingness of the message receiver to participate in the process, and uncertainty about parental and community expectations about what it means to communicate effectively.

Open, inclusive communication offers a means of removing barriers to effective communication. When contrasted with more traditional teacher-centered communication, the student-focused process places a higher premium on clear, complete, and visible definition of achievement targets; the sharing of that vision broadly throughout the classroom, school, and community; and the division of assessment responsibility. It also places heavy reliance on means of sharing information that include but go far beyond grades and test scores.

In preparing to sample new communication systems, we explored the relationship between various systems and student motivation to achieve, including issues of reward and punishment, student internal and external attributions for success and failure (locus of control), and the relationship between risk taking and the learner's sense of self-worth. I hope this exploration reveals to you the immense potential of the intrinsic motivation we can engender by communicating more effectively with students.

Exercises to Advance Your Learning

Knowledge

1. After you have had a chance to study them, list and define from memory three key steps in preparing to address the achievement dynamics that underpin effective communication in the classroom.

2. After reviewing them, list and define from memory three key steps in addressing the interpersonal dynamics of the classroom communication environment.

3. Referring to the text, identify potential barriers to effective communication about student achievement in the classroom.

4. From memory, analyze the elements of a student-centered communication environment.

5. In your own words, describe the relationship between student-centered communication and student motivation. Refer to the text as necessary to formulate your response.

Reasoning

1. Identify a system of communication about student achievement currently in use in your school. This might be a report card grading system you use in your classroom, one that a professor in your program uses, or a system of reporting test scores to decision makers. Analyze this specific attempt to communicate in terms of the six criteria of effective communication identified at the beginning of this chapter. Is it a sound system of communication? Why?

2. Compare and contrast teacher-centered and student-centered communication as defined in this chapter by identifying both the strengths and weaknesses of each kind of environment.

3. Based on this comparison, which is likely to result in greater achievement gains for students? Why?

Dispositions

1. Describe in writing the direction and intensity of your feelings about the potential role of student-centered communication in helping us fulfill our two reasons for assessing: (1) to provide dependable information for decision making, and (2) to take advantage of the assessment and communication processes to promote student success in school.

Developing Sound Report Card Grading Practices

CHAPTER ROADMAP

The first communication option we will consider is report cards and grades. As a result of studying the material presented in Chapter 15, reflecting on that material, and completing the learning exercises presented at the end of the chapter, you will know and understand the following:

1. Arguments for and against factoring achievement, aptitude, effort, and attitude into report card grades.
2. The steps in the report card grading process and the specific activities that make up each step.
3. Practical strategies for avoiding common grading problems.
4. How to evaluate grading practices in terms of the principles of effective communication about student achievement.

You will be prepared to use that knowledge to reason in the following ways:

1. Differentiate between achievement communications that do and do not satisfy the principles of effective communication.
2. Compare grading based on rank order (on a curve) with grading in terms of student competence (with preset standards).
3. Think critically about arguments for and against factoring various student characteristics into the report card grade.

By experimenting, practicing, and working with the ideas presented in this chapter, you will develop the following skill:

1. Learn to carry out the steps in effective report card grading and to avoid common problems.

And finally, as a result of studying and using the ideas expressed, I hope you will be predisposed to do the following:

1. See the need for more than the appearance of accountability for student learning in our grading systems.
2. Value more effective communication about *achievement* via grades in the future than we have attained in the past.
3. Value accurate description of student achievement in report card grades.

The objectives of this chapter do not include the creation of any products.

As a teacher, for many years, I experienced considerable anxiety wondering whether I was grading my students the "right" way. I asked myself the following questions:

- Exactly what distribution of grades am I to assign—how many As, Bs, and so on?
- Should I grade on a curve or use preset standards?
- Should my grades reflect absolute achievement at one point in time or improvement over time?
- How do I grade students who already know all the material at the beginning of the term?
- Should I grade just on ability and achievement or also consider effort and attitude?
- How am I supposed to manage all this achievement information for all these students?
- What should I do if my tests are too hard and everyone fails? What grades do I assign?
- Are my grades supposed to mean the same thing as those of others who teach the same courses? How can we achieve that?
- If we all reflect different expectations and standards in our grades, how can anyone interpret our grades accurately? How do we make any of this make sense?

My list of questions, uncertainties, and concerns seemed endless. What teacher has not wondered the same things?

If we are to use grades as an effective means of communication, each of us must come to terms with these issues. This is the subject this chapter.

Time for Reflection

Before we go further with this discussion, take a few moments to summarize your attitudes and values about the topic of grading. How do you feel about report cards and grades? List as many things as you can that are good about them. Then list as many negatives as you can. Be specific. Save your lists for later use.

Understanding Our Current Grading Environment

Before we begin to address the specifics of grading, we must understand the evolving school environment within which we grade students. Five key dimensions of that environment warrant comment, some because they are changing and some because they are not.

A Continuing Expectation of Grades

First, a huge majority of parents and communities still expect their children to be graded in school, especially at junior high and high school levels. They know, as we should too, that grades will play a role in decisions that influence students' lives. This may not always be true in the future, because we are constantly confronting the limitations of grades as a communication system. But it is true now and will be for the immediate future, at least. This means our challenge is to do the very best job we can of assigning grades.

To be sure, we are currently experiencing greater freedom to explore communication options, particularly at the elementary level. We will consider many alternatives—portfolios, checklists, rating scales, narratives, and conferences—in the final two chapters.

But we must understand that these options are different from simply changing the grading symbols we use. Elementary teachers have often said to me, "We don't use grades in our school. We use check, check plus, and check minus." Or, "We use O for outstanding, S for satisfactory, and U for unsatisfactory. So we don't have to worry about grades." The material covered in this chapter applies in these contexts, also. *Grading* is the process of abstracting a great deal of information into a single symbol for ease of communication. The only things that change in the instances just cited are the symbols used; the underlying issues remain the same.

An Evolving Mission.   In the 1990s, assigning grades in schools and classrooms has taken a new meaning. Schools used to be considered effective if they produced a rank order of students at the end of high school. We have discussed this in earlier chapters. As long as there was a valedictorian and everyone had a "rank in class," few questioned the effectiveness of the school's functioning. However, over the past two decades, as the demands of both our society and the economy have changed, we have come to understand the inadequacy of this standard of school effectiveness. The demand for higher levels of competence for larger proportions of our students has brought about a demand for schools driven by achievement—not rank order—expectations.

This change in mission carries implications for our grading practices. For decades in the American educational system, we have been demonstrating how it is possible to rank students without knowing much about the quality of the assessments or the soundness of the grading practices. Since the ritual sorting process seemed to connect to our society's need to identify a range of abilities, no one was concerned about the underlying dangers of mismeasurement and/or unsound grading practices. No one asked for a dependable rank order. Appearances sufficed. Few cared that meaningful comparison and interpretation of grades across classrooms, schools, or districts was impossible. The actual information about student achievement contained within a grade wasn't considered very important. As long as the symbols appeared to have academic rigor, schools were assumed to be effective.

But this has begun to change as society has begun to realize the limitations of ranking students. We have come to understand that, while we can assign grades and sort students without dependable assessments and sound grading practices, we cannot ensure their competence. Thus, we are forced to come to terms with the problems of mismeasurement and unsound grading. We have begun to realize that, if we are to take students from a starting place of no competence to the highest levels of competence, those contributing to student success must have constant access to dependable information about their achievement status. We have also realized that teachers must communicate with each other, with families, and with students themselves about the specifics of student achievement if we are to support a continuous progress curriculum. It is within this changing environment that we address grading practices in this chapter.

Evolving Achievement Targets

We also are experiencing rapid changes in our collective vision of the meaning of academic success. Two facets of our evolving expectations are important from a grading point of view. First, the range of our expectations is expanding with the addition of technological, health-related, and teamwork achievement targets, among others. Second, the complexity of our expectations is increasing as researchers help us understand more clearly what it means to be a good reader, writer, math problem solver, and team member, to mention a few. These changes make it necessary for teachers to gather, store, retrieve, summarize, grade, and otherwise communicate about far more achievement targets today than ever before. In short, the information processing challenges faced by the typical classroom teacher are immense. This means that we must also address grading practices from a perspective of efficiency.

Changing Student Needs

In addition, teachers must deal with the grading implications of mainstreaming special needs students. The typical teacher is facing a much broader range of academic abilities than ever before. Assessments must be planned and conducted and grades assigned in classrooms where different students are working toward the attainment of fundamentally different achievement targets. If each student succeeds, each deserves an "A." But how do we communicate the differences among those As? Is it even conceivable to individualize these communication systems to promote understanding and sound decision making? This reality places immense pressure on our traditional grading practices, and is a part of the challenging context we face in the 1990s.

The Need for Quality

As we discuss grading practices within this evolving environment, we must bear in mind our six specific standards of communication quality. If we are to communicate effectively via grades, we must start with the following:

- clearly articulated and appropriate achievement expectations
- quality assessments capable of accurately reflecting student proficiency
- the accumulation of a reservoir of dependable information regarding the achievement of each individual student
- clearly articulated and agreed on reasons for communicating achievement results
- a shared language for message sender and receiver to use in passing information
- an opportunity to share information—a time, place, and set of circumstances when message sender and receiver can attend to the information being shared

Time for Reflection

Before we proceed, please take some time to reflect about the grading process in your school world. If you are a teacher, to what extent do your grading practices meet each of these six standards of effective communication? If you are a student, to what extent do your professors' grading practices satisfy these criteria?

Selecting Targets for Grading Purposes

If we are to devise grading approaches that meet our communication needs in achievement-driven schools and that contribute to a supportive, productive, and motivating environment, the first issue we must confront is, What do we wish to communicate about? We must decide which student characteristics should be factored into report card grades.

Traditionally, we appear to have considered several factors, among them the following:

- *achievement*—those who learn more receive higher grades
- *aptitude*—those who "overachieve" in relation to their aptitude, intelligence, or ability receive higher grades
- *effort*—those who try harder receive higher grades
- *attitude*—those who demonstrate more positive attitudes receive higher grades

Of course, no two teachers will define these in the same terms, assess them in the same way, or give them the same relative weight in assigning grades. It is interesting to speculate on what the interpretability of a single letter grade is when we don't know (1) which of these elements the grader deemed important, (2) how they defined each, (3) how or how well they assessed each, and (4) what weight they gave each factor in grade computation. If we expect to communicate effectively about student achievement via grades, we must regard all these unknowns as deeply troubling. But this is just the tip of the iceberg when it comes to communicating through grades.

To illustrate what I mean, join me now in a wide-ranging and thoughtful analysis of the role in the grading process of each of the four listed factors. Here are the issues in a nutshell:

- Should achievement be a factor in grading? That is, if two students have demonstrated fundamentally different levels of attainment of your achievement expectations, should you assign them different grades?

- Should you consider the student's aptitude, intelligence, or ability in the grading process? That is, if two students have demonstrated exactly the same level of achievement—and let's say that level is right on the line between two letter grades—but you regard one as an overachiever in relation to ability and the other an underachiever, is it appropriate to assign them different grades?

- Is it appropriate to consider a student's level of effort, seriousness of purpose, or motivation in the grading process? That is, let's say two students have demonstrated exactly the same level of achievement and, again, that level is right on the line between two letter grades, but you regard one as having tried very hard while the other has not tried hard at all. Is it appropriate to assign them different grades?

- Is it proper to factor the student's attitude into the grade? Again, given two students equal in actual achievement and on a grade borderline, one of whom has exhibited a positive attitude in class and one a distinctly negative attitude, is it appropriate to assign them different grades?

Time for Reflection

Before reading on, reflect on and take a personal position on each of these questions. If possible, discuss your views with colleagues or classmates. Once you have answered each of these four questions with a yes or no, then proceed.

What are the arguments for and against factoring each of these aspects into a grade? Which set of arguments should win out, arguments for or against, given our purpose to communicate effectively? Let's consider these questions.

Achievement as a Grading Factor

If we use achievement as one basis for a report card grade, in effect, our contract with students is that those who master a larger amount of the required material—who attain more of the valued targets—will receive higher grades than those who attain less. This has long represented a foundation of our grading process.

Arguments for. One reason this factor has been so prominent in grading is that schools exist to promote student achievement. In that sense, it is the most valued result of schooling. If students achieve, schools are seen as working effectively. Grades are supposed to reflect a student's level of success in learning the required material.

Besides, students are expected to achieve in life after school. School is an excellent place to learn about this fundamental societal expectation. In addition, achievement in most academic disciplines can be clearly defined and translated into sound assessments. So we can build a strong basis for grading achievement in our assessments. In short, it can be done well, given currently available technology.

These are all compelling reasons why we traditionally have factored achievement into the report card grade, most often as the most prominent factor. Who would question the wisdom of grading in this way? Are there compelling reasons not to factor in achievement?

Arguments Against. In fact, there are. For example, what if we define achievement in complex terms that are difficult to assess well, and we inadvertently mismeasure it? Or, what if we grade student performance based on a very important term-length homework assignment that the student did not do—a well-meaning parent did, instead? If we factor the results of such assessments into the grade, that grade misrepresents real student achievement. Those who read the grade later would draw incorrect inferences about student achievement and would make inappropriate decisions.

Or, what if we lack sufficient assessment expertise in the valued target to adequately evaluate student achievement of it? Again, mismeasurement is likely and the grade might not reflect real achievement.

Or, in a more serious and more likely dilemma, what if each teacher has a different definition of the meaning of successful achievement, assesses it differently, and assigns it a different weight in the grade computation? Now our attempts to communicate about achievement are full of noise—static, not clear, meaningful signals. When this happens, grades become uninterpretable.

Besides, if we factor in achievement, isn't there a danger that perennial low achievers will never experience success in the form of high grades? For them, factoring achievement into the grade simply means more failure and a damaged sense of self-worth.

These seem to represent compelling reasons not to grade on achievement. So, which should win out—arguments for or against?

The Resolution.   The answer lies in our ability to address the arguments against factoring achievement into the grade. Let's explore this further.

Time for Reflection

Before reading on, how do these arguments balance for you? Do we grade on achievement or not? Take a stand, list your reasons, and then continue.

If we can devise and implement practices that overcome *every* argument against factoring achievement into the grade, then the argument must fall in favor of including it. In other words, it is unethical and therefore unacceptable to know that there are compelling reasons not to grade in a certain way and then simply decide to do it anyway.

So, can we address all of the arguments against factoring achievement into the grade and eliminate them?

If there is a danger of mismeasurement due to the complexity of targets. we can either simplify them, or we can participate in professional development to help us to (1) refine our vision of the target to capture its complexity, and (2) devise more accurate assessments. These actions can prevent inadvertent mismeasurement of achievement.

If the problem is a lack of assessment expertise on the part of teachers responsible for grading, this may be alleviated by providing high-quality professional development in assessment so all teachers may attain essential expertise. Or, we can work with qualified colleagues, supervisory staff, or higher-education faculty to devise sound assessments.

If problems arise because some teachers hold different definitions of achievement, we can meet to compare definitions. By airing differences of professional opinion, we can find the common ground on which to build sound grading practices.

If the problem is inevitable failure for the perennial low achiever, we can establish achievement targets that are within the grasp of each student, grading students in terms of standards that hold the promise of success for all and communicating individualized results. More about this later.

Thus, if we act purposefully to develop and implement practices that remove objections by setting clear and specific targets that are within the reach of all students, using sound assessments, we can find ample justification for including achievement in the report card grade.

But remember, it is not enough simply to acknowledge each potential problem—we must take specific, calculated action to eliminate it. Fail to act and the arguments against must win.

Aptitude as a Grading Factor

Remember the issues here: Assume two students demonstrate exactly the same level of achievement, and that level happens to be right at the cutoff between two grades. If you judge one of the students to be an overachiever in relation to expectations based on ability, aptitude, or intelligence, and judge the other to be an underachiever, is it appropriate to assign them different grades? In other words, is it appropriate to factor a judgment about a student's aptitude into the grading equation?

Arguments for.   If we consider aptitude, or ability, in the equation, we hold out the promise of success for every student—a positive motivator. And, as students gain a sense of their own efficacy, we also will gain a source of motivation. What teacher is not energized by the promise of individualized achievement targets set so as to match the capabilities of each individual student, thus ensuring each student at least the chance of academic success?

Besides, if we can identify those underachievers, we can plan the special motivational activities they need to begin to work up to their fullest potential. And we do so with no grading penalty to the perennial low achiever. This is a win-win proposition!

These are compelling arguments indeed. Factoring aptitude or ability into the grading process makes perfect sense. Who could argue against it?

Arguments Against.   Once again, there are important counterarguments. For example, the definition of this thing called *aptitude,* or sometimes *intelligence,* is far from clear. Scholars who have devoted their careers to the study of this construct and its relationship to achievement do not agree among themselves as to whether each of us has one of these or many. They disagree on whether this is a stable or volatile human characteristic, or whether it is stable at some points in our lives and unstable at others. They disagree about how this attribute (or these attributes) should be assessed (Gardner, 1993; Sternberg, 1996).

Given this uncertainty among experts, how can we who have no background presume to know any student's aptitude or intelligence? That is not to say that all students come to school with the same intellectual tools—we know they do not. But it is one thing to sense this to be true and quite another matter to assume that we possess enough refined wisdom about intelligence to be able to capture it in a single index and then manipulate that index to factor it into such an important decision as a report card grade. We do not have sufficient knowledge or assessment expertise in hand yet to justify such practices.

But even if we resolve this problem of definition, we still would face a serious assessment dilemma. Given the absence of training in aptitude assessment, even teachers with a dependable definition would face severe difficulty generating the classroom-level data needed to classify students according to their aptitude. Remember the key attributes of a sound assessment? Each would have to be met— for an attribute called aptitude—independent of achievement!

A brief comment is in order about this issue of aptitude as something separate from achievement. It is tempting to use a student's record of prior achievement as a basis from which to draw inferences about ability, intelligence, or aptitude. But, *achievement* and *aptitude* are not the same. Many things other than intellectual ability influence achievement, such as home environment, school environment, and dispositions. Inferring level of ability from prior performance is very risky. Resist this temptation.

This is precisely what makes the over-/underachiever concept so difficult to apply. Specifically, each teacher would need a formula for deciding precisely how many units of achievement are needed per unit of aptitude to be labeled an over- or underachiever—and that formula would have to treat each and every student in exactly the same manner to assure fairness. We do not possess the conceptual understanding and classroom assessment sophistication to enable us to do this.

Besides, what if we made the mistake of mislabeling a student an under-achiever? The student may be misclassified for years and suffer the consequences. Such a wrong label may well become a self-fulfilling prophecy.

Even if the label were correct, is there not a danger of backlash from the student labeled as being a bright high achiever? At some point, might this student ask, How come I always have to strive for a higher standard to get the same grade as others who have to do less? Consider the motivational implications here!

And finally there is the same "signal-noise" dilemma we faced with achievement. To the extent that different teachers define intelligence or ability or aptitude differently, assess it differently, and factor it into the grade computation equation differently, those who try to interpret the resulting grade later cannot hope to sort out the teacher's intended message. Only noise is added into our communication system.

The Resolution.   There are compelling arguments for and against factoring the student characteristic called aptitude into the report card grade. Which shall win?

Time for Reflection

Again, how do you sort these out? Take a position and state why before continuing.

The requirements for inclusion do not change. To justify incorporating aptitude or intelligence into the report card grade, we must address and remove all compelling objections through specific action. Can we devise a definition of aptitude that translates into sound assessment, that promises to treat each student equitably? Perhaps someday, but not today. There is no place for aptitude, ability, or intelligence in the report card grading equation. For now, the definition and assessment problems are insurmountable.

But, you might ask, what about all of those compelling arguments in favor of this practice? What about our desire to individualize so as to motivate student and teacher with the promise of success? What about the hope this practice could offer to the perennial low achiever? Must we simply abandon these hopes and desires?

The answer is a clear and definite *No!* But we must individualize on the basis of a student characteristic that we can define clearly, assess dependably, and link effectively to the learning process. I submit that a far better candidate—a candidate that meets all requirements while not falling prey to the problems we experience in struggling with aptitude or intelligence—is *prior achievement*. If we know where a student stands along a path to ultimate competence, we can tailor instruction to help that student take the next step.

If teachers set achievement targets based on the student's learning achievement, share that expectation with the student, and grade on mastery of knowledge, demonstrated problem-solving proficiency, performance of required skills, and/or creation of required products, then we can conceive of a continuous progress assessment and communication system based entirely on achievement. Think of it as a contract between teacher and student where targets are set at the outset and monitored continually for success.

Effort as a Grading Factor

Remember that, in this case, the issue is framed as follows: Assume two students demonstrate exactly the same level of achievement, and that level happens to be right on the borderline between two grades. If one student obviously tried harder to learn, demonstrated more seriousness of purpose, or exhibited a higher level of motivation than did the other, is it appropriate to assign them different grades? Does level of effort have a place in the report card grading equation?

Arguments for.   Many teachers include effort in their grading process for a variety of apparently sound reasons. We see effort as being related to achievement: Those who try harder learn more. So by rewarding effort with higher grades and punishing lack of effort with lower grades, we strive to promote achievement.

As a society, we value effort. Those who strive harder contribute more to our collective well-being. School seems an excellent place to begin teaching what is, after all, one of life's important lessons.

A subtle but related, and important, reason for factoring effort into the grade is that it appears to encourage risk taking—another characteristic we value in our society. A creative and energetic attempt to reach for something new and better should be rewarded, even if ultimate success falls short. And so, some think, it should be with risky attempts at achievement in school.

This may be especially important for perennial low achievers, who may not possess all of the intellectual tools and therefore may not have mastered all of the prerequisite knowledge needed to achieve. But the one thing that is within their control is how hard they try. So even if students are trapped in a tangle of inevitable failure because of their intellectual and academic history, at least they can derive some rewards for trying.

Thus, there are compelling reasons, indeed, for using effort as one basis of the grade. Could anyone argue against such a practice?

Arguments Against.   In fact, we can argue against it for many good reasons. A primary reason is that definitions of what it means to try hard vary greatly from teacher to teacher. Some definitions are relatively easy to translate into sound assessments: *Those who complete all homework put forth effort.* But other definitions are not: *Trying hard means making positive contributions to the quality of the learning environment in our classroom.* To the extent that teachers differ in their definition, assessment, and manner of integrating information about effort into the grading equation, we add noise into the grade interpretation process.

Besides, we may say we want students to participate in class as a sign of their level of effort, but who most often controls who gets to contribute in class? The teacher. How, then, do we justify holding students accountable for participating when they don't control this factor?

Further, students can manipulate their *apparent* level of effort to mislead us. If I know you grade in part on the basis of my level of effort and I care what grade I receive, you can bet that I may act in such a way as to make you think I am trying hard, whether I am or not. How can you know if I'm being honest?

From a different perspective, effort often translates into assertiveness in the learning environment. Those who assertively seek teacher attention and participate aggressively in learning activities are judged to be motivated. But what of naturally quieter students? Effort is less likely to be visible in their behavior regardless of its level. And this may carry with it gender and/or ethnic differences, yielding the potential of systematic bias in grades as a function of factors unrelated to achievement. Members of some groups are enculturated to avoid competition. Gender, ethnicity, and personality traits have no place in the grading equation.

And finally, factoring effort into the grade may send the wrong message to students. In real life, just trying hard to do a good job is virtually never enough. If we don't deliver relevant, practical results, we will not be deemed successful, regardless of how hard we try.

Besides, from the perspective of basic school philosophy, what is it we really value, achieving or achieving and knowing how to make it look like we tried hard? What if it was easy?!

The Resolution.   The balance scale tips in favor of including effort only if we can eliminate all arguments against doing so.

Time for Reflection

How do you come down on this one? How does the scale tip and why?

First, we must face the issue of what we value. If we value learning, then we must define it and build our reporting systems around it. If we value effort too, then again we must arrive at a mutually acceptable definition of it and its assessment. If we value both, why must we combine them into the same grading equation? We know how to devise reporting systems that present information on each—separately.

If the objection is to lack of consistency in underlying definitions, then we must come together to agree on clear and appropriate definitions—*and* they must account for students who need little effort to learn. There can be no penalty for them.

If the problem is poor-quality assessment of effort, we must understand and adhere to all appropriate rules: sound assessment of effort must arise from a clear target, have a clear purpose, rely on a proper method of assessment, sample effort in a systematically representative manner, and control for all relevant sources of extraneous interference. But again, if we go to all this work to create rigorous assessments, why bury the results in the far reaches of some complex grade computation equation? Why not report the achievement and effort results separately?

When students set out purposely to mislead us with respect to their real level of effort, they can seriously bias our assessment. This may be impossible to eliminate as a problem. If we address 30 students per day all day for a year and some are misleading us about their real level of effort, we may well see through it. But as the number approaches and exceeds 150 students for one hour a day and sometimes only for a few months, as it does for many middle and high school teachers, there is no way to confidently and dependably determine how hard each student is trying.

Moreover, if effort influences the grades of some, equity demands that it have the same influence on all. The assessment and record-keeping challenges required to meet this standard are immense, to say the least.

But a more serious challenge again arises from the personality issue. Less aggressive people are not necessarily trying less hard. Quiet effort can be diligent and productive. As teachers, we really do have difficulty knowing how much effort most students are putting forth. And we have few ways of overcoming this problem—especially when most of the effort is expended outside the classroom.

If you can define effort clearly, treat all students consistently, and meet the standards of sound assessment, then gather your data and draw your inferences about each student's level of effort. Just be very careful how you use those results at report card grading time. This is a mine field that becomes even more dangerous when you combine effort and achievement data in the same grade. I urge you to report them separately, if you report effort outcomes at all.

Finding Better Ways to Motivate.   We grade on effort to motivate students to try hard. We feel that if they try hard, they will learn more. For those students who care about their grades, this may work. But if we are to understand other ways to motivate, we must also consider those cases in which our leverage has lost its power. We discussed this in the previous chapter. How shall we motivate those students who could not care less what grade we assign them—those who have given up and who are just biding their time until they can get out? For them, grades have lost all motivational value. If you think they are going to respond to our admonitions that they try harder so they can raise their grade, you are being naive.

Consider this hypothetical situation: What would you do to encourage students to come to school and participate with you in the learning experiences you had designed for them if you could no longer use grades and report cards as a source of reward and punishment to control students?

Now consider these options: You might strive to sense students' needs and interests and align instruction to those. You might work with students to establish clear and specific targets so they would know that they were succeeding. In short, you could try to take the mystery out of succeeding in school.

You could be sure instructional activities were interesting and provocative—keeping the action moving, always bearing agreed targets in mind. You would share the decision-making power so as to bring them into the learning process as full partners, teaching them how to gauge their own success. In short, you would strive to establish in your students an internal locus of control over their own academic well-being. If they participate, they benefit—and they know this going in.

These ideas will work better as motivators than saying to students, "If you make it look too easy, I will lower your final grade," or, "If you convince me you are trying hard, I will raise your grade." The message we must send is, "Hard work leads to higher achievement. Higher achievement leads to good grades." This is a tough message. In effect, it says that trying hard may be important, but it may not be good enough. Just doing the work does not "get" good grades. The only thing that gets good grades is the *learning* that comes from the work.

Attitude as a Grading Factor

You understand the problem: Two students attain exactly the same level of achievement. Their semester academic average is on the cutoff between two letter grades. One has constantly exhibited a very positive attitude, while the other has been consistently negative. Are you justified if you assign them different grades?

Arguments For.   A positive attitude is a valued outcome of school, too, so anything we can do to promote it is an effective practice. People with positive attitudes tend to secure more of life's rewards. School is an excellent place to begin to teach this lesson.

Besides, this just may be the most effective classroom management tool we teachers have at our disposal. If we define positive attitude as treating others well, following classroom rules, listening to the teacher, getting work in on time, and the like, then we can use the controlling leverage of the grade to maintain a quiet, compliant learning environment.

And, once again, this represents a way for us to channel at least some classroom rewards to the perennial low achiever. As with effort, attitude is within the control of students. If they're "good," they can experience some success. Sounds good—let's make it part of the grading equation!

Arguments Against.   It is seldom clear exactly which attitudes are supposed to be positive. Are students supposed to be positive about fellow students, the teacher, school subjects, school in general, or some combination of these? Must all or just some be positive? What combinations are acceptable?

How shall we define a positive attitude? Is it positive to accept an injustice in the classroom compliantly, or is it positive to stand up for what you think is right, causing a disruption? Is it positive to act as if you like story problems in math, when in fact you're frustrated because you don't understand them? The definition of positive is not always clear.

Further, if apparent effort can be manipulated, so can apparent attitude. Regardless of my real feelings, if I think you want me to be positive to get a better grade and if I care about that grade, you can bet that I will exhibit whatever behavior you wish. Is honesty not also a valued outcome of education?

Assessment also can be a source of difficulty. It takes a special understanding of paper and pencil assessment methodology, performance assessment methods, and personal communication to evaluate affective outcomes such as attitudes. The rules of evidence for quality assessment are challenging, as you will recall from our earlier discussion of the assessment of affect. So mismeasurement is a very real danger.

Oh, and as usual, to the extent that different teachers hold different values about which attitudes are supposed to be positive, devise different definitions of positive, assess attitudes more or less well, and assign them different weights in the grading equation, we factor even more noise into our communication system.

Some pretty tough problems . . .

Time for Reflection

Once again, are you for or against? Make your stand and then read on.

The Resolution.   To decide which side of the balance sheet wins out here, we must determine which use of attitude information produces the greatest good for students. Let's say we encounter an extremely negative attitude on the part of one student about a particular school subject. Which use serves that student better: Citing your evidence of the attitude problem (gathered through a good assessment) and telling that student they had better turn it around before the end of the grading period or their grade will be lowered? Or, accepting the attitude as real and talking with the student honestly and openly about the attitude and its origins (using high-quality assessment of this disposition through personal communication) in an honest attempt to separate it from achievement and deal with it in an informed manner?

The power of attitude data lies not in its potential to help us control behavior but in our ability to promote a more positive learner, and learning environment. If we go to the difficulty of (1) defining the attitudes we want to be positive (and this can be done), (2) devising systematic, high-quality assessments of those attitudes (which can be done, too), and (3) collecting representative samples of student attitudes (an eminently achievable goal), and then fail to use the results to inform instructional design—choosing only to factor the results into grades—we have wasted an immense opportunity to help students.

And if we enlist students as partners in this process, they are likely to be even more honest with us about how they feel about their learning environment, thus providing us with even more ammunition for improving instruction. But if you think for one moment students are likely to be honest with us in communicating attitudes if they think the results might be used against them at grading time, you are again being naive.

Although we probably can overcome all of the difficulties associated with defining attitudes for grading purposes, and can overcome the assessment difficulties attendant to these kinds of outcomes, I personally think it is bad practice to factor attitudes into report card grades.

Summary of Grading Factors

If report card grades are to serve us in our transition into the era of achievement-driven schools, they *must* reflect student attainment of our valued achievement targets. For this reason, grading systems must include indicators of student achievement unencumbered with indicators of other student characteristics, such as aptitude, effort, or attitude. This is not to say that we should not report information on effort or attitude, if definition and assessment difficulties can be overcome, which is no small challenge. Under any circumstances, aptitude or intelligence or ability have no place in the grade reporting process.

Grades can reflect valued expectations—meaning *achievement*—only if we clearly define these expectations in each grading context for a given grading period, develop sound assessments for those outcomes, and keep careful records of student attainment of the achievement expectations over the grading period. In the next section, we explore these ideas in detail.

Gathering Achievement Information for Grading Purposes

If report card grades are to inform students, parents, other teachers, administrators, and others about student achievement, then we must clearly and completely articulate and assess the actual achievement underpinning each grade. To be effective, we must spell out the valued targets *before* the grading period begins. Further, we must lay out in advance an assessment plan to systematically sample those targets. While it sounds like a great deal of preparation to complete before teaching begins, it is not. And, it saves a great deal of assessment work during instruction.

Remember the great benefits of being clear about your achievement targets:

- *They set limits on teacher accountability*—you know the limits of your teaching responsibility. When the target is clear and appropriate and all of your students can hit it, you are successful as a teacher.

- *They set limits on student accountability*—they know the limits of their learning responsibility. When they can hit the valued target, they are successful as students. And the less mysterious that target is, the more serious they will be about striving to hit it.

- *Clear targets allow students to share in a great deal of the assessment work*, thus turning assessment time into valuable teaching and learning time.

Let's look at an effective and efficient six-step plan for gathering sound and appropriate achievement information for grading purposes. Figure 15–1 lists the six key steps.

Step 1: Spelling out the Big Achievement Picture

To complete a picture of the valued achievement targets for a given subject over a grading period, gather together all relevant curricular and text materials and ask four questions (they will sound very familiar):

- What is the *subject matter knowledge* that students are to master? Outline it in general terms, in writing.

- What *reasoning and problem-solving* proficiencies are they to demonstrate? Specify each of them.

- What *skills,* if any, are students to master—what things do they need to be able to do? List them.

- What *products,* if any, are they to create? Outline them.

Further, if you have a sense of the relative importance of these various targets in the overall plan for developing student competence (more about this soon), state those priorities in writing.

By the way, I do not list disposition targets here, not because they are unimportant, but because, as discussed, they do not play a role in the report card grading decision.

Later, as you actually prepare to present each unit of instruction, you will need to fill in the specific detail:

- the actual propositions in order of importance, that capture the important knowledge outcomes of that unit

- the specific kinds of reasoning to be demonstrated, again, noting priorities among them as appropriate for each unit

- key elements in successful skill performance relevant to each unit

- the nature of the products to be created and the key elements of a high-quality product

Figure 15–1
Steps in the Report Card Grading Process

1. Begin with a comprehensive set of expectations.
2. Turn that big picture into a specific assessment plan.
3. Turn the plan into assessments.
4. Turn assessments into information about achievement.
5. Summarize the information in an achievement composite for each student.
6. Convert each composite into a grade.

These will form the basis of your actual assessments. For now, simply create a general outline of the important elements of your big assessment picture—spelled out in your own words. In short, immerse yourself in this and *force yourself to impose limits on it.*

As you do this, if any part of this picture remains unclear, you have several places to turn for help: state or local curriculum goals and objectives, your text and its support materials, your principal, department chair, or colleagues, and your professional library.

Here is another productive way to think about this planning process (we have discussed this idea before): States or districts that adopt an achievement-driven mission for their schools typically begin by working with their communities to agree on a set of achievement expectations for students in their school system. From that start, then, it is up to educators, working across all grade levels, to back those expectations down into the curriculum and divide up responsibility for helping students progress smoothly through the various levels of competence. Teachers from kindergarten through 12th grade must work collaboratively with one another to plan this integrated and articulated instructional program. Only then can the progression of student growth be coordinated over the students' years of schooling. The purpose of this planning process is to be sure that you and each of your colleagues understand how your contribution will contribute to the long-term evolution of student competence. From that process you must derive a clear sense of the knowledge, reasoning, skills, and product development capabilities that are your instructional responsibility.

Step 2: Turning Your Big Picture into an Assessment Plan

Once you are clear about your targets, your report card grading challenge is clearly drawn. The next question is, How will you use assessments to effectively yet economically accumulate a reservoir of evidence about each student's attainment of those targets? That set of assessments must help you position yourself to state with confidence what proportion of the total array of achievement expectations each student has met. In other words, what specific assessments—whether they be selected response, essay, performance, or personal communication assessments in the form of homework assignments, projects, quizzes, tests, or interviews—will provide you with an accurate sense of how much of the required material each student has mastered? You need an assessment plan to determine this.

You don't need the assessments themselves—not yet. Those come later, as each unit of instruction unfolds. But you do need to know how you will take students down the assessment road, from "Here are my expectations" to "Here is your grade," making sure both you and they know how they are progressing all along that road. This assessment plan needs to satisfy certain conditions:

- It must include listings for each grade-related assessment event during the grading period:
    the achievement focus of the assessment
    when the assessment is to take place
    what assessment method you will use

In addition,

- Each assessment listed in the plan needs to supply an important piece of the puzzle with respect to the priority targets of the unit and grading period within which it occurs.

- Each assessment must accurately represent the particular targets(s) it is supposed to depict (i.e., each must be a sound assessment according to our quality criteria).

- The full array of assessments conducted over the entire grading period must accurately determine the proportion of your expectations that each student has attained.

- The entire assessment plan must involve a reasonable assessment workload for both teacher and students.

A Reality Check.   These conditions may be easier to meet than you think. The report card grading challenge is to gather just enough information to make confident grading decisions and no more. Ask yourself: How can I gather the fewest possible assessments for grading and still generate an accurate estimate of performance? I believe that most teachers spend entirely too much time gathering and grading too many assessments for *grading* purposes. Some feel they must grade virtually everything students do and enter each piece of work into the record to assign accurate report card grades. This is simply not true. With planned, strategic assessments, you can generate accurate estimates of performance very economically.

I also see many teachers operating on the shotgun principle of grading: Just gather a huge array of graded student work over the course of the grading period, and somewhere, somehow, some will reflect some of the valued targets. While this may be true in part, this approach is at best inefficient. Why not plan ahead and minimize your assessment work?

If you can zero in on the key targets and draw dependable inferences with a few unit assessments and a final exam or project assignment about student mastery of big picture targets, that's all you need to produce report card grades that reflect student achievement.

Assessments for Learning But Not for Grading.   Let's be sure to remember that grading is not the only reason for classroom assessment. We established that fact very early in our journey. We also can use assessments for diagnosing student needs, providing students with practice performing or evaluating their performance, and tracking student growth as a result of instruction.

For example, I give my students assignments every class and inform them that practice is critical for performing well on the final essay exam. Our agreement is that if they wish to hand in practice assignments for feedback, I'll be pleased to provide it. Some take advantage of this opportunity. Some do not. But there is no grade involved in this "homework for practice" process.

You need not factor into the report card grading process student performance on assessments used for purposes other than grading. Self-assessment is used for diagnosing needs. We don't grade students when they are evaluating their own needs. Practice assessments are for polishing skills, overcoming problems, and fine-tuning performance. We shouldn't grade students when they are trying to learn from their mistakes. Students need time simply to muck around with new learnings, time to discover through risk-free experimentation, time to fail and learn from it without the shadow of evaluative judgment.

Experienced teachers who read this might say, "If I don't assign a grade and have it count toward the report card grade, the students won't take it seriously—they won't do it!" This breeds exactly the kind of dependency that Kohn (1993) decried in the previous chapter. Once students come to understand that practice helps, but performance on subsequent assessments counts for the grade, I think they will learn to practice and will complete the activities. They must take responsibility for developing their own sense of control over their success. This is exactly the point Covington (1992) made, as discussed in Chapter 14, when he wrote of developing an internal sense of responsibility for one's own success. While it might take some time to break old dependencies, once our students come to understand that good grades are not the rewards for doing work but are rather a signal of their success at achieving through studying effectively, I think they will practice *as needed*—especially if that practice can take place in a supportive, success-oriented classroom.

Learning success requires a collaborative partnership, with both partners fulfilling their part of the bargain. Has that occurred? As a teacher, you can provide the supportive environment, opportunity, and means to learn. But you cannot do the learning for your students. As a teacher, you must set limits on your contribution. All you can do is be sure your students see the relationship between practice and successful performance on the assessments that contribute to their grades.

But, let's say a student fails to practice on interim assignments and performs poorly on the assessment that counts for the grade. As a teacher, how do you respond? One option is to say, "I told you so," and let it go. Another response is, "I guess you found out how important practice is, didn't you? Nevertheless, I value your learning whenever it occurs. Do you want to practice now and redo the assessment? If you do, I will reevaluate your performance—no penalties. But that reevaluation will need to fit into my schedule."

Time for Reflection

Have you ever had the opportunity to retake an exam? Did your performance change? What was the effect on your mastery of the material?

Incidentally, you can prepare for such retest eventualities by developing more than one form of your graded assessments. That may mean creating more than one set of items reflecting your tables of test specifications or more than one sample exercise for your performance assessments. Just be sure these alternate forms are parallel, that they sample exactly the same achievement targets.

Your job as a teacher is to set appropriate targets that reflect your share of the building blocks to competence and that your students can achieve, and then agree with your students and your supervisor that you will do everything ethical within your power to ensure student success.

That means there is no artificial scarcity of high grades—"Only 10 percent of my students can get an A"—no limit to the number of students who can succeed. If you want to see students rapidly become failure avoiders and hopeless failure acceptors, just set up an environment in which they actually learn a great deal but still receive low grades anyway! In a healthy, success-oriented classroom, if everyone succeeds, everyone receives a high grade. The more students believe they can succeed, the more seriously they will practice in preparation for the assessments that contribute to their grades. You need conduct only enough assessments during a grading period to identify when that learning has happened.

Step 3: From Plan to Assessments

So you begin the grading period with your assessment plan in hand. What next? You then need to devise or select the actual assessments for each unit, being sure to follow the assessment development guidelines specified in Chapters 6 through 9. You will need to create and conduct each assessment, and evaluate and record the results.

In each case where you have knowledge and problem-solving targets to assess via selected response or essay assessments, you need to devise those specific assessments around precisely defined categories of knowledge and kinds of reasoning. You can capture these in lists of objectives, tables of specification, propositions, and finally the test exercises themselves, which you may assemble into assignments, quizzes, and tests. When assessing skill and product outcomes, you need to assemble descriptions, performance criteria, exercises to elicit performance, and rating scales or checklists into performance assessments. Each component assessment fills in part of the big picture.

All assessments should also align exactly with your vision of student competence. Although you may develop some in advance, to save time later, you may develop others during instruction and involve students in the process. I know this sounds like a great deal of work, but remember five important facts:

1. This method is not nearly as much work as the shotgun approach.
2. It affords the conscientious teacher a great deal more peace of mind. When your students succeed, you will know that you have been successful.
3. Students can play key roles in specific ways spelled out earlier, thus turning nearly all of this assessment time and energy into productive learning time and energy.
4. Student motivation to learn is likely to increase—no surprises, no excuses leads to a success orientation.
5. Your plan remains intact for you to use or adapt next time, and the time after that. Thus, development costs are spread out over the useful life of your plan and its associated assessments.

A Comment on Grading Individual Assessments.   Since it is common practice to assign grades to the component assessments, such as assignments, during the grading period—not just at report card time—we need to reflect for a moment on this meaning of "grading." Think of your big picture of achievement expectations as a mosaic, with small tiles (each component assessment) coming together to tell the overall story. In fact, each component assessment represents its own small mosaic in the sense that it too is made up of its own small tiles—the exercises (e.g., test items) used to sample student achievement. If in the end you wish to draw conclusions about the proportion of your overall set of expectations each student has met, then each component assessment must help you see what proportion of its targets each student has mastered. When we combine all of these component assessment results at grade computation time (i.e., combine all of the tiles in the form of individual assessment grades into the mosaic) we create the overall picture of student achievement we need. An example presented later in the chapter will illustrate.

Given the mosaic metaphor, it should be clear to you why step two, building an assessment plan, is so critical. How do you plan instruction to help students master the mosaic if you don't know—*in advance*—how the overall picture comes together? Or even more importantly, how do you help them practice hitting targets not yet specified? This has been our theme throughout our journey together. It is relevant in the grading process, too. At no point during the grading period should either you or your students have any question what grade the student is achieving at that point in time. Both you and they should know how much of the big picture has been covered as well as how much they have mastered—based on component grades.

Further, at no point should students feel that that the grade is beyond their control. At one point in high school, my daughter informed us that her algebra teacher told her two weeks before the end of the semester that she was going to get a C on her report card regardless of how she did on the final exam. Would you like to guess how much algebra she learned after that announcement? Only students who possess some hope of succeeding are likely to succeed.

Step 4: From Assessments to Information

Obviously, the next step is to carry out your plan, developing and administering your assessments when appropriate as the grading period progresses. As the achievement information begins to come in, what should be recorded? A few guidelines follow:

- Maintain written records. Remember the fallibility of the human mind—no mental record keeping.
- Include as much detail in the accumulated records as you can. If scores result, record them as is. Don't convert them to a grade and record the grade, thus unnecessarily sacrificing information that could be useful later. Or, if a profile of performance data results, such as when you use a performance assessment with several rating scales, record the profile. Again, don't covert the information to a grade and lose valuable detail. Instead, record percent correct or actual profile ratings.

- If you are going to weight scores differently later to compute a composite index of achievement (i.e., you regard some assessments as more important than others because they reflect attainment of critical material or just cover more material) record those scores in the same units, such as percent of total available points. This is illustrated in step five.

When you have carried out your assessment plan and collected the records, the time has come to generate a composite index of achievement for conversion to a grade.

Time for Reflection

Many teachers have discovered that they can easily store, retrieve, and summarize grading records, and convert them to actual grades using their personal computers. Software packages are available that can serve as your grade book and much more. How might you find out more about these options?

Step 5: Summarizing the Resulting Information

At the end of the grading period, the recording process will result in a range of information indicating student performance on each of the components in your strategic assessment plan. This constitutes a portrait of how well each student mastered the targets that made up your big picture. The question is, how do you get a grade out of all of this information?

I urge you to rely on a consistent computational sequence for all students that you can reproduce later should you need to explain the process or revise a grade. Such a sequence helps to control personal biases, which may either inappropriately inflate or deflate a grade for reasons unrelated to actual achievement.

Please note that I am not opposed to a role for professional judgment in grading. As we established in earlier chapters, that role comes in the design and administration of the assessments used to gather information about student achievement. We need, however, to minimize subjectivity when combining indicators of achievement for grading purposes.

Combining Achievement Information.   To derive a meaningful grade from several existing records of achievement, again, each piece of information gathered should indicate the proportion of the targets each student has mastered. So, if we combine them all, we should obtain an estimate of the proportion mastered for the total grading period. Remember the mosaic? Two ways to achieve it are the percent method and the total points method.

Percent Method.   Convert each student's performance on each contributing assessment into a percent of total available points. For instance, if a selected response test has 40 items, and a student answers 30 correct, we enter 75 percent in the record. Or if a student scores all fours on six 5-point performance assessment rating scales, that totals 24 of 30 possible points, or 80 percent.

Time for Reflection

Think about the assumption being made here. If those 40 test items have been carefully selected during test development to sample a defined domain of content, then we can confidently conclude that this student probably mastered about 75 percent of that domain. Under what specific conditions is this a dependable inference? What could cause the inference to be wrong?

If the individual assessment results recorded as percentages are averaged across all assessments for a total grading period, then the result should provide an indication of the proportion of the total array of expectations for that grading period that each student has mastered. In effect, translating each score to a percentage places all on the same scale for averaging purposes and permits you to combine them in an easily interpreted manner—in terms of intended targets.

With this procedure, if you wish to give greater weight to some assessment results than to others, you can accomplish this by multiplying those scores by their weight before adding them into the overall computation. For instance, if some are to count twice as much as others, simply multiply their percentages by two before summing to arrive at an average.

Time for Reflection

Under what conditions might you assign some assessment results a higher weight than others in the grading process?

With this system of record keeping and grade computation, everyone involved can know at any particular point in time how their scores, to that date, relate to expectations. This permits students to remain aware of and in control of their success. Some teachers also ask students to assign their own grade as a means of promoting student self-evaluation. If information gathering, storage, and retrieval systems are working effectively, there should be absolute agreement between teacher and students at all times about what grade they are earning.

Total Points Method. Another way to combine information is to define the total target for a grading period in terms of a total number of points. Students who earn all or most of the points demonstrate mastery of all or most of the valued targets and earn a high grade.

In this case, each individual assessment contributes a certain number of points to the total. If you carefully plan this so the points earned on each assessment reflect their fair share of the big picture, then at the end of the grading period you can simply add up each student's points and determine what percentage of the total each student earned. That percentage of total points, then, represents the proportion of valued targets attained.

Differential weighting is possible here, too. Assign a large number of points to those assessments (such as final exams or large projects) that cover the largest proportions of the valued targets and fewer points to the assessments (such as daily assignments) that are narrower in focus.

Either of these options provides an acceptable basis for clearly communicating via report card grades about student achievement. But be careful, difficulties can arise! We discuss next some of these difficulties, and offer ways to handle them.

Some Practical Advice.   Unless you carefully develop and summarize assessments, the result may be misleading about the proportion of the total achievement picture that students have mastered. Let me illustrate.

Using the Most Current Information.   Let's say your strategic assessment plan includes five unit assessments and a comprehensive final exam that covers the entire set of targets for the grading period. And, say a particular student starts slowly, scoring very low on the first two unit assessments, but gains momentum and attains a perfect score on the comprehensive final exam—revealing, in effect, subsequent mastery of the material covered in those first two unit assessments.

The key grading question is this: Which piece of information provides the most accurate depiction of the student's real achievement at the end of the grading period—the final exam score or that score averaged with all five unit tests? If the final is truly comprehensive, averaging it with those first two unit assessments will result in misleading information.

If students demonstrate achievement at any time that, in effect, renders past assessment information inaccurate, then you must drop the former assessment from the record and replace it with the new. To do otherwise is to misrepresent that achievement.

Grading on Status Versus Improvement.   An issue many teachers struggle with is whether a grade should reflect a student's achievement status at the end of the grading period or register improvement over time. The resolution of this issue lies in understanding the immense difficulties we face in dealing with the concept of improvement.

If *improvement* means that those who gain more over time get higher grades, students who happen to arrive knowing less have an advantage. Is that fair to those who arrive knowing more? Besides, in order to grade on improvement, you need to establish a baseline by conducting a comprehensive preassessment of students on all relevant outcomes for that grading period. You are seldom able to preassess in this manner. And even if you could, you would face challenging statistical problems in dealing effectively with the undependable "gain scores" that would result.

For all of these reasons, grades should reflect the student's status in attaining the specified targets for that classroom during a particular grading period.

About Borderline Cases.   Another common problem arises when a particular student's academic average is literally right on the borderline between two grades and you just don't know which way to go. Some teachers allow factors unrelated to achievement to push the grade one way or the other. We addressed the unacceptability of that approach previously. A better way to determine such grades is to collect one or two significant pieces of achievement data during the grading process that overlap other assessments, thus double checking previous information about achievement. Hold these assessments in reserve—don't factor them into the grade. Then, if you need "swing votes," use them to help you decide which grade to assign. This keeps unrelated factors out of the grading decision and the communication system.

Grading in a Cooperative Learning Context.   With the increasing popularity of cooperative learning environments, questions often arise about how to treat the grading process. If students achieve together, how does that get factored into the grade? The simple rule is this: Grades to be assigned and communicated on report cards need to provide dependable information about the actual achievement of the individual student graded. This means that the grading process in a cooperative environment must include procedures that permit individual students to demonstrate their attainment of the prescribed targets. If there is any doubt that a score on a group performance does not reflect the achievement of any group member, then it has no place in the grade computation process.

Dealing with Cheating.   Here's another kind of grading problem: A student cheats on a test and, as punishment, is given a zero in the grade book to be averaged with other assessments to determine the semester grade.

Time for Reflection

Before you continue, reflect on this practice. In your opinion, is this an appropriate course of action? Why? Be specific.

The problem in this instance is that the zero may systematically misrepresent that student's real achievement. This is not acceptable under any circumstances. Consequently, the grade and the discipline for cheating *must* be separated from one another. The student should be retested to determine real levels of achievement and that retest score should be entered into the grade book. Cheating can and should be punished in some other way if we are to communicate accurately.

Awarding "Extra Credit."   Some teachers try to encourage extra effort on the part of their students by offering extra credit opportunities. You must be very careful of the message you send here. If grades are to reflect achievement, you must deliver the consistent message that the more you learn, the better your grade. If extra credit work is specifically designed to provide dependable information that students have learned more, then it should influence the grade assigned. But if students come to believe that merely doing the work is sufficient to attain a higher grade, then it is counterproductive.

Policies That Interfere.   Sometimes, district policy can cause serious grading problems. For instance, some districts link grades to attendance. A policy might specify that more than five unexcused absences in a given grading period must result in an F for the student, regardless of actual achievement. In the case in which a student has mastered enough of the material to receive a higher grade, this policy leads to the purposeful misrepresentation of actual student achievement, and is unacceptable. Administrative policies that mislead us about academic achievement and that interfere with the report card grading process must be avoided if we are to communicate accurately about student attainment.

Advance Notice.   Another critically important guideline to follow is to be sure all students know and understand in advance the procedures you will use to compute their grades. What assessments will you conduct, when, and how will you factor each into the process? What are students' timelines, deadlines, and important responsibilities? If students know their responsibilities in the partnership you establish with them, they have a good chance of succeeding.

Heterogeneous Grouping.   There is just one more potential problem to address for which educators simply must find an acceptable solution. How do we grade different students in the same classroom who are striving to attain fundamentally different targets? As we try to mainstream special needs students and students from diverse cultural and linguistic backgrounds, this becomes a critical issue.

In a classroom of mixed ability, for instance, one student might be working on basic math concepts, while another is moving toward prealgebra. If both hit their respective targets, each deserves an A. But those As mean fundamentally different things. How is someone reading the report cards of these two students to be made aware of this critical difference?

In my opinion, this single issue renders simple letter grades out of date and insufficient as a means of communicating about student achievement. The only solution I can find for this problem is to add more information to the reporting system, by identifying the targets covered by the grade reported. Without that detail, we cannot communicate about individual differences in the grades assigned within the same classroom.

The Bottom Line.   In developing sound grading practices for use in communicating about achievement, logic dictates that you start with a clear vision of targets, translate it into quality assessments, and always remain mindful of that big achievement picture for a given grading period. Then you must follow this simple rule (another part of the art of classroom assessment): Grades must convey as accurate a picture of a student's real achievement as possible. Any practice that has the effect of misrepresenting real achievement is unacceptable. The guidelines for avoiding the problems just discussed are summarized in Figure 15–2.

Step 6: Converting Composite Achievement Scores to a Grade

Once you have attained an average or total set of points or some other overall index of student achievement for the grading period, you face the final and in some ways most difficult decision in the grading process: What grade do you report?

Figure 15–2
Practical Guidelines for Avoiding
Common Grading Problems

- Grade on achievement of prespecified targets only, not intelligence, effort, attitude, or personality.
- Always rely on the most current information available about student achievement.
- Devise grades that reflect achievement status with respect to preset targets rather than improvement.
- Decide borderline cases with additional information on achievement.
- Keep grading procedures separate from punishment.
- Change all policies that lead to miscommunication about achievement.
- Advise students of grading practices in advance.
- Add further detail to grade report when needed.
- Expect individual accountability for learning even in cooperative environments.
- Give credit for evidence of extra learning—not just for doing extra work!

Over the years, some districts and schools have opted simply to report that final achievement average in the form of a percentage score. This has the benefit of permitting the record to convey the maximum amount of available information about a student's achievement. In doing so, no useful information is sacrificed by converting it to another scale. That's good.

But most districts require teachers to convert the academic achievement average or point total to a letter or number grade, from A to F or from 4.0 to 0. This has the effect of sacrificing a great deal of available information. For instance, a range of scores, say the ten points between 90 to 100 percent, are all transformed into just one point on the grade scale, and in effect, are made equal.

Time for Reflection

When might a student be harmed as a result of sacrificing the more precise percentage score? Here's a hint: How do we select a valedictorian?

So the key question is, How do you convert a composite index of student achievement into an accurate report card grade? Traditionally, we have accomplished this in one of the following ways:

- grading in terms of preset performance standards
- assigning grades according to the student's place in the rank order of class members

In an era of achievement or performance-driven education, only the first option makes sense. Let's explore each and see why.

Grading with Preset Standards.   Grading in terms of preset standards says, Here are the assessments that represent the achievement targets—score at this level on them and this is the grade you will receive. A set of percentage cutoff scores is set and all who score within certain ranges receive that designated grade.

Time for Reflection

Before you read on, please take just a minute to think about this kind of conversion plan. What do you think are both the strengths and weaknesses of this method?

If two important conditions are met, this method maximizes the probability of success for students. Those conditions are (1) that students possess the prerequisites to master the required material, and (2) that assessments accurately represent the targets on which you will base the grade.

One advantage of this system is that the meaning of the grade is clearly couched in the attainment of intended achievement targets. Another is that it is computationally simple—one need only know how to compute percentages and averages. Still another strength is that grades can work effectively in the context of a continuous progress curriculum. As students master prerequisites for later, more advanced work—as indicated by high grades, teachers can know that they are ready for the next stage. A fourth advantage is that grading in terms of preset standards increases the possibility that all students can succeed, if they achieve. And finally, from your perspective, if you as a teacher become more effective over time, greater student success will be reflected in a greater proportion of higher grades.

However, grading in terms of predetermined percentage cutoff scores is not without its limitations. For instance, the cutoff scores themselves are arbitrary. There is no substantive or scientific reason why 90 to 100 percent should be considered an A. This cutoff, and those used to assign other grades, represent social conventions adopted over decades. As a result, cutoffs vary from district to district, school to school, and even teacher to teacher. The range for an A in some places may be 94 to 100 percent, for example. Although these differences cannot be eliminated, we can acknowledge the lack of precision they imply.

Further, we must recognize that two assessments reflecting attainment of the same valued targets can vary greatly in difficulty. For example, you may devise two tests to cover the same material and, depending on the particular propositions selected and the way you write the items, one test could be much harder than the other. As a result, the same student might score differently on the two tests. So assessment difficulty, not just target mastery, can influence the percentage correct and therefore the grade the student attains.

Some teachers counter this problem by arbitrarily labeling the highest student score actually received on a difficult test (i.e., the highest raw score or number correct attained) as a score of 100 percent. The rest of the students' percentages are then based on that new maximum number correct. This practice might have been acceptable under circumstances in which all we wanted the grade to do was sort students. But in times when we care more about real achievement, this practice of shaving off the top of the scale can lead to a systematic misrepresentation of actual achievement, because it suggests that students mastered more of the material than they actually did. If the assessment in fact reflects truly important targets—key building blocks to later learning—then this misrepresentation can interfere with later learning.

A more acceptable way to deal with this problem is for all teachers to learn to translate clearly articulated targets into assessments that are of appropriate difficulty for their students. That is, teachers who develop assessments for report card grading must remain cognizant of their expected achievement and the differing ability levels of the students they will assess.

Grading on a Curve.   The tactic of assigning grades based on a student's place in the rank order of achievement scores within a class is commonly referred to as "grading on a curve." In its classic application, the teacher uses the composite index of achievement for each student to rank students from the highest to the lowest score. Then, counting from the top, the teacher counts off 7 percent *of the students* on the list. These students receive As. Then the next 24 percent receive Bs, and so on down to the bottom 7 percent of students, who are assigned Fs.

Another variation on this method is to tally how many students attained each score and then to graph that distribution to find natural gaps between groups of scores that appear to permit division into groups of students to whom you can then assign different grades.

These ranking methods have the strength of yielding a grade that is interpreted in terms of group performance. They also have the effect of promoting competition among students: Students will know that their challenge is to outscore the others.

But in a context in which high achievement is the goal, the limitations of such a system become far more prominent than its strengths. The percentage of students receiving each grade is not a matter of science. Again, the cutoffs are arbitrary, and once grades are assigned and recorded on the transcript, no user of that grade information will necessarily know or understand the system of cutoffs used by the grader.

Besides, it's not clear what group should be ranked for grading purposes. Is it all students in the same class at the same time? In the same school? District? In the same semester or year? Over the years? The answers to these questions can have major implications for the grade a student receives. For instance, if a student happens to fall into an extremely capable cohort, the results might be vastly different from how they would be if that same student just happens to be part of a generally lower-achieving group. So issues of fairness come into play.

Further, this system produces grades that are unrelated to real achievement. A class could, in fact, learn very little but the grade distribution could still convey the appearance that all had performed as expected. In other words, in a high-achieving group, some who actually learned a great deal but scored below the highest achievers might be doomed to receive a low grade.

And again, from your point of view as a teacher, even if your instruction improves markedly over the years, and helps more and more students master the important material, the distribution of grades will appear unchanged. That would frustrate anyone!

Teachers who develop success-oriented partnerships with students have no use for grading on a curve. They know they are not the best teacher they can be until every student attains an A—demonstrating the highest possible achievement on rigorous high-quality assessments.

A Simple Illustration

To tie all of these procedures together, let's work through a hypothetical example of a fifth-grade teacher developing grading procedures in science. The context is a self-contained classroom of 32 students.

Step 1. This teacher's comprehensive picture for this particular 10-week grading period includes knowledge, reasoning, skill, and product outcomes for three 3-week units of instruction:

- an ecology unit on wetlands
- a biology unit on amphibians
- a chemistry unit on biodegradable substances

Our teacher lists the priority achievement targets for each unit.

Step 2. The instructor decides to sample student mastery of content and most reasoning targets with three weekly quizzes in each unit and a culminating unit test, each combining selected response and essay formats.

In addition, each student will participate in a combined performance assessment for the ecology and amphibian units, in order to tap scientific process achievement targets. Each student will produce a brief research report. The combination of nine quizzes backed up with three unit tests and the report, our teacher reasons, will provide an excellent portrait of student achievement for end-of-term report card grading.

Step 3. Our teacher translates content and reasoning outcomes into tables of specifications for the short quizzes and the unit tests, making sure to include each relevant content category, both on a quiz and on a subsequent unit test. The teacher drafts lists of propositions reflecting important content to be tested, ensures their importance, then writes the required test items. As an ungraded exercise, the teacher also asks students to write some practice test questions to ask each other.

Students also prepare for the writing-based performance assessment by reading samples of previous written reports of varying quality and trying to figure out what makes a really good report. With the teacher's guidance, they then devise a solid set of performance criteria. The teacher develops the written exercise that spells out each student's research reporting responsibilities.

Step 4.   During the grading period, the teacher administers the various assessments. Some of the tests and quizzes are open-book, and call for students to know how to retrieve information; others require students to learn information outright. Some occur in class, others students take home.

The performance assessment takes place as planned, including distributing the exercise and developing the performance criteria in class, with teacher and students working together to define success. Students then draft their reports and share them in their collaborative teams with classmates. Each student gets focused feedback from teammates using the agreed-on performance criteria. They then complete the final product.

As each assessment is completed, the teacher enters information into the grade book (installed on a personal computer), regarding students' performance in terms of the percentage of total possible points on each test and quiz.

Students who score low have 2 days to study and take advantage of the regular "after-school retake," which is another version of the test or quiz that covers the same required material with different exercises. If they score higher, the new scores replace the old ones in the grade book. If they score lower, student and teacher meet to discuss why and plan further assessments together. Students who miss a test or quiz may use the after-school option to make it up.

The students' research reports are evaluated by three previously trained raters: the teacher, a high school student who volunteered to help the fifth graders conduct the wetlands study, and a member of the school's community advisory committee who works in the area of environmental science. Each applies the five 5-point rating scales.

Time for Reflection

How might the teacher, high school student, and community representative prepare themselves to apply the score scales dependably? How might they check to see if their scores are indeed consistent with one another? If the scores are not, what should they do?

Students receive detailed feedback in the form of profiles of ratings on each criterion used and written comments about their products. The grade book gets an entry for each student: the combined total of ratings converted to a percentage of the maximum possible score of 75 points (five scales, 5 points, three raters). Students disappointed with their ratings have one week to redo the work and resubmit. The teacher will reevaluate the work and enter the new score in the record. Otherwise, the old score stands.

Step 5.   The teacher has devised a specific strategy for combining all of these percentages to a composite that reflects student mastery of all relevant outcomes:

Each of the nine quizzes receives a weight of one, unit tests count as two, and the performance assessment counts five times. That means the teacher will average 20 scores—nine quiz scores, six test scores (three test scores each counted twice), and the performance assessment score counted five times—to determine an overall percentage. The teacher generates composite scores using the grade book computer, and prints summaries for each student, who checks the record of scores and the composite for any errors.

Step 6.   Our instructor transforms these composites into grades for the report card by applying a previously announced set of standards: 90 to 100 percent equals an A, and so on.

Time for Reflection

Assume you are the teacher in this illustration. You have set specific percentage cutoff scores to be used in grade determination and made them public from the beginning of the grading period. A student who scores 90 to 100 percent receives an A. One of your students ends up with an average of 89.5 percent. What grade do you assign and why?

An Illustration from Performance Assessment

In contexts where all assessments convert neatly into percent correct, where if you answer 90 percent of the items right you get an A, assigning grades by means of traditional grading rules is relatively easy. But these days, with many teachers assessing with performance assessments that result in profiles of ratings rather than single scores, conversion to grades can be somewhat more complicated. So to avoid confusion, let's consider an example of this.

Remember, to derive a meaningful grade from several samples of performance, again, each piece of information gathered should indicate the proportion of the targets each student has mastered. So, if we combine them all, we should obtain an estimate of the proportion mastered for the total grading period. Remember the mosaic? Four ways to achieve this with performance assessment ratings are the composite profile, the current profile, percent, and total points methods.

To see how these work out, consider the example of Emily's record of achievement in writing over an entire grading period, as depicted in Table 15–1. She has completed a total of 13 assignments, some of which were rated on all six analytical score scales, and some of which were only partially rated. Following are some ways to summarize all of this for conversion to a grade that represents applications of ideas offered in this chapter.

The Composite Profile Method.   This method simply stipulates that, at the end of the grading period, the pattern of analytical ratings the student has received across all assessments must take a certain form to attain a certain grade. For instance, you might stipulate that a student needs to have attained a preponderance of 5s on four

Table 15–1
Emily's Writing Assessment Record

Student's Name Emily

	Ideas and Content	Organization	Voice	Word Choice	Sentence Fluency	Conventions	Maximum Possible	Points Attained	%
Public Lab	1 2 3 4 5	1 2 3 4 5	1 2 3 4 5	1 2 3 4 5	1 2 3 (4) 5	1 2 3 4 5	5	4	80
Reports #5 & 6	1 2 3 4 5	1 2 3 4 5	1 2 3 4 5	1 2 3 4 5	1 2 3 4 5	1 2 3 (4) 5	5	5	100
Writing assessment #1	1 2 3 (4) 5	1 2 (3) 4 5	1 2 3 (4) 5	1 2 3 (4) 5	1 2 (3) 4 5	1 2 (3) 4 5	30	21	70
Computers	1 2 3 4 5	1 2 3 4 5	1 2 3 4 5	1 2 3 4 5	1 2 3 (4) 5	1 2 3 4 5	5	5	100
Amazing Ride	1 2 3 4 (5)	1 2 3 4 (5)	1 2 3 (4) 5	1 2 3 4 (5)	1 2 3 (4) 5	1 2 (3) 4 5	30	27	90
Baseball	1 2 3 4 5	1 2 3 4 5	1 2 3 4 5	1 2 3 4 5	1 2 3 (4) 5	1 2 3 4 5	5	4	80
Autobiography	1 2 3 4 5	1 2 3 4 5	1 2 3 (4) 5	1 2 3 4 5	1 2 3 4 (5)	1 2 3 4 5	10	10	100
Poster	1 2 3 4 5	1 2 3 4 5	1 2 3 4 5	1 2 3 4 (5)	1 2 3 4 5	1 2 3 (4) 5	5	5	100
Pet Essays	1 2 3 4 5	1 2 3 4 5	1 2 3 4 5	1 2 3 (4) 5	1 2 3 4 5	1 2 3 (4) 5	10	10	100
Social Studies Research	1 2 3 (4) 5	1 2 (3) 4 5	1 2 3 (4) 5	1 2 3 4 (5)	1 2 (3) 4 5	1 2 3 4 (5)	30	19	63
Science Research	1 2 3 (4) 5	1 2 3 (4) 5	1 2 3 (4) 5	1 2 3 (4) 5	1 2 3 (4) 5	1 2 3 (4) 5	30	24	80
TV Preview	1 2 3 4 5	1 2 3 4 5	1 2 3 4 (5)	1 2 3 4 5	1 2 3 4 5	1 2 3 4 5	5	5	100
Space Report	1 2 3 (4) 5	1 2 3 (4) 5	1 2 3 (4) 5	1 2 3 (4) 5	1 2 3 (4) 5	1 2 3 (4) 5	30	24	80
Rating Totals	4,1	2,2,1	4,3	4,2	2,5,2	2,2,4	200	163	88%

13 ratings of "5"

$\dfrac{163}{200} = 82\%$

440

of the six scales to earn an A. Referring to Table 15–1, Emily's ratings were predominately 4s on five of six scales, so she didn't qualify for an A.

You can establish whatever profile expectations you wish to guide transformations from ratings to grades. Just be sure that everyone involved knows and understands the conversion rules from the outset. No surprises, no excuses.

The Current Profile Method.   This method of grade determination holds that competence at the end of the grading period is everything. If a student produces samples of writing that consistently reflect a very high level of proficiency—say all 5s and 6s on the analytical scales—that student receives an "A." Another profile pattern is established for B, another for C, etc. Here is the interesting part of this option: Past performance is not averaged in. If the student produces consistent evidence of one level of proficiency, all previous records of writing achievement are deemed out of date. They no longer reflect the student's reality. The student's goal, therefore, is to be constantly striving to establish and maintain evidence of a new high level of proficiency. But remember, student profiles can decline, too, if they fail to maintain or demonstrate competence.

Referring to Table 15–1, if we were to apply this standard to Emily, only her "Space Report" would count toward the grade. Obviously, this places a great deal of emphasis on one assessment. So we must manage it very carefully. That means students will need a great deal of preparation and support leading up to it. And they will need that same kind of encouragement and support as they prepare such an important piece of work.

Understand that the profiles of analytical scale ratings established to represent each letter grade, once again, are completely up to you. They merely represent conventions of understanding between you and your students. But they must reflect clear differences in performance and everyone must know them in advance (no moving targets!). This represents the quintessential internal control grading option. At any time, students can aim as high as they wish.

The Total Points Method.   Another way to combine information is to define the overall target for a grading period in terms of a total number of points. Students who earn all or most of the points demonstrate mastery of all or most of the valued outcomes and earn a high grade.

In this case, each individual assessment contributes a certain number of points to the total. If you carefully plan this so the points earned on each assessment reflect their fair share of the big picture, then at the end of the grading period you can simply add up each student's points, and can determine what percentage of the total each student earned. That percentage of total points, then, represents the proportion of valued outcomes attained.

Refer once again to Table 15–1. The first of the summary columns at the right lists the maximum number of points attainable on rated assignments. Next, we see how many points Emily earned. When we total these, we see that her ratings earned her 163 out of 200 points during the grading period, or 82 percent. If we had stipulated that 80 to 89 percent earns a B, that is the grade Emily would receive.

Differential weighting is possible here, too. Assign a large number of points to those assessments (such as final exams or large projects) that cover the largest proportions of the valued targets and fewer points to the assessments (such as daily assignments) that are narrower in focus.

The Percent Method.   Convert each student's performance ratings on each contributing assessment into a percent of total possible points for that assignment. For instance, if a student receives two 5s and a 6 on an assignment rated on three of the 6-point analytical scales, that's 16 out of 18 points, or 88 percent. Or if a student scores all 4s on six 5-point performance assessment rating scales, that totals 24 of 30 possible points, or 80 percent. Please refer to Table 15–1 once again. The third summary column on the right shows how Emily did on each assignment in terms of the percent of total possible points. If we sum these and compute an average by dividing by 13 (the number of assessments), we see that she averaged 88 percent, a B+ in most grading systems.

If we averaged the individual assessment results recorded as percentages across all assessments for a total grading period, then the result should provide a composite indication of the proportion of the total array of expectations for that grading period that each student has mastered. In effect, translating each score to percentages places all on the same scale for averaging purposes and permits them to be combined in an easily interpreted manner—in terms of intended targets.

If some assignments are of greater importance than others, as with the total points method, then you may give those ratings greater weight in determining the grade. For instance, referring to Emily's performance in Table 15–1 one final time, let's say we felt that the five assessments rated on all six scales were the most important and so we wanted to double their weight in determining the grade. The fourth column to the right reveals the result. By counting each large assessment twice, summing the percentages and dividing this time by 18 (13 + 5) we see that Emily averaged 85 percent, or a B.

Each of these four systems of record keeping and grade computation allows everyone involved to know at any particular point in time how their performance relates to expectations. This permits students to remain aware and in control of their success. Some teachers also ask students to assign their own grade as a means of promoting student self-evaluation. But they must be ready to justify their grade with specific data. If information gathering, storage, and retrieval systems are working effectively, there should be absolute agreement between teacher and students at all times about what grades they are earning.

Each of these options provides an acceptable basis for communicating via report card grades about student achievement as reflected in performance assessments.

A Final Time-saving Thought

It troubles me deeply that so many 1990s teachers still maintain grade records the way teachers did at the turn of the century. They rely on Fred Flintstone technology—a gradebook with one line per student containing all of the test scores and assignment grades for the grading period. There is a better way. Many software producers have developed gradebook packages specifically designed for teachers to use on their personal computers. They permit easy entry, long-term accurate storage, efficient retrieval, and convenient summary functions for interim or final

Figure 15–3
Gradebook Software Packages

Aeius Gradebook
Aeius Corporation
San Jose, CA

Bobbing Gradebook
Bobbing Software, Inc.
Buda, TX

Computerized Gradebook
Electronic Courseware Systems, Inc.
Champaign, IL

First Class Gradebook
First Class Systems, Inc.
Colorado Spring, CO

Gradebook
The Academic Software Library
Raleigh, NC

Gradebook
Wren Software
Castle Rock, CO

J & S Grade Book
J & S Software, LTD
Port Washington, NY

Teacher Gradebook
Surfside Technology, Inc.
East Orleans, NA

Teacher Gradebook
Dynacomp, Inc.
Webster, NY

Teacher's Gradebook for SSTS/M
Software Technology, Inc.
Mobile, AL

Turbo Gradebook
J. Weston Walch
Portland, ME

reporting. In the hands of proficient users, these software programs can save immense amounts of time. Figure 15–3 provides a partial list of currently available products.

Chapter Summary: Making the Grade

As in all aspects of assessment addressed in this book, the key to effective report card grading is for you, the teacher, to be a master of the material your students are to learn. This permits you to translate your clear and appropriate targets into rigorous, high-quality assessments, which, in turn, you can convert to information that you may combine into fair and equitable grades.

The reference point for interpreting a grade should always be the specific material to be learned—and nothing else. Students deserve to know in advance how you will accomplish this in their class, and they need to know the standards you expect them to meet. If you are assessing characteristics other than achievement, you must follow appropriate rules of sound assessment, and should report results separately from achievement grades.

Teachers must carefully plan for gathering information for report card grades. In times when grades served only to rank students, it didn't seem to matter what those grades actually meant. Today, however, we need to produce meaningful communication about student attainment of specific competencies.

This requires a clearly stated set of grading priorities. These achievement expectations are most productively set when a faculty meets across grade levels and across classrooms within grade levels to determine the building blocks of ultimate competence and to integrate them into their classrooms—systematically dividing up responsibility for learning.

You must, however, take responsibility for assembling a strategic assessment plan for generating the information to determine which of your students attain the desired targets. You must then translate that plan into quality assessments throughout the grading period. Students serve as valuable allies in developing and using these assessments, turning assessment for grading into assessment for learning, too.

As you conduct assessments and accumulate results, you must take care to record as much detail about student achievement as is available. To be sure, nearly all of this useful detail ultimately will be sacrificed in our obsession to describe the rich complexity of student achievement in the form of a single letter grade. But don't give up the detail until you absolutely must. And when report card grading time arrives, share as much of the detail as you can with your students, so they understand what is behind the single little symbol that appears on the report card. Then boil the richness of your detail away only grudgingly.

Remember two final guidelines: (1) You need not assign a grade to absolutely everything a student produces. It's acceptable to sometimes simply use words and pictures to describe your response. Allow room to explore and grow in between grades. (2) Your challenge is not to rank students in terms of their achievement. While not all students will learn the same amounts or at the same rates and a ranking may naturally result from your work, the student's next teacher needs more information than a place in the rank order to know what to do next to assist. Remember, our goal is to communicate in ways that *help students learn.*

Exercises to Advance Your Learning

Knowledge

1. Consulting the text, identify several changes currently unfolding in schools that call for changes in grading practices.

2. Create a four-row by three-column chart listing achievement, aptitude, effort, and attitude in the rows. Review the material presented in this chapter and briefly summarize the arguments for and against factoring each into report card grades. Leave column three blank for now.

3. List the six steps in the report card grading process described in this chapter and identify the specific activities in each step.

4. Compile a two-part list of practical strategies, as spelled out in this chapter, for avoiding common grading problems. First, identify a potential problem, and then specify a remedy.

Reasoning

1. Rank the three forms of achievement communication listed below according to which are most and least likely to reflect the principles of effective communication. Why do you rank them as you do?
   A letter grade on a report card
   An anecdotal narrative description of student achievement
   A portfolio containing samples of student work

2. In column three of the chart you created for knowledge exercise 2, for each factor, explain whether you believe that the arguments for or against should win out, and briefly state why.

3. Analyze the options of grading based on rank order (i.e., on a curve) and grading in terms of student competence (i.e., preset standards) in terms of underlying assumptions about the mission of schools and the nature of student learning, as well as the specific procedures involved in each. Identify similarities and differences between these two procedures for transforming achievement information into letter grades.

4. Report card grades permit the user to create the appearance of accountability—the appearance that students have learned the required materials, whether or not they have in fact achieved. What, if anything, can we do to encourage teachers to commit to more than just the appearance of success?

Skills

1. Identify a semester- or quarter-length college or university course you have recently completed, or one school subject you recently taught for a full grading period. Choose a fairly recent educational experience so your recollections are fresh and/or you have access to notes or other instructional materials. Follow the basic steps in effective grading by completing the exercises that follow. You may delve as deeply into these exercises as you wish. If you focus on a program of study you plan to teach in the future, you could use the results to advantage as you devise your complete grading plan.

   a. List the major units of instruction that comprised this program of study—outline the course or subject matter coverage. Review two of these units and specify the key knowledge, reasoning, skill, and product targets.

   b. Using these two units as examples, and your list of the material comprising the overall coverage of this program, outline the major elements of an assessment plan that you think might accurately sample student performance for determining grades. What assessments would you use when sampling each of the targets?

c.   Create blueprints for at least two of the assessments you would use to sample student achievement.

d.   Explain in writing how you would compile information over the course of study of this material that would permit computing a composite index of achievement for a final grade.

e.   Specify how you would convert your summary of student achievement into a report card grade.

Dispositions

1.   Throughout this chapter, I have argued that it is more important for us to be able to communicate accurately about student achievement now than it has been in the past. Do you agree? Why?

2.   I also have suggested that we need to devise report card systems capable of conveying the student's grade accompanied by a note outlining the particular achievement target reflected in that grade. Do you agree? Why?

3.   Many continue to feel that students will not complete classwork without the motivation of a grade. Do you agree? Do you feel that there are other ways to motivate? If so, what are they?

4.   Some contend that report cards and grades as we know them will remain in place in schools for a long time into the future, because parents will not accept alternative communication systems. Do you agree? Why?

5.   Refer to the six keys to effective communication introduced in Chapter 14. Can report card grades, in your opinion, be made to meet these standards? If so, how? If not, why not?

Special Ongoing Assessment Project: Part 10

To conclude your special project, review each of the assessments you plan to use in your chosen unit of instruction. Stipulate in writing how you would collect achievement information during the unit (in what form(s)?) and how you plan to convert student performance into a letter grade. Answer the following questions:

- What, precisely, will this grade say about student achievement?

- What level of detail will you be sacrificing, if any, in converting to grades?

- Can you think of other ways to communicate that prevent the loss of information?

16

The Role of Portfolios in the Communication Process

CHAPTER ROADMAP

While we can meet some communication needs with report cards and grades, we are by no means restricted to this way of sharing information about student achievement. Another very popular alternative these days is a portfolio of student work. In this chapter, we will explore this option, with the goal of having you know and understand the following:

1. Why this record-keeping and communication option has become so popular.
2. The challenges that accompany the use of portfolios.
3. The active ingredients that go into a sound portfolio system.
4. The full range of possible uses of portfolios to both improve communication and enhance student achievement.
5. How to manage many of the practicalities of using portfolios in the classroom.

Further, you will be able to use this knowledge to reason and solve problems in classroom applications in the following ways:

1. Analyze a previously developed portfolio application to discern its active ingredients.
2. Compare and contrast report card grades and portfolios as means of communication about student achievement.
3. Compare and contrast different kinds of portfolios in terms of similarities and differences.
4. Infer about the kind of portfolio that is likely to fit best into a particular classroom assessment context.

5. Evaluate applications of portfolios to see if they meet standards of effective practice and are likely to promote student learning.

As a result of your study of this chapter, I hope you will become skillful at the following:

1. Developing plans for portfolio applications in your own classroom.
2. Implementing those plans in a student-involved manner to promote strong motivation and achievement among your students.

This will result in your development of one specific product: the preparation of a written plan for the development of one or more portfolios for use in your school or classroom.

And finally, you will develop the following dispositions:

1. You will come to see portfolios as a potentially valuable way to communicate about and to motivate students.
2. You will be ready to cautiously proceed in using portfolios, attending carefully to the quality of the assessments you use to evaluate student achievement.

Recently, Lewis & Clark College in Portland, Oregon, surprised many by initiating an admissions policy in which academically talented students have the opportunity to submit portfolios of their academic work instead of SAT scores and the standard admissions essay. The college explained this new portfolio policy as follows:

> If you select the Portfolio Path, we ask that you submit materials which demonstrate that you meet Lewis & Clark's criteria for admission. You might, for example, include samples of papers and exams from a variety of courses over a period of years or from a particular course through a term. In either case, we suggest you choose three to five papers which show intellectual growth and an ability to write clearly and think critically. You might also include in your portfolio science projects, complicated mathematical proofs or computer programs of your own devising, sample work from advanced placement or honors courses, programs from musical or theatrical events in which you have participated (and audio or video tapes if you have them) or photographs of artistic work. Your portfolio should contain an official high school transcript, a letter from your college counselor or principal certifying that the work submitted is your own, and at least three letters in sealed envelopes from recent teachers assessing your academic abilities. We also ask that you fill out the first page of the regular application materials. *Standardized test scores, additional recommendations from teachers and others, a statement describing your academic goals and interests, and an admissions essay are optional.* (Lewis & Clark College, 1990, emphasis added)

Clearly, Lewis & Clark is seeking a more open, rich, and flexible way for prospective students to communicate their abilities and accomplishments—a more student-involved means of sharing information.

This is only one illustration of the fact that portfolios have become the focus of many local initiatives and statewide mandates across all levels of education. While most applications are occurring in language arts contexts, such as reading and writing portfolios, other uses are emerging in math, science, and arts education. Some districts and state licensing boards are even beginning to conceive of portfolios as the basis for teacher and principal evaluation.

A *portfolio* is a collection of student work assembled to provide a representation of that student's achievement. The representation conveyed, as you might anticipate, is a function of the context: the purpose for assessing and communicating and the achievement target(s) about which we wish to communicate. Thus, the range of possible applications of portfolios in the classroom is wide indeed, as you shall see in this chapter. But first, let's set the stage with a simple definition.

The best depiction of the portfolio concept that I have seen was developed by a professional association of educators (Arter & Spandel, 1992):

> A student portfolio is *a purposeful collection of student work that tells a story about the student's efforts, progress or achievement in [one or more academic disciplines]. This collection must include student participation in selection of portfolio content; guidelines for the selection of that material; criteria for judging the merit of the work collected, and evidence of student self-reflection.* This definition supports the view that assessment should be continuous, capture a rich array of what students know and can do, involve realistic contexts, communicate to student and others what is valued, portray the process by which work is accomplished and be integrated with instruction. (p. 36)

Just as artists assemble portfolios of their work to convey their talents and journalists assemble samples of their work to represent their writing capabilities, so too can our students collect examples of their work to tell their school achievement story.

The essential difference between report card grades and portfolios as ways of communicating is that, with grades, we aspire to the most efficient way to share information and care little about details, whereas, with portfolios, we abandon concern for efficiency and seek to maintain the detail. Each form meets the information needs of different users. Let's analyze the ingredients of quality portfolios to see whose information needs they meet.

Time for Reflection

Before we continue, take a few minutes and personalize the portfolio concept. Respond in writing to the following questions. They arise out of this scenario:

You are a high school senior applying for admission to Lewis & Clark College. You have decided to take the portfolio path and so must make your case for admission into their school in your best possible terms. Please answer the following questions in order. Be sure to complete each response before proceeding to the next.

1. *What would you place in your college admissions portfolio? Just list the ingredients.*

2. *Next to each ingredient, specify briefly why you included it.*

3. *In a few sentences, can you capture the story about yourself that you were trying to tell with this portfolio?*

4. *How critical would it be for you to know the purpose for this portfolio before you put it together? Why?*

5. *How critical would it be for you to be able to anticipate the performance criteria the review committee will apply? Why?*

6. *How important would it be for you to be in charge of assembling this portfolio if this context were real? Why?*

7. *What role would your personal self-reflection play in your assembly of this portfolio, if you were really called on to tell this story?*

Save your responses for later reference.

The Popular Culture of Portfolios

The portfolio idea as it is being played out in schools these days brings with it a mixed bag of strengths, limitations, and possible applications. Without question, it is a very powerful and popular example of inclusive, student-involved communication at work in the classroom. But by the same token, portfolios can lead to counterproductive and frustrating work for both student and teacher if we don't use them wisely. Let's consider these pluses and minuses.

The Reasons for Popularity

Over the past decade, the portfolio has become one of the most popular approaches in school culture because it permits teachers to use assessments flexibly to serve several important purposes, including the following:

- Track student achievement over time to *reveal improvement* or the lack thereof. In this sense, they can be diagnostic.

- *Preserve the detailed and complex picture of student achievement* often lost when we condense everything into a report card grade.

- Afford students an excellent context within which to *take responsibility* for maintaining and tracking their own files and records of achievement. This is a critical life skill.

- *Help students learn to reflect* on and see their own improvement as achievers. This involvement has real motivational power.

- Provide important *insights into students' academic self-concepts,* academic interests, and sense of their own needs.

- Provide excellent opportunities for students to *practice their reasoning proficiencies,* analyze their own work, compare work over time, draw inferences about their growth or needs, and learn evaluative or critical thinking skills.

- Help students understand the *work production requirements of real-life situations.* That is, we can establish simulations of life beyond school or connect school experiences with real life, such as developing portfolios for job applications.

For all of these reasons, teachers experienced in using portfolios find them to be engaging for both themselves and their students.

The Challenges

With all of this encouragement, it's tempting simply to dive in and start developing and using student portfolios. But wait, there's more. Portfolio specialists Spandel and Culham (1995) remind us of three myths about portfolios that you would do well to keep in mind as you study this idea for your classroom.

Myth 1.   *Creating portfolios automatically makes you a better teacher.* Spandel and Culham advise us that it's not that simple. Without a student-centered assessment environment in place—that is, without a strong foundation underpinning the portfolio structure—this way of communicating will not automatically lead to better teaching. That means we must start with clear targets, organized in a continuous progress manner and feeding into quality assessments (i.e., sound sampling of skills and control for bias and distortion), with students as full partners in assessing and assuming responsibility for their own learning.

Myth 2.   *Portfolios are easy to manage if you're an organized person.* Being organized helps, they advise. Over time, teachers report that they become more organized about their portfolios and therefore more comfortable using them. But the lessons they learn along the way are critical to their success. Even if you're organized, it's hard work. It takes time and patience to work into this idea. If you have difficulties early on, it is not because you are disorganized. As one teacher put it, when she first started implementing this idea in her classroom, her students "had portfolios." Now two years later, her students "do portfolios" in her classroom (Austin, 1994). By the time you finish this chapter, you will know what she meant, and will understand what it takes to use them successfully.

Myth 3.   *Portfolios make learning easy for students.* "On the contrary," Spandel and Culham (1995) tell us, "Portfolios offer students a whole new set of challenges:

planning, time management, comparing, analyzing, learning to understand how to learn. What is equally true is that students can potentially gain great insight from the experience—insight equivalent to the effort they put into it" (p. 14). Our challenge as teachers is the same in this case as it has been throughout: to help students see the personal value of assuming responsibility for their learning.

Maintaining Perspective

The immense popularity of portfolios and their rapid evolution have led in some instances to an unfortunate narrowing of perspectives. As you think about and plan for possible applications of portfolios in your classroom, be cautious of the following perspectives:

Portfolio Assessment?   It is not uncommon to see reference in our professional literature to this topic as "portfolio assessment." I don't, however, think of this as an assessment concept per se. In fact, the context (purpose and target) within which we use portfolios may require that we assemble multiple assessments using different assessment formats to tell a complete story. It is the *combination* of these ingredients that underpin and give meaning to the message. So for this reason, I think of the portfolio as a communication rather than an assessment system.

Portfolios and Performance Assessment.   In addition, it is common to find the concepts of portfolios and performance assessment closely linked in current literature. When artists assemble portfolios of their work, they collect the artistic products they have created. When journalists collect samples of their articles, they too gather their work into a coherent whole. These are products. That's one kind of performance assessment. Thus, it is tempting to speak of a portfolio as relying only on performance assessment as the source of its information of student achievement. Resist that temptation. You have four forms of assessment in your repertoire: selected response, essay, performance assessment, and personal communication. We have said consistently that they are all potentially valuable contributors to the story we tell about student achievement. So they all can appear in portfolios.

Time for Reflection

Think of a grade level and achievement target that would permit the development of a portfolio that would include more than just performance assessment to accurately reflect student achievement. This should be an instance in which evidence of achievement would have to be generated and collected using a variety of different assessment methods.

Portfolios and Life Skills.   Third, the popular culture associated with portfolios often requires that they focus on life skills—proficiencies, for example, that stretch beyond school to the world of work. Some hold that portfolios should be married to the concept of "authentic" assessment, or assessment of skills required in the "real world."

While this represents one excellent application of the portfolio idea, and we should take maximum advantage of it, it is far from the only or even the most valuable application of portfolios. Opportunities abound in classrooms for portfolios to tell powerful stories about emerging academic proficiencies, such as math skills, beginning writing skills (including spelling and grammar), social interaction skills, knowledge and understanding of science, and others. These are the academic foundations that ultimately will underpin students' life skills and for this reason are very important. Portfolios can contribute to student success in developing these too, inside the academic world.

The Need for Quality Assessments.   The trend that concerns me most about portfolios is the tendency of many users to think that, just because they're using portfolios, they're assured a rich and accurate portrait of student achievement. I have met teachers, administrators, and policy makers who seem to feel that the mere presence of portfolios somehow ensures quality schools, regardless of how well they implement the idea. This is potentially very dangerous. Because any portfolio is really a collection of contributing assessments, each assessment provides part of the big picture—part of the mosaic, as you will recall from the preceding grading chapter. For this reason, *it is essential that each contributing assessment provide dependable information* about the part of the story it is intended to represent.

Just as high-quality assessments give meaning to report card grades, so too do they permit portfolios to tell rich and compelling stories about student academic growth and development. But, they can help us to communicate more effectively and thus improve schools only if they tell an accurate story. We can ensure the accuracy of the stories they tell only if we maintain a consistent commitment to our five standards of assessment quality: clear targets, clear purpose, proper methods, sound sampling, and control of bias and distortion. Poor-quality assessments will misrepresent student achievement and will place students directly in harm's way, regardless of how we communicate those results. In that sense, everything covered in parts 1, 2, and 3 of this book as a prologue to our discussion of report card grades in the previous chapter also is a prologue to our discussion of portfolios in this chapter. With these cautions foremost in our minds, then, let's explore inside the realm of the portfolio.

Analyzing the Active Ingredients in Portfolios

The definition of *portfolio* offered at the beginning of the chapter suggested that an effective portfolio system includes several specific ingredients. We'll consider these now. To start with, concentrate on building your portfolios around these six keys to success:

1. *Maintain a sharp focus.* Know your purpose for assessing and place limits on the achievement target(s) of interest.

2. *Rely on quality assessments.* Align targets and purposes to assessment methods that can deliver into portfolios the information needed.

3. *Know what story the portfolio will tell.* Develop clear guidelines for the selection of material collected in the portfolio.

4. *Rely on explicit criteria for assessing student work.* These are the standards against which you and your students will gauge success.

5. *Involve students in selecting some of that work.* Do this for the same reason that you would want to be involved in developing your own college admission portfolio—students have a stake in the story the portfolio is telling.

6. *Require periodic student self-reflection on their own achievements.* This represents the heart of the learning experience provided by portfolios.

Let's probe inside each of these keys to success for the practical lessons they teach.

Sharp Focus

The effective use of portfolios requires that we use them in a disciplined way. I have come in contact with several local and even state education agencies that like the portfolio idea so much that they simply instruct teachers to start one for each student. Envision what I call the universal, all-encompassing, "megaportfolio." Starting in primary grades, teachers accumulate evidence of achievement. Then each teacher along the way adds more, as the child's school story unfolds. Visualize a file folder that then becomes a file drawer, then a file cabinet, and then a closet full of material. Soon we've evolved to a room-sized collection, leading ultimately to the student driving a tractor trailer across the stage at high school graduation!

Sound foolish? Of course it does. And I take little solace from technology buffs who tell us not to worry about volume because we can digitize it all and place it on a computer chip the size of your thumbnail. Imagine an "electromegaportfolio," devoid of purpose. This lack of focus arises from a lack of understanding or discipline on the part of those who would conceive of such plans. If we start with no focus—no story to tell, no purpose, no clear achievement targets—we end up with an unmanageable portfolio.

To understand how to avoid this, we must visualize a different scenario. We must begin each portfolio application with a clear sense of purpose and target. During the schooling experience, students will develop and use many portfolios, each associated with a different purpose and target. Some will reflect math achievement, some reading and writing, and others science skills. Some will be more structured, some less. Some will be more student involving, some less. Some will deal with knowledge targets, others with reasoning, still others with skills or products. Their content will vary. But we hope what will remain in each student's mind is a sense that she or he is in control of her or his increasing academic competence—a strong and growing academic self-concept. My vision has teachers using portfolios flexibly and opportunistically to communicate information about student achievement and develop a sense of academic well-being. Over the years, most of these portfolio collections will end up in the student's hands after serving their purpose.

If a state, district, school, or family wants to maintain a set of portfolios containing the best, most timely evidence of a student's current level of academic achievement, such as for the award of a certificate of mastery or to qualify for graduation, that's fine. This simply means that when a student can provide compelling evidence of a new level of competence with respect to a particular achievement expectation, the old outdated evidence in that portfolio is discarded and the new material replaces it. But this again is just one of many possible ways to give the portfolio a context, a reason for being, a target to reflect, a purpose to serve, and a sharp focus.

We will return to the range of different purposes for portfolios in a later section of this chapter.

Quality Assessments

By this point in our journey, we don't need to add detail about how quality assessments form the foundation of a quality communication system. We have long since defined our five quality control criteria and discussed how to meet those standards. As we accumulate evidence of student achievement in a portfolio, we must continue to meet those standards. We can use selected response assessments if they fit the context to collect some of that information. Essay and performance assessments obviously represent viable options, too—in the hands of qualified users. Written or audio summaries may of course come into play. I know of a school in which teachers record students struggling to speak a new language and then continue recording on that same audiocassette over the years as proficiency increases. They wrap the cassettes as gifts and present them to their students at graduation along with their diploma. If they have developed a quality student-involved assessment process, students not only hear themselves improving over time, but also can articulate precisely what it is that makes each new addition to the recording better than those that preceded it. Quality assessments placed in student hands encourage achievement.

Guidelines for Selection

To merge effectively into instruction, portfolios must have a story to tell. Thus, we must plan to collect materials that can tell that story. Those plans provide students and teacher with specific guidelines for the selection of work for the portfolio. Guidelines will vary according to the purpose and target. Spandel and Culham (1995) provide us with a productive way to think of this by suggesting several structures for portfolios. These are not mutually exclusive categories, and you may blend them to fit the occasion. These structures are the celebration portfolio, the time sequence portfolio, and the status report portfolio.

The Celebration Portfolio.   A portfolio can be used as a keepsake, which you might invite students to create as a personal collection of favorite works and special academic mementos. They might use this to communicate to families the things they are most proud of or to show positive examples of their learning experiences or classroom activities.

In this case, the student's guidelines for portfolio selection are driven by this question, What do I think is really special about my work and why? This is a wonderful place for young students to begin their portfolio development experience by just collecting favorite experiences. They may then begin to categorize and cull for the really special works. The only evaluations are made by the students, according to their own vision of what's "special." No one else's standards have a place here. This is critically important.

Students can use this experience to begin to identify the attributes of special classroom work and to generate personal insights about their own meaning of quality. Over time and through interaction with you and classmates, they can begin to connect these elements of quality into a growing framework that ultimately helps them understand their own sense of what represents "good work." In this sense, the celebration portfolio—devoid of externally imposed standards—can put students in touch with their own strengths and interests, and can help them learn to make choices.

Time for Reflection

If you did a celebration portfolio of your years as an educator, what might you put in? List some things you would enter. Next to each, specify why you would include it. Then try to capture in a few sentences the story you are trying to tell.

The Time Sequence Portfolio.   Another reason to build a portfolio is to reveal changes or accomplishments in a student's academic performance over time. Two classroom applications of this idea warrant discussion, the growth portfolio and the project portfolio.

The Growth Portfolio.   The portfolio creator (the storyteller) might collect samples of work over time to show how proficiency has changed. When this is the purpose, guidelines for selection dictate that we assemble multiple indicators of the same proficiency, such as samples of writing or selections of artwork. If you recall our opening scenario in Chapter 1, Emily shared samples of her writing from the beginning of the year for the school board to review and critique. Then she wowed them with two other samples from the end of the year that revealed how much more proficient she had become. These writing samples came from her writing portfolio—a growth portfolio.

In this case, the evaluation criteria need to be held constant over time. Emily was able to discuss specific improvements in her work included in her portfolio over the year because the writing criteria—word choice, organization, sentence structure, voice, and so on—remained the same for each writing activity. This gave her a yardstick by which to see her writing progress to higher levels of competence. The motivational power of a growth portfolio can be immense.

The Project Portfolio.   Alternatively, the storyteller might depict the completion of steps in a project conducted over time. When this is the purpose, guidelines for selection dictate that the storyteller provide evidence of having completed all necessary steps in a quality manner. For example, students completing a major science project might show how they arrived at a hypothesis, how they assembled the apparatus for gathering the needed data, how they conducted the tests, the test results, and the analysis and interpretation of those results. A project portfolio is an ideal format to use to describe such work carried out over an extended period.

The evaluative judgments made in this case are based on two sets of performance criteria. The first reflect the steps students must have completed within a specified time frame. These typically provide highly structured guidelines for what to collect as proof of work completion. They teach the student lessons about the necessity of planning a task and sticking to a timeline. You might also hold students accountable for periodically reviewing progress with you. The second set focuses on the quality of work completed at each step along the way. These, of course, demand that students not merely provide evidence of having done the activity, but also provide evidence that they did it well.

One final comment regarding the time sequence portfolio: The span of time covered can range from a brief several-day project to one lasting a full year or longer, depending on the context. This is a very flexible option.

The Status Report Portfolio.   Yet another kind of story to tell by means of a portfolio can be that of having met certain preestablished standards of performance. Spandel and Culham (1995) cleverly refer to this as a "passportfolio." In this instance, the student must make a case within the portfolio for having attained certain levels of proficiency. Therefore, the intended achievement targets determine the guidelines for content selection.

Several applications of this kind of portfolio are relevant in the schooling process. The Lewis & Clark College admissions portfolio is one example. In another kind of application, the State of Oregon soon will require that students present a portfolio of evidence of having attained certain essential proficiencies to earn a certificate of mastery in high school. In a much simpler context, we might ask students to assemble evidence of having completed all requirements for the completion of a particular course. Or we might review a status report portfolio to make a course placement decision, such as, What is the next natural course in this student's progression of math instruction?

In all of these cases, the guidelines for the selection of material will probably be highly structured and driven by specific academic requirements that provide evidence that the student has mastered prerequisites and is ready to move on.

Summary of Portfolio Possibilities.   Clearly, the concept of a "megaportfolio"—a monster file of academic stuff devoid of purpose and structure—makes no sense in assessing student achievement. However, if we formulate careful guidelines for selection around focused stories to tell, we can use portfolios advantageously to integrate our students deeply into the teaching and learning process.

We can start them with celebration portfolios in early grades. We do far too little personal assessment just for the fun and memories. Such celebrations can span the school years. But we need not stop there.

We can also help students track their own academic development over time. Sometimes this might center on the growth of a particular set of proficiencies. Other times, it might track the completion of a set of required projects. Either way, the student's skills are the focus of the story.

And finally, we can tap the portfolio idea to describe students' achievement status—standards met, courses completed, requirements satisfied—descriptions that inform our decisions about appropriate next steps.

The possible combinations and permutations of these portfolio options in the classroom are infinite. And remember, both the time span covered and amount of material collected for any particular portfolio may readily vary from a little to a great deal, depending on the learning context and the teaching strategy, thus making this a very flexible communication approach.

Criteria for Evaluating Merit

As you well know by now, we need to establish criteria by which to evaluate a student's progress, whether judging the merit of writing, charting the expansion of scientific knowledge, or recording increased proficiency in speaking a foreign language. In the case of portfolios, we must remain open to a range of target possibilities, varying with the assessment format as needed.

To illustrate, if a student-teacher team decides that the best evidence of student attainment of a particular target is a score on a multiple-choice test, then the criteria used to judge merit is a high score on the test. If an essay test most accurately reflects the target, then once again, a traditional test score provides the needed information. However, with performance assessments, the applied criteria must reflect proficiency on the skills of interest or reflect the extent to which the student has met quality product standards.

Consequently, we must decide in advance and share with our students how we and they will judge merit. I continue to press the point that students can hit any target that they can see and that holds still for them. Obviously, this is equally important with portfolios, and is the essential way to link assessment and instruction.

Involving Students in the Selection Process

When you were completing the Time for Reflection for your college admission portfolio at the beginning of the chapter, I asked how important it would be for you to take responsibility for selecting the material. I'll bet you said it would be critically important for two reasons. First, you know yourself best and can best ensure the telling of a complete and accurate story. Second, selecting the content allows you to present yourself in the most positive light called for in this competitive situation.

Our students are driven, Covington (1992) tells us, by a desire to maintain and to present to the world a sense that they are academically capable. We support and encourage that positive self-image by involving students in recording their own story through their portfolios. But to make this work, they must also actively participate in selecting the work for the portfolio.

In the celebration portfolio described previously, the story is essentially the student's to tell. But there also is much room for student involvement in the time sequence and status report options. Notice that I am not saying that the student selects. Nor does the teacher. We're talking partnership here. Here's how one teacher friend of mine handles this: Her sixth graders maintain files of all work completed, one for each discipline. When it comes time to assemble the representative work for their growth portfolios in preparation for the periodic student-led parent conferences (discussed in detail in the next chapter), students and teacher meet as a team to select exemplary work. And remember, this is a growth collection, not a status report; the early material may not be very good, but is presented as a baseline from which to show improvement. This teacher wants her students to see their improvement, and she wants their parents to see it, too. Portfolios can demonstrate this very effectively.

Davies, Cameron, Politano, and Gregory (1992) advise us that we can maximize the benefits of student involvement in the selection process by having them describe what they selected and why they selected it. They recommend using a cover sheet for each portfolio entry to capture this information. For an example, see Figure 16–1.

Periodic Student Self-reflection

Of all the dimensions of portfolios, the process of self-reflection is the most important. If we are to keep our students in touch with their emerging academic selves, we must share in understandable terms our vision of what it means to succeed, provide our students with a vocabulary to use in communicating about it, and keep them in touch with the accumulating evidence of their own proficiency. One way to hold them accountable for achieving a clear sense of themselves as learners is to have them write or talk about that accumulating evidence. With portfolios, this has come to be known as *student self-reflection*.

The simple fact is that students who learn to evaluate their own achievement become better achievers through that process. They maintain contact with their own strengths and weaknesses. Figure 16–2 provides an example in two parts, an eighth-grade student's essay, "Visions of Hope," and her reflection on the quality of her work. In this essay, the author assumes the persona of a prisoner who uses her art to maintain perspective. Please read the essay carefully first, then the self-reflection. Note that the author is applying the six analytical writing assessment score scales presented in Chapter 8. As you can see, this student is in touch with her own writing proficiency.

When I chose to include this example of my writing in my portfolio I remembered that...

FICTION
- has a good story
- uses interesting language
- has a beginning, a middle, and an end
- uses a variety of sentences, both simple and complex

NON-FICTION
- gives information
- groups information under main headings
- has a table of contents
- has diagrams or pictures to give additional information

I also know that it is important that my work is neat and that it has been edited for spelling and sentence structure.

The piece of work I have chosen is...

It shows...

I want you to notice...

Please give me one compliment and ask me one question after you read my selection...

I put this in my portfolio on————————   ————————————————————
                               [date]   [signature]

Figure 16–1

Summary Sheet for Student Use in Describing Portfolio Selections

Source: From *Together Is Better: Collaborative Assessment Evaluation and Reporting* (p. 79) by A. Davies, C. Cameron, C. Politano, and K. Gregory, 1992, Winnepeg, MB: Peguis Publishers Ltd. Reprinted by permission.

VISIONS OF HOPE

I call my picture "Visions of Hope." If I'm caught with this picture, I'll be killed. But it's worth it if people outside see it. I want them to know what life was like in the camp and how we kept our hopes up.

You may be wondering how I got the materials I used in this picture. It wasn't easy. I got the materials for the prisoner figures from old pieces of uniforms that had been torn off. This was one of the easier things to get. Uniforms get torn all the time from hard work. All the people look alike because to the Nazis it doesn't matter what you look like—only what you can do. To the Nazis we are all just numbers, without faces and without names.

The buildings in the picture are black to represent evil and death. Most of the buildings, aside from the barracks, you would enter but never come out again alive. I got this cloth from an old blanket that had worn thin from overuse. The Germans didn't care if we were cold or uncomfortable, so they didn't make any real effort to mend things. Everything in our world badly needs mending, too, including our spirits.

Inside the smoke of death coming out of the smokestacks you will see the Star of David. This star represents hope. Hope for life and for living. We will never totally die as long as our hope lives on.

My picture has two borders. One is barbed wire. It symbolizes tyranny, oppression, and total loss of freedom. The barbs are shaped like swastikas to represent the Nazis, Hitler and hate. This is a symbol of true evil.

The other border, outside the barbed wire, represents all the hope and dreams that are outside the camp. The flowers, sun, moon and bright colors were all things we took for granted in our old world. Even though we can see the sun through the clouds and smoke, we can't enjoy it anymore. The feathers represent the birds we barely see or hear inside the camp. We miss the cheeriness of their voices. The tiny brown twigs are as close as we come to the trees we remember. I got the bright cloth from a dress. When new prisoners come to the camp they must take off their own clothes and put on the hated prison outfits. All the nice clothes are sent to Germans outside the camps. My job is to sort through the clothes and pick out the nice things that will be sent away. When I saw this beautiful cloth, I tore off a piece and saved it for my picture.

I hope someone finds this and remembers that we always kept our hopes alive even when they took away everything else. They could never take our hope.

Figure 16–2
Sample Student Writing and Author's Self-reflection
Source: "Vision of Hope," a sample of writing and self-reflection by Nikki Spandel. Reprinted by permission.

Helping Students Get Started.   Sometimes it's helpful to initiate students into self-reflection by posing some simple questions for them to reflect about, such as the following (adapted from Arter & Spandel, 1992):

- Describe the steps you went through in completing this assignment. Did this process work and lead to successful completion or were there problems? What would you change next time?

REFLECTION

This piece has always been one of my favorites. It shows not only what I can do as a writer, but as an artist as well. I knew very little of the Holocaust before working on this project. It was almost impossible for me to believe how brutal people could be. It both frightened and horrified me. In my written piece and my picture, I tried to capture that horror but also the courage which kept many people going. I also tried hard to imagine how it would really feel to be imprisoned, locked away from the things and the work and the people I loved. I don't know if anyone can really imagine this without living it, but this project made me think.

In **Ideas and Content,** I gave myself a 5. I thought my ideas were clear, and I thought I created a vivid picture of an artist trying to keep his work alive.

I would also give myself a 5 in **Organization.** My opening does a good job of leading the reader into my paper, especially with the dramatic and honest statement: "If I'm caught with this picture I'll be killed." I want the reader to know right away what is at stake.

My **Voice** is not as strong as I would have liked it to be. It is hard to take on the voice of another person. I am pretending to be someone else, not myself. I guess I just haven't had enough practice at this. Also, my natural voice tends to be humorous, and clearly, this is the most serious of topics. Anyway, I just did not find quite the voice I wanted, and I gave myself a 4.

I gave myself a 5 in **Word Choice.** The language is simple and natural. I did not try to impress the reader with words they might not understand. Also, I tried to capture the mood of what it would be like to live in a concentration camp and think how the people who lived there might talk. What words would they use?

My **Sentence Fluency** was pretty strong. You will notice that I vary my sentence beginnings a lot. That's one of my strengths. It's smooth, whether you read it silently or aloud. I think a few sentences are a little short and choppy, though. Some sentence combining would help. So I rated myself a 4 on this trait.

In **Conventions** I would rate myself a 5. I have always been strong in this trait. Conventions are fairly easy for me, if I think about them, especially with the aid of a computer. I can catch most grammatical errors, and I use a spell checker. I also read through my paper when it's finished to make sure it sounds just right. Rating myself on these traits is very helpful. It allows me to see how I'm doing as a writer, and to see my work as it really is. I think the traits give you a way of teaching yourself.

Figure 16–2, *continued*

- Did you receive feedback along the way that permitted you to refine your work? Describe your response to the feedback offered—did you agree or disagree with it? Why? What did you do as a result of this feedback?

- What makes your most effective piece of work different from your least effective? What does your best work tell you about where you have improved and where you need further work?

- What are the strengths of your work in this project (or this series of works)?

- What aspects still need more work? What kind of help will you need?

- What impact has this project had on your interests, attitudes, and views of this area?

These and other related questions can be very helpful in beginning self-reflection. It's human nature to experience some difficulty being constructively analytical and self-critical, at least at first. As we established earlier, this is risky business for most, and especially for those with a history of academic failure. Covington (1992) reminds us that students will go to great lengths to maintain a positive internal sense of academic ability—even to the point of denying or being unable to see, let alone face, the flaws in their work. For this reason, guided practice is a necessity.

It may be helpful for your students to see you model the process by reviewing, analyzing, and self-evaluating some of your own work. Or, consider having the whole class collaborate as a team to compose a hypothetical self-reflection to a particular project. This is the best way I know to show students that your classroom is a safe place within which to risk trying. Either success or problems point the direction—not to a judgmental grade, but to a specific path to each student's improvement.

What Makes a Good Self-reflection?   In effect, self-reflection is a kind of student performance. Therefore, it too can be the focus of a performance assessment. In fact, remember the strategy discussed in the performance assessment chapters (Chapters 8 and 11) of having students contrast samples of outstanding and poor-quality performance to uncover key differences? Consider involving older students (mature middle schoolers and high schoolers) in a similar process to discover the key elements of an effective self-reflection. To minimize the risk to students, make up high- and low-quality reflections of some of your work and have students do the contrasting, devising criteria for evaluating their own reflections. Plan to engage students over time in the process of refining their visions of a good self-reflection as needed.

For those who need more specific guidance, consider these key dimensions. But remember, their relevance will vary with the activity (adapted from Arter & Spandel, 1992):

- *Coverage*—Does the reflection address all relevant criteria? Make a checklist of them, and work with the students to review their self-reflection and check them off.

- *Accuracy*—Are students developing an accurate sense of their achievement or growth? Compare your evaluations with theirs. Discuss similarities and differences of perspective.

- *Specificity*—Does the reflection include examples to support points made in the self-reflection? Work with students to identify or develop them.

- *Integration*—Have students appropriately synthesized important insights into broader conclusions about their achievement? Work with them to be sure they understand how to draw this kind of inference (excellent practice using an important form of reasoning).

- *Revelation*—Does self-reflection bring students to new insights about their learning? Discuss these new insights with your students.

One teacher I know has translated these guidelines into a simple checklist students complete after each required self-reflection. Soon, she reports, these activities become second nature to her students.

Summary of Active Ingredients

When portfolios are merged seamlessly into instruction, students and teacher can be partners in the process of transforming evidence of student achievement into a picture of the student's current achievement status or growth. Figure 16–3 lists the keys to successful portfolios.

Time for Reflection

Early in the chapter, I told you of a teacher whose students "had portfolios." But after she developed some experience with the idea, she now reports that her students "do portfolios." Now that you've read most of the chapter, what do you think she meant?

Dealing with Some Practicalities

As I work with teachers exploring classroom applications of portfolios, several questions seem to come up over and over. I recently sat down with Casey, our high school teacher friend and a skilled and experienced user of portfolios, to discuss them.

Time for Reflection

In the following section, after you read each question and before you read Casey's response, take just a minute to think through how you would answer it. Then compare your responses to Casey's.

Figure 16–3
Key Ingredients in a Quality Portfolio Application

1. Keep all eyes on the right achievement target(s).
2. Never lose sight of the need for quality assessments.
3. Be sure you and your students know the story the portfolio is to tell.
4. Be sure students get to tell at least some of that story.
5. Rely on explicit criteria in evaluating student work.
6. Require periodic student self-reflections.

AUTHOR: Casey, how can a teacher get started with portfolios?

CASEY: Start small. In primary grades, a simple celebration portfolio can ease students into the process. Turn next to an application of a growth portfolio. But keep it simple—a narrow, sharply focused target over a brief time span. Leave the status portfolio for later. That's the one I use, but I teach in high school.

And, you know, I really notice a difference in my students' comfort level when they come to my class with prior portfolio experience. Those who began with them very early plunge with confidence into my project assignment. I wish all my students arrived with that kind of experience and confidence.

The way several colleagues and I got started was to make a commitment to conducting student-led parent conferences [see Chapter 17]. Then we used the portfolio to help students prepare evidence of their achievement to share with parents. My particular application of the idea takes the form of a course project. Over the grading period, each student has to complete all the project steps and keep a portfolio of evidence of the nature and quality of their work.

AUTHOR: How much time does it take?

CASEY: It varies. As the scope of the target(s) of interest, the time span of the portfolio, and the complexity of the evidence accumulated increase, so will the commitment. But as the maturity and experience of students go up, they learn to handle most of the work—and to enjoy it.

The greater role the students play, the more feasible the idea becomes. But all teachers have to tailor their use of portfolios to fit their resources.

AUTHOR: You teach high school and face 150 students a day in different classes. Is this idea really feasible for you?

CASEY: You bet! But you have to be crafty about it. As I said, my performance assessment for my social studies classes requires my students to complete a project. Their work culminates either in a final product or a final presentation that meets certain standards of quality. I expect each student to keep a project (time sequence) portfolio containing evidence of having completed all of the steps in the assignment. I count on heavy student involvement in all phases of the work. Subject to my approval and within certain parameters that I lay out, students identify the target(s) of interest to them, plan the time sequence of project activities, specify the nature of the final product, assist in devising the performance criteria used to evaluate their work, work in teams to apply those criteria (both for interim revisions and the final product), and maintain complete and accurate records along the way.

At first I was astounded, and I continue to be impressed with their willingness and ability to assume responsibility. My major hassle is forcing them to narrow their target and keep to a schedule. The only way I can make the whole thing feasible, given my teaching load, is to stagger these project assignments across courses throughout the school year.

AUTHOR: Can students really manage their own portfolios? What if they cheat?

CASEY: Yes they can manage them, as long as I provide leadership and insist on those timelines.

And do you know what really minimizes cheating? The weekly written self-reflection I require. Students first share them with their study teammates, then put them in their portfolios, where I get to read them. If you don't know where you are in your project and don't know what you're talking about, it's very hard to bluff. It stands out like a sore thumb.

Cheating becomes an interesting issue here. Students can copy someone else's test paper, sneak in a crib sheet, have someone else do their homework for them, and even forge grades on assignments before returning them to the teacher. In my years of teaching, I've seen it all.

But students know that it's impossible to sneak by in the student-involved assessment activities we use in my classes. Those who prepare and deliver stand tall; those who don't, stand out.

And do you know what really minimizes cheating? The weekly written self-reflection I require. Students first share them with their study teammates, then put them in their portfolios, where I get to read them. If you don't know where you are in your project and don't know what you're talking about, it's very hard to bluff. It stands out like a sore thumb.

My students know that I am expecting to see increasing sophistication over time on their part. It's as if each self-reflection is more demanding than the one preceding it. Everyone seems to acknowledge that there are no excuses in this classroom. It may sound crazy, but I believe that the value of cheating declines in their minds. If students understand that they have the opportunity to watch themselves get better, cheating loses its luster. There's no percentage in it.

Besides, my students quickly learn through the grapevine that they simply can't bluff in the conference with their parents and me at the end of the project, where any attempt to misrepresent their own achievement will be transparent. I ask tough questions in front of their families. They know they're responsible for giving good answers. And you know, I can see the pride in their eyes when they deliver quality.

AUTHOR: How do you convert portfolio work to a grade?

CASEY: We work as a class to devise a set of project performance criteria. Before anyone starts the project, I share examples of good and bad ones from past classes, and we work as a team to identify the differences between them. We establish and define our keys to success, and formulate performance rating scales. Frankly, there is a great deal of similarity among the scales developed by my different classes, but that's because I lead their development. My expectations are not open to negotiation. But, I find that student involvement in this process buys ownership on their part. And, I am flexible regarding the vocabulary we use to describe our standards. My students truly have important input.

I then base the grade on the quality of the final product or presentation at the end of the project. We establish and agree on the target in advance, and we define levels of proficiency that equate to different grades. Work completed during the project is only important as it relates to the quality of the final product. No one gets credit for just doing the work.

Typically, we have five or six 5-point rating scales. Students know from the start what ratings will receive an A, a B, and so on. They know they must set their own aspirations and work accordingly. There's no mystery here.

AUTHOR: Who owns the portfolios?

CASEY: My students. When their purpose is served, students can take them home.

However, the district is discussing the idea of a graduation portfolio. That would require the maintenance of a portfolio of the most current evidence of student achievement of a specified set of expectations for high school graduation. This might take on the stature of an official transcript and might need to be given the security status of traditional academic records. For a period of time, the district may need to hold these.

AUTHOR: Who has access to your portfolios?

CASEY: These are academic records, just like report cards. Therefore, all normal privacy rights are in force. Only me, my students, their families, and school officials have access, unless families grant permission for others to see them.

AUTHOR: Where do you store all of these portfolios?

CASEY: With their owners: my students. They can be responsible for this. If they wish, they can use a file cabinet accessible in my room at school. But, the agreement is that each portfolio is private property.

I have heard that there are some electronic portfolio software packages coming on the market. Several teachers who use portfolios have formed an ad hoc committee to investigate this option for the district for the future.

AUTHOR: Thanks, Casey.

CASEY: My pleasure. I recommend the portfolio idea to other teachers. Once you and your students get used to it, it's a real time saver, and a great motivator.

About Those Electronic Portfolios. There are some promising new developments on the horizon with respect to storing student portfolios. A number of computer software developers have created and are refining packages that permit classroom teachers to help students develop electronic portfolios. These purport to allow easy entry of traditional academic records (student background, grades, etc.), as well as actual examples of student work, including everything from written products to color videos with sound. Easy retrieval also is possible using networked personal computers. A partial list of currently available systems appears in Figure 16–4.

Figure 16–4
Electronic Portfolio Software Packages

Abacus Instructional Management Systems
NCS/ABACUS
Portland, OR

Classroom Manager
CTB Macmillan/McGraw-Hill
Monterey, CA

Electronic Portfolio
Learning Quest
Corvallis, OR

Electronic Portfolio
Scholastic
Jefferson, MO

Grady Profile
Aurbach and Associates
St. Louis, MO

Learner Profile
Sunburst
Pleasant, NY

On Track
Addison-Wesley Longman
Reading, MA

Standard Tracker
IPS Publishing
Vancouver, WA

The Assessor
Software America
Chicago, IL

Teacher Instructional Mapping
   and Management System (TIMMS)
Synectics Co.
Seattle, WA

Tycho—Teacher Information Manager
AMS, Inc.
Fairfax, VA

Chapter Summary: Speaking Through Portfolios

Portfolios offer a detailed way of communicating about student achievement. In this case the communication arises out of collecting and displaying actual examples of student work. Unlike grades, portfolios maintain the detail needed to tell a complete story of a student's achievement. This does not mean that they should replace grades, but rather that we should see them as serving different but nonetheless important purposes.

Portfolios have gained immense popularity in recent years because of their potential as a teaching tool that offers many opportunities for student involvement. Portfolios diagnose student needs and reveal improvement over time. They can encourage students to take responsibility for their own learning, track that learning, and gain an enhanced sense of academic progress and self-worth. Portfolios help students learn to reflect on their own work, identify strengths and weaknesses, and plan a course of action—critically important life skills. And finally, they give students opportunities for practicing important and useful reasoning and problem-solving skills.

But with all these pluses, many tend to underestimate the complexity of the portfolio development process. They take very careful planning and dedication. The hard work can pay off with immense achievement and motivational dividends if we implement them in calculated small steps. Think big, act small; one step at a time. Unfortunately, many have drowned in the sea of student papers collected to serve a policy maker's mandated megaportfolio system. We can avoid such problems by preparing carefully.

As we have seen, we may use portfolios in diverse ways to support student achievement. But all require careful attention to some key ingredients: focused achievement targets (as usual!), quality assessments (as usual!), a clear sense of the achievement to be described with students as partners in the telling, clear judgmental criteria (as usual!), and an expectation of periodic student self-reflection. The possibilities of student involvement in this kind of communication are bounded only by the imagination of the users (meaning you and your students).

Exercises to Advance Your Learning

Knowledge

1. After reviewing this chapter, identify in your own words why portfolios have become so popular in schools in the 1990s.

2. List what you believe to be the major challenges teachers face in their use of portfolios and identify why each is a challenge.

3. Commit to memory the six active ingredients that go into a sound portfolio system

and why each is so essential to our success in using them.

4. Create a chart, labeling each line with one of the four types of portfolios discussed in this chapter: celebration, growth, project, and status report. Add four columns headed by these questions: What story will the portfolio tell? What kinds of evidence must it contain? How will we evaluate the information? How does this portfolio type connect to our instruction? Referring to

the text, within each cell of this four-by-four chart, briefly answer each question for each portfolio type.

5. In the last section of the chapter, Casey and I discussed a few practicalities of portfolio use in the classroom. Referring to the text, list each question raised in that section, and next to each, answer it in the briefest possible manner—a word or phrase, if possible.

Reasoning

1. Identify a local professional artist (perhaps a graphic artist or an art teacher) and discuss the artist's portfolio with her or him. Analyze the portfolio in terms of the six active ingredients discussed in this chapter. Are they all accounted for?

2. Compare and contrast report card grades and portfolios as means of communication about student achievement. How are they alike and different? What do those similarities and differences tell you about the information users likely to be well served by each?

3. If you were to replace your parent-teacher conferences with student-led parent conferences, what type of portfolio would you have students develop? Why? If you were helping students to prepare portfolios to certify completion of high school graduation requirements, what kind would you help them develop? Why?

4. If you are currently teaching, find an application of the portfolio idea in your school district and evaluate it in terms of the standards of quality outlined in this chapter. If you are in training and not yet teaching, go to a local school district near you and ask if they might permit you to see portfolios in action in their schools. Evaluate that application in terms of the standards of effective portfolio practice outlined herein.

Skills

1. Develop a small-scale, but specific, plan for a portfolio application in your classroom. Specify purpose and target(s). Identify the story to be told and possible assessments for inclusion. How might students be involved in the telling? What criteria might apply? How might you weave the process of student self-reflection into your plan?

2. If and when possible, put your plan into action, just on a small scale. Evaluate your implementation and draw conclusions about the potential of portfolios for enhancing the motivation and achievement of your students.

Dispositions

1. Some states are requiring that administrators assemble professional portfolios in preparation for being considered for certification. Some teacher training programs assist their new graduates in assembling portfolios to assist them in securing their first jobs. Some practicing teachers are relying on professional portfolios to help them progress to new jobs. Why do you think all of these developments are happening? Do these sound to you like sound applications of portfolios? Why? What do they tell you about the power of this means of communicating about accomplishments? What do you think might be the problems with these applications of the portfolio idea?

2. Teachers often report that the design and implementation of portfolios are hard work—at least to start with, until students can shoulder their share of the responsibility. As a result, some reject the idea as a viable option in their classrooms and never try it. How challenging do you feel this idea might be to implement in your classroom? What advice might you offer to

those who are teetering on the edge of experimenting with portfolios that would encourage them to experiment?

3. Other teachers dive right into the portfolio idea, implementing with abandon and never looking back at issues of quality portfolios and quality assessments within their portfolios. If you were the supervisor of such a teacher who wanted to get them to develop a stronger sense of responsibility for the quality of this work, how might you do this?

Reports and Conferences That Highlight Achievement

CHAPTER ROADMAP

Our journey through the realm of student-involved communication continues in this chapter with a diversity of examples intended to reveal the range of possibilities available to you. As a result of studying the material presented in Chapter 17, reflecting on that material, and completing the learning exercises presented at the end of the chapter, you will come to know and understand the following:

1. The strengths, limitations, and keys to successful use of three forms of written reports on student achievement that stretch beyond grades: rating scales, narrative reporting, and continuous progress reporting.

2. The benefits, challenges, and keys to successful implementation of three forms of conferences that can serve to deliver accurate and complete information about student achievement.

In addition, you will be prepared to use that knowledge to reason as follows:

1. Analyze currently existing communication systems to understand their component parts.

2. Compare and contrast the communication options to uncover important similarities and differences.

3. Draw inferences about which system of communication is most likely to be effective in which classroom contexts.

4. Evaluate communication systems such as those discussed in this chapter to see if they meet standards of quality and to determine how they might be improved.

You will become skillful at the following:

1. Developing plans for applications of these communications options in your own classroom.

2. Implementing those plans in a student-involved manner to promote strong motivation and achievement on the part of your students.

You will be able to use these skills to develop products in the form of written plans for the integrated use of these options in your school or classroom.

And finally, you will develop the following dispositions:

1. You will come to see these written and conference-based options as potentially valuable ways to communicate about and to motivate students.

2. You will be prepared to proceed with caution in your use of these options, attending always to the quality of the assessments used to tell the achievement story.

"The tablecloths are out, cookies arranged, lemonade cooling, and I'm eating supper—frozen yogurt." Terri Austin, a sixth-grade teacher from Fairbanks, Alaska, begins to tell us what it's like in her classroom the evening of student-parent conferences. Let's listen to the rest of her story.

It's 5:45. Will they come? No matter how many times I do this, I always wonder if families will show up.

At 5:50, Frank and his mom arrive early. He's all polished, clean shirt and hair combed. As she sits at a table by the window, he quickly finds his portfolio, joins her and begins.

At 6:00, the room fills quickly, Ruth and her mother drink lemonade while looking at the class photographs on the bulletin board.

Chuck says, "Pick a table, mom." She picks one with a purple tablecloth. Chuck smiles and says, "Oh yeah, you like purple. Would you like some refreshments?" After his mother and brother are seated, Chuck goes to pick up cookies and drinks.

Dennis and his father come in. Dennis's father is still in his military uniform. They find a table by the window. As Dennis shares his work, his father smiles. The father leans closer to Dennis, so they see the paper at the same time.

With his mother sitting across from him, Chuck goes over each paper very carefully. Occasionally, she looks over Chuck's head and smiles at me.

Greg and his mom speak Spanish as they look at the papers together.

Darrin's father rushes in with his family trailing behind. His father asks, "Mrs. Austin, what time are we?" "I scheduled the time wrong," Darrin apologizes. I say, "It's OK. There are no set times. Just find a table and begin." They stop at the refreshment table as Darrin finds his portfolio.

I hear Greg explaining his summary sheet in Spanish.

Steve, his mom, and an unknown lady and child arrive. At the end of the conference, I find out the women is a neighbor who heard about "Steve's portfolio" and wanted to see it. So Steve invited her to his conference.

Darrin's mom catches my eye and smiles. She listens to Darrin read [one of his papers].

On their way out the door, I talk with [Hope's] family. They are very pleased with Hope's work. Her mom has tears in her eyes as she tells me how proud she is of Hope. (Austin, 1994, pp. 66–67)

Thus, Terri introduces us to the idea of student-led parent conferences. In this case, we combine the strengths of student-teacher conferences and parent-teacher conferences into a rich and engaging learning experience for students. Terri and her students spend a great deal of time both preparing information about student achievement and preparing to share it with parents. Sometimes they rely on checklists and rating scales to collect information for the conference. Other times they use personal narrative. Still further, in Terri's classroom, the last topic of conversation in the student-led conference is the grades that appear on the student's report card. But the personal conference with families adds a depth of communication about student growth and development over time that is unattainable with any of these written options.

After the conferences, Terri checked with her students to see if they thought the hard work and preparation were worth it for them. She was startled at the strength of student feelings:

ANNE: I think it really does make a difference. It's definitely easier because you know the outcome of the conference and you don't get the jitters and all worried wondering about the outcome. It teaches you responsibility. You also learn while you're getting ready. I admit it is hard but you are also satisfied knowing you can prepare a conference like a teacher can.

DAVE: Yes, it does make a difference. It is fun and a new experience. I learned patience and responsibility. I learned to tell the truth and to talk about my grades.

SAMANTHA: I have learned that I could explain myself and my grades. It also teaches me to take my time. I learned that I could do more things if I tried because I thought I never could have done them. I also learned that it is a better way to get in touch with your parents.

PHILIP: I learned I can find trust within my grades and show responsibility as in how to make the most of my grades.

MARY: It's scary sometimes.

AARON: It's a very good method.

RICK: I know a lot more about what's going on. Otherwise I don't know what the teacher has said about me. I feel a lot more comfortable doing this. I know my grades and my papers, I seem to know what's going to happen and how I'm doing in school. I'm fair to myself.

DAVID: I learned that I do things that I've never done before and that I can make mistakes sometimes.

MRS. A: Would you recommend this type of conference to other students and teachers?

           [Everyone agrees they would.]

MRS. A: What do you think? Should we continue this procedure for the rest of the year?

           [All agree they should.]

MELISSA: Yes. I think parents understand things better when their child answers their questions. Also, we know the answers to all the questions. Maybe a teacher-parent conference wouldn't answer all the questions. (Austin, 1994, pp. 27–28)

Any doubt about the power of Terri's way of setting clear goals, compiling evidence of goal attainment in portfolios, and preparing students to share information about their own achievement is erased when we read this kind of comment from a parent:

> The transformation of Jason as a student has been remarkable, from an F and C– student to an A and B student. We cannot help but believe that a great deal of the credit must go to the manner in which class materials are presented and the curriculum is organized. Jason certainly has become more focused on his capabilities rather than his limitations. The general emphasis on responsibility for one's own actions and performance has also been most beneficial. Jason was a very frustrated young man in [his former school] and has had a tendency to place blame on others rather than accepting responsibility for his own choices. The last portion of this year has brought welcome changes in this respect. Though not always the most conscientious student, he puts forth serious effort on his studies and assumes responsibility for the results of his efforts. We believe that the "writing classroom" environment has been crucial to Jason's educational development, self-examination and personal growth. (Austin, 1994, p. 48)

I hope this vignette encourages you to explore open, inclusive, student-involved ways of communicating. In this chapter, the final stage of our journey together, I will share an array of ideas for communicating about student achievement that stretch far beyond our traditional teacher-centered, report card grade ways of communicating—and beyond the traditional parent-teacher conference. But remember, my point is not to negate those ways of sharing information; rather, is it to offer additional possibilities.

I present six alternative communication ideas. Three represent applications of written reports of student achievement that promise to capture greater detail about that achievement: rating scales, narrative reporting, and continuous progress reporting. The other three represent productive conference strategies that promise not only to enhance the scope of the communication, but also to affect student understanding and motivation: these include student-teacher conferences, teacher-parent conferences, and finally student-led parent conferences, perhaps the most exciting innovation in school-to-home communication conceived in recent decades. As you proceed through this final chapter, you will understand why it is fitting that we end our journey together with a discussion of these topics.

Be advised from the outset that these alternative means of recording, summarizing, and sharing information do not represent panaceas that promise to deliver us from our communication challenges. Each option presents its own unique and special problems. And, to be sure, each requires every bit as much work as report cards and grades. However, I believe that we can markedly increase our positive impact on the achievement of our students by implementing some of these strategies.

And finally, never lose sight of the fact that these communication systems, just like report cards and portfolios, require the use of high-quality assessments as the basis for gathering accurate information about student achievement. No one has succeeded as yet in inventing a communication alternative capable of converting misinformation into accurate information.

Detailed Written Reports

The reporting alternatives described below permit us to maintain and share very detailed messages about student achievement. The illustrations cross grade levels, from primary to elementary to junior high and high school. Each offers special features worthy of your consideration.

Rating Scale Example: Effective Kindergarten Communication

In Ann Arbor, Michigan, under the public schools' "Success for All Kindergarten Students" initiative, kindergarten faculty developed the 27 achievement targets spelled out in Figure 17–1, a written report to parents. This form provides the basis for periodic communication about student achievement during the school year, and reflects the expectations that form the basis of a much more complete assessment and communication system. While space limits will not permit the presentation of the whole package, Figure 17–2 provides insight into the level of information provided to parents to help them understand the ratings they receive in the report.

Name _____ **Teacher** _____ **School** _____

Key
Not Yet
Developing
Achieving
Not Applicable at this time

	Fall				Winter				Spring			
	NY	Dev	Ach	NA	NY	Dev	Ach	NA	NY	Dev	Ach	
1. Responsible for Own Learning												
2. Positive Self-esteem												
3. Response to Teacher-Directed Activities												
4. Self-control												
5. Social Interaction												
6. Responds to Oral Language												
7. Concepts of Print												
8. Concepts of Books: How They Work												
9. Concepts of Story: How a Story Works												
10. Positive Attitude Toward Own Reading												
11. Positive Attitude Toward Own Writing												
12. Recognizes Words/Logos-Environmental Print												
13. Communicates Through Speaking												

14. Recognizes Most Letters of the Alphabet											
15. Reproduces (by Copying) Most Letters of the Alphabet											
16. Reproduces First Name by Memory and Last Name by Copying											
17. Names Eight Colors											
18. Identifies Four Shapes											
19. Counts to 20 or Above											
20. Numeral Recognition											
21. Number Families/4											
22. Counts Aloud a Set of 12 Objects											
23. Instant Number Recognition											
24. Sorts and Classifies Objects: Two Attributes											
25. Measurement: a. Estimates Length											
b. Measures Length											
26. Graphing a. Creates a Graph											
b. Interprets a Graph											
27. Patterns a. Extends Patterns											
b. Creates Patterns											

Figure 17–1

Ann Arbor Public Schools' Kindergarten Report to Parents

Source: From "Success for All Kindergarten Students" (n.p.) by Department of Research, Ann Arbor Public Schools, 1993, Ann Arbor, MI: Author. Reprinted by permission of the publisher.

479

Name _____

Teacher _____

School _____

ATTENDANCE	Fall	Winter	Spring
Half Days Absent	___	___	___
Times Tardy	___	___	___

	Not Yet 1	Developing 3	Achieving 5
1. Responsibility for Own Learning	Rarely attends to lessons taught. Completes task with one-to-one teacher help.	Inconsistent attention to lessons taught. Needs occasional help in order to complete task.	Shows interest in and is involved in classroom activities. Completes tasks independently, seeking help only when necessary.
2. Positive Self Esteem	Often demonstrates a negative attitude toward self and others.	Needs continued support to develop positive relationships with self and others.	Communicates a positive attitude toward self and others
3. Response to Teacher-directed Activities	Cannot follow most directions. Needs one-to-one help in most areas to complete work.	Sometimes needs extra reinforcement to follow directions and/or complete work.	Follows directions and is able to work independently in most areas.
4. Self-control	Demonstrates inappropriate behavior in the classroom and on the playground	Needs frequent reminders to follow school and classroom rules.	Independently follows school and classroom rules.

	Not Yet 1	Developing 3	Achieving 5
5. Social Interaction	Cannot solve social problems with peers without adult help.	Is developing more positive responses to peers.	Solves social problems with peers independently.
6. Responds to Oral Language	Unaware of what speaker is saying in a group setting. Responds to a word or two from the speaker but does not relate to general topic. Needs teacher assistance with 2-step directions.	Sometimes loses track of what is being said. Responds to speaker in a limited manner. Uses help in responding to 2-step directions.	Listens well in a group setting. Responds to speaker indicating understanding of topic. Understands and follows 2-step directions.
7. Concept of Print	*Such as:* Does not know what a letter or word or number is. Unaware that words convey the meaning. Cannot recognize own name.	*Such as:* Sometimes unclear about differences among letters, words, and numbers. Inconsistently tracks left to right.	Knows what letters, words, and numbers are. Knows that words convey the meaning. Tracks from left to right. Recognizes own name.
8. Concepts of Books and How They Work	*Such as:* Incorrectly uses book. Cannot locate words. Does not know where book begins or ends.	*Such as:* Shows inconsistent knowledge of how a book works.	*Such as:* Turns pages front to back. "Reads" from left to right, top to bottom. Can point to title and text.

Figure 17–2

Detailed Performance Criteria for Parents

Source: From "Success for All Kindergarten Students" (n.p.) by Department of Research, Ann Arbor Public Schools, 1993, Ann Arbor, MI: Author. Reprinted by permission of the publisher.

To produce these reports, teachers are trained to apply a complete set of performance criteria, such as those shown in Figure 17–3. These targets and performance criteria provide an excellent basis for communicating about student development at any point, or in terms of student growth over time. Note the various pieces that come together here: a set of expectations to guide communication, a message sender's version to facilitate encoding, a form for use in sending the message, and a message receiver's version to assist in interpreting the message. Both teachers and parents report more complete and satisfying conferences because they share this common frame of reference and thus have more specific material to discuss.

Time for Reflection

Based on what you have seen of this communication system, what do you anticipate would be its biggest limitations? Can you see any way(s) around the potential problems you identify?

Dealing with the Practicalities. As you consider this option, remember that Ann Arbor is succeeding with this project because the entire kindergarten team of teachers collaborated in developing the achievement targets, creating the performance rating system, and implementing the communication system. It represents the collective wisdom and teamwork of many experienced professionals. This kind of backing and commitment is required to make such a system work.

Another important key to successfully using this kind of communication system is that teachers *must* be trained to make dependable ratings of student performance. That training takes time and effort. Resources must be allocated to make it possible. However, to the extent that the teachers who are to use the system play a role in its development, training costs can be minimized.

This system provides a high level of detail about student achievement. Although users report that the performance criteria become second nature and easy to rate with practice and experience, we would be naive to think such records are easy to create and deliver at conference time. Because the report is detailed, communicating results can be time consuming.

Narrative Reporting Example: Elementary Communication

Another way to forge a stronger communication link between school and home is to use narrative descriptions of student learning. Rather than grades, to convey meaning, Catlin Gabel School in Portland, Oregon uses this method in its elementary and middle school. The philosophy that guides the evaluation system is effectively summarized in the school's policy statement:

We maintain that the student is the unit of consideration, and that our commitment is to create conditions within our school that serve to develop each student's fullest powers as an individual and as a group member. Further, we hold that any system of evaluation ought to:

1. enhance intrinsic motivation for learning.
2. help students take increasing responsibility for their own learning and be active partners in the learning process through continual self-evaluation.
3. serve as a means for direct, sensitive communication between the teacher and student and the teacher and family.
4. focus on the specific strengths and weaknesses of individual students and provide prescriptive as well as descriptive information. (Catlin Gabel School, n.d., p. 18)

This philosophy, as the following illustrates, is intrinsic to the way Catlin Gabel staff communicate about student achievement with parents:

> The [elementary school faculty] chooses to write narrative reports rather than issue letter grades because it enables faculty to convey specific information about a child's strengths, weaknesses, progress and problems, as well as suggest strategies for improvement and enhancement. In addition, it provides a vehicle to impart information about a child's motivation, attitudes toward learning, special interests, socialization skills, and emotional tone. The written evaluation also allows the teacher to describe facets of an individual's intellectual and emotional development and compare children to themselves rather than to their peers. Finally, it provides content for conferences, which promotes dialogue between home and school and contributes to the sense of partnership that we seek to develop between student and teacher. (Catlin Gabel School, n.d., p. 28)

The nature and quality of the communication that results is clearly seen in the sample Catlin Gabel narrative report presented in Figure 17–4, a description of a hypothetical fourth-grade student.

This carefully crafted description reflects a clear vision of achievement, clear criteria and standards, and a vivid sense of how this student relates to those expectations. This report demonstrates how we can use written descriptions and samples of student work, in addition to grades and scores, to communicate about student achievement.

However, the potential value of narrative reporting doesn't stop here. While I find few teachers doing it, we also can deliver very engaging and highly motivating narratives to our students. Figure 17–5 illustrates.

Time for Reflection

What are some of the potential limitations of written narrative description? As you identify problems, see if you can identify possible remedies.

Dealing with the Practicalities.   The major drawback of these kinds of reports, obviously, is the time required to prepare them. High student-teacher ratios may

1. Responsibility for Own Learning.

Not Yet	Developing	Achieving
Such as:	*Such as:*	*Such as:*
Shows little interest in classroom activities.	Participates with teacher motivation and/or direction.	Shows interest in and is involved in classroom activities.
Cannot complete task without one-to-one assistance.	Needs occasional help or reinforcement in order to complete task.	Completes task independently, seeking help only when necessary.

2. Positive Self-esteem.

Not Yet	Developing	Achieving
Such as:	*Such as:*	*Such as:*
Demonstrates a negative attitude/behavior toward self and others:	Needs continued support to develop positive relationships with self and others.	Communicates a positive attitude toward self and others.
• makes such statements as: *"Nobody likes me," "I can't do this."*	Occasionally uses negative language and behavior.	Is proud of own accomplishments, (e.g., *"I can do this," "I like this"*).
• uses put-downs,	Increasing willingness to try new things.	Willing to try new things.
• is aggressive.	Is learning to accept mistakes as part of the learning process.	Accepts mistakes as part of the learning process rather than blaming self for the problem.
May appear to		Shows confidence in self when approaching hard tasks.
• resist new things,		
• be withdrawn,		
• have poor eye contact,		
• have unexpressive facial expression,		
• be unresponsive		

3. Response to Teacher-directed Activities.

Not Yet	Developing	Achieving
Such as:	*Such as:*	*Such as:*
Complains during teacher-directed activity.	Needs extra support to follow directions and/or complete work.	Willingly participates in teacher-directed activities.
Ignores teacher.	Responds reluctantly when given instructions.	Pays attention during class discussions.
Is easily distracted.	Occasionally pays attention.	Makes connections with concepts being taught.
Is often not on task during learning activity times.	Often needs reminders.	Attends to tasks independently.
Has trouble going from one activity to another.	Moves from one activity to another with teacher giving advanced warning.	Completes learning activities.
		Asks and answers questions.
		Follows directions; moves easily from one activity to another.

4. Self-control

Not Yet	Developing	Achieving
Such as:	*Such as:*	*Such as:*
Does not follow school and classroom rules.	Needs to be reminded to follow school and classroom rules.	Independently follows school/classroom rules.
Inappropriate use of materials and equipment.	Frequent reminders to use equipment and materials appropriately.	Uses equipment and materials appropriately.
Does not clean up after self.	Often reminded to clean up after self.	Assists others with correct use of materials and equipment.
Has tantrums, cries easily, strikes out at others when frustrated.	Beginning to deal with frustrations.	Independently cleans up after self.
Demonstrates inappropriate behavior during "circle" time:	Occasionally demonstrates inappropriate behavior during "circle" time.	Deals with frustrations in appropriate ways:
• talking,	Needs several reminders to change inappropriate behavior.	• uses language,
• playing with objects,		• seeks help when needed,
• daydreaming,		• sets reasonable limits for self.
• constant movement.		Listens attentively during "circle" time.
Needs many reminders to change inappropriate behavior.		Responds positively when reminded of inappropriate behavior.

Figure 17–3

Detailed Performance Criteria for Parents

Source: From "Success for All Kindergarten Students" (n.p.) by Department of Research, Ann Arbor Public Schools, 1993, Ann Arbor, MI: Author. Reprinted by permission of the publisher.

ABC Lower School
June, 1990
Fourth Grade
Teacher's Name

Joan Student

Joan is determination and strength presented in a lively package. This strong-willed student has contributed much to her peers in her fourth-grade year. From her they have learned the importance of fighting for one's point of view. Joan is never wanting for an opinion on any subject. It is easy for her to express her viewpoint. On occasion she takes the opposite point of view solely for the pleasure of differing from the group consensus. Where she has made considerable growth this year is in her willingness to consider the ideas of others. She has learned to back away from a stance when she sees that it is unreasonable or in error. This has helped Joan progress academically because she has become more open to the learning process—the give and take of ideas. Joan is a motivated and independent student who cares deeply that the work she pursues is meaningful. She has grown in her ability to engage fully in an assignment, and has learned that revising an idea only enhances its content.

"I am the Emperor's garden/With a plum tree by my side/The blossoms bloom in the sunlight/while the fragrance is carried by a gentle breeze . . . " Joan has the soul of a poet. She creates strong, vivid images of lovers willing to die for their love, souls tortured by war or gentle gardens peaceful in the sunlight. She allows whole worlds to come alive with her writing. As the year has progressed she has learned how to return to her writing and flesh out her images to make them even more dramatic. Joan has shown great tenaciousness in her willingness to revise a piece, searching for the exact words to make the images strong. She is developing the writer's gift of seeing detail, recognizing its significance, and then understanding how to weave all that she envisions into a finely crafted piece of writing.

Joan has broadened her vocabulary and added many new concepts and words to her knowledge base. This has helped her comprehension improve as the year has progressed. She has taken on increasingly difficult books and relishes the specific details. Joan prefers to read books that are challenging in their content and posses valuable issues with which to grapple. However, she still struggles with jumping to conclusions on first glance of a passage. It is the subtler levels of comprehension that still present her with a challenge. If her interpretation of the information is incorrect, as it sometimes is, she finds it difficult to backtrack and clarify her ideas. The format of reading group,

Figure 17–4
Sample Student Report
Source: From "Sample Student Report" (n.p.) by Catlin Gabel School, 1990, Portland, OR: Author.
Copyright 1990 by Catlin Gabel School. Reprinted by permission.

render this option impractical for many teachers. However, if the narrative is intended for delivery to parents, how about if students and teachers work as partners to compose the letter? Shared work resulting in positive achievement for the student, shared planning and preparation of the narrative to assist the teacher, open and effective student-involved communication for families, and shared credit for doing a good job! Sounds like a win-win-win situation.

In addition, as always, we must center the narrative message on the relevant achievement targets. We must take care to transform those targets into rigorous where the content of a book is carefully analyzed, has helped her to see when she needs to readjust her ideas. There were many incidents where Joan discovered that what she thought was occurring was in error. The growth has occurred in her willingness to accept this and go back to the book to discover where she made the misinterpretation. She needs continued encouragement to ask herself if what she is interpreting from the reading makes sense with what she knows of the details of the book. It would help her to continue reading over the summer with the opportunity to discuss with an adult the content of the books. It would be helpful if she could even take a reading course over the summer.

It was a challenge for Joan to work cooperatively on the Japanese research. Being paired with another strong-willed student gave her both frustration and rewards. Together they explored the topic of Kabuki theater, and they designed a well organized presentation that thoroughly covered the topic. Joan was a very captivated audience during our Japanese unit. She found every experience fascinating and worked hard to glean as much from the study as she could. She was very observant during the Seattle trip, making connections whenever possible. Her determination and passion for knowledge brought her many insights into the culture of the Japanese.

Joan has a solid understanding of the whole-number operations, has mastered multidigit multiplication and long division with remainders. She has secured most of her multiplication tables and she has become quick and proficient at solving mental math problems. As she has grown in her ability to sustain academic effort, Joan has brought perseverance to story problems. She is more likely to struggle with a problem, try a variety of strategies and adjust until she finds the tactic that works. She has added many problem solving techniques to her repertoire. Joan has a good conceptual understanding of fractions and decimals. She has built for herself a fine foundation from which to learn and grow mathematically.

Joan has many successes to celebrate this year. Not all have come easily but her willingness to grow has brought her great satisfaction as a learner. She is a serious student who cares about the quality of her work. She is conscientious about deadlines. Not only has her academic understanding broadened but her social world has expanded. No longer is she on the fringes trying to find an entry into the group. She is a fully vested member of a wide social network with many friends from which to choose. She has come a long way in her fourth-grade year.

Joan, we will miss your determination and voice next year. We hope you have an adventure-filled summer that includes special times with family and friends. Please come next door and check in often so we can keep track of your continued progress.

assessments and write about specific achievement results. In other words, we must maintain a clear focus on achievement. To use this option productively, users must regard these reports as far more than "free writing time," when they can say whatever comes to mind about the student. The issue in narrative reports is, What does it mean to be academically successful, and how did this student do in relation to those expectations?

The only way this kind of communication can become practical for a teacher is with careful planning and record keeping. At the time of the writing, all relevant

October 17

Dear Sarah,

The beginning of the year is a time to get to know each other, find out what you know and find the best way that I can aid your learning. For that reason, I've done lots of watching. The thing that struck me most about you is that you are a reader. You read every single minute you aren't doing something else. Today I watched you read during lunch. You were so intent in the story, you hardly noticed what you were eating. You also smoothly read out loud with much expression. You read many kinds of materials, from fairy tales, picture books to long novels like *Maniac McGee*. Your writing reflects your reading ability. Your text flows smoothly from one idea to the next. Tied into all of this are your art ideas. The pictures from *Peppermint in the Parlor* and *Princess Bride* show that you can listen and create pictures from what you hear.

I love it when you share your ideas in class. You always add much to the discussion. You are a strong performer. During our musical performance last week, you knew all your lines and followed stage directions well. I could tell that you have been in front of an audience before. You had the same quality of work when you were one of the presidential candidates. You knew your platform and your issues.

Your work shows that you are a disciplined student. You always know your poem and it's evident that you studied for the several tests we've had. You think through problems. An example of this is gathering and organizing data and creating a highly readable graph. I know that along with breaking some school records, you go to gymnastics three times a week.

You are a good strong student. I'm really proud of all that you have learned this quarter.

Love,

Mrs A

Figure 17–5
Sample Narrative Report in the Form of a Letter to a Sixth Grader
Source: Reprinted from *Changing the View: Student-led Parent Conferences* (p. 55) by T. Austin. Copyright in 1994 by Heinemann, Portsmouth, NH. Reprinted by permission of the publisher.

information to be factored into the report must be readily available. The framework for the report must be completely spelled out. And to the extent possible, modern information processing technology should be brought to bear. For example, you might develop a template for narrative reporting on your personal computer. Within this general outline, then, you might merely need to enter essential details.

Remember, however, that narrative reporting places a premium on being able to write well. Teachers or students who have difficulty communicating in writing will find a narrative system frustrating to use and will not use it well. Obviously, the sample report shown in Figure 17–4 is very well written. If you feel that you might need help improving your own writing skills for purposes of preparing these reports, I recommend Spandel and Stiggins (1996), *Creating Writers: Linking Assessments and Writing Instruction, 2nd ed.* While this book is intended primarily for teachers who teach writing, it assumes that teachers who are themselves proficient writers will do the job better than those who are not. If you study the parts of the book that define the basic elements of good writing and learn to apply them, your narratives will work just fine. In addition, you will learn some valuable lessons about good writing to share with your students, regardless of the grade or subject(s) you teach.

Continuous Progress Reporting Example: Communication Through the School Years

Teachers in Victoria, Australia have devised yet another kind of reporting scheme that develops a continuous record of student progress through a series of specifically defined and progressively linked targets (Ministry of Education and Training, 1991). They call these records *profiles* and describe them as follows:

> Profiles are a means of reporting on a student's progress and achievement in key areas of learning. Profiles consist of a series of short descriptive statements, called indicators, arranged in nine levels of achievement called bands. These describe, in order of difficulty, significant skills and knowledge that students must learn to become proficient. A student's progress can be charted over these bands. English Profiles show student progress and achievement in the key areas of reading, writing and spoken language. (p. 7)

The spoken language bands are identified in Figure 17–6, from A at the beginning to I on the high-performance end. In addition, Figure 17–7 illustrates one kind of parental reporting form used, focusing on spoken language band C. Note that it highlights the band the student is working on at the time of reporting, and includes prior and following proficiencies for context. Teachers enter brief comments for the record regarding student progress and achievement.

Time for Reflection

What seem to you to be the strengths of this system compared to the two preceding ones? What apparent limitations do you identify? Can you suggest specific remedies for potential problems?

Dealing with the Practicalities.   This kind of reporting overcomes some, but not all, of the shortcomings of the systems described previously. First, it minimizes the amount of narrative the teacher must enter. This saves time. Second, it reduces the range of achievement targets and levels over which the teacher must comment, focusing on the particular forms of achievement on which the student is working. This, too, saves time. Third, a concrete record of progress is generated, with cumulative reports of bands of achievement. This helps with interpretation. Fourth, this is quite a comprehensive and carefully articulated communication system, with the span of achievement covered ranging from elementary levels through high school. This makes the system valuable in contexts where students are expected to make continuous progress in acquiring an interlaced series of outcomes across grade levels.

But there remains the challenge of defining, sharing, and being able to dependably assess the various levels of achievement reflected in the bands. These will take

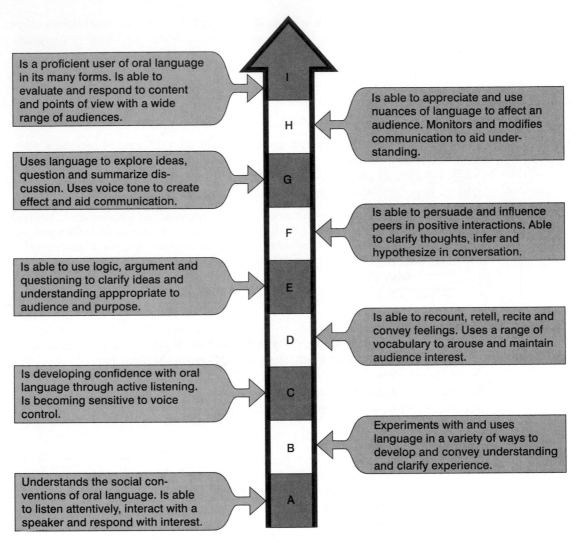

Figure 17–6

The Spoken Language Bands

Source: From *English Profiles Handbook* (n.p.) by the Schools Program Division, Ministry of Education and Training, Victoria, Australia, 1991. Reprinted by permission of the publisher.

considerable investment. Their development and implementation across the curriculum requires that teachers meet across grade levels from primary grades through high school to articulate a continuous progress curriculum—that is, to divide up responsibility for helping students make smooth transitions through the various levels of proficiency. Given our historic lack of communication across classrooms within the same building, let alone across grade levels, opening channels of communication across *both* grades and buildings will test our resolve.

But imagine the nature and quality of the open, inclusive, student-involved communication environment we could achieve with such bands in place and with

ENGLISH PROFILE—SPOKEN LANGUAGE

School _____   Class_____

Name_____
                                                                Teacher's Assessment
Language Spoken At Home _____   Contexts And Comments   Date

SPOKEN LANGUAGE BAND B

Use of Oral Language
Makes short announcements clearly. Tells personal anecdotes
in discussion. Retells a story heard in class, preserving the
sequence of events. Accurately conveys a verbal message to
another person. Responds with facial expressions. Responds
with talk when others initiate conversation. Initiates conversation
with peers. Holds conversation with familiar adults. Asks what
unfamiliar words mean. Uses talk to clarify ideas or experience.

Features of Oral Language
Reacts (smiles, laughs, etc.) to absurd word substitutions.
Demonstrates an appreciation of wit. Reacts (smiles, laughs)
to unusual features of language (such as rhythm, alliteration
or onomatopoeia).

SPOKEN LANGUAGE BAND C

Use of Oral Language
Makes verbal commentary during play or other activities with
concrete objects.

Speaks confidently in formal situations (e.g., assembly, report to
the class).

Explains ideas clearly in discussion.

Discusses information heard (e.g., dialogue, news item, report).

Based on consideration of what has already been said, offers
personal opinions.

Asks for repetition, restatement, or general explanation to clarify
meaning.

Features of Oral Language
Sequences a presentation in a logical order.

Gives instructions in a concise and understandable manner.

Reads aloud with expression, showing awareness of rhythm
and tone.

Modulates voice for effect.

Nods, looks at speaker when others initiate talk.

Figure 17–7
English Profile—Spoken Language
Source: From *English Profiles Handbook* (n.p.) by the Schools Program Division, Ministry of Educa-
tion and Training, Victoria, Australia, 1991. Reprinted by permission of the publisher.

SPOKEN LANGUAGE BAND D

Use of Oral Language
Tells personal anecdote, illustrating in a relevant way the issue being discussed. Recounts a story or repeats a song sponta-neously. Retells scenes from film or drama. Offers predictions about what will come next. Recites poems. Asks questions in conversation. Has a second try at something to make it more precise. Arouses and maintains audience interest during formal presentations (e.g., report to class, announcements).

Features of Oral Language
Uses range of vocabulary related to a particular topic. Maintains receptive body stance in conversation. Speaks in a way that conveys feelings (while keeping emotions under control).

OTHER INDICATIONS

Figure 17–7, *continued*

everyone able to accurately assess student progress through them. Imagine the power of a portfolio system (including extensive use of student self-reflection on their improvement as achievers) when used in conjunction with such a continuous progress curriculum. And finally, imagine the learning power brought to bear if the student is the primary record keeper.

Conference Formats That Enhance Communication

In addition to these expanded modes of written communication, we can also open new vistas in communicating about student achievement if we begin to make exten-sive use of three practical conferencing strategies: focused student-teacher confer-ences, traditional parent-teacher conferences, and student-led parent conferences.

In the first case, teacher and student share a common vision and definition of academic success that allows them to share focused discussions of the student's progress. Some teachers are using these strategies to transform their classrooms into workshop settings. We'll look inside such a classroom here.

The second case brings parent and teacher together to share information on student achievement. While this kind of conference has long been a standard part of schooling, we'll put some new spins on the idea to bring the student into the process.

The third case—student-led parent conferences—in effect, takes advantage of the benefits of both of the other strategies, adding some special pluses of its own. Further, it overcomes many of their weaknesses, although it brings its own challenges. With this approach, as we learned from Terri Austin at the beginning of the chapter, the primary responsibility for communicating about expectations and progress shifts from teacher to student. We'll explore some practical guidelines for using this option, review benefits to students and parents, and share some reactions from users.

Student-Teacher Conferences

A classroom learning environment turns into a workshop when the teacher shares the vision of achievement with students and then sets them to work individually or in groups in pursuit of the designated target. In this setting, the teacher becomes a consultant or coach, working one-on-one or in groups to improve students' performance. This permits a kind of individualization that works very well when students are at different levels of achievement, such as in the development of their math or writing proficiencies. Much of the communication between teacher and student occurs in conference—one-on-one between teacher and student.

According to experienced writing instructor Vicki Spandel, who uses this idea in writing instruction, a conference is both an excellent means of communicating achievement information to students and an effective teaching device (Spandel & Stiggins, 1990). Conferences give students personal attention. Besides, the students who are reticent to speak out in class often will come forth in conference. As a result, that two-way communication so essential to effective instruction can take place. And finally, according to Spandel, the conference provides an excellent context in which to provide specific feedback. Teachers can provide commentary on student performance and students can describe what is and is not working for them.

To understand the kind of dialogue that can emerge from this idea, read the example of student writing provided in Figure 17–8. A conference is about to take place between teacher and student focusing on this work. Ed, the teacher, has been holding conferences with his students since the beginning of the school year. It is now January. He tries to confer with each student every 2 to 3 weeks, and, though it takes a fair amount of time, he feels that the payoff is worth it. The dynamics of the conferences are changing a bit. In the beginning, the teacher had to ask lots of questions. Now, students usually come to a conference with things to say.

Jill, the student, has never been an exceptional writer. Until recently, she didn't like to write and wrote only when forced. She didn't like talking about her writing, and her most frequent comment was, "I can't write."

At first, she didn't want to speak about her writing. The last two conferences, however, have been somewhat different. Jill is beginning to open up. She is writing

My Dog

Everyone has something important in their lives and the most important thing to me, up to now, has been my dog. His name was Rafe. My brother found him in an old barn where we were camping in a field near my grandpa's house. Somebody had left him there and he was very weak and close to being dead. But we nursed him back to health and my mom said we could keep him, at least for a while. That turned out to be for ten years.

Rafe was black and brown and had a long tail, floppy ears, and a short, fat face. He wasn't any special breed of dog. Most people probably wouldn't of thought he was that good looking but to us he was very special.

Rafe kept us amused a lot with funny tricks. He would hide in the shadows and try to spook the chickens but they figured out he was just bluffing so he had to give up on that one. When Rafe got hit by a truck I thought I would never stop crying. My brother misses him too, and my mom, but no one could miss him as much as I do.

Figure 17–8

A Sample of Jill's Writing

Source: Adapted from *Creating Writers: Linking Assessment and Writing Instruction* (p. 105) by V. Spandel and R. J. Stiggins, 1990, White Plains, NY: Addison-Wesley Longman. Copyright 1990 by Longman Publishing Group. Reprinted by permission of the publisher.

more on her own. She keeps a journal. She is still, however, reluctant to voice opinions about her own writing; she looks to her teacher for a lead. In the dialogue shown in Figure 17–8, they are talking together about a paper Jill wrote about her dog, Rafe.

"Pretty terrible, huh?" she asks him.

"What do you think of it?" he asks, tossing the question back to her. She doesn't answer right away, but Ed doesn't break the silence. The seconds tick by. Ed waits.

"I don't like the ending," Jill volunteers at last.

"Tell me why."

"Well, it just stops. The whole thing just doesn't tell how I really feel."

"How do you feel?"

She thinks for a minute. "Oh, it isn't like I miss him all the time. Some days I don't think about him at all. But then—well, it's like I'll see him at the door, or I'll see this shadow dashing around the side of the barn. Sometimes when we cook out, I think about him because he used to steal hotdogs off the grill, and one time my dad yelled at him when he did that and he slipped and burned one of his feet real bad."

"Now there's the real Jill and Rafe story beginning to come out! You're telling me about Rafe in your real personal voice and I sense some of your feelings. When you wrote about Rafe, did you speak like that? Let's read part of your writing again."

After doing so, Jill comments, "Pretty blah, not much me!"

"If you did write like you were speaking, how do you think it might read?"

"Like a story, I guess."

"Try it and let's see what happens. Talk to me about Rafe in your own personal voice. Besides, stealing hotdogs off the grill conjures up a funny picture—doesn't it? Those are the kinds of mental pictures great stories tell. When I can picture what you're saying, that's ideas. You're giving the story some imagery and focus that I like very much. What kind of imagery do you see in this writing?"

They scan the piece again. Jill says in a low voice, "No images here—just facts."

"How about if you think up and write about some of those personal things you remember about Rafe?"

"Do you think I should?"

"Well, when you were talking, I had a much better sense of you in the story—of how much you missed your dog and how you thought about him."

"I think I could write about some of those things."

"How about if you give it a try, and we'll talk again in about a week?"

"How about the spelling, punctuation, and sentences? Were those okay?" Jill asks.

"Let's leave that 'til later. Think about the ideas, the organization, the voice. We'll come back to the other."

"I don't want any mistakes, though," she confesses.

"But is this the right time to worry about that?"

"I don't know; I just don't want to get a bad grade."

"Okay," Ed nods. "Suppose we agree that for now, we'll just assess the three traits I mentioned: ideas, organization, and voice."

"That's all?"

Ed nods again. "And if you decide you want to publish this paper in the school magazine . . . "

"We can fix the other stuff, right?"

"You will have time to fix it, yes."

Time for Reflection

In your opinion, what are the keys to making conferences like this work? What are some of the barriers to effective conferences? How might you remove these barriers?

Dealing with the Practicalities.   Those who have turned classrooms into workshops tell us that conferences need not be long. A great deal of information can be communicated in just a few minutes. However, thoughtful preparation is essential. It is best if both students and teacher examine student work beforehand with performance criteria in mind and prepare focused commentary.

Good listening is essential. If you prepare a few thoughtful questions in advance, you can draw insight out of students, triggering their own self-reflection. Effective conferences don't rely on the traditional one-way mode of communication. Rather, they work best when teachers share both the control of the meeting and the responsibility for directing the communication.

Over time, and with experience in conferences, it will become easier to open the dialogue because both you and your students will become more at ease with each other. Over time, students also will become more familiar with your expectations and they will develop both the conceptual frameworks and vocabulary needed to communicate efficiently with you about their progress. So begin with modest expectations and let the process grow.

Parent-Teacher Conferences

We would be remiss if we failed to insert the traditional parent-teacher conference into our discussion of effective ways to communicate. As students, we tended to be the "odd person out" of these meetings—often left wondering what was really said about us. And any experienced teacher has been on the other side of the desk too, obviously knowing what was said, but wondering if we said the right things and if we were understood. We can deliver quality messages with this option, however, if we lay down a strong foundation.

Analyzing the Benefits.   Parent-teacher conferences offer three specific advantages over report card grades as means of communication. They permit us to do the following:

1. Retain and share a sufficiently high level of detail to provide a rich picture of student achievement. In effect, they provide a personal way to share the checklists, rating scales, and narratives discussed previously.

2. Ask follow-up questions to determine if we have succeeded in communicating. We can provide additional detail and explanation as needed to be sure the message gets through. Parents can ask questions to eliminate uncertainty.

3. Plan jointly with families to blend school and home learning environments for maximum productivity. In some cases, that means we can find out what may be going wrong with a student's home environment and urge adjustments in that environment.

But these advantages should not lead us necessarily to infer that conferences should replace report cards or any other record-keeping or communication option. Rather, we can use our various communication options in combination—with part of our conference time being used to explain grades, checklists, ratings, or other symbols, for example.

Anticipating the Challenges.   Of course, challenge number one is time. Parent-teacher conferences take a great deal of time to prepare for and to conduct. Every family must get its share of one-on-one time with you. For junior high and high school teachers working with large numbers of students, again, this option may not be feasible.

Challenge number two is that of devising a jargon-free, family-friendly vocabulary and interpersonal manner to use in describing student achievement to parents. If we pile on a great deal of technical language delivered in an aggressive style, we will have difficulty connecting.

Challenge number three is encouraging parental participation in the conferences. Some families care more about their children than do others. Some have busy lives, and competing priorities always seem to win. Some parents feel vulnerable in parent-teacher conferences, especially if things aren't going well in school for their child. There is always the chance in their minds that you might accuse them of failing to support your teaching efforts. Even though *you* know you would never do that, they don't know it for sure.

Challenge number four is helping students to come through conference time with academic self-concepts intact. This can be risky stuff for our students. If they're left wondering what was really said about them—as they usually are—the effect can be uncertainty, frustration, and even anger. At the very least they will be left with the impression that they aren't important enough in this communication equation to warrant a role.

For any one or all of these reasons, if we use parent-teacher conferences as our means of message delivery, we can be in danger of failing to communicate effectively with students and with some families.

Dealing with the Practicalities.   We can meet these challenges and take maximum advantage of this conference format if we follow some simple, straightforward procedures:

STEP 1   Establish a clear and complete set of achievement expectations.

STEP 2   Transform those expectations into quality assessments and gather accurate information.

STEP 3   Carefully summarize that information for sharing—via grades, checklists, rating scales, narrative, portfolios, or test scores.

STEP 4   Conduct a *student-teacher* conference to review all of this material before conducting the parent-teacher conference. This permits the student to understand the message delivered. In fact, imagine a classroom in which this step was unnecessary because steps 1 to 3 were carried out in a student-centered manner, with targets clarified and shared, students involved deeply in the accumulation of achievement evidence, and students as partners in developing the portfolio that will be the topic of discussion at the parent-teacher conference. The motivational and achievement benefits of such a partnership might be considerable.

STEP 5   Schedule and conduct the parent-teacher conference. By the way, imagine the kind of ongoing communication link that we might forge with parents if we had our continuous progression of achievement targets organized into bands like the previous Australian illustration. We'd have concrete ways to show parents both how their child is doing with respect to our expectations and, if necessary, in relation to other students of like age or grade.

STEP 6   Ask for a written follow-up reflection from parents presenting their impressions of the achievement and progress of their child.

Student-led Parent Conferences

Of all the communication possibilities available to us, the one that excites me the most places the student at the heart of the communication process itself: student-led parent conferences. Notice immediately that I did not label this "student-involved parent-teacher conferences." I used the label "student-led" to emphasize the need to hold students accountable for telling at least some of their own achievement story.

Be advised that this is a more complex communication option than either of the other two conference types. However, the payoff for the added work can be impressive, to say the least.

Exploring the Benefits.   Among the positive effects reported by teachers who use this idea are the following:

1. *A much stronger sense of responsibility for their own learning among students.* When our students understand that, down the road, they (not you) will be telling their own success (or lack of success) story, they realize that there is no escaping accountability. They realize very quickly that, if they have nothing to share at that meeting by way of success, they are going to be very uncomfortable. This can be a strong motivator. And once they have some positive experience with this process and develop confidence in themselves, they become even more motivated to do well at it.

2. *A much stronger sense of pride within students* when they do have a success story to share at conference time. It feels good to be in charge of a meeting in which you're the star of a winning team.

3. *A different and more productive relationship between students and their teachers.* When that conference takes place, if that student has nothing by way of success to share, the student won't be the only one who will be somewhat embarrassed. In this sense, students and teachers become partners in the face of a common challenge. Both need to succeed—together. This can be very beneficial to student achievement.

4. *Improved student-parent relationships.* Many families report that their conversations about student achievement extend far beyond the conference itself—sometimes weeks beyond. Often what emerges from the meeting is a sense of mutual interest in student projects, along with a shared language that permits ongoing interaction. School-family partnerships can flourish under these circumstances.

5. *An active, involved classroom environment built on a strong sense of community.* Students take pride not only in their own accomplishments and their ability to share them, but also in the opportunity to help each other prepare for and succeed at their conferences. A team spirit—a sense of community—can emerge and this can benefit the motivation and achievement of all.

6. *A reduction in relevance or value of cheating.* Not only is it difficult to misrepresent one's achievement when concrete evidence will be presented at the conference, but also, students seem less interested in cheating (as mentioned in Chapter 16). What can emerge is a greater sense of honor and honesty related to their heightened sense of responsibility for and pride in actually achieving.

7. *The development of important leadership skills.* Coordinating and conducting a student-led parent conference requires that the student schedule the meeting, invite participants, handle the introductions, organize and present information to the group, and follow up to discern meeting results. These are important life skills.

8. *Greater parental participation in conferences.* Many schools report that a far higher percentage of parents show up to be part of conferences when students are the leaders. You can probably anticipate why this might be the case. If you are a parent, which invitation is more likely to bring you to a meeting: a mimeographed note from your child's teacher with a date and time filled in stuck to the refrigerator, or your child standing in front of you looking up with those eyes reminding you that the conference is tomorrow and she will be in charge and "You're going to be there, right?"

Further, parents who experience difficulty themselves in school and for whom things may not be going well sometimes think that you might accuse them of being a bad parent if they come to a parent-teacher conference. That can be reason enough to avoid the meeting. When their child is to lead the meeting, this risk seems to be reduced in their minds.

Facing the Challenges.   At the same time, this idea of student-led conferences is not without its downside risks. For example, it's not easy for some teachers to share control with students. This requires a kind of trust teachers typically don't grant to their students. When we give up control in this way, we cannot always be absolutely sure what will happen. If difficulties arise, they arise in a fishbowl and some pretty important people will see them. That's scary.

Further, it should be clear that the presentation of student-led conferences is just the tip of a pretty big iceberg. You buy the whole environment or none of it. This is a hollow communication concept if it is not founded in a student-centered classroom environment. We cannot simply plug in student-led parent conferences in a traditional teacher-centered assessment environment, where students have little idea what the expectations are or how they are doing with respect to those targets. I recently spoke with a parent who's third-grade daughter "got caught" between two adults talking about her. The child was scared before and during the event, according to her mom. She had no idea what was happening, was given no responsibility during the meeting, and had a completely negative experience. This was a good idea badly implemented and one mother was left very cold about the whole idea. We must set students up to succeed at the conferences over the long haul or such conferences are not worth conducting. But from the teacher's perspective, it can be very scary to contemplate such far-reaching changes.

A corollary challenge is finding the time to prepare for and manage such conferences. Most teachers plan for at least 30-minute conferences. This is especially difficult for junior high or high school teachers, who might face 150 students a day. First, be careful about how you think about time used in this context. There is a strong tendency to think of it as time lost to instruction. Nothing could be further from the truth. The time spent preparing to confer turns into highly focused teaching and learning time.

Beyond this, we need to creatively manage the logistics of conferencing. Many teachers report that they can have students conducting several conferences at one time, once those students have experience running conferences. In addition, high school teachers I know limit conferences to one or two courses per grading period, thus spreading them across the year. In fact, one teacher I know asks that conferences last at least one hour, with only the first 30 minutes taking place in the classroom. The remainder is to take place at home, and students are responsible for reporting back in writing about how the rest of the conference went. To a person, her students report that conferences stretched far beyond the required hour.

But perhaps the most difficult challenges faced by those who would place students in charge of these conferences arise when the student comes from a dysfunctional family. The easiest version of this problem occurs when parents simply fail to show up. More difficult versions have parents showing up and being abusive in any of a number of ways.

Time for Reflection

How might we maximize the chances that parents will show up by actions we and our students take during the planning stages of the conference? Further, if parents or other invited guests fail to arrive for the conference, how might we handle this in a manner that keeps the student's ego intact? Think about this for a moment before reading on.

Some teachers I know cover the very rare occurrence of parents failing to show up by having a backup "listener" available on conference day. It might be a former teacher, the principal, a janitor, or someone from the cafeteria staff. The only requirement is that the listener be someone whose opinion of him or her the student cares about. When this condition is satisfied, the student can present enthusiastically and take pride in her or his achievements. It's okay to reschedule too, if the listener scheduled cannot make it.

Keys to Success.   We overcome these challenges only by attending to some simple fundamental conditions. To make this idea work, we need the following:

- students who care enough and are risk takers enough to be willing to evaluate their own learning in front of their parents
- teachers who are willing to take the risk of stepping aside and letting their students take charge, just as a coach helps the players learn the game and then places them on the field or court to play the game themselves
- achievement targets that have been clearly and completely defined, woven into instruction, and used as the basis for an open communication system
- both teacher and students who share a common language for talking about attainment of each important target
- students who have had time to learn about, to prepare for, and to practice their leadership roles

When these conditions are satisfied and students take the lead in evaluating their learning, many good things occur. For example, because student and teacher must work closely together to prepare for the conference, it builds a greater amount of individual attention into the instructional process. This gives students a greater sense of their own importance in the classroom.

Time spent planning and preparing for student-led parent conferences becomes high-quality teaching and learning time. Students work to understand the vision of success, master the language needed to communicate about it, learn to describe their achievements, and evaluate their own strengths and weaknesses. Is this not the essence of a productive learning environment? Besides, as they prepare for the meeting, students might organize demonstrations, set up exhibitions, and/or develop other documentary evidence of success. It is difficult to envision more engaging student learning experiences.

A great deal of positive motivation can result—for all conference participants. As students and teachers prepare, the meaning of success becomes increasingly clear. Clearly defined goals are easier to attain. As evidence of success is compiled, a sense of being in control can emerge for students, spurring them to greater heights—especially in the hope that they might be able to achieve those last-minute gains that will impress their parents even more. Parents acquire new understanding of their children, and of the teacher. In short, the stakes change for students, and so does their opportunity to succeed.

Dealing with the Practicalities.   Here are the steps in the student-led parent conference process:

STEP 1   Establish the relevant achievement targets, be sure all students and parents are aware of them, and plan instruction around their achievement.

STEP 2   Convert those expectations into quality assessments and use those assessments to help students build portfolios of quality evidence of their own achievement. Note that these can be either growth or status report portfolios, depending on your wishes.

STEP 3   While the evidence is building, keep the channels of communication open with the student's family. This might involve the use of a "take-home" portfolio or a take-home journal that students use to keep their parents informed of progress during instruction. Ask parents to respond to you in writing about their impressions of progress or about any concerns they may have.

STEP 4   As conference time approaches, convene a student-teacher conference to assemble the conference portfolio. Work as a team to select the material needed to tell the desired story.

STEP 5   Model a student-led conference for your students. Role-play a good one and a bad one, so they can see what make them work well. Be absolutely sure students know their role (as leader), your role (as coach), and their parents' role (as interested listeners and questioners). Be sure your students understand that we strive for a natural conversation among conferees—an interaction about accomplishments that includes examples, questions, answers, and sharing.

You might consider engaging your students in the collaborative process of developing performance criteria for a good conference. Remember the chapters on performance assessment design? We started by brainstorming critical elements, then we clustered them into major categories and labeled and defined the categories. Next we analyzed and compared cases of vastly different quality to devise rating scales or checklists to capture the essential differences between the two. Your students can build such criteria for good student-led conferences.

STEP 6   Provide opportunities for students to practice their conference presentations in teams using the above-mentioned performance criteria to provide feedback and offer suggestions for improvement.

STEP 7   Establish the time period during which the conferences are to take place. Permit students to select their own specific presentation time—again, not less than 30 minutes. Make them responsible for inviting participants, and for following up the invitation to be sure all are informed.

STEP 8   When the event happens, be sure students welcome all participants, handle introductions, review the objectives of the meeting, coordinate meeting events, handle follow-up communications, and summarize results. If we have prepared carefully, conferences should unfold productively with few surprises.

STEP 9   Offer parents an opportunity for a one-on-one meeting with you, the teacher, if they wish—just in case there are any personal, family, or risky issues that need attention. The vast majority of parents will decline, but it is good to offer. Incidentally, one teacher I know frames the conference this way: It will last 30 minutes, with the student leading the first 20 minutes. The final 10 minutes is intended for teacher and parents alone, unless the parents invite the student to remain. Almost all do.

STEP 10   Solicit a follow-up written review from parents. You might develop a simple reaction questionnaire that allows parents to participate in planning their child's future goals. Students can take responsibility for collecting this feedback and can be partners in its interpretation and use.

STEP 11   Debrief your students on the entire experience. Discuss it as a group or have students evaluate the experience by writing about it. What facets worked and what needs improvement? Be sure you and they learn the important lessons this process teaches both about academics and students' personal reactions.

At the time of this writing, virtually every teacher I have spoken with across the country who has carefully prepared for and conducted student-led parent conferences has found it to be a compellingly positive experience. Figure 17–9 shares the thoughts of two sixth-grade teachers (Arnold & Stricklin, 1993, personal communication) on their experiences with student-led conferences. Refer to Figure 17–10 for a concise summary of the key points made in this section about student-led parent conferences.

With a combined 35 years of teaching experience, we have rarely found a more valuable educational process than student-led conferences. During preparation the students experienced goal setting, reflected upon their own learning, and created a showcase portfolio.

Once underway, the conferences seem to have a life of their own. We, the teachers, gave up control and became observers, an experience that was gratifying and revealing. It validated our growing belief that students have the ability to direct their own learning and are able to take responsibility for self-evaluation. For many of our students, we gained insights into individual qualities previously hidden from us in the day to day classroom routine.

Students blossomed under the direct and focused attention of their parents. In this intimate spotlight, where there was no competition expect that which they placed on themselves, they stepped for a moment into the adult world where they took command of their own convergence as well as their own development. Parents were surprised and delighted at the level of sophistication and competence their children revealed while sharing personal accomplishments.

In order to refine and improve this process, we surveyed both students and parents. Parents were emphatic in their positive response to student-led conferences, with most requesting that we provide this type of conference more often. Students, even those at risk and with behavior problems, overwhelmingly responded with, "We needed more time; a half an hour was not enough."

Figure 17–9
Teacher Commentary on Experience with Student-led Conferences
Source: By Harriet Arnold and Patricia Stricklin, 1993, Central Kitsap School District, Washington. Reprinted by permission of the authors.

Figure 17–10
Student-led Parent Conferences
in a Nutshell

Benefits

1. Stronger sense of accountability among students

2. Stronger sense of pride in achievement among students

3. More productive student-teacher relationship

4. Improved student-parent relationship

5. Stronger sense of classroom community

6. Reduced value of cheating

7. Development of leadership skills among students

8. Greater parental participation in conferences

Challenges

1. The uncertainty of sharing control with students

2. The need to adopt a completely student-centered philosophy

3. The amount of time required to prepare and present conferences

4. The logistical challenges of organizing for conferences

5. The difficulties that can arise with dysfunctional families

Keys to Success

1. Students willing and able to risk

2. Teachers willing and able to step aside

3. Clear targets known to all

4. A shared language for talking about targets and their achievement

5. A commitment of time to learn, prepare, and practice

A Final Thought About Your Communication Challenge

If we want our students to use feedback about their achievement as the basis for academic improvement, they need to be able to hear and accept the truth about their current achievement. When that truth is positive, this may not be a problem. But when it is negative—particularly when it seems to always have been negative—acceptance of the message can be difficult. Students can and often do find ways to brush these messages aside, to rationalize them, to discredit the source, or to find some other way to escape. Some might call this human nature. The problem is, however, that in a learning community, such avoidance is immensely counterproductive.

And so, we must be mindful of conditions that we may need to satisfy for students to really listen to and accept negative information about themselves. For instance, students may need to learn to develop certain attitudes and perspectives to be able to receive and act on such messages. They may need to see themselves as key players in the search for information about their own achievement. In addition, students may need assistance in developing a sufficiently strong academic self-concept so they can acknowledge their shortcomings and not feel defeated. Further, students must see the provider of the feedback as credible, honest, and helpful. And finally, they must come to see the benefits of the message very quickly, so they can muster the resources needed to act purposefully.

From the other point of view, the giver of the feedback (you) must be able to present it constructively, delivering a clear and focused message using understandable language. You must be able to communicate acceptance of students while critiquing their achievement. They must know that you are evaluating their achievements—not them as people. Even more importantly, you must help students understand that you share a common mission: greater student achievement.

Clearly, it is no simple task to communicate to students that they have missed the target but still have the hope of success and reason to stay motivated. But as a teacher-communicator, that is exactly what you must do. The suggestions offered in previous chapters for clearly defining the meaning of academic success, assessing it well, and transforming the results into quality information are intended to help you fulfill this most important of your responsibilities.

Chapter Summary: Finding Effective Ways to Communicate

We have reviewed and discussed six alternative ways to communicate about student achievement. Three of these alternatives rely on greater detail in written reports. One conveys information in the form of checklists or rating scales that describe all of the key elements in successful performance. Another relies on extended narrative description to describe student performance. The third is a hybrid of the first two structured to accommodate continued progress reporting. Like report cards, these options result in enduring records of performance. These options trade a more labor-intensive recording method for much higher-resolution pictures of achievement than can be obtained with grades on report cards.

We also explored three communication systems that rely on direct contact among students, teachers, and parents in the classroom assessment process. One uses workshop conferences to exchange information between teachers and students. Another is the traditional parent-teacher conference, expanded to permit more student involvement. The third places students in charge of their parent conferences. All require that students understand expectations well enough to be able to converse about them. They also permit students the opportunity of gathering and communicating information about their own achievement. Proficient assessors and communicators rapidly become better performers.

We must continue to explore, develop, and implement these kinds of communication systems as our achievement targets become more numerous, complex, and individualized. Implementation will be made easier as modern information-processing technology evolves and we learn new ways to apply it to the art of assessment. In the meantime, for the immediate future, we will most often use these alternatives in conjunction with or parallel to report card grading systems.

The methods of conveying information reviewed in this chapter hold the promise of allowing students to tell their own story about their own academic success. That, in and of itself, represents one of the most powerful learning experiences we can offer them.

As educators, our mission is to work ourselves out of a job—that is, to take our students to a place where they don't need us anymore. Any students who leave school still needing to rely on their teacher to tell them they have done well in order to know that has not yet learned to hit the target, because they cannot see the quality of their own performance. We must turn our standards over to them so as to make them independent of us. Only then can we assure ourselves that we have helped our students become the lifelong learners they will need to be in the twenty-first century.

As Tom Armstrong asked me recently, "How will our students know how to take maximum advantage of what they have to offer if they don't know who they are?" (1995, personal communication). Covington (1992) speaks in these same tones: "Indeed, at its best, education should provide students with a sense of empowerment that makes the future 'real' by moving beyond merely offering children plausible alternatives to indicating how their preferred dreams can actually be attained" (p. 3). We can fulfill this mission only if we rely on student-centered classroom assessment combined with student-involved communication.

This ends our journey together through this book. I hope our journey has helped you to understand your classroom assessment challenges and solutions more clearly. Please do not permit your personal professional journey to end here, however. I implore you to continue your professional development in assessment by exploring the following readings, and others listed in the references section. When you have put into practice all we have discussed during our journey, return to these readings to enrich your learning.

Thank you for traveling with me and best wishes in becoming the best teacher you can become.

For Further Reading

Follow-up readings on assessment methods:

Linn, R. L., & Gronlund, N. E. (1995). *Measurement and Assessment in Teaching* (7th ed.). Englewood Cliffs, NJ: Merrill/Prentice Hall. When you have put into practice all of the principles of sound assessment described in this book and are ready for more, Linn and Gronlund will take you to the next level of application.

Wiggins, G. (1993). *Assessing Student Performance*. San Francisco: Jossey-Bass. This book provides a thoughtful reexamination of the role of assessment in American education and advocates' reliance on a variety of assessment methods. It is a book on assessment philosophy more than on assessment practice.

Essential readings on the relationship of assessment to student motivation:

Kohn, A. (1993). *Punished by Rewards*. New York: Houghton Mifflin. Kohn provides a thought-provoking analysis of extrinsically and intrinsically motivating ways to encourage students to engage in academically productive work. Management of rewards and punishments will not suffice in school. He offers alternatives.

Covington, M. (1992). *Making the Grade: A Self-worth Perspective on Motivation and School Reform*. New York: Cambridge University Press. The author offers a comprehensive treatment of the correlates of student motivation to strive for academic excellence. Many of the points he makes have implications for how we assess students and how we communicate with them about assessment results.

Practical references on student involvement in assessment and communication:

Austin, T. (1994). *Changing the View: Student-led Parent Conferences.* Portsmouth, NH: Heinemann. An authentic storyteller has prepared a teacher's handbook on setting up and conducting student-involved communications. You can read this in two hours and learn so much!

Davies, A., Cameron, C., Politano, C., & Gregory, K. (1992). *Together Is Better: Collaborative Assessment, Evaluation and Reporting.* Winnepeg, MB: Peguis. The authors provide a practical guide to the design and completion of student-involved communications. You can follow their path to success with this way of communicating.

Spandel V., & Culham, R. (1995). *Putting Portfolio Stories to Work.* Portland OR: Northwest Regional Educational Laboratory. This handbook offers more practical advice on how to set up and use portfolios than anything else I've seen. These authors are teachers talking directly to teachers.

Must reading on the topic of assessing reasoning and problem solving:

Marzano, R., Pickering, D., & McTighe, J. (1993). *Performance Assessment Using the Dimensions of Learning.* Alexandria, VA: Association for Supervision and Curriculum Development. This book provides many examples of performance assessment exercises and scoring criteria for assessing reasoning and problem-solving proficiency.

Paul, Richard (1995). *Critical Thinking: How to Prepare Students for a Rapidly Changing World.* Santa Rosa, CA: Center for Critical Thinking. This is a very big book, full of very important ideas. When it comes to understanding what it means to be a clear thinker, there is no better or more important reference.

Anyone who teaches students to write needs to study the following:

Spandel, V., & Stiggins, R. J. (1996). *Creating Writers: Linking Assessment and Writing Instruction* (2nd ed.). White Plains, NY: Addison-Wesley Longman. This is a teacher's guide to integrating student-involved writing assessment into the teaching and learning process.

Exercises to Advance Your Learning

Knowledge

1. Make a three-column-by-three-row chart on a large sheet of paper. Reviewing the text, on this chart identify the strengths, limitations, and keys to successful use of the three forms of written reports on student achievement discussed in this chapter: rating scales, narrative reporting, and continuous progress reporting.

2. On the same kind of chart, identify the benefits, challenges, and keys to successful implementation of the three conference forms discussed.

Reasoning

1. Focus on the system of communication used in your school or in the college or university in which you study. Evaluate that system in terms of the keys to effective communication. In your opinion, does it represent a sound system? Why?

2. If you are able to identify problems within the system evaluated in reasoning exercise 1, how might they be overcome?

3. Return to the charts you completed for knowledge exercises 1 and 2 and identify similarities and differences among the

written and conference-based communication alternatives you have analyzed.

4. Some who have experimented with alternative communication systems have met with parental resistance. Parents wanted report cards and grades, as they had received when they were in school. If you developed a sound communication system in your school and were confronted with this kind of resistance, how would you respond? Why?

Skills and Products

1. Develop a written plan for the implementation of at least one written and one conference-based communication system in your classroom. Be sure to detail your objectives, procedures, and how you would evaluate the effectiveness of your implementation.

2. Implement your plans, being sure to note any important changes in the motivation of your students.

Dispositions

1. Do you see these written and conference-based options as potentially valuable ways to communicate about and to motivate students? Why?

2. Throughout Part 4 of this book, I have urged you to proceed with caution in your use of these options, attending always to the quality of the assessments used to tell an accurate achievement story. In other words, I have argued, vague targets poorly assessed in a manner that excludes students from the assessment process will lead to grades, portfolios, written reports, and conferences that are more ritual than substance. Do you agree with me? Why?

References

Alberta Education. (1994). *Science performance assessment and standards: Just do it!* St. Albert, Alberta, Canada: Author.

Alberta Education. (1995). *Oral communication evaluation.* Edmonton, Alberta, Canada: Author.

American Council of Teachers of Foreign Language. (1989). *Oral proficiency interview: Tester training manual.* Yonkers, NY: Author.

American Psychological Association. (1985). *Standards for educational and psychological testing.* Washington, DC: Author.

Anderson, L. W. (1981). *Assessing affective characteristics in the schools.* Needham, MA: Allyn & Bacon.

Ann Arbor Public Schools. (1993). Success for all kindergarten students. Ann Arbor, MI: Department of Research Services.

Arter, J., & Spandel, V. (1992). Using portfolios of student work in instruction and assessment. *Educational Measurement: Issues and Practice, 11*(1), 36–44.

Austin, T. (1994). *Changing the view: Student-led parent conferences.* Portsmouth, NH: Heinemann.

Barbour, C., & Barbour, N. (1997). *Families, schools, and communities; Building partnerships for educating children.* Upper Saddle River, NJ: Merrill/Prentice Hall.

Baron, J. B. (1991). Strategies for the development of effective performance exercises. *Applied Measurement in Education, 4*(4), 305–318.

Berk, R. A. (Ed.). (1986). *Performance assessment: Methods and applications.* Baltimore, MD: Johns Hopkins University Press.

Bloom, B. S., Englehart, M. D., Furst, E. J., Hill, W. H., & Krathwohl, D. R. (Eds.). (1956). *Taxonomy of educational objectives: Handbook 1, cognitive domain.* New York: McKay.

Bloom, B. S., Hastings, J. T., & Madaus, G. F. (1971). *Handbook on formative and summative evaluation of student learning.* New York: McGraw-Hill.

Bond, L., & Roeber, E. (1995). *State student assessment program database, 1992–1993.* Oakbrook, IL: North Central Regional Educational Laboratory and Washington, DC: Council of Chief State School Officers.

Catlin Gabel School. (n.d.). *Student evaluation criteria policy manual.* Portland, OR: Author.

Catlin Gabel School. (1990). Sample student report. Portland, OR: Author.

Condry, J. (1977). Enemies of exploration: Self-initiated versus other-initiated learning. *Journal of Personality and Social Psychology, 35,* 459–477.

Corvallis School District. (n.d.). *Outcomes and performance statements.* Corvallis, OR: Author.

Covington, M. (1992). *Making the grade: A self-worth perspective on motivation and school reform.* New York: Cambridge University Press.

Davidson, L., Myford, C., Plasket, D., Scripp, L., Swinton, S., Torff, B., & Waanders, J. (1992). *Arts propel: A handbook for music.* Princeton, NJ: Educational Testing Service.

Davies, A., Cameron, C., Politano, C., & Gregory, K. (1992). *Together is better: Collaborative assessment, evaluation and reporting.* Winnipeg, MB: Peguis.

Dunbar, S. B., Koretz, D. M., & Hoover, H. D. (1991). Quality control in the development and use of performance assessments. *Applied Measurement in Education, 4*(4), 289–304.

Fort Hays Educational Development Center (1994). *Science rating scales.* Hays, KS: Author.

Gable, R. (1986). *Instrument development in the affective domain.* Boston: Kluwer-Nijhoff.

Gable, R., & Wolf, M. (1993). *Instrument development in the affective domain.* Norwell, MA: Kluwer.

Gardner, H. (1993). *Frames of mind: The theory of multiple intelligences.* New York: Basic Books.

Haertel, E., Farrara, S., Korpi, M., & Prescott, B. (1984). *Testing in secondary schools: Student perspectives.* Paper presented at the annual meeting of the American Educational Research Association, New Orleans.

Hoskyn, J., & Quellmalz, E. (1993). *Multicultural reading and thinking program resource notebook.* Little Rock, AR: Arkansas Department of Education.

Hunkins, F. P. (1995). *Teaching thinking through effective questioning.* Norwood, MA: Christopher-Gordon.

Illinois State Board of Education. (1995). *Performance assessment in mathematics: Approaches to open-ended problems.* Springfield, IL: Author.

Iowa Testing Program. (1996). *Iowa Tests of Basic Skills Interpretation Guide.* Chicago, IL: Riverside Publishing Co.

Kohn, A. (1993). *Punished by rewards.* New York: Houghton Mifflin.

Lewis & Clark College. (1990). Press release on new admissions initiatives. Portland, OR: Author.

Lindquist, E. F. (1951). Preliminary considerations in objective test construction. In E. F. Lindquist (Ed.), *Educational measurement* (pp. 4–22). Washington, DC: American Council on Education.

Linn, R. L., & Gronlund, N. E. (1995). *Measurement and evaluation in teaching* (7th ed.). Englewood Cliffs, NJ: Merrill/Prentice Hall.

Marzano, R. J. (1992). *A different kind of classroom.* Alexandria, VA: Association for Supervision and Curriculum Development.

Marzano, R. J., Pickering, D. J., & McTighe, J. (1993). *Performance assessment using the dimensions of learning.* Alexandria, VA: Association for Supervision and Curriculum Development.

Messick, S. (1989). Validity. In R. L. Linn (Ed.), *Educational measurement* (3rd ed.) (n.p.). Englewood Cliffs, NJ: Merrill/Prentice Hall.

Ministry of Education and Training, Victoria. (1991). *English profiles handbook: Assessing and reporting students' progress in English.* Melbourne, Australia: Ministry of Education and Training, Victoria, School Programs Division.

National Council of Teachers of Mathematics (1989). *Curriculum and evaluation standards for school mathematics.* Reston, VA: Author.

Neill, D. M., & Medina, N. J. (1991). Standardized testing: Harmful to educational health. *Phi Delta Kappan, 73,* 688–697.

Norris, S. P., & Ennis, R. H. (1989). *Evaluating critical thinking.* Pacific Grove, CA: Critical Thinking Books & Software.

Novak, J. D., & Gowin, D. B. (1984). *Learning how to learn.* New York: Cambridge University Press.

Oregon Department of Education. (1994). CIM outcome: Apply science and mathematics. Salem, OR: Office of Assessment and Technology, Oregon Department of Education.

Paul, R. (1995). *Critical thinking: How to prepare students for a rapidly changing world.* Santa Rosa, CA: Foundation for Critical Thinking.

Pinnell, G. S., Pikulski, J., Wixson, K. K., Campbell, J. R., Gough, P. B., & Beatty, A. S. (1995). *Listening to children read aloud.* Washington, DC: Office of Educational Research and Improvement, U.S. Department of Education.

Quellmalz, E. (1987). Developing reasoning skills. In J. B. Baron & R. J. Sternberg (Eds.), *Teaching thinking skills: Theory and practice.* New York: W. H. Freeman.

Quellmalz, E. (1991). Developing criteria for performance assessments: The missing link. *Applied Measurement in Education, 4*(4), 319–332.

Quellmalz, E., & Hoskyn, J. (1988). Making a difference in Arkansas: The multicultural reading and thinking project. *Educational Leadership, 45,* 51–55.

Rowe, M. B. (1978). Specific ways to develop better communications. In R. Sund & A. Carin (Eds.), *Creative questioning and sensitivity: Listening techniques* (2nd ed.) (n.p.). Englewood Cliffs, NJ: Merrill/Prentice Hall.

Scates, D. E. (1943). Differences between measurement criteria of pure scientists and of classroom teachers. *Journal of Educational Research, 37*, 1–13.

Shavelson, R. J., & Stern, P. (1981). Research on teachers' pedagogical thoughts, judgments, decisions, and behavior. *Review of Educational Research, 41*(4), 455–498.

Skinner, B. F. (1974). *About behaviorism.* New York: Alfred A. Knopf.

Skinner, E. A., Wellborn, J. G., & Connell, J. P. (1990). What it takes to do well in school and whether I've got it: A process model of perceived control and children's engagement and achievement in school. *Journal of Educational Psychology, 82*, 22–32.

Smith, M. L., & Rottenberg, C. (1991). Unintended consequences of external testing in elementary schools. *Educational Measurement: Issues and Practice, 10*(4), 7–11.

South Kitsap School District. (n.d.). *South Kitsap school district outcomes.* Port Orchard, WA. Author.

Spandel, V. (1994). *Seeing with new eyes: A guidebook on teaching and assessing beginning writers.* Portland, OR: Northwest Regional Educational Laboratory.

Spandel, V., & Culham, R. (1995). *Putting portfolio stories to work.* Portland, OR: Northwest Regional Educational Laboratory.

Spandel, V., & Stiggins, R. J. (1990). *Creating writers: Linking assessment and writing instruction.* White Plains, NY: Addison-Wesley Longman.

Spandel, V., & Stiggins, R. J. (in press). *Creating writers: Linking assessment and writing instruction* (rev. ed.). White Plains, NY: Addison-Wesley Longman.

Sternberg, R. J. (1996). Myths, countermyths, and truths about intelligence. *Educational Researcher, 25*(2), 11–16.

Stiggins, R. J., & Conklin, N. F. (1992). *In teachers' hands: Investigating the practices of classroom assessment.* Albany, NY: State University of New York Press.

Swartz, M., & O'Connor, J. R. (1986). *Exploring American history.* Englewood Cliffs, NJ: Globe.

Wade, S. E. (1990). Reading comprehension using thinkalouds. *Reading Teacher, 43*(7), 442–451.

Ward, A. W. (1991). *Item banking and item banks.* Daytona Beach, FL: Techné Group.

Washington Commission on Student Learning. (n.d.). *Washington State's classroom assessment competencies for teachers.* Olympia, WA: Author.

Weiner, B. (1974). *Achievement motivation and attribution theory.* Morristown, NJ: General Learning Press.

Wiggins, G. (1989). A true test: Toward more authentic and equitable assessment. *Phi Delta Kappan, 703*–713.

Wiggins, G. (1993). *Assessing student performance.* San Francisco: Jossey-Bass.

Zola, J. (1992). Middle and high school scored discussions. *Social Education, 56*(2), 121–125.

Index

ABACUS, 123
Academic self-concept, 328
Accountability
as communication barrier,
390–392
of students, 52–53, 422
of teachers, 50–52, 422
testing, 350–351
Achievement assessments, 43–70
and aptitude, 416
and communication, 68–69
community involvement in,
63–64
debate about expectations, 48
definition of, 13–14
and dispositions, 60
and grading, 410, 412, 413–414
and knowledge, 55–57
mental state of, 80
methods of, 75, 81
mission of, 45–50
performance exercises, 184
and product assessments, 59
professional preparation for,
61–63
and reasoning assessments,
57–58
and skills assessments, 58–59
and teacher's challenge, 48–50
and team effort, 64–66
Achievement information, gathering for grading, 422–444
Achievement stages for writers,
291–293
ACT Assessment Program, 350,
361–362
Administration of assessments,
differences in, 35
Affect in dispositions, 327–330
and attitudes, 327–328

and interests, 328
and locus of control, 328–329
and motivation, 328
and values, 328
variations of, 329–330
Alberta Education, 298, 300
American College Testing Pro-
gram, 361–362
American Council on the Teaching of Foreign Languages
(ACTFL), 310, 311
American Psychological Association, 33
Analytical reasoning, 260
Analytical scoring, 185, 208
Anderson, L. W., 327, 328, 330
Ann Arbor Public Schools,
477–482
Aptitude
and achievement, 416
as grading factor, 412, 415–417
Arnold, Harriet, 503
Arter, J., 449, 461
Artistic performance assess-
ments, junior high, 301,
304–305
Arts Propel, 301, 304, 306
Assessment literacy, 7–10, 106
Assessments
context of, 23–24
expertise, 94, 106–107
as learning, 18–19
methods. See Methods
vs. standardized tests, 30–36
At-risk youth programs, 47–48
Attitudes
and affect, 327–328
grading on, 412, 420–422
Attribution theory, 398
Austin, T., 475, 476

Barbour, C., 64
Barbour, N., 64
Baron, J. B., 204, 290
Barriers to assessments, 91–108
assessment expertise as, 94,
106–107
community beliefs as, 93,
99–102
emotions as, 93, 94–98
and essay assessments, 171
and performance assessments,
217, 218
and selected response assessments, 143
time as, 93–94, 102–106
Barriers to communication,
390–394
accountability as, 390–392
and message receiver, 392–393
parent or community expectations as, 393–394
time as, 392
Behaviorism, 396
Berk, R. A., 178
Bias
in performance assessments,
215
in standards, 16–17
Bloom, B. S., 134, 259
Bond, L., 360
Borderline cases, grading,
431–432
Brainstorming, in performance
assessments, 194–195

Cameron, C., 459, 460
Catlin Gabel School, Portland,
Oregon, 482–486
Causal attributions in communi-
cation, 398–399

Cause/recall propositions, 130–131

Celebration portfolios, 456

Cheating, in report card grading, 432

Checklist option in essay scoring, 169

Classroom assessments vs. standardized tests, 30–36

Collaborative tests, 38

College admissions testing programs, 350, 361–362

College Board, 361–362

Communication, 11, 223–248, 383–405. *See also* Conferences; Grading; Portfolios; Reports, written
  and achievement, 68–69
  as assessment, 78
  barriers to, 390–394
  context of, 234–239
  and continuous progress curriculum, 65
  and conversations, 245–246
  and discussions, 227–228, 242–243
  and dispositions, 233–234, 341–342
  environment of, 236, 387–390
  and filters, 229–230
  and honesty, 236
  integrating assessments into instruction, 246–248
  and interviews, 241–242
  and journals and logs, 244–245
  and knowledge assessments, 231–232
  and language, 235, 388–389
  and oral tests, 243–244
  and personality, 235
  and quality assessments, 228–231, 239, 385–387
  and questions, 240–241, 246, 247
  and reasoning assessments, 232, 270–271
  and records, 236
  and sampling, 230–231, 236–239
  sharing, 387–389
  and skills and product assessments, 233
  and standardized tests, 364
  and student involvement, 83, 246–248, 394–396
  and subjectivity, 229–231
  and time, 235–236
  understanding of, 390
  and verbal fluency, 235

Community
  as assessment barrier, 93, 99–102
  awareness of standardized tests, 377
  as communication barrier, 393–394
  involvement in achievement assessment, 63–64

Comparative reasoning, 261

Composite achievement scores, 433–437

Composite profile performance assessments, 439–440

Computers, 122–123
  software, 123, 443–444, 468

Condensing and performance assessment development, 195

Condry, J., 397

Conferences, 492–504
  and communication, 241–242
  parent-teacher, 496–498
  student-led, 498–504
  student-teacher, 493–496

Conklin, N. F., 12, 34, 54, 100, 178

Connell, J. P., 399

Content knowledge, 82–83

Continuous progress reporting, 489–492

Conversations, 245–246

Cooperative learning, 432

Covington, Martin V., 399–402, 426, 459, 463

Creating Writers: Linking Assessments and Writing Instruction (Spandel and Stiggins), 488

Criterion-referenced tests, 35, 346–347, 358
  large-scale assessments, 355

Critical spirit behaviors, 340

Critical thinking, 84, 276–278

Culham, R., 451, 455, 457

Current profile method, 441

Curriculum
  continuous progress, 65
  expanded, 103

Davidson, Lyle, 301, 306

Davies, A., 459, 460

Decision-making, 24–30

Declarative knowledge, 55

Detail stage for writers, 293

Diaries, 244–245

Discussions
  and assessment process, 227–228
  and communication, 227–228, 242–243
  and performance assessments, 312–315
  scored, 226

Dispositions, 319–343
  and achievement, 60
  and affect, 327–330
  and assessment methods, 87–88, 330–342
  and communication, 233–234, 341–342
  and essay assessments, 87, 160
  importance of, 321–323
  and performance assessments, 190–191, 337–341
  and questionnaires, 333–337
  and selected response assessments, 121
  and standards, 323–326

Distortion, in standards, 16–17

Drawing stage for writers, 292

Dunbar, S. B., 178

Educational Testing Service, 362

Effort as grading factor, 412, 417–420

Electronic portfolios, 468

Elementary level
  communication narrative reports, 482–489
  math skills assessments, 298–299
  performance assessments, 298–301

Emotions, as barriers to assessments, 93, 94–98
Englehart, M. D., 259
Ennis, R. H., 58, 276–279, 338
Environment of communication, 236, 387–390
Errors in judgment, 215–217
Essay assessments, 77, 149–173
  barriers to, 171
  context of, 155, 161–162
  development of, 161–170
  and dispositions, 87, 160
  feedback on, 154–155
  impact on students and teachers, 155
  and instruction integration, 171–172
  and knowledge assessments, 82, 157–158
  planning of, 162–164
  and problem-solving, 85
  process of, 154
  and product assessments, 159–160
  and reasoning assessments, 85, 158–159, 269–270
  and sampling, 163–164
  scoring of, 154, 168–170
  and skills assessments, 159
  and standardized tests, 363
  subjectivity in, 156–157
  tables of specifications in, 162–163
Evaluative thinking, 84
Experimentation stage for writers, 292
Extra credit, in grading, 432

Failure-accepting students, 399, 401–402
Failure-avoiding students, 399–401
Feedback, in essay assessments, 154–155
Fill-in items, 77, 133, 137, 141
Filters, in communication, 229–230
Focused purpose, in standards, 14–16
Foreign languages, 310–312

Fort Hays Educational Development Center, 299
Furst, E. J., 259

Gable, R., 334
Gardner, H., 415
Goals, assessment, 32–33
Gowin, D. B., 283
Grade equivalent scores, 371–374
Grading, 407–444
  on achievement, 410, 412, 413–414
  advance notice of, 433
  on aptitude, 412, 415–417
  assessment plans for, 424–427
  on attitude, 412, 420–422
  and borderline cases, 431–432
  and changing student needs, 410–411
  and cheating, 432
  and composite achievement scores, 433–437
  composite profile method of, 439–440
  and cooperative learning, 432
  current profile method of, 441
  on curve, 436–437
  definition of, 409
  on effort, 412, 417–420
  and extra credit, 432
  gathering achievement information for, 422–444
  and heterogeneous grouping, 433
  percent method of, 429–430, 442
  and performance assessments, 439–442
  and planning, 424–427
  and policies, 432–433
  with preset standards, 435–436
  and quality assessments, 411
  and ranking order, 409–410
  software packages for, 443–444
  on status vs. improvement, 431
  total points method of, 430–431, 441–442
Gregory, K., 459, 460
Gronlund, N. E., 138
Growth portfolios, 456–457

Haertel, E., 12
Hastings, J. T., 134
Heterogeneous grouping, 433
Higher-order thinking labels, 257
High school performance assessments, 310–315
  discussion skills, 312–315
  foreign language, 310–312
Hill, W. H., 259
Holistic scoring, 185, 208
Honesty and communication, 236
Hoover, H. D., 178
Hoskyn, J., 279–280, 282
Hunkins, F. P., 246, 247

Illinois State Board of Education, 295, 297, 298
Independence stage for writers, 293
Inferential reasoning, 261–262
Inferential thinking, 84
Instruction
  and essay assessments, 171–172
  integrating assessments into, 246–248
Instructional objectives as test plans, 127
Integrated Reading Performance Record (IRPR), 294
Intelligence, 415
Interests and affect, 328
International assessments, 351–352
Interpersonal activity, 17–18
Interpretation of assessment results, 35
Interpretive exercises, 138–139
Interviews and communication, 241–242
Iowa Test of Basic Skills, 374
IPS Publishing, 123

Journals and logs, 244–245
Judgment errors in performance assessments, 215–217
Junior high performance assessments, 301–310
  artistic performance, 301, 304–305
  math skills, 305, 308–310

Kansas Science Assessment, 299,
301, 302–303
Kindergarten rating scale,
477–482
Knowledge
content, 82–83
declarative, 55
Knowledge assessments, 55–57
and communication, 231–232
and essay assessments, 82,
157–158
and performance assessments,
188–189
and reasoning assessments, 257
and selected response assessments, 119
and skills assessments, 58–59
Kohn, A., 397, 426
Koretz, D. M., 178
Krathwohl, D. R., 259

Labeling, 257, 394
Labor-intensive assessments,
103–104
Language
and communication, 235,
388–389
foreign language performance
assessments, 310–312
spoken language bands,
490–492
Large-scale assessments,
355–362. *See also* Stan-
dardized tests
college admissions testing,
361–362
criterion-referenced tests, 355
local, 357
national, 360–361
norm-referenced tests, 355
published achievement tests,
357–358
state, 358–359, 360
Learned helplessness, 402
Learning in classroom assessments, 18–19
Learning logs, 245
Lewis & Clark College, 448, 457
Lifelong learning of teachers, 62
Life skills and portfolios, 452–453

Linn, R. L., 138
Linquist, E. F., 178
Literature for achievement
assessments, 63
Local large-scale assessments,
357
Locus of control, 398
and affect, 328–329

Madaus, G. F., 134
Marzano, R. J., 55, 58, 201, 259,
270
Matching items, 77, 137, 142
Math skills assessments
elementary level, 298–299
junior high, 305, 308–310
Oregon project, 305,
308–310
primary grades, 295–298
McTighe, J., 55, 201, 270
Medina, N. J., 32
Message receivers, 392–393
Messick, S., 17
Methods, 74–88
and assessment plans, 75–76
classroom assessments vs. standardized tests, 34–35
and communication, 78
and essay assessments, 77
and performance assessments,
77–78
and product assessments,
86–87
and selected response assessments, 76–77
and standards, 16
Ministry of Education, Alberta,
Canada, 312, 314
Motivation, 328
Multiple-choice items, 76, 133,
135–136, 141
Myford, Carol, 301, 306

Narrative reports, elementary
level, 482–489
National Assessment of Educational Progress (NAEP),
294, 351, 360–361
National assessments, 351–352,
360–361

National Computer Systems
(NCS), 123
National Council of Teachers of
Mathematics (NCTM), 305
Neil, D. M., 32
Norm-referenced tests, 35, 346,
355, 358, 359
Norris, S. P., 58, 276–279, 338
Novak, J. D., 283

Objective testing science, 31
Objective tests. *See* Selected
response assessments
O'Connor, J. R., 168
Open-book tests, 38
Optical scanning for scoring, 123
Oral Proficiency Interview, 310
Oral tests, 243–244
Oregon math assessment project,
305, 308–310
Outcomes and performance state-
ments, 66–67, 68

Parents' expectations as communication barriers, 393–394
Parent-teacher conferences,
496–498
Partnerships, in performance
assessments, 198–199,
217–219
Passportfolio, 457
Paul, Richard, 58, 258, 266,
272–275, 282
Percent correct scores, 68
Percentile rank scores, 368–371
Percent method, grading,
429–430, 442
Performance assessments, 77–78,
104, 175–220
barriers to, 217, 218
and bias, 215
and brainstorming, 194–195
and condensing, 195
and contrasting, 196–197
criteria for, 192–200
definition of, 196
and dispositions, 190–191,
337–341
in elementary grades, 298–301
math skills, 298–299

science, 299–301
exercises, 179, 183–184,
    200–207
and grading, 439–442
in high school, 310–315
    discussion skills, 312–315
    foreign language, 310–312
judgment errors, 215–217
in junior high, 301–310
    artistic performance, 301,
        304–305
    math skills, 305, 308–310
and knowledge assessments,
    188–189
and partnerships, 198–199,
    217–219
and portfolios, 452
in primary grades, 291–298
    math skills, 295–298
    reading, 294–295
    writing skills, 291–293
and product assessments, 190,
    287–316
and quality assessments,
    186–191, 290–291
raters, 211
and reasoning assessments,
    189–190, 270
refining, 198
and scoring, 184–186,
    208–211
and skill assessments, 190,
    287–316
and standardized tests,
    363–364
subjectivity of, 186–188
and success, 181
Personality and communication,
    235
Pickering, D. J., 55, 201, 270
Pinnell, G. S., 294, 295
Planning
    and assessment methods,
        75–76
    and essay assessments,
        162–164
    and grading, 424–427
    and selected response assess-
        ments, 124–128
Plasket, Donna, 301, 306

Policies and grading process,
    432–433
Politano, C., 459, 460
Portfolios, 79, 447–469
    challenges of, 451–452
    definition of, 449
    electronic, 468
    evaluation of, 458
    getting started, 461–463
    and life skills, 452–453
    and performance assessments,
        452
    popularity of, 450–451
    and quality assessments, 453,
        455
    selection of, 455–459
    and students, 458–464
Portland, Oregon, Levels Test,
    357
Practice tests, 38
Primary grades performance
    assessments, 291–298
    math skills, 295–298
    reading skills, 294–295
    writing skills, 291–293
Problem-solving, 84–86, 201
    and essay assessments, 85
    proficiency of, 58
Procedural knowledge, 55–56
Process portfolios, 457
Product assessments
    and achievement assessments,
        59
    and assessment methods,
        86–87
    and communication, 233
    and essay assessments,
        159–160
    and performance assessments,
        190, 287–316
    and selected response assess-
        ments, 120–121
Professional preparation for
    achievement assessments,
        61–63
Profiles, 489
Propositions
    and selected response assess-
        ments, 133–140
    in test plans, 130–131

Published achievement tests,
    357–358

Quality assessments. See also
    Standards
    barriers. See Barriers
    classroom assessment vs. stan-
        dardized tests, 33–34
    and communication, 228–231,
        239, 385–387
    and grading, 411
    and performance assessments,
        186–191, 290–291
    and portfolios, 453, 455
Quellmalz, E., 58, 199, 259,
    279–280, 282, 290
Questionnaires
    and dispositions, 333–337
    and selected response formats,
        334–336
    and written responses, 336
Questions
    and communication, 240–241,
        246, 247
    and reasoning assessments,
        266–268

Ranking by achievement
    and grading, 409–410
    and students, 45–47
Rating scales
    and essay assessments,
        169–170
    for kindergarten, 477–482
    and performance assessments,
        185, 211
Raw scores, 367–368
Readiness stage for writers, 292
Reading
    performance assessments,
        294–295
    proficiency of students, 122
Reasoning assessments, 57–58,
    253–284
    analytical, 260
    classifying, 261
    and communication, 232,
        270–271
    comparative, 261
    elements of, 272–273

Reasoning assessments, *continued*
  and essay assessments, 85, 158–159, 269–270
  evaluating, 262
  and higher-order thinking labels, 257
  inferential, 261–262
  and knowledge assessments, 257
  Norris-Ennis framework for, 276–279
  and performance assessments, 189–190, 270
  and performance criteria, 274–275
  and problem-solving, 84–86
  proficiency of, 271–276
  Quellmalz framework for, 279
  and questions, 266–268
  relationships among parts, 262–265
  and selected response assessments, 119–120, 268–269
  and student-involved assessments, 279–284
  and students as natural thinkers, 258
  synthesizing, 260–261
Recording results in performance assessments, 184–186, 208–211
Record-keeping
  and assessments, 104–106
  and communication, 236, 386–387
Report card grading. *See* Grading
Reports, written, 477–492
  continuous progress, 489–492
  narrative, 482–489
  rating scales, 477–482
Response journals, 244
Rewards and punishment, 396–398
Riverside Publishing, 374
Roeber, E., 360
Roles, classroom assessments vs. standardized tests, 32–33
Rottenberg, C., 32

Sampling
  and communication, 230–231, 236–239
  and essay assessments, 163–164
  and performance exercises, 204–205, 207
  and standardized tests, 365–366
  and standards, 16
  in test plans, 128–129
Scates, Robert, 31–32, 348
Scholarship testing, 350
Scholastic Assessment Test (SAT), 361–362
School-related values, 328
Schools, U.S., evolution of, 45–50
Science performance assessments, 299–301
Scientists and teachers, training differences between, 31
Scored discussions, 226
Scoring. *See also* Standardized test scores
  analytical, 185, 208
  composite achievement, 433–437
  in essay assessments, 154, 168–170
  holistic, 185, 208
  in performance assessments, 184–186, 208–211
Scripp, Larry, 301, 306
Scriven, 18
Seeing With New Eyes (Spandel), 291
Selected response assessments, 76–77, 113–146
  barriers to, 143
  context of, 122–123
  development, 122–142
  and dispositions, 121
  formats of, 137–138, 140–142
  importance of, 116–118
  and knowledge assessments, 119
  and planning, 124–128
  and products assessments, 120–121
  and propositions, 133–140
  and questionnaires, 334–336

  and reasoning assessments, 119–120, 268–269
  selecting test material, 128–132
  and skills assessments, 120
  and standardized tests, 362–363
  and students, 144–145
  and teacher's judgment, 116
  technology use in, 122–123
Selection
  of material to test, 128–132
  of portfolios, 455–459
Self-worth, student, 399–402
Shavelson, R. J., 12
Short answer fill-in items, 77
Skills assessments, 86
  and achievement assessments, 58–59
  and communication, 233
  and essay assessments, 159
  and knowledge assessments, 58–59
  and performance assessments, 190, 287–316
  and product assessments, 233
  and selected response assessments, 120
Skinner, B. F., 396
Skinner, E. A., 399
Smith, M. L., 32
Software
  for electronic portfolios, 468
  for grading, 443–444
  for tests, 123
Sound assessments, definition of, 33
Spandel, Vicki, 291, 449, 451, 455, 457, 461, 488, 493, 494
Spoken language bands, 490–492
Standardized tests, 12, 345–378
  accountability testing, 350–351
  vs. classroom assessments, 30–36
  and communication, 364
  community awareness of, 377
  and contradictions, 352–353
  development of, 364–367
  and essay assessments, 363
  history of, 347–352

methods of, 362–364
national and international,
    351–352, 360–361
and performance assessments,
    363–364
and sampling, 365–366
and scholarship and college
    admissions testing, 350
and selected response assess-
    ments, 362–363
and statewide testing, 351
and student well-being, 32,
    374–377
and teacher implications,
    374–378
test batteries, 350
users of, 356
Standardized test scores, 367–374
grade equivalent, 371–374
percent correct, 68
percentile rank, 368–371
raw scores, 367–368
stanine, 371
Standards, 14–17
bias and distortion in, 16–17
and dispositions, 323–326
focused purpose of, 14–16
methods of, 16
and performance assessments,
    184, 290–291
and sampling, 16
Stanford University, 12
Stanine scores, 371
State standardized tests, 351,
    358–359, 360
Status report portfolios, 457
Stern, P., 12
Sternberg, R. J., 415
Stiggins, R. J., 12, 34, 54, 100,
    178, 488, 493, 494
Stricklin, Patricia, 503
Student dispositions. *See* Disposi-
    tions
Student-involved communication,
    246–248, 394–396
Student-led conferences, 498–504
Students
and accountability, 52–53, 422
as assessment users, 12–13,
    217–219

changing needs of, 410–411
and failure, 51, 399–402
as natural thinkers, 258
and portfolios, 458–464
ranking by achievement of,
    45–47
and reasoning assessments,
    279–284
and sampling, 163–164
self-reflection of, 459–464
well-being of, 374–377
workplace competence of,
    47–48
Student-teacher conferences,
    493–496
Subjective scoring, 215–217
Subjectivity
and communication, 229–231
in essay assessments,
    156–157
performance assessments,
    186–188
Success-oriented students,
    399–400
Swartz, M., 168
Swinton, Spence, 301, 306
Synthesizing reasoning, 260–261

Table of test specifications
for essay assessments, 162–163
for selected response assess-
    ments, 124–127
Take-home tests, 38
Teachers
accountability of, 50–52, 422
and achievement assessments,
    48–50
judgment role of, 116
and objective tests, 46
and standardized tests,
    374–378
team effort of, 64–66
training in assessments, 31,
    62–63, 100–101
workload of, 53
Teaching and assessments,
    18–19, 36–39
Team effort, teachers, 64–66
Technological change in schools,
    49

Technology use in assessments,
    122–123
Tests
and accountability, 350–351
backword analysis in, 142
batteries, 350
history in assessments, 46
norming, 366
planning, 124–128
Time
as assessment barrier, 93–94,
    102–106
and communication, 235–236
as communication barrier, 392
in test taking, 122
Time sequence portfolios,
    456–457
Torff, Bruce, 301, 306
Total points method of grading,
    430–431, 441–442
Training, of scientists and teach-
    ers, 31
True/false items, 76, 133,
    136–137, 141

U.S. schools, evolution of, 45–50
Users, of standardized tests, 356

Verbal fluency, 235
Victoria, Australia, Ministry of
    Education and Training,
    489

Waanders, Janet, 301, 306
Wade, S. E., 364
Ward, A. W., 123
Washington State Commission on
    Student Learning,
    106–107
Weiner, B., 398, 399
Welborn, J. G., 399
Wiggins, G., 178
Workplace competence of stu-
    dents, 47–48
Writing skills
and performance assessments,
    291–293
and product assessments, 160
Written responses, question-
    naires, 336

About the Author

Richard J. Stiggins, B.S., M.A., Ph. D., is founder and president of the Assessment Training Institute, Inc., Portland, Oregon, a service agency devoted to supporting teachers as they face the day-to-day challenges of classroom assessment. He received his bachelor's degree in psychology from the State University of New York at Plattsburgh, master's degree in industrial psychology from Springfield (MA) College, and doctoral degree in education measurement from Michigan State University. Dr. Stiggins began his assessment work on the faculty of Michigan State before becoming director of research and evaluation for the Edina, Minnesota, Public Schools and a member of the faculty of educational foundations at the University of Minnesota. In addition, he has served as director of test development for the American College Testing Program, Iowa City, Iowa, as a visiting scholar at Stanford University, and as director of the Centers for Classroom Assessment and Performance Assessment at the Northwest Regional Educational Laboratory, Portland, Oregon. He has also served on the graduate faculties of the University of Minnesota, Minneapolis, Minnesota, and Lewis and Clark College, Portland, teaching educational measurement and program evaluation courses for teachers and administrators.

Rick has synthesized two decades of classroom assessment research into a wide ranging set of practical professional development materials and experiences for educators at all levels. The foundational research is summarized in his book *In Teachers' Hands: Investigating the Practice of Classroom Assessment* (Albany, New York: SUNY Press, 1992). He has also collaborated with Vicki Spandel to offer practical strategies for teachers in *Creating Writers: Linking Assessment and Writing Instruction, 2nd Ed.* (New York: Addison-Wesley Longman, 1996). Rick has also developed a series of classroom assessment training videos distributed through the Assessment Training Institute.